Contents

List of figures

About the editors

Avi Brisman is an Associate Professor in the School of Justice Studies at Eastern Kentucky University and an Adjunct Associate Professor in the School of Justice at Queensland University of Technology. He is the author of *Geometries of Crime: How Young People Perceive Crime and Justice* (Palgrave Macmillan, 2016). He is also co-author, with Nigel South, of *Green Cultural Criminology: Constructions of Environmental Harm, Consumerism, and Resistance to Ecocide* (Routledge, 2014); co-editor, with Nigel South, of the *Routledge International Handbook of Green Criminology* (2013); and co-editor, with Nigel South and Rob White, of *Environmental Crime and Social Conflict: Contemporary and Emerging Issues* (Ashgate, 2015). His forthcoming publications include *Water, Crime and Security in the Twenty-First Century: Too Dirty, Too Little, Too Much*, co-authored with Bill McClanahan, Nigel South and Reece Walters (Palgrave Macmillan); *Environmental Crime in Latin America: The Theft of Nature and the Poisoning of the Land*, co-edited with David Rodríguez Goyes, Hanneke Mol and Nigel South (Palgrave Macmillan); and *Introducción a la Criminología Verde: Conceptos para la Comprensión de los Conflictos Socioambientales* (translated as *Introduction to Green Criminology: Concepts for an Understanding of Socio-Environmental Conflicts*), co-edited with Hanneke Mol, David Rodríguez Goyes and Nigel South (Editorial TEMIS S.A.) – the first Spanish-language volume on green criminology. In 2015, he received the Critical Criminologist of the Year Award from the American Society of Criminology, Division on Critical Criminology.

Eamonn Carrabine is a Professor in the Department of Sociology at the University of Essex. His books include *Crime in Modern Britain* (co-authored, 2002); *Power, Discourse and Resistance: A Genealogy of the Strangeways Prison Riot* (2004); and *Crime, Culture and the Media* (2008), while the textbook he co-authors with colleagues from the University of Essex, *Criminology: A Sociological Introduction* (2014), is now in its third edition. He has recently completed a book on *Crime and Social Theory*, which will be published by Palgrave, and he currently holds a Leverhulme Trust Major Research Fellowship to research his project, 'The Iconography of Punishment: From Renaissance to Modernity', which began in 2015 and will run for three years. He is a Fellow of the Academy of Social Sciences, and in 2012 was awarded the Radzinowicz Memorial Prize for his article 'Just Images' published in the *British Journal of Criminology*. With Michelle Brown, he has co-edited the forthcoming *Routledge International Handbook of Visual Criminology*, and together they edit the journal *Crime, Media, Culture*.

Nigel South is a Professor in the Department of Sociology and Director of the Centre for Criminology at the University of Essex, UK, and is also an Adjunct Professor in the School of Justice at Queensland University of Technology, Brisbane. He is a Fellow of the Academy of Social Sciences and in 2013 received a Lifetime Achievement Award from the American Society of Criminology's Division on Critical Criminology. He has published widely on green criminology, drugs and crime, and policing. With Avi Brisman he is co-author and co-editor of a number of books, and with Eamonn Carrabine, co-author (with others) of *Criminology: A Sociological Introduction* (Routledge, 2014, 3rd edition).

Notes on contributors

Robert Agnew is Samuel Candler Dobbs Professor of Sociology at Emory University.

Biko Agozino is a Professor in the Department of Sociology at Virginia Polytechnic Institute and State University.

Martin A. Andresen is a Professor in the School of Criminology and Director of the Institute for Canadian Urban Research Studies at Simon Fraser University.

Bruce A. Arrigo is a Professor in the Department of Criminal Justice and Criminology at the University of North Carolina at Charlotte.

Matthew Ball is a Senior Lecturer in the School of Justice at Queensland University of Technology.

Gregg Barak is a Professor in the Department of Sociology, Anthropology and Criminology at Eastern Michigan University.

Kimberly L. Barrett is an Assistant Professor in the Sociology, Anthropology and Criminology Department at Eastern Michigan University.

Anthony Beech is a Professor in the School of Psychology and Head of the Centre for Forensic and Criminological Psychology at the University of Birmingham.

Piers Beirne is a Professor in the Department of Criminology, Economics and Sociology at the University of Southern Maine.

Joanne Belknap is a former President of the American Society of Criminology, a Professor in the Department of Ethnic Studies at the University of Colorado at Boulder, and an Adjunct Professor in the School of Justice at Queensland University of Technology.

Nachman Ben-Yehuda is a Professor in the Department of Sociology and Anthropology at the Hebrew University of Jerusalem.

Colleen M. Berryessa is a PhD candidate in the Department of Criminology at the University of Pennsylvania.

Joel Best is a Professor in the Department of Sociology and Criminal Justice at the University of Delaware.

Shane Blackman is Professor of Cultural Studies in the School of Media, Art and Design at Canterbury Christ Church University.

Kristie R. Blevins is an Associate Professor in the School of Justice Studies at Eastern Kentucky University.

Benjamin Bowling is a Professor and Acting Dean of the Dickson Poon School of Law at King's College London.

Nicholas Branic is a doctoral student in the Department of Criminology, Law and Society at the University of California, Irvine.

Michelle Brown is an Associate Professor in the Department of Sociology at the University of Tennessee.

Phil Carney is a Lecturer in the School of Social Policy, Sociology and Social Research at the University of Kent.

Kerry Carrington is a Professor in and Head of the School of Justice, Faculty of Law at Queensland University of Technology.

Leonidas K. Cheliotis is an Assistant Professor in the Department of Social Policy at the London School of Economics and Political Science.

Heith Copes is a Professor in the Department of Justice Studies and the Director of Graduate Studies in Criminal Justice at the University of Alabama at Birmingham.

Chris Cunneen is a Professor in the School of Social Sciences at the University of New South Wales and an Adjunct Professor at the Cairns Institute, James Cook University.

Elliott P. Currie is a Professor in the Department of Criminology, Law and Society at the University of California, Irvine and an Adjunct Professor in the School of Justice at Queensland University of Technology.

Graham Davies is an Emeritus Professor in the Department of Neuroscience, Psychology and Behaviour at the University of Leicester.

Pam Davies is an Associate Professor in the Department of Social Sciences at Northumbria University.

Albert de la Tierra is a PhD candidate in sociology at the CUNY Graduate Center, and a lecturer of sociology at Hunter College and the John Jay College of Criminal Justice.

Walter S. DeKeseredy is the Anna Deane Carlson Endowed Chair of Social Sciences, Director of the Research Center on Violence, and a Professor in the

Department of Sociology and Anthropology at West Virginia University, as well as an Adjunct Professor in the School of Justice at Queensland University of Technology.

Geert Dhondt is an Assistant Professor in the Department of Economics at the John Jay College of Justice, City University of New York.

Joseph F. Donnermeyer is a Professor Emeritus in the School of Environment and Natural Resources at The Ohio State University and an Adjunct Professor with the Research Center on Violence at West Virginia University and the School of Justice at Queensland University of Technology.

Deborah Drake is a Senior Lecturer in the Department of Social Policy and Criminology at the Open University.

Adam J. Duso is a graduate student in the Department of Criminal Justice and Criminology at the University of North Carolina at Charlotte.

Meredith Edelman is a PhD student in the School of Regulation and Global Governance at Australian National University.

Karen Evans is a Senior Lecturer in the Department of Sociology, Policy and Criminology at the University of Liverpool.

David P. Farrington is an Emeritus Professor of Psychological Criminology at the Institute of Criminology, Cambridge University.

Luis A. Fernandez is a Professor in the Department of Criminology and Criminal Justice in Northern Arizona University.

Jeff Ferrell is a Professor in the Department of Sociology and Anthropology at Texas Christian University and a Visiting Professor of Criminology in the School of Social Policy, Sociology and Social Research at the University of Kent.

Michael Fiddler is a Senior Lecturer in the Department of Law at the University of Greenwich.

Peter Fussey is a Professor in the Department of Sociology at the University of Essex.

Emily Gaarder is an Associate Professor in the Sociology-Anthropology Department at the University of Minnesota Duluth.

David Gadd is a Professor in the Centre for Criminology and Criminal Justice in the School of Law at the University of Manchester.

Carole Gibbs is an Associate Professor in the School of Criminal Justice at Michigan State University.

Erich Goode is an Emeritus Professor in the Department of Sociology at the State University of New York (SUNY) at Stony Brook.

Meredith L. Gore is an Associate Professor in the Department of Fisheries and Wildlife and the School of Criminal Justice at Michigan State University.

Cecil E. Greek is an Associate Professor in the Department of Sociology at the University of South Florida.

Gill Green is a Professor in the School of Health and Human Sciences at the University of Essex.

Penny Green is a Professor in the Department of Law at Queen Mary, University of London.

Olivia K. Ha is a PhD candidate in the School of Criminology at Simon Fraser University.

Matthew Hall is a Professor at Lincoln Law School at the University of Lincoln.

Steve Hall is a Professor in the School of Social Sciences, Business and Law at Teesside University.

Mark Halsey is a Professor of Criminology in the Centre for Crime Policy and Research, Flinders University.

Joseph A. Hamm is an Assistant Professor in the Environmental Science and Policy Program and School of Criminal Justice at Michigan State University.

Lynn Hancock is a Senior Lecturer in the Department of Sociology, Policy and Criminology at the University of Liverpool.

Nathan Harris is a Visitor in the School of Regulation and Global Governance at Australian National University.

Keith Hayward is a Professor of Criminology in the Faculty of Law at the University of Copenhagen.

Kathryn (Kate) Henne is an Assistant Professor in the Department of Sociology and Legal Studies at the University of Waterloo.

Dick Hobbs is a Professor in the Institute of Cultural Studies at Western Sydney University, Emeritus Professor at the University of Essex, and an Associate Fellow of the Royal United Services Institute.

Russell Hogg is a Professor in the School of Justice at Queensland University of Technology.

Clive R. Hollin is an Emeritus Professor in the Department of Neuroscience, Psychology and Behaviour at the University of Leicester.

Gordon Hughes is a Professor in the School of Social Sciences at Cardiff University.

Wim Huisman is a Professor in the Department of Criminal Law and Criminology at Vrije Universiteit Amsterdam.

Scott A. Hunt is a Professor in the School of Justice Studies at Eastern Kentucky University.

Ben Hunter is a Senior Lecturer in the Department of Law at the University of Greenwich.

Jonathan Ilan is a Senior Lecturer in the Department of Sociology at City, University of London.

Tony Jefferson is an Emeritus Professor in the School of Social Science and Public Policy at Keele University and an Adjunct Professor in the School of Justice at Queensland University of Technology.

Gary Jensen is an Emeritus Professor in the Department of Sociology at Vanderbilt University.

Helen Johnston is Reader in Criminology in the School of Education and Social Sciences at the University of Hull.

Victor E. Kappeler is a Foundation Professor in the School of Justice Studies and Dean of the College of Justice and Safety at Eastern Kentucky University.

Andrew Krebs is a doctoral student in the Department of Sociology at the University of Texas at Austin.

Charis E. Kubrin is a Professor in the Department of Criminology, Law and Society at the University of California, Irvine.

Gloria Laycock is a Professor of Crime Science in the Jill Dando Institute at University College London.

John Lea is an Honorary Professor of Criminology at the University of Roehampton.

Martine Synnøve Bergersen Lie holds a master's degree in criminology from the Department of Criminology and Sociology of Law at the University of Oslo, and is currently working with the Norwegian Animal Protection Alliance.

Shichun Ling is a doctoral student in the Department of Criminology at the University of Pennsylvania.

Randy K. Lippert is a Professor in the Department of Sociology, Anthropology and Criminology at the University of Windsor.

Michael J. Lynch is a Professor in the Department of Criminology at the University of South Florida.

Nick Malleson is an Associate Professor in the School of Geography at the University of Leeds.

Shadd Maruna is Professor of Criminology at the University of Manchester.

Roger Matthews is a Professor in the School of Social Policy, Sociology and Social Research at the University of Kent.

Mackenzie McBride is a graduate student in the Department of Criminal Justice and Criminology at Georgia Southern University.

James W. Messerschmidt is a Professor in the Department of Criminology, Economics and Sociology at the University of Southern Maine.

Gareth Millington is a Senior Lecturer in the Department of Sociology at the University of York.

Pat O'Malley is Distinguished Honorary Professor, College of Arts and Social Sciences, Australian National University.

Ken Pease is a Visiting Professor of Crime Science in the Department of Security and Crime Science at University College London and in the Department of Social Sciences at Loughborough University.

Hal Pepinsky is a Professor Emeritus in the Department of Criminal Justice at Indiana University Bloomington.

Stephen Pfohl is a Professor in the Sociology Department at Boston College.

Chad Posick is an Assistant Professor in the Department of Criminal Justice and Criminology at Georgia Southern University.

Gary W. Potter is a Professor in the School of Justice Studies and Associate Dean of the College of Justice and Safety at Eastern Kentucky University.

Scott Poynting is an Adjunct Professor in the School of Psychology and Social Sciences at Western Sydney University and in the School of Justice at Queensland University of Technology.

Lois (Lo) Presser is a Professor and Associate Head of the Department of Sociology at the University of Tennessee.

Adrian Raine is the Richard Perry University Professor in the Departments of Criminology, Psychiatry, and Psychology at the University of Pennsylvania.

Robert Reiner is an Emeritus Professor in the Law Department at the London School of Economics and Political Science.

Claire M. Renzetti is the Judi Conway Patton Endowed Chair for Studies of Violence Against Women in the Center for Research on Violence Against Women, and Professor and Chair of the Department of Sociology at the University of Kentucky.

Jose Rivera is a doctoral student in the Department of Education at California State University, San Bernardino.

Louie Rivers III is an Assistant Professor in the Department of Forestry and Natural Resources at North Carolina State University.

Melissa Rorie is an Assistant Professor in the Department of Criminal Justice at the University of Nevada, Las Vegas.

Jeffrey Ian Ross is a Professor in the School of Criminal Justice and a fellow at the Center for International and Comparative Law and a fellow at the Schaefer Center for Public Policy at the University of Baltimore.

Lee E. Ross is an Associate Professor in the Department of Criminal Justice at the University of Central Florida.

Vincenzo Ruggiero is a Professor in the Department of Criminology and Sociology at Middlesex University.

Sveinung Sandberg a Professor in the Department of Criminology and Sociology of Law at the University of Oslo.

Judah Schept is an Associate Professor in the School of Justice Studies at Eastern Kentucky University.

Susie Scott is a Professor in the Department of Sociology at the University of Sussex.

Phil Scraton is a Professor in the School of Law at Queen's University Belfast.

Sarah Senker is a chartered psychologist with a PhD in health and human sciences, and Director of ATD Research & Consultancy, Ltd.

Damien Short is a Reader and Director of the Human Rights Consortium at the School of Advanced Study at the University of London.

Joe Sim is a Professor in the School of Humanities and Social Science at Liverpool John Moores University.

Martha J. Smith is an Associate Professor at the School of Community Affairs at Wichita State University.

Jennifer Snyder is a doctoral student in the Department of Sociology and Criminal Justice at the University of Delaware.

Ragnhild Sollund is a Professor in the Department of Criminology and Sociology of Law at the University of Oslo.

Dale C. Spencer is an Assistant Professor in the Department of Law and Legal Studies at Carleton University.

Peter Squires is a Professor in the School of Applied Social Sciences at the University of Brighton.

Juan Tauri is a Lecturer in the School of Health and Society at the University of Wollongong.

Stephen G. Tibbetts is a Professor in the Department of Criminal Justice at California State University, San Bernardino.

Stephen Tomsen is a Professor at the Institute for Culture and Society at Western Sydney University.

Emily I. Troshynski is an Assistant Professor in the Department of Criminal Justice at the University of Nevada, Las Vegas.

Jackie Turton is a Professor in the Department of Sociology at the University of Essex.

Judith van Erp is a Professor of Public Institutions at Universiteit Utrecht.

Reece Walters is a Professor in the School of Justice and Director of the Crime and Justice Research Centre at Queensland University of Technology.

Mark Warr is a Professor in the Department of Sociology at the University of Texas at Austin.

Craig Webber is an Associate Professor in the Division of Sociology, Social Policy and Criminology in the University of Southampton.

Sophie Westenra is a Research Fellow at the Dickson Poon School of Law at King's College London.

Elizabeth Whalley is a PhD candidate in the Department of Sociology at the University of Colorado at Boulder.

Rob White is a Professor in the School of Social Sciences at the University of Tasmania.

Christopher R. Williams is a Professor in the Department of Criminal Justice Studies at Bradley University.

Simon Winlow is a Professor in the School of Social Sciences, Business and Law at Teesside University.

Anne Worrall is an Emerita Professor in the School of Social Science and Public Policy at Keele University.

Adam Zwickle is an Assistant Professor in the Environmental Science and Policy Program and School of Criminal Justice at Michigan State University.

Preface

The Routledge Companion to Criminological Theory and Concepts (the '*Companion*') is a resource designed for all – from undergraduate and graduate students to seasoned academics. Its goal is to introduce a wide range of criminological theories and conceptual themes, explaining their emergence, context (historical, social, disciplinary/institutional), evolution and current status. Thus, the *Companion* serves as a study guide to assist introductory students in their understandings of key theories and concepts and their relationship to each other (especially for those students whose primary text is a reader); as a reference starting point for advanced students (as evidenced, in part, by a list of 'Further reading' at the end of each essay); as a 'memory-jogger' or 'refresher' for scholars and researchers; and as a snapshot of the present and a bit of crystal ball-gazing for the future.

Comprehensive in scope and content, and drawing on the expertise of contributors from around the world, the *Companion* contains authoritative essays written by leading scholars in the field with considerable international reputations. Each theory or concept is encapsulated in a short essay (approximately 1,500 words) and each essay serves as a stand-alone 'chapter' in one of the following six historical or thematic parts (each of which begins with a short introduction):

Part 1   Foundations of criminological thought and contemporary revitalizations
Part 2   The emergence and growth of American criminology
Part 3   From appreciation to critique
Part 4   Late critical criminologies and new directions
Part 5   Punishment and security
Part 6   Geographies of crime

The essays in Parts 1 and 2 are organized somewhat chronologically to reflect some of the intellectual history, development and genealogy of criminological thought (as illustrated in 'A Map of Criminological Theory Development' on pp. 144–5); the essays in Parts 3–6, which present theories and concepts that emerged at various overlapping periods, are organized alphabetically. In an effort to acknowledge and underscore that, over time, a good number of theories increasingly coexisted and developed in complementary, critical or synergistic fashion, clear cross-referencing provides readers with signposts to earlier and later developments, to critiques and to associated theoretical directions described in other essays.

In order to allow readers to grasp concepts, theories and topics from the start, each essay adopts somewhat of a pyramid structure, with an overview at 'the top' opening out into further detail and additional directions. The beginning of each essay sets out a very clear definition or description of the theory or concept in order to convey its significance so that the reader can immediately grasp its criminological importance. That said, not all of the essays contain all of the same kind of content, but each endeavours to provide:

- the historical, intellectual and social context regarding the theory or concept;
- the key dimensions of the theory or concept;
- the development of and changes shaping the theory or concept and its treatment in the literature;
- the current status of the theory or concept (e.g., cutting edge? alive and well? dead or dying? an historical relic?) and how it is employed and applied today (if relevant); and
- future development and directions (if relevant).

With relatively short essays, contributors have dispensed with summaries or conclusions at the end. In an effort to make the pieces accessible and engaging, contributors have offered simple, clear, crisp pieces without sub-headings or footnotes/endnotes, and with minimal quotations. The essays are not embellished, and evidence is presented and summarized without referring to every single publication related to it. The authors have sought to avoid bias so that, as a work of reference, readers can expect to find all major, serious points of view in a concise but balanced account of a theory or concept. Readers are directed to additional works ('Further reading') that elaborate points made in the individual essays, offer complementary approaches or represent competing perspectives.

The idea for the *Companion* originated from a conversation between Tom Sutton, Senior Editor for Criminology at Routledge, and us at the Annual Meeting of the American Society of Criminology in Atlanta in November 2013. Although we were initially hesitant about undertaking such a monumental endeavour in a market flush with criminological theory books, with Tom's encouragement we realized we had an opportunity to produce a volume sensitive to the rich (and growing) intellectual history of criminological thought that would be broader than some texts, more focused than others and more thematically oriented than still others. As we developed our proposal and began contacting potential contributors, our list of theories and concepts grew. Thus, the *Companion* contains more than 100 essays by close to 150 authors. We are grateful to Tom for his ongoing support; to Hannah Catterall (Editorial Assistant for Criminology at Routledge) for her assistance, enthusiasm and patience; and to our contributors for their time, effort and work. Finally, an International Visiting Fellowship in the Department of Sociology at the University of Essex allowed Avi to come to Colchester in Spring 2017 so that the three of us could complete the project. Our hope is that as criminology continues to flourish and develop, future editions will reflect yet further new ideas.

Avi Brisman
Eamonn Carrabine
Nigel South
Colchester, Essex, UK
April 2017

A rendezvous subject? A fragmented discipline?

An introduction to *The Routledge Companion to Criminological Theory and Concepts*

Criminology refers to the study of the *nature, extent, causes* and *consequences* of acts and omissions that are proscribed by a region's criminal code. It also includes inquiries and considerations of our individual and collective responses to harmful and lawbreaking behaviour; the *meaning* of crime to those who engage in such behaviour and are affected by it; and the ways in which crime is depicted, described, discussed and portrayed by the media.

Although the term criminology is often attributed to the Italian law professor Raffaele Garofalo in the late nineteenth century (see Lanier and Henry 2010:16, citing Garofalo 1914), the study of crime at the individual and societal level preceded Garofalo by more than a century. In general, contemporary *criminology* differs from the study of *criminal justice* in that the latter is often conceptualized as the study of crime *control* approaches, philosophies, policies and practices used by governments – specifically, law enforcement officers and agencies, courts and systems of corrections – in order to uphold social order. *Criminal justice* centres on *preventing* and *mitigating* crime, as well as on *sanctioning* those who violate criminal laws.

Like *criminal justice, victimology* is a relatively recent field, tracing its origins to the mid-twentieth-century work of Hans von Hentig (1948) and Benjamin Mendelsohn (1963) (see Walklate 2007). Schafer (1977:35) refers to victimology as the 'reverse of criminology' insofar as victimology pertains to the study of who becomes a victim (and who does not); who is labelled a 'victim' and who identifies as such; the ways in which victims are victimized; how much harm they suffer; their role in criminal acts and omissions; and their rights and roles in the criminal justice system.

Finally, *crime science* is the newest of these related fields, having emerged since the mid-1990s (see Laycock 2005). Unabashedly committed to reducing crime (rather than studying it as a social phenomenon), it focuses on *crime* rather than *criminals*, and seeks to employ experimental approaches and scientific principles.

While *criminology*, *criminal justice*, *victimology* and *crime science* represent discrete areas, there is obviously some overlap – and, indeed, this volume recognizes as much with explicit essays entitled 'Crime science' and 'Victimology', as well as with a sprinkling of *types* of crimes with theoretical implications or resonance (e.g., 'Financial crime', 'Genocide and ecocide', 'Hate crime', 'Organized crime', 'State crime', 'State-corporate crime' and 'White-collar crime'). That said, our focus is primarily *criminological* – and on the study of crime as a social phenomenon (as opposed to a legal or forensic one). The preponderance of these essays, then, attempt to shed light on questions of *why people commit crimes*, as well as why people do not.

With this disciplinary backdrop, a word about *theory* is in order. In daily parlance, we often use the word theory to mean a guess or a set of ideas based on a wide range of support to account for or explain a situation or to justify a course of action. Examples might include: 'My theory for why the Chicago Cubs finally won the World Series is that . . .' or 'I have a theory as to what is wrong with English football and why the national team keeps failing in the World Cup'. In the academic world, *theory* means something a little different. A narrow conception of theory would be an explanation of a circumstance or happening based on experimentation, systematic observation and reasoning. A narrow view of *criminological theory*, then, would be a group of ideas that purport to offer a causal explanation of crime. If, however, we consider *theory* as encompassing ideas and tools for describing and analysing *why* things are as they are; *who* engages in various behaviours, patterns and practices; and *how* we do – or might – interpret and ascribe meaning to those behaviours, patterns and practices (and to the consequences thereof), then criminology is much more elaborate and rich, and its influence and impact far more substantial (Brisman 2014:24). In other words, a notion of *criminological theory* that includes ideas about *interpretation*, in addition to *explanation and prediction* – indeed, a *criminology* that is a marriage of humanistic and scientific ways of thinking about crime (Wilson 2014:107) – is one that we find more robust, rewarding and, well, *interesting*. That said, we recognize that many students, professors and contributors to this volume may hold a less expansive definition of *theory*. In an effort, then, to avoid claims that a particular approach does not merit the title of 'theory' – and in an attempt to prevent assertions that a certain orientation demands inclusion as a 'theory' – we have elected to call this volume *The Routledge Companion to Criminological Theory and Concepts* (and thus leave it to others to decide which essays describe 'theories' and which cover 'concepts').

Putting aside the question of what *theory* is – or should be – we would be remiss if we did not acknowledge that criminology is unique among academic disciplines in that it studies a single topic (broadly conceived, crime/harm) from a variety of perspectives rather than a range of topics from a common perspective, as anthropology, psychology and sociology do (see Agnew 2011:13; Cullen et al. 2014:1; see also Brisman 2012a; Carrabine 2016). As Cullen and colleagues (2014:1) explain:

> In biology, for example, Charles Darwin's theory of evolution provides the organizing framework that virtually all serious scientists embrace. Economists as a field share the assumption that human behavior is self-interested and based on rational choice – the pursuit of benefits over costs. Both biologists and economists disagree among themselves a great deal and develop different ideas about how the world operates, but they tend to do so within the parameters of an overriding paradigm.

Criminology, in contrast, lacks a prevailing paradigm to which most scholars subscribe. Over the years, various perspectives have gained popularity, fallen out of favour and then received renewed interest and enthusiasm (as we attempt to demonstrate in 'A Map of Criminological Theory Development' on pp. 144–5). Cohn and Iratzoqui (2016) have found that the most highly cited works in five major international criminology journals have been in the areas of developmental and life-course criminology and criminal careers, but whether this trend will continue remains to be seen, and debates will persist over whether such studies really reflect scholarly influence. Perhaps, then, we should not be surprised that Barak (2003:219) has observed that there is rarely 'any type of integration or accommodation between establishment and anti-establishment criminologies', while DeKeseredy (2011:57) has claimed that '[c]riminology is fragmented and academic criminology is under siege'.

We recognize that 'social problems like crime . . . will not be solved through the use of any single lens' (O'Connor 2015:175). We also take inspiration from Friedrichs (1996:123), who has proposed that 'a plurality of perspectives and approaches has the . . . potential to reach the largest number of people', while Michalowski (1996:9) has suggested that 'we can best arrive at useful truth by telling and hearing multiple versions of the same story'. If criminology is to continue to enjoy being a 'rendezvous' subject or discipline rather than a fragmented one – as various scholars have suggested (Downes 1988; Hayward and Young 2004) – then we would encourage the type of pluralism proffered by Friedrichs and Michalowski and others.

Before turning to the entries in this volume, one final word is in order. In his influential book on *desistance* (or the processes by which former offenders discontinue their involvement in criminal activities and create new lives for themselves), Maruna writes:

The creation of bogeymen may serve a distinct social purpose. If there is no common enemy, no Them, perhaps there can be no Us. Yet creating a Them also essentially relieves Us from having to examine ourselves for signs of deviance. If crime is something that wicked people do, we need not worry that our own behavior is wrong. Despite occasional transgressions, we do not expect to be treated like 'some kind of common criminal.' In the black-and-white world of good guys and bad guys, one is either a good person who makes some forgivable mistakes or a common criminal who deserves no sympathy.

[. . .]

[T]he myth of the bogeyman has its most profound influence in societies passing through uncertain times.

(2001:5, citing Irwin 1985)

Arguably, around the world, the first twenty years of the twenty-first century have been uncertain and volatile, and we are witnessing increasing expressions of 'Us' vs. 'Them' (with only vague notions of what constitutes 'Us' – or 'Them'). While there are frequently assertions of 'Us-es' and 'Thems' in criminology, and while we may lack optimism for a unified criminology along the lines of Agnew (2011) – and even question its desirability (see Brisman 2012a, b) – we think criminology has much to offer in distinguishing 'occasional transgressions' from 'pure wickedness', 'forgivable mistakes' deserving sympathy from unconscionable horror, and deviance 'from within' from deviance 'from without'. In sum, we agree with Matthews (2014:30) that '[t]heory should never be an end in itself but a tool for analyzing substantive social problems', and we hope that the ideas in this volume can help.

References

Agnew, Robert. 2011. *Toward a Unified Criminology: Integrating Assumptions about Crime, People, and Society*. New York and London: New York University Press.

Barak, Gregg. 2003. Revisionist History, Visionary Criminology, and Needs-Based Justice. *Contemporary Justice Review* 6(3): 217–25.

Brisman, Avi. 2012a. Review of *Toward a Unified Criminology: Integrating Assumptions about Crime, People, and Society*. *Theoretical Criminology* 16(4): 525–7.

Brisman, Avi. 2012b. *Toward a Unified Criminology: Integrating Assumptions about Crime, People, and Society*: A Commentary. *Journal of Theoretical and Philosophical Criminology* 4(2): 54–64.

Brisman, Avi. 2014. Of Theory and Meaning in Green Criminology. *International Journal of Crime, Justice and Social Democracy* 3(2): 22–35.

Carrabine, Eamonn. 2016. Changing Fortunes: Criminology and the Sociological Condition. *Sociology* 50(5): 847–62.

Cohn, Ellen G., and Amaia Iratzoqui. 2016. The Most Cited Scholars in Five International Criminology Journals, 2006–10. *British Journal of Criminology* 56(3): 602–23.

Cullen, Francis T., Robert Agnew, and Pamela Wilcox. 2014. *Criminological Theory: Past to Present* (5th edn). New York and Oxford: Oxford University Press.

DeKeseredy, Walter S. 2011. *Contemporary Critical Criminology*. London and New York: Routledge.

Downes, David. 1988. The Sociology of Crime and Social Control in Britain, 1960–1987. *British Journal of Criminology* 28(2): 175–87.

Garofalo, Raffaele. 1914. *Criminology*. Translated by Robert Wyness Millar. Boston: Little, Brown.

Friedrichs, David O. 1996. Critical Criminology and Progressive Pluralism: Strength in Diversity for These Times. *Critical Criminology* 7(1): 121–8.

Hayward, Keith J., and Jock Young. 2004. Cultural Criminology: Some Notes on the Script. *Theoretical Criminology* 8(3): 250–73.

Irwin, J. 1985. The Return of the Bogeyman. Keynote lecture at the meeting of the American Society of Criminology, November, San Diego, CA.

Lanier, Mark M., and Stuart Henry. 2010. *Essential Criminology* (3rd edn). Boulder, CO: Westview.

Laycock, Gloria. 2005. Defining crime science. In *Crime Science: New Approaches to Preventing and Detecting Crime*, Melissa J. Smith and Nick Tilley, eds, pp. 3–24. Cullompton, UK: Willan.

Maruna, Shadd. 2001. *Making Good: How Ex-Convicts Reform and Rebuild Their Lives*. Washington, DC: American Psychological Association.

Matthews, Roger. 2014. *Realist Criminology*. Basingstoke: Palgrave Macmillan.

Mendelsohn, Benjamin. 1963. The Origin of the Doctrine of Victimology. *Excerpta Criminologica* 3(3): 239–44.

Michalowski, Raymond J. 1996. Critical Criminology and the Critique of Domination: The Story of an Intellectual Movement. *Critical Criminology* 7(1): 9–16.

O'Connor, Patricia E. 2015. Telling moments: narrative hot spots in accounts of criminal acts. In *Narrative Criminology: Understanding Stories of Crime*, Lois Presser and Sveinung Sandberg, eds, pp. 174–204. New York and London: New York University Press.

Schafer, Stephen. 1977. *Victimology: The Victim and His Criminal*. Reston, VA: Reston.

von Hentig, Hans. 1948. *The Criminal and His Victim*. New Haven, CT: Yale University Press.

Walklate, Sandra (ed.). 2007. *Handbook of Victims and Victimology*. Cullompton, UK: Willan.

Wilson, Jeffrey R. 2014. Shakespeare and Criminology. *Crime Media Culture* 10(2): 97–114.

Part 1

Foundations of criminological thought and contemporary revitalizations

Part 1 Introduction

The earliest theories of crime reflected religious and spiritual beliefs – ideas based on theological understanding of the battle between Good and Evil. Crime was thought to be the result of supernatural forces: people engaged in crime because they were possessed by forces of Evil or had submitted to the temptations of Satan. According to such a 'demonic perspective,' crime was considered an offence against God (or gods or some other deity or deities) and brutal, corporeal punishment was inflicted in order to 'purify' those guilty of crime.

This approach continued into the 1700s, when it was challenged by Enlightenment thinkers Cesare Beccaria and Jeremy Bentham (often considered the father of *utilitarianism*). Drawing on the ideas of the philosopher Thomas Hobbes, what has become known as the Classical School of criminology criticized the demonic perspective and its attendant forms of punishment, arguing instead that: individuals exercise free will in making their decisions; individuals are rational beings who pursue their own interests by attempting to maximize their pleasure and minimize their pain; and individuals may engage in crime in pursuit of their self-interests unless they are deterred by the threat of swift, certain and appropriately severe punishments.

Classical criminology predominated for about a century – from the late 1700s to the late 1800s. Rising crime rates (despite changes in the legal system and punishment inspired by the Classical School) and emerging evidence that punished offenders might be *more*, rather than *less*, inclined to continue their criminal ways led to criticisms of classical criminology. Most notably, Cesare Lombroso, an Italian physician, argued that criminals are anything *but* normal, rational individuals who choose to offend in pursuit of their self-interests. Rather, drawing on Charles Darwin's theory of evolution, Lombroso contended that criminals are 'atavistic' in their origin – savages living in a primitive state. Through physical examinations of criminals, Lombroso developed a list of traits that, he maintained, could be employed to differentiate 'born criminals' from others.

Lombroso's individualistic theory of crime held sway into the first half of the twentieth century, when changing demographics in the United States caused criminologists and sociologists to examine social environments. Subsequent trait studies also failed to find that physical features could distinguish criminals from non-criminals, and that biological factors could lead directly to crime. For these reasons, along with concerns over the policy implications of Lombroso's ideas (eugenics through selective breeding and sterilization), biological theories fell out of favour. By the mid-1950s, sociological theories had come to dominate criminology, and, by and large, most attempts to explain crime are sociological in orientation (see Part 2: The emergence and growth of American criminology).

In the intellectual history of criminology, the popularity of various theories has tended to ebb and flow. While both Beccaria and Lombroso argued that crime is caused by *natural* rather than *supernatural* forces, and while both Beccaria's classical criminology and Lombroso's biological explanations became unfashionable, their influence endures.

Beccaria's assertions that offenders are rational thinkers who freely elect to engage in crime serve as the basis for many legal systems. The aspiration of 'blind justice' – that the law should be applied equally to everyone – also comes from classical criminology, as do contemporary attempts to enhance the certainty and severity of punishment. Moreover, criminological research and scholarship in the mid-1980s to the present has revived interest in classical theory (see the essays on 'Rational choice' and 'Deterrence' in this part), while many 'control' theorists (see Part 2) regard classical theory as essentially early control theory.

Although no serious criminologist would consider criminals to be 'genetic throwbacks' à la Lombroso, positivist criminologists owe much to the path forged by Lombroso. Use of a scientific approach to the study of criminals has become one of the primary strategies employed by contemporary criminologists. In addition, technological innovations in brain imaging and genetics have contributed to the re-emergence of biological and individual trait theories of crime. A growing number of criminologists today have endeavoured (and continue) to attempt to consider background and situational factors across an individual's lifetime in their explanations of crime, as well as interweaving biological, psychological and sociological theories.

1.1 Religion, spirituality and crime

Stephen Pfohl

The earliest theories of crime are religious theories – ideas rooted in theological beliefs about warring supernatural forces in a cosmic battle between good and evil. God-fearing people who obey divinely ordained laws are pictured as pious or saintly, while criminals who transgress God's commandments are viewed as sinners. Religious viewpoints also envision the causes of lawbreaking in supernatural terms. Evildoers are imagined as succumbing to demonic temptation and deserving of divine punishment. Sinful criminal acts have also occasionally been attributed not to the guilty mind (*mens rea*) of an offender but to the notion that she or he has become 'possessed' by a demonic spirit. In such cases, religious officials may perform rites of exorcism to expel the demon rather punish the possessed offender. While rooted in a religious theory of demonic 'indwelling,' the idea that someone may commit a crime because he/she is possessed foreshadows later secular criminological viewpoints, particularly the idea that 'criminally insane' offenders, 'labouring under a defect of reason' when committing a crime, should be committed for psychiatric treatment rather than held legally responsible and punished.

Another feature of religious theories involves crime's cosmic consequences. This is due to the fact that crime, like everything else, is believed to take place in an enchanted world of invisible spiritual connections. Crime's effects are thus never limited to individual injury, but impact the universe as a whole. Especially egregious crimes may throw the entire cosmic order out of balance until evildoers are brought to justice and spiritual communion is restored. Religious viewpoints on crime such as this, while hegemonic in medieval thought, found little currency in the modern capitalist/colonial era. Indeed, from the late eighteenth century to the present, a plethora of criminological theories, while competing for influence with each other, have each explained crime in unabashedly secular terms.

While naturalistic theories are today taken for granted by most criminologists, religious interpretations have not disappeared entirely. Think only of how crime is theorized by media-savvy evangelical Christian organizations such as the US-based *The Moral Majority*. For decades, groups like the Moral Majority have painted a picture of crime, delinquency, drug abuse and mass incarceration as signs of immorality and widespread spiritual malaise. Accordingly, for crime control to be effective, society must first undergo widespread spiritual revival. Messages to this effect are repeated daily in fundamentalist Christian churches and media, and by televangelists such as Reverend Jerry Falwell, a founder of the Moral Majority and Liberty University in Lynchburg, Virginia. For 50 years Falwell hosted the weekly *Old Time Gospel Hour*, a highly influential conduit for conservative Christian thought and politics, watched by millions.

Falwell's fierce religious criminology was nowhere more on display than in the immediate aftermath of the terrorist attacks of September 11, 2011. Conversing on TV with Reverend Pat Robinson, another influential televangelist, Falwell interpreted the attacks as a sign that God had lifted his 'curtain of protection' and allowed the United States' enemies 'to give us what we probably deserve.' Robinson concurred, pointing the finger with Falwell at those 'who've got to bear some of the burden of this' – people who 'mock God' but 'God will not be mocked': 'abortionists,' 'pagans,' 'feminists,' 'gays and lesbians,' civil libertarians and secular humanists of various stripes.

For further evidence of the continuing influence of religious theories one need venture no further than the other side of the 9/11 attacks. The attacks were, after all, accounted for in explicit religious terms by the jihadists who perpetrated them. Citing the 'evils' of a US foreign policy that allegedly targeted Muslims, Al-Qaeda theorist Osama Bin Laden claimed that the attacks were carried out with God's blessing in defence of Islam. Although Bin Laden's theology of terror has been condemned by leading Islamic scholars the globe over, Salafist justifications for extreme violence against 'infidels' are again being offered by **terrorists** aligned with *Daesh* or the self-declared Islamic State (IS/ISIS).

See Chapter 4.19 Institutional/ anti-institutional violence

Conservative religious interpreters of the three Abrahamic religions – Judaism, Christianity and Islam – often cite related scriptural grounds for harsh punishment of criminals. Consider the Old Testament precept of 'an eye for an eye' or *lex talionis*, a principle advocated by righteous adherents of all three monotheistic religions – although dispensed with by Jesus' New Testament proclamation of God's love and forgiveness. Thus, a thief's hand should be cut off, as should the penis of a rapist; and the tongue of a liar and the heart of a traitor should be cut out. Someone who takes another's life is said to deserve the same. Bloody punishments of this sort convey strong religious messages and were said to give criminals a glimpse of the hell that awaited them in the afterlife (Newman 1978: 46).

The predominant story of crime told by Abrahamic religions has also been a **patriarchal** story; and the orthodox legal codes of Jews, Christians and Muslims are replete with negative images of women as second-class citizens in the spiritual realm or, worse yet, as temptresses who lead men to sin. The opening chapters of *Genesis*, the first book of the Bible, provide a template for this criminological displacement of women. Eve – seduced by the wily Serpent (a pre-monotheistic Mesopotamian symbol of the Earth as a sacred 'Mother of All the Living') – tempts Adam with fruit from the tree from which God had forbidden them to eat. Eve's treachery, we are taught, resulted in humankind's first crime – and banishment from Paradise. In this way, making Eve an archetype figure for 'original sin' casts a negative theological shadow on women, making women a target for men's religious fears and fervours, resentments and suspicion. But nowhere in Occidental history was criminal law used more viciously in the service of patriarchy than during the so-called **'witch craze'** of the sixteenth and seventeenth centuries.

Medieval Christianity had for centuries coexisted with popular animistic beliefs revering nature as a sacred mother or goddess. While Christians residing in royal courts and urban enclaves typically embraced a more doctrinaire version of monotheism, peasants everywhere across Europe mixed the 'old religion' of 'Mother Earth' with the newer rites of 'God the Father.' This changed drastically in the late fifteenth century as inquisitors at the helms of church and state joined in a war against the crime of 'witchcraft.' The resulting campaign of terror took its theory from a papal bull issued by Innocent VIII in 1484 and was buttressed by the 1487 publication of the *Malleus Maleficarum*, a notorious guide for hunting witches authored by two Dominican monks. Citing the depiction in *Genesis* of Eve's primordial temptation of Adam, *Malleus Maleficarum* took aim at women, claiming, as did St. Augustine, that women's sexuality represented a pernicious 'gateway to the devil' (Kramer and Sprenger 1487/1971). For two centuries this misogynous handbook guided the persecution of European animists. A related religious logic was used to justify violence against the original inhabitants of Europe's colonies, where, under the auspices of 'cross and crown,' conquerors likened the animism of indigenous people to devil-worship and dealt with it accordingly, sometimes by **genocidal means**.

Eighty per cent of those accused, tortured and burnt at the stake for witchcraft in Europe were women (Barstow 1994). Common victims included midwives, single women, older women, women who practised healing and those who loved in excess of the patriarchal religious codes of the time. Accused witches were stripped naked and their hair shaved. They were then tortured, many to the 'third degree' by terrifying devices such as 'the pear,' a forceps-like metallic instrument heated red-hot and inserted into the mouth, vagina or anus. Others who were accused convulsed in terror when held

See Chapter 4.26
Patriarchy and
crime

See Chapter 3.7
Folk devils

See Chapter 4.13
Genocide and
ecocide

underwater so long they thought they were drowning – an early version of what we today call 'water boarding.' Subject to escalating pain, tortured women sometimes confessed to wild patriarchal fantasies about insatiable female lust and having sex with the Devil.

Other forms of religious punishment for crime were more symbolic, resulting more in shame than pain. A baker found to have short-weighted a buyer's loaves was punished by having bread tied around his neck. A fishmonger convicted of selling bad fish was fitted with a stinky collar of decayed smelts. Heretics who sang the praises of Judaism were forced to eat pork in public. 'Scolds' convicted of gossiping had their tongues cooled by a public dunking. Women found guilty of adultery were made to walk around with a shaved head or with a 'scarlet letter' draped over their garments.

Not all religious theories are as righteous or hurtful when imagining punishment. 'Liberation theologies' and fervent beliefs about justice, equality and human dignity have inspired campaigns to outlaw slavery and human trafficking, secure civil rights, abolish the death penalty, reduce poverty, provide sanctuary for undocumented immigrants, promote restorative justice and combat environment crime. Beliefs about God's mercy also animate 'faith-based' ministries that comfort prisoners and assist former inmates re-entering society.

Criminologists have also occasionally supplemented naturalistic theories with lessons drawn from religion or spirituality. Richard Quinney, an influential Marxist theorist of the inequities of crime control in capitalist societies, is a case in point. Quinney (1980) later incorporated elements of 'prophetic theology' and 'religious socialism' into a holistic critical framework attentive to both social justice and spiritual resonance. A related amalgam of material and spiritual concerns, including lessons drawn from Buddhism, has influenced calls for **restorative justice** and **peacemaking criminology** (Hadley 2001; Pepinski and Quinney 1991).

See Chapter 5.15 Restorative justice; Chapter 3.12 Peacemaking in criminology

While theories based on a supernatural viewpoint are no longer dominant, it is nevertheless important that criminology remain alert to the continuing influence of religion, especially in today's global society, where digitalized ideas and affects traverse the planet at the speed of light. Here occidental viewpoints about law, society and justice enter into conversation with coevolving perspectives of many sorts, some of which religiously refuse the separation between natural and supernatural judgements about crime that has been a feature of modern criminology since its inception. To converse effectively with religious viewpoints in this context, it may be necessary for criminology to supplement its modern analytic methods with modes of inquiry more closely attuned to spiritual resonance (or dissonance) and the impact this may have on crime. Developments such as this await future dialogue between theorists in criminology and religious studies.

References

Barstow, Anne Llewellyn. 1994. *Witchcraze: A New History of the European Witch Hunts.* San Francisco: Pandora.

Hadley, Michael L. 2001. *The Spiritual Roots of Restorative Justice.* Albany: State University of New York Press.

Kramer, Heinrich, and James Sprenger. 1487/1971. *The Malleus Maleficarum.* Translated by Montague Summer. New York: Dover.

Newman, Graeme. 1978. *The Punishment Response.* Philadelphia: Lippencott.

Pepinski, Harold E., and Richard Quinney (eds). 1991. *Criminology as Peacekeeping.* Bloomington: Indiana University Press.

Quinney, Richard. 1980. *Providence: The Reconstruction of Social and Moral Order.* New York: Longman.

Further reading

Armstrong, Karen. 1993. *A History of God: The 4000-Year Quest of Judaism, Christianity and Islam.* New York: Ballantine Books.

Goodstein, Laurie. 2001. Falwell's Finger-Pointing Inappropriate, Bush Says. *New York Times*, 15 September: A15.

Pfohl, Stephen. 2007. *Left Behind: Religion, Technology and Flight from the Flesh.* Victoria, Canada: CTheory Books/New World Perspectives.

Pfohl, Stephen. 2009. *Images of Deviance and Social Control: A Sociological History* (2nd edn). Long Grove, IL: Waveland Press.

Phillips, John A. 1984. *Eve: The History of an Idea.* San Francisco: Harper & Row.

Sjöö, Monica, and Barbara Mor. 1987. *The Great Cosmic Mother: Rediscovering the Religion of the Earth.* San Francisco: Harper & Row.

Classical criminology

Piers Beirne

The approach described here is variously termed 'classical criminology', 'classical theory', 'classical **deterrence** theory', 'Enlightenment criminology' and 'administrative criminology'. That it still goes under so many names suggests how difficult it might be to identify its precise content. On two features in its landscape, however, there is much agreement, at least in the Anglophone world of criminal law and criminology. One is that its theoretical inclinations were first expressed in the respective writings of the Milanese nobleman and lawyer Cesare Beccaria (1738–94) and the English jurist Jeremy Bentham (1748–1832). The other is that it continues to be identified – mistakenly or not – as much by its core belief in the doctrine of free will and its recommendations for the reform of criminal law as by its alleged polar opposite, namely, positivist criminology.

See Chapter 1.17
Deterrence

Beccaria owes his pioneering reputation almost exclusively to the 47 rambling chapters of his short treatise entitled *On Crimes and Punishments* (*Dei delitti e delle pene*, henceforth *OC&P*). The first copies were printed in Livorno, Italy, and circulated anonymously in the summer of 1764. Beccaria's *OC&P* was a product of the Italian Enlightenment – a humanist plea for the reform of criminal law; for the supremacy of the rule of law; and for the right of the individual to be free from abuse by unjust and arbitrary power. *OC&P*'s major tenets about the nature of political power and the role of criminal law in a modern enlightened society are as follows:

■ The right to punish originates not in religion or the divine right of kings, but in a voluntary social contract between a sovereign state and its citizenry. According to this social contract, citizens must sacrifice a small portion of their liberty to the state in return for protection from usurpations of power, whatever their source. The rule of law is the condition by which 'independent and isolated men come together in society. Wearied by living in an unending state of war and by a freedom rendered useless by the uncertainty of keeping it, [they] unite in society' (Beccaria 1764:9).

■ The only persons who may be punished are those who have violated criminal law.

■ The practice of judicial torture (i.e., interrogation through the infliction of physical pain) should be abolished.

■ The death penalty should be abolished because it is not effective in deterring crime. Deterrence can succeed only through moderate and prolonged punishment – namely, through imprisonment. A life sentence is a sufficiently intense substitute for the death penalty, and it includes all the necessary ingredients needed to deter even the most hardened criminal.

■ For punishment to act as a deterrent to crime, it must be prompt, certain and proportionate to the seriousness of the crime as measured by the harm that it does to society.

■ It is better to prevent crimes than to punish them.

To those who desired that law and punishment should follow humane enlightenment, Beccaria's *OC&P* was an instant success. Its radical proposals appealed not only to many legal philosophers and reform-minded lawyers – like William Blackstone in England and a young John Adams in colonial America – but also to a large cross-section of educated society. Beccaria's followers included benevolent and not so benevolent despots such as Gustav(us) III of Sweden, Catherine II of Russia and Empress Maria Theresa of Austria. Despite its popularity, in 1766 *OC&P* was placed on the papal *Index Prohibitorum* and banned for its 'extreme rationalism'. Immediately thereafter, however, *OC&P* exercised great influence in the enactment of classical legal codes in Austria, Denmark, France, Poland, Prussia, Russia and Sweden. In the fledgling United States, both the Constitution and the Bill of Rights adopted Beccarian principles.

Nevertheless, *OC&P* shares with many Enlightenment treatises the fact that its meaning does not always strike with immediate clarity. Its surface messages obviously drew inspiration from the humanism of the French *philosophes*, especially Montesquieu's advocacy for just laws in *De l'esprit des lois*. At the same time, the vivid humanism decorating *OC&P*'s every page was a mask behind which some of Beccaria's other arguments lie hidden. This is not altogether surprising – opponents of the *ancien régime* had good cause to fear prosecution for heresy in the inquisitorial ecclesiastical courts. Reformist authors like Beccaria therefore minimized personal risk by using a number of avoidance strategies, including anonymous authorship, frontispieces with phoney places of publication, secret printing presses and an underground network for the distribution and sale of books and pamphlets.

Aside from the humanist influence of Montesquieu's writings, many of Beccaria's militant ideas had another, largely unacknowledged source. This was the emerging 'science of man', especially as it was formulated in the widely read book *System of Moral Philosophy* of 1755, by the Scottish philosopher Francis Hutcheson. Hutcheson's new science appears in two chief ways in *OC&P*. First, at numerous points in his text, Beccaria argues that if criminal law were to serve as an effective deterrent to crime, then its rules of evidence and scale of punishment must be applied with mathematical precision and predictability. Would-be criminals should thereby be forced to make an accurate 'association of ideas' between crime and punishment. Such a deterministic calculus implicitly challenged one of the very pillars of Roman Catholicism – namely, the doctrine of free will (about which Montesquieu also had great misgivings). Second, Beccaria indicated in *OC&P*, however primitively, that criminals and criminal activity should be understood causally, in material and social terms rather than purely individualistic ones. He suggested, for example, that '[t]heft is generally the crime of poverty and desperation, the crime of that unhappy section of men to whom the perhaps "terrible" and "unnecessary" right to property has allowed nothing but a bare existence' (1764:53). Pursuing this logic, Beccaria therefore favoured the idea that the strategy of deterrence should operate in tandem with the peaceful acquisition of property through the free economic marketplace of capitalism. Thus, he argued that while commerce and the ownership of goods are not the goal of the social contract, they can be a means of achieving it. As such, he was most enthusiastic about economic competition between countries: it is 'the most humane sort of war and more worthy of reasonable men' (ibid.:8).

The author of the other great cornerstone of classical criminology was Jeremy Bentham, Beccaria's greatest disciple. Like Beccaria, Bentham (1780) believed that the path to effective government lay in the coupling of deterrence with the **utilitarian** principle of the greatest happiness to the greatest number of people. The happiness, the pleasure and the security of individuals, Bentham held, are the sole ends that laws should protect and promote. Because criminals are **rational actors** who consciously calculate the profits and losses that arise from the commission of a crime, lawmakers must ensure that the pleasure derived from crime is outweighed by the pain of punishment.

See Chapter 1.3
Utilitarianism

See Chapter 1.18
Rational choice

This utilitarian doctrine led more or less directly to Bentham's invention of the Panopticon – a three-storey circular building around the entire circumference of which the inmates' cells were positioned. (In the eighteenth century a rough version of this all-seeing inspection house was built in Philadelphia, with others also planned in this period in France and Ireland.) Each cell contained one inmate. Each inmate was isolated from the others by partitions. In this way, inmates were encouraged to commune with God. Prison guards ('Inspectors') looked out on each inmate from a central round tower. So that the inmates could not see the guards, the tower windows were draped with blinds. The inmates were thus seen but could not see.

See Chapter 5.11
Panopticism

To these architectural principles Bentham added a strict regimen of visits by prisoners to the prison chapel for moral and religious instruction. Every minute of the prisoners' day was subject to discipline, order and isolation – all with the aim of moral reformation of character. Bentham urged that, for the construction of a well-regulated and orderly society, the principle of **panopticism** should be extended from prisons to workhouses for the poor, and to factories, madhouses, hospitals and schools.

Classical criminology's legacy, though enormous, is thoroughly ambiguous. Does it offer a sound basis for the rights of the individual (Ferrajoli 2015)? Or is it, rather, neither enlightened nor humanitarian but authoritarian (Foucault, 1979:73–103)? Inevitably, one has to marvel that Bentham failed to specify how his inspectorate would be inspected, and by whom.

References

Beccaria, Cesare. 1764/1995. *On Crimes and Punishments and Other Writings*. Edited by Richard Bellamy. Translated by Richard Davies. Cambridge: Cambridge University Press.

Bentham, Jeremy. 1780/1973. *An Introduction to the Principles of Morals and Legislation*. New York: Hafner.

Ferrajoli, Luigi. 2015. Two Hundred and Fifty Years since the Publication of *On Crimes and Punishments:* The Currency of Cesare Beccaria's Thought. *Theoretical Criminology* 16(5): 501–19.

Foucault, Michel. 1979. *Discipline and Punish: The Birth of the Prison*. Translated by Alan Sheridan. New York: Vintage.

Further reading

Beirne, Piers. 1993. *Inventing Criminology: Essays on the Rise of 'Homo Criminalis'*. Albany: State University of New York Press.

Hutcheson, Francis. 1755. *A System of Moral Philosophy*. Glasgow: Foulis.

Utilitarianism

Eamonn Carrabine

Every time a court imposes a sentence, it emphatically declares, in both a physical and symbolic sense, the sovereignty of the political power from which it draws judicial authority. But the punishment of offenders raises profound questions regarding human rights, civil liberties and social justice because punishment will always involve the loss of some basic rights and, in the case of the death penalty, extinguishes the most fundamental: the right to life. A key issue that immediately arises is what gives any social institution the moral right to inflict deliberate suffering on wrongdoers? There are a number of common and competing justifications which have come to revolve around the central problem of reconciling punishment as state coercion alongside a valuing of individual autonomy. The oldest known justification is a system of vengeance whereby revenge is considered a social duty in societies governed by shame, while the earliest documented response to checking the vindictive passions is also to be found in the classical Greek pantheon where the Erinyes (or Furies in later Roman mythology) dispensed justice.

Modern philosophical thinking insists that punishment is justified 'as it protects the freedom of individual citizens to go about their lives safe from the threat of crime' (Duff and Garland 1994:3), while individual rights are advocated as essential defences against the abuse of power by the state. The competing justifications for punishment are rooted in opposing ideas of what the purpose of punishment should be, and fall into two distinctive groups: those who see the aim of punishment as the prevention of future crimes are generally referred to as *reductivist*, while those who look to the past to punish crimes already committed are typically known as **retributivist**. In practice,

See Chapter 5.16
Retribution

however, most criminal justice systems fashion quite contradictory justifications so that the different rationalities often uncomfortably co-exist, and tensions between the two perennially arise. For instance, in many criminal justice systems it is recognized that the pursuit of **crime prevention** (as a general good) must be subject to the specific constraints of procedural justice so that the innocent are not deliberately punished or the guilty excessively punished. These tensions between the crime control and due process orientations of criminal justice are often compared to pendulum shifts between two competing sets of values, with neither quite dominating the other, but the balance between them changing.

See Chapter 6.2
Community safety

Reductivism justifies punishment on the grounds of its alleged future consequences. These arguments are supported by the form of moral reasoning known as utilitarianism. Although the origins of utilitarian thinking can be found in the fifth-century BC in Plato's dialogues with Protagoras, a Thracian philosopher (Walker 1991:142), this moral theory was most famously advanced by Jeremy Bentham (1748–1832) as he argued that moral actions are those which produce 'the greatest happiness of the greatest number' of people (1787). For **punishment to reduce future crimes**, the pain and unhappiness caused to the offender must be 'outweighed by the avoidance of unpleasantness to other people in the future – thus making punishment morally right from a utilitarian point of view' (Cavadino and Dignan 2002:34). By pointing to a future or greater 'good', reductivist principles focus on the instrumental 'ends' of punishment. In doing so, utilitarian justifications of punishment make two further important appeals: 'that human well-being matters and that moral rules ought to be evaluated in light of their effect on human well-being' (Matravers 2000:5).

See Chapter 1.2
Classical
criminology

Utilitarian philosophy establishes appropriate behaviour – 'what is good to do' – on the grounds of social usefulness, and it judges actions by their consequences. It stipulates that 'the good' is human happiness, not some abstract metaphysical property like the idea of 'natural rights', which Bentham famously dismissed as 'nonsense on stilts' or an empirically unknowable object, as in the will of God. Bentham's intention was to establish the law on a rational basis, which for him meant the facts of pleasure and pain rather than the vague fictions of natural rights – ideas driving much social reform in the nineteenth century. As revolutionaries replaced aristocrats on the guillotine in the years after the French Declaration of the Rights of Man and Citizen, the executions provided 'a practical refutation of its claim that "rights" were natural, let alone inalienable and sacred' (Robertson 2000:5). Bentham mounted an influential liberal attack on natural rights and the conservative disposition of natural law that upheld unjust legal systems, which became a pivotal force driving social reform in the nineteenth century.

By pointing to a future or greater 'good', the focus is on the instrumental 'ends' of punishment. On this basis, it is argued that future crime can be reduced by a number of strategies – such as deterring potential offenders, reforming actual criminals or by keeping actual or potential offenders out of circulation. For Bentham, the only rights were legal rights: 'legitimate, enforceable rights come not from nature but from laws duly passed by the supreme authority of the state' (Feldman 2002:25) and are justified by arguments of social utility. Utilitarianism thereby inspired a 'positive rights' tradition grounded in the legal **positivism** that continues to be influential in human rights and other areas of the law.

See Chapter 1.4
Positivism

The utilitarian justification of punishment is that the wrong experienced by the offender is outweighed by the compensating good effects for overall human well-being. The avoidance of further crime can be achieved through a number of strategies, such as:

- **deterring** potential criminals;
- reforming actual criminals; or
- keeping actual or potential offenders **out of circulation**.

See Chapter 1.17
Deterrence

See Chapter 5.9
Incapacitation

Utilitarian philosophy also informed Bentham's famous **Panopticon** prison design in 1787. The innovative idea was that inspection would be continuous from a central watchtower, but the inmates would not know whether they were being watched in their peripheral cells because of a series of blinds shielding the inner tower. Bentham's elaborate machinery was set to 'grinding rogues honest', and he readily acknowledged that it was an omniscient 'way of obtaining power, power of mind over mind' – and thus a potent magnification of his own philosophy. Critics not only worried about the tyranny exemplified in the design, but also disliked Bentham's insistence that the panopticon could be run as a profitable commercial business – and it was this latter objection that ultimately led to the rejection of his plans. Nevertheless, significant elements of his design have informed subsequent prisons. Notable examples include Millbank (1816) and Pentonville (1842) in England, while Joliet (1858) in Illinois became a model for prisons in the United States; and the Isle of Pines prison built in Cuba in the 1920s is closely structured on panoptic principles.

See Chapter 5.11
Panopticism

Bentham (1787:40) also thought that the Panopticon was 'applicable to any sort of establishment in which persons of any description are to be kept under inspection', and this included 'prisons, houses of industry, work-houses, poor-houses, manufactories, mad-houses, lazarettos, hospitals and schools'. Of course, it was Foucault who took these proposals as evidence of an attempt to punish more efficiently and extensively to create a disciplined society, through the techniques of **surveillance**, classification and examination. These new institutional spaces were crucial places managing the upheavals rendered by rapid industrialization and spiralling population growth. The new disciplinary mode of power, which the prison was to represent, belonged to an economy of power quite different from that of the direct, arbitrary and violent rule of the past. Power in capitalist society had to be exercised at the lowest possible cost, both economically and politically, while its effects had to be intensified and extended throughout the social apparatus. Ignatieff's analysis of the rise of the modern prison situates the new institution in a more Marxist understanding

See Chapter 5.19
Surveillance

See Chapter 5.1
Abolitionism;
Chapter 5.5
Decarceration;
Chapter
3.3 Critical
criminologies;
Chapter
3.9 Marxist
criminologies

of class conflict at the time of the Industrial Revolution. On this reckoning, the penitentiary offers a vision of social order that can discipline the urban poor; and Ignatieff contends that the hardening of penal policy in the first half of the nineteenth century was an effort to contain the social disruptions associated with rising unemployment and new class divisions – an argument that continues to hold sway with proponents of **abolitionism** as well as with **critical criminologists** and **Marxist criminologists**. All in all, then, the values and operations of criminal justice systems today still reflect considerations (and dilemmas) born out of utilitarianism – although in a context in which various forms of moral reasoning have been subject to greater critique and questioning.

References

Bentham, Jeremy. 1787. Panopticon. In *The Works of Jeremy Bentham*. New York: Russell.

Cavadino, Michael, and James Dignan. 2002. *The Penal System: An Introduction* (3rd edn). London: Sage.

Duff, Antony, and David Garland (eds). 1994. *A Reader on Punishment*. Oxford: Oxford University Press.

Feldman, David. 2002. *Civil Liberties and Human Rights in England and Wales* (2nd edn). Oxford: Oxford University Press.

Matravers, Matt. 2000. *Justice and Punishment: The Rationale of Coercion*. Oxford: Oxford University Press.

Robertson, Geoffrey. 2000. *Crimes against Humanity: The Struggle for Global Justice*. London: Penguin.

Walker, Nigel. 1991. *Why Punish?* Oxford: Oxford University Press.

Further reading

Cantarella, Eva. 2001. Private Revenge and Public Justice: The Settlement of Disputes in Homer's Iliad. *Punishment and Society* 3(4): 473–83.

Carrabine, Eamonn. 2006. Punishment, rights and justice. In *Rights: Sociological Perspectives*, Lydia Morris, ed., pp. 191–208. London: Routledge.

Duff, R.A. 1996. Penal Communications: Recent Work in the Philosophy of Punishment. *Crime and Justice: A Review of Research* 20: 1–97.

Foucault, Michel. 1977. *Discipline and Punish: The Birth of the Prison*. Harmondsworth: Penguin.

Ignatieff, Michael. 1978. *A Just Measure of Pain: The Penitentiary in the Industrial Revolution, 1750–1850*. London: Macmillan.

Scarre, Geoffrey. 2002. *Utilitarianism*. London: Routledge.

Positivism

Kristie R. Blevins

The positive (or positivist) school of thought suggests that human behaviour is shaped by structural and/or individual factors that can be identified through scientific research methods. Unlike the **classical school**, which assumes that individuals have free will and will act in a way that maximizes pleasure and minimizes pain, positivism assumes that behaviour is determined, at least in part, by internal and/or external factors acting upon individuals. Early sociological positivists focused primarily on structural factors and behaviour, while early positivist criminologists concentrated largely on biological factors and crime. Today, both sociological and biological positivists generally recognize that criminal behaviour is the result of a complex interaction between a variety of social, psychological and biological variables.

See Chapter 1.2 Classical criminology

The French philosopher Auguste Comte is considered one of the forefathers of the field of sociology and the school of positivism. In *Cours de Philosophie Positive*, Comte discussed three phases of social evolution, the last of which was the positive (or scientific) stage, during which individuals could use science to identify and remedy social problems. He stressed that there must be a connection between theory and practice – that the scientific method should be used to test ideas about society. His ideas were accepted by scholars such as Émile Durkheim, who worked to elevate sociology to the level of legitimacy enjoyed by the 'hard' sciences. Although Durkheim recognized individual consciousness, he focused on larger society through institutions and structural social forces. Comte (1830) embraced the importance of the scientific method, including impartial observations, in discovering how factors such as education, religion, laws, poverty and the division of labour can influence society, norms and social relationships.

Early criminological positivists explored the relationship between biological characteristics and crime. One of the founders of the positive school of criminology was Italian physician Cesare Lombroso, who in the late 1800s theorized that criminals had distinguishing physical traits (e.g., enormous jaws, strong canines, prominent zygomae, strongly developed orbital arches) that could be identified via scientific methods. Initially, he focused almost exclusively on biological traits, but later revised his theory to include environmental forces such as laws, government structure, climate, tariff policies, the price of grain, banking practices and church organization. These ideas were expanded by other Italian positivists, such as Enrico Ferri (1967).

Although the Italians' work was instrumental in the development of the positive school of criminology, it was criticized for a lack of statistical sophistication in the research methods used. Charles Goring (1913), an English physician, addressed this problem in his research involving 3,000 criminals. Using an expert statistician to perform the analyses, he studied almost 100 physical features of English convicts and a control group of non-criminals. Results published in 1913 indicated that there were differences in body weight and stature between the groups, but Goring concluded that there was not a specific physical type for criminals. In 1940, William Sheldon published findings from his study of the body types and behaviours of young males. He found that delinquents tended to be mesomorphic, and his findings were supported by the Gluecks' (1950) physical comparisons of delinquent and non-delinquent males in the 1940s – at a time when sociological theories were coming to dominate the discipline of criminology. Most biological researchers, however, ultimately recognized that environmental and biological factors probably interact to influence behaviour.

See Chapter 1.9 Personality theory; Chapter 1.15 Forensic psychology

During the late 1800s and early 1900s, research involving **psychological variables** and their impact on criminal behaviour became prominent. For example, Sigmund Freud (1923) identified components of the human psyche, how they develop, and how they function and interact to influence individual decisions and ultimately behaviour. Likewise, researchers began to explore the relationship between intelligence and criminal behaviour. Henry Goddard (1914) studied intelligence levels of inmates, and found that most inmates had low IQs and below average functioning. Other investigators linked insanity, psychosis and other psychological/personality disorder with criminal behaviour.

Results of early biological and psychological studies played a major role in shifting criminal justice policy from concentrating on *crimes* to the actual *criminals*. Accordingly, causes of crime came to be seen as rooted primarily within individual offenders. These views led to programmes and laws intended to remove genetic defects and improve the quality of humans, all as part of what is known as the eugenics movement. Such programmes included psychosurgery and sterilization of some offenders to attempt to 'fix their defects' or keep them from passing their defects on to future generations. Long prison sentences also became a popular way to incapacitate offenders who could not be 'rehabilitated' through physical or psychological procedures. In addition, some regions in both Europe and the United States implemented laws that prohibited marriage between individuals of different races in order to prevent the production of biologically inferior offspring.

During the mid-twentieth century, pure biological or psychological positivist models subsided and were largely replaced with positivist theories that drew from a variety of disciplines, especially sociology. Scholars began to realize that causes of crime are likely a combination of individual (e.g., biological, psychological) and environmental (sociological) factors. For instance, some of the most significant criminological theories posit that crime is learned through social interaction with others. Edwin Sutherland pioneered this **social learning** movement when he published his theory of **differential association** in 1924. Although later researchers such as Albert Bandura, Robert Burgess and Ronald Akers have presented modified theories, social learning theories generally suggest that criminal behaviour is learned through a process of interaction and communication with individuals in groups, the same way any behaviour is learned. The behaviour itself – as well as the attitudes, rationalizations and motives for the behaviour – is learned through a process of observation and reinforcement, and a person will likely engage in illegal activities if he or she develops an excess of definitions favourable to criminal behaviour. The behavioural learning, however, may be mediated by psychological factors such as attention and retention of the behaviour observed and its consequences.

See Chapter 2.5 Social learning theory; Chapter 2.4 Differential association

Social **control theories** also are widely used to explain criminal behaviour. While some scholars argue that social control theories are not positivistic in nature because they explain why people do *not* commit crime, others contend that they are positivistic because the scientific method can be used to identify who is most likely to participate in criminal behaviour. For example, Travis Hirschi's (1969) social control theory suggests that strong bonds to society – through attachment to prosocial others, involvement in non-criminal activities, commitment to convention and belief in societal laws and norms – will prevent criminal behaviour. A little more than two decades later, Hirschi, along with Michael Gottfredson (1990), proposed a general theory of crime that identified self-control as a primary mechanism in the pathway to crime or conformity. While this general theory of crime has received considerable support in empirical studies, researchers point out that levels of self-control may be influenced by factors such as education, socialization by parents and others, and some biological factors.

See Chapter 2.6 Control theories

There are also positivist theories that focus on strain and crime. For instance, Robert Merton, who in the late 1930s explored the relationship of culture, social structure and **anomie**, theorized how people will adapt and behave when faced with the gap between the normative goal of achieving wealth and the lack of means for attaining that goal. In essence, Merton argued, those without legitimate means to achieve their goals will experience strain and may react with criminal behaviour. Others have taken this idea of strain and expanded it to explain individual behaviour. For example, Robert Agnew's

See Chapter 2.3 Anomie

See Chapter 2.9
General strain
theory

general **strain theory** specifies that criminal behaviour may result when individuals are unable to cope legally with strains such as the failure to achieve positively valued goals, the presentation of noxious stimuli and/or the removal of positively valued stimuli.

The theories described above do not comprise an exhaustive list of positivist criminological theories. The positive school of criminology contains numerous theories that seek to explain crime at both the micro and macro levels. There are, however, at least two commonalities among all positivist criminological theories. First, positivists assume that crime is caused primarily by factors or forces acting upon an individual, meaning that individuals do not possess pure free will. Thus, the focus is on *individual offenders* rather than *the crimes they commit*. This assumption stands in opposition to the classical school view that individuals have free will and will act based on their personal calculations of benefits and costs of behaviours. Second, positivists believe in using the same scientific method that is used in the natural sciences. That is, positivists seek to use objective research methodology and analyses when examining factors that might be associated with criminal behaviour.

See Chapter 1.17
Deterrence

See Chapter
1.5 Biological
criminology

Given that positivism assumes that the scientific method can be used to identify causes of criminal behaviour, it offers a sanguine outlook for preventing and addressing crime. Contrary to the classical school ideology of **deterrence** through equal punishments for those committing the same crime, positivism holds that such punishments alone will not be effective in preventing future crime. Instead, the positive school suggests that the best ways to approach crime include rehabilitation and crime prevention efforts that address criminogenic risk factors. For example, if low levels of education and high levels of unemployment are shown to be significant in predicting criminal behaviour, then rehabilitation and crime prevention programmes should include educational and vocational components. The challenge is to identify social, psychological and **biological variables** that are correlated with criminal behaviour, and to develop rehabilitation and prevention programmes that effectively target and change these criminogenic factors.

References

Comte, Auguste. 1830. *Cours de Philosophie Positive*. Paris: Bachelier.

Ferri, Enrico. 1967/1884. *Criminal Sociology*. New York: Agathon.

Freud, Sigmund. 1923. *The Ego and the Id*. New York: Norton.

Glueck, Sheldon, and Eleanor Glueck.1950. *Unraveling Juvenile Delinquency*. New York: Commonwealth Fund.

Goddard, Henry H. 1914. *Feeble-Mindedness: Its Causes and Consequences*: New York: Macmillan.

Goring, Charles. 1913. *The English Convict: A Statistical Study*. London: Her Majesty's Stationery Office.

Gottfredson, Michael R., and Travis Hirschi. 1990. *A General Theory of Crime*. Stanford, CA: Stanford University Press.

Hirschi, Travis. 1969. *Causes of Delinquency*. Berkeley: University of California Press.

Sheldon, William H. 1940. *The Varieties of Human Physique*. New York: Harper and Brothers.

Further reading

Akers Ronald L. 1991. Self-Control as a General Theory of Crime. *Journal of Quantitative Criminology* 7(2): 201–11.

Jeffery, Clarence R. 1956. The Structure of American Criminological Thinking. *Journal of Criminal Law, Criminology, and Police Science* 46(5): 658–72.

Lilly, J. Robert, Francis T. Cullen, and Robert A. Ball. 2002. *Criminological Theory: Context and Consequences* (3rd edn). Thousand Oaks, CA: Sage.

Vold, George B., and Thomas J. Bernard. 1986. *Theoretical Criminology* (3rd edn). New York: Oxford University Press.

Wagner, Helmut R. 1963. Types of Sociological Theory: Toward a System of Classification. *American Sociological Review* 28(5): 735–42.

1.5 Biological criminology

Chad Posick and Mackenzie McBride

Criminology is interdisciplinary – drawing on insights from diverse fields ranging from economics and sociology to biology and psychology. Some of the first perspectives on why people engage in criminal, or antisocial, behaviour were biological in nature – placing the 'blame' on the human mind and body. These perspectives dominated the explanation of criminal behaviour until the early 1900s, when sociological criminology built its stronghold on the field, a stronghold which it has since maintained for decades. It appears, however, that criminology is returning to its roots – pulling biology back into the explanation of crime alongside sociological or environmental explanations.

One of the earliest theories of crime was based on physiognomy, which began with the assumption that physical characteristics – especially facial features – could reveal a person's temperament. In 1586, Giambattista della Porta published *De Humana Physiognomonia*, in which he compared the anatomy of human and animal faces. Johann Kaspar Lavater, influenced by della Porta, became the first modern practitioner to investigate physiognomy on a scientific basis. In his *Essays on Physiognomy*, written in 1878, he insisted he could determine a person's temperament from their face. For example, long foreheads indicate knowledge, and short ones volatility. While facial features quickly became an outdated way of determining behaviour, the practice remained into the twentieth century when Sir Francis Galton studied mugshots in the hopes of identifying the 'criminal look' using facial features. His interest in heredity led him to coin the term 'eugenics' used to describe the science of selective breeding to improve the physical and mental characteristics of human beings (Rafter 2008).

Similar to physiognomy, German physician Franz Joseph Gall believed that physical differences of the skull – bumps, indentations and shape – could be linked to personality traits, characteristics and abilities. This idea led to the development of phrenology in the late 1700s, when he developed a system of 27 different faculties that he believed could be attributed to specific areas of the skull.

Following Gall, Johann Spurzheim systemized Gall's six volumes of work into English in *The Physiognomical System of Drs. Gall and Spurzheim.* He insisted that the destructive propensity differs in intensity among people: some are indifferent to animals' pain, others enjoy seeing animals killed and some have an irresistible desire to kill. To demonstrate that the propensity to kill is due to an innate biological defect in the function of mental organization, he used the story of a murderous fiddler who played songs at Dutch weddings and later confessed that he killed 34 people simply because the bloodshed brought him great joy (Rafter 2008).

In colonial times in America, people attributed antisocial behaviour to **demonic possession and sin**. Benjamin Rush turned this idea on its head, and investigated crime as a natural phenomenon rather than sin. In his 1839 book *The Influence of Physical Causes upon the Moral Faculty,* he focused on the types of serious repeat criminal behaviour that psychiatrists would later consider moral insanity. Rush insisted that people are born with moral faculty or the capacity in the human mind to distinguish and choose between good and evil. One can be born with a defective moral faculty, or damage due to physical causes such as fever, poor diet, too much sleep or the climate can lead to moral deficiency.

See Chapter 1.1 Religion, spirituality and crime

At the turn of the nineteenth century, Philippe Pinel studied mentally ill patients who lacked signs of hallucinations or psychosis, yet were lashing out violently; he called this condition *manie sans delire* – madness without delusions. His research led him to believe that the mind could become ill without a corresponding illness in the brain.

In 1835, James Cowles Prichard's *A Treatise on Insanity* standardized the psychiatric term 'moral insanity'. He held that the morally insane are logical in their thought processes and display great ingenuity in justifying their misconduct. He also assumed that they constantly plot against others without provocation and are extremely irascible. In 1885, Daniel Hack Tuke, drawing on Prichard's ideas, used moral insanity to explain the case of W.B., a young man who bullied other youth and sadistically tortured and killed other animals, specifically a prized horse belonging to his neighbour, without experiencing even a bit of remorse (Rafter 2008).

Cesare Lombroso, credited by some as the father of criminology (or, at least, the father of the **Positive School** in criminology) first published his text *The Criminal Man* in 1876, in which he argued that criminals were biologically different from the rest of society, having certain physical characteristics – large

See Chapter 1.4 Positivism

jaws, high cheekbones, scanty beard or baldness – that distinguished them from non-criminals. He declared that 'born criminals' are 'atavists', whose very existence makes them dangerous. Later, he identified two other types of criminals – the insane criminal and the criminaloid. Insane criminals possess some physical characteristics but are not born criminals; instead, they become criminal as result of the brain, which upsets their moral nature. Criminaloids have no physical characteristics of born criminals, but occasionally engage in criminal behaviour due to environmental influences (Rafter 2008).

Richard Dugdale and his research on the Jukes family inspired Lombroso's later work. In his 1877 book *The Jukes,* Dugdale traced the relatives of six original jail inmates back seven generations. He was not focused on evolution, but on the inheritance of degeneration. Later, in 1912, Henry Goddard set out to show that feeble-mindedness is inherited by conducting a pedigree study of a family he named the 'Kallikaks'. He and his assistant conducted 'eugenic field research' by tracking down Martin Kallikak's two very different lines of descendants – one from an illicit liaison with a 'feeble-minded' girl and the other from a respectable girl who was raised in a good family. The majority of the 'bad branch' of relatives were criminals, while the reputable family had only a few mentally degenerate members. Goddard demonstrated these results in a heredity chart, which seemed to prove that feeble-mindedness and normal intelligence are inherited as unit characteristics.

In the mid-twentieth century, Earnest A. Hooton, William Sheldon and Eleanor and Sheldon Glueck established 'constitutional theory'. These research-ers believed that the cause of crime could be discovered in how the body was constituted or formed. Sheldon's work *The Varieties of Human Physique* (1940), presented three types of physique called 'somatotypes'. 'Endomorphs' are soft and round with a laid-back personality. 'Ectomorphs' are skinny with intro-verted personalities. 'Mesomorphs' are solid and muscular, with an aggressive personality. He concluded that the mesomorphic body type was the most likely to generate criminal behaviour.

In 1950, the Gluecks conducted studies comparing the physiques of delin-quents and non-delinquents, and concluded that mesomorphy was more predominant among the delinquents. In 1956, the Gluecks examined the data further, including other sociological variables and traits. They concluded that there is not one specific pattern of physical and sociological traits to predict delinquency (Rafter 2008).

Although early biological theories have been mostly discredited, current scientific research is showing the promise of biology in predicting antisocial behaviour. **Neuroscience** attributes criminality (or antisociality) to disease or abnormality of the brain and central nervous system. Neurophysiology includes two types of research – psychophysiology and neuroimaging – that relate the brain's prefrontal cortex to antisocial behaviour. The electroencepha-logram (EEG) is a psychophysiological test that indicates that criminals are more slowly aroused than non-criminals. Similarly, antisocial people have low resting heart rates and weak skin conductance responses (Portnoy et al. 2014).

See Chapter 1.16
Neurocriminology

Using brain imaging technologies such as computer tomography (CT), magnetic resonance imagining (MRI), positron emission tomography (PET) and functional magnetic resonance imagining (fMRI) researchers have identified physical deformations and functional abnormalities that correlate with aggressive and antisocial behaviours (Raine 2013). Similarly, researchers are studying neurotransmitters and their impact on antisociality – a condition that possibly triggers personal and social pathologies. The levels of neurotransmitters in our brain are partly genetic, but also fluctuate due to environmental factors. Deficits in serotonin increase impulsivity and aggression; imbalance of dopamine is linked to attention disorders, drug addiction and aggressive behaviour; and an imbalance of norepinephrine can lead to impulsivity, aggression and increased sensation-seeking.

Contemporary behavioural genetics includes research on families, twins and adoptees in order to examine the influence of genes and the environment separately. The family studies methodology dates back to Richard Dugdale and 'the Jukes', and various studies have followed providing evidence of an association between genetics and family lines of crime. However, these family studies hardly considered environmental influences; consequentially, twin and adoption studies emerged. The results of twin studies consistently show that genes *and* nurture, in the form of unique environments, both have some impact on criminal behaviour.

Today, researchers are focusing on molecular genetics, in which they examine particular genes that may predispose individuals to criminal behaviour. 'Epigenetics', the study of how environmental factors can influence gene function without changing DNA sequences, is also a promising avenue to study antisociality. Epigenetic modifications are the result of genes switching on and off due to challenges faced in the physical and social environment or the internal chemical environment (Walsh et al. 2012). These studies help demonstrate why no one is doomed to be a criminal, but how nature and nurture interact, creating risk factors that lead to criminal behaviour.

References

Portnoy, Jill, Adrian Raine, Francis R. Chen, Dustin Pardini, Rolf Loeber, and J. Richard Jennings. 2014. Heart Rate and Antisocial Behavior: The Mediating Role of Impulsive Sensation Seeking. *Criminology* 52(2): 292–311.

Rafter, Nicole. 2008. *The Criminal Brain: Understanding Biological Theories of Crime.* New York: New York University Press.

Raine, Adrian. 2013. *The Anatomy of Violence: The Biological Roots of Crime.* New York: Vintage.

Walsh, Anthony, Hailey Johnson, and Jonathan D. Bolen. 2012. Drugs, Crime, and the Epigenetics of Hedonic Allostasis. *Journal of Contemporary Criminal Justice* 28(3): 314–28.

Further reading

Anderson, Gail S. 2006. *Biological Influences on Criminal Behavior*. Boca Raton, FL: CRC Press.

Ellis, Lee. 1982. Genetics and Criminal Behavior: Evidence through the End of the 1970s. *Criminology* 20(1): 43–66.

Fishbein, Diana H. 2001. *Biobehavioral Perspectives in Criminology*. Belmont, CA: Wadsworth/Thomson Learning.

Nelson, Randy Joe (ed.). 2005. *Biology of Aggression*. New York: Oxford University Press.

Rowe, David C. 2002. *Biology and Crime*. Los Angeles, CA: Roxbury.

Walsh, Anthony. 2009. *Biology and Criminology: The Biosocial Synthesis*. New York: Routledge.

Pathology

Eamonn Carrabine and Nigel South

In bio-medical terms, pathology would refer to the scientific study of organic diseases, their causes and symptoms (hence the role of the 'pathologist'). The term has been used far more extensively, however, from more flexible applications across the human and natural sciences to adoption for metaphorical and descriptive purposes in **literature and film**. The notion of the 'pathological' is powerful, suggesting morbidity and abnormality, with associations of disease, infection and deterioration, and is therefore employed in various ways, for example as a diagnosis, an explanation or a comment on a situation or context.

See Chapter 4.15
Gothic criminology

Psychiatry has defined the 'psychopath' in clinical terms, and historically variants of criminology have also adopted this usage. Hervey Cleckley's *The Mask of Sanity* (1941) is usually regarded as popularizing the term psychopath in the professional and public spheres. In the **biological and psychological** versions, pathology may originate in hormonal imbalances, a disturbed mental state or genetic disorder (which may then be inherited by subsequent generations).

See Chapter 1.5
Biological
criminology;
Chapter 1.11
Biosocial theory

Use of **positivist** methods of investigation is associated with the establishment of pathology as a reputable description and explanation. Work in this vein did not necessarily reflect a crude biological determinism, and the influence of environment, family and education was accepted by some such as Enrico Ferri (1856–1929) in his work on criminal psychology. Others, however, such as Charles Buckman Goring (1870–1919), argued that 'the real cure' for crime 'lay in the regulation of the reproduction' of criminal traits – 'namely: feeble-mindedness, epilepsy, insanity, and defective social instinct'

See Chapter 1.4
Positivism

(Driver 1957:523) – and as many as 32 US states once had laws for the compulsory sterilization of people deemed 'feeble-minded', 'moronic' and otherwise undesirable as parents (see Editorial 2012).

The translation of the language of organic, medical pathology to the social body – society – has become a powerful descriptor and metaphor regarding social threats of various kinds, indicating forms of social disease that require 'treatment', control, purging, quarantine or cleansing. Such language can, of course, be employed as if scientifically neutral and humane, yet disguise inhumane and immoral actions driven by prejudice and bias.

The functionalist biological/organic model of society is found in much classic sociology, from Auguste Comte and Herbert Spencer to Emile Durkheim and, later, Talcott Parsons. Durkheim, and others, elaborated a theory of social functionality based on equilibrium. If individuals conform to the social norms of expected behaviour, this social balance is maintained; but when social rules and moral expectations are eroded or break down, then social disorganization follows, and a pathological condition arises within society termed **anomie**. Durkheim's study of suicide was an exercise in demonstrating how pathological social conditions could fail to support and anchor an individual such that they turn to suicide. This form of analysis saw society as a social 'body' which, analogous to the human body, could suffer disease, breakdown and dysfunction in society.

See Chapter 2.3
Anomie

More individualist or essentialist views have described examples of deviance or 'social disease' and social pathology as affecting individuals (Lemert 1951; Wootton 1959); and the later term, 'sociopathy', combined the social and the individual, signalling the performance of **antisocial behaviour** as an expression of personality disorder. The North American sociologist Charles Wright Mills was an early critic. In an influential study of the professional ideology of social pathologists, Mills denounced how they regarded deviance as a kind of diseased state and unhealthy maladjustment. Here he insisted that those sociologists who focus on deviation from norms as an instance of social disorganization were blinded to the fundamental problems posed by power and the larger historical context. Instead, he argued that the concept of social deviation was rooted in a particular vision of middle-class morality that advocated piecemeal reform and operated as a conservative 'propaganda for conformity' (Mills 1943/63:549). He returns to this theme in *The Sociological Imagination*, where the field is located in a discussion of 'liberal practicality' (Mills 1959:85), which is both apolitical and un-sociological. For Mills this perspective espoused a narrow-minded ideal of Protestant, small-town America that too often focused on individual failings at the expense of social structure.

See Chapter 5.2
Antisocial
behaviour

In the British context, and written at around the same time, Barbara Wootton's (1959) *Social Science and Social Pathology* was a major intervention, debunking the myths of value-free social science and demolishing the pretensions to expertise of the medical, psychiatric and social-work professions colonizing how antisocial behaviour was understood. The rise of psychiatry, Wootton observed, had led more people to be diagnosed as mentally ill; and, while some of this labelling undoubtedly had beneficial effects, it also ignored the social causes of mental and social distress. In this she anticipated the anti-psychiatry movements of the 1960s and echoed themes then being developed by Thomas Szasz – that attributions of mental illness, like deviance in general, involve moral and political judgements too often disguised by psychiatric labels. Neither denied the pain, discomfort or distress associated with mental illness, but insisted that it was a serious mistake to classify many psychological conditions and problems as a form of illness.

In a similar vein, Wootton exposed the dangers of the criminological tradition that had devoted itself to predicting delinquency, and exposed how notions like the 'problem family' were irrevocably linked to eugenic class prejudice. On publication, the book provoked defensive reactions from the professions demolished across 400 pages of text but by attempting to situate criminal conduct in a broader social setting, the clear implication was that many social problems were produced by cultural conflicts in highly differentiated societies – and in this the book can be regarded as anticipating the radical criminology that subsequently followed. Wootton's contribution to the development of the social sciences does not always receive the full attention it deserves, and in many respects she shares with Mills an impassioned commitment to the role of **public intellectual**, challenging conventional wisdoms and shaping the political landscape.

See Chapter 4.31
Public criminology

The view of the dysfunctional or deviant individual embraces the idea of the body and mind as vulnerable to diseases and disorders such as alcoholism, drug addiction or madness – pathologies that *act upon* the body. Alternatively, deviant or illegal behaviours may be seen as *evidence of* pathology: lack of internal restraints regarding aggression, lack of conscience and empathy for others, uncontrolled aggression, compulsions regarding lying or gambling, sexual dysfunction, abnormality or promiscuity – all are common examples in twentieth-century criminology. Racism and the attribution of specific biological characteristics and inferior status to certain people have also evoked a 'science' of pathology to excuse or explain the necessity for slavery or programmes of 'social hygiene', for example, designed to remove 'undesirables' and ensure the purity and health of a population or nation through **genocide**.

See Chapter 4.13
Genocide and
ecocide

This approach is also related to the medicalization of various social behaviours (Conrad 1992) and related forms of social and legal control, justified in some cases by reference to medical works such as the *Diagnostic and Statistical Manual of Mental Disorders* (DSM). Many examples of such pathologization and medicalization have been subsequently criticized as forms of **social control** representing bias and prejudice, and lacking genuine scientific foundation. The diagnostic category of 'homosexuality' as a mental illness is a classic example, viewed until the 1970s by psychiatrists, psychologists and psychoanalysts as a form of psychopathology, but removed from the DSM classifications in 1973 as cultural change and empirical evidence undermined the basis for this view.

See Chapter 5.18
Social control

In some contemporary sociologically and psychoanalytically influenced assessments of modern life and the effects of consumer culture and globalization, pathology may also be employed as a term signalling cultural dislocations and unhappiness, reflected in narcissism, fragmentation, broken relationships, miscommunication and so on. Young's (1999) notion of a bulimic, exclusionary and 'othering' society is based on an analysis of the ubiquity of ontological insecurity and the construction of criminals as pathological and as 'human pollutants'. This analysis is influenced by the work of the anthropologist Mary Douglas, whose classic work, *Purity and Danger* (1966), highlighted the reactions of societies and social groups to that which is not in its proper place or out of order, identifying common features of such responses and the ways in which they are justified, notably by reference to danger and pollution. Specific variations are produced in different cultural conditions and contexts, but the elements of these share common features.

See Chapter 1.16
Neurocriminology

While the study of, and interest in, pathology *qua* pathology has fallen out of favour, new directions in **neurocriminology** have garnered much interest and seek to identify associations between neurobiological markers and risk of offending, developing risk-assessment techniques in relation to particular offenders such as psychopaths.

References

Cleckley, Hervey. 1941. *The Mask of Sanity: An Attempt to Clarify Some Issues about the So-Called Psychopathic Personality.* St. Louis, MO: C.V. Mosby.

Conrad, Peter. 1992. Medicalization and Social Control. *Annual Review of Sociology* 18: 209–32.

Douglas, Mary. 1966. *Purity and Danger: An Analysis of the Concepts of Pollution and Taboo.* London: Routledge and Kegan Paul.

Driver, Edwin. 1957. Pioneers in Criminology XIV: Charles Buckman Goring (1870–1919). *Journal of Criminal Law, Criminology and Police Science* 47(5): 515–25.

Editorial. 2012. Truth and Atonement in North Carolina. *New York Times*, 29 April: SR10.

Lemert, Edwin. 1951. *Social Pathology: A Systematic Approach to the Theory of Sociopathic Behaviour.* New York: McGraw-Hill.

Mills, Charles Wright. 1943/63. The professional ideology of social pathologists. In *Power, Politics and People: The Collected Essays of C. Wright Mills*, Irving Horowitz, ed., pp. 525–52. New York: Oxford University Press.

Mills, Charles Wright. 1959. *The Sociological Imagination.* Oxford: Oxford University Press.

Wootton, Barbara. 1959. *Social Science and Social Pathology.* Oxford: Macmillan.

Young, Jock. 1999. *The Exclusive Society: Social Exclusion, Crime and Difference in Late Modernity.* London: Sage.

Further reading

Bauman, Zygmunt. 1991. *Modernity and the Holocaust.* Cambridge: Polity Press.

Fuchs, Thomas. 2007. Fragmented Selves: Temporality and Identity in Borderline Personality Disorder. *Psychopathology* 40(6): 379–87.

Harris, Jonathan. 1998. *Foreign Bodies and the Body Politic: Discourses of Social Pathology in Early Modern England.* Cambridge: Cambridge University Press.

Schouten, Ronald, and James Silver. 2012. *Almost a Psychopath: Do I (or Does Someone I Know) Have a Problem with Manipulation and Lack of Empathy?* Center City, MN: Hazelden.

1.7 Psychopathy

Shichun Ling and Adrian Raine

Psychopathy is a clinical condition characterized by a constellation of affective, antisocial, lifestyle and interpersonal characteristics and traits. Individuals with psychopathic traits are more likely to exhibit aggressive, violent and antisocial behaviour, and have higher criminal recidivism rates than their non-psychopathic counterparts, with the prevalence of psychopathy much higher in prison settings (approximately 20–25 per cent) compared to the general population (approximately 0.5–1 per cent) (Patrick 2006). Psychopathy is more common in males than females, which could be due to differences in behavioural manifestation of psychopathy and antisociality (Patrick 2006) – such as increased physical aggression toward others for males and increased relational aggression or self-injurious behaviour for females. While there is some evidence that there may be differences in the manifestation of psychopathy across ethnicities (Patrick 2006), a meta-analysis found no meaningful differences in core psychopathic features between black and white people (Skeem et al. 2004). Whether it is lower in East Asian samples is an unresolved issue.

There is no official diagnosis of psychopathy in the *Diagnostic and Statistical Manual of Mental Disorders* (5th edition, DSM-5), the standard classification of mental disorders by medical professions in the United States, or in the International Statistical Classification of Diseases and Related Health Problems (ICD), an international standard classification system developed by the World Health Organization (WHO) for diseases and other health-related issues. Antisocial personality disorder (APD) is perhaps the closest equivalent to psychopathy. Previous literature, however, suggests that approximately 90 per cent of psychopathic offenders would meet the DSM criteria for APD but only approximately 25 per cent of those diagnosed with APD would meet the criteria for psychopathy, thus engendering a debate as to whether APD and psychopathy are two distinct conditions with differences in aetiology and epidemiology (Patrick 2006). Moreover, the criteria for APD have previously been found to be more associated with the social deviance aspect of psychopathy rather than the core personality features of psychopathy (Patrick 2006), thus suggesting there is utility in differentiating psychopathy from APD. Narcissistic personality disorder has been another DSM diagnosis associated with psychopathic features, although it has been associated more with the interpersonal and personality features of psychopathy than the social deviance aspects (Patrick 2006).

To date, the most widely used validated criterion for assessing adult psychopathy is Robert Hare's revised Psychopathic Checklist (PCL-R). The PCL-R uses a semi-structured interview supplemented by an individual's case history information to rate each individual on a 20-item, 3-point (0, 1, 2) scale based upon the extent to which each item applies to a given person. The PCL-R is comprised of two correlated factors: Factor 1 reflects interpersonal and affective deficits (e.g., manipulativeness, lack of empathy/remorse/guilt) and Factor 2 reflects socially deviant and antisocial behaviours (e.g., impulsivity, early behavioural problems). In addition to the clinical PCL-R, there are alternative methods of measuring psychopathic features that rely on self-report, such as the Psychopathic Personality Inventory (PPI) and Levenson's Primary and Secondary Psychopathy Scale (LPSP). There have also been scales derived from the PCL-R to diagnose childhood or youth psychopathy, such as the Child Psychopathy Scale (CPS) and the Hare Psychopathy Checklist: Youth Version (PCL: YV). Yet, there are still issues with the measurement and conceptualization of psychopathy, such as whether to use clinical or self-reports for assessment or whether antisocial behaviour is a symptom or consequence of psychopathy (Patrick 2006).

The aetiology of psychopathy and psychopathy-related traits likely reflects interactions between **biological predispositions** and environmental risk factors. For example, adoptees with an antisocial biological mother may be more likely to develop callous-unemotional behaviours that could contribute to the development of psychopathy; but the risks of developing these callous-unemotional behaviours are buffered if these individuals receive positive reinforcement from their adoptive mother (Hyde et al. 2016). Behavioural genetic and twin studies have found appreciable genetic influences as well as moderate non-shared environmental influences on the development of psychopathy (Patrick 2006). A meta-analysis examining behaviour genetic studies of psychopathy estimated that additive genetic influences account for approximately 49 per cent of the variance in self-reported psychopathy, while non-shared environmental factors accounted for the remaining 51 per cent of the variance (Patrick 2006).

See Chapter 1.5
Biological
criminology

Brain-imaging studies have found that individuals with psychopathic features have impairments in brain regions such as the amygdala and the

See Chapter 1.16
Neurocriminology

orbitofrontal cortex (OFC). Higher psychopathy in violent offenders has been linked with smaller amygdala volume, reduced amygdala functioning and impaired OFC functioning (Patrick 2006). Because the amygdala is involved in emotion processes, the formation of emotional memory and instrumental learning, and the OFC is involved in decision-making and reward-seeking behaviour, dysfunction in these two brain regions is thought to contribute to the development of psychopathy by impairing emotional and moral development.

Previous literature has also suggested that there may be neurochemical and genetic differences between psychopaths and non-psychopaths. Decreased serotonin levels are related to self- and other-directed aggression, and are closely associated with behaviours that develop into adult antisocial behaviour, including impulsivity and aggression in adult psychopaths. Prior research suggests serotonergic deficits are more closely associated with impulsive-antisocial aspects of psychopathy. Relatedly, low levels of MAOA, a major enzyme for breaking down brain serotonin, has been associated with sensation-seeking traits, aggression, criminality and **antisocial behaviour** (Patrick 2006) which have been found in psychopaths.

See Chapter 5.2
Antisocial
behaviour

See Chapter 2.1
Chicago School;
Chapter 2.2 Social
disorganization
theory

See Chapter 2.4
Differential
association;
Chapter 2.5 Social
learning theory;
Chapter 2.6
Control theories

In addition to biological risk factors, **environment** likely plays a role in the development of psychopathy. In fact, correlates of psychopathy include both familial factors and extra-familial factors. Previous research has suggested that familial factors such as minimal parental supervision, paternal rejection and childhood maltreatment (e.g., physical, emotional, and sexual abuse as well as neglect) are related to the development of psychopathic traits (Cooke et al. 1998). Research also suggests that extra-familial factors such as **delinquent friendships** or living in a **high-crime neighbourhood** are implicated in the manifestation of psychopathy and of antisocial behaviour (Patrick 2006).

Psychopathic individuals tend to be resistant to treatment and rehabilitation, with less time in treatment and fewer benefits gained from received treatment than non-psychopathic individuals (Patrick 2006). Group therapy, for example, has been found ineffective, and may actually increase violent recidivism as such therapeutic settings may give psychopaths more information that can be used to improve manipulation. There have also been attempts at using pharmacological treatments for the treatment of psychopathy or psychopathic symptoms. Oxytocin treatments have been proposed because oxytocin has been thought to promote prosocial behaviour. There have been inconsistent results, however, as some studies show elevated oxytocin levels in psychopathic individuals, while other studies show an oxytocin deficiency. Nevertheless, there are certain treatment methods that hold potential. Intensive treatments that are tailored to the emotional, cognitive and motivational styles of children and adolescents with elevated callous-unemotional traits, for example, may effectively reduce both the level of callous-unemotional traits and the severity of their behavioural problems (Frick et al. 2014) that might otherwise progress to adult psychopathy.

Future studies may be improved by investigating the mechanisms by which well-correlated risk factors such as heart rate or sex contribute to psychopathic predisposition. Distinguishing between subtypes of psychopathy to determine whether treatments have differential effects would also be a useful endeavour. Finally, it would be beneficial to explore potential protective factors that could buffer adverse situations that could otherwise lead to psychopathy.

References

Cooke, David J., Adelle E. Forth, and Robert D. Hare (eds). 1998. *Psychopathy: Theory, Research and Implications for Society*. Dordrecht, Netherlands: Springer.

Frick Paul J., James V. Ray, Laura C. Thornton, and Rachel E. Kahn. 2014. Can Callous-Unemotional Traits Enhance the Understanding, Diagnosis, and Treatment of Serious Conduct Problems in Children and Adolescents? A Comprehensive Review. *Psychological Bulletin* 140(1): 1–57.

Hyde, Luke W., Rebecca Waller, Christopher J. Trentacosta, Daniel S. Shaw, Jenae M. Neiderhiser, Jody M. Ganiban, David Reiss, and Leslie D. Leve. 2016. Heritable and Nonheritable Pathways to Early Callous-Unemotional Behaviors. *American Journal of Psychiatry* 173(9): 903–10.

Patrick, Christopher J. (ed.). 2006. *Handbook of Psychopathy*. New York: Guilford Press.

Skeem, Jennifer L., John F. Edens, Jacqueline Camp, and Lori H. Colwell. 2004. Are There Ethnic Differences in Level of Psychopathy? A Meta-Analysis. *Law and Human Behavior* 28(5): 505–27.

Further reading

Blair, R. James R. 2013. Psychopathy: Cognitive and Neural Dysfunction. *Dialogues in Clinical Neuroscience* 15(2): 181–90.

Glenn, Andrea L., and Adrian Raine. 2014. *Psychopathy: An Introduction to Biological Findings and Their Implications*. New York: New York University Press.

Kiehl, Kent A., and Morris B. Hoffman. 2011. The Criminal Psychopath: History, Neuroscience, Treatment, and Economics. *Jurimetrics* 51(4): 355–97.

Raine, Adrian. 2013. *The Anatomy of Violence: The Biological Roots of Crime*. New York: Pantheon.

Thompson, Dennis F., C.L. Ramos, and J.K. Willett. 2014. Psychopathy: Clinical Features, Developmental Basis and Therapeutic Challenges. *Journal of Clinical Pharmacy and Therapeutics* 39(5): 485–95.

Wynn, Rolf, Marita H. Høiseth, and Gunn Pettersen. 2012. Psychopathy in Women: Theoretical and Clinical Perspectives. *International Journal of Women's Health* 4(1): 257–63.

1.8 Learning theory

Clive R. Hollin

See Chapter 2.4
Differential
association;
Chapter 2.5 Social
learning theory

There are three distinct variations of learning theory – **learning through association**, learning through consequences and **social learning theory** – that may be applied to formulate an explanation of criminal behaviour.

Learning through association: The Nobel Prize-winning Russian physiologist Ivan Pavlov (1849–1936) famously demonstrated, in a process now called *classical conditioning*, how the behaviour of dogs can be prompted by a learned association between a specific stimulus, such as a light or a sound, and the arrival of food. The importance of Pavlov's work is that it moved thinking about the causes of behaviour away from internal processes as seen with, say, Freud's **psychoanalytical theory**, to environmental determinants of our actions. Some of the early American criminologists may have been familiar with Pavlov's work, as implied by Edwin Sutherland's (1883–1950) differential association theory, first published in 1939 and which Donald Cressey (1919–87) subsequently developed and refined (Sutherland and Cressey 1974). Differential Association Theory is notable because it viewed criminal behaviour as a *learned* behaviour, with the learning taking place in a social context.

See Chapter 1.10
Psychoanalytic
perspectives

Learning through consequences: While influenced by Pavlov, the unfolding of behaviourism in American universities had its roots in the work of figures such as Edward Thorndike (1874–1949) and John B. Watson (1878–1958). It was the American psychologist B.F. Skinner (1904–90), however, who framed the principles of *operant learning* to clarify how behaviour is acquired and maintained through its effects on the environment (Skinner 1974). Thus, behaviour *operates* on the environment to bring about change which may be rewarding or aversive for the individual concerned. Behaviours acquired or maintained over time by their rewarding consequences are, by definition, being *reinforced*; a behaviour which decreases in frequency over time is, by definition, being *punished* by its consequences (note that, here, unlike its meaning in everyday use, the idea of 'punishment' is not the same as the administration of physical pain or strict prison regimes).

In operant learning, the focus is on the individual such that different individuals will have their own unique histories of reinforcement and punishment. While people may belong to particular social groups or **subcultures**, there will nonetheless be differences between individuals in their **learning within their family, peer group, school and other environments**. This aspect of the theory explains how, even within ostensibly similar environments, there are some people who commit criminal acts and others who do not.

See Chapter 3.17
Subculture

See Chapter 2.2
Social
disorganization
theory

Skinner called the relationship between behaviour and its consequences a *contingency*. There are two types of reinforcement contingency: *positive reinforcement*, when the consequence of the behaviour *gains* a reward; and *negative reinforcement*, when behaviour *avoids* an aversive consequence. There are also two punishment contingencies: *positive punishment*, where the consequences of the behaviour are aversive; and *negative punishment*, when the consequence of the behaviour is the removal of something the individual finds rewarding. Skinner noted that behaviour does not occur at random: environmental cues, antecedent to the behaviour, signal when a given behaviour may be reinforced or punished. Thus, *A*ntecedent conditions indicate that a particular *B*ehaviour will result in certain *C*onsequences: these three elements form a *three-term contingency*.

Jeffery (1965) used operant theory to frame differential reinforcement theory. If criminal behaviour, such as theft, is seen as an operant behaviour, it may be prompted by antecedent conditions, such as an open window or an unlocked car, and maintained by the rewarding consequences of material gain. The rewarding consequences of crime can also be social in nature, as with peer approval and group status or, more rarely, causing other people to suffer. Thus, the material and social consequences can positively reinforce the criminal behaviour. Alternatively, the gains from theft may have the consequence of avoiding the effects of poverty, or the use of physical force can be an effective means to overcome victim resistance. In these instances, negative reinforcement contingencies act to maintain criminal behaviour. Criminal behaviour can bring about aversive consequences – such as being arrested, loss of liberty and family breakdown – which may reduce, that is punish, the frequency of the criminal behaviour.

Thus, differential reinforcement theory holds that an individual is likely to behave in a criminal manner when he/she is in an environment where he/she has previously been reinforced for such behaviour. Any previous aversive consequences will not have been sufficiently aversive to control or prevent the behaviour.

A (misplaced) criticism of operant theory is that it ignores the role of thoughts and feelings. The development of social learning theory highlighted the central role of cognitive and emotional processes in learning.

Social learning theory: The American psychologist Albert Bandura (1977) formulated social learning theory, which includes reinforcement in an operant sense but gives added emphasis to the role of cognition in learning. (The term *cognitive-behavioural* follows this line of theorizing.) Social learning theory holds that, as well as being acquired through reinforcement by external consequences, new behaviours may follow from observing the actions of other people (or *models*). The observational learning involved in the acquisition of criminal behaviour takes place primarily in three contexts. First, the behaviour modelled within families by parents and siblings; second, in the context of the peer group; and/or third, by the images shown in films, television and computer games. Yet further, social learning theory introduces the notion of *motivation* to amplify the operant notion of reinforcement. Bandura describes three types of motivation:

(i) *external reinforcement* as in operant theory;
(ii) *vicarious reinforcement*, when an individual's actions are motivated by observing the reinforcement or punishment of someone else's behaviour;
(iii) *self-reinforcement*, which refers to the motivational force of the individual's own sense of pride or achievement in his/her actions.

See Chapter 4.10
Emotions

Social learning theory has heralded interest in the role of **emotion** in criminal acts. In particular, attention has focused on the interplay between anger and acts of violence, with the American social psychologist Raymond Novaco making a significant contribution (Novaco and Welsh 1989). Novaco's model of angry violence begins with environmental cues – typically the words and actions of other people – which the individual perceives and appraises, sometimes wrongly, as hostile and threatening. These perceptions may produce a state of physiological and psychological arousal which the person labels as 'angry'. The interplay between cognition and rising anger intensifies the hostility of the appraisal of the situation so that the individual ultimately acts aggressively. In turn, an aggressive act may prompt a reaction from others present, eventually escalating to verbal and physical violence. Social learning theory maintains its position of pre-eminence, particularly among applied psychologists – although other paradigms based on neuroscience are increasingly popular.

The criticisms of accounts of criminal behaviour based on learning theory mostly focus on what is *not* explained by this approach. Thus, Rutter and Giller (1983) erroneously suggest that learning theories do not take account of sex differences, age changes and developmental factors in the aetiology of offending. These criticisms often neglect the basic point that, with its focus on the individual, learning theory does not seek to formulate general rules to account for specific acts, such as theft or the behaviour of antisocial adolescents. Further, this approach does not attempt to offer wide-ranging explanations of the relationship between culture or social structure and crime as found elsewhere in mainstream criminology. Thus, learning theories primarily work at an individual level, emphasizing each individual's uniqueness in terms of their learning history and their patterns of reinforcement and punishment contingent upon their previous criminal acts.

At a philosophical level, as with **personality theory**, learning theories raise the conundrum of whether our actions are determined by environmental contingencies or whether we have recourse to free will in deciding upon our actions. Indeed, at the point at which social learning theory gives cognition a critical role in causing behaviour, so the quandary between 'external' and 'internal' causality returns to centre stage.

See Chapter 1.9
Personality theory

References

Bandura, Albert. 1977. *Social Learning Theory*. New York: Prentice Hall.

Jeffery, C.R. [Clarence Ray]. 1965. Criminal Behavior and Learning Theory. *Journal of Criminal Law, Criminology and Police Science* 56(3): 294–300.

Novaco, Raymond W., and Wayne N. Welsh. 1989. Anger disturbances: Cognitive mediation and clinical prescriptions. In *Clinical Approaches to Violence*, Kevin Howells and Clive R. Hollin, eds, pp. 39–60. Chichester: Wiley.

Rutter, Michael, and Henri Giller. 1983. *Juvenile Delinquency: Trends and Perspectives*. Harmondsworth: Penguin.

Skinner, B.F. [Burrhus Frederic]. 1974. *About Behaviourism*. London: Cape.

Sutherland, Edwin Hardin, and Donald R. Cressey. 1974. *Principles of Criminology* (9th edn). Philadelphia: Lippincott.

Further reading

Akers, Ronald L. 1973. *Deviant Behavior: A Social Learning Approach*. Belmont, CA: Wadsworth.

Akers, Ronald L., and Wesley G. Jennings. 2009. The social learning theory of crime and deviance. In *Handbook on Crime and Deviance*, Marvin D. Krohn, Alan J. Lizotte, and Gina P. Hall, eds, pp. 103–20. New York: Springer.

Glenn, Andrea L., and Adrian Raine. 2014. Neurocriminology: Implications for the Punishment, Prediction and Prevention of Criminal Behaviour. *Nature Reviews Neuroscience* 15(1): 54–63.

Hollin, Clive R. 2013. *Psychology and Crime: An Introduction to Criminological Psychology* (2nd edn). Hove: Routledge.

Modgil, Sohan, and Celia Modgil (eds). 1987. *B.F. Skinner: Consensus and Controversy*. New York: Falmer Press.

Nietzel, Michael T. 1979. *Crime and Its Modification: A Social Learning Perspective*. Oxford: Pergamon Press.

1.9 Personality theory

Clive R. Hollin

See Chapter 1.8
Learning theory

A range of **psychological theories**, including several variants of personality theory, has been applied to give an account of why an individual may behave in an antisocial or criminal manner. With regard to terminology, the word 'personality' can take on various meanings within mainstream psychology. It can be used in the general sense of referring to a grand theory – as, say, with Freud's **psychoanalytic theory** – or it can be used specifically to refer to those theories that fall under the rubric of personality theory. It is the latter sense in which it is used here.

See Chapter 1.10
Psychoanalytic
perspectives

In personality theory, an individual's actions are understood as the product of internal processes. These internal processes, which constitute personality, remain consistent over time so that the individual has a stable predisposition to act in a particular way. In one tradition within personality theory, these stable internal processes are termed *traits*. The most influential trait theory was formulated by Hans Eysenck (1916–97) and is based on the proposition that genetic inheritance bestows individual differences in the functioning of the cortical and autonomic nervous systems. This **biological variation** determines the capability to *condition* to environmental stimuli (in the sense of learning by association or Pavlovian conditioning), thereby playing a role in a child's socialization and the development of what Eysenck termed a *conscience*.

See Chapter 1.5
Biological
criminology

Eysenck (1959) defined two personality dimensions, *extraversion* (E) and *neuroticism* (N), with each dimension a composite of specific inter-correlated traits. Thus, for example, E is composed of traits that include being sociable, active and sensation-seeking; while N encompasses anxiety, shyness and emotionality. Eysenck and Eysenck (1968) added a third dimension, *psychoticism*

(P), which is comprised of traits such as aggression, egocentricity and lack of empathy.

Personality dimensions are conceptualized as a continuum such that extraversion ranges from high (extravert) to low (introvert), neuroticism from high (neurotic) to low (stable), and psychoticism simply from high to low. The distribution of personality dimensions across the population is such that the majority of people cluster at the centre of the continuum, with the minority divided between the upper and lower extremes.

Eysenck (1959) proposed a biologically based explanation for E and N. The extravert is cortically *under*-aroused and so seeks to increase his/her levels of cortical arousal through behaviour that is characterized by impulsivity, risk-taking and thrill-seeking. The introvert is cortically *over*-aroused and so avoids stimulation and excitement, so maintaining a reserved demeanour. As conditionability is related to levels of *both* E and N in combination, stable introverts (Low N–Low E) condition best; stable extraverts (Low N–High E) and neurotic introverts (High N–Low E) condition at a mid-level; and neurotic extraverts (High N–High E) condition least well. Psychoticism, initially intended to differentiate the personality traits underlying psychosis rather than neurosis, was later seen by Eysenck as analogous to psychopathy. High P is associated with traits such as a lack of feeling for others, sensation-seeking and aggression. Psychometric tests, such as the Eysenck Personality Inventory, are designed to provide a measure of personality.

Eysenck (1964) applied his theory to explain criminal behaviour, refining his approach over time (Eysenck and Gudjonsson 1989). The basis of Eysenck's theory of criminal behaviour is that as High E–High N produces poor conditionability, so those with this combination of personality traits will be least well socialized and therefore over-represented in offender populations. The Low E–Low N group is best socialized, and so is predicted to be under-represented among offenders. High E–Low N and Low E–High N groups are at a mid-level, and so will appear in both offender and non-offender groups. Psychoticism (P) is seen as particularly related to aggressive offences.

Eysenck's theory of criminal behaviour has generated a substantial body of empirical research. A typical study by McGurk and McDougall (1981) used cluster analysis to examine the patterns of P, E, and N scores in delinquents and non-delinquents. They found that both groups contained the Low E–High N and High E–Low N combinations, but the combinations predicted to be related to criminal behaviour – High E–High N and High P–High E–High N – were evident only in the delinquent sample. The Low E–Low N combination was, as predicted, found only in the non-delinquent group. Subsequent studies have attempted to replicate the McGurk and McDougall study, with varying degrees of exactness of match to Eysenck's theory.

The balance of empirical evidence, particularly with younger offenders, tends to support Eysenck's position on the relationship between personality and crime. Eysenck has acknowledged that there are, as with any theory, limitations: the theory is not applicable to all crime and all criminals, and the emphasis on conditioning does not include other types of learning which may be important in socialization.

Eysenck's theory has been superseded by the Five Factor Model, sometimes referred to as the 'Big Five' (McCrae and Costa, 1997). The Big Five personality factors are: (1) Neuroticism/Emotional Stability; (2) Extraversion; (3) Openness to Experience; (4) Agreeableness; and (5) Conscientiousness. The first two factors are similar to Eysenck's E and N, while the third relates to imagination and artistic feeling, the fourth to altruism and the fifth to self-discipline; agreeableness and conscientiousness may be inversely related to Eysenck's P.

There is markedly less research investigating the relationship between the Big Five and criminal behaviour than is the case with Eysenck's theory. The trends in the research suggest that, compared to non-delinquents, young offenders are significantly lower with regard to agreeableness, conscientiousness and openness, but higher on extraversion. Yet further, three broad traits have been identified as persistently occurring in association with antisocial behaviour: these 'Big Three' traits are extraversion-sociability, neuroticism-**emotionality** and impulsivity-disinhibition.

See Chapter 4.10
Emotions

Cale (2006) reported a meta-analysis of the relationship between personality and **antisocial behaviour**. The results indicated that across the Eysenck personality types, the Big Five and the Big Three, impulsivity-disinhibition has the strongest association with antisocial behaviour. Cale also noted that the strength of the association in individual studies was moderated by several factors, including the age of the sample.

See Chapter 5.2
Antisocial
behaviour

There are two levels of criticism of personality theory when applied to explain criminal behaviour. The first stems from within psychology in that in offering an explanation for behaviour, personality theories pay undue attention to individual factors, both biological and psychological, and insufficient attention to **environmental**, particularly social, factors. The second level of criticism of personality theory is from criminology, as expressed by Taylor et al. (1973), who state two fundamental points of disagreement (specifically with Eysenck's theory, but their arguments can be taken more generally with respect to personality theory). First, they take issue with Eysenck's **biological positivism** in which human action is seen to be determined and law-governed. In contrast, Taylor and colleagues express the view that the interaction between the individual and his/her environment, indeed his/her society, is a dynamic, fluctuating process. Second, Taylor et al. stress the significance of 'meaning' in their view of human nature, such that account must be taken of the meaning that criminal behaviour has for the individual offender. The philosophical contrast is evident: on the one hand, human behaviour is determined by biological and social forces; on the other, we are active, **rational agents** seeking to comprehend our social world and construct our own destiny.

See Chapter 2.1
Chicago School;
Chapter 2.2 Social
disorganization
theory

See Chapter 1.4
Positivism

See Chapter 1.2
Classical
Criminology;
Chapter 1.18
Rational choice

In summary, while personality theory no longer has the dominance it once enjoyed within mainstream psychology, it does nevertheless continue to receive some attention. The aspects of personality initially described by

Eysenck remain predominant in attempts to account for criminal behaviour from within the wider church of personality theory.

References

Cale, Ellison M. 2006. A Quantitative Review of the Relations between the 'Big 3' Higher Order Personality Dimensions and Antisocial Behavior. *Journal of Research in Personality* 40(3): 250–84.

Eysenck, Hans J. 1959. *Manual of the Maudsley Personality Inventory*. London: University of London Press.

Eysenck, Hans J. 1964. *Crime and Personality*. London: Routledge & Kegan Paul.

Eysenck Hans J., and Sybil B.G. Eysenck. 1968. *Manual for the Eysenck Personality Inventory*. San Diego: Educational and Industrial Testing Service.

Eysenck, Hans J., and Gisli H. Gudjonsson. 1989. *The Causes and Cures of Criminality*. New York: Plenum.

McCrae, Robert R., and Paul T. Costa. 1997. Personality Trait Structure as a Human Universal. *American Psychologist* 52(5): 509–16.

McGurk, Barry J., and Cynthia McDougall. 1981. A New Approach to Eysenck's Theory of Personality. *Personality and Individual Differences* 2(4): 338–40.

Taylor, Ian, Paul Walton, and Jock Young. 1973. *The New Criminology: For a Social Theory of Deviance*. London: Routledge & Kegan Paul.

Further reading

Eysenck, Hans J. 1977. *Crime and Personality* (3rd edn). London: Routledge & Kegan Paul.

Eysenck, Hans J. 1996. Personality and Crime: Where Do We Stand? *Psychology, Crime and Law* 2(3): 143–52.

Hollin, Clive R. 2013. *Psychology and Crime: An Introduction to Criminological Psychology* (2nd edn). Hove: Routledge.

Jones, Shane E., Joshua D. Miller, and Donald R. Lynam. 2011. Personality, Antisocial Behavior, and Aggression: A Meta-Analytic Review. *Journal of Criminal Justice* 39(4): 329–37.

Maltby, John, Liz Day, and Ann Macaskill. 2013. *Personality, Individual Differences and Intelligence* (3rd edn). Harlow: Pearson Education.

1.10 Psychoanalytic perspectives

Tony Jefferson

Psychoanalytic theory has gone through many iterations since Freud, its founding father, but what all share is a belief that human behaviour is a product of unconscious desires as well as conscious intentions, which will sometimes be in conflict. Its core notion is thus a conflicted subject not fully known to itself; not the rational 'man' presumed by economics and **rational choice theory** but a subject riven by **emotions** and feelings that the reasoning mind attempts to make sense of or to defend itself against if these prove too painful or anxiety-invoking. 'Irrational' behaviour (which includes many crimes as well as neuroses) is thus its speciality.

See Chapter 1.18
Rational choice

See Chapter 4.10
Emotions

There are three relevant moments in the history of psychoanalytic theorizing: the initial, traditional, instinct or drive-based theorizing of Freud himself, centred on the individual; the shift from the idea that the unconscious is founded on sexuality or desire (the instinctual pursuit of bodily pleasure) to the notion that it is founded on relations with objects/others (initially the mother's breast) which enabled a more social, intersubjective version of the individual to emerge; and the work of the Frankfurt School, which, in attempting to link a Freudian subject with Marx's political economy, developed the idea that social structure and personality were indissolubly connected, thus producing a fully social reading of the individual.

In thinking about the first of these moments, the simplest formulation of Freud's theory is probably the notion that civilization is built on the renunciation of instincts. At the individual level, understanding how the infant at the mercy of his/her instincts becomes socialized entails the concept of a conscious self (or 'ego') constantly caught between instinctual desires and the demands of social living. The internalization of the latter (Freud's 'super-ego' or conscience) is accompanied by the repression of instinctual impulses, which are thereby rendered unconscious. These repressed libidinal and destructive instincts (the 'id') are thereafter inaccessible to consciousness directly but may manifest indirectly as neurotic symptoms (e.g., hysteria, slips of the tongue, phobias, 'acting out'), which can become disabling. Psychoanalysis as a practice was a series of techniques designed to bring to consciousness the previously unconscious: to 'read' the symptom back to its unconscious roots. For some criminologists inspired by these ideas between the 1920s and the 1960s, crime, too, became a symptom to be decoded: a manifestation of an underlying **pathology**.

See Chapter 1.6 Pathology

Although Freud was clear that normality and pathology constituted the ends of an inclusive continuum rather than marking a divide, his work was focused on the pathological (neuroses or psychoses) and used the language of perversion in describing sexual pathologies. Unsurprisingly then, those criminologists attempting to work with Freud's ideas saw (some) crime as a pathological manifestation of intra-psychic conflict. Repressed sexuality, guilt about sexuality, failures of super-ego development, for example, could all produce 'complexes' or pathologies that might eventuate in criminality, according to criminologists like M. Hamblin Smith (a prison medical officer) and Edward Glover (founder of the Portman Clinic and a founding editor of what became the *British Journal of Criminology*). Although Glover pointed to the use of psychoanalysis beyond understanding offenders – noting how punitive attitudes reflected the needs of punishers, for example – and to the affinities between psychopathy and normality, this early work is now generally dismissed (not without cause) as individualistic (offender-focused), normative, correctionalist and **biologically deterministic**: characteristics that became anathema to the emergent, critical criminological theorizing of the 1960s and 1970s.

See Chapter 1.5 Biological criminology

If this early period constituted the brief heyday of psychoanalysis within criminology, since around 1960 (on both sides of the Atlantic), psychoanalytic approaches to crime have been at best marginal and largely ignored within criminology, where sociology became the dominant discipline. Consequently, interest in the criminal subject waned. But feminist interest in 'the personal is political', together with the relational turn in psychoanalysis (associated, in the UK, especially with the work of Melanie Klein and, with a somewhat different provenance, in the US with figures such as Jessica Benjamin and Nancy Chodorow), has stimulated a psychoanalytically informed psychosocial approach within criminology that may yet provoke a revival of interest in **psychoanalytic concepts**. Similarly, the work of the Frankfurt School, especially that of Erich Fromm, has undergone a mini-revival.

See Chapter 4.30 Psychosocial criminology

John Bowlby constitutes a unique, transitional figure between the first and the second moment of psychoanalytic theorizing. His early work, *Forty-Four*

Juvenile Thieves (1946), belongs thematically and chronologically with that of Hamblin Smith and Glover. It explored the link between prolonged separation from the mother (or substitute) in infancy and various 'disturbed' outcomes, including the production of a group of 'affectionless' delinquents. His later, better-known, work on attachment theory – a product of the 1970s – drew upon evolutionary biology, ethology (the idea of imprinting), developmental psychology and cybernetics as well as psychoanalysis, although he distanced himself from both Freud and Klein. What unites both periods of his work is his sustained, empirically driven attention to the issue of mother (or her substitute)–child relations and the different kinds of attachment associated with positive and negative child development. Much debated and contested, ideas associated with attachment theory remain hugely influential. Whether or not they can strictly be called psychoanalytic is moot. Be that as it may, such ideas are all but absent from the criminological imagination.

Klein's major revision of Freud, our second moment, was to make object-relating, not sexuality, key to understanding the neonate – a conceptual move that placed the mother, not the father, centre stage. Relating first to the part-object of the maternal breast produces anxiety (because it is not always available when wanted), which, in turn, produces phantasies of love and hate driven by the primitive defence mechanisms of splitting and projection. 'Bad', hateful feelings are split off from 'good' ones (in phantasy) and projected onto the mother's breast, thus externalizing the persecutory anxiety. Klein called this the 'paranoid-schizoid' position. Once the baby learns to perceive the mother as a whole object who is the source of both love and hate, and to live with the resulting ambivalence, then the baby is said to have entered the depressive position. But neither position is absolute or confined to relations with the mother: the paranoid-schizoid defences of splitting and projection remain generally available and will continue to be drawn upon at anxious moments, especially by those whose early attempts at projecting out the 'bad' have been rebuffed – i.e., not introjected (taken in/accepted) by the mother and successfully 'contained' (or detoxified).

One area in particular where Kleinian-inspired work has had some contemporary impact is racism. The notion of defensively splitting off unwanted 'bad' parts of the self and projecting them onto the racially/ethnically different 'Others' who then become the phantasized carriers of such disavowed negative attributes is key to understanding, at the personal level, the (irrational) negative prejudices and hatred sustaining the racist imagination. Because racism also signifies at the social level (ideologically/discursively), this is an area where **psychosocial criminology** too has a contemporary presence.

See Chapter 4.30
Psychosocial
criminology

The relational psychoanalytic work of Benjamin and Chodorow tends to start with Freud's Oedipus complex, as gender is one of their key areas of interest. Their critical look at the Oedipus complex (a concept that Klein virtually replaced with her notions of paranoid-schizoid and the transition to the depressive position) led to significant revisions. Benjamin's key idea, that Freud's traditional version of the Oedipus complex (that boys renounce their desire for their mothers in favour of identification with their fathers under the threat of castration), is one of many possible outcomes, and is the least desirable. This is because it is, in effect, a defensive repudiation of femininity. This idea – masculinity as a renouncement of femininity – has impacted contemporary studies of **masculinity** (if only marginally) and criminology (given the close affiliation of traditional masculinity with violence).

See Chapter 4.21
Masculinities,
structure and
hegemony

The work of the Frankfurt School, especially its influential work on racism, constitutes our third moment. Erich Fromm's (1941) classic wartime study of fascism theorized the notion of the 'authoritarian character' as the personality structure most conducive to fascism. Nine years later, his colleagues were able, through a mammoth research study, to confirm it empirically (Adorno at al. 1950). Rejecting Freud's instinctually based starting point for the idea that individual nature is always a cultural product, Fromm attempted to show how the predominant character structure of any particular historical period is shaped by the prevailing socio-economic conditions: how the new individualistic freedoms of capitalism produced new fears and anxieties that led to the development, in the case of the moment of fascism, of an authoritarian character structure. By this he meant a normalized sadomasochism uniting both masochistic submission (to authority) and sadistic domination (of weaker outsiders/deviants).

Fromm's other directly relevant criminological writings appeared only recently in English, in an edited volume dedicated to the contemporary relevance of his work for critical, **feminist** and **peacemaking criminology** in particular (Anderson and Quinney 2000). As well as discussing the psychology of the criminal, Fromm's papers also introduce the notion of the punitive society: the idea that the state's commitment to a punitive criminal justice system, despite its obvious failure to ameliorate crime, serves primarily educative and legitimating purposes. This anticipates **critical criminology** by some 40 years. Moreover, such a punitive system, he argued, also provides an opportunity to satisfy the aggressive and sadistic impulses of the masses – impulses that would otherwise be directed at their rulers (a psychoanalytic insight that might yet enrich thinking about **moral panics**).

Chapter 3.6
Feminist
criminologies;
Chapter 3.13
Radical feminism;
Chapter 4.26
Patriarchy and
crime

See Chapter 3.12
Peacemaking in
criminology

See Chapter 3.3
Critical
criminologies

See Chapter 3.10
Moral panic

Harry Stack Sullivan, a one-time colleague of Fromm, has recently had his interpersonal relational psychoanalytic approach resurrected in understanding certain forms of murder (Stein 2007). In particular, Stein uses Sullivan's notion of the defence of 'dissociation', and shows how it is used by those suffering serious childhood trauma and abuse, and in certain situations, can culminate in murder. From South Africa, Duncan Cartwright's (2002) work on rage murder has similarities. In the UK, the book on murder by Hyatt-Williams (1998), one-time chair of the Adolescent Department at the Tavistock Clinic, brings us back to Klein.

References

Adorno, Theodor, Else Frenkel-Brunswik, Daniel Levinson, and R. Nevitt Sanford. 1950. *The Authoritarian Personality*. New York: Harper & Row.

Anderson, Kevin, and Richard Quinney (eds). 2000. *Erich Fromm and Critical Criminology: Beyond the Punitive Society*. Urbana: University of Illinois Press.

Bowlby, John. 1946. *Forty-Four Juvenile Thieves*. London: Balliere, Tindall and Cox.

Cartwright, Duncan. 2002. *Psychoanalysis, Violence and Rage-Type Murder: Murdering Minds*. London: Brunner-Routledge.

Fromm, Erich. 1941. *Escape from Freedom*. New York: Farrar and Rinehart.

Hyatt-Williams, Arthur. 1998. *Cruelty, Violence and Murder: Understanding the Criminal Mind*. London: Karnac.

Stein, Abby. 2007. *Prologue to Violence: Child Abuse, Dissociation and Crime*. Mahwah, NJ: Analytic Press.

Further reading

Benjamin, Jessica. 1998. *Shadow of the Other: Intersubjectivity and Gender in Psychoanalysis*. London: Routledge.

Freud, Sigmund. 1973. *Introductory Lectures on Psychoanalysis*. Harmondsworth: Penguin.

Frosh, Stephen. 1997. *For and Against Psychoanalysis*. London: Routledge.

Minsky, Rosalind. 1998. *Psychoanalysis and Culture: Contemporary States of Mind*. Cambridge: Polity.

Biosocial theory

Stephen G. Tibbetts

Biosocial theories of crime can be defined as those perspectives that emphasize the interaction between **physiological dispositions** and **environmental conditions** that affect the likelihood of criminality in individuals. This perspective is generally considered an inherently interdisciplinary approach that is designed to integrate and synthesize information from many diverse fields of research to form a more coherent understanding of criminality. This category of theories is also commonly known as the 'nature via nurture' or 'biology X environment interaction' perspective.

See Chapter 1.5 Biological criminology

See Chapter 2.1 Chicago School; Chapter 2.2 Social disorganization theory

The biosocial perspective grew out of the early history of criminology in the nineteenth century – influenced by craniometry, phrenology and physiognomy – and, perhaps most importantly, by Cesare Lombroso, often considered the 'father of criminology', who emphasized the **genetics/physiology** of certain individuals as well as their environment. Many of these theories became popular among researchers and policymakers due to the societal beliefs in social Darwinism and eugenics at the time – particularly that some groups of individuals were inferior to others. Although these perspectives emphasized physiological differences between people, most of them also recognized the importance of social context in their theoretical frameworks. Still, these theoretical frameworks were eventually discredited for various reasons, including their strong emphasis on biology, their relative lack of an equal focus on social and other environmental factors, and their public policy implications (e.g., mandatory sterilization).

See Chapter 1.5 Biological criminology

Towards the latter half of the twentieth century, however, more modern perspectives were proposed that reflected the concepts and methodology of studying the interactions between individuals' physiology and their environmental contexts that either suppressed or encouraged (or 'triggered') the biological dispositions some individuals possessed toward criminality. Many of these more modern biosocial models were informed by research in other disciplines, such as anthropology, medicine and psychology. The integration of such diverse areas of study has resulted in the basic assumption of biosocial theory that genes and environment tend to work in tandem such that disadvantaged environments tend to enhance antisocial gene expression.

Perhaps the most seminal of these more modern biosocial perspectives is that of behavioural genetics, which is primarily concerned with examining variation among groups of twin pairs in order to estimate the relative contributions of shared environments, unshared environments and genetics toward the development of criminality. Such studies have gone a long way to helping place the heritability estimates for antisocial behaviour at approximately 0.50 (i.e., 50 per cent). In other words, the proportion of variance due to genetic effects for underlying traits in a given population in a specific environment is about half of the explained variance.

Additional studies have examined observed physiological factors that appear to be different in chronic, habitual offenders as compared to 'normal' persons (non-offenders). For example, one of the most established differences revealed by these studies is that of heart rate. Empirical studies consistently have found that chronic offenders have a significantly lower heart rate than that of non-offenders, and thus they need more excitement – such as killing another individual – in order to be aroused (Armstrong and Boutwell 2012). This observed difference in heart rate is one manifestation of how serious offenders often seem to not worry much about apprehension and punishment, which has implications for reducing their anti-social behaviour.

Another category of studies has examined specific genes (or variations of such genes), often referred to as molecular genetic studies, most of which examine the effects certain gene polymorphisms have on criminality from the functioning of the nervous system via **neurotransmitters**. For example, the most researched of these types of gene-specific predictors are those of certain allele categories of MAO-A and the DRD2/DRD4 polymorphisms. The MAO-A variation has consistently been linked to lower levels of the neurotransmitter serotonin, as well as to higher levels of the hormone testosterone – both of which predispose an individual to criminality (Tibbetts 2014). It is the coupling of the MAO-A polymorphism with a disadvantaged environment (e.g., child neglect/abuse) that produces the most significant effect (Raine 2013), however. The DRD2 and DRD4 polymorphisms have been consistently implicated in the development of criminality due to the effect on levels of the neurotransmitter dopamine; once again, it is not *the fact* that certain individuals have this type of gene variation which affects criminality, but *the extent* to which those genetic polymorphisms interact with disadvantaged environmental factors (Beaver 2009). There are other genetic variations that are being investigated currently.

See Chapter 1.16
Neurocriminology

The biosocial theoretical perspective has a number of strengths and weaknesses. By far the greatest strength of the biosocial model is that it inherently includes a very broad scope of factors – both physiological and environmental – that can include virtually any and/or all potential predictors of criminality that may be important in understanding criminality. After all, nearly any biological factor can be investigated in this model, as can nearly all environmental factors; and then, importantly, so can the many types of interactions potentially resulting from their coupling (or multivariate interactions) that can occur among the many variables from physiology and the environment. This is a primary strength, and makes the biosocial perspective an inherently general theoretical framework. Another important strength of this approach is that it requires researchers in this area to examine the research findings of all other relevant fields of study (e.g., medicine, psychology).

Unfortunately, the very characteristics that are the strengths of the biosocial perspective can also be seen as the major weaknesses or criticisms of the theoretical model. Namely, the biosocial framework lacks parsimony, which is commonly regarded as an important quality in most 'good' theories of human behaviour. As most theoretical texts point out, the more simple a theory the better – because it can be better understood and more easily tested and, ultimately, be far easier to apply for policy purposes. The biosocial theoretical model is inherently complex and defies a simple framework, largely due to the fact that there are literally thousands of potentially important physiological factors to be accounted for, as well as perhaps even more environmental factors that can be implicated in criminality; and this is further complicated by the many thousands of possible interaction effects among these various potential factors.

Another primary criticism of biosocial theory largely stems from the many criminologists that have traditionally been trained exclusively in the social/environmental realm, and have virtually no knowledge or background in doing biological-related research. They simply do not understand basic concepts or methodology regarding how biological factors are studied, let alone how they can be applied to criminal behaviour. The field of criminology is well known to have been dominated by sociology since the latter part of the twentieth century. Thus, there has been a very obvious backlash by many respected criminologists, likely because they are protecting what they see as their intellectual turf. Still, science is inherently based on constantly questioning and seeking, and for this reason the biosocial framework has survived and even thrived in recent years.

There is recent empirical research that backs up this new emphasis on the biosocial perspective: specifically, a 2008 study by Ellis and his colleagues that sampled 387 leading experts in the field and asked them to rank the most important theories for explaining serious criminal offending. This study showed that biosocial theory was ranked 6th by these experts, and that this perspective had moved up significantly compared to a very similar study conducted approximately one decade earlier. Furthermore, the research on biosocial theory has increased even more since the time of this study. Specifically, Tibbetts (2014) has noted that, in examining the abstract entries in databases such as Criminal Justice Abstracts and PsycINFO, the rate of entries has increased exponentially in most recent years.

Regarding future developments in biosocial theory, far more work must be done to explore the many biological and environmental factors that are important in the causes of criminal offending, as well as to examine the many types of bivariate and multivariate interactions that occur between these factors. The knowledge on biosocial interactions is growing faster than ever before. There are, however, many factors and interactions that have not been studied to date, such as those regarding actual precise genes that are involved with neurotransmitter levels correlated with criminality. So far only a few have been discovered (e.g., the DRD2 gene), but many more must be examined to see if they are implicated in the development of a predisposition toward antisocial tendencies. These future studies will likely enhance the empirical validity of the biosocial perspective, as well as build a more comprehensive understanding of the development of criminality among individuals.

References

Armstrong, Todd, and Brian Boutwell. 2012. Low Resting Heart Rate and Rational Choice: Integrating Biological Correlates of Crime in Criminological Theories. *Journal of Criminal Justice* 40(1): 31–9.

Beaver, Kevin M. 2009. *Biosocial Criminology: A Primer*. Dubuque, IA: Kendall Hunt.

Ellis, L., Jonathon A. Cooper, and Anthony Walsh. 2008. Criminologists' Opinions about Causes and Theories of Crime Delinquency: A Follow-Up. *The Criminologist* 33(1): 23–6.

Raine, Adrian. 2013. *The Anatomy of Violence: The Biological Roots of Crime*. New York: Pantheon.

Tibbetts, Stephen G. 2014. Prenatal and perinatal predictors of antisocial behavior: Review of research and interventions. In *Criminological Theory: A Life-Course Approach* (2nd edn), Matt DeLisi and Kevin M. Beaver, eds, Chapter 2. Burlington, MA: Jones and Bartlett.

Additional reading

Beaver, Kevin M., and Anthony Walsh (eds). 2011. Biosocial criminology. In *The Ashgate Research Companion to Biosocial Theories of Crime*, Kevin M. Beaver and Anthony Walsh, eds, Chapter 1. Farnham: Ashgate.

Brennan, Patricia A., and Adrian Raine. 1997. Biosocial Bases of Antisocial Behavior: Psychophysiological, Neurological and Cognitive Factors. *Clinical Psychology Review* 17(6): 589–604.

DeLisi, Matt, Kevin M. Beaver, Michael G. Vaughn, and John Paul Wright. 2010. Contemporary retrospectives on biosocial theories. In *Criminological Theory:*

Readings and Retrospectives, Heath Copes and Volkan Topalli, eds, pp. 74–84. New York: McGraw-Hill.

Rowe, David. 2001. *Biology and Crime*. Los Angeles: Roxbury.

Tibbetts, Stephen G. and Alex R. Piquero. 1999. The Influence of Gender, Low Birth Weight, and Disadvantaged Environment in Predicting Early Onset of Offending: A Test of Moffitt's Interactional Hypothesis. *Criminology* 37: 843–78.

Wright, John Paul. 2009. Biosocial criminology. *Oxford Bibliographies Online*. http://www.oxfordbibliographies.com/view/document/obo-9780195396607/obo-9780195396607-0015.xml. Accessed 23 January 2017.

Wright, John Paul, Stephen G. Tibbetts and Leah E. Daigle. 2014. *Criminals in the Making: Criminality across the Life Course*. Thousand Oaks, CA: Sage.

1.12 Developmental criminology

David P. Farrington

See Chapter 5.2
Antisocial
behaviour

Developmental criminology is concerned with the development of offending and **antisocial behaviour** from the womb to the tomb, and especially with continuity and change throughout life. It also focuses on the effects of risk and protective factors, and life events, at different ages on the course of development.

See Chapter 1.13
Life-course theory

Developmental criminology is similar to **life-course criminology** in many respects, and the two are commonly linked in developmental and life-course criminology (DLC). While there are many overlaps, there are some differences in emphasis between the two areas. In general, developmental

See Chapter 1.8
Learning theory

criminology (as exemplified by the work of Terrie Moffitt) is grounded in **psychology** and focuses more on the onset of offending and the influence of risk and protective factors in childhood and adolescence. In contrast, life-course criminology (as exemplified by the work of Robert Sampson and John Laub) is

See Chapter 5.6
Desistance

grounded in sociology and focuses more on **desistance** and on the influence of life events in adulthood.

At least up to the 1970s, criminologists carried out cross-sectional surveys and tried to draw conclusions about the causes of offending from comparisons between individuals. For example, in investigating whether unemployment was a cause of offending, crime rates of unemployed individuals would be compared with crime rates of employed individuals. The main problem, however, was that unemployed individuals differed from employed individuals in numerous uncontrolled factors that might cause offending.

In contrast, developmental criminologists carry out prospective longitudinal surveys, which are important in avoiding retrospective bias in reporting and in calculating prospective probabilities (e.g., the probability of a juvenile delinquent becoming an adult criminal). Importantly, they investigate comparisons within individuals. For example, offending during unemployment periods is compared with offending during employment periods for the same individual. In this comparison, each person acts as his or her own control, so all individual factors (e.g., impulsiveness, intelligence) are held constant. These types of within-individual comparisons yield much more convincing evidence about causal effects.

Developmental criminology began with the classic American longitudinal studies of Sheldon and Eleanor Glueck and William and Joan McCord. These were soon followed by longitudinal studies in the UK (by Israel Kolvin and by Donald West and David Farrington), in Scandinavia (by David Magnusson and Lea Pulkkinen), in Canada (by Marc Le Blanc and Richard Tremblay) and in New Zealand (by Phil Silva and David Magnusson). The 1980s proved to be the golden age for the initiation of American longitudinal studies (Farrington 2015a).

In the best longitudinal surveys, information is obtained repeatedly from different sources, including the participants themselves, their parents, their teachers, their peers and official (criminal and health) records. Since convictions are only the 'tip of the iceberg' of offending, it is important to compare official records with self-reports of offending to estimate the 'scaling-up factor'. For example, in the Pittsburgh Youth Study, there were over 30 self-reported offences for every conviction. Most longitudinal researchers focus on statistical analyses, but some present detailed case histories from childhood to adulthood. Researchers who study desistance are most likely to use qualitative methods.

Whatever their background, most longitudinal researchers investigate not only violence and property crime but also many other topics – including drug use, alcohol use, drink driving, reckless driving, smoking, gambling, sexual behaviour, relationship problems, employment problems, educational problems, and mental and physical health. Many researchers have concluded that offending is only one element of a larger syndrome of antisocial behaviour that tends to persist from childhood to adulthood and from one generation to the next. The challenge is how to interrupt this persistence, and a number of longitudinal studies (e.g., the Montreal project of Richard Tremblay) have tested the effectiveness of an experimental intervention designed to achieve this.

Many longitudinal researchers have proposed DLC theories to explain their findings (Farrington 2005). In most cases, their theories were highly influenced by their data. For example, Terrie Moffitt analysed the Dunedin study of over 1000 three-year-old children who were followed into their 30s. Her more psychological theory distinguished life-course-persistent and adolescence-limited offenders, and emphasized childhood risk factors for life-course-persistent offending. In contrast, Robert Sampson and John Laub analysed the Gluecks' study of 500 delinquent males and focused on their adult years, roughly from age 30 to age 70. Their more sociological theory emphasized informal social control by adult social institutions such as marriages and jobs, and aimed to explain desistance.

In studying the development of offending, the most important phenomenon is the age–crime curve. In most times and places, the aggregate rate of offending increases up to a peak in the teenage years (usually) and then decreases more gradually in the 20s and beyond. In general, the age–crime curve for males is more sharply peaked than the curve for females, which is flatter and has a higher average age of offending. The age–crime curve for individuals, however, may be very different from the aggregate curve. In recent years, inspired by the work of Daniel Nagin, there has been a great deal of interest in identifying different offending trajectories.

Following the work of Alfred Blumstein, developmental criminology is very concerned to advance knowledge about criminal careers (Piquero et al. 2007), which have an age of onset, a duration and an age of desistance. During their careers, offenders commit a variety of crimes with a particular frequency per year. Most offenders are versatile, but a minority (e.g., child sex offenders) are more specialized. There is little evidence of escalation in the seriousness of offending during criminal careers.

The major risk factors for male offending are well known and highly replicable in longitudinal studies (Farrington 2015b). They include:

- individual factors (e.g., high impulsiveness, low achievement);
- parental factors (e.g., young or criminal parents);
- child-rearing factors (e.g., poor parental supervision, physical punishment);
- **socio-economic factors** (e.g., low family income, large family size, broken families);
- peer factors (e.g., **associating with delinquent peers**);
- school factors (e.g., attending a high delinquency-rate school); and
- **neighbourhood factors** (e.g., living in a high-crime area).

See Chapter 2.6 Control theories

See Chapter 2.4 Differential association; Chapter 2.5 Social learning theory

See Chapter 2.2 Social disorganization theory

While a great deal is known about risk factors that predict the onset of offending, less is known about risk factors for other criminal career dimensions such as frequency, duration, specialization or escalation.

The extent to which risk factors have causal effects is not clear. For example, in the Pittsburgh Youth Study, peer delinquency was the strongest correlate and predictor of a boy's delinquency (between individuals), but it did not predict within individuals. In other words, changes in peer delinquency from one wave to the next did not predict changes in delinquency (for the same individual) from one wave to the next. In contrast, parental factors such as poor parental supervision and low involvement of the boy in family activities predicted the boy's delinquency both between and within individuals. Because the concept of a cause requires that a change in a factor within individuals predicts a change in delinquency within individuals, it was concluded that parental factors might be causes of delinquency but peer delinquency was not. Because most offences by young people are committed with other young people, peer delinquency is probably an indicator rather than a cause of delinquency.

There is today a great deal of interest in protective factors against delinquency, but much less is known about these. Protective factors are defined either as factors that predict a low rate of offending or as factors that predict a low rate of offending among people in a risk category. The first type of protective factor is not necessarily the 'other side of the coin' to a risk factor. For example, in the Pittsburgh Youth Study, high achievement predicted a low probability of delinquency, but low achievement did not predict a high probability of delinquency (compared with average achievement). The second type of protective factor has important implications for intervention. For example, in the Cambridge Study, living in poor housing was a risk factor for delinquency, but boys who were living in poor housing and receiving good child-rearing had the same probability of delinquency as boys who were living in good housing. Therefore, the protective factor of good child-rearing nullified the risk factor of poor housing, suggesting that parent training to improve child-rearing might be effective in reducing the delinquency of boys living in poor housing.

There has been a great deal of research on the influence of later-life events on the course of development of offending, and the life event that has been studied most is getting married. Longitudinal research shows that offending by males decreases after they get married (compared with matched males who did not get married), and, conversely, that offending increases after males become separated or divorced. Other important life events that have been studied include cohabiting with a romantic partner, having a first child, moving house, obtaining a steady job and joining the military forces.

The most exciting recent development is the extension of a number of longitudinal studies into the third generation, by following up the children of the original children (see e.g., Farrington et al. 2015). Many DLC researchers are now focused on investigating, explaining and preventing the intergenerational transmission of offending and antisocial behaviour. Also, with longer follow-ups, many researchers are now investigating desistance and offending by people in their 40s and older, and discovering that there is a lot more offending by older people than was previously believed. The most important advances in the near future will probably focus on protective factors and within-individual analyses. Also, there are now large-scale and extensive longitudinal studies of the development of female offending, which will throw more light on this relatively neglected topic. Better knowledge from new longitudinal studies should lead to better theories and more effective interventions.

References

Farrington, David P. (ed.). 2005. *Integrated Developmental and Life-Course Theories of Offending*. New Brunswick, NJ: Transaction.

Farrington, David P. 2015a. Prospective Longitudinal Research on the Development of Offending. *Australian and New Zealand Journal of Criminology* 48(3): 314–35.

Farrington, David P. 2015b. The developmental evidence base: Psychosocial research. In *Forensic Psychology* (2nd edn), David A. Crighton and Graham J. Towl, eds, pp. 161–81. Chichester: Wiley.

Farrington, David P., Maria M. Ttofi, Rebecca V. Crago, and Jeremy W. Coid. 2015. Intergenerational Similarities in Risk Factors for Offending. *Journal of Developmental and Life-Course Criminology* 1(1): 4862.

Piquero, Alexis R., David P. Farrington, and Alfred Blumstein. 2007. *Key Issues in Criminal Career Research: New Analyses of the Cambridge Study in Delinquent Development*. Cambridge: Cambridge University Press.

Further reading

Carlsson, Christoffer, and Jerzy Sarnecki. 2016. *An Introduction to Life-Course Criminology*. London: Sage.

Farrington, David P. 2002. Developmental criminology and risk-focussed prevention. In *The Oxford Handbook of Criminology* (3rd edn), Mike Maguire, Rodney Morgan and Robert Reiner, eds, pp. 657–701. Oxford: Oxford University Press.

Gibson, Chris L., and Marvin D. Krohn (eds). 2013. *Handbook of Life-Course Criminology: Emerging Trends and Directions for Future Research*. New York: Springer.

Liberman, Akiva (ed.). 2008. *The Long View of Crime: A Synthesis of Longitudinal Research*. New York: Springer.

McGee, Tara R., and Paul Mazerolle (eds). 2015. *Developmental and Life-Course Criminological Theories*. Farnham: Ashgate.

Morizot, Julien, and Lila Kazemian (eds). 2015. *The Development of Criminal and Antisocial Behavior: Theory, Research and Practical Applications*. New York: Springer.

Life-course theory

1.13

Stephen G. Tibbetts and Jose Rivera

Life-course perspectives on crime can be defined as those that emphasize the examination of individuals over their lifetimes. More specifically, this perspective examines the onset of criminality, as well as when individuals increase or desist in the frequency and/or seriousness of the crimes they commit. Life-course theories of criminality have become one of the most researched perspectives among theorists for explaining criminality in recent years, and support for this theoretical approach to understanding criminal behaviour has grown exponentially in current research.

The life-course perspective can trace its roots to the work by Sheldon and Eleanor Glueck (1950) in which they studied over a thousand young boys/ men, emphasized a multifactor approach that examined almost all aspects of their **development**, and applied such data to predicting their delinquency and adult criminal behaviour. Due to the dominance of sociological perspectives after World War II, however, this multifactor line of research soon fell out of favour for research for many years. In the 1970s and early 1980s, the life-course perspective experienced a rebirth in attention by several cohort studies, such as those by Wolfgang and colleagues (1972), as well as one by West and Farrington (1973) and another by Shannon (1982), with each of them showing that approximately 6–8 per cent of all habitual offenders were responsible for committing over 80 per cent of all violent crimes. Furthermore, such research pointed out that most traditional theories of crime focused on *teenagers*, and, while this is the period in which most individuals who offend commit their

See Chapter 1.12
Developmental
criminology

crimes, there were many more pieces to the puzzle for understanding and explaining criminal offending. This was a key advance in the understanding of offenders and how they are distributed in society. Specifically, there are a handful of offenders, statistically speaking, who commit the vast majority of serious violent crimes – and they offend before and after teenage years.

In the mid- to late-1980s, the life-course perspective received more attention due to a significant report by Alfred Blumstein et al. (1986), who edited a volume about career criminals and criminal careers for the US National Academy of Sciences which advanced the perspective significantly and provided a clearer framework for examining individuals' criminality over their life-course. Blumstein and his colleagues presented a new formulaic notation and diagrams for depicting individuals' criminal behaviour, as well as clearly defining the meanings of key concepts in the life-course perspective. These include *onset*, *prevalence*, *frequency*, *seriousness*, and *desistance*.

See Chapter 5.6
Desistance

In the 1990s, Robert Sampson and John Laub (1993) expanded the life-course perspective not only by utilizing and re-examining the Gluecks' data, but also by proposing a theoretical framework for explaining the results of the data. Specifically, they created a theory based on *transitions* and *trajectories* occuring in an individual's life that affect everything they do – especially criminal behaviour. Transitions (or turning points) are single but significant life events, such as getting a new job or getting married. A series of transitions tend to form a trajectory (or pathway) over at least one extended developmental period of the life-course. Often, earlier trajectories create a cumulative effect that predisposes individuals into further trajectories toward criminality at later stages of life.

In the early 1990s, perhaps the most insightful life-course perspective was proposed by Terrie Moffitt (1993), who presented a developmental taxonomy that not only clearly identified two types of offenders but also gave different causal explanations for why they commit crime. Specifically, she distinguished two types of offenders, which she labelled as *adolescence-limited offenders* (those who primarily offend only during their teenage years or early 20s) and *life-course persistent offenders* (those who start offending very early and continue throughout their life). Importantly, Moffitt claimed that the reasons or causes for their offending differ greatly. The adolescence-limited offenders are normal, and commit relatively minor crimes during their teenage years due to peer-influence and trying to be more 'adult-like' by engaging in acts that make them seem older. On the other hand, the life-course persistent offenders start offending very early on (before the age of 10) and continue to commit crime throughout their life; their offending is caused by an interaction between biological predispositions toward criminality and disadvantaged environments.

See Chapter 1.5
Biological
criminology

See Chapter 2.6
Control theories

Biological predisposition factors, such as low birth weight, low IQ, delivery complications at birth (e.g., anoxia), can vary greatly. **Disadvantaged environment factors** – such as an absent father, an abusive household, poverty/low socio-economic status – can also differ greatly. Regardless of the reasons for either biological predisposition or disadvantaged environment, the point is that it is the combination of biological predispositions and maladaptive environments that causes individuals to become life-course, chronic offenders.

Many studies have since drawn on Moffitt's developmental taxonomy. Such studies have examined the interaction of various physiological problems with social/familial factors and how they combine to predict which individuals will become life-course-persistent offenders (i.e., chronic, habitual criminals). Specifically, a number of studies have found that infants with a low birth weight, when born into a poor family, have a much higher likelihood not only of having an early onset of criminal behaviour but also of becoming habitual offenders and continuing their criminal behaviour into adulthood. Similar findings have been recorded for other physiological maladies (such as the mother smoking during pregnancy) that interact with a variety of social disadvantages (such as the father being absent from the household during the early years of development).

On the other hand, most studies show that desistance from criminal behaviour is typically marked by primary life-events, or transitions, that encourage individuals to stop offending. Research has shown that the key events most likely to reduce criminal offending are: getting married; gaining employment in a stable job; moving to a better neighbourhood; and joining the military. It is important to note that the life-course perspective puts much effort into research on how and why people *desist* from criminal behaviour, and not just explaining why certain individuals commit crime *in the first place* or become chronic offenders. After all, the more we can learn about why people stop committing crime, the more we can understand and intervene in cases in which individuals do not reduce or stop offending.

The most significant weakness of the life-course perspective is that it is very broad, and can likely include many hundreds, if not thousands, of factors in both the physiological and psychological realm, as well as thousands of concepts in the sociological area. Not only does this make the perspective very difficult to test and validate empirically, but it is also in stark contrast to far more parsimonious theories, such as that of low self-control theory, which includes only a handful of primary concepts in its framework. The fact that life-course perspectives include far more potential factors in explaining the highly complex phenomenon of criminal behaviour can also be seen as a strength rather than a weakness.

Despite its weaknesses, in recent years the life-course perspective has become one of the highest-ranked theories for explaining serious crime. Specifically, a study published in *The Criminologist* in 2008 showed that life-course theory ranked second (below social learning theory) in a survey of over 380 criminologists who were asked which theoretical perspective was best for explaining serious crime among adults. This was a huge increase in ranking from previous studies, and shows how the life-course perspective is gaining popularity in terms of ranking by experts. Much of this increase in ranking is likely due to scholars embracing the biosocial approach, which examines

See Chapter 2.5
Social learning theory

See Chapter 1.11
Biosocial theory

interactions among physiological factors with maladaptive social problems. As noted recently by scholars such as John Wright and colleagues (2015), it is the interaction of biological and social factors that provides the most insight into understanding and predicting the development of criminality among individuals, as well as changes in the prevalence, frequency, seriousness and desistance of such behaviour – which is the essential goal of research in the life-course perspective.

References

Blumstein, Alfred, Jacqueline Cohen, Jeffrey A. Roth, and Christy Visher. 1986, *Criminal Careers and Career Criminals*. Washington, DC: National Academy Press.

Glueck, Sheldon, and Eleanor Glueck. 1950. *Unraveling Juvenile Delinquency*. Cambridge, MA: Harvard University Press.

Moffitt, Terrie. 1993. Adolescence-Limited and Life-Course-Persistent Antisocial Behavior: A Developmental Taxonomy. *Psychological Review* 100(4): 674–701.

Sampson, Robert, and John Laub. 1993. *Crime in the Making: Pathways and Turning Points Through Life*. Cambridge, MA: Harvard University Press.

Shannon, Lyle W. 1982. *Assessing the Relationship of Adult Criminal Careers to Juvenile Careers: A Summary*. Washington, DC: Government Printing Office.

West, Donald J., and David. P. Farrington. 1973. *Who Becomes Delinquent? Second Report of the Cambridge Study in Delinquent Development*. London: Heinemann.

Wolfgang, Marvin E., Robert M. Figlio, and Thorsten Sellin. 1972. *Delinquency in a Birth Cohort*. Chicago: University of Chicago Press.

Wright, John Paul, Stephen G. Tibbetts, and Leah Daigle. 2015. *Criminals in the Making: Criminality over the Life-Course*. Thousand Oaks, CA: Sage.

Further reading

DeLisi, Matt, and Kevin M. Beaver. 2014. *Criminological Theory: A Life-Course Approach* (2nd edn). Burlington, MA: Jones & Bartlett.

Ellis, L., Jonathon A. Cooper, and Anthony Walsh. 2008. Criminologists' Opinions about Causes and Theories of Crime and Delinquency: A Follow-Up. *The Criminologist* 33(1): 23–6.

Experimental criminology

Melissa Rorie

Experimental criminology 'seeks to promote and improve the use and development of experimental methods in the advancement of criminological theory and evidence-based crime policy' (ASC 2013). Randomized experiments are the principal and preferred method for meeting a fundamental goal of scientific research – establishing a causal relationship – and randomized controlled trials (RCTs) are the best way to develop, improve and evaluate programmes; prevent programmes from causing unintended harms; and enhance theoretical as well as policy-relevant research (Welsh et al. 2013). The use of RCTs in the field of criminology, however, continues to provoke debate about whether they are appropriate or desirable, and they are rarely employed – compared to the frequent use of other methods such as surveys or secondary data analysis.

Of course, **experimental designs** *have*, at times, been incorporated into criminological research since the 1930s. The first criminological study to employ this method was the Cambridge-Somerville Youth Study, which randomly assigned disadvantaged youth to a treatment programme in which they received academic tutoring, medical treatment and mentoring. This study, led by Joan McCord, found that the programme did not have a beneficial effect on youth's short-term delinquency outcomes, and that those youths who attended a summer camp as part of treatment *increased* the likelihood of criminal behaviour as they entered adulthood. Despite strong evidence that RCTs

See Chapter 1.4
Positivism

can more accurately evaluate programme impact, RCTs were rare until the 1980s. Since then, many studies have employed random methods, including:

- the Newark Foot Patrol Experiment
- the Minneapolis Domestic Violence Experiment
- the Minneapolis 'Hot Spots' Patrol Experiment
- the Moving to Opportunity Experiment
- the Boot Camp Correctional Program Evaluation.

Recently, criminological experiments have become more popular in the United States (Farrington 2013) because of successful implementations receiving widespread attention; strong advocacy for the method by renowned criminologists; and the creation of organizations for the purpose of such advocacy (Weisburd et al. 2013), as well as research funding being increasingly linked to the use of such methods. In addition to encouraging more frequent use of the method, experimental criminologists have been improving experimental designs in a variety of ways. Recent studies have increasingly:

- used multiple sites/replications;
- recruited larger samples;
- used self-report as well as official records to assess changes in outcomes;
- employed more refined analyses of outcomes;
- conducted long-term follow-up assessments;
- reported effect sizes when writing up results (as opposed to just reporting statistical significance);
- used 'intent to treat' analyses to overcome differential attrition problems (as opposed to merely assessing differences between treatment completers and non-completers) (Welsh et al. 2013).

Establishing a truly causal relationship between variables is a fundamental goal of research. There is a consensus among researchers that experimental designs improve internal validity and reduce selection bias (Heckman and Smith 1995). Four main characteristics of this research strategy make it best suited for establishing causality:

1. *The deliberate manipulation of the independent variable* strengthens confidence that the change in outcomes was actually due to the manipulation (i.e., that an association exists) if this manipulation produces a change in the dependent variable.
2. *The measurement of the dependent variable* after *manipulation of the independent variable* makes it clear that the treatment evoked change in the outcome, and not the other way around.
3. *The presence of a comparison group that does not experience the manipulation but is otherwise treated exactly like the treatment group.* Having this control group demonstrates what would happen under the same circumstances

but in the absence of a treatment (i.e., rules out potentially confounding factors).

4. *The random assignment to the comparison or manipulation group* allows researchers to assume that no background characteristics influenced membership in the treatment group and, therefore, that the control and treatment groups have similar characteristics (see, e.g., Weisburd 2010; Weisburd et al. 2013).

The usefulness of RCTs has been illustrated in comparisons with quasi-experimental and non-experimental designs, and RCTs are better able to rule out selection effects and more accurately depict the programme's impact. Weisburd (2010) also points out that the amount of 'variance explained' using quasi- and non-experimental designs is low. He warns that many potentially confounding variables are missing from such designs, and that researchers are dismissing the systematic nature (and importance) of these missing variables.

There are instances when randomly assigning individuals to receive treatment is not considered feasible or ethical. Furthermore, although there is a consensus that RCTs improve internal validity, they are not without methodological limitations. Five commonly cited limitations in the literature include: experiments are simplistic/artificial; cost (experiments are expensive); randomization may not always be complete; selection bias is not completely eliminated; and RCTs may not be appropriate with certain populations.

The highly controlled nature of experiments (especially in laboratories) makes it difficult to determine whether the treatment being studied would have the same effect under real-world conditions, without the supervision of a programme designer or researcher. RCTs also tend to tell us *when* a programme is effective, but are often unable to tell us *why* it is effective (Heckman and Smith 1995), which is important for supporting causal claims.

Compared to other methods, it is more expensive and more time-intensive to implement an RCT. Such costs are especially problematic for underfunded criminal justice agencies that are already pressured to provide direct services with limited budgets.

The main benefit of RCTs comes from random assignment to treatment or control conditions; but projects frequently encounter difficulties implementing randomization. For example, it can be difficult to get cooperation from practitioners when they perceive a specific individual in the 'control group' to be particularly deserving of a treatment. Although randomization should allow one to assume that the treatment and control groups are equivalent prior to the treatment, this assumption should (if feasible) be verified with a pre-treatment assessment. It is also imperative to protect against possible 'contamination' effects: if individuals in the treatment group and the control group are able to communicate with one another (e.g., in the waiting room of a probation office) about their unique experiences, this may impact the findings (Weisburd et al. 2013).

Even when randomization is successful, Sampson (2010) argues that it does not necessarily 'solve' issues with selection bias. It is often difficult to recruit participants that know they may not receive the treatment; those who opt in to the experiment itself are likely to be different from the people who did not choose to participate in the research. Even for those people participating, there is a chance they will drop out (if the program requires more time and effort than the control condition), or if they do stay enrolled in the program, they may not comply with all requirements. This 'differential attrition' will make the previously equivalent treatment and control groups appear very different at the end of the study.

Finally, RCTs may not be appropriate for all populations (e.g., reluctant subjects, resistant practitioners, underfunded agencies) or research topics. It is unlikely that a judge would agree to randomly assign someone to jail as opposed to probation for the sake of scientific knowledge. When a researcher is unable to randomly assign people to groups, it is still possible and desirable to create treatment and control groups that are as similar as possible prior to the treatment. Research designs that attempt to create equivalent groups, but do not randomize, are called 'quasi-experimental' designs (QEDs). QEDs use statistical methods, time-series analyses, matching strategies, natural experiments and other approaches to produce equivalency in relevant characteristics prior to treatment implementation. Although QEDs improve causal inference in many ways, they are still unable to rule out confounding influences from unmeasured variables (Weisburd 2010).

Despite the limitations of the method, experimental criminologists continue to demonstrate the usefulness of RCTs for crime scholarship. Of course, it is important not to see RCTs as the *only* way to conduct research, but as a strong component that can be integrated with or used alongside QEDs and non-experimental methods to gain confidence in findings regarding a research question. As scientists, criminologists benefit from examining research questions using a variety of methods. 'Mixed-methods' studies that use both quantitative methods (such as an experiment) and qualitative methods (such as observations) are useful for understanding not only *whether* an intervention worked but also *why* the intervention worked (Sampson 2010). Randomized experimental designs are an integral part of the field's ability to build knowledge and create programmes to reduce the harm caused by crime as well as harm caused by society's responses to crime.

References

ASC. 2013. American Society of Criminology Division of Experimental Criminology, http://expcrim.org. Accessed 19 January 2016.

Farrington, David P. 2013. Longitudinal and Experimental Research in Criminology. *Crime and Justice* 42(1): 453–527.

Heckman, James J., and Jeffrey A. Smith. 1995. Assessing the Case for Social Experiments. *Journal of Economic Perspectives* 9(2): 85–110.

Sampson, Robert J. 2010. Gold Standard Myths: Observations on the Experimental Turn in Quantitative Criminology. *Journal of Quantitative Criminology* 26(4): 489–500.

Weisburd, David. 2010. Justifying the Use of Non-Experimental Methods and Disqualifying the Use of Randomized Controlled Trials: Challenging Folklore in Evaluation Research in Crime and Justice. *Journal of Experimental Criminology* 6(2): 209–27.

Weisburd, David, Anthony Petrosino, and Trevor Fronius. 2013. Randomized experiments in criminology and criminal justice. In *Encyclopedia of Criminology and Criminal Justice*, Gerben Bruinsma and David Weisburd, eds, pp. 4283–91. New York: Springer.

Welsh, Brandon C., Anthony A. Braga, and Gerben J.N. Bruinsma. 2013. New Perspectives and Developments in Experimental Criminology. *Policing* 7(4): 411–18.

Further reading

Berk, Richard A. 2005. Randomized Experiments as the Bronze Standard. *Journal of Experimental Criminology* 1(4): 417–33.

Farrington, David P., and Brandon C. Welsh. 2005. Randomized Experiments in Criminology: What Have We Learned in the Last Two Decades? *Journal of Experimental Criminology* 1(9): 9–38.

Lum, Cynthia, and Sue-Ming Yang. 2005. Why Do Evaluation Researchers in Crime and Justice Choose Non-Experimental Methods? *Journal of Experimental Criminology* 1(2): 191–213.

Rorie, Melissa, Bethany Backes, and Jaspreet Chahal. 2014. Services for IPV Victims: Encouraging Stronger Research Methods to Produce More Valid Results. *National Institute of Justice Journal* 274: 25–32.

Sherman, Lawrence W. 2007. The Power Few: Experimental Criminology and the Reduction of Harm. *Journal of Experimental Criminology* 3(4): 299–321.

Sherman, Lawrence W. 2009. Evidence and Liberty: The Promise of Experimental Criminology. *Criminology and Criminal Justice* 9(1): 5–28.

Weisburd, David. 2000. Randomized Experiments in Criminal Justice Policy: Prospects and Problems. *Crime and Delinquency* 46(2): 181–93.

1.15 Forensic psychology

Graham Davies and Anthony Beech

'Forensic psychology' is a term used to cover the broad and growing area of psychological research and practice at the interface between psychology and law. It embraces both research on the characteristics, management and treatment of offenders (*criminological psychology*) and the application of psychological knowledge and theory to the processes of law and the courts (*legal psychology*). The use of the term to describe both these areas is a relatively recent coinage, and one not without controversy (Blackburn 1996). In terms of what forensic psychology is, it is best described by what forensic psychologists do, which (according to Davies and Beech 2012), includes:

- piloting and implementing treatment programmes for offenders;
- generating research evidence to support penal policy and practice;
- undertaking assessments of risk for violent and sexual offenders;
- assessment of domestic violence and family issues;
- treating offenders with drug or alcohol problems;
- writing reports and giving evidence in court;
- advising parole boards and mental health tribunals;
- crime analysis and offender profiling;
- conducting experimental and field studies on the reliability of witnesses;
- advising on interview techniques with suspects and vulnerable witnesses;
- **counter-terrorism** policy and hostage negotiation.

See Chapter 4.19 Institutional and anti-institutional violence

The goals, origins, evolution and guiding theories of criminological and legal psychology are rather different, and deserve to be treated separately. For both facets of the discipline, theory is inextricably linked with practice.

Criminological psychology stems from the important link between psychology and criminal behaviour long recognized in common law. It is reflected in the legal principle of *mens rea* or 'guilty mind', meaning that an individual cannot be guilty of a crime unless he or she carries out the act both wilfully and intentionally. **Early theories** of criminal behaviour emphasized the **heritability of criminal behaviour**, reflected in the work of the Italian criminologist Cesare Lombroso (1835–1909). Of course, criminological psychology has developed tremendously since this time, noting the importance of environmental factors. The application of psychological theories, starting with the **psychodynamic** ideas of Sigmund Freud and his successors, has had a significant influence on conceptions of many aspects of everyday life, including crime.

See Chapter 1.4 Positivism; Chapter 1.5 Biological criminology

See Chapter 1.8 Learning theory; Chapter 1.10 Psychoanalytic perspectives

The psychologist, psychiatrist and psychoanalyst John Bowlby (1907–90) argued that separation of mother and child during the second to sixth months of life had permanent, damaging consequences for a child's later development and well-being (in terms of attachment to others and self) and could, in a number of cases, lead to the individual becoming a criminal in later life (Bowlby, 1969). Here, attachment can be broadly defined as the process by which an infant has an inborn biological need to maintain close contact with its parents/primary carers. Therefore, an individual's attachment style can be seen as a set of enduring characteristics for making sense of one's life experiences and interactions, in that the relationship between infant and primary caregiver provides a model for future interpersonal and intimate relationships. This model is maintained irrespective of whether the relationship between the individual and their primary caregiver/s in childhood was positive or negative. It is a model for an individual's future social interactions, whether primarily about approach or avoidance of others or, *in extremis*, criminal behaviour.

As for more recent applications of theory to treat offenders, the emergence of cognitive psychology encouraged the integration of internal processes, such as thoughts and emotions, into behaviourist learning theory. This integration is most clearly seen in the development of **social learning theory** by the psychologist Albert Bandura. Bandura's approach aimed to change internal processes (i.e., cognitions) as well as overt behaviour, giving rise to the term 'cognitive-behavioural treatment' (CBT) and the associated methods of therapy. CBT interventions have become increasingly popular for use with offenders. For example, the psychologist Raymond Novaco emphasized the central importance of anger in understanding some forms of violence. As a result, the use of anger-control treatments has become widespread with violent offenders. Similarly, in sex-offender treatment, CBT is the mainstay of such interventions. Similarly, a social-learning/CBT approach has also been successfully adapted for the treatment of those with intellectual disabilities.

See Chapter 2.5 Social learning theory

Legal psychology, by contrast, traces its origins to Wilhelm Wundt (1832–1920), the father of experimental psychology. Students of Wundt were responsible for early research on psychological factors influencing the accuracy and reliability of judicial processes. The American psychologist James M. Cattell (1860–1944) demonstrated the unreliability of memory for events from the recent past and the tenuous link between witness confidence and accuracy. Cattell's findings excited the interest of the French psychologist Alfred Binet (1857–1911), who conducted some of the earliest investigations into suggestibility in children. Another pupil of Wundt, Hugo Münsterberg (1863–1916), wrote the first book in English on psychology and law: *On the Witness Stand* (1911). In addition to questioning the reliability of eyewitness testimony, the book discussed the role psychology might play in the detection of deception, false confessions, the impact of leading questions in court and the development of effective interviewing procedures for witnesses.

Despite this promising beginning, little if any research on legal psychology was conducted for over a half a century. Münsterberg's bombastic tone alienated lawyers, and experimental psychology veered off on a reductionist track under the influence of the behaviourist theories of J.B. Watson (1878–1958) with their exclusive focus on the study of stimulus, response and reinforcement. Today, however, thanks to the rise of cognitive psychology – with its renewed emphasis on mental processes as a basis for understanding human behaviour in the real world – all the topics raised by Münsterberg are the subject of extensive research, of which the area of witness memory is the most prominent (Davies and Beech 2012).

The doyen of modern legal psychology is Elizabeth Loftus. She draws on the theoretical ideas of Sir Frederic Bartlett (1886–1969), who had argued that remembering did not involve passive reproduction of the 'fixed lifeless traces' of the behaviourist model, but rather, an active, mental reconstructive process based on accumulated knowledge which fuses individual experiences into a single whole (termed a 'schema' by Bartlett). Across a range of evidential settings, Loftus and colleagues have demonstrated that witnesses find great difficulty in testifying accurately about a specific incident because they so readily introduce additional material into their evidence based upon what they have seen, heard or reflected upon subsequently: so-called 'post-event information' (Loftus 2005). Unlike Münsterberg, Loftus has found the US courts more receptive to expert testimony from a psychologist, and she and her followers have regularly appeared in high-profile cases regarding the potential unreliability of memory, where the testimony of an eyewitness forms the key element of the prosecution case.

Such testimony is controversial, however, not least because of shifting theoretical conceptions of the nature of memory. Are *all* memories inevitably unreliable? Some memory theorists (such as Endel Tulving) argue that memories, once stored, are not lost, but just become inaccessible, overlaid by more recent stored experiences. However, provided the right cue or prompt is given, the original memory can be retrieved. These conflicting theories of how memory functions have led to 'battles of experts' in the criminal courts.

One key area concerns the status of 'recovered memories' – the emergence in adulthood of vivid and often distressing personal memories, typically from childhood, of which the individual claims no previous awareness. In the Franklin murder trial in 1990, Loftus for the defence faced psychiatrist Lenore Terr for the prosecution. The prosecution's case was that Franklin's daughter had witnessed her father murdering a schoolfriend nearly 30 years previously, but had only recently recovered the memory. Terr argued that such recovered memories were commonplace in therapeutic work, while Loftus argued that old memories become less rather than more reliable over time, and that there was no scientific evidence to support the concept of memory recovery following repression. The jury found Franklin guilty, but the verdict was later reversed on appeal. By this time, Loftus had demonstrated that it was possible for individuals to generate detailed, but entirely fictitious, memories of events from the past, through the use of suggestion. Such rigorous courtroom examination of research and theories can only assist the development of a robust and rigorous legal psychology.

References

Blackburn, Ronald. 1996. What *Is* Forensic Psychology? *Legal and Criminological Psychology* 1(1): 3–16.

Bowlby, John. 1969. *Attachment and Loss: Attachment.* New York: Basic Books.

Davies, Graham, and Anthony Beech. 2012. *Forensic Psychology: Crime, Justice, Law and Interventions.* Chichester: Wiley.

Loftus, Elizabeth F. 2005. Planting Misinformation in the Human Mind: A 30-Year Investigation of the Malleability of Memory. *Learning and Memory*, 12(4), 361–6.

Further reading

Adler, Joanna R., and Jacqueline M. Gray. 2010. *Forensic Psychology: Concepts Debates and Practice.* Abingdon: Willan.

Brown, Jennifer M., and Elizabeth A. Campbell. 2010. *The Cambridge Handbook of Forensic Psychology.* Cambridge: Cambridge University Press.

Loftus, Elizabeth F., and Katherine Ketcham. 1994. *The Myth of Repressed Memory.* New York: St. Martin's Press.

Novaco, R.W., Renwick, S. and Ramm, M. (2012). *Anger treatment for offenders.* Chichester: Wiley-Blackwell.

Ward, Tony, Devon Polaschek, and Anthony R. Beech. 2006. *Theories of Sexual Offending.* Chichester: Wiley.

Neurocriminology

Colleen M. Berryessa and Adrian Raine

Significant advances in neuroscience in recent years have led to new understandings of how brain and other neurophysiological factors play a role in the development and increased risk of offending and antisocial behaviour. Neurocriminology seeks to apply principles, methods and insights garnered from the field of neuroscience to the study of what causes crime, as well as how to best predict, prevent and manage criminal behaviour and its consequences (Raine 2013). Yet, importantly, neurocriminology does *not* suggest that the study of the causes and management of criminal behaviour should be isolated to just neurobiological factors. Neurocriminology argues that crime can be only partially explained and scientifically studied by looking at social and **environmental factors**, and that neurobiological factors play a meaningful role in the causes and prevention of criminal behaviour. Thus, in order to fully understand and study crime as a phenomenon, neurobiological factors and their roles in these processes also need to be studied (Raine 2013).

See Chapter 2.1 Chicago School; Chapter 2.2 Social disorganization theory; Chapter 2.6 Control theories

Nineteenth-century Italian psychiatrist Cesare Lombroso has been heralded as the founding father of neurocriminology. Applying principles from **biological positivism**, he argued that criminal behaviour was caused by brain abnormalities which could be visually observed by looking at an individual's facial and cranial characteristics, or their *stigmata*. To Lombroso, criminals were 'throwbacks' to primitive humans, and were incapable of following the complex rules of society due to their 'born' criminality. Although Lombroso tested his theory empirically, it was largely based on his preconceived

See Chapter 1.4 Positivism; Chapter 1.5 Biological criminology political motivations and discriminations towards different ethnicities, as well as flawed research methods such as small, biased samples and the absence of control groups (Wolfgang 1961). Yet, although Lombroso's phrenologist theories have been dismissed, the study of how crime is influenced by neurobiological factors – and how this should be factored into managing, predicting and preventing it – has persisted into the modern day. Contemporary research in neurocriminology has been driven largely by recent and emerging advances in neuroscience techniques and methods since the mid-1980s, which have provided better and more rigorous methods, compared to Lombroso's day, to study the relationships between neurobiological functioning and antisocial behaviour.

As such, modern neurocriminology focuses on brain-imaging in particular, and, more generally, other technologies measuring hormonal and neurophysiological functioning to document neurobiological influences on criminal and antisocial behaviour. Current neurocriminological research, which predominantly uses cross-sectional, correlational research designs, encompasses three main areas of inquiry: brain imaging, neurochemistry and neurophysiology. Brain-imaging techniques such as magnetic resonance imaging (MRI) and functional magnetic resonance imaging (fMRI) have been utilized to study how the structure and function of specific brain areas are associated with criminal and antisocial behaviour. To date, the most replicated neural correlate associated with antisocial behaviour has been reduced functioning of the prefrontal cortex, including the dorsolateral prefrontal cortex (associated with impulsivity, sustained attention and cognitive flexibility), the anterior cingulate cortex (associated with rewards, emotion processing and impulsivity) and the orbitofrontal cortex (associated with emotion, judgement and learning). An association between structural and functional abnormalities of the amygdala (a brain structure associated with fear-conditioning and emotion) and adult **antisocial behaviour**, including **psychopathy**, is also a reasonably well-replicated finding (Raine 2013).

Studies on the relationship between antisocial behaviour and neurochemistry – the study of neurochemicals, neurotransmitters and hormones – have demonstrated relationships between levels of specific hormones or neurotransmitters and antisocial behaviour; low levels of cortisol (a stress hormone) and high levels of testosterone (a male sex hormone) have been associated with increased antisocial and aggressive behaviour, as well as significantly lower than normal levels of serotonin (a neurotransmitter associated with impulse control and aggression). The relationship between neurophysiology – the study of nervous-system functioning – and antisocial behaviour has been studied by measuring physiological differences between antisocial individuals and healthy control groups. One of the best-replicated findings to date is low resting heart rate. Poor autonomic functioning and fear-conditioning are associated with, and to some extent predictive of, criminal offending (Gao et al. 2010).

These three main areas of neurocriminological study have helped shed light on how certain neurobiological characteristics might increase one's risk of

See Chapter 5.2
Antisocial
behaviour

See Chapter 1.6
Pathology; Chapter
1.7 Psychopathy

developing criminal or antisocial behaviour. Not only is this research relevant to studying the causes of crime, but it also has potential legal and philosophical implications regarding the prediction, prevention and punishment of criminal behaviour and its consequences. Philosophically, neurocriminological findings have led to questions of whether such research – documenting a relationship between biological characteristics and crime – implies biological determinism, potentially affecting perceptions of **free will**, human agency and leading to the **removal of an antisocial individual's responsibility** for his antisocial actions due to his/her neurobiological abnormalities. Legally, neurocriminology may create implications in three areas: predicting criminal behaviour; how criminal behaviour is punished; and for providing knowledge on how to best treat or intervene regarding criminal behaviour in the criminal justice system (Glenn and Raine 2014). This nexus of neurocriminological research and implications for the law is known as the sub-discipline of *neurolaw*.

See Chapter 1.2
Classical
criminology
See Chapter 5.9
Incapacitation

First, neurocriminological findings may help predict future criminal behaviour by augmenting the predictive value of existing methods of **risk assessment**, such as actuarial instruments. As neurotechnologies improve and findings are replicated in the future, neurocriminological findings reporting an association between neurobiological markers and an increased risk for offending may be integrated into risk-assessment models for certain types of offenders (e.g., psychopaths) or for specific types of offending behaviour (e.g., sexual offending). Initial structural and functional MRI research has provided preliminary evidence that brain abnormalities can predict future offending over and above social, demographic and behavioural risk factors (Pardini et al. 2014).

See Chapter 6.7
Risk

Second, findings in the neurocriminological literature may affect perceptions regarding how to punish criminal behaviour. Neurocriminological evidence suggesting a relationship between neurobiological characteristics and criminal offending, and its potential presentation in court to a judge or jury making sentencing decisions, has been discussed as potentially influencing punishment in two ways. Neurocriminological findings may be viewed as an aggravator to punishment, meaning knowledge of an individual's biological characteristics and his/her association with offending behaviour may lead a judge or jury to believe that an individual is less amenable to treatment or intervention because he/she is 'biologically broken'. This may lead to a more punitive prison sentence in order to protect the public from the danger a biologically broken offender is thought to represent. Conversely, neurocriminological findings might be thought of as a mitigator to punishment: a judge or jury making sentencing decisions may believe that an offender's biological characteristics, and his/her perceived direct association with his/her offending behaviour, make him/her less morally responsible for his/her actions because he/she is biologically broken and his/her agency was compromised by his/her predisposing neurobiological characteristics. This may result in a mitigated criminal sentence.

Unfortunately, there are no rigorous data regarding if and how neurocriminological evidence has been perceived as either a mitigator or aggravator in court. Yet, it is known that the large majority of cases of this type of evidence being presented in court in recent years have been offered as mitigating factors during sentencing in capital cases by the defence. This is largely due to the fact that guidelines on the types of mitigating factors that jurors are allowed to consider in capital cases are extremely lax. In non-capital cases, judges are guided by standards that provide rules of evidence regarding what is considered admissible evidence in court proceedings; yet, they are not guided as to how much weight should be given to neurocriminological evidence or how it should be factored in decision-making during sentencing, leaving judges to interpret whether the evidence should be considered as either mitigating or aggravating. Hence, courts are given much leeway in deciding how this evidence should influence punishment decisions (Morse and Newsome 2013).

Third, research in neurocriminology may lead to the development of better methods of treating or intervening in offending and antisocial behaviour, either before or after criminal behaviour has occurred. Interventions informed by neurocriminological findings, which could be cost-savers compared to existing criminal sentences or rehabilitative methods, might range from brain or neuroscientific interventions or manipulations; to pharmacological or medical treatments; to nutritional supplements or mindfulness training to affect neurobiological attributes or abnormalities associated with antisocial behaviour. Yet, how and when it might be ethical to intervene has been another widely discussed issue, especially in relation to interventions that might potentially label individuals with biological attributes associated with antisocial behaviour before they exhibit any antisociality (Raine 2013).

Ultimately, as it further emerges and develops as a sub-discipline, the field of neurocriminology should continue to play a meaningful role in illuminating the causes and management of criminality. The future directions of neurocriminology include: the development of more advanced neuroscience techniques to examine the relationships between neurobiological attributes and antisocial behaviours; more effective interventions or treatments to ameliorate these neurobiological risk factors; the use of these findings in identifying and developing more effective modes to both predict and curb criminal **recidivism**; and further implications of presently unidentified neurocriminological findings for a range of complex ethical, philosophical and legal issues.

See Chapter 5.13
Recidivism

References

Gao, Yu, Adrian Raine, Peter H. Venables, Michael E. Dawson, and Sarnoff A. Mednick. 2010. Association of Poor Childhood Fear Conditioning and Adult Crime. *American Journal of Psychiatry* 167(1): 56–60.

Glenn, Andrea L., and Adrian Raine. 2014. Neurocriminology: Implications for the Punishment, Prediction and Prevention of Criminal Behaviour. *Nature Reviews Neuroscience* 15(1): 54–63.

Morse, Stephen J., and William T. Newsome. 2013. Criminal responsibility, criminal competence and criminal law prediction. In *A Primer on Criminal Law and Neuroscience*, Stephen J. Morse and Adina Roskies, eds, pp. 150–78. Oxford: Oxford University Press.

Pardini, Dustin A., Adrian Raine, Kirk Erickson, and Rolf Loeber. 2014. Lower Amygdala Volume in Men Is Associated with Childhood Aggression, Early Psychopathic Traits, and Future Violence. *Biological Psychiatry* 75(1): 73–80.

Raine, Adrian. 2013. *The Anatomy of Violence: The Biological Roots of Crime*. New York: Pantheon.

Wolfgang, Marvin E. 1961. Pioneers in Criminology: Cesare Lombroso (1835–1909). *Journal of Criminal Law, Criminology, and Police Science* 52(4): 361–91.

Further reading

Rafter, N. 2008. *The Criminal Brain: Understanding Biological Theories of Crime*. New York: NYU Press.

Raine, Adrian. 2002. Biosocial Studies of Antisocial and Violent Behavior in Children and Adults: A Review. *Journal of Abnormal Child Psychology* 30(4): 311–26.

Raine, Adrian, and Yaling Yang. 2006. Neural Foundations to Moral Reasoning and Antisocial Behavior. *Social Cognitive and Affective Neuroscience* 1(3): 203–13.

Umbach, Rebecca, Colleen M. Berryessa, and Adrian Raine. 2015. Brain Imaging Research on Psychopathy: Implications for Punishment, Prediction, and Treatment in Youth and Adults. *Journal of Criminal Justice* 43(4): 295–306.

Deterrence

Avi Brisman and Eamonn Carrabine

Many criminological theories are 'deterministic' in the sense that they consider crime to be the result of forces outside of an individual's control (e.g., individual traits, disorganized communities, various strains). Such deterministic perspectives on crime have dominated criminological theory since the late 1880s. In contrast, according to **classical criminology**, which preponderated in criminological theory in the eighteenth and much of the nineteenth centuries, individuals *choose* to engage in crime based on a careful calculation or **rational** consideration of the costs and benefits associated with crime. In other words, from a 'classical' perspective, individuals participate in criminal activities because they believe that the benefits of doing so will outweigh the costs.

See Chapter 1.2 Classical criminology

See Chapter 1.18 Rational choice

Deterrence is based on the idea that humans will naturally violate the law if they are able to do so, and that crime can subsequently be discouraged if members of the public fear the punishment they may receive if they break the law. The concept of deterrence owes much to classical criminology (and the ideas of Cesare Beccaria, 1738–94) and **utilitarianism** (and the ideas of Jeremy Bentham, 1748–1832), which maintained that people attempt to maximize their pleasure and minimize their pain. Indeed, Beccaria argued that individuals will engage in crime *unless* punishments are *swift*, *certain* and *appropriately severe* (proportional). Original formulations distinguished between two types of deterrence: *specific deterrence* and *general deterrence*.

See Chapter 1.3 Utilitarianism

Specific deterrence is aimed at the known offender. It is the idea that punishing someone for an offence will reduce the likelihood of further offending *by that person*. In other words, specific deterrence contends that punishment is appropriate because it will reduce the chance of crime by those *specific individuals* who had committed the crime and who are punished for doing so.

General deterrence, in turn, targets the entire population. It is the idea that punishment discourages crime among people in the broader public. In other words, general deterrence contends that punishment is appropriate because it will reduce the chance of crime *by other people*, such as those who have not committed (a) crime but have contemplated doing so.

Both specific and general deterrence operate under a set of assumptions. With respect to specific deterrence, the assumption is that increasing the *severity* of punishment will further reduce crime – that more severe punishments are more effective at diminishing the incidence of crime than less severe punishments. But such an approach does not consider the possibility that severe punishments may have the opposite effect – of increasing the likelihood of subsequent crime – such as when an individual is **incarcerated and learns from other offenders** and/or is **labelled a felon** and/or suffers increased **strain** as a result of punishment. Moreover, punishment may not deter individuals from committing further crime if they are not rational – if they are impulsive or experience high negative emotionality. Indeed, specific deterrence fails to recognize the innumerable reasons and motivations for committing crime, as well as the fact that some offenders may not contemplate or care about the consequences of their actions for themselves or others.

See Chapter 2.4 Differential association; Chapter 2.5 Social learning theory; Chapter 2.7 Techniques of neutralization; Chapter 3.8 Labelling theory; Chapter 2.9 General strain theory

With respect to general deterrence, the assumption is that increasing the certainty and severity of punishment will reduce offending in the general population. But this presupposes that people possess some degree of awareness of the certainty and severity of punishment. In fact, many people may have little idea as to the certainty and severity of punishment, and may overestimate the chance of getting caught and receiving a harsh sanction.

Some question the stark distinction between specific deterrence (which essentially deals with *direct experience of punishment*) and general deterrence (which essentially deals with *indirect experience of punishment*). As Stafford and Warr (1993) point out, some people are subject to both specific and general deterrence in that they have both direct and indirect experiences of punishments. For example, someone may have both direct (personal) experience of punishment and may have observed or otherwise have knowledge of punishment received by others. Moreover, Stafford and Warr contend, a more complete notion of deterrence must also consider *punishment avoidance*: some individuals may have committed offences and not received a punishment, or may be aware of others who have committed offences for which they have not been punished. As such, Stafford and Warr (1993:126) submit, 'most people are likely to have a mixture of indirect and direct experience with punishment and punishment avoidance'.

A reconceptualized deterrence theory, then, must consider:

■   direct experiences of punishment (whether an individual has been punished for any crimes he/she has committed);

- indirect experiences of punishment (whether an individual is aware of others who have been punished for their offences);
- direct experiences of punishment avoidance (whether an individual has avoided punishment for crimes committed); and
- indirect experiences of punishment avoidance (whether an individual is aware of others who have avoided punishment for their infractions).

Because all of these factors will influence estimates of the certainty and severity of punishment, a reconceptualised deterrence theory can account for both the impact of specific and general deterrence on both individuals and populations, and the compatibility of deterrence theories with contemporary learning theories.

There is a long history of governments introducing severe punishments through claims that harsher penalties will produce special deterrence effects. The results, however, are modest at best. For instance, the introduction of 'short, sharp, shock' regimes into detention centres for young offenders in England and Wales by the Conservative government in the early 1980s proved to have no better post-release reconviction scores than centres operating the normal regime. In the United States, deterrence-based approaches to punishment became popular in the 1970s, 1980s and 1990s, when the criminal justice system began to eschew rehabilitation and endeavoured instead to control crime through severe determinate sentencing schemes, such as 'three strikes and you're out' measures and mandatory waiver provisions that tried certain juvenile offenders in adult courts. As a result, **prison populations** in the United States skyrocketed (see, e.g., Kovandzic et al. 2004).

See Chapter 5.5
Decarceration

The 'success' of deterrence-based punishment approaches has been called into question. For example, the popular American 'boot camps' of the 1990s, based on the aggressive training regimes of US Marines, 'have not been shown to be at all effective in discouraging reoffending' (Dunbar and Langdon 1998:10). In addition to such empirical doubts over the effectiveness of such strategies, there are also more general moral objections raised against individual deterrence, as it can:

- be used to justify punishing the innocent as what matters is the communication of the penalty (Duff 1996:3);
- allow for punishment in excess of that deserved by the offence; and
- be primarily concerned with offences that might be committed in the future rather than with the offences that have actually been committed (Hudson 2003:25).

See Chapter 3.12
Peacemaking
in criminology;
Chapter 5.14
Reintegrative
shaming; Chapter
5.15 Restorative
justice; Chapter 5.6
Desistance

With the economic downturn in the first decade of the twenty-first century, many parts of the United States began to rethink the financial feasibility of punitive practices and policies. Accordingly, states are beginning to review their overreliance on deterrence-based strategies to the exclusion of **less punitive and less expensive sentencing schemes** and approaches.

References

Duff, Raymond. 1996. Penal Communications: Recent Work in the Philosophy of Punishment. *Crime and Justice: A Review of Research* 20: 1–97.

Dunbar, Ian, and Anthony Langdon. 1998. *Tough Justice: Sentencing and Penal Policies in the 1990s*. London: Blackstone.

Hudson, Barbara. 2003. *Understanding Justice: An Introduction to Ideas, Perspectives, and Controversies in Modern Penal Theory* (2nd edn). London: Sage.

Kovandzic, Tomislav V., John J. Sloan III, and Lynne M. Vieraitis. 2004. 'Striking Out' as Crime Reduction Policy: The Impact of 'Three Strikes' Law on Crime Rates in U.S. Cities. *Justice Quarterly* 21(2): 207–39.

Stafford, Mark C., and Mark Warr. 1993. A Reconceptualization of General and Specific Deterrence. *Journal of Research in Crime and Delinquency* 30(2): 123–35.

Further reading

Becker, Gary S. 1968. Crime and Punishment: An Economic Approach. *Journal of Political Economy* 76(2): 169–217.

Kleck, Gary, Brion Sever, Spencer Li, and Marc Gertz. 2005. The Missing Link in General Deterrence Research. *Criminology* 43(3): 623–60.

Klepper, Steven, and Daniel Nagin. 1989. The Deterrent Effect of Perceived Certainty and Severity of Punishment Revisited. *Criminology* 27(4): 721–46.

Piliavin, Irving, Craig Thornton, Rosemary Gartner, and Ross L. Matsueda. 1986. Crime, Deterrence, and Rational Choice. *American Sociological Review* 51(1): 101–19.

Piquero, Alex R., and Greg Pogarsky. 2002. Beyond Stafford and Warr's Reconceptualization of Deterrence: Personal and Vicarious Experiences, Impulsivity, and Offending Behavior. *Journal of Research in Crime and Delinquency* 39(2): 153–86.

Rational choice

Martha J. Smith

Rational choice theory in criminology is often considered a direct descendant of the **classical theories** of Cesare Beccaria and Jeremy Bentham, which focus on the importance of the benefits (or **utility**, Bentham) and costs (or punishment, Beccaria) of crime in the decision-making of self-interested or rational actors. While acknowledging the influence of classical cost-and-benefit theories on economic rational choice models, however, Clarke and Cornish (1985) – the leading proponents of 'rational choice' theory in criminology since the mid-1980s – sought to provide a broader, more nuanced view of the role of rationality in criminal decision-making than was found in either classical or **deterrence theories**. In developing their rational choice perspective (as they later termed their approach), they synthesized concepts from criminology, economics, psychology and sociology to provide more dynamic, situationally grounded models covering a range of policy-relevant decisions about crime involvement and commission. In doing this, they also wanted to move the focus of criminological theory away from (1) traditional conceptions of offending behaviour as being sick or **pathological**; and (2) attempts to identify factors leading to an offender's criminal disposition or propensity to offend, which tended to overemphasize early **lifetime influences** at the expense of later ones.

See Chapter 1.2
Classical criminology

See Chapter 1.3
Utilitarianism

See Chapter 1.17
Deterrence theory

See Chapter 1.6
Pathology

See Chapter 1.13
Life-course theory

Cornish and Clarke (2008:24) set out six core concepts related to the rational choice perspective (RCP):

- 'Criminal behaviour is purposive.'
- 'Criminal behaviour is rational.'

- Criminal decision-making is specific for each type of crime.
- Decisions regarding the commission of crime can be classified as being related to offender involvement or to the crime event itself.
- 'Involvement' in crime relates to the initial decision to offend (initial involvement), to decisions about continuing to commit crime (habituation), and to those about stopping (desistance).
- Crime events are made up of unfolding stages and decisions.

In their view, purposes can be instrumental or emotional, and they do not have to be laudable, make sense to the general populace, or even necessarily be criminal. Rationality – albeit often 'limited' or 'bounded' by factors such as the decision-maker's intelligence, skills, nerve or level of intoxication (together with constraints of time, information and resources) – is assumed to be the primary means or mechanism used by offenders to move toward achieving their goals or purposes. The assumption of rationality among potential offenders has an added benefit for policymakers. It provides at least a minimal framework for predicting some of the types of factors that an offender might assess when seeking to achieve his or her purpose.

Crime-specificity is considered important because not all crimes meet a particular offender's purposes, and not all offenders have the intelligence, nerve or skills to commit all crimes. Different crimes fulfil differing needs and purposes, and have diverse requirements in terms of actions, skills, etc. This need for crime-specific analyses leads to the recognition of what Cornish and Clarke later term the 'choice-structuring' properties of the crime – a concept they first used in 1987 to analyse the likelihood that preventive measures would result in the displacement of the crime to a different time, place, victim, method or crime type.

Previous research by Clarke (on absconding from approved schools), Cornish (on gambling) and others suggested the importance of considering the 'situation' in which decisions were made. 'Situation' broadly conceived can be seen as part of RCP's early recognition of the potential utility of specifying a series of contexts, phases or stages that might involve different types of situational factors in the decision-making processes of offenders. Building on this, Clarke and Cornish produced specific models for each of three stages of involvement in a crime (starting, continuing and stopping) and for the unfolding of a crime event.

This 'situational' approach brought the focus of inquiry to factors closer to offenders' decision points. For example, the *initial involvement* model focused on aspects of the person and the situation, and stopped at the decision as to readiness to offend. The *habituation model* looked at factors that would tend to influence decisions to continue offending, while the *desistance model* detailed factors that might lead someone to decide to stop offending. The *event model* initially described a basic model of factors that might be important in carrying out a crime. Later, Cornish (1994) developed an approach using the concept of 'scripts' to elaborate a more detailed sequential unfolding of actions for modelling crime events, which also allowed planners to link situational crime prevention (SCP) measures to each offender action.

RCP was not the only theory in the mid-1980s looking at the factors influencing crime-event situations; nor was it the only theory influencing the development of SCP. Both the crime pattern theory (sometimes also referred to as environmental criminology) of Pat and Paul Brantingham, and routine activity theory, proposed by Lawrence Cohen and Marcus Felson, highlighted time, place and actor convergence in relation to crime events. All are concepts used in SCP analyses. In keeping with the original purpose of the approach, RCP has been used extensively for SCP research and policymaking, targeting a broad set of crimes from burglary to terrorism, wildlife poaching and cybercrime.

These situational crime-prevention efforts have been aided by the series of classifications of SCP measures devised by Clarke and others to highlight the mechanisms employed to block or reduce offending. The most recent iteration of these classification schemes identifies 25 techniques (see Cornish and Clarke 2003). The first three categories of preventive techniques involve measures that increase the effort of offenders, increase the risks of offending and reduce the rewards of the crime – all factors recognized as potentially important influences on decision-making in RCP. Often working in tandem with SCP efforts, research using the crime-script approach has recently proliferated and now includes analyses of a wide range of diverse crimes, from interactive crimes such as child sexual abuse and robbery to more traditional acquisitive crimes such as cigarette smuggling.

While the RCP framework continues to provide guidance for practical research and crime-preventive purposes, it has been subject to a number of different types of criticism. For example, early critics claimed that the original rational choice theory was not a true 'theory'. Clarke and Cornish addressed this by adopting the term 'perspective', emphasizing RCP's heuristic value and making it clear that it did not claim to have a testable series of propositions. In response to criticism from Akers (1990) that RCP was nothing new and was, in fact, subsumed by social learning theory, Cornish (1993) not only highlighted its differences from other existing theoretical approaches, but also claimed that it was a 'meta-theory', – i.e., an underlying theory of action. In addition, Cornish argued that RCP was the best among several candidates (including social learning theory) to be the meta-theory for all criminological theorizing. He saw RCP's assumption of 'bounded' rationality as a particularly useful safeguard against views of criminal behaviour as necessarily pathological or outside the ordinary. This assumption of the value of bounded rationality in the RCP, however, has not been universally accepted.

Criticisms of the bounded rationality component of RCP have occurred repeatedly since the mid-1980s. They tend to fall into three general categories (for examples, see Further reading):

See Chapter 6.2
Community safety

See Chapter 6.10
Space, place and crime

See Chapter 6.8
Routine activity theory

See Chapter 4.19
Institutional and anti-institutional violence

See Chapter 4.16
Green criminology

See Chapter 6.4
Cybercrime

1. criminal behaviour (or some criminal behaviour) is not rational;
2. assuming rationality is not an accurate picture of the mental processes involved because it does not take emotions or 'affect' into account; and
3. 'rationality' is not needed as long as the choice is situational.

The first type of criticism focuses either on so-called 'expressive crimes', such as assault, or on the nature of modern offending among some groups responding to modern culture. Cornish and Clarke's response to this type of criticism has been to suggest that the purposive aspects of the behaviour (i.e., its instrumental goals within an emotive framework) or the processual aspects of the doing of the behaviour may be analysed in terms of RCP (as a heuristic device) and lead to useful crime-preventive outcomes. The second type of criticism – that RCP is not an accurate depiction of the mental processes at work in decision-making – was one noted by Clarke and Cornish (1985) in their discussion of the heuristic aspects of their approach to a 'good enough' theory. More recently, Cornish and Clarke (see Further reading) have taken a 'show me' approach to this claim, one in which they ask critics to demonstrate the advantage of using other types of decision-making models for SCP. The incorporation of the script approach into RCP and the expansion of the table of SCP techniques by Cornish and Clarke in 2003 are examples of how infrequently they have changed the theory (Clarke 2013). The third type of criticism – that rationality is not needed in the RCP – can be seen as risking the incorporation of **pathological** conceptions of criminal behaviour into SCP.

See Chapter 1.6
Pathology

References

Akers, Ronald L. 1990. Rational Choice, Deterrence and Social Learning Theory in Criminology: The Path Not Taken. *Journal of Criminal Law and Criminology* 81(3): 653–76.

Clarke, Ronald V. 2013. Affect and the reasoning criminal: Past and future. In *Affect and cognition in criminal decision making*, Jean-Louis Van Gelder, Henk Elffers, Danielle Reynald, and Daniel Nagin, eds, pp. 20–41. London and New York: Routledge.

Clarke, Ronald V., and Derek B. Cornish. 1985. Modeling Offenders' Decisions: A Framework for Research and Policy. *Crime and Justice* 6: 147–85.

Cornish, Derek B. 1993. Theories of action in criminology: Learning theory and rational choice approaches. In *Routine Activity and Rational Choice*, Ronald V. Clarke and Marcus Felson, eds, pp. 351–82. New Brunswick, NJ: Transaction Press.

Cornish, Derek B. 1994. The Procedural Analysis of Offending and Its Relevance for Situational Prevention. *Crime Prevention Studies* 3: 151–96.

Cornish, Derek B., and Ronald V. Clarke. 2003. Opportunities, Precipitators and Criminal Decisions: A Reply to Wortley's Critique of Situational Crime Prevention. *Crime Prevention Studies* 16: 41–96.

Cornish, Derek B., and Ronald V. Clarke. 2008. The rational choice perspective. In *Environmental Criminology and Crime Analysis*, Richard Wortley and Lorraine Mazerolle, eds, pp. 21–47. London and New York: Routledge.

Further reading

Bouhana, Noemie. 2013. The Reasoning Criminal vs. Homer Simpson: Conceptual Challenges for Crime Science. *Frontiers in Human Neuroscience* 7: 1–6.

Cornish, Derek B., and Ronald V. Clarke. 1987. Understanding Crime Displacement: An Application of Rational Choice Theory. *Criminology* 25(4): 933–47.

Cornish, Derek B., and Ronald V. Clarke. 2016. The rational choice perspective. In *Environmental Criminology and Crime Analysis* (2nd edn), Richard Wortley and Michael Townsley, eds, pp. 29–61. Abingdon and New York: Routledge.

Coyne, Michelle A., and John E. Eck. 2015. Situational Choice and Crime Events. *Journal of Contemporary Criminal Justice* 31(1): 12–29.

Hayward, Keith. 2007. Situational Crime Prevention and Its Discontents: Rational Choice Theory versus the 'Culture of Now'. *Social Policy and Administration* 41(3): 232–50.

Part 2

The emergence and growth of American criminology

Part 2 Introduction

As noted in the Introduction to Part 1, Lombroso's individualistic theory of crime – and his assertions that the seeds of crime rest *within* people – dominated criminological thought into the twentieth century. Changing demographics in the United States – notably, African-Americans moving from rural parts of the South to urban areas in the North and immigrants from Europe settling in East-Coast and later Midwestern cities – led a group of researchers in Chicago to examine whether theories regarding urban growth and expansion could be helpful in explaining rates of crime and delinquency. In particular, Clifford Shaw and Henry McKay, who worked at the Institute for Social Research in Chicago, hypothesized that the combination of persistent poverty, rapid population growth, heterogeneity and transiency could disrupt core social institutions (e.g., family) that influence children's moral values, and that crime and delinquency would be higher in these *socially disorganized* areas than in neighbourhoods that were more affluent and stable. Shaw and McKay found that, over time, rates of crime by area were relatively the same, leading them to conclude that the key to understanding crime could be found not in examining the biological features of *individuals*, but in the traits of *neighbourhoods*.

Shaw and McKay did not, however, really demonstrate *how* social disorganization *caused* crime and delinquency – a task left to progenitors and promoters of differential association and social learning theories, as well as control theorists. Moreover, Shaw and McKay also painted a rather idyllic picture of life outside inner cities – a perspective challenged by rural criminologists (see Part 6). For a variety of reasons, then, by the 1960s, Shaw and McKay's theory of social disorganization had lost some of its allure. But we should not view their work as a historical relic. Like Lombrosian-inspired ideas about the role of biology, Shaw and McKay's work was revived and extended in the 1980s. In addition, their research begat two theoretical traditions (which, like many siblings, have become rivals): differential association/social learning theories and control theories.

Edwin Sutherland's theory of *differential association* posits that criminal behaviour is not innate but learned – in much the same way that most other human behaviour is learned. Sutherland's differential association theory, however, did not specify the mechanisms by which such behaviour is learned – an endeavour undertaken by Ronald Akers's *social learning theory*, which is much broader than that of Sutherland.

In essence, Sutherland's work, as well as that of Akers, suggested how individuals in socially disorganized areas (as well as those in other areas) might learn the attitudes favourable to and the techniques of crime. Travis Hirschi's control theory augmented Shaw and McKay's assertions that crime and delinquency could be linked to the attenuation of (parental) control in inner cities. Subsequent permutations – e.g., containment theory, social bond theory, self-control theory – all concern the ways in which various types of control relate to illegal behaviour. More broadly, they ask not why do people commit crime, but why do people *not* commit crime – or what frees people to commit crime?

A middle sibling, so to speak, between differential association/social learning theories and control theories would be Gresham Sykes and David Matza's *techniques of neutralization*, which are before-crime and after-the-fact excuses for engaging (or having participated) in crime. Sykes and Matza's perspective is a *learning theory* in that these justifications are learned from others; it is a *control theory* because these rationalizations do not motivate crime but liberate individuals, so to speak, to engage in activities that satisfy their desires and perceived needs.

It must be stressed that Shaw and McKay, and those who followed in their footsteps, were not the only ones to reject Lombrosian thought in the first half of the twentieth century. The work of Dutch criminologist Willem Bonger in the second decade of the twentieth century produced a Marx-influenced thesis that capitalist modes of production breed crime, which would later inspire future generations of critical criminologists (see Part 3). It was the work of Robert Merton (in the late 1930s), however, and subsequent revisions by various criminologists that would represent another prominent dimension of American criminological thought. Merton's *anomie theory* attempted to explain why some societies, such as the United States, had higher crime rates than others – a perspective further refined during the 1980s and 1990s. Merton's *strain theory*, focused on trying to understand why some individuals and groups within society (rather than society *as a whole*) are more likely to engage in crime and delinquency than others. In its classic form, the theory was attacked in the late 1960s and early 1970s, but revised in approaches such as *relative deprivation* and *general strain theory*.

In sum, the sociological explanations of crime described in this introduction arose as a reaction to Lombroso and have exerted enormous influence on the development of criminological thought: notable here are differential association/social learning theories and control theories (coming from the Chicago School and social disorganization theory) and the tradition of anomie/strain (coming from Merton). While a good deal of criminological theoretical research extends these lineages, contemporary biologically-infused approaches or hybrids (described in Part 1) and critical perspectives, owing much to Bonger (and described in Parts 3 and 4), then gained traction and expanded the scope of and interest in criminology.

Chicago School

Charis E. Kubrin and
Nicholas Branic

The Chicago School is particularly known for its work in the early twentieth century when it hosted a variety of influential sociological perspectives, reflecting the collective research of visionary scholars affiliated with the Department of Sociology at the University of Chicago. The Chicago School profoundly changed how many social scientists studied human behaviour, creating an iconic intellectual legacy that began at the end of the nineteenth century and that continues to the present day. One hallmark of early Chicago School scholars was their intellectual diversity: insights from sociology, anthropology, human ecology, social psychology and geography permeated their work. The Chicagoans also utilized a wide range of methodological approaches, including case studies, ethnographic fieldwork, participant observation, geographic mapping and statistical analysis. Especially in the formative years, influential figures such as Ernest Burgess, Ellsworth Faris, Robert Park, Louis Wirth and Florian Znaniecki, among others, produced an important collection of ideas that paved the way for later scholarship.

A second wave of the Chicago School succeeded the early Chicagoans in the decades following World War II, cultivating further developments in thought. With the rise of this 'second' Chicago School, scholars such as Howard Becker, Erving Goffman and Anselm Strauss propelled symbolic interactionism and social psychology to the forefront of sociological theorizing on human behaviour.

To fully understand the Chicago School requires a socio-historical discussion of its origins and the context within which it emerged. Chicago began as a small town of approximately 4,000 residents in 1833, but experienced rapid changes near the turn of the century. By 1890, the city's population had reached 1 million; by 1910, it had surpassed 2 million. The primary drivers behind this exponential growth were industrialization, urbanization and immigration, which attracted a new and highly diverse population into the ever-expanding city. The migration of emancipated African-Americans travelling north in search of a better life in the years following the Civil War also contributed to the city's growing diversity. These processes vastly transformed Chicago, producing great cultural, religious and ethnic heterogeneity among its residents. This churning metropolis served as the unique setting for emerging Chicago School scholars, who examined how the ever-changing nature of the city impacted its neighbourhoods and residents. This approach was a vast departure from prevailing approaches of the time, such as **biological**, **psychological** and **rational choice** orientations, which emphasized more individualistic explanations.

See Chapter 1.4 Positivism; Chapter 1.5 Biological Criminology; Chapter 1.8 Learning theory; Chapter 1.10 Psychoanalytic perspectives; Chapter 1.2 Classical criminology; Chapter 1.18 Rational choice

To Chicago School scholars, the city provided an ideal environment to explore human behaviour, social interaction and dynamic processes. Robert Park and Ernest Burgess, in particular, encouraged their students to perceive the city as a 'social laboratory' where they could carry out their research. Both Park and Burgess had backgrounds in human ecology, and applied concepts derived from plant and animal ecology to their observations of Chicago city life. This approach led them to theorize the city as a complex ecological web of interrelated social structures and processes. Using this framework, they examined how the environment and individual human action interrelated, an interest of key predecessors such as Georg Simmel, and observed how these contextual relationships changed over time as the city evolved. In particular, they theorized the growth of a city in terms of ecological competition – similar to natural ecosystems – and introduced concepts such as 'dominance', 'invasion' and 'succession' to describe patterns of residential migration across neighbourhoods. Humans coexisted within a system of symbiotic and competitive relationships, they argued, vying for scarce and desirable resources and space within the city.

Park and Burgess also developed their concentric zone theory to account for different environmental conditions across Chicago neighbourhoods. Near the commercial centre of the city, or the Central Business District, they observed deteriorated, disinvested areas in what they called the 'zone in transition'. These areas had high rates of poverty, residential turnover and population heterogeneity, which they argued disrupted the core social institutions of society, reduced social ties among residents and inhibited social control within the neighbourhood. Park and Burgess defined this condition as 'social disorganization'. They observed improving conditions in areas progressively further from the core ('zone of workingmen's homes', 'residential zone', 'commuters' zone'), with the most desirable communities found in suburban areas outside the city. Consistent with the idea of ecological competition, Park and Burgess discovered that those who were able to relocate away from the inner-city neighbourhoods would do so, while those without sufficient resources remained in socially disorganized neighbourhoods.

Two other Chicago School researchers, Clifford Shaw and Henry McKay, later adapted and applied Park and Burgess's concentric zone theory to the study of delinquency in their influential work *Juvenile Delinquency in Urban Areas* (1942). Adopting an ecological approach, Shaw and McKay used official data – Cook County juvenile court records in particular – to create maps of the city, including *spot maps* to demonstrate the location of various social problems, most notably juvenile delinquency; *rate maps* that divided the city into blocks of 1 square mile and showed the population by age, gender, ethnicity, etc.; and *zone maps* demonstrating that the major social problems clustered near the city centre, in line with Park and Burgess's concentric zone theory (Bursik 2012). In addition to accumulating decades' worth of official data, Shaw collected life histories, supplemented by personal interviews, from males referred to juvenile court. He used these data to flesh out the processes emphasized by the **social disorganization model**, especially the cultural and peer group elements that were impossible to study with official data.

See Chapter 2.2
Social
disorganization
theory

Of course, this important work by Park, Burgess, Shaw and McKay does not fully account for the wide range of scholarship produced by the Chicago School. Other scholars researched everything from taxi dance halls, which were becoming big business in Chicago as the city grew and expanded (Cressey 1932), to how urban geography shapes gangs, discovering that neighbourhoods in flux were more likely to produce gangs (Thrasher 1929); from the rise of organized crime in Chicago (Landesco 1929) to the social and economic hardships faced by the city's homeless (Anderson 1923). This work and the work done by other Chicago School scholars subsumed both a wide variety of substantive and methodological orientations.

Collectively, the Chicago School studies generated valuable findings. First, the research revealed that crime and delinquency co-occurred with other social problems, including poverty, residential turnover and population heterogeneity. This co-occurrence implied a connection between the social and economic conditions of places and crime rates. Second, the research showed that some areas in the city exhibited consistently high rates of crime and delinquency regardless of the characteristics or nationalities of the residents living therein. This finding suggested that crime and delinquency stemmed from the social conditions of neighbourhoods rather than the ethnic composition of residents.

Beyond these findings, the field has inherited several broader principles from the Chicago School. We are reminded, for example, that context matters. In the words of Andrew Abbott (1997:1152), 'All social facts are located in contexts' and 'No social fact makes any sense abstracted from its context in social (and often geographic) space and social time'. A related principle is that contexts are dynamic; they shift and evolve over time. The work of the Chicago School clearly emphasized change rather than fixed social structure. We are also encouraged to pay close attention to process. Short (1971) argues that, more than any of the several 'schools' and styles of sociology that developed during the formative years of the discipline, the Chicago School developed a sensitivity to process – ecological processes, organizational and institutional processes, processes of identity formation and groups – by which we function as human beings. Finally, a key insight of the Chicago School was the value of eclectic methods in research. When paired, both qualitative methodologies – especially those used in naturalistic observation – and quantitative ones were ideally suited for the study of urban, social phenomena. This ethnographic closeness to the data, combined with quantitative measures, brought great richness and depth to the Chicago work.

References

Abbott, Andrew. 1997. Of Time and Space: The Contemporary Relevance of the Chicago School. *Social Forces* 75: 1149–82.

Anderson, Nels. 1923. *The Hobo: The Sociology of Homeless Men*. Chicago: University of Chicago Press.

Bursik, Robert J. 2012. The Chicago School of Criminology. Oxford Bibliographies Online. http://oxfordbibliographiesonline.com. Accessed January 2017.

Cressey, Paul G. 1932. *The Taxi-Dance Hall: A Sociological Study in Commercialized Recreation and City Life*. Chicago: University of Chicago Press.

Landesco, John. 1929. *Organized Crime in Chicago*. Chicago: Illinois Association for Criminal Justice.

Shaw, Clifford R., and Henry D. McKay. 1942. *Juvenile Delinquency and Urban Areas: A Study of Rates of Delinquents in Relation to Differential Characteristics of Local Communities in American Cities*. Chicago: University of Chicago Press.

Short, James F. Jr. 1971. *The Social Fabric of the Metropolis: Contributions of the Chicago School of Urban Sociology*. Chicago: University of Chicago Press.

Thrasher, Frederick Milton. 1929. *The Gang*. Chicago: University of Chicago Press.

Further reading

Becker, Howard S. 1999. The Chicago School, So-Called. *Qualitative Sociology* 22(3): 3–12.

Bulmer, Martin. 1984. *The Chicago School of Sociology: Institutionalization, Diversity, and the Rise of Sociological Research*. Chicago: University of Chicago Press.

Faris, Robert E.L. 1967. *Chicago Sociology: 1920–1932*. San Francisco: Chandler.

Park, Robert E., Ernest W. Burgess, and Roderick McKenzie. 1925. *The City*. Chicago: University of Chicago Press.

Plummer, Ken (ed.). 1997. *The Chicago School: Critical Assessments*. London: Routledge.

Shaw, Clifford R. 1930. *The Jack-Roller: A Delinquent Boy's Own Story*. Chicago: University of Chicago Press.

2.2 Social disorganization theory

Michael J. Lynch and Kimberly L. Barrett

Social disorganization theory is one of the oldest and most prominent macro-level theories of crime. Emile Durkheim was the first to draw attention to the ways in which social disorganization could affect the level of crime in society – an idea that was developed more extensively in the early twentieth century by the **Chicago School** theorists. Social disorganization theory was prominent from the 1930s to the 1950s when interest declined until it was rekindled in the 1980s. Today it remains one of the most widely employed macro-level theories concerning the spatial distribution of crime.

See Chapter 2.1
Chicago School

In his 1895 book *The Rules of Sociological Method*, Durkheim proposed that crime was normal, meaning that all societies had some type and level of crime and that these were related to social organization. Thus, changes in the level of crime were due to changes in society's social organization. In particular, rapid social change could produce significant changes in the level of crime in society as such a society might become increasingly disorganized, promoting a condition he called **anomie** or normlessness (Agnew 2006; Merton 1938; Messner and Rosenfeld 2013). Under such conditions, anomie/normlessness caused people's desires to become uncontrolled, in turn promoting crime. Durkheim did not fully develop this idea, and in various other works (e.g., *The Division of Labor in Society*, 1893; *Suicide*, 1897; *Moral Education*, 1925) he explored further social factors that impacted on crime in society.

See Chapter 2.3
Anomie

Social disorganization theory was more fully developed by Chicago School writers in the 1910s and 1920s, being particularly associated with Robert E. Park, Ernest W. Burgess and Roderick D. McKenzie's 1925 book *The City* (which was an extension of Park's 1915 article 'The City', published in the *American Journal of Sociology*). Park and colleagues proposed that cities were like organisms and that they developed in an evolutionary manner. Using Chicago as a model, Park et al. argued that as a city grows from the centre outward, similar activities cluster together and form zones (in Chicago, those zones were comprised of five concentric circles, but the concentric zone model does not apply to all cities, and later researchers found unique development patterns for other cities). As the city grows, these zones can overlap and compete with one another, producing both social organization and the emergence of social disorganization. Park et al. were the first to suggest that this growth process, with the forms of social disorganization it could cause, was one of the factors that generated crime, and that crime would be higher in disorganized as opposed to organized communities.

The idea that social disorganization affected crime was further advanced by Clifford Shaw and Henry McKay in their 1942 book *Juvenile Delinquency in Urban Areas*. Shaw and McKay suggested that crime was a normal response to abnormal conditions, and hypothesized that crime would therefore be highest in the most socially disorganized urban areas. Socially disorganized areas not only had high rates of crime and delinquency, but also elevated rates of poverty, ethnic heterogeneity, signs of physical deterioration (urban decay) and population change/residential mobility. Shaw and McKay argued that urban areas with such characteristics could be labelled as 'zones of transition', and that those transitions caused an area to become socially disorganized. From their observations of delinquency in Chicago over time, they suggested that it was the nature of social order in a community (i.e., whether a community was organized or disorganized) rather than the people who lived in a community that was the source of crime, suggesting that certain parts of the city itself are more prone to crime than others.

Social disorganization was traditionally viewed as a characteristic of the social structure of an area rather than as a characteristic of the people who lived there, although this observation has not always been widely accepted and numerous criminological theories posit that the characteristics of individuals have something to do with the causes of crime. Missing from the social disorganization argument was a theory specifying *how* the structural characteristics of areas caused people's behaviour to change. As such, in the 1960s, the theory of social disorganization began to fall out of favour but it was revived in the 1980s by research conducted by Robert Bursik and Robert J. Sampson, who suggested that social disorganization impacted people's behaviour by weakening social institutions and processes of informal social control in communities (Bursik 1988; Sampson 1985; Sampson and Groves 1989). Thus, social disorganization was reconceptualized as producing weak **social bonds** that, in turn, contributed to higher rates of crime. Numerous studies

See Chapter 2.6
Control theories

followed, examining groups within communities that suffered from social disorganization and exhibited weak bonds as well as forms of ineffective informal social control. Other studies examined community *collective efficacy* – the willingness of residents to exercise informal social control, driven by a sense of solidarity, mutual trust and support of one another – which became one of the dominant topics in social disorganization research (Sampson et al. 1997).

In recent years, a number of studies related to social disorganization have re-examined the effect of community migration, and especially immigration, on crime. Here, the question is whether immigration and the concentration of immigrants within a community have an adverse impact on crime (Sampson 2008). Recent studies suggest that immigration reduces crime, perhaps because of the types of informal social control that immigrant groups transfer to their new communities.

Social disorganization theory has also led to the development of a concept called *community disadvantage*. Disorganized communities have numerous structural disadvantages. One of these is the differential distribution of social capital across communities. Social capital is a broad concept; it includes an assessment of the types of social networks within communities, and can also include *cultural capital*, such as the presence and quality of educational institutions. In the modern social disorganization view, communities with low social capital have low collective efficacy, disrupted systems of informal social control and limited resources to constrain the behaviours of community residents.

Another important set of studies related to social disorganization theory has been undertaken by John Hipp, drawing attention to how community inequality, racial and ethnic heterogeneity and other social disorganization constructs affect neighbourhood crime rates (e.g., Hipp et al. 2009). Recently,

See Chapter 4.16
Green criminology

green criminologists have also suggested that community disorganization relates to the presence of green/environmental crimes and environmental injustice in communities (Stretesky et al. 2013). In the green criminological view, community social disorganization is seen as one consequence of how economic production and pollution is distributed across cities; social disorganization within communities, then, is a consequence of economic organization which concentrates community disadvantages within low-income and minority communities, making them the primary locations of green crime and

See Chapter 4.11
Environmental
justice and
victimology

environmental injustice (Jarrell et al. 2014; Jarrell and Ozymy 2012). The uneven distribution of environmental hazards across communities related to community racial, ethnic and class composition is also part of the study of environmental justice.

Many studies now examine how various dimensions of neighbourhood structures can affect crime and delinquency. The older Chicago School ecological models have been replaced by more extensive illustrations of how community structures affect the ways in which people living within those communities behave, and the social disorganization approach continues to stimulate quite a diverse body of criminological work. In 2003, Charis Kubrin and Ronald Weitzer took stock of conceptual and methodological developments in recent social disorganization studies, and recommended several new directions for future tests of the theory. For example, they noted that the use of dynamic models, examinations of reciprocal effects and assessments that account for spatial interdependence have facilitated a more thorough understanding of social disorganization theory. They also recommend additional ethnographic research as well as refinement in the measurement of social disorganization theory's key variables. With respect to future work, Kubrin and Weitzer (2003) suggest that examinations of social disorganization theory should consider the role of culture, formal social control and political economy. Recent works that are heavily informed by political economic theories have begun to examine intersections between social and ecological disorganization. Exploration of these intersections, addressing methodological considerations and inclusion of significant mediating and moderating variables represent promising directions for the growing body of scholarship on communities and crime.

References

Agnew, Robert. 2006. *Pressured into Crime: An Overview of General Strain Theory*. New York: Oxford University Press.

Bursik, Robert J. 1988. Social Disorganization and Theories of Crime and Delinquency: Problems and Prospects. *Criminology* 26(4): 519–52.

Hipp, John R., George E. Tita, and Lyndsay N. Boggess. 2009. Intergroup and Intragroup Violence: Is Violent Crime an Expression of Group Conflict or Social Disorganization? *Criminology* 47(2): 521–64.

Jarrell, Melissa L., Michael Lynch, and Paul B. Stretesky. 2014. Green criminology and green victimization. In *The Routledge Handbook of International Crime and Justice Studies*, Bruce A. Arrigo and Heather Y. Bersot, eds, pp. 423–44. Abingdon: Routledge.

Jarrell, Melissa L., and Joshua Ozymy. 2012. Real Crime, Real Victims: Environmental Crime Victims and the Crime Victims' Rights Act (CVRA). *Crime, Law and Social Change* 58(4): 373–89.

Kubrin, Charis E., and Ronald Weitzer. 2003. New Directions in Social Disorganization Theory. *Journal of Research in Crime and Delinquency* 40(4): 374–402.

Merton, Robert. 1938. Social Structure and Anomie. *American Sociological Review* 3(5): 672–82.

Messner, Steven F., and Richard Rosenfeld. 2013. *Crime and the American Dream* (5th edn). Belmont, CA: Wadsworth.

Sampson, Robert J. 1985. Neighborhood and Crime: The Structural Determinants of Personal Victimization. *Journal of Research in Crime and Delinquency* 22(1): 7–40.

Sampson, Robert J. 2008. Rethinking Crime and Immigration. *Contexts* 7(1): 28–33.

Sampson, Robert J., and W. Byron Groves. 1989. Community Structure and Crime: Testing Social-Disorganization Theory. *American Journal of Sociology* 94(4): 774–802.

Sampson, Robert J., Stephen W. Raudenbush, and Felton Earls. 1997. Neighborhoods and Violent Crime: A Multilevel Study of Collective Efficacy. *Science* 277(5328): 918–24.

Stretesky, Paul B., Michael A. Long, and Michael J. Lynch. 2013. *The Treadmill of Crime: Political Economy and Green Criminology*. New York: Routledge.

Further reading

Bursik, Robert J. 2006. Rethinking the Chicago School of criminology: a new era of immigration. In *Immigration and Crime: Ethnicity, Race, and Violence*, Ramiro Martinez Jr and Abel Valenzuela Jr, eds, pp. 20–35. New York: New York University Press.

Sampson, Robert J. 1986. Effects of Inequality, Heterogeneity, and Urbanization on Intergroup Victimization. *Social Science Quarterly* 67(4): 751–66.

Sampson, Robert J. 2012. *Great American City: Chicago and the Enduring Neighborhood Effect*. Chicago: University of Chicago Press.

Sampson, Robert J., and William J. Wilson. 1995. Toward a theory of race, crime, and urban inequality. In *Crime and Inequality*, John Hagan and Ruth D. Peterson, eds, pp. 37–54. Stanford, CA: Stanford University Press.

Shaw, Clifford R., and Henry D. McKay. 1942. *Juvenile Delinquency and Urban Areas: A Study of Rates of Delinquency in Relation to Differential Characteristics of Local Communities in American Cities*. Chicago: University of Chicago Press.

Steenbeek, Wouter, and John R. Hipp. 2011. A Longitudinal Test of Social Disorganization Theory: Feedback Effects among Cohesion, Social Control, and Disorder. *Criminology* 49(3): 833–71.

Anomie

Eamonn Carrabine

Now regarded as one of the of the 'founding fathers' of sociology, Émile Durkheim (1858–1917) was a French social theorist who, more than any other at the time, placed crime, law and punishment at the centre of the sociological enterprise. Anomie is the central concept in his account of the consequences of a breakdown in cultural regulation and institutional structure, resulting in a sense of futility, emptiness and dislocation among members of a society experiencing such a collapse of normative order. Although often discussed alongside Marx's concept of alienation, anomie describes a somewhat different social condition. It is most fully developed in Durkheim's classic study *Suicide* (1897/2002), which sought to demonstrate the power of sociological analysis by showing how such an apparently individualistic decision (to take one's own life) could be explained by social forces.

Based on his empirical work, Durkheim argued that variations in suicide rates among Protestant and Catholic countries could be explained by differences in the levels of social *integration* and *regulation* they displayed. Integration he defined through the strength of attachment a person has to social groups, which he measured on a scale from 'egoism' to 'altruism'. Regulation refers to the extent to which group norms control individual desires, which he also measured on a different scale – from 'anomie' to 'fatalism'. All four (egoism, altruism, anomie and fatalism) led to distinctive types of suicide. 'Anomic suicide' resulted from a lack of normative regulation, caused by the spread of limitless desires and the inability to achieve them. In contrast, 'fatalistic suicide' occurs when normative regulation is so constraining that there is no freedom of choice, resulting in acceptance or resignation among members of such societies, so that suicide in this context is still an expression of collective values.

Durkheim found that Protestants had a consistently higher rate of suicide than Catholics, and that this variation was due to the different degrees of social cohesion each group encouraged: the 'only essential difference between Catholicism and Protestantism' is that the latter permits a greater degree of 'free inquiry' than the former (Durkheim 1897/2002:157). Consequently, it was the lack of a common credo in Protestantism that made it a less strongly integrated church than its Roman Catholic counterpart. He then suggested that this explanation accounted for the even lower suicide rates of Jews who, in response to the hostility directed against them, established strong community ties that practically eliminated individual differences, and thereby secured a high degree of unity, solidarity and integration among members. It also explained why, of all the notable Protestant countries, England has the lowest suicide rate, as it had the most 'integrated' of Protestant churches.

Durkheim's ideas were developed by Robert Merton, who became one of the most instrumental North American sociologists of the twentieth century. His thinking was steeped in the classical sociological tradition of the nineteenth century, which he innovatively fused and enlarged to address contemporary concerns. This is exemplified in his famous essay 'Social Structure and Anomie', which became one of the most important essays in American sociology, not least because it highlighted how deviance and crime were rooted in the class structure of society (Merton 1938). Drawing from the traditions established by both Durkheim and Marx, Merton's 'strain theory' of criminal behaviour emphasized the importance of 'structural frustration' in the specific context of American culture between the wars.

See Chapter 2.8
Market society and
crime

For Merton, the defining characteristic of the post-Depression 1930s was the malaise produced by the tension between the **American Dream** (based on an egalitarian ideology that anyone can make it, with enough hard work) and the actual reality of extreme economic inequality – where there are only limited legitimate opportunities for achieving the kind of material success that is so culturally exalted. Merton's central thesis is that the disjuncture between culture (the values placed on symbols of success, which are inevitably monetary) and structure (only a few had the means to acquire such prosperity) gives rise to a 'malintegration' at the core of American society (Merton 1938:673). In developing his argument, Merton reworks the concept of anomie, which in Durkheim's original formulation referred to a lack of normative regulation, to describe various forms of deviant conduct generated in the United States.

Merton described four very different individual responses to such structural strain: 'innovation', 'ritualism', 'retreatism' and 'rebellion' – each depending on the wider context. As he put it (1938:679–80, emphasis in original):

> [Al] Capone represents the triumph of amoral intelligence over morally prescribed "failure" when the channels of vertical mobility are closed or

narrowed *in a society which places a high premium on economic affluence and social ascent for* all *its members.*

Some maintain that Merton has shifted the meaning of anomie away from the radical implications of the term as used by Durkheim, but there is a very clear sense in which he grounds his analysis in a more Marxist understanding of social contradictions and the commodity fetishism American society produces. In particular, Merton was keenly aware of the power of advertising and the role of conspicuous consumption in sustaining an intense, competitive pressure on people to keep acquiring status symbols.

Merton wrote the paper early in his career at Harvard, where he worked with Talcott Parsons, and both were key figures in promoting a functionalist school of sociology that thrived from the 1930s up to the late 1960s in the United States. Significantly, Merton was quite hostile to Parsons' abstract way of theorizing, preferring instead what he later dubbed 'middle-range theory' – and his essay on anomie can be seen as an exemplar of this approach. For much of this time, the piece was widely accepted and highly regarded; and then, from the early 1960s, it began to be criticized as part of a broader movement against functionalism. Here the importance the perspective attached to stable social systems, dominant cultural goals and deterministic role structures came under attack for its inability to explain social change, make sense of conflict and teleological forms of explanation (that is, where the observed social action is tautologically explained through its purpose). Consequently, functionalism was tainted with an inherent conservative disposition, so that the concept of anomie was increasingly marginalized and regarded as somewhat dated. It was in **subcultural theory** that the Mertonian legacy was to persist most influentially among ardent followers.

See Chapter 3.17
Subculture

One of these followers was Albert Cohen (1955), who in *Delinquent Boys* advanced the concept of subculture to insist that the social world of the juvenile delinquent provides an alternative means of acquiring recognition and respect among disadvantaged youth. Although the term 'subculture' had been used by anthropologists since the 1870s, it is Cohen who is often credited as the first to systematically apply it to delinquency. For Cohen, subcultures typically borrow elements from the dominant culture, but rework them in distinctive ways. The prefix 'sub' highlights the way the groups are subordinate, subversive or subterranean, and thereby viewed as beneath, but still within a wider culture. Accordingly, the gang was defined as a subculture with a value system at odds with mainstream culture, distinguished by specialized vocabulary, shared beliefs and distinctive fashions. Subcultures were then regarded as collective solutions to the structural problems posed by class location and the experience of anomie. Cohen pioneered the idea that boys became delinquent through a process of 'status frustration'. In schools especially, he noted that boys from deprived backgrounds often found them alienating places as they were judged against prevailing middle-class standards.

Against these standards, some children are doomed to fail, as their cultural differences do not prepare them for school life. In their frustration, working-class boys invert the values of the school (achievement, hard work, planning for the future and deferring gratification) and develop an exaggerated hostility toward it. Through a process of 'reaction formation', academic success is redefined and the vices of the middle classes become virtues in the working-class gang: hedonism, maliciousness, disrespect of property and pursuit of instant pleasures are among the defining features of this milieu.

Drawing on Merton, Cohen described three different responses working-class boys could adopt: the 'college boy solution' offers the bright 'conformists' a way of achieving upward mobility; 'stable corner boys' are 'retreatists' who accept their inferior position and adjust to middle-class values without attaining them; while the 'delinquent subculture' is for the 'innovators' who invert the rules of respectable society and reject them. *Delinquent Boys* was written in the midst of post-war anxieties over urban gang delinquency, and gave rise to a whole raft of studies in the 1950s and 1960s testing and modifying various elements of the theory in various metropolitan settings (Cloward and Ohlin 1961, Short and Strodtbeck 1967) as well as prison (Clemmer 1958; Sykes 1958).

An early critic of Cohen was David Matza (1964, 1969), who objected to the sharp distinction drawn between the criminal and the law-abiding, and argued that subcultural theorists are mistaken in seeing the relationship between the values embodied in delinquent subcultures and the conventional mainstream as set in opposition. There are many points of 'subterranean convergence' and 'conventional culture' is often not quite as 'conventional' as it is made out to be (Matza 1964:36–7). It consists not only of ascetic puritanism, middle-class morality, the boy-scout oath and so forth, but is also hedonistic, frivolous and exciting – especially where toughness is equated with masculinity, as in cowboy frontier mentality, or the Bohemian celebration of demi-monde excess.

See Chapter 3.5 Drift

A key component of his theory of **drift** is that boys can commit delinquent acts when their commitment to the moral order is weakened, which is accomplished through **'techniques of neutralization'** (Sykes and Matza 1957)

See Chapter 2.7 Techniques of neutralization

that operate to deflect disapproval from authority figures. The process of drift helps explain the fluid, episodic character of much delinquency and why there is such an alluring pull to make things happen in a mundane world.

It must be said that the idea of there being a structural tension produced by market inequalities and the failure of apparently meritocratic systems to deliver social mobility and social status remains an important one. As Young (2004:553) wrote, the 'Mertonian notion of contradiction between culture and structure has run throughout all my work, from *The Drugtakers* onwards'. An incarnation of anomie was further revived in the 1990s in the guise of **general strain theory**, which is a telling indication of the strength of these ideas.

See Chapter 2.9 General strain theory

References

Clemmer, Donald. 1958. *The Prison Community*. New York: Rhinehart.

Cloward, Richard, and Lloyd Ohlin. 1961. *Delinquency and Opportunity: A Theory of Delinquent Gangs*. London: Routledge & Kegan Paul.

Cohen, Albert. 1955. *Delinquent Boys: The Culture of the Gang*. New York: Free Press.

Durkheim, Émile. 1897/2002. *Suicide*. London: Routledge.

Matza, David. 1964. *Delinquency and Drift*. New York: Wiley.

Matza, David. 1969. *Becoming Deviant*. Englewood Cliffs, NJ: Prentice Hall.

Merton, Robert K. 1938. Social Structure and Anomie. *American Sociological Review* 3(5): 672–82.

Short, James, and Fred Strodtbeck. 1967. *Group Process and Gang Delinquency*. Chicago: University of Chicago Press.

Sykes, Gresham. 1958. *The Society of Captives*. Princeton, NJ: Princeton University Press.

Sykes, Gresham, and David Matza. 1957. Techniques of Neutralization: A Theory of Delinquency. *American Sociological Review* 22(6): 664–70.

Young, Jock. 2004. Crime and the Dialectics of Inclusion/Exclusion. *British Journal of Criminology* 44(5): 550–61.

Further reading

Carrabine, Eamonn. 2017. *Crime and Social Theory*. Basingstoke: Palgrave Macmillan.

Katz, Jack. 1988. *The Seductions of Crime*. New York: Basic Books.

Messner, Steven F., and Richard Rosenfeld. 2013. *Crime and the American Dream* (5th edn). Belmont, CA: Wadsworth.

2.4 Differential association

Andrew Krebs and Mark Warr

Differential association is a theory of how individuals learn to engage in criminal behaviour. Originally formulated by Edwin Sutherland, it is among the most well-known theories in criminology and has been part of the field for more than seventy-five years and been tested hundreds of times. Sutherland also provided concepts such as **white-collar crime** and the professional criminal, which are central to modern criminology.

See Chapter 4.41
White-collar crime

See Chapter 2.1
Chicago School

Sutherland was initially influenced by the **Chicago School** of sociology, and was a proponent of the multiple-factor approach to crime, which viewed criminal behaviour as a product of multiple causes – age, broken homes, mental disorder, race, social class and urban or rural location. In time, however, Sutherland grew dissatisfied with this approach and sought a more coherent account of crime, one in which individual offending was a result of the normative conflict that characterizes many modern industrial societies. The first explicit statement of differential association appeared in the third edition of his *Principles of Criminology* (1939). The final statement of the theory in the fourth edition (1947) took the form of nine propositions (each followed by brief elaborations or clarifications):

1. Criminal behaviour is learned.
2. Criminal behaviour is learned in interaction with other persons in a process of communication.

3.   The principal part of the learning of criminal behaviours occurs within intimate personal groups.

4.   When criminal behaviour is learned, the learning includes: (a) techniques of committing the crime, which are sometimes very complicated, sometimes very simple; and (b) the specific direction of motives, drives, rationalizations and attitudes.

5.   The specific direction of motives and drives is learned from definitions of the legal codes as favourable or unfavourable.

6.   A person becomes delinquent because of an excess of definitions favourable to violation of law over definitions unfavourable to violation of law.

7.   Differential association may vary in frequency, duration, priority and intensity.

8.   The process of learning criminal behaviour by association with criminal and anti-criminal patterns involves all of the mechanisms that are involved in any other learning.

9.   While criminal behaviour is an expression of general needs and values, it is not explained by those general needs and values because non-criminal behaviour is an expression of the same needs and values (Sutherland 1947).

Sutherland's theory was radical when it first appeared because it rejected popular **biological theories of crime** in favour of a strongly sociological approach to crime. Sutherland argued that criminal behaviour is not innate or a result of personal or private experience; instead, it is *learned* behaviour, in the same way that most other human behaviour is learned – arising from interaction with other human beings in intimate groups. This interaction conveys knowledge or techniques of committing crimes, as well as definitions of the legal codes as 'favourable or unfavourable', which in turn dictate 'motives, drives, rationalizations, and attitudes' that promote lawbreaking (Sutherland 1947).

See Chapter 1.5 Biological criminology

   Sutherland's theory is an unabashedly social explanation of crime, and it can also be described as a naturalistic theory, meaning that it does not turn to unique or special causes to explain criminal behaviour in relation to other forms of human behaviour – the mechanisms of learning that explain any behaviour also apply to criminal behaviour. Although most modern tests of differential association have focused on peer influence, the theory recognizes a wide range of individuals (e.g., peers, parents, teachers, classmates, church members, co-workers) who offer 'definitions' (attitudes or meanings) favourable or unfavourable to the violation of law.

   Many criminologists believe that strong empirical support for differential association can be found in the fact that one of the best predictors of criminal behaviour known to criminologists is the number of delinquent friends an individual has (Warr 2002), a correlation observed in scores of studies from the 1950s to the present (see Matsueda 1988) using various research designs and sources (self-reports, official records, perceptual data, criminal records) concerning subjects and friends. Moreover, delinquent behaviour is largely committed by juveniles acting in groups, which appears to support (but is not required by) Sutherland's position.

Sceptics, however, question whether this correlation actually supports or even bears on the theory of differential association. Drawing on the sociological principle of homophily (people make friends with people who are similar to themselves), they argue that the causal direction between delinquency and friends runs in the opposite direction from that implied by peer influence. People do not become delinquent because they acquire delinquent friends; instead, they acquire delinquent friends after they themselves have become delinquent. As the Gluecks (1950) famously suggested, 'birds of a feather flock together'. Today, the question of causal direction – social selection versus socialization – remains a central and often heated issue among criminologists (Matsueda and Anderson 1998).

Among Sutherland's nine propositions, the most critical is the sixth, sometimes referred to as the 'theory of differential association', which suggests that 'A person becomes delinquent because of an excess of definitions favourable to violation of law over definitions unfavourable to violation of law.' In essence, Sutherland proposed that delinquency is the result of attitude transference, whereby the attitudes or knowledge of one individual are socially transmitted to another. Many investigators, however, have found that the effect of friends' attitudes on adolescents is small in comparison to that of friends' *behaviour*, which has a more direct impact than through changing attitudes: i.e., adolescents are much more sensitive to the *behaviour* of their friends than their *attitudes*.

Criminologists have also challenged Sutherland's seventh proposition, which suggests that the process of differential association may vary in frequency, duration, priority and intensity. Specifically, Warr (1993) examined the effects of priority (or the age at which associations occur) and duration on self-reported delinquency at age 17 using data from the National Youth Survey and found two dimensions of friendships (priority and duration) are not entirely independent because adolescents who acquire delinquent friends are likely to retain them – and thus those who acquire such friends at younger ages (greater priority) will tend to have longer histories of delinquent friendships (greater duration). The two elements cannot be regarded as entirely independent components of differential association. Taken as a whole, Warr's findings can be summarized this way: the cumulative number of years in which an adolescent has delinquent friends has a positive effect on his or her current behaviour. Among adolescents with the same duration of delinquent friendships, however, those who acquire delinquent friends *most recently* are those who are most prone to delinquency. Warr's findings regarding priority may surprise some, but are consistent with modern **social learning theory**, with its emphasis on reinforcement, extinction and modelling or imitation.

Burgess and Akers (1966) restated Sutherland's theory of differential association in the terminology of operant conditioning, a then developing branch

See Chapter 2.5
Social learning
theory

of **behavioural psychology** associated with B.F. Skinner that emphasized the relation between behaviour and reinforcement. Akers has subsequently developed and tested a social learning approach to the explanation of crime, emphasizing the role of reinforcement (both positive and negative) in criminal behaviour and the effect of 'the relative frequency, amount and probability of past, present, and anticipated rewards and punishments perceived to be attached to the behavior' (Akers 1998:66).

See Chapter 1.8 Learning theory

The key to social learning theory is the idea that behaviour is learned through social sources of reinforcement. A young girl learns to put away her toys after playing with them because her mother praises her and hugs her for doing so (positive reinforcement), or because she sees her sister picking up her toys (imitation or modelling), or because she sees her sister being praised by her mother (vicarious reinforcement). Although the mechanisms may differ, social learning theory is much like differential association in stressing the social sources of learning when it comes to human behaviour – including criminal behaviour.

The empirical evidence for social learning theory is extensive and overwhelmingly positive, although it has been criticized as somewhat limited in scope, concentrating as it does on tobacco, alcohol and other drug use, and on relatively minor forms of deviance (see Gray et al. 2015). Because social learning theory was derived from the theory of differential association, Akers goes so far as to say that the two theories are one and the same, and it may be the case that differential association can be wholly, or partially, subsumed under social learning theory. If so, it would not diminish the historical impact of Sutherland's work in criminology or sociology, and it would be consistent with Sutherland's search for a general theory of human behaviour that would explain legal behaviour as fully as illegal behaviour.

References

Akers, Ronald L. 1998. *Social Learning and Social Structure: A General Theory of Crime and Deviance*. Boston, MA: Northeastern University Press.

Burgess, Robert, and Ronald L. Akers. 1966. A Differential Association-Reinforcement Theory of Criminal Behavior. *Social Problems* 14(2): 336–83.

Glueck, Sheldon, and Eleanor Glueck. 1950. *Unraveling Juvenile Delinquency*. New York: Commonwealth Fund.

Gray, Andrew C., Keith F. Durkin, James T. Call, Holly J. Evans, and Wade Melton. 2015. Differential Association and Marijuana Use in a Juvenile Drug Court Sample. *Applied Psychology in Criminal Justice* 11(1): 1–8.

Matsueda, Ross L. 1988. The Current State of Differential Association Theory. *Crime and Delinquency* 34(3): 277–306.

Matsueda, Ross L., and Kathleen Anderson. 1998. The Dynamics of Delinquent Peers and Delinquent Behavior. *Criminology* 36(2): 269–308.

Sutherland, Edwin H. 1947. *Principles of Criminology* (4th edn). Chicago: Lippincott.

Warr, Mark. 1993. Age, Peers, and Delinquency. *Criminology* 31(1): 17–40.

Warr, Mark. 2002. *Companions in Crime*. Cambridge: Cambridge University Press.

Further reading

Akers, Ronald L. 1985. *Deviant Behavior: A Social Learning Approach*. Belmont, CA: Wadsworth.

Jennings, Wesley G., George E. Higgins, and Ronald L. Akers. 2013. Examining the Influence of Delinquent Peer Association on the Stability of Self-Control in Late Childhood and Early Adolescence: Toward an Integrated Theoretical Model. *Deviant Behavior* 34(5): 407–22.

Reiss, Albert J. 1986. Co-offender influences on criminal careers. In *Criminal Careers and 'Career Criminals'*, Vol. 2, Alfred Blumstein, Jacqueline Cohen, Jeffrey Roth, and Christy Visher, eds, pp. 121–60. Washington, DC: National Academy Press.

Warr, Mark, and Mark Stafford. 1991. The Influence of Delinquent Peers: What They Think or What They Do? *Criminology* 29(4): 851–66.

Social learning theory 2.5

Gary Jensen

Social learning refers to a theory of human behaviour emphasizing social relationships. Although it has been elaborated in detail in psychology, the theory is widely known in criminology as a blend of psychological and sociological perspectives designed to explain variations in crime over time and among people, settings and societies. The theory addresses the acquisition and maintenance of and changes in criminal behaviour, as well as learning processes that inhibit criminal behaviour. In its most recent form, the theory has been extended to explain macro- as well as micro-processes facilitating crime.

Beginning as early as the 1920s, sociological theories of crime had adopted the view that criminal behaviour is learned in the same manner as other forms of behaviour, and that support for such a view could be found both in ecological patterns of crime and delinquency and in case studies of individuals and groups. A sociologist, Edwin Sutherland, published his ground-breaking book, *Principles of Criminology*, in 1924. By 1939, he had developed a set of propositions that emphasized the role played by 'conflicting definitions' of appropriate and inappropriate conduct in a complex society, and **'differential association'** with people communicating such definitions. Applied to delinquency, the central proposition of differential association was simply that a person 'becomes delinquent because of an excess of definitions favorable to violation of law over definitions unfavorable to violation of law' (Sutherland 1947:7). Definitions were the symbolic messages communicated in everyday interaction with significant others such as parents, peers and teachers.

The two traditions – psychological development of a social learning theory of human behaviour and sociological development of criminological

See Chapter 2.4
Differential
association

theories emphasizing normal learning processes – proceeded rather independently until the mid-1960s. Ronald Akers (a sociological criminologist) teamed with Robert Burgess (a sociologist trained in operant theory) to modify Sutherland's principles using the terminology and principles of modern behaviourism. This 'differential-association-reinforcement' theory of criminal behaviour became the foundation for a perspective in criminology that Akers later elaborated as a 'social learning theory' of deviant behaviour (1973).

See Chapter 1.8
Learning theory

In the development and application of the theory, Akers drew not only on Skinnerian principles of operant theory but also drew extensively on the **work of psychologists** working in the tradition established by Miller and Dollard, especially Albert Bandura. Bandura extended the study of modelling and vicarious learning mechanisms to adolescent aggression in 1959, and published *Aggression: A Social Learning Analysis* in 1973. The focus on aggression facilitated Akers's integration of social learning mechanisms identified by psychologists with mechanisms of symbolic learning and differential social interaction as key features of a social learning theory of crime.

Whereas Sutherland's differential association theory argued that criminal behaviour is learned in interaction with others, it did not specify the mechanisms by which such behaviour is learned. Akers endeavoured to reformulate and extend Sutherland's theory by proposing four distinct mechanisms as the central features of social learning processes: 1) differential association; 2) definitions; 3) differential reinforcement; and 4) imitation. *Differential association* refers to the process whereby an individual is exposed to normative definitions that are favourable or unfavourable to illegal or law-abiding behaviour. It has both behavioural interactional and normative dimensions and thus can be understood as time spent interacting or observing other people distinguishable in their physical and verbal behaviour.

The other three mechanisms encompass the major processes through which people affect one another. *Definitions* are the attitudes or meanings one attaches to given behaviour – the orientations and rationalizations that define the commission of an act as right or wrong, good or bad, desirable or undesirable, justified or unjustified. When interaction involves attempts to teach or convey the attitudes, values, norms and beliefs appropriate for a particular social role that type of interaction can be called socialization and it encompasses the 'definitional' learning distinguished by Akers. The third mechanism through which associations affect behaviour is *differential reinforcement*, defined by Akers and Sellers (2004:87) as 'the balance of anticipated or actual rewards and punishments that follow or are consequences of the behavior'. The fourth mechanism, *imitation*, refers to engagement in behaviour after the observation of similar behaviour in others. When a person copies a behaviour because it has yielded rewarding outcomes or prevented negative outcomes for someone else, this type of observational learning can be called vicarious reinforcement modelling, or imitation.

Akers has expanded his version of the theory to include both 'micro' and 'macro' issues in the form of a 'social structure-social learning theory (SSSL)'.

The macro version of the theory includes differential social organization, differential location in the social structure, differential social location and **social disorganization**/conflict. The social learning principles applied at the micro level are a mediating process through which social structure has an effect on criminal and delinquent behaviour. When the causal logic of social learning theory is extended to the macro level and applied to violence, the resulting perspective focuses on characteristics of societies that impede or undermine cultural and political consensus and conventional institutional relationships but enhance unregulated interaction in peer groups, situational opportunities to engage in, or be a **victim** of, crime, and the development of sustained tendencies for people to resolve interpersonal conflicts through violent action (Jensen 2007).

See Chapter 2.2
Social
disorganization
theory

See Chapter 4.39
Victimology

At the turn of the twenty-first century, there had been over one hundred empirical tests of Akers's theory and, were tests of closely related theories added, there would be hundreds of additional studies relevant to one or another feature of that perspective (see Akers and Jensen 2006). The number of relevant studies could easily exceed 1000 when considering investigations of:

- continuity in crime across settings attributed to imitation, socialization and differential reinforcement;
- the influence of distinctive variations in values, norms and beliefs in the generation and perpetuation of crime;
- the effects of shifts in social interaction and relationships over the life course;
- specific learning mechanisms such as imitation and modelling; and
- the separable mediating effect of peer group interaction when other variables' support for the theory are controlled.

When applications of versions of social learning to family treatment and juvenile offenders are considered (Gerald Patterson, Oregon Social Learning Center) the perspective gains even more support.

With a huge variety of tests of the basic social learning model and features of that model, a call for more tests is not likely to excite scholars interested in crime. Rather, the focus in extending research on social learning theory and crime should be on those topics where little research has been conducted. It is time to return to the integration of sociological and psychological perspectives that was central to the original advocacy of the theory in the 1940s and Akers' reformulation in the 1970s. The key emphasis for the theoretical and empirical development of social learning theory should be on micro–macro transitions and the perplexing complexities involved in linking ideas about social structure and culture to the theory. At present, when the logic and concepts involved in social learning theory at lower levels of aggregation are extended to macro-level variations, they apply to a wide range of known patterns over time and space, and appear to generate more empirically valid models than current alternatives (Akers and Jensen 2006).

In addition to extending the SSSL model, variations in the relative importance and form of learning mechanisms in distinct categories of people need to be explored. For example, it has been demonstrated that the relatively small association of measures of social class or social status with delinquency can reflect countervailing mechanisms. Privilege can help advantaged youth avoid formal sanctions, and family income can facilitate involvement in approved activities that actually provide the freedom and opportunity for crime. At the same time, commitments to long-term goals and other constraints imposed by social advantage can inhibit involvement in crime. Not only does social learning theory encourage an examination of potentially countervailing learning mechanisms, it also promotes a thorough consideration of the balance of complex contingencies of reward and cost when attempting to explain variations among groups. No other verified theoretical framework in criminology considers as many intricacies as social learning theory.

References

Akers, Ronald L. 1973. *Deviant Behavior: A Social Learning Approach*. Belmont, CA: Wadsworth.

Akers, Ronald, and Gary Jensen. 2006. Empirical status of social learning theory: Past, present, and future. In *Taking Stock: The Status of Criminological Theory*, Vol. 15, Frances T. Cullen, John Paul Wright, and Kristie R. Blevins, eds, pp. 37–76 New Brunswick, NJ: Transaction Publishers.

Akers, Ronald, and Christine S. Sellers. 2004 *Criminological Theories: Introduction, Evaluation, and Application* (4th edn). Los Angeles, CA: Roxbury.

Bandura, Albert. 1973. *Aggression: A Social Learning Analysis*. Englewood Cliffs, NJ: Prentice Hall.

Jensen, Gary F. 2007. Social learning and violent behavior. In *The Cambridge Handbook of Violent Behavior and Aggression*, David Flannery, Alexander Vazonsyi, and Irwin Waldman, eds, pp. 636–46. New York: Cambridge University Press.

Sutherland, Edwin H. 1947. *Principles of Criminology* (4th edn). Chicago: Lippincott.

Further reading

Akers, Ronald L. 1990. Rational Choice, Deterrence, and Social Learning Theory in Criminology: The Path Not Taken. *Journal of Criminal Law and Criminology* 81(3): 653–76.

Payne, Alison A., and Steven Salotti. 2007. A Comparative Analysis of Social Learning and Social Control Theories in the Prediction of College Crime. *Deviant Behavior* 28(6): 553–73.

Pratt, Travis C., Francis T. Cullen, Christine S. Sellers, L. Thomas Winfree, Tamara D. Madensen, Leah E. Daigle, Noelle E. Fearn, and Jacinta M. Gau. 2010. The Empirical Status of Social Learning Theory: A Meta-Analysis. *Justice Quarterly* 27(6): 765–802.

Rotter, Julian B., June E. Chance, and E. Jerry Phares. 1972. *Applications of a Social Learning Theory of Personality*. New York: Holt, Rinehart and Winston.

Winfree, L. Thomas, Jr, Teresa Vigil-Backstrom, and G. Larry Mays. 1994. Social Learning Theory, Self-Reported Delinquency, and Youth Gangs: A New Twist on a General Theory of Crime and Delinquency. *Youth and Society* 26(2): 147–77.

2.6 Control theories

Kristie R. Blevins

Early theories of crime attempted to explain why individuals engage in deviant acts. Regardless of whether the assumption of human nature was based on free will (**classical school**) or determinism (**positivist school**), and whether primary theoretical concepts were based on hedonistic calculus or religious, biological, psychological, sociological or economic factors, theorists sought to identify variables that would increase the likelihood people would commit illegal acts. In the mid-1900s, a different approach to criminology emerged in the form of the control perspective, which asks a different question: Why do people conform to conventional laws and norms?

Unlike traditional theories of criminal behaviour, control theories do not seek to explain why people commit crimes or delinquency; rather, they attempt to explain why people do *not* engage in deviant behaviour – why they follow societal laws and norms. The underlying assumption of control theories is that all people have some motivation for deviant behaviour and that they will engage in such acts if not for controls that compel them to conform. The key premise is that people will conform when such controls are present, but that crime and delinquency are possible outcomes when the controls are not developed adequately or when they are somehow weakened.

The control perspective did not appear in a vacuum. Many control theories borrowed concepts from conventional theories of individual behaviour and were heavily influenced by societal factors and social functions identified in theories such as **anomie** and those based in the **Chicago School**. For example, increasing social distance, collapse of the community and the weakening

See Chapter 1.2
Classical
criminology

See Chapter 1.4
Positivism

See Chapter 2.3
Anomie

See Chapter 2.1
Chicago School

impact of families – all factors identified as part of **social disorganization theory** – may play a role in levels of social control.

See Chapter 2.2 Social disorganization theory

Early control theories sought to identify sources of restraints against deviant behaviour. Reiss (1951) posited that social and personal controls are important in the prevention of delinquency. He speculated that primary groups – including family, neighbourhood and school – are responsible for providing social control over children and helping them to develop personal controls. Key components in effective controls include the adolescent identification with family members and acceptance of societal norms. In addition, levels of restraint are increased when adult family members are able to meet the needs of children and provide enough supervision and control, without over-controlling a child.

Nye's (1958) extended version of control theory recognized that a variety of social groups could provide restraints, but that families are most important in providing social control for adolescents. Nye asserted that there were different types of social controls – direct control, internalized control, indirect control or control through alternative means of needs satisfaction – and that each type of control, while important in and of itself, was also interconnected. For example, if legitimate immediate needs are satisfied legally, only small amounts of direct, internal and indirect control are needed to produce conformity to laws and societal norms.

Reckless (1961) expanded the control perspective further with his *containment theory*, where he acknowledged that everyone could face certain factors, such as low socio-economic status, that push people toward crime, as well as issues such as deviant peers that pull people toward illegal acts. According to containment theory, though, these 'pushes' and 'pulls' are kept in check by inner and outer containments that serve as controls. External containments include conventional social controls, while inner containments involve constructs, such as frustration tolerance, legitimate goals and acceptance of societal laws and norms. A lack of, or deterioration of, one or both types of containment will increase the chances of someone committing a deviant act. Although both types of containment are important, inner containment is especially significant, as adolescents with high levels of inner containment tend to commit fewer delinquent acts, even in areas with high rates of delinquency.

Finally, Sykes and Matza's (1957) **techniques of neutralization** posited that deviant youths actually did accept societal laws and norms. Delinquents, however, have learned techniques by which they can temporarily neutralize the rules, which makes it easier to violate them. They specified five techniques of neutralization: denial of responsibility, denial of injury, denial of the victim, condemnation of the condemners, and the appeal to higher loyalties. When adolescents implement one or more of these techniques, they experience a greater sense of freedom to violate the laws to which they conform the majority of the time. In 1964, Matza advanced the theory by acknowledging that neutralization made delinquency possible, but that something more drives the actual behaviour – that delinquents have to have some level of preparation

See Chapter 2.7 Techniques of neutralization

See Chapter 3.5
Drift

to give them the ability to perform the act, and desperation that provides the need to commit the act. He went on to describe many adolescents as in a state of **drift** between delinquency and non-delinquency, especially during their teenage years when controls become relaxed because of elements such as decreased parental supervision and typically little responsibility in terms of employment or accountability for other individuals.

Each of the control theories described above has its own merits, but control theory garnered much more attention with Hirschi's (1969) *social bond theory*. Hirschi identified family and school as the two main systems that help juveniles connect with conventional society, and distinguished four major social bonds. The first bond, *attachment*, is likely the most important, and involves relationships with parents and teachers. *Commitment* is the second bond, and includes dedication to positive short- and long-term goals. If an individual has a high level of commitment, deviant behaviour carries more risk. The third bond is *involvement* – the amount of time devoted to pro-social activities. The last social bond is *belief*, which is the degree to which someone agrees with society's laws. Each of the four bonds is important in establishing social control, but they are not mutually exclusive.

Twenty years after the publication of Hirschi's social bond theory, Gottfredson and Hirschi (1990) developed a modern *control theory* – a general theory of crime based on what empirical studies had revealed about crime and criminals. For example, it was known that criminals and delinquents sought short-term gratification through risk-taking, excitement and often small amounts of cash that could, at least temporarily, help relieve frustrating conditions. They also recognized that many deviants do not specialize in certain types of crime; they simply engage in deviant activities when they are presented with the opportunity to do so. Consequently, an individual's level of self-control – a mechanism of control that ultimately comes from within – is the key factor in determining whether someone will conform or turn to deviance. Individuals with high levels of self-control are able to resist breaking the law or engaging in other deviant behaviour. Self-control, however, is not something individuals have from birth. Rather, self-control is taught and instilled in children during their early years through good parenting and exposure to pro-social models. Inadequate parenting practices lead to low self-control, which children might exhibit at an early age by taking risks, being impulsive and showing insensitivity to others. Children with low self-control grow up to be adults with low self-control, and are most likely to engage in delinquency and criminal behaviour as they grow.

Tittle's (1995) *control-balance theory*'s central premise is that every individual is subject to some level of control, but that individuals also exercise some level of control over their situations. There is a balance when these types of control are equal; but other control ratios, in the forms of control deficits or control surpluses, may result in conditions that make delinquency and crime more likely to occur. Put simply, Tittle created a continuum with seven categories. Three categories on the left represent *repression* and are associated with *control deficits*. Minor and serious conventional crimes are explained by these categories on the left. The middle category on the continuum signifies *a balance of control*, in which deviant behaviour is least likely. The right side of the continuum has three categories based on *autonomy*, which is associated with a *control surplus* and, often, white-collar crimes. Tittle, however, went on to identify a complex causal chain that involved many variables that are interconnected in many ways. Therefore, some social scientists have argued that this theory is so complicated that it is nearly impossible to test.

Another modern control theory is Colvin's (2000) *differential coercion theory*. Colvin distinguished between *interpersonal coercion*, intended to create conformity through the threat of punishment or withdrawal of some positive stimuli or support mechanism, and *impersonal coercion*, which results from societal stresses such as low socioeconomic status. He established that non-coercive methods serve as better controls than coercion, and that children who are consistently exposed to non-coercive types of control are least likely to engage in delinquency. Conversely, children who are exposed to inconsistent coercive methods of control are likely to engage in delinquency because those methods may create a sense of unfairness or degradation, and may inhibit the formation of both social bonds and self-control that would serve to prevent deviant behaviour

Control theories, in general, have been subjected to many empirical tests. Most of these studies provide support for at least some elements of the theories, but control theories have been criticized on a number of grounds. First, critics argue that control theories focus on very general, minor and occasional deviant acts; they do not typically address chronic offenders or individuals who commit serious crimes. Second, self-report surveys of general populations are the most common method of testing control theories. Opponents claim there are not enough deviants in these general populations to produce meaningful results. The third criticism is that the **control perspective** is better at explaining juvenile delinquency than adult criminality. Fourth, and perhaps most importantly, specific control theories have been criticized for not including variables shown to be important in other theories. For example, self-control theory does not account for compelling empirical evidence that strong social bonds to employment and marriage are associated with reduced recidivism rates; nor does it address the social factors that could influence a parent's ability to provide the type of parenting that results in high levels of self-control. Still, the support that has been given to the control perspective offers promise for criminal justice policies and programmes that serve to prevent delinquency and crime, and to rehabilitate individuals who have engaged in deviant behaviour. Such policies do not focus on **incapacitation** or **retribution**; instead, they should be based on strengthening family units and parenting skills, as well as improving positive social integration through educational programmes, involvement in school activities, employment networks and pro-social community activities.

See Chapter 1.13
Life-course theory

See Chapter 5.9
Incapacitation

See Chapter 5.16
Retribution

References

Colvin, Mark. 2000. *Crime and Coercion*. New York: St. Martin's Press.

Gottfredson, Michael R., and Travis Hirschi. 1990. *A General Theory of Crime*. Stanford, CA: Stanford University Press.

Hirschi, Travis. 1969. *Causes of Delinquency*. Berkeley: University of California Press.

Matza, David. 1964. *Delinquency and Drift*. New York: Wiley.

Nye, F. Ivan. 1958. *Family Relationships and Delinquent Behavior*. New York: Wiley.

Reckless, Walter C. 1961. *The Crime Problem* (3rd edn). New York: Appleton-Century-Crofts.

Reiss, Albert J., Jr. 1951. Delinquency as the Failure of Personal and Social Controls. *American Sociological Review* 16(2): 196–207.

Sykes, Gresham M., and David Matza. 1957. Techniques of Neutralization: A Theory of Delinquency. *American Sociological Review* 22(6): 664–73.

Tittle Charles R. 1995. *Control Balance: Toward a General Theory of Deviance*. Boulder, CO: Westview Press.

Further reading

Britt, Chester L., and Michael Rocque. 2016. Control as an Explanation of Crime and Delinquency. In *The Handbook of Criminological Theory*, Alex R. Piquero, ed., pp. 182–208. New York: Wiley.

Lilly J. Robert, Francis T. Cullen, and Richard A. Ball. 2002. *Criminological Theory: Context and Consequences* (3rd edn). Thousand Oaks, CA: Sage.

Pratt, Travis C., and Francis T. Cullen. 2000. The Empirical Status of Gottfredson and Hirschi's General Theory of Crime: A Meta-Analysis. *Criminology* 38(3): 931–64.

Topalli, Volkan, George E. Higgins, and Heith Copes. 2014. A Causal Model of Neutralization Acceptance and Delinquency: Making the Case for an Individual Difference Model. *Criminal Justice and Behavior* 41(5): 553–73.

Vazsonyi, Alexander T., and Li Huang. 2015. Hirschi's Reconceptualization of Self-Control: Is Truth Truly the Daughter of Time? Evidence from Eleven Cultures. *Journal of Criminal Justice* 43(1): 59–68.

Techniques of neutralization

Heith Copes and Shadd Maruna

Those who contemplate deviant or criminal behaviour are often constrained from doing so because of the potential for experiencing guilt or developing a negative self-image. Overcoming these internal controls is necessary for the successful commission of deviance and crime. While scholars have developed numerous **theories** to explain how people overcome the moral hurdles of crime, perhaps none have been as well received as Sykes and Matza's (1957) neutralization theory. According to the theory, norm-violators seek to free themselves of the guilt and potential negative self-image associated with their actions by pre-emptively using linguistic devices (i.e., techniques of neutralization) that nullify the corresponding guilt. The use of such neutralization techniques is what allows offenders to start and maintain criminal and deviant careers.

See Chapter 2.6
Control theories

Sykes and Matza's theory emerged as a critique of subcultural theories that were popular at the time of their writings. **Subcultural theorists** posited that delinquency was the result of lower-class boys rebelling against the dominant social order. Those adhering to a delinquent subculture were thought to reject middle-class standards and replace them with a delinquent set of values. Sykes and Matza disagreed with this contention, arguing that subcultural theorists overstated the extent to which delinquents adopted subcultural values and rejected conventional ones. They argued that lower-class delinquent gang members retain some commitment to the dominant value system of

See Chapter 3.17
Subculture

society, despite their delinquency. As evidence of this claim, Sykes and Matza pointed to the fact that delinquents show respect and admiration for honest, law-abiding others; make clear distinctions about who can and cannot be victimized; and participate in conventional activities (e.g., church, school and family activities).

This commitment to the dominant social order complicates social norm violations because doing so can instil guilt or shame in the actor. It is this guilt – and its potential for producing a negative self-image – that dissuades most people from engaging in crime. Thus, those participating in criminal behaviour under such conditions must find ways to neutralize the corresponding guilt associated with norm violations. This can be done by using neutralization techniques that blunt the moral force of the law and minimize the guilt of criminal participation. Through the use of these techniques, social and internal controls that serve to inhibit criminal behaviours are nullified, which allows individuals to engage in delinquency without damaging their self-image. In this way, offenders can remain committed to the dominant normative system and interpret their deviant actions as acceptable, if not proper.

In their original formulation, Sykes and Matza outlined five techniques of neutralization that allow youths to engage in delinquency. These neutralization techniques include:

- *denial of responsibility* – claiming one's behaviours are accidental or due to forces beyond one's control;
- *denial of injury* – claiming that no one was hurt or that harm was not intended;
- *denying the victim* – arguing that some victims acted improperly and are thus deserving of one's punishment or retaliation;
- *condemnation of the condemner* – focusing on the motivations or behaviours of those who disapprove of them, claiming their condemners are hypocrites; and
- *appeal to higher loyalties* – claiming one's behaviour is consistent with the moral obligations of a specific group to which they belong.

As the theory has been expanded to different types of offenders and offences scholars have described new techniques, including the *defence of necessity*, the *claim of normality*, the *claim of entitlement, metaphor of the ledger* and *justification by comparison* (Cromwell and Thurman 2003; Klockars 1974). While there are likely many more undiscovered neutralizations, some argue that describing the full range of neutralizations is not important. What is important is the function of neutralization techniques (what they *do*), rather than the specific varieties in which they come.

In their original formulation of the theory, Sykes and Matza state that techniques of neutralization must precede deviant behaviour. This statement makes two crucial claims about the techniques of neutralization that are often overlooked in empirical work evaluating the theory. First, there is a specific chronological sequence of neutralizations and delinquent behaviour. Neutralizations are not just *a posteriori* rationalizations. Instead, they precede crime, otherwise the guilt and potential negative self-images would act as deterrents. Second, Sykes and Matza emphasize that this order does not imply a deterministic or causal relationship. Neutralization techniques enable crime but do not require it. Neutralization enables drift by freeing the individual from the moral bind of law and order. Once set in a state of drift, a person can drift among competing normative systems.

Neutralization theory has been widely accepted and researched in criminology. Research on the theory typically occurs in two forms. The most common type uses qualitative methods to illustrate how neutralizations are used by deviant actors. This research provides insights into how offenders understand and make sense of their crimes. Interviews with a diverse array of offenders suggest that all rely on neutralizations when committing their crimes. Such research is published with regularity, and confirms the importance of techniques of neutralization for committing crime. This type of research shows that the use of neutralizations is not pathological. Rather, they are a common way people make sense of their actions.

The second form of neutralization research consists of quantitative assessments. This research typically finds a weak, but positive, relationship between acceptance of neutralizations and participation in delinquency. Overwhelmingly, this type of research involves questionnaires that ask participants to self-report their acceptance of neutralization beliefs and their delinquent and criminal behaviour. The bulk of this research has used cross-sectional designs, which limits researchers' abilities to determine if neutralizations precede criminal behaviour.

While longitudinal designs are ideal for disentangling the sequential relationship of neutralizations and crime, relatively few have used such designs. Morris and Copes (2012) applied a structural equation modelling approach to five waves of data from the Denver Youth Survey. They found that earlier neutralizing had a significant effect on later neutralizing, and a modest effect on later delinquency. Similarly, Topalli et al. (2014) found that early acceptance of neutralizing beliefs was predictive of later offending (and future neutralization acceptance). Thus, there is limited, but supportive, longitudinal research suggesting that neutralization acceptance contributes to crime and delinquency over the life-course.

Recently, some scholars have sought to determine the stability of neutralizing beliefs. Using trajectory analysis, this research suggests that adolescents vary in their acceptance of neutralizations and that these groups are relatively stable, at least throughout adolescence (Topalli et al. 2014). In addition, the neutralizing groups are positively correlated with delinquency groups: those in high neutralizing groups tend to be in the high delinquency groups.

Despite the popularity of this theory, researchers have offered few theoretical advancements for it, other than adding to the list of neutralizations. One advancement is the idea that neutralization theory is best understood as an

See Chapter 5.6
Desistance

explanation of persistence or **desistance** in offending rather than a theory of onset of offending (Maruna and Copes 2005). The argument is that neutralizations may not be powerful enough to allow offenders to commit their first crimes, especially serious offences. But once an actor commits a crime, the use and acceptance of neutralizations allows him or her to continue offending (i.e., neutralizations allow for persistence). In addition, if the acceptance of neutralizations is important for maintaining criminal involvement, then the rejection of neutralizations may lead to desistance. Such ideas are supported by research on the psychological components of desistance.

A second major refinement is the idea that neutralizations are not limited to violations of conventional norms (Topalli 2005). Ethnographic research shows that persistent street offenders seldom experience guilt when committing serious forms of crime, and thus do not neutralize their criminal actions. These offenders do, however, offer up excuses and explanations (i.e., neutralizations) when they violate subcultural norms, such as when they snitched or failed to retaliate when wronged. Thus, the range of the theory can be expanded to included violations of all held values.

Even with over fifty years of research on neutralizations, there is still much that is not known about the theory. There are certainly many questions left to ask about neutralizations and their role in criminality. Issues that are still in question include how neutralizations change as offenders age; how acceptance of neutralizations varies by the background and cultural make-up of those who elicit them; and whether neutralization acceptance is a stable characteristic of people. For such a seemingly simple theory, there is still much to learn.

References

Cromwell, Paul, and Quint Thurman. 2003. The Devil Made Me Do It: Use of Neutralizations by Shoplifters. *Deviant Behavior* 24(6): 535–50.

Klockars, Carl B. 1974. *The Professional Fence*. New York: Free Press.

Maruna, Shadd, and Heith Copes. 2005. What Have We Learned From Fifty Years of Neutralization Research? *Crime and Justice: A Review of Research* 32: 221–320.

Morris, Robert G., and Heith Copes. 2012. Exploring the Temporal Dynamics of the Neutralization/Delinquency Relationship. *Criminal Justice Review* 37(4): 442–60.

Sykes, Gresham, and David Matza. 1957. Techniques of Neutralization: A Theory of Delinquency. *American Sociological Review* 22(6): 664–70.

Topalli, Volkan. 2005. When Being Good is Bad: An Expansion of Neutralization Theory. *Criminology* 43(3): 797–835.

Topalli, Volkan, George Higgins, and Heith Copes. 2014. A Causal Model of Neutralization Acceptance and Delinquency: Making the Case for an Individual Difference Model. *Criminal Justice and Behavior* 41(5): 553–73.

Further reading

Cressey, Donald. 1953. *Other People's Money: Study in the Social Psychology of Embezzlement*. New York: Free Press.

Maruna, Shadd. 2001. *Making Good: How Ex-Convicts Reform and Rebuild Their Lives*. Washington, DC: American Psychological Association.

Matza, David. 1964. *Delinquency and Drift*. New York: Wiley.

Scott, Marvin B., and Stanford M. Lyman. 1968. Accounts. *American Sociological Review* 33(1): 46–62.

Market society and crime

Elliott P. Currie

The central thesis of criminological theories of market society is that societies that emphasize the pursuit of private gain over all other social ends are inherently prone to higher levels of crime. Market theories distinguish between that core concept of the 'market society' and the conventional idea of a 'free market economy'. Twenty-first-century capitalist societies are characterized by a deep and complex interweaving of private profit-seeking and state facilitation and support. Although these are not 'free market societies' in the conventional sense, they are organized demonstrably around the central principle of private gain, and, in the age of deregulation and the spread of **'neoliberal'** ideology and social policy, increasingly so – some more than others. Theories of the market and crime argue that high levels of both 'street' and institutional crime are a predictable cost of those social arrangements. In that sense, these theories fall within the body of criminological thought that seeks to link the 'micro' level of individual action with the pervasive effects of global social and economic forces. Market theories share a number of elements with the **'institutional anomie'** perspective, but their historical roots and theoretical assumptions are significantly different.

See Chapter 4.24
Neoliberalism

See Chapter 2.3
Anomie

The idea that the growth of market values and institutions breeds predatory and violent behaviour has a long history, beginning with early critics of a newly emerging market capitalism in the seventeenth and eighteenth centuries. But it appears in a more focused and empirically grounded way in the writings of Marx and Engels, and especially in Engels' classic mid-nineteenth-century exploration *The Condition of the Working Class in England*. Though **Marxian theories** are often perceived as viewing crime rather narrowly through the lens of class, Engels' perspective is actually far broader, addressing the multiple adverse impacts of a social order that is not only harshly unequal and depriving, but also insecure, chaotic and neglectful. Observing English cities in the 1840s, he saw:

See Chapter 3.9
Marxist
criminologies

> Everywhere barbarous indifference, hard egotism on one hand, and nameless misery on the other, everywhere social warfare . . . everywhere reciprocal plundering under protection of the law, and all so shameless, so openly avowed, that one . . . can only wonder that the whole crazy fabric still holds together.
>
> (Engels 1950:64–5)

Nineteenth-century capitalism, in Engels' view, bred crime – as well as alcoholism and other related social ills – in several mutually reinforcing ways. On the most basic level, it generated a new kind of poverty that was especially destructive to family and personality because it was largely unbuffered by traditional communal supports. 'Want,' Engels wrote, 'leaves the working man the choice between starving slowly, killing himself speedily, or taking what he needs where he finds it . . . And there is no cause for surprise that most of them prefer stealing to starvation and suicide' (1950:154). But that level of 'want' also fostered a deep sense of injustice and alienation that weakened whatever bonds of loyalty and commitment workers felt toward the larger social order. This toxic mix of deprivation and alienation was compounded by the fundamental personal insecurity that Engels (and Marx) regarded as a central feature of the experience of the modern proletariat – indeed, as a part of the very definition of this new social class. Describing the worker under modern capitalism as a 'playball to a thousand chances', Engels argued that the practical inability to plan or control their future leads to a narrowing of attention to the present, aggravating the profound demoralization that can lead to both drinking and criminality.

That central theme of 'demoralization' continued in what is arguably the most thorough and systematic early attempt to draw out the links between market capitalism and crime – the Dutch criminologist and activist Willem Bonger's (1916) massive study *Criminality and Economic Conditions*. Bonger's aim was not to isolate the impact of particular economic ills like poverty or unemployment on crime, but to explore the consequences of 'the present economic system' as a whole. In his view, what most characterized late nineteenth and early twentieth-century capitalism was its historically unprecedented devotion to the pursuit of profit as a central organizing principle. That fundamental orientation bred what Bonger (following Engels) called 'egoism', and weakened 'the social instincts in man'. The essentially predatory and calculating values of the market came to suffuse the culture of modern capitalist societies, encouraging rapacity and heedlessness at the top and demoralization at the bottom. Bonger's analysis concluded on a note of cautious optimism: the condition of the working class had already begun to improve, largely as a result of growing consciousness and class action on the part of working people; and, to the extent that this improvement continued – both in material conditions and in the sense of solidarity – crime would decrease accordingly.

See Chapter 2.6
Anomie

See Chapter 2.6
Control theories

See Chapter 2.2
Social
disorganization
theory

See Chapter 2.5
Social learning
theory

In contrast to much later criminological thinking in which a variety of relatively narrow explanations of crime are pitted against each other (**anomie** versus '**control**', **social disorganization** versus **social learning**), these early expressions of market theory are holistic, encompassing many of what are now seen as competing perspectives at once, and blurring conventional distinctions between individual and society, culture and structure, 'micro' and 'macro'. And they are adamantly systemic approaches, firmly situating crime as one kind of response to broader, historically specific social conditions. Those qualities appear as well in more recent versions of market theory which began to emerge in the context of the intellectual and political ferment of the 1960s. Thus, Ian Taylor, Paul Walton and Jock Young, in their seminal book *The New Criminology* (1973), called for a 'political economy of criminal action' that would 'deal with society as a totality', and that call bore fruit around the world.

Similar perspectives emerged in the United States, beginning in the 1980s, prompted in part by the need to develop a framework for understanding why American rates of serious violent crime were so much higher than those of comparable advanced industrial societies. In this view, it was not accidental that the United States was both the advanced society where the forces of the 'market' were least buffered by 'countervailing mechanisms of social obligation and support' and the one with by far the worst levels of serious violent crime (Currie 1985). In line with the multilayered perspective of Engels and Bonger, it was argued that several mutually sustaining aspects of market societies worked in concert to breed predatory and brutal behaviour. Societies organized around market values tended to destroy stable livelihoods; to increase social deprivation and inequality; and, simultaneously, to erode the sustaining capacity of families and communities, as well as undercut public sources of social support. At the cultural and psychological level, market society bred what (following Engels' 'barbarous indifference' and Bonger's 'egoism') was described as a materialistic, neglectful and 'hard' culture in which the sense of social obligation and solidarity was submerged. And, at the political level, market society often worked, over time, to close off other avenues of political and social action, and in that way encouraged individual crime as a default response to deprivation and alienation. Finally, in the American context especially, the market-driven deregulation of the sale of firearms was an inescapable element of this complex mix (Currie 1997).

In England, similarly, John Lea and Jock Young's *What Is to Be Done About Law and Order* argued in the 1980s that, despite enormous changes since the nineteenth century, crime remained deeply linked to the 'core dynamics of capitalism'. Though absolute poverty of the kind Engels observed in the mid-nineteenth century was no longer the lot of most people, the problem of exclusion from the 'glittering prizes of capitalist society' remained 'endemic'. That continuing exclusion was exacerbated by the fact that the **relatively deprived** were marginalized from 'legitimate channels for redressing the balance' – suggesting, again, that it is the *combination* of deprivation and insecurity with the absence of more productive channels for taking action against them that is the most fertile ground for criminality. As Lea and Young (1984:88) put it, 'discontent where there is no political solution leads to crime'.

See Chapter 2.10 Relative deprivation

How has this perspective fared in the light of experience and empirical research? Both historical developments and careful research strongly support the central argument that unshackled market priorities breed predation and violence. The broad patterns of distribution of violent crime around the world closely track the contours of global market society. The societies with the worst levels of violence are those where extremes of market-driven inequality and marginalization are most evident; and, within the smaller group of advanced industrial societies, it is the United States – with the widest extremes of inequality and the most minimal commitment to social provision – that appears as an 'outlier', particularly with respect to gun violence. Quantitative research has consistently affirmed that what Messner and Rosenfeld (1997) call 'political restraint of the market' is associated with lower levels of violent crime. Studies of the trajectory of crime in societies undergoing rapid transition to a market economy confirm the connection from another angle: the sudden 'marketization' of the economy in Russia, China and some countries of Eastern Europe in the late twentieth century, for example, was associated with striking rises in crime, driven by rapid economic dislocation, unemployment and deepening poverty. Qualitative studies of communities hit hard by market-driven economic and social transformation put a human face on these processes. Research by Steve Hall, Simon Winlow and Craig Ancrum (2008) in the north of England, for example, powerfully illustrates the shifts in values and behaviour that have resulted from both the material and cultural effects of deindustrialization and the erosion of traditional working-class communities.

Future work in this vein might involve applying the principles of market theory to the unique contexts of specific societies or regions. In the United States, for example, the social and personal impact of relatively unrestrained market forces is deeply intertwined with a distinct history of racial subordination, and the American crime problem cannot be adequately understood without taking that history into account. But the breadth of evidence that crime is a predictable human cost of the growth and spread of market values and institutions has troubling implications for the quality of life in the contemporary global economy, and suggests that this body of theory will be relevant for a long time to come.

References

Bonger, Willem. 1916. *Criminality and Economic Conditions*. Boston: Little, Brown.

Currie, Elliott. 1985. *Confronting Crime: An American Challenge*. New York: Pantheon.

Currie, Elliott. 1997. Market, Crime, and Community: Toward a Mid-Range Theory of Post-Industrial Violence. *Theoretical Criminology* 1(2): 147–72.

Engels, Friedrich. 1950. *The Condition of the Working Class in England in 1844*. London: Allen & Unwin.

Hall, Steve, Simon Winlow, and Craig Ancrum. 2008. *Criminal Identities and Consumer Culture*. Cullompton, UK: Willan.

Lea, John, and Jock Young. 1984. *What Is to Be Done About Law and Order*. Harmondsworth: Penguin.

Messner, Steven F., and Richard Rosenfeld. 1997. Political Restraint of the Market and Levels of Criminal Homicide: A Cross-National Application of Institutional Anomie Theory. *Social Forces* 75(4): 1393–416.

Taylor, Ian, Paul Walton, and Jock Young. 1973. *The New Criminology: For a Social Theory of Deviance*. London: Routledge.

Further reading

Currie, Elliott. 2013. The Market Economy and Crime. In *The Oxford Handbook of Criminological Theory*, Francis T. Cullen and Pamela Wilcox, eds, pp. 424–39. Oxford and New York: Oxford University Press.

Taylor, Ian. 1999. *Crime in Context: A Critical Criminology of Market Societies*. Cambridge: Polity.

General strain theory

Robert Agnew

General strain theory (GST) states that people engage in crime because they experience certain strains or stressors (Agnew 1992, 2006, 2012). These strains can lead to a range of negative emotions, such as anger. These emotions, in turn, can create pressure for corrective action, and some people cope through crime. Crime may be a way to reduce or escape from strains (e.g., theft to obtain needed money, running away to escape abusive parents). Crime may be a way to seek revenge against the source of strain or related targets; and crime may be a way to reduce the negative emotions that result from strains (e.g., illicit drug use to feel better). Not all individuals respond to strains with crime, however. Criminal coping is most likely among those who lack the ability and resources to cope in a legal manner, have little to lose from crime and are disposed to crime. General strain theory traces its origins to Merton's (1938) theory of social structure and anomie; but while **anomie** theories focus on normlessness in the larger society, general strain theory focuses on the experience of aversive events and conditions or strains. This entry describes: (a) the strains most likely to result in crime; (b) why strains cause crime; and (c) the factors that increase the likelihood of criminal coping.

See Chapter 2.3 Anomie; Chapter 2.8 Market society and crime

'Strains' refer to events and conditions that are disliked by individuals. Strains fall into three general categories. Individuals may lose something they value, such as money, property or a romantic partner. Individuals may be treated in a negative or aversive manner by others. For example, they may be verbally or physically abused by family members, peers or employers. And individuals may be unable to achieve their goals, such as their monetary and status ambitions. There are hundreds of particular strains, as reflected in inventories of stressful life events, chronic stressors and daily life hassles. But not all strains lead to crime. For example, many juveniles dislike their parents' imposition of rules and sanctions for misbehaviour; but, unless the rules are unreasonable or the sanctions overly harsh, these parental actions reduce rather than increase the likelihood of crime (Agnew and Brezina 2015). Those strains most likely to cause crime have four characteristics: (i) they are high in magnitude or strongly disliked; (ii) they are seen as unjust; (iii) they are associated with low social control; and (iv) they are conducive to criminal coping (Agnew 2006).

Strains that are high in magnitude are severe (e.g., a serious assault as opposed to a minor insult). They are of long duration, frequent and expected to continue into the future. And they threaten the *core* goals, needs, values, activities and/or identities of the individual. Strains that are seen as unjust involve the voluntary and intentional violation of relevant justice rules. For example, they are seen as underserved or they involve treatment that is very

See Chapter 2.6
Control theories

different from that received by similar others. Strains that are low in **social control** involve weak bonds to conventional others and low direct control or supervision. Parental rejection, for example, is associated with low control because it involves a weak bond to parents and low levels of parental supervision.

Finally, certain strains are conducive to crime because they are readily resolved through crime. For example, that strain involving a desperate need for money is readily resolved through crimes such as theft, drug-selling and prostitution. But that strain involving the natural death of a parent is not easily resolved through crime. Also, some strains are conducive to crime because they involve exposure to others who model crime, reinforce crime, teach beliefs favourable to crime or otherwise encourage crime. Individuals who are abused by their parents, for example, are exposed to violent paradigms and implicitly taught that violence is an appropriate way to respond to certain problems.

Drawing on these characteristics, GST predicts that the following strains are especially likely to cause crime:

- parental rejection;
- erratic, very strict, excessive and/or harsh discipline by parents, school officials, employers and police (e.g., use of humiliation/insults, threats, screaming, physical punishments);
- child abuse and neglect;
- negative secondary school experiences (e.g., low grades, negative relations with teachers);
- abusive peer relations;
- work in the secondary labour market (e.g., jobs that are unpleasant, poorly paid, have few benefits);
- chronic unemployment;
- marital problems (e.g., frequent conflict, verbal and physical abuse);
- criminal victimization;

- residence in very poor communities plagued by problems such as crime and incivilities;
- economic problems (e.g., inability to feed or clothe oneself or one's family, difficulty paying bills);
- homelessness;
- discrimination;
- the inability to achieve certain goals (e.g., thrills/excitement, autonomy, masculine status, the desire for much money in a short period of time).

Research indicates that these strains increase the likelihood of crime, with certain of these strains – such as parental rejection and criminal **victimiza-tion** – among the leading causes of crime (Agnew 2006, 2012; Kubrin et al. 2009). Such research supports the central proposition of GST – that certain strains increase crime – and is the main reason why GST is one of the leading theories of crime.

See Chapter 4.39
Victimology

These strains increase crime for several reasons (Agnew 2006, 2012). Most notably, they lead to a range of negative emotions, such as anger, frustration and depression. These emotions create pressure for corrective action. Individuals feel bad and want to do something about it, and crime is one method of coping. Anger is said to be especially conducive to crime, particularly crime directed at other individuals. Anger energizes the individual to take action, creates a desire for revenge, reduces concern for the consequences of one's behaviour and impedes efforts at legal coping, such as negotiation. While other negative emotions may also result in crime, research suggests that negative emotions, particularly anger, partly explain the effect of strains on crime (Agnew 2006, 2012).

Strains may also increase crime for other reasons (see Agnew 2006, 2012). Strains frequently reduce social control. Most strains involve negative treatment by others, including parents, teachers and employers. For example, parents may reject or harshly sanction their children; teachers may fail students and treat them in a demeaning manner; and employers may humiliate, exploit or terminate employees. Such strains reduce bonds to conventional others and institutions. Further, strains may reduce direct control and the belief that crime is wrong because they weaken ties to conventional others and institutions. Strains also increase the likelihood that individuals will join criminal groups, which they view as a solution to strains. For example, individuals frequently join gangs in an effort to achieve their economic and status goals (Agnew and Brezina 2015). Also, strains can foster the development of beliefs favourable to crime. For example, juveniles who are regularly victimized by others often conclude that violence is a justified response to the threats they face. Finally, strains lead to the development of traits conducive to crime, particularly irritability (Agnew 2006).

While the exposure to certain strains increases the likelihood of crime, most people who experience such strains do *not* cope through crime. Rather, they cope in a legal manner. For example, someone who is bullied by peers at school might cope by trying to convince their peers to stop their bullying, avoiding the peers, reporting the peers to teachers or the police, or trying to ignore the bullying. The research on coping indicates that there are a variety of ways to cope with strains, only some of which involve crime. A central question for GST, then, is why are some people are more likely than others to cope through crime? GST states that criminal coping is more likely among those with:

- poor coping skills and resources, including poor problem-solving and social skills, low socioeconomic status, low self-efficacy, and traits such as negative emotionality and low constraint;
- low levels of conventional social support;
- low levels of social control, including direct control, bonds to conventional others and institutions, and amoral beliefs;
- criminal associates, including delinquent peers and gang members;
- beliefs favourable to criminal coping, such as the belief that one should respond to insults and disrespectful treatment with violence;
- exposure to situations where the costs of crime are low and the benefits are high, such as residence in a community where the police seldom sanction offenders.

There has been some research on whether these factors influence or condition the response to strains. Taken as a whole, the research results are mixed. For example, some studies find that strains are more likely to lead to crime among those with delinquent peers, while other studies do not. Several reasons have been offered for these mixed results (see Agnew 2006, 2013). Most notably, it has been argued that criminal coping is unlikely unless strained individuals score high on *several* of the above factors, such that they have a strong propensity for criminal coping and are in circumstances conducive to criminal coping. More research is needed here, however.

References

Agnew, Robert. 1992. Foundation for a General Strain Theory of Crime and Delinquency. *Criminology* 30(1): 47–87.

Agnew, Robert. 2006. *Pressured Into Crime: An Overview of General Strain Theory*. New York: Oxford University Press.

Agnew, Robert. 2012. General strain theory. In *Handbook on Crime and Deviance*, Marvin D. Krohn, Alan J. Lizotte, and Gina P. Hall, eds, pp. 169–85. New York: Springer.

Agnew, Robert. 2013. When Criminal Coping is Likely: An Extension of General Strain Theory. *Deviant Behavior* 34(8): 653–70.

Agnew, Robert, and Timothy Brezina. 2015. *Juvenile Delinquency: Causes and Control*. New York: Oxford University Press.

Kubrin, Charis E., Thomas D. Stucky, and Marvin D. Krohn. 2009. *Researching Theories of Crime and Deviance*. New York: Oxford University Press.

Merton, Robert K. 1938. Social Structure and Anomie. *American Sociological Review* 3(5): 672–82.

Further reading

Agnew, Robert, Francis Cullen, Velmer Burton, David Evans, and Gregory Dunaway. 1996. A New Test of Classic Strain Theory. *Justice Quarterly* 13(4): 681–704.

Brezina, T., and Robert Agnew. 2013. General strain and urban youth violence. In *The Oxford Handbook of Criminological Theory*, Francis T. Cullen and Pamela Wilcox, eds, pp. 143–59. Oxford: Oxford University Press.

Broidy, Lisa, and Robert Agnew. 1997. Gender and Crime: A General Strain Theory Perspective. *Journal of Research in Crime and Delinquency* 34(3): 275–306.

Eitle, David. 2010. General Strain Theory, Persistence and Desistance among Young Adult Males. *Journal of Criminal Justice* 38(6): 1113–21.

Slocum, Lee Ann. 2010. General Strain Theory and Continuity in Offending over Time. *Journal of Contemporary Criminal Justice* 26(2): 204–23.

Craig Webber

See Chapter 3.14
Realism and left
idealism

Relative deprivation is a concept central to the **left realist** tradition of criminology. It is founded on the idea that anyone can feel deprived of something no matter where he/she is in the social hierarchy. Therefore, it extends further than the idea of absolute deprivation, which posits that only those at the bottom of the social structure suffer the most. In left realist criminology, relative *economic* deprivation represented the central cause of crime because it could explain crime committed by anyone in the social hierarchy, rich or poor.

See Chapter 2.3
Anomie

Relative deprivation, as conceptualized by the left realists, derives from the **anomie** tradition of the sociologist Robert K. Merton, but has been more fully and explicitly outlined in *The American Soldier* by Stouffer and colleagues (1949) and *Why Men Rebel* by T.R. Gurr (1970). Its most complete elaboration is by W.G. Runciman in *Relative Deprivation and Social Justice* (1966). Runciman's account of the theory is the one that has had more influence on later research, especially in the field of social psychology. Nevertheless, despite Runciman being a graduate student of Merton, his 1966 study was only briefly mentioned in the left realist use of the concept (see Webber 2007 for a full discussion of this). The following, therefore, outlines the theory as it was elaborated by Runciman.

Runciman's *Relative Deprivation and Social Justice* might be described as a combination of theory, historical analysis and survey. It should not be thought of as the definitive discussion of relative deprivation because others had used the term before Runciman. Moreover, Runciman does not discuss relative deprivation in relation to its effects on crime and incivilities. Nevertheless, Runciman is important for a number of reasons, not least of which is his relationship to Merton, and it is no surprise to see some similarity between their work. The most significant aspect of relative deprivation theory is the way it can supersede the polarized debate between the left and right of the political and academic spectrum. This debate on the link between the cause of crime and social class followed two distinct and diametrically opposed paths. Marxist/ socialist commentators emphasized poverty as a motivation for crime and the agents of capitalism as responsible for criminalizing the poor, at the same time as ignoring or legitimizing crime and deviance committed by the powerful – what is sometimes referred to as **white-collar crime**. Those on the right, on the other hand, focused on the individual's volition or **psychological/ biological impairments** rather than capitalism. Moreover, the representation of class in both of these debates is primarily one of imposition of pre-existing definitions and metrics. Runciman's survey focused on self-defined class position, so comparisons could be made between the self-elected class position and that which would be imposed when reference was made to economic indicators and occupations, such as in a census. Such a methodology allows the actor to subjectively place himself/herself within a stratified hierarchy, arguably a more accurate reflection of how people perceive themselves.

See Chapter 4.41 White-collar crime

See Chapter 1.5 Biological criminology; Chapter 1.8 Learning theory

Runciman set out to answer two related questions: 'what is the relation between institutionalized inequalities and the awareness or resentment of them?' and 'which, if any, of these inequalities ought to be perceived and resented – whether they are or not – by the standards of social justice?' (1966: 3–4). Runciman was concerned with identifying the circumstances that led to feelings of resentment, and highlighted three main sources of relative deprivation: class position, power and education. Frustration within one category does not necessarily mean frustration in the other two categories, Runciman explained. Unlike Merton's **opportunity theory** (1938), Runciman argued that 'Relative deprivation should always be understood to mean a *sense* of deprivation; a person who is "relatively deprived" need not be "objectively" deprived in the more usual sense that he [*sic*] is demonstrably lacking something' (1966:10–11, emphasis in original).

See Chapter 6.6 Opportunity theory

Runciman's conceptualization provides a broader framework and, in so doing, could be characterized as a synthesis between Durkheim's emphasis on the effects of anomie on the better off and Merton's emphasis on the poor. Runciman's theory combines several key components. The first aspect of the theory that needs addressing is the relative/absolute distinction. To be 'relatively deprived', a person need not be suffering deprivations that are harmful to his/her existence, as is the case in many definitions of absolute deprivation. Thus, relative deprivation applies to those who are poor and those who are rich and everyone in between. For example, someone (Person A) earning the average income for his/her country might compare himself/herself to someone else (Person B) earning the same salary, but feel deprived because Person B seems better able to invest his/her money in a house that appreciates in value more than does Person A's home. In other words, Person A has a home, warmth, food and a stable job but feels relatively deprived when compared to

Person B. The closeness of match between the comparative reference groups is also important because the theory predicts that we rarely compare ourselves to others who are far removed from our position. For example, a homeless person might not compare himself/herself to royalty and feel deprived, but might do so if comparing himself/herself to another homeless person.

The second main issue is the idea that we compare ourselves to other comparative reference points. These can be at the individual level, so that one person compares himself/herself to another person and adjudges himself/herself deprived in one or more dimensions, such as wealth, happiness or health. This is referred to as *egoistic relative deprivation* by Runciman. When someone feels relatively deprived as a member of a group when he/she compares that group to another group, Runciman refers to this as *fraternalistic relative deprivation*.

The fundamental question is when do we make comparisons? And what determines whether or not we feel deprived of something when we do make a comparison? In other words, when do we feel that the glass is half empty and when is it half full? Ultimately, relative deprivation is a subjective, rather than objective, sense of being deprived. One of the interesting aspects of the theory is identifying those who do not feel deprived but possibly should, and those who we might not expect to feel deprived but do.

As a central explanation for crime in left realism, relative deprivation suffered by being linked to such a well-known, and therefore critically explored, school of criminology. Its success has been outside criminology, where it has been rendered a key empirical tool of social psychology and political science. Relative deprivation fell out of fashion rather than becoming irrelevant as left realism became superseded by other approaches.

Despite being a central element of left realism, the application of relative deprivation theory has been more fully explored within social psychology, especially in social identity theory and self-categorization theory. In this regard, relative deprivation has been inverted so that the processes through which individuals or groups arrive at a sense of well-being or injustice have become more important than the outcome of deprivation. Deprivation might now be only one possible outcome, along with satisfaction or anger – or, indeed, *any* other **human emotion**. The social psychological approaches have also seen some use within criminology. This is especially apparent in the literature on procedural justice (Tyler and Blader 2003).

See Chapter 4.10
Emotions

One aspect that might make the theory more applicable today is the rise of the cult of celebrity alongside hyper-commercialism. This has meant that many more comparative reference groups that once might have been regarded as non-comparative – such as everyday people becoming television celebrities, pop stars or Internet millionaires – now seem quite realistic and achievable to many people. The Web has accelerated this trend, while at the same time allowing for more reference groups to become available for comparison. Indeed, the technologies that power this trend towards a seemingly democratic free-for-all – computers, tablets and smartphones, and the necessary availability of fast broadband connectivity – are themselves key contributors to feelings of relative deprivation if one is unable to afford access to such technologies either through cost, location or knowledge.

References

Gurr, Ted Robert. 1970. *Why Men Rebel*. Princeton, NJ: Princeton University Press.

Merton, Robert K. 1938. Social Structure and Anomie. *American Sociological Review* 3(5): 672–82.

Runciman, Walter G. 1966. *Relative Deprivation and Social Justice*. London: Routledge & Kegan Paul.

Stouffer, Samuel A., Edward A. Suchman, Leland C. DeVinney, Shirley A. Star, and Robin M. Williams, Jr. 1949. *The American Soldier: Adjustment during Army Life*. Princeton, NJ: Princeton University Press.

Tyler, Tom R., and Steven R. Blader. 2003. The Group Engagement Model: Procedural Justice, Social Identity, and Cooperative Behavior. *Personality and Social Psychology Review* 7(4): 349–61.

Webber, Craig. 2007. Revaluating Relative Deprivation Theory. *Theoretical Criminology* 11(1): 97–120.

Further reading

Lea, John, and Jock Young. 1993/1984. *What Is to Be Done about Law and Order?* London: Pluto.

Young, Jock. 1992. Ten points of realism. In *Rethinking Criminology: The Realist Debate*, Jock Young and Roger Matthews, eds, pp. 24–68. London: Sage.

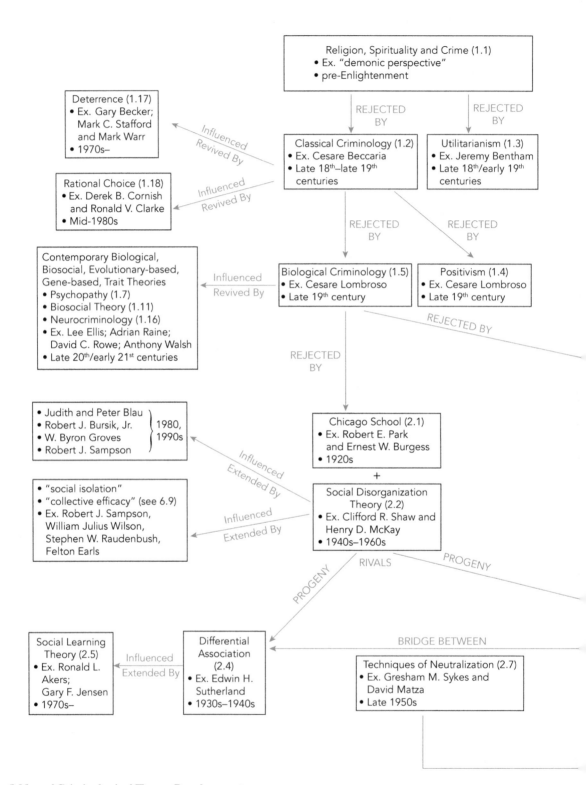

Religion, Spirituality and Crime (1.1)
• Ex. "demonic perspective"
• pre-Enlightenment

REJECTED BY

REJECTED BY

Deterrence (1.17)
• Ex. Gary Becker; Mark C. Stafford and Mark Warr
• 1970s–

Influenced Revived By

Classical Criminology (1.2)
• Ex. Cesare Beccaria
• Late 18th–late 19th centuries

Utilitarianism (1.3)
• Ex. Jeremy Bentham
• Late 18th/early 19th centuries

Rational Choice (1.18)
• Ex. Derek B. Cornish and Ronald V. Clarke
• Mid-1980s

Influenced Revived By

REJECTED BY

REJECTED BY

Contemporary Biological, Biosocial, Evolutionary-based, Gene-based, Trait Theories
• Psychopathy (1.7)
• Biosocial Theory (1.11)
• Neurocriminology (1.16)
• Ex. Lee Ellis; Adrian Raine; David C. Rowe; Anthony Walsh
• Late 20th/early 21st centuries

Influenced Revived By

Biological Criminology (1.5)
• Ex. Cesare Lombroso
• Late 19th century

Positivism (1.4)
• Ex. Cesare Lombroso
• Late 19th century

REJECTED BY

REJECTED BY

• Judith and Peter Blau
• Robert J. Bursik, Jr.
• W. Byron Groves
• Robert J. Sampson
} 1980, 1990s

Influenced Extended By

Chicago School (2.1)
• Ex. Robert E. Park and Ernest W. Burgess
• 1920s

+

• "social isolation"
• "collective efficacy" (see 6.9)
• Ex. Robert J. Sampson, William Julius Wilson, Stephen W. Raudenbush, Felton Earls

Influenced Extended By

Social Disorganization Theory (2.2)
• Ex. Clifford R. Shaw and Henry D. McKay
• 1940s–1960s

PROGENY

RIVALS

PROGENY

Social Learning Theory (2.5)
• Ex. Ronald L. Akers; Gary F. Jensen
• 1970s–

Influenced Extended By

Differential Association (2.4)
• Ex. Edwin H. Sutherland
• 1930s–1940s

BRIDGE BETWEEN

Techniques of Neutralization (2.7)
• Ex. Gresham M. Sykes and David Matza
• Late 1950s

A Map of Criminological Theory Development

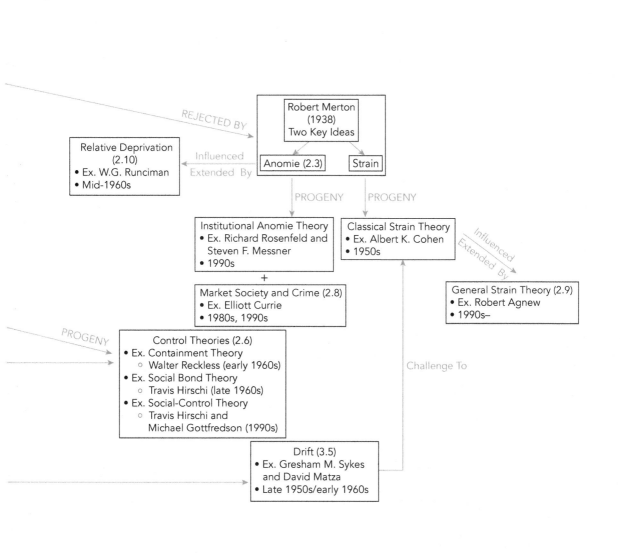

Part 3

From appreciation to critique

Part 3 Introduction

The chapters in this section of the book reflect a period when what had become the 'traditional' assumptions and rules of 'criminology' were, if not 'in retreat', at least not 'in fashion'. In ascendance was, first, a 'sociology of deviance', which itself subsequently (and indeed quite quickly) felt the harsh edge of critique – not from the 'old' criminology but from several versions of 'new criminologies'. These sources of challenge and dissent in the field were given momentum by widespread social change and increased appreciation of the significance of con-flict and power. In the US, the civil rights movement inspired many to call for a challenge to embedded prejudices, prohibitions and power structures. Protests and demonstrations took place in many countries against the US presence in Vietnam, against nuclear weapons, against governments – in short, against 'the establishment'. In the 1960s, expressions of the need for 'alternatives' multiplied as counter-narratives articulated what was wrong with politics, the economy, the universities, dominant morality and so on.

Objectivity, scientific categorization and the trappings of positivism were attacked. Causality was questioned and taken-for-granted assumptions about what actually constitutes 'crime' or 'deviance' were challenged. The argument followed that so much of what is treated as crime and deviance was defined as such because of societal reaction and the application of negative and stig-matizing labels, not because of qualities inherent to the actions so 'labelled'. Critical reassessment and scepticism framed exciting new work, and studies of the powerless and marginalized flourished. The impact of media, families, police and 'the system' in creating 'outsiders' became the focus, rather than seeking explanations of 'why' individuals might be in a position to be labelled criminal or deviant. This was not all new, but it seemed to mark a radical turning point: notions of crime, deviance, justice and law were socially constructed.

Significantly, the seed of a further source of critique was now sown. By empha-sizing the social construction of pathologies and categories, the unfairness of labels and stigmatization and the plight of the powerless and the 'underdog', these new radical deviancy theorists, ethnographers and investigators brought 'power' into question. 'Who' controlled the systems of designation and dis-paragement, policing and punishment? 'Why' did gross inequalities persist throughout societies, but particularly in the operation of the criminal justice system? And why did the study of deviance and criminology seem to make little difference – perhaps even contributing to justifications for social control?

Radical analysis rapidly turned to examination of the material underpinnings of capitalism – the exploitation of the working class and the marginalized – and to the crimes of the powerful. The significance of economic power, media manipulation and forces of conflict and control became central to a 'new criminology'. Oddly – and shamefully – it took some time before widespread criminological attention was directed to the most sizeable group typically experiencing economic disadvantage and exclusion from power: women. As a feminist criminology developed, it created its own substantial and influential body of work as well as its own debates and diverse directions. It also influenced and shaped wider criminology, although the question 'by how much?' remains open. Critical criminology also continued to diversify, with various strands: some that brought together subcultural and Marxist theories; some that set themselves against the state and called for abolition of coercive systems of control; and others that argued for an alternative approach and a 'realist' engagement with the politics and problems of victimization and crime control. As such, it might be more proper to think of 'critical criminolog*ies*' instead of '*a* critical criminology'.

See Chapter 3.8
Labelling theory

See Chapter 4.8
Cultural
criminology

See Chapter 2.1
Chicago School

3.1 Appreciative criminology

Avi Brisman

Appreciative criminology is an approach that endeavours to grasp – and thus *appreciate* – the social world from the perspective of the individual or group of individuals whose acts, behaviours, customs and practices have been **labelled** 'criminal' or 'deviant' by the dominant culture. Although the term 'appreciative criminology' rarely appears in the criminological lexicon as such, the appreciative orientation has a rich history in criminology and sociology; is integral to ethnographic methodologies (which are important to **cultural criminology**); and holds the untapped potential to forge linkages between criminology and anthropology, law, legal history and socio-legal studies.

In describing the emergence of the **Chicago School**, Hayward (2004:94) notes the Chicagoans' 'two ostensibly very contrasting innovations: the celebrated concentric circle map of the city, and the development of a more interactive, street-level approach to the problem of crime that sought to understand the deviant lifestyle from the "inside"'. Whereas the research undertaken by Clifford Shaw and Henry McKay was, in Hayward's (2004:95) words, 'largely the product of abstracted demographic analyses, the plotting of juvenile delinquency court statistics onto Burgess's concentric circle model', the Chicagoans 'also employed a more proactive, phenomenologically and culturally inspired approach to *street life*'. According to Hayward (2004:95):

This sensitive approach to the study of urban life/delinquency ushered in a new era of social science research practice, systematising ethnographic methods such as participant observation, the first-hand interview and the individual case history. This approach to the study of crime – initially oriented to the city environment – later became known as the 'appreciative' tradition (see Matza 1969: 24–40, 70–73).

In *Becoming Deviant*, Matza (1969) describes an appreciative 'attitude', 'posture' or 'view' to studying deviant subcultures – one that attempts to understand their social world through their own eyes. It is important to note, however, that before Matza, researchers affiliated with the Chicago School were examining urban subcultures from the point of view of those being studied.

Appreciative criminology possesses both theoretical and methodological dimensions. Theoretically, appreciative criminology reflects **interactionism's** polyvocality – its concern for multiple, equally valid social perspectives – as well as interactionism's assertions that such perspectives are constructed and produced through our relations with other actors in everyday life. Because interactionism eschews the notion of external truths and grand theories regarding the causes of individual behaviour – and because it focuses on how people experience and create their social worlds – the interactionist framework stresses the importance of observing individuals in their normal, everyday lives. Thus, methodologically, interactionism – and hence appreciative criminology – relies on ethnography for data collection.

See Chapter 3.18 Symbolic interactionism

For criminologists with a sociological background, this raises questions about whether conducting value-free research is possible (or even desirable) – issues encapsulated in the famous debate on 'taking sides' between Howard Becker and Alvin Gouldner (see Further reading below). For criminologists with an anthropological orientation, an appreciative criminology implicates 'cultural relativism' – the notion that a people's customs and values should be analysed – and must be understood – in reference to *their own* histories and in terms of the cultures of which they are a part, and *not* according to the values of another culture.

While cultural relativism requires suspending judgement in order to understand the logic and dynamics of other cultures and refraining from viewing the actions of other people simply in terms of the degree to which they correspond with the researcher/observer's notions of right and wrong, it is distinct from *moral relativism* – the idea that because no universal standard of behaviour exists, people should not judge behaviours as 'good' or 'bad'. As such, an appreciative criminology that adopts or subscribes to cultural relativism necessitates *suspending* judgement but not *dispensing* with it entirely, for it is possible to understand other cultures without approving of (all of) their cultural practices. Using the anthropological technique of cultural relativism can then assist appreciative criminologists in recognizing that our own culture is only one design for living among many in the history of humankind, and that it has emerged under a particular set of historical practices rather than being the inevitable end result of human social evolution. Like anthropology, then, appreciative criminology can offer the dual promise of adding to the understanding of human diversity (and humans' widely different views about what is proper, necessary and moral), while also offering a cultural critique of our own society.

Both theoretically and methodologically, appreciative criminology reflects important aspects of **cultural criminology**, especially in its notion of *criminological verstehen*. As Ferrell (1999:400) explains, the concept of criminological verstehen 'denotes a field researcher's subjective appreciation and empathic understanding of crime's situated meanings, symbolism, and emotions, in part through the sorts of directly participatory research that can foster a methodology of attentiveness'.

See Chapter 4.8
Cultural
criminology

While Ferrell and other cultural criminologists laud the benefits of adopting an empathic stance towards the participants in their studies of subcultural domains and of endeavouring to develop an emotional understanding of the (often dangerous) experiences that define and accompany criminality, they have been criticized for their glorification of individuals engaged in criminal behaviour – a concern that would extend to appreciative criminology. Cultural criminologists, however, acknowledge that the idea of criminological verstehen challenges principles of research 'objectivity', but respond by asking: 'if the meaning of crime is largely constructed in the immediacy of its experience, how else are criminologists to investigate and understand it?' (Ferrell 2009:163).

An appreciative approach – whether from cultural criminological, ethnographic or interactionist perspectives – has also endured criticisms for its reliance on 'criminals/deviants' for information (who may under- or over-report their involvement in illegal activities); its lack of generalizability (given small sample sizes); the risks of failing to consider macro-level structural inequalities; and the **reality of crime and its consequences for victims**. But here, too, an appreciative criminology might well reject the critiques premised on the purported superiority of objective 'science', embracing the very aspects that other theoretical and methodological approaches seek to avoid.

See Chapter 3.14
Realism and left
idealism

One potential avenue for future research in appreciative criminology might entail venturing into the venues where systems of social control construct and reconstruct various cultural practices as crime. Thus, an appreciative criminology might attempt to draw linkages to legal scholarship on judicial toleration of and respect for alternative normative worlds (see, e.g., Cover 1983) and the role of empathy in jurisprudential philosophy and judicial decision-making (see, e.g., Menkel-Meadow 1992). Much like anthropologists, appreciative criminologists might also help articulate the benefits and drawbacks of the 'culture defence' in criminal cases (see, e.g., Bovenkerk and Yesilgöz 2004), thereby affording them an opportunity to engage in praxis or contribute to a **public criminology**.

See Chapter 4.31
Public criminology

References

Bovenkerk, Frank, and Yucel Yesilgöz. 2004. Crime, ethnicity and the multicultural administration of justice. In *Cultural Criminology Unleashed*, Jeff Ferrell, Keith Hayward, Wayne Morrison, and Mike Presdee, eds, pp. 80–96. London: GlassHouse Press.

Cover, Robert M. 1983. Nomos and Narrative. *Harvard Law Review* 97: 4–68.

Ferrell, Jeff. 1999. Cultural Criminology. *Annual Review of Sociology* 25: 395–418.

Ferrell, Jeff. 2009. Crime and culture. In *Criminology* (2nd edn), Chris Hale, Keith Hayward, Azrini Wahidin, and Emma Wincup, eds, pp. 157–75. New York: Oxford University Press.

Hayward, Keith J. 2004. *City Limits: Crime, Consumer Culture and the Urban Experience*. London: GlassHouse Press.

Matza, David. 1969. *Becoming Deviant*. Englewood Cliffs, NJ: Prentice Hall.

Menkel-Meadow, Carrie. 1992. The Power of Narrative in Empathetic Learning: Post-Modernism and the Stories of Law; a Review-Essay Based on Patricia J. Williams's *The Alchemy of Race and Rights: Diary of a Law Professor. UCLA Women's Law Journal* 2(0): 287–307.

Further reading

Becker, Howard S. 1967. Whose Side Are We On? *Social Problems* 14(3): 239–47.

Ferrell, Jeff. 1997. Criminological *Verstehen*: Inside the Immediacy of Crime. *Justice Quarterly* 14(1): 3–23.

Ferrell, Jeff, and Mark S. Hamm (eds). 1998. *Ethnography at the Edge: Crime, Deviance, and Field Research*. Boston: Northeastern University Press.

Ferrell, Jeff, Keith Hayward, and Jock Young. 2015. *Cultural Criminology: An Invitation* (2nd edn). Thousand Oaks, CA: Sage.

Gouldner, Alvin W. 1969. The Sociologist as Partisan: Sociology and the Welfare State. *American Sociologist* 3(2): 103–16.

Renzetti, Claire M. 2012. Feminist perspectives in criminology. In *The Routledge Handbook of Critical Criminology*, Walter S. DeKeseredy and Molly Dragiewicz, eds, pp. 129–37. Abingdon and New York: Routledge.

Shaw, Clifford R. 1930. *The Jack-Roller: A Delinquent Boy's Own Story*. Chicago: University of Chicago Press.

The Birmingham Centre for Contemporary Cultural Studies

Eamonn Carrabine

The Centre for Contemporary Cultural Studies ('CCCS' or 'the Centre') was established at the University of Birmingham in England in 1964 by Richard Hoggart (then a professor of English). It was his deputy, Stuart Hall, who would guide it through its most influential period in the 1970s that saw the introduction of innovative approaches to culture, politics and society. With never more than three staff members, two research fellows and forty postgraduate students, the work produced here, much of it collectively, was crucial to the development of cultural studies as an interdisciplinary field in Britain and elsewhere.

See Chapter 3.17
Subculture

See Chapter 2.1
Chicago School

The **subcultural tradition**, as it evolved through the **Chicago School** up to the CCCS, always sought to portray subcultures as distinctive social worlds – deviant, disenfranchised and unconventional, but forming ties with others sharing similar values, practices and geographies. At root, what is emphasized in the subcultural tradition are the social aspects of difference and affiliation in increasingly pluralized, fragmented societies. The subcultures group working at the CCCS in the 1970s established an approach that was framed by broader theoretical debates. These were a lively and volatile mix of 'two paradigms' shaping the overall cultural studies project: one is often termed 'culturalism' and is a distinctly British perspective associated with socialist historians and literary critics, while 'structuralism' is the second paradigm and was strongly influenced by European thinkers where the 'linguistic turn' proved seismic (Hall 1980). With respect to the latter, the legacy of the Italian Marxist theorist and interwar communist activist Antonio Gramsci – especially his concept of 'hegemony' – would have a profound influence on Stuart Hall's thinking. Also decisive were developments in **critical criminology, symbolic interactionism** and **labelling studies** – all of which, in various ways, insisted that deviance was not so much an *action* but a *transaction* given a particular meaning by those with the power to define. These different strands enabled subcultures to be understood in new ways – no longer in terms of a frustrated readjustment to dominant middle-class values, but as a defiant opposition to them.

See Chapter 3.3
Critical
criminologies

See Chapter 3.18
Symbolic
interactionism

See Chapter 3.8
Labelling theory

The rise of spectacular youth subcultures in post-war Britain were read as signifying the predicament of social change and distilling the bitter dynamics of class conflict in the shift to a modern, consumer society. In the key collection *Resistance through Rituals* (Hall and Jefferson 1975), which is informed by developments in Marxism (most notably from Althusser and Gramsci), the various subcultures discussed in the book are seen as attempts to 'win back space' by challenging the status quo. This resistance is played out not with sticks and stones and in the streets, but in the fields of leisure and consumption, so that it ultimately fails to challenge broader structures of power. This theme is developed in Paul Willis's *Learning to Labour* (1977), an ethnographic study of how a 'counter-school culture' among a group of working-class 'lads' ultimately serves to prepare them for menial, unskilled employment, and thereby reproduces inequalities.

The meanings of subcultural style are explored with considerable verve by Hebdige (1979) through a mix of textual analysis and case studies where the interest in the working class is retained, but is now situated in the subversive potential of Continental avant-garde aesthetics. Although Hebdige saw subcultures as creative and mobile sites of resistance in their innovative and improvised use of objects, they were also vulnerable to two kinds of 'incorporation'. One is through the 'commodity form', where the styles become mass-produced commodities and part of conventional, mainstream fashion. The second is the 'ideological form', and here Hebdige (1979:97) is attentive to the ways 'folk devils' are defined as 'deviant' in the media, but also to the subtler processes in which their threat is tamed: 'the Other can be trivialized, naturalized, domesticated' or 'transformed into meaningless exotica . . . consigned to a place beyond analysis.' The lasting impact of his book, and the CCCS approach more generally, is to pit youth subcultures against the incorporating logics of mass culture.

Critics were quick to dispute the political significance attached to subcultures in the approach, and were troubled by the elitist focus on the original, authentic moment at the expense of any sense of a 'lived' culture and lacking authentic, ethnographic depth. Others found fault with the tendency to romantically read youth style as internal to the group, with commercialization only coming later, which, they argued underestimates the way changes in youth subcultures are manufactured by culture industries. Concerns were also raised over the preoccupation with white, male and working-class subcultures, where the celebration of the spectacular ignored the racism and sexism in them. The **Marxist** emphasis on class was contested by **feminists** at the Centre, most notably Angela McRobbie (1981), who highlighted how Willis and Hebdige had implicitly privileged **masculinity** and ignored relationships in the family, households and sexuality. Working-class culture is not just the school and workplace, McRobbie contended; it also includes the bedroom and breakfast table, indicating how writing women into subcultural arguments radically changes them. Indeed, much of her work ever since has been a sustained, gendered interrogation of social change and a tracking of how consumerism borrows some of feminism's central concerns while at the same time diluting and undermining their critical meaning and impact.

See Chapter 3.9
Marxist
criminologies

See Chapter
3.6 Feminist
criminologies;
Chapter 3.13
Radical feminism

See Chapter 4.21
Masculinities,
structure and
hegemony

The relative neglect of ethnicity is a criticism that needs to be addressed in more detail, not least since Hall and his colleagues had begun to track the politics of race in their major work, *Policing the Crisis* (Hall et al. 1978). Likewise, Hebdige (1979:45) had a keen eye for the cross-cultural exchanges between black and white communities, seeing 'played out on the loaded surfaces of British working-class youth cultures, a phantom history of race relations since the War'.

The very 'Englishness' of the cultural studies project remained unexamined until Paul Gilroy (1987:12) condemned the 'morbid celebration of England and Englishness from which blacks are systematically excluded' in the discipline. By this point, it is also clear that Hall (1996) was turning from a preoccupation with class and ideology to the 'politics of difference' and 'hyphenated identity'. He became critical of claims that forms of national identity are unified and integrated, insisting that the category of 'black subject' can no longer serve as the basis of identity politics under these fragmented circumstances.

Gilroy's position also hardened and denounced essentialist accounts of black cultural formations, insisting they produce 'camp mentalities' echoing not only fascism but also the commercialization of African-American music and urban, ghetto styles. Here new claims of ethnic authenticity chime with twenty-first-century corporate multicultural commodification: when 'hip-hop's marginality' becomes 'as official and routinized, as its overblown defiance, even if the music and its matching life-style are still being presented – marketed – as outlaw forms' (Gilroy 2000:180). His critique of exclusivist bio-politics is also extended to the ways the black body is coded as either 'super human' in the black athlete or as 'less than human' in the violent black criminal. Notions of 'ghettoness' have become synonymous with forms of transgressive 'otherness'; but Gilroy's more recent work has turned to the ways people live together in multicultural cities, which he describes as 'convivial culture' where forms of tolerance jostle with racism, providing fresh insights into the relationships between the metropolis, colony and the 'immigrant' (Gilroy 2004).

In significant respects, this focus on identity and difference was bound up with broader changes across the intellectual landscape, where the era of 'the Post' came to characterize these new times: post-colonialism, post-feminism, post-Fordism, post-Marxism, **post-structuralism** and, looming over all, the **postmodern**. In *Hiding in the Light*, Hebdige sets out to overcome the weaknesses of subcultural analysis by exploring debates over postmodernism. Early on, we learn that this will be an 'obituary' for his initial 'theoretical models' where the 'idea of subculture-as-negation grew up alongside punk, remained inextricably linked to it and died when it died', so the opening chapters constitute his 'attempt at a farewell to youth studies' (Hebdige 1988:8). This idea was subsequently picked up by Redhead (1997) and others, who argued that the subcultural moment had now passed into history (between the death of punk and the rise of rave later in 1980s), and that the movement to 'club cultures' required fresh postmodern theorizing – where terms like 'tribe', 'scene' and 'lifestyle' have been advanced to deal with the problems associated with subcultural theory. The suggestion is that these terms are better equipped to capture the proliferation, fragmentation and individualized character of contemporary youth cultures.

See Chapter 4.29
Post-structuralism
and criminology

See Chapter 4.28
Postmodern
and constitutive
criminologies

Others criticized CCCS subcultural approaches for over-relying on theoretical abstraction at the expense of empirical data. In response, the mid-1990s onwards has seen the growth of 'post-subcultural' studies emerge to address the criticisms associated with the Birmingham tradition (Sweetman 2013). These new perspectives have difficulties of their own, not least since the outright rejection of this past leaves a 'valorizing of individual consumption' that fails to grasp 'the generation or articulation of deviance as social experience' (Blackman 2014:506). In many respects, the rise of **cultural criminology** over this same time period can be seen as a response to the questions initially posed at Birmingham, though the tensions exposed by these developments are far from being resolved (Carrabine 2016).

See Chapter 4.8
Cultural
criminology

References

Blackman, Shane. 2014. Subculture Theory: An Historical and Contemporary Assessment of the Concept for Understanding Deviance. *Deviant Behavior* 35(6): 496–512.

Carrabine, Eamonn. 2016. Changing Fortunes: Criminology and the Sociological Condition. *Sociology* 50(5): 847–62.

Gilroy, Paul. 1987. *There Ain't No Black in the Union Jack: The Cultural Politics of Nation and Race*. London: Unwin Hyman.

Gilroy, Paul. 2000. *Between Camps: Nations, Cultures and the Allure of Race*. London: Penguin.

Gilroy, Paul. 2004. *After Empire: Melancholia or Convivial Culture*. London: Routledge.

Hall, Stuart. 1980. Cultural Studies: Two Paradigms. in *Media, Culture and Society* 2(1): 57–72.

Hall, Stuart. 1996. New ethnicities. In *Stuart Hall: Critical Dialogues in Cultural Studies*, David Morley and Kuan-Hsing Chen, eds, pp. 442–51 London: Routledge.

Hall, Stuart, and Tony Jefferson (eds). 1975. *Resistance through Rituals*. London: Hutchinson.

Hall, Stuart, Chas Critcher, Tony Jefferson, John Clarke, and Brian Roberts. 1978. *Policing the Crisis: Mugging, the State and Law and Order*. London: Macmillan.

Hebdige, Dick. 1979. *Subculture: The Meaning of Style*. London and New York: Routledge.

Hebdige, Dick. 1988. *Hiding in the Light*. London: Comedia.

McRobbie, Angela. 1981. Settling accounts with subcultures: a feminist critique. In *Culture, Ideology and Social Process: A Reader*, Tony Bennett, Graham Martin, Colin Mercer, and Janet Woollacott, eds, Chapter 4. London: Batsford/Open University Press.

Redhead, Steve. 1997. *Subculture to Clubcultures*. Oxford: Blackwell.

Sweetman, Paul. 2013. Structure, Agency, Subculture: The CCCS, *Resistance through Rituals*, and 'Post-Subcultural' Studies'. *Sociological Research Online* 18(4): 22. www.socresonline.org.uk/18/4/22.html. Accessed 23 January 2017.

Willis, Paul. 1977. *Learning to Labour*. Farnborough: Saxon House.

Further reading

Carrabine, Eamonn. 2017. *Crime and Social Theory*. Basingstoke: Palgrave Macmillan.

Jenks, Chris. 2004. *Subculture: The Fragmentation of the Social*. London: SAGE.

Turner, Graeme. 2002. *British Cultural Studies* (3rd edn). London and New York: Routledge.

Critical criminologies 3.3

Walter S. DeKeseredy

There is no single critical criminology. Rather, there are critical criminologies with different origins that use different methods and reflect diverse political beliefs. Thus, 'critical criminology' serves as an umbrella term for concepts, interpretations and theories about crime, deviance and social control – united in a shared belief that crime is:

> rooted in economic, social, and political inequalities, along with social class divisions, racism and hate, and other forms of segmented social organization, reinforced and rationalized by culturally derived relativistic definitions of conforming, deviant, and criminal actions, which separate, segregate, and otherwise cause governments at all levels everywhere to differentially and discriminately enforce laws and punish offenders.
>
> (Donnermeyer 2012:289)

Critical criminologists of various stripes view hierarchical social stratification and inequality along class, ethnic, **gender, patriarchal and racial lines** as the major sources of crime and as the key factors that shape societal reactions to violations of legal and social norms. Yet, 'there is no party line' and many heated scholarly and political debates occur within critical criminological circles (Currie 2008:vii).

Regardless of their particular pasts, different orientations or geographical homes – critical criminology is, indeed, an *international* endeavour – most critical criminologists share unyielding opposition to draconian means of **social control**. The main goal is not just reform in and of the criminal justice

See Chapter 3.6 Feminist criminologies; Chapter 4.26 Patriarchy and crime; Chapter 3.13 Radical feminism; Chapter 4.7 Critical race theory

See Chapter 5.18 Social control

See Chapter 5.1
Abolitionism;
Chapter 4.1
Anarchist
criminology

See Chapter 4.24
Neoliberalism

See Chapter 3.14
Realism and left
idealism; Chapter
4.38 Ultra-realism

See Chapter 4.16
Green criminology;
Chapter 4.11
Environmental
justice and
victimology;
Chapter 4.13
Genocide and
ecocide

See Chapter 6.9
Rural criminology

See Chapter 4.5
Corporate crime;
Chapter 4.36 State
crime; Chapter
4.37 State-
corporate crime;
Chapter 4.41
White-collar crime

See Chapter 3.1
Appreciative
criminology

See Chapter 4.19
Institutional and
anti-institutional
violence

See Chapter 3.9
Marxist
criminologies

system (or, for some, **abolition**), but to broaden social democracy and equality through radical structural and cultural changes – *social justice* rather than just justice in the *criminal justice* system. In the current **neoliberal** era, such changes face obstacles, so most critical scholars and activists propose progressive, short-term solutions to crime while simultaneously pursuing major transformations (e.g., **left realists**, **ultra-realists**).

Just as critical criminologists do not all share a specific political ideology or research agenda, they are not wedded to any particular research method – although many use qualitative techniques such as biography, content analysis, critical crime history, deconstruction, ethnography, and inductive and deductive reasoning. These are used to gather and analyse data on a variety of topics, from violence against women in public and private places, to racist police practices, to **environmental crimes and harms**, to **rural crime**, to **crimes of the powerful**. In so doing, many such critical criminologists try to maintain a balance between an indictment of various structural and institutional relations and a sensitivity to the relationship between knowledge and power.

Critical criminologists do not shy away from a commitment to the socially, politically and economically disadvantaged, and often consider those harms that may not be proscribed by law. Thus, in response to Becker's (1967) query, 'Whose side are we on?', critical criminologists have developed an interest in and **appreciation** of victims of human rights violations; un- and under-skilled workers who are chronically unemployed (e.g., because major corporations have relocated), people lacking adequate social services (e.g., child care, health care); and targets of state **terrorism**, such as those unjustly imprisoned in Guantanamo Bay. Critical criminologists seek to broaden the definition of crime to include these harms (Schwendinger and Schwendinger 1975). Accordingly, many critical criminologists are practitioners (e.g., working for non-profit organizations, government agencies) and in recent decades have influenced numerous organizations that struggle for social justice, such as the Sentencing Project in the US and Penal Reform International in England.

While critical criminology's roots are widespread, some progressive scholars trace their lineage to **Marxism and Marxist thought**. Orthodox Marxists, however, argue that Marxist theory cannot be applied to the study of crime and law, and there may be some truth to such assertions. Still, many – especially those who produced theories of crime and its control in the 1970s and early 1980s – relied on Marxist analyses of capitalist society and defined themselves as *radical criminologists*. Works such as those by Quinney (1974), Pearce (1976) and Chambliss (1975) were important for their contribution to a sociological understanding of crime and the administration of justice, and some critical scholars still apply Marxist perspectives to criminological problems.

Lea (2010:23) sensitizes us to the fact that Marx and Engels may be long gone but the 'general perspective on crime' derived from them 'has a particular salience for the present situation.' Others agree and predict that Marx and Engels' work will remain relevant within critical criminology in light of major global economic crises, the rapidly increasing gap between the 'haves' and 'have-nots' and staggering levels of unemployment among people attempting to enter the workforce and earn a living wage.

There were several reasons for replacing the term *radical criminology* with *critical criminology*, one of which is that, starting in the mid-1980s, a number of younger or newer criminologists, especially feminists, were also challenging mainstream criminology from perspectives that were not Marxist in orientation. In the United States, many of these academics and activists ultimately helped create the American Society of Criminology's Division on Critical Criminology (DCC) in Chicago in 1988 – although, arguably, the term 'critical criminology' was formally introduced in 1975 by Taylor, Walton and Young with the publication of their anthology *Critical Criminology*. Regardless of when and where the name *critical criminology* was first crafted, the fact remains that there are numerous variants of critical criminological thought, and new types continue to emerge.

What will the future bring? Perhaps, we will see rich empirical support for the hypothesis that 'the impact of critical criminology will increase exponentially in years ahead, perhaps at some point even coming to overshadow mainstream forms of analysis' (Friedrichs 2009:217). One thing we do know for sure is that critical criminology is now characterized by much international collaboration and intellectual cross-fertilization. It is essential to always remember that most critical scholarly and political projects are, to quote Currie (1985:vii), 'to a much greater extent than is usually recognized, the products of collective effort'. In addition, whatever directions critical criminologists take in the years to come, they will always owe much to their predecessors, such as these pioneers who passed away in recent years: William Chambliss, Stan Cohen, Stuart Hall, Barbara Hudson, Geoffrey Pearson, Mike Presdee, Nicky Rafter, Julia Schwendinger, Ian Taylor and Jock Young.

References

Becker, Howard S. 1967. Whose Side Are We On? *Social Problems* 14(3): 239–47.

Chambliss, William J. 1975. Toward a Political Economy of Crime. *Theory and Society* 2(2): 167–80.

Currie, Elliott. 1985. *Confronting Crime: An American Challenge*. New York: Pantheon.

Currie, Elliott. 2008. Preface. In *Critical Criminology: Issues, Debates, Challenges*, Kerry Carrington and Russell Hogg, eds, pp. vii–ix. Portland, OR: Willan.

Donnermeyer, Joseph F. 2012. Rural crime and critical criminology. In *The Routledge Handbook of Critical Criminology*, Walter S. DeKeseredy and Molly Dragiewicz, eds, pp. 290–302. London: Routledge.

Friedrichs, David O. 2009. Critical criminology. In *21st Century Criminology: A Reference Handbook*, Vol. 1, J. Mitchell Miller, ed., pp. 210–18. Thousand Oaks, CA: Sage.

Lea, John. 2010. Karl Marx (1818–83) (and Frederick Engels (1820–95)). In *Fifty Key Thinkers in Criminology*, Keith Hayward, Shadd Maruna, and Jayne Mooney, eds, pp. 18–24. Abingdon: Routledge.

Pearce, Frank. 1976. *Crimes of the Powerful: Marxism, Crime and Deviance*. London: Pluto.

Quinney, Richard. 1974. *Critique of Legal Order*. Boston: Little, Brown.

Schwendinger, Herman, and Julia R. Schwendinger. 1975. Defenders of order or guardians of human rights? In *Critical Criminology*, Ian Taylor, Paul Walton, and Jock Young, eds, pp. 113–46. London: Routledge.

Taylor, Ian, Paul Walton, and Jock Young. 1973. *The New Criminology*. London: Routledge.

Further reading

DeKeseredy, Walter S. 2011. *Contemporary Critical Criminology*. London: Routledge.

DeKeseredy, Walter S., and Molly Dragiewicz (eds). 2012. *Routledge Handbook of Critical Criminology*. London: Routledge.

DeKeseredy, Walter S., and Molly Dragiewicz (eds). 2014. *Critical Criminology, Volumes 1–4*. London: Routledge.

Hall, Steve, and Simon Winlow. 2015. *Revitalizing Criminological Theory: Towards a New Ultra-Realism*. London: Routledge.

Reiman, Jeffrey, and Paul Leighton. 2013. *The Rich Get Richer and the Poor Get Prison* (10th edn). Boston: Allyn & Bacon.

Taylor, Ian, Paul Walton, and Jock Young (eds). 1975. *Critical Criminology*. London: Routledge.

Walton, Paul, and Jock Young (eds). 1998. *The New Criminology Revisited*. London: Macmillan.

Winlow, Simon, and Rowland Atkinson (eds). 2013. *New Directions in Crime and Deviancy*. London: Routledge.

Defiance theory

Avi Brisman

In the context of criminology, *defiance* refers to 'the net increase in the prevalence, incidence, or seriousness of future offending against a sanctioning community caused by a proud, shameless reaction to the administration of a criminal sanction' (Sherman 1993:459). 'Specific' or 'individual' defiance is the reaction of one person to his/her own punishment, while 'general' defiance is the reaction of a group or collectivity to punishment directed at one or more of its members. Defiance can be 'direct' – a crime committed against a sanctioning agent – or 'indirect' – 'the displaced just deserts committed against a target vicariously representing the sanctioning agents' that provoked the reaction (Sherman 1993:459). To understand how defiance relates to and differs from other mechanisms by which sanctions may (or may not) affect crime, it is necessary to situate *defiance theory* within a brief intellectual history of criminological thought.

Most criminological theories seeking to explain the aetiology of crime and delinquency begin with the *offender*. These theories can, in turn, be divided into biological and sociological explanations – with the former pointing to factors *inside* the individual that can lead to crime and the latter identifying dynamics and environments *outside* the individual that can increase the likelihood of crime. The exceptions are **biosocial theories** of crime, which emphasize the interaction between physiological dispositions and environmental conditions that affect the likelihood of criminality in individuals.

Labelling or *social reaction* perspectives eschew using the offender as the starting point of analysis. Instead, such perspectives suggest that researchers examine not the acts and omissions of individual offenders, but the behaviours

See Chapter 1.11
Biosocial theory

See Chapter 3.8
Labelling theory

of those who react to, label or sanction those who commit transgressions of the law. Implicit in this approach is the idea that the criminal justice system and other mechanisms of social control can *contribute* to crime, rather than curb it.

Labelling and social reaction theories grew in popularity in the 1960s and early 1970s. Given the social upheaval of the times (e.g., civil rights demonstrations, prison riots, the Vietnam War, Watergate), a theoretical orientation critical of state power and intervention was widely appealing. But in the late 1970s and early 1980s, interest in labelling and social reaction perspectives waned: critics pointed to their empirical weaknesses and attention turned to **life-course theories**.

See Chapter 1.13
Life-course theory

Lawrence Sherman's defiance theory seeks to explain the conditions under which punishment reduces, increases or has no effect on crime, and he begins by asserting that the common question in criminology and public policy – 'Does punishment control crime?' – should be replaced by a more useful one: 'under what conditions does each type of criminal sanction reduce, increase, or have no effect on future crimes?' (1993:445). While modern criminology has been preoccupied with the problem of *crime causation*, the 'conceptual core' of criminology – dating back to **Beccaria** – is the *science of sanction effects*, which, Sherman maintains, 'requires explicit theories of those effects, not just modified theories of crime causation' (1993:446).

See Chapter 1.2
Classical
criminology

Deterrence and labelling theories have dominated the study of sanction effects, requiring a choice between the two. Sherman notes (1993:446, 447), however, that three new theories have emerged to resolve the stalemate:

See Chapter 1.17
Deterrence

See Chapter 5.14
Reintegrative
shaming

■ Braithwaite's (1989) theory of **reintegrative shaming**, which suggests that sanctions can be either 'reintegrative' (if they focus on the *act*) or 'stigmatizing' and 'disintegrative' (if they shame and reject the *actor*);
■ Tyler's (1990) study of compliance and the distinction he draws between sanctions that citizens perceive as fair and those viewed as unfair; and
■ Scheff and Retzinger's (1991) sociology of pride and shame (the 'master emotions') that dominate individuals' responses to sanctions (experienced and vicarious) – responses that vary, in part, with individuals' social bonding to the 'sanctioning agent' and to society more generally.

Sherman's defiance theory represents an attempt to integrate these three theories into one theory that accounts for many of the facts of diverse sanction effects.

Sherman identifies four key concepts in the emotional response to sanctioning experiences (1993:448):

1. the *legitimacy* granted by the sanctioned offender to the sanctioning agent's behaviour, related more to whether the offender is treated with respect and experiences procedural fairness than the morality the agent represents (drawing on Tyler's (1990) study of *procedural justice*);

2. the *social bond* that the offender may or may not have with the sanctioning agent, the community represented and other degrees of attachment (drawing on Scheff and Retzinger 1991);

3. the *shame,* which the offender acknowledges, denies or rejects and which, in response, repairs or results in the weakening of social bonds with the sanctioning agent and/or community (drawing on Braithwaite 1989); and

4. the *pride,* as felt by the offender following any sanction: 'social solidarity with the relevant community or isolation from that community as an "unconquerable soul"' (Henley [1875] 1954).

These concepts, Sherman submits, allow a three-pronged, falsifiable statement of a defiance theory based on the ways in which sanctions provoke future *defiance* of the law, act as future *deterrence* to lawbreaking, and become *irrelevant* to future lawbreaking.

According to Sherman, defiance occurs under four necessary conditions. First, the offender perceives the criminal sanction as unfair because the sanctioning agent behaved in a disrespectful manner or the sanction is seen as 'arbitrary, discriminatory, excessive, undeserved, or otherwise objectively unjust' (1993:460, 461). Second, the offender is poorly bonded to or alienated from society – specifically, the sanctioning agent or community represented. Third, the offender defines the sanction as stigmatizing in a way directed at him/her rather than the *lawbreaking act*. Fourth, the offender denies or refuses to recognize the shame that the sanction has, indeed, caused him/her to suffer. For Sherman, the key is the relationship of shame to the **social bond** (see also Bouffard and Piquero, 2010:228).

See Chapter 2.6
Control theories

Sherman's defiance theory predicts three reactions to a punishment perceived as unfair – *irrelevance*, *deterrence* or *defiance* (although, as he acknowledges, it may be more powerful a predictor of predatory crimes than of retreatist offences). When a poorly bonded individual perceives a sanction to be unfair but accepts the accompanying shame, the sanction may be irrelevant or a deterrent to future offending. On the other hand, when a poorly bonded individual denies the shame that he/she experiences as a result of a sanction that he/she deems unfair and stigmatizing, he/she is likely to respond with defiance and rage, and to participate in future offending. When a well-bonded individual – one with a strong(er) 'stake in conformity' – perceives a sanction to be unfair but accepts the accompanying shame, the sanction will likely have a deterrent effect. On the other hand, when a well-bonded individual denies the shame that he/she experiences as a result of a sanction that he/she feels is unfair and stigmatizing, the sanction will likely be irrelevant rather than a deterrent because, as Bouffard and Piquero (2010:229) explain, 'the perceived unfairness of the sanction and the failure to accept the shame that accompanies the sanction will essentially nullify any deterrent effect produced by the strong bond'.

In sum, defiance theory integrates differential effects of sanctions and is closely related to both deterrence and labelling perspectives. It recognizes the potential criminogenic impact of stigmatizing sanctions (especially among offenders with weak social bonds), while highlighting the role of shame (which may elicit different individual reactions based on levels of social bonding). Defiance theory also involves perceptions of procedural justice.

While defiance theory does not provide a complete explanation for criminal behaviour – and while social reaction is often the *result* rather than the *cause* of crime and deviance – defiance theory lends support to assertions that sanctions can be crafted in ways that are not criminogenic. In this way, defiance theory can be seen as endorsing **restorative justice** approaches, where the state serves as a partner working with the victim and offender rather than as an adversary. Ultimately, defiance theory's long-term viability will be linked to the extent to which it attends to early life and trajectories of (continuity in and desistance from) offending – i.e., within a life-course perspective (see Bouffard and Piquero 2010) – as well as considering other phenomena, such as concentrated disadvantage and poverty and structural inequalities.

See Chapter 5.15
Restorative justice

References

Bouffard, Leana Allen, and Nicole Leeper Piquero. 2010. Defiance Theory and Life Course Explanations of Persistent Offending. *Crime and Delinquency* 56(2): 227–52.

Braithwaite, John. 1989. *Crime, Shame and Reintegration*. Cambridge: Cambridge University Press.

Henley, William E. [1875] 1954. Invictus. In *The Victorian Age: Prose, Poetry, and Drama* (2nd edn), John W. Bowyer and John L. Brooks, eds. New York: Appleton-Century-Crofts.

Scheff, Thomas J., and Suzanne M. Retzinger. 1991. *Emotions and Violence: Shame and Rage in Destructive Conflicts*. Lexington, MA: Lexington Books.

Sherman, Lawrence W. 1993. Defiance, Deterrence, and Irrelevance: A Theory of the Criminal Sanction. *Journal of Research in Crime and Delinquency* 30(4): 445–73.

Tyler, Tom R. 1990. *Why People Obey the Law*. New Haven: Yale University Press.

Further reading

Belvedere, Kimberly, John L. Worrall, and Stephen G. Tibbetts. 2005. Explaining Suspect Resistance in Police–Citizen Encounters. *Criminal Justice Review* 30(1): 30–44.

McCluskey, John D., Stephen D. Mastrofski, and Roger B. Parks. 1999. To Acquiesce or Rebel: Predicting Citizen Compliance with Police Requests. *Police Quarterly* 2(4): 389–416.

Paternoster, Raymond, and Alex Piquero. 1995. Reconceptualizing Deterrence: An Empirical Test of Personal and Vicarious Experiences. *Journal of Research in Crime and Delinquency* 32(3): 251–86.

Paternoster, Raymond, and Sally Simpson. 1996. Sanction Threats and Appeals to Morality: Testing a Rational Choice Model of Corporate Crime. *Law and Society Review* 30(3): 549–83.

Paternoster, Raymond, Robert Brame, Ronet Bachman, and Lawrence W. Sherman.

1997. Do Fair Procedures Matter? The Effect of Procedural Justice on Spouse Assault. *Law and Society Review* 31(1): 163–204.

Piquero, Alex, and Raymond Paternoster. 1998. An Application of Stafford and Warr's Reconceptualization of Deterrence to Drinking And Driving. *Journal of Research in Crime and Delinquency* 35(1): 3–39.

Piquero, Nicole Leeper, and Leana Allen Bouffard. 2003. A Preliminary and Partial Test of Specific Defiance. *Journal of Crime and Justice* 26(1): 1–21.

3.5 Drift

Jeff Ferrell

The concept of drift denotes a social situation characterized by dislocation and disorientation, or a social process whose trajectory is radically uncertain. Such situations and processes are often associated with those individuals and groups who have in some way become disengaged from the larger social order. Various criminological theories attempt to account for these social dynamics and to analyse their connection to crime, deviance and delinquency.

See Chapter 2.1 Chicago School

One foundational perspective on drift emerged roughly a century ago in the work of sociologists Georg Simmel and **Robert Park**. Writing about 'the stranger', Simmel described the sort of person who relocates to a new community but never fully becomes a part of it – a person who remains ready to depart as needed. The stranger's latent mobility, Simmel argued, creates an odd mix of proximity and remoteness within the new community, and produces for the stranger a subversive sort of perceptual freedom; with the stranger's actions freed from customary attachments, the stranger is able to assess his new situation in a more general and comparative manner. Drawing in part on Simmel's work, Park explored migration and marginality, and likewise suggested that migration serves to liberate those involved in it from the conventions of custom, thereby sparking a cosmopolitan orientation towards new ideas and interpretations. Park argued that the migrant begins to see the world from which he/she came with a certain detachment; and, arriving as a newcomer in a new world, the migrant acquires a double estrangement from the taken-for-granted security of the familiar, past and present. Park here proposed a radical epistemology of drift, and one that is radically sociological as well – a comparative epistemology by which the drifter, on the move between social settings, comes to see the social construction of convention, and to *see past it* as well. Dislocation and disruption can certainly spawn desperation, but, as Simmel and Park suggested, they can also produce alternative ways of understanding the world – a kind of drifting liberation through which new worlds can be undertaken.

A second, parallel orientation to the perspective on drift proposed by Simmel and Park developed from the work of Émile Durkheim and from **Robert Merton's adaptation of Durkheim's analysis.** Durkheim's classic sociological concept of anomie denotes a breakdown of social order – a rupture in moral regulation – such that members of society are left in a state of ill-defined identity and normless uncertainty. Here, Durkheim suggests that disruptions of social structure can produce extremes of cultural estrangement and disorientation, and with them a drift away from the social foundations of everyday society. Pushing further still to understand drift as a social phenomenon, Merton emphasizes that the impetus toward normative disorientation can be located not only in social crisis, but also within the structure of society itself. As part of the everyday social order, a society offers its members culturally approved aspirations and legitimate means to achieve them. If the mismatch between these two is sufficiently great, however – if the strain of unattained and unattainable aspirations is deeply enough felt – then the social order carries within itself the potential for producing members afflicted by desperation and moral drift. As Merton emphasizes, those so afflicted remain free to choose any number of adaptations to this strain. Among these adaptations are those that can generate various forms of criminality.

See Chapter 2.3 Anomie; Chapter 2.9 General strain theory

Within the history of criminological theory, the most fully developed model of normative uncertainty, drift and crime has come from Gresham Sykes and David Matza (1957). On one level, their model proposes to explain how would-be delinquents manage to **temporarily neutralize** their bonds to a shared moral order, with successful neutralization then leaving them free to drift toward delinquent behaviour. Yet, on another level, Sykes and Matza's model proposes a critical theory of the shared moral order itself. They argue that the seeming solidity and consistency of the collective moral order is illusory; in reality, it is haunted by cultural contradictions, interpretive ambiguity and situational flexibility. In neutralizing their bonds to this ambiguous social order, then, potential delinquents draw on the same moral ambiguities already circulating through social life – ambiguities that operate as shared cultural constructions rather than flawed individual beliefs. For Matza and Sykes (1961; Matza 1964), the social and moral order incorporates its own contradictions – and so, as with Merton, the prerequisites for its own crime and deviance. Like Simmel's strangers and Park's migrants, Sykes and Matza's potential delinquents notice and negate taken-for-granted cultural assumptions, developing along the way a sort of critical exteriority. But, like Merton's strained subjects, theirs is nonetheless an ironic operation in which the social order's own contradictions become the lever for drifting from it.

See Chapter 2.7 Techniques of neutralization

In developing this model, Sykes and Matza were challenging Albert Cohen's theory of subculturally grounded delinquency: if for Cohen, delinquency takes shape and endures within oppositional delinquent subcultures, for Matza and Sykes, it emerges in a more uncertain and episodic manner. Yet, writing as they were at the height of America's post-World War II power and success, with its presumed normative consensus and social stability, Matza and Sykes were also arguing against the validity of this very characterization. Amid this alleged success and stability, they noted, distinctions between moral and immoral, between legal and criminal, were nonetheless fluidly ambiguous – and so drift away from moral constraint was latent in this compromised moral order, awaiting only the neutralizations of the potential delinquent. Then, as now, the structural contradictions promoting drift lurk underneath the shiny surface of society: the everyday uncertainty of dominant ethical claims; the suspicious flexibility of allegedly absolute legal codes; the ongoing violation of supposedly inviolable religious commandments. The potential delinquent does not create these contradictions, Matza and Sykes emphasized, but he/she does notice them and act on them, putting them to use in an attempt to elude, if only episodically, existing social constraints. For Sykes and Matza, then, drift emerges from a cultural milieu of moral ambiguities and subterranean values – and with this drift comes the possibility of crime and delinquency.

Together, the work of Merton, Matza and Sykes begins to suggest an integrated criminological theory of drift. For Matza and Sykes – and for Merton – the normative order of contemporary society is itself anomic, both at the level of the structural and cultural contradictions that Merton charted and within the milieu of everyday moral compromise that Sykes and Matza exposed. Like Merton, Sykes and Matza (1957) speculate that drift away from moral constraint may be more pronounced for those most afflicted by the discrepancy between collective social goals and inadequate means to achieve them; then again, they say, it may be that such drift occurs episodically across the social spectrum. In any case, the gap between goals and activity – the strained relationship between ideals and daily life – produces the possibility of drift into crime and delinquency. Significantly, for Merton as for Sykes and Matza, this drift may lead elsewhere as well; drift is, after all, less a causal equation than an uncertain trajectory that retains aspects of agency and autonomy. But if crime is the result, Sykes, Matza and Merton are clear as to its social and cultural origins.

Taken together with Park and Simmel's approach, then, the work of Merton, Sykes and Matza produces a useful sociology and criminology of drift. Arriving from outside the social order or emerging from inside it, the drifter is both the consequence and the carrier of cultural liminality. A stranger in a strange land, the drifter lives in between – between places past and present, between marginality and belonging, between conventionality and criminality, and within the spaces left open by ambiguity and contradiction. In response to the contemporary crisis in global inequality and migration, Ferrell (2012) has recently revisited this criminology of drift, suggesting that these interstitial spaces are now multiplying, and that drift is now emerging as the defining trajectory of late modern social life. Combining earlier sociological and criminological approaches with more geographic orientations, he has shown how spatial and normative drift intersect and amplify – in part due to contemporary policing strategies that exacerbate drift as they endeavour to control it. He has also explored emerging subcultures and illicit social movements that increasingly embrace drift, and form drifting communities, as strategic resistance to these same global developments.

If the criminological question is the place of the individual inside or outside the legal order, the concept of drift continues to offer some distinctly uncertain and revealing answers.

References

Ferrell, Jeff. 2012. Outline of a criminology of drift. In *New Directions in Criminological Theory*, Steve Hall and Simon Winlow, eds, pp. 241–56. London: Routledge.
Matza, David. 1964. *Delinquency and Drift*. New York: Wiley.
Matza, David, and Gresham Sykes. 1961. Juvenile Delinquency and Subterranean Values. *American Sociological Review* 26(5): 712–19.
Sykes, Gresham, and Matza, David. 1957. Techniques of Neutralization: A Theory of Delinquency. *American Sociological Review* 22(6): 664–70.

Further reading

Debord, Guy. 1958. Theory of the Dérive. www.bopsecrets.org/SI/2.derive.htm. Accessed 23 January 2017.
Durkheim, Émile. 1964 [1893]. *The Division of Labor in Society*. New York: Free Press.
Ferrell, Jeff. 2012. Anarchy, Geography and Drift. *Antipode* 44(5): 1687–704.
Merton, Robert K. 1938. Social Structure and Anomie. *American Sociological Review* 3: 672–82.
Park, Robert. 1928. Human Migration and the Marginal Man. *American Journal of Sociology* 33(6): 881–93.
Simmel, Georg. 1971 [1908]. The stranger. In *Georg Simmel: On Individuality and Social Forms*, Donald Levine, ed., pp. 143–9. Chicago: University of Chicago Press.

3.6 Feminist criminologies

Claire M. Renzetti

Feminism, as both a paradigm to analyse and explain social relations and a social movement to bring about social change, enjoyed a resurgence in the 1960s and 1970s which came to be known as the **'second wave' of feminism** to distinguish it from the feminist movement of the late 1800s and early 1900s. As with much political and social activism of this period, university campuses were important centres for feminist theorizing and activity. Students and academics, especially women, questioned how their disciplines, along with social institutions and social relations more generally, were explicitly or implicitly reproducing gender inequality. In criminology, this introspection and critique led to the development of perspectives that differed in important ways, but all of which are considered feminist and share a set of core principles that include:

See Chapter 3.13
Radical feminism

- Gender is the socially constructed expectations or norms that prescribe attitudes and behaviour for women and men, which are usually dichotomously organized as femininity and masculinity, respectively, and are transmitted and reproduced through socialization.
- Gender is a basic organizational element of social life and social structure, embedded in all social institutions and everyday social interactions; that is, societies and social life are fundamentally gendered.
- Every society has a gender structure that typically functions as a system of social stratification, differentially valuing the traits and behaviours associated with women and men, respectively.
- The gender structure of most societies in the world today is **patriarchal**

See Chapter 4.26
Patriarchy and
crime; Chapter
4.21 Masculinities,
structure and
hegemony

– one in which men dominate women and what is considered masculine is more highly valued than what is considered feminine. This differential valuing is called sexism and manifests as gender discrimination.

■ Criminology, like other academic disciplines, has developed and continues to function within the patriarchal gender structure and, therefore, reflects it by, for example, historically excluding women and girls from most criminological studies and from the field itself.

Beginning in the 1970s, then, feminist criminologists drew attention to gender biases in criminological theories and research, and to widespread sexism in the discipline and in the criminal justice system with regard to offenders and victims, as well as academics, professionals and practitioners. Feminist criminologists have sought to redress this exclusion and discrimination in varied ways, explaining criminal offending and **victimization**, along with institutional responses to these problems, as fundamentally gendered, and emphasizing the importance of influencing public policy to alleviate discrimination and oppression. There is, however, no single, unitary feminist perspective in criminology. There is instead a diversity of feminist criminologies, including liberal feminist criminology, radical feminist criminology and black and multiracial feminist criminology.

See Chapter 4.39 Victimology

One focus of liberal feminist criminologists has been explaining gender differences in criminal offending. For example, emancipation theory maintained that although females historically have committed significantly less crime than males, women's 'liberation' would result in a dramatic increase in female offending because women and girls would be afforded opportunities, both legitimate and illegitimate, previously available only to men (Adler 1975). Although emancipation theory received little empirical support, it did draw more attention to women's offending, and challenged other feminist criminologists to further explore gender differences in offending.

Power-control theory, another liberal feminist perspective, focuses on differential gender socialization to explain differences in male and female offending, and posits that the relative power of fathers and mothers in families (and how this translates into familial decision-making and differential socialization and social control of male and female children) results in variations in rates of male and female juvenile offending (Hagan 1989). Empirical support for this proposition has been equivocal at best, but it has prompted many feminist criminologists to more closely examine family relationships and gendered differences in both criminal offending and victimization.

Liberal feminists, more generally, have lobbied for legislation to outlaw gender discrimination and mandate equal rights for women and men in all areas of social life, e.g. for laws that forbid discrimination in educational institutions that receive government funding or that prohibit discrimination in hiring, benefits and other employment decisions. In the United States, such reforms have contributed to the dramatic increases in female criminology, criminal justice and law students and faculty, as well as increases in the number of women police and corrections officers, lawyers and judges since the 1960s. Although all feminist criminologists appreciate these significant changes, some maintain that legislative strategies alone are insufficient to ensure gender equity – and equity for **racial and ethnic minorities**, the poor, the **LGBTQ community** and other groups that have historically experienced discrimination in criminology and the legal system. For these feminist criminologists, more fundamental changes in the social structure are necessary to produce equity.

See Chapter 4.7
Critical race
theory

See Chapter 4.32
Queer criminology

Radical feminist criminologists begin with the assumption that gender inequality is the most fundamental form of oppression, and that women are the most oppressed social group in virtually any society; men, regardless of social class or race or ethnicity, enjoy gender privilege at the expense of women. Men preserve male dominance and female subordination through control of women's sexuality and the threat or actual use of violence. Pornography, sexual assault, sexual harassment, battering and other forms of gender-based violence all serve to preserve men's power and women's relative powerlessness. Remedying this fundamental inequality requires greater change than simply prohibiting sex discrimination; it requires the destruction of **patriarchy**.

See Chapter 4.26
Patriarchy and
crime

Radical feminist criminologists have focused less on women as offenders and more on women as victims, seeking to understand the causes and consequences of violence against women and the failure of the criminal justice system to protect women from men's violence. This research has demonstrated that perpetration of, and victimization by, violent crime is gendered. Although men are more likely than women to perpetrate violent crime and to be victimized by it, radical feminist criminologists have documented the alarming frequency of violence against women throughout the world, the multitude of forms this takes and the fact that women are most likely to be victimized by someone they know, rather than by a stranger (MacKinnon 1989).

Although the work of radical feminist criminologists has been instrumental in reforming criminal justice practices and developing specialized services with regard to female victims of gender-based violence, this perspective has been criticized for portraying the criminal legal system too simplistically as an instrument of male domination, and for characterizing all men as dominant and oppressive and all women as subordinated and powerless. According to critics, this overlooks the efforts of pro-feminist men and downplays women's agency in resisting victimization; it also gives gender oppression primacy, overlooking or downplaying other forms of oppression. While all men may enjoy gender privilege, many men experience the oppression of other men's race and class privilege. Similarly, not all women are equally at risk of gender-based violence; some women, especially poor women, are significantly more vulnerable.

Both liberal feminism and radical feminism have been criticized for assuming that the experiences of white, middle-class, heterosexual women are the normative standard. Women criminologists of colour have been instrumental in showing how various social locating factors – gender, race, ethnicity, social class, sexuality, age, national origin, physical ability – are structured hierarchically with differential power and privilege attached to each rung of each hierarchy. But these hierarchies do not operate side by side; rather, they overlap and intersect to form a 'matrix of domination' (Collins, 2000). All social actors experience the hierarchies of gender, race, ethnicity, class and so on simultaneously; that is, everyone is gendered, raced, classed, etc. – although in any given situation one or two of these social locations may be more salient than the others. These interlocking inequalities shape individual identities, interactions between individuals and across groups, and access to opportunities, rewards, privileges and power. Consequently, all people experience privilege as well as oppression; no one enjoys total privilege or suffers total oppression.

Black and multiracial feminists have undertaken criminological research that documents how **intersecting inequalities** based on gender, race, class, age and sexuality construct and constrain the life experiences of various groups of women and men, including their experiences as criminal offenders and as crime victims. The greatest contributions of black and multiracial feminist research to the discipline have arguably been in the areas of violent crime and criminal justice processing. Traditionally, for example, criminologists approached the question of how extra-legal factors affect criminal justice processing, such as disparities in the sentencing of offenders, by analysing one variable at a time (e.g., race) while controlling for other variables (e.g., gender). In contrast, black and multiracial feminist criminologists have examined such issues as how racial stereotypes may condition gender stereotypes among judges and juries, resulting in racialized *and* gendered sentencing outcomes. Thus, black and multiracial feminist criminologists challenge their colleagues to move beyond the conceptualization of gender, race and other social locators as simply 'control variables' and understand how these hierarchies of inequality intersect to produce differential opportunities and outcomes for different groups of offenders and victims.

See Chapter 4.20
Intersectionality

Space constraints do not allow for a discussion of the many other **feminist criminological perspectives**, such as **Marxist feminism**, socialist feminism, **left realist feminism** and **postmodern feminism**. Together with the feminist criminological perspectives presented here, these theories have clearly enriched the discipline of criminology and had a significant impact on the criminal legal system. Feminist criminologists are now expanding the conceptualization of intersecting inequalities to include gender experiences of state crimes such as terrorism and human rights violations (Barberet 2014). Although some observers argue that feminist criminologies continue to be marginalized within the discipline, feminist criminologists will undoubtedly continue to refine their theoretical perspectives and broaden the scope of the field.

See Chapter 3.13
Radical feminism

See Chapter 3.9
Marxist
criminologies

See Chapter 3.14
Realism and left
idealism

See Chapter 4.28
Postmodern
and constitutive
criminologies

References

Adler, Freda. 1975. *Sisters in Crime*. New York: McGraw-Hill.
Barberet, Rosemary. 2014. *Women, Crime and Criminal Justice: A Global Inquiry*. London: Routledge.
Collins, Patricia H. 2000. *Black Feminist Thought* (2nd edn). New York: Routledge.

Hagan, John. 1989. *Structural Criminology*. New Brunswick, NJ: Rutgers University Press.

MacKinnon, Catharine A. 1989. *Toward a Feminist Theory of the State*. Cambridge, MA: Harvard University Press.

Further reading

Jones, Nikki. 2010. *Between Good and Ghetto: African American Girls and Inner-City Violence*. New Brunswick, NJ: Rutgers University Press.

Potter, Hillary. 2008. *Battle Cries: Black Women and Intimate Partner Violence*. New York: New York University Press.

Renzetti, Claire M. 2013. *Feminist Criminology*. London: Routledge.

Renzetti, Claire M., Susan L. Miller, and Angela R. Gover (eds). 2013. *Routledge International Handbook of Crime and Gender Studies*. London: Routledge.

Smart, Carol. 1976. *Women, Crime and Criminology*. London: Routledge.

Folk devils

Nachman Ben-Yehuda

Stanley Cohen characterized folk devils as 'visible reminders of what we should not be. The identities of such social types are public property' (1972:10). Folk devils are thus people whose very existence is socially constructed as posing a negative challenge and a grave threat to morality and who, as a result, provoke feelings of fear (as indeed the reference to the devil implies). Folk devils must therefore be easily identifiable and made to be salient in the public sphere and mind. The concept of folk devils is primarily associated with **moral panics** (Cohen 1972; Goode and Ben-Yehuda 2009) and with concepts of **fear**, morality and deviance.

See Chapter 3.10
Moral panic

See Chapter 5.7
Fear of crime

Moral panics refer to a common social phenomenon where an increased interest in and fear of what is described as a moral threat to the well-being and future of a culture is generated. The construction of such a threat typically exaggerates the supposed moral danger, and those who allegedly present the danger are typically described as folk devils. Characteristic issues involving folk devils have been drug use, witchcraft, Satanism, sex trafficking, hit-and-run car accidents, mugging, AIDS, terror and, of course, crime more generally.

Fear – and fear of moral challenges particularly – lies at the heart of the social construction of folk devils. Indeed, the idea that our societies are characterized by a 'culture of fear' has caught the attention of a few scholars. In 1997, Frank Furedi pointed out that members of modern societies are exposed to messages that we live in a chronic situation of being constantly 'at some form of risk'. Furedi interprets this as a reflection of changed values about how to face dangers and situations containing risks. Barry Glassner (1999) concurs, but asks why and how some Americans are so afraid of the wrong things. He provides a long list of the 'things' that are made to provoke such exaggerated fears, including illicit psychoactive substances, road rage and teen moms. Culturally produced exaggerated fears are thus one main cornerstone on which the social construction of folk devils rests.

As Glassner pointed out, the fear of becoming a victim of crime is one of the central pillars of the culture of fear. Literature on the fear of crime is plentiful and growing, both views and research. Criminals tend to be prime candidates for being viewed as folk devils. A distinction needs to be made here between the perception of crime and the fear generated by this perception, on the one hand, and the actual probability of becoming a victim, on the other. While these two do not necessarily match, when one perceives that the probability of becoming a victim is high – regardless of the actual risk – anxiety and fear of crime will be magnified.

An interesting and relevant issue here is what gives people a sense of the magnitude of the risk of being victimized by folk devils? The media – no doubt – play a pivotal role here. Media reports, framing and agenda settings give crime high priority. 'If it bleeds – it leads' is a dictum to which media editors and journalists seem to cling. News reports, choice of words, place of specific items in the news as well as the tone of the reports (the 'music' as some editors like to state) help to crystallize an emotional response to a socially constructed threat of **victimization** perpetrated by folk devils. The media can – and do – emphasize reporting violent crimes (e.g., murder, rape, bodily attacks), in proportional frequencies that generally tend to far exceed those of police reports. This journalistic framing tends to create an impression of saliency of these events, and in many people's mind this saliency 'translates' into frequency – that is, that these violent crimes are common and that victimization is a real and frequent hazard. And, indeed, Robert Reiner titled his 2007 review of the media and crime 'Media Made Criminality'. Almost by definition, folk devils star in these constructions. One interesting and ironic moral twist here is the infrequent reversal construction of some folk devils as heroes (Kooistra 1989). Most prominent here were such figures as Robin Hood, Bonnie and Clyde and Billy the Kid.

That criminals have become popular folk devils is obvious. One main reason is that the behaviour of criminals challenges morality. In fact, one needs to remember that the very definition of what is crime is a political decision by relevant political legislatures and is based on moral considerations – that is, moral legislation. In this context, the social construction of folk devils needs to be viewed as an instrumental social mechanism that can be, and is, used to delineate moral boundaries (Ben-Yehuda 1985) between right and wrong, desirable and undesirable, good and bad. In this sense, and in a more popular parlance, the fear of crime is fear from 'the dark side of the force'.

In the past, powerful social groups were able to construct others – real or imaginary – as folk devils. Such constructions typically meant that folk devils were stigmatized and demonized, and thus their quality of life was severely damaged. In past, less complex cultures, socially constructing folk

See Chapter 4.39
Victimology

devils tended to be a one-way street. Two modern developments changed this. One is that the spread and availability of the new media (e.g., Facebook, blogs, WhatsApp, etc.) have made it much easier to create folk devils and diffuse them in much clearer and faster ways into the public scene. The other is that, as Ben-Yehuda (1990) and McRobbie (1994) have pointed out, in more varied and complex societies, characterized by a multiplicity of cultural cores (Ben-Yehuda 2013), processes of reversed 'deviantization' and stigmatization can be observed – and we can now witness candidates for the position of folk devils fighting back. Moreover, in such complex cultures socially constructing folk devils has become a competition issue among various groups that use their power and concepts of morality to try to bestow folk devil status on 'others'.

Many potential moral and physical threats may exist in our mind as we go about our daily business. Some of these threats are genuine and real, others are pure constructions of our innovative mind, and some are exaggerations of real or imaginary threats. Feelings of being threatened will typically increase levels of concern and anxiety, and some may escalate to the level of a panic reaction. Such reactions need not be expressed by immediate and actual physical action. Not every panic is generated by an imminent physical and concrete threat. Panics can be generated by an idea and reacted to by responses that are not instantaneous. Witch-hunts are a good illustration.

While many illustrations for creating folk devils exist, one of the very best is probably the European witch craze of the fifteenth to the seventeenth centuries (Ben-Yehuda 1985). Up to about the fifteenth century, social attitudes towards practising witchcraft were mixed. Magic could be used for beneficial purposes (e.g., blessing growing agricultural products) or for negative outcomes (e.g., cursing a hated neighbour). Moreover, witches had a powerful position vis-à-vis **supernatural deities**. Controlling spells or using amulets, for example, could actually force deities to do certain things. Towards the end of the fifteenth century, three major transformations took place. One was that witchcraft became identified only with negative outcomes. A demonological theory developed which suggested that God and Satan locked horns in a struggle for controlling the universe, and that witchcraft was a practice used by the devil. Two was that humans became part of the struggle. Three was that because only the devil was capable of satisfying the endless sexual appetite of women, women became the primary target of witch-hunts because witches supposedly exchanged sexual favours from the devil in return for corrupting the world. The result of this abstruse development was that thousands of women were tortured and killed based on suspicions of practising witchcraft in the devil's service. These witch-hunts ended in the seventeenth century. Clearly, the European witch-hunts constructed women as folk devils. The belief in the above-mentioned demonological perception, coupled with the lack of adequate political power of the victims, made the widespread suffering and mass murder of thousands of women a grim reality. More recent illustrations for constructions of folk devils include users of illicit psychoactive

See Chapter 1.1 Religion, spirituality and crime

substances and the persecution of suspected communists during the 'red scare' in the USA or of Jews and others during the Nazi reign of Germany.

References

Ben-Yehuda, Nachman. 1985. *Deviance and Moral Boundaries: Witchcraft, the Occult, Science Fiction, Deviant Sciences and Scientists*. Chicago: University of Chicago Press.

Ben-Yehuda, Nachman. 1990. *The Politics and Morality of Deviance: Moral Panics, Drug Abuse, and Reversed Stigmatization*. Albany: State University of New York Press.

Ben-Yehuda, Nachman. 2013. *Atrocity, Deviance, and Submarine Warfare: Norms and Practices during the World Wars*. Ann Arbor: University of Michigan Press.

Cohen, Stanley. 1972. *Folk Devils and Moral Panics*. London: MacGibbon & Kee.

Furedi, Frank. 1997. *Culture of Fear*. London: Cassell.

Glassner, Barry. 1999. *The Culture of Fear*. New York: Basic Books.

Goode, Erich, and Nachman Ben-Yehuda. 2009. *Moral Panics: The Social Construction of Deviance* (2nd edn). Oxford: Blackwell.

Kooistra, Paul G. 1989. *Criminals as Heroes*. Bowling Green, OH: Bowling Green State University Popular Press.

McRobbie, Angela. 1994. Folk Devils Fight Back. *New Left Review* 203: 107–16.

Reiner, Robert. 2007. Media-made criminality: The representation of crime in the mass media. In *The Oxford Handbook of Criminology*, Mike Maguire, Rod Moran, and Robert Reiner, eds, pp. 302–37. Oxford: Oxford University Press.

Further reading

Carrabine, Eamonn. 2008. *Crime, Culture and the Media*. Cambridge: Polity.

Greer, Chris (ed.). 2010. *Crime and the Media*. London: Routledge.

Potter, Gary W., and Victor E. Kappeler (eds). 2006. *Constructing Crime: Perspectives on Making News and Social Problems*. Prospect Heights, IL: Waveland Press.

Labelling theory

Dale C. Spencer

Labelling theory emerged in the post-World War II period and reached its height of popularity in the 1960s and 1970s. The 'Labelling School,' as it is known by both its advocates and detractors, is concerned with how deviance and crime are created through social processes of definition and rule-generation and interactions between and with individuals and organizations, including agents and agencies of social control (Becker 1963). Whether viewed as a full social theory (see Schur 1971) or a perspective (see Plummer 1979, 2011), labelling theory stresses how processes and reactions to deviant behaviour affect the development of deviant self-concepts among those who transgress the law or a given norm. This is all to say that 'deviance', both in terms of broader definition and self-concept, is an outcome of continuous and dynamic processes of social interaction.

Labelling theory is rooted in **symbolic interactionism** and phenomenology, with George Herbert Mead and Alfred Schutz, respectively, serving as the primary intellectual progenitors. At an ontological level, early labelling theorists rejected the notion that there is an inner core of the self, or that deviance is a characteristic internal to some individuals and not others. At the epistemological level, labelling theory rejected the positivistic nomothetic project, insisting that it is impossible to remain neutral in studying crime and that one must 'take sides', aligning with the value positions of the people being studied (see Becker 1967). Methodologically, ethnographic research of and on outsiders (e.g. Polsky 1969) has been favoured, in order to understand participants in terms of how they experience and make sense of their worlds.

See Chapter 3.18
Symbolic
interactionism

Frank Tannenbaum and Edwin Lemert were key contributors to the development of labelling. Tannenbaum initially suggested the concept of *dramatization of evil* to show how the first label affixed to someone who transgresses a law or norm is particularly salient: tagging and identifying a person as 'criminal' has an impact on his/her consciousness, and will influence the labelled person's future actions. Lemert subsequently presented the concepts of 'primary' and 'secondary deviation'. Primary deviation is a singular act that involves only minor implications for the person's identity, and the corresponding consequences do not lead to a symbolic reorganization of the deviator's way of life. Secondary deviation refers to the deviant behaviour and the social roles assumed by the deviator. That is, the criminalized act sets into motion ongoing processes of defence, attack and/or adaptation by the deviator to the overt and covert problems manifested by the social reaction to primary deviation. Both Tannenbaum and Lemert pointed to the effects of the labelling and to the social reactions to the labels.

The name most commonly associated with labelling is Howard Becker. In a book that took over a decade to complete, *Outsiders: Studies in the Sociology of Deviance* (1963), Becker outlines his position on labelling theory. In relation to *Outsiders*, Becker introduces a number of concepts that have been formative for understanding social problems. One concept that Becker develops is the notion of *master status* (see also, Hughes 1945), which points to how the label of deviance tends to migrate from a single event or cue related to actual, suspected or alleged behaviour to a more general picture of a person. For example, the person may become known as a thief or a paedophile. This interpretive framework also leads to the labelled individual being the subject of what labelling theorists called *retrospective interpretation*, which includes the mechanisms by which reactors come to view deviators or those suspected of deviating from the norm in a completely different way. For example, in terms of someone accused or convicted of a sexual offence, reactors will reinterpret their past interactions with, or what is known of, that person and point to clues that explain this person's sexual offence – and, consequently, confirm that he or she was a sexual deviant all along.

Guided by the work of Erving Goffman, labelling theory has also been concerned with the centrality of stereotyping in terms of its effects on societal understandings of identities and character traits, as well as its impact on deviancy and social control. Stereotyping, in this sense, relates to identity and deviance in two main ways. First, it serves as a facet of mental ordering whereby an individual can reasonably anticipate the actions of others or, at the least, organize his/her disposition to a stereotyped other. In relation to a given deviant identity, mental ordering involves a selective perception of the other, which involves negative imputation, inaccurate assessments and negative social reaction.

See Chapter 3.7 Folk devils; Chapter 3.10 Moral panic
Labelling theory also takes seriously the role of the mass media in contributing to definitions of deviance and drawing the attention of the public to crime. A key concept in this regard is **deviancy amplification**, which

illustrates how minor occurrences of deviant behaviour can be inflated in the mass media, with this amplification provoking imitation from others, thereby creating a mutually reinforcing loop of deviance. This leads to a solidification of deviant identity and **subculture** through reactions to, and repression of, deviant behaviour by manifold agents and agencies. Two dynamic processes are at play in deviancy amplification. First, there is an intensification of the deviancy of the subject through reinforcing and magnifying his/her deviant values. Second, through the shift in the way of life and world of the deviator, the deviant person comes to embody the stereotypical deviant identity. The result of these processes is that media fantasy manufactures reality.

See Chapter 3.17
Subculture

Analytically overlapping with deviancy amplification, labelling theorists utilize the concept of *role engulfment*. This explains the tendency of those labelled to become caught up in the deviant role and take on this deviant identity as an important element in their general personal identity. The person's behaviour then becomes increasingly organized around his/her deviant role, and the cultural expectations related to that role become prioritized over other social expectations and become part of his/her overall way of life. For example, a gang member may become engulfed in his/her role in the gang and that, in turn, will become his/her way of life. Concomitantly, an individual's affiliation with gang subculture works as a defence mechanism in relation to broader society and various agents of control.

Another key concept that is related to labelling is *status degradation ceremonies*. Coined by Harold Garfinkel in the mid-1950s, this concept captures the ongoing communicative work directed towards converting an individual's identity into an identity lower in the relevant group's scheme of social types. Moral indignation and shame are integral to conditions of status degradation, which are contingent on particular times and spaces. While public denunciations can take place outside of the courts, legal proceedings serve as potent degradation ceremonies where the accused are publicly degraded by professional degraders – lawyers and judges – as an occupational practice. Status degradation ceremonies serve to reaffirm public reactions to a given form of deviation and those who transgress formal norms and laws.

Labelling theory has experienced a resurgence in popularity, due in large part to the critical scholarship falling under the rubric of **cultural criminology**. Cultural criminology assumes the anti-essentialism of labelling theory by interrogating the processes related to the formation of deviant labels, and promotes understanding at the level of meaning of criminalized populations. Furthermore, cultural criminology has taken up the **anti-positivist** banner, calling for ethnographic understanding of crime and wrongdoing. While cultural criminology draws on other theoretical perspectives, its reliance on labelling theory reveals the enduring influence of this *oeuvre* in critical criminology.

See Chapter 4.8
Cultural
criminology

See Chapter 1.4
Positivism

John Law and John Urry (2004) have demonstrated how social scientists not only describe the social world, but also enact it. They point to labelling theory as a prime example of such a phenomenon that quickly became current and broadly influential in social and political debates. This has resulted in manifold contemporary consequences: for example, it has played a part in attempts to avoid labelling and stigmatization of the marginalized, critiques of total institutions and broader policies of deinstitutionalization. As a paradigm in criminology, labelling theory serves as a prime example of how criminology can positively influence **public debate**.

See Chapter 4.31
Public criminology

References

Becker, Howard. 1963. *Outsiders: Studies in the Sociology of Deviance*. New York: Free Press.

Becker, Howard. 1967. Whose Side Are We On? *Social Problems* 14(3): 239–47.

Hughes, Everett. 1945. Dilemmas and Contradictions of Status. *American Journal of Sociology* 50(5): 353–9.

Law, John, and John Urry. 2004. Enacting the Social. *Economy and Society* 33(3): 390–410.

Plummer, Ken. 1979. Misunderstanding labelling perspectives. In *Deviant Interpretations*, David Downes and Paul Rock, eds, pp. 85–121. Oxford: Martin Robertson.

Plummer, Ken. 2011. Labelling theory revisited: Forty years on. In *Langweiliges Verbrechen (Boring Crimes)*, Helge Peters and Michael Dellwing, eds, pp. 83–103. Wiesbaden: Springer.

Polsky, Ned. 1969. *Hustlers, Beats, and Others*. New York: Anchor Press.

Schur, Edwin. 1971. *Labeling Deviant Behavior: Its Sociological Implications*. New York: Harper & Row.

Further reading

Becker, Howard (ed.). 1964. *The Other Side: Perspectives on Deviance*. New York: Free Press.

Garfinkel, Harold. 1956. Conditions of Successful Degradation Ceremonies. *American Journal of Sociology* 61(5): 420–24.

Goffman, Erving. 1963. *Stigma: Notes on the Management of Spoiled Identity*. Englewood Cliffs, NJ: Prentice Hall.

Scheff, Thomas. 1975. *Labeling Madness*. Englewood Cliffs, NJ: Prentice Hall.

Schur, Edwin. M. 1969. Reactions to Deviance: A Critical Assessment. *American Journal of Sociology* 75(3): 309–23.

Marxist criminologies

John Lea

Karl Marx and Friedrich Engels produced no general criminology. They saw crime neither as 'the mere violation of right and law' (Marx and Engels 1845:358) nor as an epiphenomenon lacking 'ontological reality' (Hulsman 1986), but as the concretization of specific configurations of conflicts arising from capitalist development. Marx's famous discussion of the criminalization, by the Rhineland parliament, of popular wood-gathering rights, deconstructs crime as a class struggle between the aspirant Rhineland bourgeoisie seeking extension of capitalist relations to the forests and a peasantry defending customary rights to gather fallen wood. Marx also wrote about the dispossession of the rural masses from the land and their criminalization as beggars and vagabonds (1867: 915) as part of the long period of 'primitive accumulation' (the accumulation of wealth which later functions as capital) from the medieval period towards the eighteenth century. Engels, meanwhile, produced well-known graphic portrayals of crime as the expression of poverty and desperation during the early stages of English industrial capitalism (Engels 1845).

What holds all these disparate accounts together is not a 'Marxist criminology' devoted to the study of crime as a singular phenomenon, but the location of the particular types and dynamics of crime and criminalization in the process of capitalist development. Thus, while it is an exaggeration to say that 'crime and deviance vanish into the general theoretical concerns and the specific scientific object of Marxism' (Hirst 1975:204), attempts to produce a 'Marxist criminology' usually remain at the level of rather abstract generalizations such as the operation of criminal justice (usually) in the interests of the ruling class, or crime as driven (for the poor) by despair or (for the wealthy) by an excess of greed. It is more accurate to speak of Marxist *criminologies* rather than a single criminology – a 'criminologically sensitive Marxism' in which specific types of criminalization in particular historical situations are to be related to the overall development of capitalism as a system of exploitation.

Marxist social theory is currently undergoing renewal in the context of the intensifying global economic and social crisis. A focus on the role played by crime and criminalization in that crisis is important. The initial task is that of mapping out the stages of capitalist development in terms of the different varieties of criminality that appear as a feature of each period.

The first, long pre-capitalist period of 'primitive accumulation' is the context for Marx's brief mention of medieval criminalization of the poor. This theme inspired Chambliss's (1960) study of English and US vagrancy laws, while Marx's Rhineland discussion inspired studies of eighteenth-century 'social crime' as resistance by the poor to advancing capitalist market society (Hay et al. 1975). These features – and some of their associated forms of criminality – continue well into the present period, especially at the **imperialist periphery** of capitalist development in the **global south**.

A second period begins with the early stages of industrial capitalism. Marx's work on alienation (loss of control by the working class of its own labour and the product thereof) complemented Engels' (1845) acute observations of urban criminality of the poor (theft and interpersonal – including family – violence) as a response to powerlessness, dehumanization and poverty. Engels' themes inspired the Dutch criminologist Willem Bonger (1905), who stressed the criminogenic effects of **anomie**, egoism and lack of social support. This theme was further developed by more recent Marxist-inspired criminologists who have linked criminality to the denial of recognition (to the poor) in capitalist society, and is relevant to understanding structural youth unemployment and the 'precariatization' of work.

The next period (in Europe) – from the later nineteenth century culminating in the welfare state, and including two world wars – is one of capitalist stabilization. The state assumes the role of 'general capitalist', acting even against the interests of individual capitals and making concessions to organized labour to stabilize the system as a whole while at the same time protecting imperialist plunder. There are two important developments regarding crime. First, the state begins to respond to **corporate crime**. With the rise of joint stock as the basis of capital formation, the need to protect investors from fraud becomes important. The struggle to 'humanize' the bourgeoisie itself and to criminalize especially banking fraud is never successful and leads to constant retaliation from powerful sections of capital and from the need to support national sections of capital against foreign competitors in imperial expansion. This contradiction is highlighted in the present financial crisis. Second, the stabilization of the working-class community leaves most urban 'street' criminality – and much traditional organized crime – moving towards a weakened, peripheral deviance to be rehabilitated as productive labour. The welfare state

See Chapter 4.27
Postcolonial
criminology

See Chapter 4.34
Southern theory

See Chapter 2.3
Anomie; Chapter
2.8 Market society
and crime

See Chapter 4.5
Corporate crime;
Chapter 4.37 State-
corporate crime

marks the period of maximum plausibility for orthodox criminologies and rehabilitative penal welfare.

This brings us to the present period of gathering social and economic crisis that in many ways evokes a return to the earlier nineteenth century. Characteristics include: global social inequality; the precariatization of labour and marginalization of the poor; and the destruction of urban infrastructures and of natural environments in the interests of capitalist profit. Migration, pollution and war combine with weak state organization in many areas of the global south, while industrialized states shift away from welfare, class compromise and the regulation of some aspects of capital, towards neoliberalism, security and protection for elites.

The politics of criminalization is an important element of this crisis. The financial crash of 2008 revealed widespread fraud by leading banks and corporations, yet little by way of prosecution by states. In a similar manner, the merging of legal and illegal enterprise processes – as evidenced in drug-trafficking as a capital source for legitimate business, bribery by arms traders, alliances between mining corporations and warlord and terrorist regimes in the global south – all point to the search for 'innovatory' cost-reduction methods to overcome falling profit rates. Similar considerations apply to the increasingly blurred distinction between crime, war and political action as leading states come to justify execution (by drone) without trial of 'terrorists' and illegal mass surveillance in the name of security while periodically joining cyber-criminals in hacking attacks on other states.

A similar blurring process is under way at the level of street crime. Falls in theft and burglary due to technological crime prevention are increasingly compensated by rising interpersonal violence and gang organization with links to drug-trafficking. Meanwhile, neoliberal post-welfare states are returning to older notions of the poor as a 'dangerous class' through strategies amounting to criminalization of the poor as a whole – as welfare recipients, unemployed, homeless. Crime control blurs into the general management of the poor through workfare, surveillance and the increasing de facto criminalization of poverty and a growing population surplus to the needs of capital accumulation. Most radical criminologists, irrespective of whether they identify as Marxists, would agree the need to relate these developments in crime and its control to the dynamics of capitalist development.

What Marxism provides, therefore, is not 'yet another criminological theory'. Rather, many aspects of Marxist theory can be deployed to provide a context: an account of the historical processes and social antagonisms in terms of which conflicts over crime and criminalization can be understood. This is always the outcome of particular concrete situations, but related ultimately, or 'in the last instance', to the requirements of the profitability of capital and the management of the social crises produced when it falters.

See Chapter 4.16 Green criminology; Chapter 4.3 Conservation criminology; Chapter 4.11 Environmental justice and victimology

See Chapter 4.19 Institutional and anti-institutional violence

See Chapter 5.17 Security and counter-security; Chapter 5.19 Surveillance

See Chapter 6.2 Community safety

See Chapter 4.24 Neoliberalism

References

Bonger, Willem. 1905/1969. *Criminality and Economic Conditions*. Bloomington: Indiana University Press.

Chambliss, William. 1960. A Sociological Analysis of the Law of Vagrancy. *Social Problems* 12(1): 67–77.

Engels, Friedrich. 1845/1975. The condition of the working class in England. In Karl Marx and Frederick Engels, *Collected Works*, Vol. 4. London: Lawrence & Wishart.

Hay, Douglas, Peter Linebaugh, John Rule, E.P. [Edward Palmer] Thompson, and Cal Winslow. 1975. *Albion's Fatal Tree: Crime and Society in Eighteenth Century England*. London: Allen Lane.

Hirst, Paul. 1975. Marx and Engels on law, crime and morality. In *Critical Criminology*, Ian Taylor, Paul Walton, and Jock Young, eds, pp. 203–32. London: Routledge & Kegan Paul.

Hulsman, Louk. 1986. Critical Criminology and the Concept of Crime. In *Abolitionism: Towards a Non-Repressive Approach to Crime*, Herman Bianchi and René van Swaaningen, eds, pp. 25ff. Amsterdam: Free University Press.

Marx, Karl. 1867/1976. *Capital: A Critique of Political Economy*, Vol. 1. Harmondsworth: Penguin.

Marx, Karl, and Friedrich Engels. 1845/1965. *The German Ideology*. London: Lawrence & Wishart.

Further reading

Chambliss, William, and Milton Mankoff (eds). 1976. *Whose Law? What Order? A Conflict Approach to Criminology*. New York: Wiley.

Cowling Mark. 2008. *Marxism and Criminological Theory: A Critique and a Toolkit*. Basingstoke: Palgrave Macmillan.

Lea, John. 2002. *Crime and Modernity*. London: Sage.

Lea, John. 2010. Karl Marx (1818–83) (and Frederick Engels (1820–95)). In *Fifty Key Thinkers in Criminology*, Keith Hayward, Shadd Maruna, and Jayne Mooney, eds, pp. 18–24. Abingdon: Routledge.

O'Malley, Pat. 1987. Marxist Theory and Marxist Criminology. *Crime and Social Justice* 29: 70–87.

Quinney, Richard. 1977. *Class, State, and Crime*. New York: David McKay.

Moral panic

Erich Goode

Humans have always felt, expressed and acted upon misplaced or exaggerated feelings of anxiety, fear, preoccupation or resentment that certain minor or non-existent agents threaten to undermine their well-being, way of life or their very existence. But from time to time, typically as a result of the conjunction of unusually difficult circumstances or sudden social change, a substantial number of the members of many societies become *intensely* concerned about a specific putative threat; they accuse certain agents of causing their suffering, and scapegoat or punish them to eliminate the presumed source of the trouble and, with it, their own fears and concerns. In other words, people virtually everywhere have made mountains out of molehills; invented enemies who have done no, or relatively little, wrong; told cautionary tales to warn listeners about the supposed wrongdoing and potential harm; and spoken against, chastised and/or criminalized the actions of the supposed wrongdoers. The content of these charges has varied from one society to another and throughout time, but the *mechanism* of making accusations – socially constructing the role of the evildoer, getting emotionally riled about imagined persecutions or minor offences or harms, and sanctioning the appropriate offenders – is a pan-historic, universal process. Many of these panics have resulted in new criminal legislation or in stricter enforcement of existing legislation; hence, the 'moral panic' represents a topic of interest to criminologists.

For at least a century and a half, several authors have independently used the precise words, 'moral panic', to indicate just such a process. For instance, in a work on revolution published in 1869, one Edgar Quinet fashioned the term, but it possessed no analytic traction and produced no intellectual progeny.

See Chapter 5.7
Fear of crime

What the earliest commentators did *not* do was construct a conceptual and theoretical argument explaining *why* the moral panic is significant and how it is linked to the sociologist's and criminologist's theoretical and empirical concerns. In contrast, Jock Young (1971) and Stanley Cohen (1972) not only used the appellation but also explained why such outbreaks occur, what conditions encourage them and how they are linked to the social structure. Moreover, their writings stimulated commentary and research on the moral panic that has been continuous since they launched it, and remains vigorous to this day. The name and the concept of moral panic have been assimilated by the popular press, and have entered the vocabulary of the general public.

A moral panic is *an outbreak or occurrence of a scare or intense concern about a threat or putative threat by agents, deviants, or 'folk devils', who, as a result of their supposed wrongdoing, are said to be responsible for menacing a society's culture, way of life, security, or central values*. To qualify as a panic, this concern must be expressed, manifested or conveyed in behaviour, including speech acts, and the accusations expressed in that concern must be *disproportional* to the objective harm or potential harm of the threat. Claims made by moral panic actors include inventing harmful actions; pointing fingers at agents supposedly responsible for the harm; and exaggerating the extent of the harm caused, the number of its victims, the monetary damage and the inevitability of harm inflicted by the action, as well as misattributing cause-and-effect sequences between putative agents and the harm they inflict and the absence of evidence supporting claims of harm. During moral panics, audiences are *sensitized* to any and all harms that stipulated deviants or **folk devils** might cause, and seize upon even flimsy evidence to support such claims (Goode and Ben-Yehuda 2009:22, 25, 28, 138). And, as its title indicates, moral panics are about *moral* issues – matters of right and wrong, good and bad, righteousness and immorality.

See Chapter 3.7
Folk devils

Fear or concern need not grip the entire society to qualify as a moral panic. Micro- and meso-panics (small and medium-sized ones) – those that overtake and are acted upon by specific communities or by particular social sectors – also qualify as panics. It is unlikely that a sufficiently large sector of the public considers a threat so plausible, and so monstrous, that it generates substantial concern among a majority. Hence, when we investigate panics or scares, we have to ask ourselves: '*Who* fears the putative threat?' '*Who* is concerned about it?' 'What categories or social circles of the society react to it?' Instead, panics may break out in some communities but not others; in certain collectivities but not among people of all categories or sectors. Only a very few panics seize hold of the society at large; typically, we can localize intense concern to identifiable social groupings or circles, or to particular communities or locales. But *to* those affected sectors, communities, circles or collectivities, the threat constitutes an importunate and immediate danger about which something has to be done. In the designated collectivities, such exaggerated concerns *are* moral panics, albeit not macro ones.

Moral panics tend to be transitory. A particular threat erupts, grows in intensity and magnitude, then declines in strength, and may even evaporate altogether. This time span, arc or trajectory may take a few months or a few years, but a defining element of moral panics is their volatility. A few panics leave a more or less lasting legacy, however, in the form of attitudes, traditions, habits, legislation, police practices, perhaps a vocabulary. But most moral panics disappear without a trace, or become absorbed into more generic concerns.

The moral panic is expressed and conveyed by one or more identifiable sets of actors, audiences or 'stations': the *media*, the population at large or *general public*, *action groups* or social movement organizations, *politicians and legislators* and/or *law enforcement*. Each of these sets of actors or stations expresses concern in its own way:

- the media by publishing or broadcasting stories about a given issue and slanting these stories in a certain way;
- the public at large through expressing their views in opinion polls, by voting and by discussing the matter with one another;
- social-movement organizations whose membership mobilizes, rallies, protests, marches, lobbies, raises money for the cause, recruits new members, petitions and so on;
- politicians and legislators by proposing and sometimes passing laws; and
- the police and judges by strengthening ties with one another, increasing the intensity of surveillance and zealousness against violators, harassing suspects, violating their civil rights and liberties and/or convicting them on less than compelling evidence.

The concept of the moral panic has proven to be a huge academic success. Ben-Yehuda and Goode (2013:33) demonstrated that the number of references to works with 'moral panic' and 'moral panics' in their titles, as measured by seven separate citation counts, increased multiple times with each succeeding decade from the 1970s to 2000–09. Given this trend, it seems likely that the total citation count during the second decade of the 2000s will tell the same story. According to Jason Ditton (2007), the moral panic 'has been far and away the most influential sociological concept to have been generated in the second half of the twentieth century'. Young's and Cohen's work initiated an era of looking at the dynamics of defining social problems, creating and constructing categories of deviance, and passing and enforcing the criminal law in an original way. In the words of Chas Critcher (2003:10): 'A whole new social problem had been defined' by the moral panic. By the 1970s, the moral panic was an idea whose time had come. Jock Young and Stanley Cohen planted the seed of intellectual promise, and it has grown into a fine and sturdy tree indeed.

References

Cohen, Stanley. 1972. *Folk Devils and Moral Panics: The Creation of the Mods and Rockers*. London: MacGibbon & Kee.

Critcher, Chas. 2003. *Moral Panics and the Media*. Buckingham, UK: Open University Press.

Ditton, Jason. 2007. Folk Panics and Moral Devils. Unpublished paper.

Goode, Erich, and Nachman Ben-Yehuda. 2009. *Moral Panics: The Social Construction of Deviance* (2nd edn). Malden, MA and Oxford: Wiley-Blackwell.

Goode, Erich, and Nachman Ben-Yehuda. 2013. The genealogy and trajectory of the moral panic concept. In *The Ashgate Research Companion to Moral Panics*, Charles Krinsky, ed., pp. 23–35. Burlington, VT and Farnham, UK: Ashgate.

Young, Jock. 1971. The role of the police as amplifiers of deviancy, negotiators of reality and translators of fantasy: Some consequences of our present system of drug control as seen in Notting Hill. In *Images of Deviance*, Stanley Cohen, ed., pp. 27–61. Harmondsworth, UK: Penguin.

Further reading

Cohen, Stanley. 2002. Moral panics as cultural politics: introduction to the third edition. In Stanley Cohen, *Folk Devils and Moral Panics* (3rd edn). London and New York: Routledge, pp. vii–xxxvii.

Critcher, Chas, Jason Hughes, Julian Petley, and Amanda Rohloff (eds). 2013. *Moral Panics in the Contemporary World*. London: Bloomsbury.

de Young, Mary. 2004. *The Day Care Ritual Abuse Moral Panic*. Jefferson, NC: McFarland.

Hadju, David. 2008. *The Ten-Cent Plague: The Great Comic Book Scare and How It Changed America*. New York: Farrar, Straus, & Giroux.

Macek, Steve. 2006. *Urban Nightmares: The Media, the Right, and the Moral Panic over the City*. Minneapolis: University of Minnesota Press.

Morgan, George, and Scott Poynting (eds). 2012. *Global Islamophobia: Muslims and Moral Panic in the West*. Farnham, UK and Burlington, VT: Ashgate.

Newsmaking criminology

Gregg Barak

Newsmaking criminology is fundamentally about criminologists actively engaging in the narrative framing and reframing of ideas about crime and justice. These frames – cognitive and cultural, for example – may be as different as those associated with 'habitual criminals,' 'zero tolerance' or the 'war on terror', and each represents a conceptual narrative device that academicians, politicians and policymakers use to move their ideas forward in the world of crime and crime control. Compared to other practitioners, politicians or pundits, newsmaking criminologists are armed with an understanding of the workings of mediated culture as well as with a history of crime and the administration of justice as these, for example, interact in real time with the changing dynamics of class, race and sexuality.

Newsmaking criminology appreciates that 'courts of public opinion' increasingly tell stories of crime and justice victimization through social media, such as Black Lives Matter – the activist movement working toward law enforcement and criminal justice reform that arose in the US following the shooting of African-American teen Trayvon Martin by George Zimmerman, whom a jury acquitted of all criminal charges in 2013. Catalysed by social media, this movement has picked up momentum with subsequent killings of several unarmed African-Americans who have died at the hands of law enforcement in 2014. Newsmaking criminologists simultaneously report on, contextualize, interpret and tell their own stories as well as assessing the

See Chapter 5.17
Security and
counter-security

See Chapter 4.7
Critical race
theory

See Chapter 3.3
Critical
criminologies;
Chapter 3.6
Feminist
criminologies;
Chapter 3.9
Marxist
criminologies;
Chapter 3.13
Radical feminism;
Chapter 4.26
Patriarchy and
crime

See Chapter 4.33
Social harm/
zemiology

criminality (or not) of the actions and inactions taken by means of both substantive law and procedural justice as well as by 'analogous social injury'. Thus, newsmaking criminologists may be in a better position than other criminologists and other newsmaking commentators, or the public at large, to engage the dominant narratives of crime and justice circulating in both public and private spaces. Accordingly, newsmaking criminologists may be regarded as engaging in ongoing struggles to demystify and reconstruct the prevailing beliefs, images and representations of crime and justice for academic, private and public consumption. Indeed, as an applied area of criminological practice, newsmaking criminologists use a Gramscian approach to hegemony and class struggle (Barak 1988).

See Chapter 4.31
Public criminology

The roots of newsmaking criminology may be traced back to what Gouldner (1976:34) described as doing 'newspaper sociology' or participating in the **public** sphere. Two decades later, Barak (2006:268) defined newsmaking criminology as those 'processes whereby criminologists use mass communication for the purposes of interpreting, informing, and altering the images of crime and justice, crime and punishment, and criminals and victims'. Today, the concept of newsmaking criminology as a mode of intervening in criminological, legal and public discourse involves not only the older print, radio and television media, but also the still-evolving forms of social media, such as those used by the Black Lives movement described above – from Facebook to Twitter, to streaming live video recorded from mobile devices. To offer another example, feminists use blogs, Tumblr and Twitter feeds to provide alternative narratives that have the potential to move beyond the hegemonic discourses of mainstream media. These forms of feminist discourse may also resist the backlash effects of 'manist,' misogynous or anti-feminist blogs and Twitter accounts more generally (Hasinoff 2015).

See Chapter 4.28
Postmodern
and constitutive
criminologies

From a **constitutive approach to crime and justice**, Henry (1994:288) views newsmaking criminology as a habitual practice of 'replacement discourse' and newsmaking criminologists as 'actively challenging silences, identifying omissions, and . . . resurrecting the eliminated through participating in the making of news stories about crime'. Methodologically, Henry has identified four basic styles of doing newsmaking criminology. These include: (1) disputing data: the criminologist as expert; (2) challenging journalism: the criminologist as journalist; (3) self-reporting: the criminologist as subject; and (4) confronting media: the criminologist as educative provocateur.

The practice of newsmaking criminology requires both the empirical examination of crime and justice discursive representations through newsmaking and/or entertaining processes, as well as engagement in producing and distributing alternative representations of crime and justice. These activities are demanding and, since the mid-1980s, only a relatively small number of criminologists in several countries scattered around the world have practised newsmaking criminology. The contemporary relevance and importance of newsmaking criminology as a praxis, however, is underscored further by the continued absence of criminologists as public intellectuals, and by the social reality that whenever issues of crime and justice break out into public discussions, especially in the United States, the criminological voices of expertise are generally absent from the mass-mediated discursive and narrative constructions of crime and justice. Those criminologists who use any or all of the styles of newsmaking, and who consciously intervene at the intersections of criminal science, policymaking and media discourse, do so by engaging in a variety of media and as a means of participating in the production and distribution of newsworthy and/or entertainment-worthy criminology. These interventions can happen wherever offline territories and/or online virtual landscapes delving into law, power and justice converge in the mediation of everyday social and hyper-reality – the latter consisting of crime and justice techno-cultural simulations that actually blur the boundaries between fiction and non-fiction, as well as between factual myths and social realities.

Perhaps more importantly, whether hegemonic narratives are about **Wall Street looting**, police shootings of unarmed marginal males, or gender or ethnic asymmetry in domestic and street violence, most of these stories are decontextualized and are indifferent to structures of power, inequality and hierarchy. Accordingly, unless newsmaking criminologists are conscious of the dominant narratives and are prepared to challenge these regimes of truth – by bringing contexts of power back into the discussion and by moving the public discourse beyond often simplistic binary confrontations – there is always the danger or risk that these criminologists will end up conforming to and becoming fodder for 'infotainment' criminology (Buckingham 2004).

See Chapter 4.5 Corporate crime; Chapter 4.12 Financial crime

Newsmaking criminology is also sensitive to the discipline's absence of widespread or serious study of the **crimes of the powerful**: namely, those harms and injuries emanating not only from governmental and corporate suites, but also from the more fundamental crimes of the economy attributed to capital accumulation, exploitation and reproduction. From this perspective, newsmaking criminology not only seeks to discover the scientific truth and distinguish fact from fiction, but also endeavours to pursue agenda-setting or claimsmaking of its own. In this sense, newsmaking criminology represents a form of objective activism that enters the private, public and professional frays as exercises in better framing of complex social realities and policymaking. To engage in this type of academic research and social intervention is to knowingly aim at narrowing the rather large gap between public as well as professional perceptions and the best available scientific evidence, on the one hand, and at demystifying and reframing the mass representations of the dominant modes and tropes of crime and criminal justice that surround the production and distribution of both news and entertainment, on the other hand.

See Chapter 4.37 State-corporate crime

References

Barak, Gregg. 1988. Newsmaking Criminology: Reflections on the Media, Intellectuals, and Crime. *Justice Quarterly* 5(4), 565–87.

Barak, Gregg. 2006. Newsmaking criminology. In *The Sage Dictionary of Criminology*, Eugene McLaughlin and John Muncie, eds, p. 269. Thousand Oaks, CA: Sage.

Buckingham, Judith. 2004. 'Newsmaking' Criminology or 'Infotainment' Criminology? *Australian and New Zealand Journal of Criminology* 37(2), 253–75.

Gouldner, Alvin. 1976. *The Dialectics of Ideology and Technology: The Origins, Grammar, and Future of Ideology*. New York: Seabury.

Hasinoff, Amy. 2015. *Sexting Panic: Rethinking Criminalization, Privacy, and Consent.* Urbana: University of Illinois Press.

Henry, Stuart. 1994. Newsmaking criminology as replacement discourse. In *Media, Process, and the Social Construction of Crime: Studies in Newsmaking Criminology*, Gregg Barak, ed., pp. 287–318. New York and London: Garland.

Further reading

Barak, Gregg. 2007. Doing Newsmaking Criminology from within the Academy. *Theoretical Criminology* 11(2): 191–207.

Shelton, Donald, Young Kim, and Gregg Barak. 2006. A Study of Juror Expectations and Demands Concerning Scientific Evidence: Does the 'CSI Effect' Exist? *Vanderbilt Journal of Entertainment and Technology Law* 9(2): 331–68.

Shelton, Donald, Young Kim, and Gregg Barak. 2009. An Indirect-Effects Model of Mediated Adjudication: The *CSI* Myth, the Tech Effect, and Metropolitan Jurors' Expectations for Scientific Evidence. *Vanderbilt Journal of Entertainment and Technology Law* 12(1): 1–43.

Stevens, Dennis. 2010. *Media and Criminal Justice: The CSI Effect*. Burlington, MA: Jones & Bartlett.

Zeppa, Carolyn, and Gregg Barak. 2015. Theft of a Nation: Show Bible and Pilot Script. A one-hour serial drama on the financial crimes of the powerful. Registered by the Writers Guild of America, 22 March.

Peacemaking in criminology

Hal Pepinsky

'Peacemaking' first became recognized in criminology through the work of Fuller (1988) and Pepinsky and Quinney (1991). It emerged as a traditional practice of **indigenous peoples** around the world, as in Navajo peacemaking courts in the US; in 'conferencing' in New Zealand and Australia, which built on Maori and Australian aboriginal traditions; and around the world in programmes emanating from indigenous and religious traditions which came to be described as **'restorative justice'**, which includes **victim–offender mediation** or reconciliation. Peacemaking has been extended to working with prisoners and guards (Braswell et al. 2008), and may also draw upon religious/spiritual inspiration.

See Chapter 4.18
Indigenous
criminology

See Chapter 5.15
Restorative justice

See Chapter 4.39
Victimology

Structurally, in all religious and spiritual traditions, peacemaking is seen as facing and coming to terms with others and/or with problems in 'circles'. 'Peacemaking circles' are an indigenously inspired formal way of airing and attempting to resolve all manner of violent disruptions of human relations, including but not limited to those that might otherwise be prosecuted as crimes. In circle processes, people take uninterrupted turns saying what they think needs to be said, often by passing a 'talking' piece or stick from one speaker to the next, until everything everyone feels the need to say has been said, commonly ending in a formal understanding or agreement as to who will do what next.

The circle represents a form of human interaction where no one exercises more power over others than anyone else, and where all participants' concerns are weighed and accommodated equally, as in the process of handling international disputes. Fisher and colleagues (2011) refer to this as 'getting to yes', and describe such interactions as moving from positions to interests – what in legal parlance is often referred to as 'mediation'.

Proponents of peacemaking argue that violence among humans and with the habitat they share is like the waste and contamination created by straightening and dredging a meandering, well-fed river (Pepinsky 1991). With an adequate water source, rivers normally shift course back and forth, and as they do so they deposit silt (including the filtering out of waste solids before they accumulate), control flooding and support a variety of plants and animals from midstream to their banks. When we straighten and dredge a river to facilitate commerce, life within the river dies and toxins accumulate. Proponents of peacemaking consider this to be the very way we approach people we treat as 'criminals': because of a course of action they have taken, we try to straighten them out, whether for their own good as rehabilitation or to make them do as we tell them. Ironically, our determination to stop and change each other amounts to using violence to 'solve' the 'crime' problem of people getting what they want regardless of the threat and harm it does to others. The way we brand and treat 'offenders' reflects the culture of violent responses to violence at large, implicit in the notion of 'giving consequences' or 'holding' people 'accountable' or 'responsible' for misdeeds, which manifests itself most pervasively in adult guardians' relations with children. In criminology and criminal justice, as in all our relations, peacemaking is the applied study of how to break these cycles of violence.

Peacemaking postulates that, as we experience and understand how it works and how it feels to build trust, peacemaking at one level of our experience may be generalized to noticing, imagining and finding ways of making peace elsewhere in our lives – by analogy, via empathy. Peacemaking entails offering a safe space in which fear, loss, anger and regret can be safely, honestly and openly expressed and heard. In our open and trustworthy relationships, this is a normal and regular way in which people's moments of hurting and being hurt by one another get resolved as relations change course. Violence becomes a problem as parties to interaction become fixated on reaching an objective regardless of adverse effect on or resistance by others, and become fixated on staying on course. Often, however, the trauma caused by violence cannot be resolved among parties involved, either because they are passing strangers or because victims have escaped the violence by leaving violent relationships. In these cases, even where violence has been prolonged and extreme, as in sexual sadism, the trauma can be relieved by those who hear their suffering, believe the violence is real and offer victims a feeling of safety, belonging and understanding. This enables traumatized victims to become healed survivors.

In all cases at all levels of chronic or acute resistance to violence that entail counter-resistance, or attempts to restore order as in reaction to crime, peacemaking (as in diplomacy) focuses on balancing the opportunity for all involved to have turns to speak and to listen without interruption – literally to balance the opportunity to be heard and to hear, and, as in victim–offender mediation, without name-calling. As a fellow mediator once remarked, if you 'trust the process', given time and safe space, people generally come to their own terms, replacing distrust and anger with feelings of safety and mutual control (see Pepinsky 1991:143–92).

What applies to making peace with those we define as criminals and those we blame for it or suspect of it, as in formal mediation or circle settings, applies to making peace informally: enabling those hurt by the exercise of power over them to be heard safely, with the opportunity for those who are blamed to respond without retaliating (as by using confessions or admissions to justify 'consequences'). In religious and spiritual traditions, the underlying transformative force – the human magnetism – is commonly known as 'love' or 'compassion'. The requirements are space and place in conflicts which involve ourselves; to transcend establishing who commands and who obeys social order; to sort out differences as peers – all of which may be learned and practised in the face of conflict in any of our relations.

The most culturally entrenched violence is found in establishing and maintaining social order by asserting that adults should be in charge of children. This is reflected in the common wisdom of criminologists and criminal justice and mental health practitioners that **adolescent, underclass men** are particularly prone to 'crime' and interpersonal violence. At one end of the spectrum of violence, survivors of chronic, severe sexual assault and terror reflect the fact that adults may not know better than children what love and mutual learning require. From any position of power and authority over others, the faith that drives peacemaking remains agnostic to who has more to learn from whom about what is to be feared and what to do about it. In moments of conflict, the will to balance discourse over conflict transcends the power to command and duty to obey.

See Chapter 4.21
Masculinities,
structure and
hegemony

Systematic differences in levels of violence and propensity to make peace can sometimes be seen across political cultures. For instance, incarceration rates are at world-record levels in the United States, and remarkably low in Norway. Correspondingly, at dinner parties in the United States, children are commonly seated by themselves apart from adults, while in Norway children are typically seated with adults, who make a point of involving children in dinner-table conversation. In primary school, students in the United States address teachers by last name (family name) and title (Ms, Mrs, Mr), while Norwegian schoolchildren are on a first-name basis with their teachers. In academic seminars in the United States, participants are generally invited to ask 'questions', and discussion is often dominated by senior or male participants, while in Norway facilitators ask for 'comments' and take note of those who signal a desire to speak, to ensure that all participants have an equal opportunity to speak. In the United States, directors on corporate boards are typically those experienced in management, while by law in Norway, corporate boards are half comprised of workers' representatives.

In sum, the study and practice of peacemaking treats violence in all our relations as an imbalance in who defines the issues and the response; the deeply rooted structural imbalance in what we define as crime and whom we treat as offenders is a case in point.

References

Braswell, Michael, John Fuller, and Bo Lozoff. 2008. *Corrections, Peacemaking, and Restorative Justice*. Cincinnati: Anderson Publishing.

Fisher, Roger, William Ury, and Bruce Patton. 2011. *Getting to Yes: Negotiating Agreement without Giving In* (3rd edn). New York: Penguin.

Fuller, John, 1988. *Criminal Justice: A Peacemaking Perspective*. Boston: Allyn & Bacon.

Pepinsky, Hal. 1991. *Peacemaking: Reflections of a Radical Criminologist*. Bloomington: Indiana University Press.

Pepinsky, Hal, and Richard Quinney. 1991. *Criminology as Peacemaking*. Bloomington: Indiana University Press.

Further reading

Boyes-Watson, Carolyn. 2008. *Peacemaking Circles and Urban Youth: Bringing Justice Home*. St. Paul, MN: Living Press.

Consedine, Jim. 1999. *Restorative Justice: Healing the Effects of Crime*. Lyttleton, NZ: Ploughshares Press.

McClanahan, Bill, and Avi Brisman. 2015. Climate Change and Peacemaking Criminology: Ecophilosophy, Peace and Security in the 'War on Climate Change'. *Critical Criminology* 23(4): 417-31.

Pranis, Kay. 2005. *The Little Book of Circle Processes: A Newfold Approach to Peacemaking*. New York: Good Books.

Pranis, Kay. 2008. *Peacemaking Circles: From Crime to Community*. St. Paul, MN: Living Press.

Yazzie, Robert, and James W. Zion. 1996. Navajo restorative justice: the equality of law and justice. In *Restorative Justice: International Perspectives*, Burt Galaway and Joe Hudson, eds, pp. 157–73. Monsey, NY: Criminal Justice Press.

Radical feminism

3.13

Kerry Carrington

There has never been a unified **feminist** approach to researching gender and crime (Gelsthorpe 1990:90), as the contribution by Claire Renzetti in this companion well illustrates. Critical of early liberal feminist attempts to add women to criminology, radical feminist analysis argued that the discipline was beyond redemption, questioning the key concepts, methods of inquiry and claims to neutrality of criminology. This theoretically informed body of feminist scholarship rejected the **positivist** research methods that had dominated mainstream criminology, and encouraged the outright rejection of criminology's core disciplinary assumptions that were based on the observations of men (Cain 1990; Naffine 1997). The distinguishing features of radical feminist engagement with criminology can be summarized as follows.

First, radical feminist scholars argued that criminology was a form of phallocentricism. Following broader developments in radical feminist theory – and in particular the influence of French feminism – this radical feminist agenda promoted a revolutionary scepticism about phallocentric modes of inquiry engendered in disciplines such as criminology, history, psychology, sociology and science, more generally. For over a hundred years, criminology had been almost entirely oblivious to the fundamental gendered differences in criminal offending (Cain 1990:11). As Naffine (1997:36) suggested, criminology had been so phallocentric that it had failed completely to even question the masculinity of criminology or the maleness of criminality. Criminology and feminism were therefore oxymorons – irreconcilable contradictory enterprises (Britton 2000:58).

See Chapter 3.6
Feminist
criminologies

See Chapter 1.4
Positivism

See Chapter 4.9
Deviant knowledge

Second, radical feminist scholars called for **transgressive knowledge** about women, gender, and crime to be generated from outside the discipline of criminology (Cain 1990). To be truly transgressive, radical feminist scholarship had to detach itself from the positivist research methods of criminology that had persistently failed to render visible the largely privatized harms endured by women at the hands of mostly men (Renzetti 2013). They argued that such 'methods cannot convey an in-depth understanding of, or feeling for, those being researched and that they often ignore sex or gender differences or look at them without considering mediating variables' (Gelsthorpe 1990:90).

Third, radical feminism questioned the separation of objectivity from subjectivity and rejected criminology's claims to be scientific, value free and completely devoid of interpretation. They argued that all research contains the exercise of power, and that elements of subjectivity are embedded in the framing of research questions. Radical feminist researchers attempted to disentangle the exercise of power from the act of doing research by adopting reflexive methodologies.

Fourth, radical feminism assumed that as knowledge is sexualized, the history of the human sciences has been masculine, and consequently feminist ways of knowing and doing research have been historically subjugated, repressed and disqualified (Harding 1987). Given this sexualized history of knowledge, the priority of radical feminism was to make visible and intelligible the formerly invisible voices and experiences of women as **victims** and offenders. The choice of topic then tended to follow logically – the study of women as gendered subjects (Hudson 2000:185). For the most radical of feminists, this led to the adoption of *standpoint feminist* methodologies. Standpoint feminism attempted to construct feminist ways of knowing based largely on experience, leading to a preference for qualitative research and a total rejection of '**masculinist ways of knowing**' (Cain 1990; Gelsthorpe 1990:86; Naffine 1997:45–8).

See Chapter 4.39
Victimology

See Chapter 4.21
Masculinities,
structure and
hegemony

While radical feminist critiques of criminology were insightful and correct about the discipline's gender-blindness, the position had its own conceptual weaknesses. In order to make the argument that criminology was inherently phallocentric, radical feminist scholarship universalized women as a homogeneous category (Naffine 1997). They presumed that commonalities shared among the female sex made it possible to analyse women as a singular unitary subject of history (see, e.g., Allen 1990:88). This leaves 'radical feminism open to charges of essentialism and reductionism' (Walklate 2004:43). Women were assumed to be one undifferentiated category, despite their astonishing historical, cultural, socio-economic, ethnic and racial diversity. As women are situated differentially in relation to the operation of criminal justice, radical standpoint feminist methodologies that assumed a commonality (or fixed essence) among women and a universal subjectivity among men constructed fictive subjectivities whose statuses before criminal justice and the law were quite diverse (Carrington 2015). Those who are particularly vulnerable to criminalization tended to come from public housing, new migrant, Aboriginal and other poor neighbourhoods, as studies of female offending have repeatedly shown (see, e.g., Carrington 1993). Consequently, there was no single universal essential female subject to be 'uncovered' through radical feminist standpoint methodologies.

Ironically, radical feminism narrowed the feminist gaze to gendered power relations and structures and the analysis of female oppression and male **patriarchy**. Like much of criminology, radical feminists confined their analysis to the treatment of domestic issues by local criminal justice agencies. The placeless and timeless unified female subject of history, politics and culture posited in these essentialist radical feminist theories was a fictional one that overlooked, excluded or marginalized women of colour, race and non-Anglo origin (Carrington 2015). Femininity became a universal construct abstracted from the specificity and variability of women's real and ethnically diverse experiences across time, class, space, history, religion, economics, culture and geo-politics. This kind of radical feminism was accused of being theoretically isolationist, reformist and obsessed with white 'middle-class concerns' (Carrington 2015; Naffine 1997; Renzetti 2013; Walklate 2004). At the time of the demise of radical feminism and rise of black feminism and intersectionality, Carol Smart noted that 'Feminism had to abandon its early frame-work and to start to look for other ways to think which did not subjugate other subjectivities' (1990:83). That, it did (see Renzetti this volume).

See Chapter 4.26
Patriarchy and crime

See Chapter 4.20
Intersectionality

References

Allen, Judith. 1990. *Sex & Secrets: Crimes Involving Australian Women Since 1880.* Melbourne: Oxford University Press.

Britton, Dana. 2000. Feminism in Criminology: Engendering the Outlaw. *Annals of the American Academy of Political and Social Science* 571: 57–76.

Cain, Maureen. 1990. Towards Transgression: New Directions in Feminist Criminology. *International Journal of the Sociology of Law* 18(1): 1–18.

Carrington, Kerry. 1993. *Offending Girls: Sex, Youth and Justice.* Sydney: Allen & Unwin.

Carrington, Kerry. 2015. *Feminism and Global Justice.* London: Routledge.

Gelsthorpe, Loraine. 1990. Feminist methodologies in criminology: A new approach or old wine in new bottles. In *Feminist Perspectives in Criminology*, Loraine Gelsthorpe and Allison Morris, eds, pp. 89–106. Buckingham: Open University Press.

Harding, Sandra, ed. 1987. *Feminism & Methodology.* Bloomington, IN: Indiana University Press.

Hudson, Barbara. 2000. Critical reflection as research methodology. In *Doing Criminological Research*, Victor Jupp, Pamela Davies, and Peter Francis, eds, pp. 175–89. London: Sage.

Naffine, Ngaire. 1997. *Feminism and Criminology.* Sydney: Allen & Unwin.

Renzetti, Claire. 2013. *Feminist Criminology.* London: Routledge.

Smart, Carol. 1990. Feminist approaches to criminology – or postmodern women meets atavistic man. In *Feminist Perspectives in Criminology*, Lorraine Gelsthorphe and Allison Morris, eds, pp. 70–84. Buckingham: Open University Press.

Walklate, Sandra. 2004. *Gender, Crime and Criminal Justice.* London: Routledge.

Further reading

Barberet, Rosemary. 2014 *Women, Crime and Criminal Justice: A Global Enquiry*. London and New York: Routledge.

Daly, Kathleen, and Lisa Maher (eds). 1998. *Criminology at the Crossroads: Feminist Readings in Crime and Justice*. New York: Oxford University Press.

Grosz, Elizabeth. 1989. The in(ter)vention of feminist knowledges. In *Crossing Boundaries: Feminisms and the Critique of Knowledges*, Barbara Caine, Elizabeth Grosz, and Marie de Lepervanche, eds, Sydney: Allen & Unwin.

Rafter, Nicole Hahn, and Frances Heidensohn (eds). 1995. *International Feminist Perspectives Criminology*. Buckingham: Open University Press.

Realism and left idealism

Roger Matthews

Realist criminology and left idealism represent two major strands of **critical criminology**, sharing a number of features but also representing opposing stances. Both question the concept of 'crime', seeing it as a social and political construct, and express a concern for social justice as well as a commitment to naturalism, while arguing for direct engagement with the lived reality of the subjects studied (Young 1979, 1994).

Viewing crime as a process of social construction means that what is defined as 'crime' changes over time and in different locations. Consequently, realists and left idealists argue for the deconstruction of the concept of crime and for its examination in relation to the context in which it is used: crime should be demystified; illusions and misconceptions regarding social processes should be removed; and the process of 'ideology critique' should be pursued to expose falsehoods, misconceptions and one-sided accounts. Thus, the focus on crime tends to be broader than that presented by conventional criminology. Both of these versions of critical criminology argue that examination of crime should not be restricted to street crime, but should also include **white-collar crime, corporate malpractice and state crime**, as well as expressing a commitment to social justice and human rights, and a commitment to fighting against forms of oppression, discrimination, suffering and abuse. Arguably, it is these normative concerns that distinguish critical criminology from, and provide an alternative to, conventional criminology. In order to defend the

See Chapter 3.3 Critical criminologies

See Chapter 4.41 White-collar crime; Chapter 4.36 State crime; Chapter 4.37 State-corporate crime rights and liberties of the marginalized, disadvantaged and the more vulnerable sections of society, both realism and left idealism seek to actively engage with these groups in order to better understand their experiences, motives and constraints. This requires the adoption of some form of qualitative methodology that involves an interpretative stance, rather than reducing those under study to statistical artefacts.

Aside from points of convergence, however, there are also significant points of divergence. The main points of opposition lie in competing views of how the issue of crime is constructed; the role of the **victim** and public opinion; the analysis of power and the state; the choice of methods; and, crucially, the nature of intervention.

See Chapter 4.39
Victimology

While both realists and left idealists agree that crime is a complex construct that needs to be critically deconstructed rather than simply taken for granted in the way that many mainstream criminologists tend to do, there is little agreement about the status and significance of the concept. For the most part, left idealists see crime as a product of social reaction and the **labelling** of certain forms of behaviour engaged in by marginalized groups in certain contexts. Other left idealists see crime as a form of resistance to the inequities of the capitalist system, or as a response to boredom or a lack of legitimate opportunities. There is a tendency, however, according to some critics, for left idealists to romanticize those convicted of crime, seeing them as the vanguard of the struggle against oppression and disadvantage (O'Brien 2005). In its more extreme forms, left idealism claims that crime control is little more than a mechanism for regulating and disciplining the poor and the marginalized.

See Chapter 3.8
Labelling theory

Realists, in contrast, argue that crime, like all other social phenomena (such as 'race' and the 'family'), is a social construct. Crime, they suggest has a material reality and a discernible social impact. Rather than seeing crime as a conflict between the rich and the poor, realists argue that crime is intra-class. Thus, for the most part, crime is seen as conflict between the 'underclass' and the working class. Realists also make the point that what is counted as 'crime' is a product of the interplay of four elements: the offender, the victim, public opinion and the state. In this way, they operate with what they refer to as 'the square of crime' (Lea 1992). Thus, for realists, crime cannot be simply wished away, and they argue that it constitutes a serious problem for the more vulnerable sectors of society. Criminal victimization, it is suggested, compounds the range of social problems that the working class already have to endure.

There are some left idealists who want to abandon the notion of 'crime' altogether, seeing it as too restrictive, while the uncritical focus on recorded crime, they argue, encourages criminologists to inadvertently participate in the regulation and disciplining of marginalized populations. Instead of focusing on crime, some left idealists have suggested that we should operate with a broader notion of '**harm**' in order to encourage researchers to pay more attention to those forms of victimization that occur outside the framework of the criminal justice system. It is argued that such harms are more socially and personally damaging than the forms of crime represented by criminal statistics (Hillyard et al. 2004).

See Chapter 4.33
Social harm/
zemiology

A central point of difference between realists and left idealists lies in their respective views on the nature of power and the state. For left idealists, the state tends to be depicted as profoundly authoritarian and a direct agent of capitalist exploitation and control. The law is seen to represent and defend the interests of the powerful. The police are seen as 'agents of social control', while imprisonment is a punishment that is reserved almost exclusively for the poor and the marginalized.

From a generally conspiratorial perspective, there is a tendency among left idealists to reject all forms of law, to limit police powers and to campaign for the **abolition** of imprisonment. These institutions and organizations are to be replaced, it is suggested, by the formation of alliances among marginalized groups, while the task of the criminologist is to expose the inadequacies and failings of the criminal justice system. Left idealists are reluctant to engage in reforming the criminal justice system, and argue that engaging in reform may well serve to re-legitimize the existing system. Consequently, they argue for a commitment to 'the unfinished' – that is, the formation of demands without specifying concrete alternatives.

See Chapter 5.1 Abolitionism

For realists, in contrast, who claim to take crime and criminal justice seriously, there is an emphasis on the formation of alternatives and the obligation to work both 'in and against' the state. For realists, the state is seen not only as an instrument of social control but also as an agency that plays a productive and protective role, particularly for the actual and potential victims of crime. The aim, realists argue, is to develop and extend these positive attributes of state power and to limit some of its less desirable practices. In relation to the police, for example, the aim is to make the police a more democratic and accountable organization that is better able to protect the weak and the vulnerable while reducing malpractice and discrimination (Lea and Young 1984).

There are significant differences between realists and left idealists in terms of methods of investigation. Although both perspectives are generally critical of positivist approaches and favour qualitative forms of analysis designed to engage directly with those under study, there are important differences in the type of information sought and the purpose of empirical investigation. Left idealists tend to favour ethnographic forms of inquiry usually involving detailed interviews or employing forms of participant observation. Studying this material normally involves discourse or narrative analysis coupled with some form of observation aimed at eliciting the meanings and motivation of those under study, or giving them voice.

While such accounts can provide rich detail, there is a danger that they can become overly descriptive and focus on the particular and the unique. In this way, there is a tendency for these accounts to descend into a form of empiricism from which it is difficult to make meaningful generalizations. In contrast, realists place a great emphasis on causality and the need to explain social change (Sayer 2010). Realists are interested in trying to explain the relation between different social phenomena with the aim of providing explanations rather than pure descriptions.

For realists, the importance of providing causal explanations is intertwined with the desire to formulate useful interventions and to contribute to social reform. Explaining how and why things work is seen as important, as is the development of viable alternatives. Realists argue that there is a need to aim for a 'joined-up' approach that effectively links theory, method and policy (Matthews 2014). For this reason, realists tend to reject the left idealist commitment to 'the unfinished' and to forms of abolition as utopian and unrealistic. In reply, left idealists argue that realists can all too easily become pragmatists and apologists for the perpetuation of an oppressive and inequitable system of social control.

In sum, these two approaches represent different branches of critical criminology; and for those drawn towards critical rather than conventional criminology, the choice between these two forms of critical criminology lies in the different conceptions of crime, power and the state, as well as the role of intervention and social reform. The difficult theoretical and strategic question that arises, however, is whether these two approaches – with their various points of convergence and divergence – could be synthesized into a form of critical criminology that draws on the strengths of both approaches (Matthews 2014).

References

Hillyard, Paddy, Christina Pantazis, Steve Tombs, and Dave Gordon. 2004 *Beyond Criminology: Taking Harm Seriously*. London: Pluto.

Lea, John. 1992. The analysis of crime. In *Rethinking Criminology: The Realist Debate*, Jock Young and Roger Matthews, eds, pp. 69–94. London: Sage.

Lea, John, and Jock Young. 1984. *What Is to Be Done About Law and Order?* London: Pluto.

Matthews, Roger. 2014. *Realist Criminology*. London: Palgrave Macmillan.

O'Brien, Martin. 2005. What is Cultural about Cultural Criminology? *British Journal of Criminology* 45(5): 599–612.

Sayer, Andrew. 2010. *Method in Social Science: A Realist Approach* (2nd edn). London: Routledge.

Young, Jock. 1979. Left idealism, reformism and beyond: From new criminology to Marxism. In *Capitalism and the Rule of Law*, Bob Fine, Richard Kinsey, John Lea, Sol Picciotto, and Jock Young, eds, pp. 11–28. London: Hutchinson.

Young, Jock. 1994. Incessant chatter: Recent paradigms in criminology. In *The Oxford Handbook of Criminology* (2nd edn), Mike Maguire, Rod Morgan, and Robert Reiner, eds, pp. 69ff. Oxford: Oxford University Press.

Further reading

Cohen, Stanley. 1998. *Against Criminology*. New Brunswick, NJ: Transaction Books.

Mathieson, Thomas. 1974. *The Politics of Abolition*. London: Martin Robertson.

Matthews, Roger. 2009. Beyond 'So What?' Criminology: Rediscovering Realism *Theoretical Criminology* 13(3): 341-62.

Pawson, Ray, and Nick Tilley. 1997. *Realistic Evaluation*. London: Sage.

Schwendinger, Herman, and Julia Schwendinger. 1975. Defenders of order or guardians of human rights? In *Critical Criminology*, Ian Taylor, Paul Walton, and Jock Young, eds, pp. 113–46. London: Routledge.

Young, Jock. 1992. Ten points of realism. In *Rethinking Criminology: The Realist Debate*, Roger Matthews and Jock Young, eds, pp. 24–68. London: Sage.

3.15 Social constructionism

Joel Best and Jennifer Snyder

Social constructionism explores the ways that individuals, through social interaction, assign meaning to the world around them. Specifically, social constructionism focuses on understanding how certain social phenomena come to be accepted as reality. A social constructionist approach to crime argues that behaviour is not objectively or inherently criminal, but rather, specific behaviours have been constructed as crimes though social interaction. Social constructionists are therefore not concerned with any objective quality of crime. Instead, they are interested in the processes through which those in positions of power and control come to define certain behaviours and individuals as criminal.

Berger and Luckmann's *The Social Construction of Reality* is the foundational American work on sociological constructionism. The authors argue that the sociology of knowledge 'must first of all concern itself with what people "know" as "reality" in their everyday, non- or pre-theoretical, lives' (1967:15). This reality is not an objective reality; instead, certain social phenomena are constructed as 'truth' through a process of objectification in which knowledge in everyday life is taken for granted and mistaken as inevitable or independent of the social processes that create it. Thus, the constructionist perspective has its origins in phenomenology, which concerns the structure of common-sense knowledge in everyday life; ethno-methodology, which examines the methods by which everyday interactions produce a shared reality; and **symbolic interactionism**, which emphasizes the role of social interaction in the construction of meaning.

The social constructionist perspective informs much of the research on deviance and social problems. For instance, **labelling theory** argues that what

See Chapter 3.18
Symbolic
interactionism

See Chapter 3.8
Labelling theory

defines a behaviour as deviant is not its objective qualities, but the societal reaction to the behaviour and the subsequent label placed upon it, just as studies of **moral panics** examine emerging concerns about threats to the social order. Constructionist social problems theory addresses the processes through which certain social conditions are constructed and accepted as social problems. Because social problems are social constructions, scholars study them as a social process: 'the activities of individuals or groups making assertions of grievance and claims with respect to some putative conditions' (Spector and Kitsuse 1977:75). Therefore, the emphasis of social problems is not on objective conditions but on the claims made about a condition by interested parties or claimsmakers: an individual or group that presents an argument, or claim, that some behaviour is problematic and should be seen as criminal – what the deviance literature calls moral entrepreneurs. In studies of social problems and moral panics, the social constructionist perspective is deeply concerned with the roles played by claimsmakers, the media and policymakers in constructing social problems (Best 2013).

See Chapter 3.10
Moral panic

By rejecting objective definitions of a crime, the social constructionist is able to focus on the process through which certain troubling conditions or behaviours come to be defined as crimes. A key player in this process is the claimsmaker. In recent years, discrimination, mobile phone use while driving, juvenile delinquency, the use of lethal force by the police, cyber-bullying and countless other troubling social conditions have been the subjects of claims calling for criminalization. Such claims can originate from activists, experts, the media or officials.

Not all claims successfully capture the attention of the general public and lawmakers, however. The **media** is an essential component in ensuring that claims about crimes are heard by a wide audience, and many claimsmakers seek extensive media coverage to promote their cause. This means that the media's choices about which claims to cover help shape the agendas of the public and policymakers. Media coverage helps drive public opinion, which in turn influences policymaking.

See Chapter 3.11
Newsmaking
criminology;
Chapter
4.8 Cultural
criminology

The existence of claims, media coverage and even public concerns does not guarantee the construction of a particular behaviour as a crime. Legislative policymakers must pass laws that designate behaviours as unlawful or illegal. When crime is socially constructed, behaviours are *criminalized*.

Definitions of crime vary over time and space. A particular behaviour may be criminalized, only later to be decriminalized or legalized. Similarly, what is considered criminal can vary across jurisdictions; there are differences not just between countries, but also among smaller jurisdictions. Temporal or geographic variation in the constructions of a particular crime may include different interpretations of its causes, how it is operationally defined, its seriousness and so on. Shifts in social constructions are central to understanding the history of any crime.

A further key element of the social constructionist approach to crime involves examining how individuals are processed through the criminal justice system. Once a crime is part of the criminal code, it becomes a label that can be applied to particular individuals. The agents of the criminal justice system – police officers, prosecutors and defence attorneys, judges, individuals who work in probation, parole and prison, and so on – are social problems workers (Best 2013). Their work involves determining whether particular individuals have committed crimes and, if so, what should be done with these criminals. Inevitably, this involves considerable discretion, as demonstrated by ethnographies of policing, courtrooms and other corrections sites. There is, for example, a very large literature addressing whether race – theoretically irrelevant to the criminal justice process – affects criminal-justice workers' judgements.

These workers reconstruct the meanings of behaviours by deciding to treat some as instances or cases of criminal activity. That is, criminal-justice workers must determine whether particular individuals or behaviours are truly instances of some crime on the books. Police officers have to decide whether the individuals they encounter on the street should be arrested; a prosecutor has to then determine whether those same individuals should be charged with crimes; and then a fact-finder (judge or jury) must declare that the case has been proven – a process that constructs people as criminals.

Criminal-justice processing does not occur in a vacuum. Criminal-justice workers may be subject to various external pressures: activists, experts, the media, politicians and **victims** all may call for changes in how crime is handled. There may be demands that the criminal-justice system is insufficient, as during a moral panic when people charge that the police are not doing enough; but there may also be claims that the system is excessive, when critics insist that police are overreacting. Still others argue that the existing laws are misguided – for example, that treatment, not punishment, should be the response to activities currently classified as crimes. Such claimsmaking can lead to yet another round of reconstructing some crime.

See Chapter 4.39
Victimology

Social constructionism questions aspects of criminology that are typically taken for granted. It views definitions of and reactions to crime as accomplishments, rather than treating them as normal or natural. Constructionism has no particular political agenda: there are constructionist studies that offer appreciative assessments of, say, how reformers altered the criminal justice system, and other analyses that are quite critical of particular claims. In either case, the constructionist analysts understand that people can and do alter how crime is understood and addressed. Such analyses can be grounded in different assumptions. Some simply seek to understand how crime is constructed: how do individuals become activists campaigning for a new crime category; how do the media portray crime; how are criminal laws passed; how do criminal-justice workers apply those laws in particular cases? But often, constructionists' analyses are underpinned by critiques: this is what is right or wrong with activists' claims, with media coverage, with lawmaking or law enforcement. Such analyses become social problems claims in their own right; calls for changes – whether cracking down or easing up – in how crimes are constructed. While only a small proportion of criminologists identify themselves as constructionists, virtually all of them incorporate some constructionist thinking in their work.

Throughout its rich history, the social constructionist perspective has had an important impact on the way that crime is understood and studied. This perspective offers the compelling viewpoint that crime is defined not by any objective or inherent qualities, but by individuals engaging in a complex process of social construction.

References

Berger, Peter, and Thomas Luckmann. 1967. *The Social Construction of Reality*. New York: First Anchor Books.

Best, Joel. 2013. *Social Problems* (2nd edn). New York: Norton.

Spector, Malcolm, and John Kitsuse. 1977. *Constructing Social Problems*. Menlo Park, CA: Cummings.

Further reading

Becker, Howard. 1963. *Outsiders*. New York: Free Press.

Cohen, Jeffrey W., and Robert A. Brooks. 2014. *Confronting School Bullying: Kids, Culture, and the Making of a Social Problem*. Boulder, CO: Lynne Rienner.

Goode, Erich and Nachman Ben-Yehuda. 2009. *Moral Panics: The Social Construction of Deviance* (2nd edn). Oxford: Blackwell.

Jenkins, Philip. 1998. *Moral Panic: Changing Concepts of the Child Molester in Modern America*. New Haven, CT: Yale University Press.

Jenness, Valerie, and Ryken Grattet. 2001. *Making Hate a Crime: From Social Movement to Law Enforcement*. New York: Russell Sage Foundation.

Parsons, Nicholas L. 2014. *Meth Mania: A History of Methamphetamine*. Boulder, CO: Lynne Rienner.

Potter, Gary W., and Victor E. Kappeler. 2006. *Constructing Crime: Perspectives on Making News and Social Problems* (2nd edn). Long Grove, IL: Waveland.

3.16 Stigma

Gill Green and Sarah Senker

The term 'stigma' is widely used in a variety of contexts, but there is consensus that the stigmatized are pejoratively regarded and devalued by wider society. A stigma is a mark of shame that communicates to others the fact that a person is not able to fulfil social and cultural role expectations. The origin of the concept of stigma as a failure to fulfil one's ascribed role stems largely from Erving Goffman's (1963) work *Stigma: Notes on the Management of Spoiled Identity.* For Goffman, stigma is not an essential feature of an attribute, like a visible physical mark such as a severe facial burn, but rather it emerges as a result of social reactions to such attributes. In addition to physical marks, non-physical characteristics, such as homosexuality or alcoholism, have also, at times, become objects of stigma. Goffman cast stigma as a **socially constructed** deviance **label** and, in the majority of studies that followed, stigmatizing characteristics, such as being identified as 'a criminal', were interpreted as social deviance. Thus, stigma is a social product generated by social interactions in which potentially stigmatizing attributes may affect interactions between the 'normal' and 'the (stigmatized) other'. As Goffman (1963:5) explains, 'we believe the person with a stigma is not quite human'. Thus stigma has the capacity to 'spoil' the social interaction, and the stigmatized person becomes 'the cripple', 'the junkie' – and who they are as individuals may get lost in the label.

Stigma varies along a number of dimensions, including degree of disruptiveness, aesthetic qualities, cause or origin, changes over time, the degree of peril held for others and concealability. The stigma of being identified as 'a criminal' is primarily linked to 'cause' and 'degree of peril' because criminal behaviour is perceived to be controllable and criminals are therefore perceived

See Chapter 3.15
Social
constructionism

See Chapter 3.8
Labelling theory

as blameworthy. Those engaging in criminal behaviour are also often viewed as untrustworthy and a source of potential danger to others.

To identify the key ingredients that lead one individual or group of people to stigmatize others, Link and Phelan (2001) identified the following stigma trajectory:

- Labelling: Human differences are noted and labelled, e.g., someone is seen to break the law and is therefore labelled as a lawbreaker and a criminal.
- Stereotyping: The labels are imbued with negative stereotypes, e.g., the criminal is perceived to be untrustworthy, anti-social and dangerous.
- Othering: Labelled persons are clearly categorized as 'other' or 'them' in order to clearly separate 'them' from 'us' – e.g., criminals are different to those of 'us' who live a law-abiding life.
- Status loss: Labelled persons are perceived by others and by themselves as devalued and inferior – e.g., criminals are less valued members of society.
- Discrimination: Labelled persons experience discrimination leading to rejection and exclusion – e.g., this person has a criminal record and we will not therefore offer them a job.
- Power: Stigma will only emerge if there is a clear power differential between 'us' and 'them'.

Numerous instances of 'stigma in action' have been studied. For example, substance-misusing offenders may be ostracized not only as a result of their criminal behaviour and 'offender' label but also due to their presumed dependence on mind-altering substances. Those 'addicted' to drugs are frequently presented as 'mindless, drug-crazed criminals and carriers of disease' (McIntosh and McKeganey 2002:2), with the commonly used term 'getting clean' aligning addiction with dirtiness and impurity. Where criminality may be seen by wider society as a choice, the additional behaviour of substance misuse can render individuals as 'unpredictable' and 'unmanageable', further excluding them from wider society and limiting their engagement or integration within the parameters of 'normality'. Substance-misusing offenders may attempt to confront or challenge their stigmatization with proclamations of having an 'illness' and therefore 'being helpless' to change their behaviour, but this may serve to isolate them further. It is important to note that stigma towards substance-misusers can stem from others within the drug-using cohort as well as from non-users, including drug-dealers (Rhodes et al. 2007). Substance-misusers who do not commit criminal offences to fund their habit may look unfavourably upon those who do (Radcliffe and Stevens 2008).

The strengths and weaknesses of the concept of 'stigma' have been discussed widely. The traditional focus on individuals' limitations and micro-level social interaction has been challenged, particularly by those espousing the social model of illness, which locates the 'problem' not in the individual but in the oppressive social environment that systematically excludes stigmatized groups. The focus is not upon the 'spoiled individual' but on the collective disadvantage and exclusion that he/she encounters – and this has now been replicated in recent sociological literature. In response, the stigma concept has been broadened, and scholars studying 'stigma' now engage with social structures, discrimination and power differentials. This shift is associated with the growth of the service-user movement and anti-stigma activism, which seeks to redress structural disadvantage and discrimination (defined as 'unfair treatment'). Accordingly, some question whether the stigma concept is still useful.

Structural constraints may compound stigma. For example, criminal-justice responses to substance-misusing or other offenders with backgrounds of low socio-economic status and poor educational attainment may reflect individualized ideas of recovery that fail to consider the sociological reasons why someone has become involved in drug-use and offending in the first place (e.g., trauma, lack of opportunity, homelessness). Despite challenges to stigma as a concept, in practice, it still retains its power to devalue a person's identity, whether following the reactions of others or due to internalization of standards held by wider society. Consequences may include self-hatred and shame, social withdrawal, impediments to employment and social relationships, and general curtailment of life opportunities. Stigma and shame resulting from

See Chapter 5.13 Recidivism

drug-use and offending may produce an unhelpful **cycle of behaviour** for the individual in various ways (Radcliffe and Stevens 2008).

References

Goffman, Erving. 1963. *Stigma: Notes on the Management of Spoiled Identity*. Englewood Cliffs, NJ: Prentice Hall.

Link, Bruce, and Jo Phelan. 2001. Conceptualizing Stigma. *Annual Review of Sociology* 27: 363–85.

McIntosh, James, and Neil McKeganey. 2002. *Beating the Dragon: The Recovery from Dependent Drug Use*. Harlow: Prentice Hall.

Radcliffe, Polly, and Alex Stevens. 2008. Are Drug Treatment Services Only for 'Thieving Junkie Scumbags'? Drug Users and the Management of Stigmatised Identities. *Social Science and Medicine* 67(6): 1065–73.

Rhodes, Tim, Louise Watts, Sarah Davies, Anthea Martin, Josie Smith, David Clark, Noel Craine, and Marion Lyons. 2007. Risk, Shame and the Public Injector: A Qualitative Study of Drug Injecting in South Wales. *Social Science and Medicine* 65(3): 572–85.

Further reading

Green, Gill. 2009. *The End of Stigma? Changes in the Social Experience of Long-Term Illness*. Abingdon: Routledge.

Jones, Edward. E. et al. 1984. *Social Stigma: The Psychology of Marked Relationships*. New York: Freeman.

Parker, Richard, and Peter Aggleton. 2003, HIV and AIDS-Related Stigma and Discrimination: A Conceptual Framework and Implications for Action. *Social Science and Medicine* 57: 13–24.

Scambler, Graham. 2004 Re-Framing Stigma: Felt and Enacted Stigma and Challenges to the Sociology of Chronic and Disabling Conditions. *Social Theory and Health* 2(1): 29–46.

Uggen, Christopher, Jeff Manza, and Angela Behrens. 2004. 'Less than the average citizen': Stigma, Role Transition and the Civic Reintegration of Convicted Felons. In *After Crime and Punishment: Pathways to Offender Reintegration*, Shadd Maruna and Russ Immarigeon, eds, pp. 261–94. Cullompton, UK: Willan.

3.17 Subculture

Shane Blackman

Subculture refers to a set of behaviours, customs, ideas, practices and values that belong to a social group that is distinct from, but integrally related to, the whole culture of society. For criminological theory, the concept subculture is an explanatory tool to understand behaviour defined as deviant by the main culture. This means that a subculture may be in opposition to what is seen as normal by the dominant culture, which can make a subculture appear to be transgressive, hostile and perceived as a threat. Because subcultures celebrate difference, they attract attention due to the value placed on authenticity. This give subcultures an edge; it makes them real through attachment and identity. Subcultures have been consistently identified through the **adoption of style** (e.g. related to music or clothing) most closely associated with young adults. As a result, the market has always expressed a fascination with subcultures and also found ways to exploit them, either producing commodities for subcultures or using subcultures to sell products not directly connected to them.

See Chapter 4.8
Cultural
criminology;
Chapter 3.2
Birmingham
Centre for
Contemporary
Cultural Studies

See Chapter 4.24
Neoliberalism

There is a tense contradiction between authenticity within subculture and the use of subculture as a marketable tool to make capital through mass-market production. Under **neoliberal capitalism**, all subcultures experience commercialization through a process of incorporation, which results in economic reward for entrepreneurs rather than young adults who are the bearers of the subculture. This means that subcultures are a pillar of global capitalism and profit renewal, while at the same time subcultures may project images of resistance and destruction. This is the live context of subculture as a marketable tool, where certain practices of a subculture may be illegal, deviant or criminal, such as drug use, but the commercial support system is highly profitable and legitimate. The state is then faced with the problem of order and control whereby subcultural practices appear to be promoted within the economy, contemporary media and advertising industry.

There is a long history and theoretical complexity to the different theories of subculture. For a century, within sociology and criminology, different paradigms – including **positivism**, structural-functionalism, behaviourism, **symbolic interactionism**, **Marxism** and **postmodernism** – have produced distinct theories of subculture incorporating ideas from different disciplines, such as anthropology, biology, **psychoanalysis** and **psychology**. One disciplinary issue is that subculture sits between two major explanations of behaviour which see subcultural activities as either 'deviant' or 'normal.' The 'deviant' is usually theorized in terms of pathology as a dysfunctional minority, such as a drug-consumer, and the 'normal' is seen as part of the 'everyday', belonging to the majority who do not consume drugs. The contemporary application of subculture in modern criminology is informed and shaped by each paradigm, which employs subculture in either an active or passive sense.

Broadly, there have been five major theoretical elaborations of subculture. Each theory contains degrees of relevance and usage in contemporary society. During the early part of the twentieth century at the **Chicago School** of Sociology, Robert Park and Ernest Burgess endeavoured to build on Durkheim's aspiration to establish sociology as a distinct discipline. For Park and Burgess, one key area of study was deviance within the community, while at the same time they sought to explore the legitimacy of qualitative research methods. As a result, the Chicago School commissioned Vivien Palmer (1928:73) to write a manual, titled *Field Studies in Sociology*, to teach research methods which specified that one of the key objectives is to collect 'maps of subcultural groups' demonstrating 'basic differences in people's mode of life which leads to clear cut variations in their customs, attitudes and behaviour patterns'. Hence the study of deviant subcultures was located within the development of qualitative fieldwork studies at the Chicago School of Sociology.

In contrast, during the 1920s in Britain, subculture became identified with biological and psychological theories that sought to explain deviance within a broader understanding of the eugenics movement, which described young adults in subcultures as 'sub-normal.' The Wood Report (1929) – written by intellectual figures such as E.O. Lewis and Cyril Burt, who were influenced by the evolutionary theories of Cesare Lombroso – saw subcultures as 'young delinquents.' This **positivist** understanding of deviance defined young people in subcultures through degrading and discriminatory labels. Such **biological** and psychological explanations of the cause of deviance quickly became the basis for understanding the role of subculture in alcoholism, criminality and unemployment as a form of abnormality. The understanding of subcultures as a social evil within British society was not replicated in American sociological work on deviance at the Chicago School of Sociology, however. Instead, early work by Nels Anderson, Paul Cressey, Clifford Shaw, Edwin Sutherland and Frederic Thrasher – as well as by female researchers at Hull House, including

See Chapter 1.4
Positivism

See Chapter 3.18
Symbolic
interactionism

See Chapter 3.9
Marxist
criminologies

See Chapter 4.28
Postmodern
and constitutive
criminologies

See Chapter 1.10
Psychoanalytic
perspectives

See Chapter 1.8
Learning
theory; Chapter
1.15 Forensic
psychology

See Chapter 2.1
Chicago School

See Chapter 1.4
Positivism

See Chapter 1.5
Biological
criminology

Jane Addams and Annie MacLean – sought to understand delinquency within its social, economic, cultural and community context as a feature of normality within an urban context.

From the 1930s to the 1950s, with the dominance of structural functionalism as the leading paradigm in sociology and criminology, Robert Merton's theory of **anomie** became a major disciplinary influence in understanding the position of subculture. Merton argued that the theory of subculture derived its origin and legitimacy from structural functionalism through the work of Albert Cohen (1956). Cohen's theory of the delinquent subculture fused Merton's theory of anomie with Freud's theory of 'reaction formation' to describe deviance as a collective solution to the social problems experienced by working-class young adults to enable them to achieve social mobility. For both Merton and Cohen, the **American Dream** is key to understanding deviant subcultures, which invert the normal goals of success. A weakness of this theory was that it could only explain working-class deviance resulting from status frustration, in contrast to middle-class youth who already possessed status. This discriminatory social class theory became the orthodox approach to explain the generation of deviance until the 1970s.

See Chapter 2.3 Anomie

See Chapter 2.8 Market society and crime

During the late 1960s, criminologists at the British National Deviancy Conference – including Stan Cohen, David Downes, Paul Rock, Laurie Taylor and Jock Young – alongside theorists at the **Centre for Contemporary Cultural Studies** (CCCS) based at the University of Birmingham, such as Stuart Hall, Dick Hebdige, Tony Jefferson and Paul Willis, began to develop a British theory of labelling which criticized the functionalist theory of subculture. Phil Cohen's (1972) *Subcultural Conflict and Working Class Community* brought the ideas of Claude Lévi-Strauss on 'myth', Louis Althusser on ideology and Jacques Lacan on 'imaginary relations' to bear on the concept of subculture. It then became possible to interpret subcultures within a complex Marxism – to magically resolve social contradictions through multiple narratives of bricolage formed of style, symbols and ritual.

See Chapter 3.2 Birmingham Centre for Contemporary Cultural Studies

Subcultures are interpreted at an ideological rather than material level; as a result, subcultures offer symbolic solutions at the level of leisure. The CCCS approach of Hall and Jefferson (1975) in *Resistance Through Rituals* is to present subcultures as a literary text to interpret multiple levels of meaning. Through a complex theoretical elaboration of style, resistance, bricolage, homology and hegemony, the CCCS championed the agency of youth subcultures to enable their practices to be seen as non-pathological social and cultural expressions of refusal and resistance. Deviance could be interpreted through a semiotic lens as recreational activities, and even upheld as a marker of class-consciousness. Building on Phil Cohen's argument that subcultural practices should be seen as separate from criminality, the CCCS developed a theory of subculture in which acts of deviance are viewed not as a social problem but as a signifier of subcultural identity.

The criticism of the CCCS theory for its light focus on gender and race and overly heavy preoccupation with social class ushered in a series of critiques from within a **postmodern** perspective defined as 'postsubcultural' (Bennett 2011). The new focus on locality, spatiality, fluidity and individual identity of the postsubculturalist theory moved away from modernist constraint and claimed that subcultures make their own biographies. A new theoretical foundation based on ideas derived from Jean Baudrillard, Michel Maffesoli and Max Weber was proposed in order to break away from a more Marxist understanding of subculture. This postsubcultural critique has been all-encompassing, calling for the creation of new terms such as neo-tribe, life style and scene. The postmodernist rejection of subculture has been at the level of critique and assertion. The call for more focus on individual consumer creativity to forge identity and lifestyle has enabled subcultural expression to show more diversity. Postsubcultural theory retains value when focused on individualistic consumer identities. The cost of this postmodern understanding of subcultural practices as free from the constraints of social class, gender and ethnic identity, however, has resulted in an analysis where authenticity and agency has been removed from young adult commitment within subcultures. The marginalization of material issues of social class and structural inequalities has weakened the position of postsubcultural theory to explain collective subcultural practices of resistance, deviance and transgression.

See Chapter 4.28 Postmodern and constitutive criminologies

For criminology the debate over subcultural terminology is not a minor issue because the term retains explanatory power at both individual and collective levels of society. Cultural criminology, with its focus on creativity within deviance, can address how individual 'ordinary youth' take up degrees of subcultural identification and at the same time examine the real lives and collective responses of participants in subcultures under conditions of contemporary social and economic austerity. Theoretically, subculture is a reservoir of ideas, histories and practices for its bearers to respond to contradictory societal issues of discrimination, gender, ethnicity and social class.

References

Bennett, Andy. 2011. The Post-Subcultural Turn: Some Reflections 10 Years On. *Youth Studies* 14(5): 493–506.

Cohen, Albert. 1956. *Delinquent Boys: The Culture of the Gang.* London: Collier-Macmillan.

Cohen, Phil. 1972. Subcultural Conflict and Working Class Community. *CCCS Working Papers in Cultural Studies* (University of Birmingham) 2: 5–51.

Hall, Stuart, and Tony Jefferson (eds). 1975/2006. *Resistance Through Rituals: Youth Subcultures in Post-War Britain.* London: Hutchinson.

Palmer, Vivien Marie. 1928. *Field Studies in Sociology: A Student's Manual.* Chicago: University of Chicago Press.

Further reading

Blackman, Shane. 2004. *Chilling Out: The Cultural Politics of Substance Consumption, Youth and Drug Policy*. Maidenhead: Open University Press.

Blackman, Shane. 2014. Subculture Theory: An Historical and Contemporary Assessment of the Concept for Understanding Deviance. *Deviant Behavior* 35(6): 496–512.

Griffin, Christine. 2011. The Trouble with Class: Researching Youth, Class and Culture beyond the 'Birmingham School'. *Youth Studies* 14(3): 245–59.

Hart, Christopher (ed.). 2010. *The Legacy of the Chicago School of Sociology*. Poynton, UK: Midrash.

Merton, Robert K. 1938. Social Structure and Anomie. *American Sociological Review* 3(5): 672–82.

Skelton, Tracey and Gill Valentine (eds). 1998. *Cool Places: Geographies of Youth Cultures*. London: Routledge.

Williams, J. Patrick. 2011. *Subcultural Theory*. Cambridge: Polity Press.

Symbolic interactionism

Susie Scott

Symbolic interactionism (SI) is a micro-sociological perspective that focuses on small-scale, often face-to-face, encounters between social actors and on the meanings they attach to their behaviour. It considers 'society' not as a fixed structure but as a dynamic process, constructed and produced through interactions in everyday life. Norms, rules, routines and rituals shape social behaviour and create the appearance of order, but this is a precarious accomplishment that can be challenged by deviance. Individual identities emerge out of social interaction and are negotiated through our relations with other actors, which can involve power struggles as well as harmonious cooperation.

In contrast to sociological realist and **positivist** approaches, SI does not attempt to discover objective truths about the external 'real' world, such as the social causes of individual behaviour. Instead, it focuses on subjective realities: how people experience and make sense of their situations to create social worlds. This reflects an interpretivist epistemology, based upon the Weberian principle of *verstehen*: the **interpretive understanding of social action**. This is in common with other micro-level perspectives like phenomenology, ethnomethodology and **social constructionism**. SI adopts the philosophy of pragmatism, analysing how people orient their action towards objects, which can be symbolic as well as material: for example, ideas, language and categories. Methodologically, this translates into a preference for qualitative research and empirical studies: observing the everyday lives of particular groups or social environments.

See Chapter 1.4
Positivism

See Chapter 3.1
Appreciative
criminology;
Chapter 4.8
Cultural
criminology

See Chapter 3.15
Social
constructionism

See Chapter 2.1
Chicago School

See Chapter 2.2
Social
disorganization
theory

SI grew out of North American sociology in the twentieth century, and is famously associated with the **Chicago School**, whose figureheads included William Thomas, Robert Park, Ernest Burgess, Louis Wirth and Everett Hughes, Howard Becker, Anselm Strauss and Erving Goffman. During the interwar period, Chicago was undergoing rapid social transformation and seemed a natural laboratory in which to study how **urbanization, migration and poverty** affected ordinary people's everyday lives. Ethnographic field studies examined social problems like crime and deviance through the experiences of what Becker (1963) called the 'underdogs' of society: those who were powerless, marginalized or disadvantaged. This resulted in classic studies of immigrants, homeless people, criminal gangs and juvenile delinquents.

Although the Chicago School predominated, SI is a wider theoretical umbrella, encompassing different approaches and branches. The short-lived Iowa School leant towards positivist, statistical analyses of social behaviour, while the structural branch of SI focuses on normative patterns of interaction. Goffman's dramaturgical theory, discussed below, is often considered a variant of SI. Meanwhile, interaction ritual theory, inspired by Goffman (and, before him, Durkheim), studies how mundane social situations follow a ritualistic format through which actors demonstrate adherence to shared values. For example, the conversational exchanges of greetings and farewells symbolically express respect and deference.

A foundational concept in SI is the social self. Mead (1934) argued that mind, self and society were all interconnected parts of the same process: just as individual action can create social change, so do social experiences shape personal identity. Selfhood is a relational, communicative process whereby we understand who we are by comparing ourselves to significant or generalized others. Mead emphasized the mind's reflective capacity for perspective-taking when he described the social self as an internal conversation between two phases. The 'I' was a subjective, impulsive agent, while the 'Me' was an objectified image of oneself, from an external perspective. 'Taking the role of the other' was an important skill learned through childhood socialization. A related notion is Cooley's (1902) looking-glass self, which had three elements: imagining how we appear to others; imagining how they might judge us; and resultant self-feelings, such as pride or shame. Thus, in a situation, we can consider alternative courses of action and their likely social consequences.

It was Herbert Blumer (1969) who consolidated the theory of symbolic interactionism, proposing three key principles: people act towards social objects on the basis of meanings; these meanings arise out of social interaction; and they can be modified by interpretation. Blumer said that we communicate through symbolic gestures, such as language, whose meanings are mutually understood. In contrast to Mead's individualistic 'act', Blumer described joint action whereby actors build and make sense of scenes collaboratively.

This reflects another key concept in SI, the 'definition of the situation' (Thomas and Thomas 1928). When actors encounter one another in a situation, they try to interpret what is going on, their respective roles and how the action will proceed. They may have different understandings and (mis-)perceptions that struggle to be reconciled. This is only a provisional construction, a working consensus, but it feels subjectively real and has pragmatic consequences for interaction. Strauss (1978) developed a related theory of 'negotiated order' whereby actors tacitly cooperate by following unspoken rules, norms and expectations, and sanctioning each other's deviant behaviour. This happens particularly in organizational settings such as the workplace, but also in shared public spaces like the swimming pool.

Social identities are performed and presented to others in everyday situations. Goffman's (1959) dramaturgical theory used a theatrical analogy to suggest that people are like actors, playing roles and presenting different characters to the audiences they encounter in each scene. We have 'frontstage' regions where we give these public performances, and private, 'backstage' regions where we retreat to relax out of character (for example, compare a store's shopfloor to its staffroom). Most interaction takes place in the frontstage region, which may be decorated with scenery and material prop objects to create a certain image: think of a university lecture hall, with its tiered seats and majestic podium. Goffman argued that this 'self-presentation' was carefully designed, involving strategic skills of 'impression management', such as idealization (giving a prototypical role performance that can be easily recognized) and mystification (keeping audiences away from the backstage region to prevent them from discovering our secrets).

The impressions we consciously try to 'give' may be undermined by those we unwittingly 'give off', however, resulting in embarrassment. Here, Goffman emphasized the importance of dramaturgical *team-mates*, or fellow actors, who step in to repair awkward situations and keep the show running. These rituals of *facework* can be defensive (saving one's own face) or protective (saving someone else's), as well as avoidant (pre-emptive) or corrective (retrospectively reparative). For example, we may use humour to reassure a team-mate that their mistake does not matter, while polite forms of talk (such as apologies, requests and disclaimers) help us avoid causing offence.

Identity is not only a performance but also a process, negotiated through social relations over the life-course. People are described as not simply 'being' but rather 'becoming' social types, in an ongoing, never-finished process. Strauss (1969) called these journeys of self-identity 'career trajectories': a linear sequence of stages punctuated by key biographical moments. Ceremonial rites of passage mark the transition to a new stage of identity (e.g. getting married or graduating college), while epiphanous 'turning points' are experiences that change the way we see ourselves (e.g. desisting from crime after being in prison). *Moral careers* are those that involve social judgement and have what Goffman called 'fateful' consequences for identity, such as becoming a psychiatric patient. *Deviant careers* are a variant of these, involving labelling and stigma. This idea was influential to **labelling theory** in the 1960s–1970s sociology of deviance. Lemert outlined a socially mediated passage from primary

See Chapter 3.8
Labelling theory

to secondary deviance, and Becker (1963) showed how peer groups change the meaning attached to an activity (e.g. drug-taking), leading the actor through a series of 'progressive commitments' to a deviant identity.

SI has faced criticism for being too focused on the mundane, everyday, micro-level and neglecting wider, structural issues of power, inequality and conflict. Defenders of the perspective, however, argue that it does theorize exactly these things, albeit in a different way. Moreover, it makes such abstract concepts easier to grasp by grounding them empirically and showing how they play out through social interaction.

SI has certainly stood the test of time, with an enduring appeal and continuing relevance. Alice Goffman's (2014) contemporary ethnography of a socially deprived Philadelphia neighbourhood showed how young black men experienced life 'on the run' from a technological web of police surveillance and arrest warrants. Through her rich descriptions of the daily interactions and encounters (both mundane and dramatic) between these men and their friends, families and neighbours we gain a deeper understanding of what it means to inhabit their particular social world. Such interpretive depth and meticulously focused analysis are hallmark features of the SI perspective.

References

Becker, Howard S. 1963. *Outsiders: Studies in the Sociology of Deviance*. New York: Free Press.

Blumer, Herbert. 1969. *Symbolic Interactionism: Perspective and Method*. Englewood Cliffs, NJ: Prentice Hall.

Cooley, Charles H. 1992/1902. *Human Nature and the Social Order*. New Brunswick, NJ: Transaction.

Goffman, Alice. 2014. *On The Run: Fugitive Life in an American City*. Chicago: University of Chicago Press.

Goffman, Erving. 1959. *The Presentation of Self in Everyday Life*. Harmondsworth: Penguin.

Mead, George H. 1934. *Mind, Self and Society*. Chicago: University of Chicago Press.

Strauss, Anselm L. 1969. *Mirrors and Masks*. London: Martin Robertson.

Strauss, Anselm L. 1978. *Negotiations: Varieties, Contexts, Processes and Social Order*. San Francisco: Jossey-Bass.

Thomas, William I., and Dorothy S. Thomas. 1928. *The Child in America*. New York: Alfred Knopf.

Further reading

Charon, Joel. 2007. *Symbolic Interaction: An Introduction, an Interpretation, an Integration* (9th edn). Englewood Cliffs, NJ: Prentice Hall.

Scott, Susie. 2009. Re-Clothing the Emperor: The Swimming Pool as a Negotiated Order. *Symbolic Interaction* 32(2): 123–45.

Sumner, Colin. 1994. *The Sociology of Deviance: An Obituary*. Buckingham: Open University Press.

Part 4

Late critical criminologies and new directions

Part 4 Introduction

This section is the largest in the book, and encompasses new intellectual turns and interpretations of the shifting character of modernity, as well as an explosion of theoretical energy and conceptualization.

For whatever reason, in recent years, criminology has grown enormously in popularity among students and, correspondingly, the number of academic and professional criminologists has increased substantially. The number of monographs, textbooks, journals and conferences has multiplied, and the intellectual life of the subject has seen astonishing vigour, productivity and excitement. Context remains important, of course, and the world has been changing too, with implications and consequences for crime, dissent, control and disputation relating to the use and abuse of power.

A number of interweaving influences have had particular impact on criminology. For example, the intensification of consumerism and widening of commodification remind the 'have-nots' of the imbalance between their aspirations and their opportunities to achieve them through legal channels. Criminology has long engaged with such status frustration, blocked opportunities and relative deprivation, but the context now is one dominated by processes of globalization and a new precariousness of employment, community life and personal security. Globalization is fed by the profit made possible by the movement of production to take advantage of low-paid workers and opportunities for the exploitation of natural resources. Criminology has taken an interest in all of this – from the cultural, gendered, sexual and emotional worlds of consumption, communications and mobility, to analysis of the erosion of human rights and degradation of the natural environment. It has also noted how the present is partly shaped by the legacies of the past, such as colonialism, and the power imbalances between the global north and the global south.

Economies have become subject to a dominant narrative of neoliberalism accompanied by trends toward deregulation, increased reliance on self-policing by businesses, and state support for corporate expansion and privatization of services. Within criminology, the study of crimes 'from above' and committed by those in positions of trust – state-corporate crime and state crime, corporate, white-collar and financial crimes – has flourished. New sources of 'threat' – such as terrorism, transnational organized crime and emotively drawn 'links' between immigration and crime – are perfect topics for a visual culture, contributing to the swelling of support for populist conservatism, as evidenced by Brexit and the election of Donald Trump to the presidency of the United States. It seems perhaps – as post-structuralists and postmodernists suggest – that many people today experience the world in terms of uncertainties, loss of confidence in 'society' and absorption into the preoccupations of the self.

Criminology has attempted to engage with such trends, and has also sought to articulate what its role should be. For some, this might be as a 'public criminology' or a new 'post-criminology' field entirely. Others make the case for new theoretical directions, as well as arguing for a broadening of criminological imaginations and horizons: for example, to consider social harm alongside crime, and human rights alongside victimization. More broadly, many might agree that the future criminological agenda is unfolding around us and reflects what some have identified as the general malaise of late modernity.

Anarchist criminology

Luis A. Fernandez and Geert Dhondt

Anarchist criminology is founded on an uncompromising critique of law, power and the state as it relates to crime and harm. It calls for solutions to criminological problems through decentralized, collaborative and community-embedded approaches. Anarchist criminology has loose and expansive boundaries, and has close kinship to other theories, including **postmodernism**, **feminism**, **abolitionism** and **radical criminology**. What makes anarchist criminology distinct is its connection to the long history of anarchist thought dating back at least two millennia, with a critical tradition that emphasizes mutual aid, cooperation, direct democracy and a deep distrust of authority. Generally, anarchist criminology has commitments to:

- a strong critique against state-based solutions to harm, including punishment and incarceration;
- understanding and resisting state subjugation of marginalized populations;
- collective decision-making and direct democracy;
- autonomy and inclusion of all beings;
- mutual aid, cooperation and relationships based on equal footing; and
- the pursuit of freedom, equality and resistance to unequal power relations via direct action and participatory methodological approaches.

To understand fully the commitments of anarchist criminology, one has to start with anarchism itself.

The word 'anarchy' has at least two definitions that exist in parallel but contrast sharply in meaning. One perspective on anarchy points to the absence of a ruler, resulting in chaos and brutality. Originating at least from the time of Thomas Hobbes (1588–1679), this position serves as the primary justification for sovereignty and government. For instance, Hobbes argued that surrendering our 'natural' rights to a sovereign enters us into a 'social contract' that guarantees civil liberties and protection from harm. Without this social contract, he argued, life would be 'solitary, poor, nasty, brutish and short'. A second perspective on anarchy as a political thought challenges the notion that systems without rulers descend into chaos. Rather, such anarchists argue that humans can (and should) function without authority, be it governmental or otherwise, because it is government that produces the most harm. Such anarchism, in contrast to Hobbes's perspective, imagines a society without the need of a social contract – one that is organized on a voluntary, cooperative basis and not through coercion or compulsion. Suffice it to say here that anarchism, at its broadest level, is against the centralization of authority, and for mutual aid, cooperation and collective decision-making on equal footing.

Anarchist criminology, then, is rooted in the second conception of anarchy outlined above. It is steeped in the political philosophy of nineteenth- and early twentieth-century anarchist thinkers such as William Godwin (1756–1836), Michael Bakunin (1814–76), Peter Kropotkin (1842–1921) and Emma Goldman (1869–1940), who launched forceful attacks at state authority and the notion of legality itself. For instance, Godwin (1987) argued that government is a corrupting force, instilling ignorance in the population through the institution of law, private property and marriage. For Godwin, justice could never derive from state-administered punishment or regulation. Bakunin (1980) was equally critical of the state and its laws. Yet his critique extended to hierarchical relations of power, which he saw as the exercise of privilege enforced through state sanctions. To mitigate the force of the state, Bakunin argued for an anti-authoritarian position that rejected any form of authority that takes power over working-class people. This stance even included a rejection of Karl Marx himself, because Bakunin saw Marx's 'dictatorship of the proletariat' as one more form of hierarchical authority. Kropotkin (1898) carried his critique of the law even further. He argued not just for the abolition of privilege, prisons and all forms of hierarchies, but also for the very obedience to the law. He famously stated that, instead of saying 'Respect the law', we should say 'Despise law and all its Attributes!' Instead of 'Obey the law', anarchists should 'Revolt against all laws!'. Equally powerful, Goldman forcefully introduced gender into the anarchist equation, fighting for women's political and reproductive rights. She embraced direct action and spent several years in prison for breaking the law by handing out condoms to women on the streets.

These anarchist critiques of the state, law and authority (as well as a tendency toward direct action) are present within anarchist criminology. In fact, some suggest that the basic outline of anarchist criminology is already present in Bakunin, Goldman, Godwin and Kropotkin because they called for the elimination of state punishment, prisons and the rule of law. Regardless, anarchist criminology took hold in the late 1970s and 1980s, and continued to grow in the 1990s and 2000s. The approach developed in reaction to traditional forms of criminology and to Marxist theory. Whereas Marxists sought to dismantle capitalism and replace it with socialism, anarchists viewed this move as another form of hierarchical domination. As such, anarchist criminologists challenged hierarchical tendencies in the analysis of crime, seeking solutions that were outside law enforcement, courts and other state institutions. Accordingly, theorists like Hal Pepinsky, Larry Tifft and Denis Sullivan proposed an anarchist approach free of existing hierarchical agencies that depend on state sponsorship and legitimacy. Instead, they called for decentralized systems – ones negotiated within local communities that address individual and collective harm. Pepinsky (1978) also proposed collective negotiation based on a communist anarchist framework that emphasizes **peacekeeping** as the main instrument in reducing harm. Tifft and Sullivan (1980) argued that solutions to social problems should come from responsive social interactions that bypass the state. In these instances, the use of an anarchist lens moved the focus away from criminal behaviour and toward the reduction of harm via collective endeavours outside state institutions.

See Chapter 3.12
Peacemaking in
criminology

In the 1990s, anarchist criminologists embraced a more cultural approach that was in part influenced by postmodern theory. Scholars like Jeff Ferrell, for instance, described crime not only as a **social construction** but also as a symbolic system that censures large portions of marginalized populations, resulting in the reproduction of unequal structural conditions. Ferrell (1994) argued that the role of the criminal justice system is not just punitive, but also defines and manufactures a criminal subject. Examining how the legal system redefined graffiti as criminal activity, Ferrell demonstrated how legal statutes, law enforcement and the courts criminalize specific behaviour because they occur within less powerful populations.

See Chapter 3.15
Social
constructionism

Anarchist criminology continued to grow in the 2000s, with other scholars picking up the approach to study other areas in criminology. In his book *Lost in Space*, Randall Amster (2008) examined how the legal system criminalized the homeless population through local regulatory measures to 'clean' and 'sanitize' urban spaces to facilitate middle-class comfort and consumption. In *Policing Dissent*, Luis Fernandez (2008) scrutinized how law enforcement controls political dissenters, describing how the law, courts and police function to reduce resistance to economic globalization. Embedded within anarchist criminology, these authors continue to demonstrate how state institutions produce criminality and are generally in line with the expansions of the criminal justice system.

See Chapter 4.16
Green
Criminology;
Chapter 4.35
Speciesism and
theriocide

See Chapter 3.6
Feminist
criminologies;
Chapter 3.13
Radical feminism;
Chapter 4.26
Patriarchy and
crime

See Chapter 4.32
Queer criminology

More recently, scholars continue to use anarchist criminological concepts in a constant search for liberation and justice in various spheres, including **animal rights**, **environmentalism**, **feminism** and **queerness**. In the end, we can say that anarchist criminology is a loose assortment of intentions, desires and attempts to challenge and dismantle domination and enhance liberation. The approach borrows from various fields, but makes a unique contribution to criminology. These contributions include: a) enough flexibility to allow scholars to innovate; b) a strong foundation in liberatory values; c) a scholarly focus away from criminal behaviour and toward the production and maintenance of and resistance to subjugation; and d) a presentation of alternative ways to reduce harm.

References

Amster, Randall. 2008. *Lost in Space: The Criminalization, Globalization, and Urban Ecology of Homelessness*. New York: LFB Scholarly.

Bakunin, Mikhail Aleksandrovich. 1980. *Bakunin on Anarchism*. Montreal: Black Rose.

Fernandez, Luis. 2008. *Policing Dissent: Social Control and the Anti-Globalization Movement*. New Brunswick, NJ: Rutgers University Press.

Ferrell, Jeff. 1994. Confronting the agenda of authority: Critical criminology, anarchism, and urban graffiti. In *Varieties of Criminology: Readings from a Dynamic Discipline*, Gregg Barak, ed., pp. 161–78. Westport, CT: Praeger.

Godwin, William. 1987. *Enquiry Concerning Political Justice and Its Influence on Morals and Happiness*. Harmondsworth: Penguin.

Kropotkin, Pëtr. 1898. *Law and Authority*. San Francisco: Free Society.

Pepinsky, Harold E. 1978. Communist Anarchism as an Alternative to the Rule of Criminal Law. *Crime, Law and Social Change* 2(3): 315–34.

Tifft, Larry, and Dennis Sullivan. 1980. *The Struggle to Be Human: Crime, Criminology, and Anarchism*. Sanday, Orkney: Cienfuegos Press.

Further reading

Ackelsberg, Martha. 2013. Preface. In *Queering Anarchism: Addressing and Undressing Power and Desire*, C.B. Daring, J. Rogue, Deric Shannon, and Abbey Volcano, eds, pp. 1–4. Edinburgh: AK Press.

Amster, Randall, Abraham DeLeon, Luis A. Fernandez, Anthony J. Nocella II, and Deric Shannon (eds). 2009. *Contemporary Anarchist Studies: An Introductory Anthology of Anarchy in the Academy*. London: Routledge.

Ben-Moshe, Liat. 2013. Disabling Incarceration: Connecting Disability to Divergent Confinements in the USA. *Critical Sociology* 39(3): 385–403.

Brisman, Avi. 2011. Vandalizing Meaning, Stealing Memory: Artistic, Cultural, and Theoretical Implications of Crime in Galleries and Museums. *Critical Criminology* 19(1): 15–28.

Ferrell, Jeff. 1997. Against the law: Anarchist criminology. In *Thinking Critically about Crime*, Brian MacLean and Dragan Milovanovic, eds, pp. 146–54. Vancouver: Collective Press.

Nocella II, Anthony J. 2015. Anarchist criminology against racism and ableism and for animal liberation. In *Anarchism and Animal Liberation: Essays on Complementary Elements of Total Liberation*, Anthony J. Nocella II, Richard J. White, and Erika Cudworth, eds, pp. 40–58. Jefferson, NC: McFarland.

Sullivan, Dennis, Larry Tifft, Georgia Gray, John Laub, and Michael Buckman. 1980. Let the Water Be Wet, Let the Rocks Be Hard: Anarchism as a Sociology of Quality of Life. *Humanity and Society* 4(4): 344–62.

4.2 Chaos criminology

Christopher R. Williams

With origins and initial application in mathematics and the physical sciences, 'chaos theory' is typically used to refer to a collection of interrelated principles and ideas that have been employed to examine qualitatively the behaviour of systems that are complex, sensitive to initial conditions, and nonlinear in their behavioural tendencies. Though these principles and ideas are often exploratory in nature and tentative in conclusion, criminologists have utilized some (e.g., attractors, the 'butterfly effect', fractal geometry, self-organization) to assess critically the inherent epistemological limitations to the study of crime and the practice of criminal and civil justice. They have formed conceptual inroads toward understanding – at least metaphorically – the ways in which stable systems advance into disorderly dynamics; the intricate forms of order that exist within apparent disorder; and the emergence of order from disorder.

Chaos theory illuminates how things – systems – change over time. Such systems are referred to as 'dynamical', and include everything from weather systems to stock markets, to human communities and the human brain. Specifically, chaos theory is relevant for the study of those dynamical systems that are 'nonlinear' in their behavioural tendencies – those for which the 'outputs' of the system can be disproportional to the 'inputs', or for which a change in one variable does not produce a proportional change in related variables. Because human beings and the societies they constitute are complex, dynamical systems comprised of infinitely vast numbers and types of intersecting and interacting variables, the principles and tools employed to understand nonlinear dynamical systems in mathematics and the physical sciences arguably hold value for the study of individual and social systems as well (e.g., Walters 1999).

Some of the most significant and widely discussed implications of chaos theory for the social and behavioural sciences are epistemological in nature, involving questions of what we can know and how we can know it. As with other social sciences, traditional (**positivist**) criminology has historically subscribed to the logic and method of the Newtonian (i.e. mechanistic) scientific paradigm in which order, certainty, stability and linearity featured prominently. Mechanistic science has been criticized for attempting to reduce natural and social systems to a collection of 'clock-like' isolable parts, the proper identification and measurement of which would allow for causal explanation, predictability and the possibility of control. If we can know, according to this logic, the initial conditions of a system and the fixed laws that govern its behaviour, we can predict accurately and with certainty its outcomes or future behaviour.

See Chapter 1.4
Positivism

Informed by several significant discoveries in the natural sciences (e.g., Einstein's theory of relativity, Heisenberg's uncertainty principle, quantum mechanics), theorists working within the chaos, complexity or nonlinear dynamical systems paradigm draw attention to the fundamentally uncertain and unpredictable nature of complex systems, including human beings and the social systems within which they exist. Chaos theory problematizes causal-mechanistic models of explanation and the reductionist tendencies of traditional social science, instead emphasizing uncertainty, instability, nonlinearity and qualitative understanding of dynamical behavioural patterns rather than lawful mechanisms and simplified causal accounts.

The inherent complexity and 'sensitivity' of nonlinear dynamical systems would seem to have important implications for how we construct theoretical models and empirical investigations of crime. Chaos theory may help elucidate some of the fundamental flaws in and shortcomings of existing theoretical models, such as over-prediction and the inability to account for behavioural differences between similarly situated individuals or groups. Because seemingly small variables can produce changes that magnify over time to produce significant changes to system behaviour – a phenomenon referred to as 'sensitive dependence on initial conditions' or the butterfly effect – theoretical models of crime that focus only or primarily on immediate and 'visible' variables will miss the 'small' ones that may be, over time and through interactions with other variables, impacting systems in large ways (e.g., Williams 1999).

The kinds of systems that criminologists typically study – individuals, groups, neighbourhoods – are complex, open systems. Simply, this means that they consist of numerous interacting parts, and also interact with and are influenced by other external systems. Think, for example, of the ways in which biological systems, social systems and ecosystems not only are comprised of countless interacting and interdependent parts, but also exist in a state of mutual influence with one another. As such, the variables on which conventional criminology has most often focused in its search for causal priority can be thought of as existing under conditions of mutual causality and influence, and are themselves often effects of other effects. Chaos theorists reject the notion of mechanical causality, instead understanding events as emergent products of complex histories, relationships and present contexts. Within complex, nonlinear dynamical systems, often no single variable has causal priority; rather, events are outcomes of complex interactions occurring within and between interrelated systems. At the very least, this logic suggests a need for further intra- and interdisciplinary conceptual integration in future efforts to understand crime, law and justice (see Robinson and Beaver 2009).

In a more applied context, chaos theory implies limitations to our efforts to know and predict future outcomes. The notion of sensitivity to initial conditions illuminates and provides context for our inability to predict behaviour beyond the immediate future with an acceptable degree of accuracy. Importantly, however, assessments of risk and dangerousness have become critical components of the criminal justice system, impacting everything from bail decisions to the civil commitment of sexually violent predators. Chaos theory cautions us to be sensible about the level of accuracy we can ever expect to attain with such undertakings. It also implies a necessary prudence when utilizing predictive assessments, whether clinical or statistical, to inform decisions that impact the liberty interests of individuals in criminal and civil contexts (e.g., Williams 2008). The same finding of sensitivity to seemingly small inputs, however, has also been adopted by **postmodern and constitutive criminologists** as a conceptual tool for promoting affirmative social change. Small inputs can, at the right time and under the right conditions, prompt an iterative dynamic which over time results in larger, transformative kinds of changes (e.g., Milovanovic 2002).

See Chapter 4.28 Postmodern and constitutive criminologies

Other ideas associated with chaos theory such as 'attractors', 'fractals' and 'self-similarity' (that describe patterns of order within systems) and 'self-organization' (which describes the emergence of orderly dynamics from disorderly states) have worked their way into criminological models as well. Self-organization, for instance, is a process by which adaptive, orderly patterns appear from periods of disorder or disruption without external imposition or strict guidance. Self-organizing processes occur in various kinds of systems, including mathematical, chemical, biological and social. These patterns result from iterations and feedback within the system and, thus, order is considered an emergent property of the system rather than something imposed upon the system. Notions of self-organization and adaptability have been utilized by those interested in the qualitative study of social change and institutional change, as well as the dynamics of individual change such as recovery from substance abuse.

Whether chaos theory can be regarded as a 'theory' or is better considered a collection of 'tools' or metaphors remains a matter of debate. In addition, the mathematical and scientific foundations of chaos theory, its breadth and lack of coherent structure for integrations and applications in the social sciences have meant that its inroads remain largely uncharted. Developments in the study of complexity and nonlinear dynamical systems have been celebrated as ushering in a new paradigm within the natural and physical sciences;

whether that paradigmatic shift is realized in criminology and the social and behavioural sciences remains to be seen.

References

Milovanovic, Dragan. 2002. *Critical Criminology at the Edge: Postmodern Perspectives, Integration, and Applications*. Westport, CT: Praeger.

Robinson, Matthew, and Kevin Beaver. 2009. *Why Crime? An Interdisciplinary Approach to Explaining Criminal Behavior*. Durham, NC: Carolina Academic Press.

Walters, Glenn. 1999. Crime and Chaos: Applying Nonlinear Dynamic Principles to Problems in Criminology. *International Journal of Offender Therapy and Comparative Criminology* 43(2): 134–53.

Williams, Christopher. 2008. Predictive Efficacy and the Preventive Detention of Dangerous Sexual Offenders: Contributions from Nonlinear Dynamical Systems Theory. *Critical Criminology* 16(3): 185-96.

Williams, Franklin. 1999. *Imagining Criminology: An Alternative Paradigm*. New York: Garland.

Further reading

Gleick, James. 2008. *Chaos: Making a New Science*. New York: Penguin.

Milovanovic, Dragan. 1997. *Chaos, Criminology, and Social Justice: The New Orderly (Dis)Order*. Westport, CT: Praeger.

Pycroft, Aaron, and Clemens Bartollas (eds). 2014. *Applying Complexity Theory: Whole Systems Approaches to Criminal Justice and Social Work*. Bristol: Policy Press.

Urry, John (ed.). 2005. Special Issue on Complexity. *Theory, Culture, and Society* 22(5).

Williams, Christopher, and Bruce Arrigo. 2002. *Law, Psychology, and Justice: Chaos Theory and the New (Dis)order*. Albany: State University of New York Press.

Williams, Christopher, and Bruce Arrigo. 2004. *Theory, Justice, and Social Change: Theoretical Integrations and Critical Applications*. New York: Kluwer.

Conservation criminology

Carole Gibbs, Meredith L. Gore, Joseph A. Hamm, Louie Rivers III and Adam Zwickle

Conservation criminology is a research framework developed at Michigan State University (MSU) to advance multi- and interdisciplinary research on environmental risks (criminal or not) that occur at the intersection of social and ecological systems (Gibbs et al. 2010). Though the term was originally used by Herbig and Joubert (2006), the MSU framework is distinct in that it integrates the fields of criminology and criminal justice, conservation and natural resource management, and **risk** and decision science to expand the scope of **environmental problems** typically examined by criminologists. It also seeks to connect criminology to other physical and social sciences to increase the range of theoretical perspectives and interventions that may be used to address environmental problems.

See Chapter 6.7
Risk

See Chapter 4.16
Green criminology

The conservation criminology framework flows from the premise that using multiple disciplines better advances efforts to understand and address environmental issues than relying on a single discipline. For example, the risk and decision sciences provide a systematic method of assessing environmental impacts beyond violations of law. Technical risk-assessments of the probability of exposure to a harm multiplied by the severity if exposure occurs (Kasperson et al. 1988) can be integrated with public perceptions of risk to identify environmental risks. Theoretically, the needs of all stakeholders can inform the process of evaluating and taking actions to address those risks. Risks with a nexus to issues of compliance or justice (e.g., **environmental justice**, the aftermath of natural disasters) and environmental crimes are included under the domain of conservation criminology.

See Chapter 4.11 Environmental justice and victimology

In addition to drawing upon these disciplines to expand the scope of inquiry, the connection to these (and other) disciplines also increases understanding of, and the range of solutions to address, environmental problems. In some instances, criminological theories, such as **deterrence**, and **conflict-based perspectives**, may help explain environmental issues. These theoretical perspectives also suggest ways to address these problems, such as through the use of sanctions or fundamental changes to the structure of society. For other environmental problems, however, theoretical perspectives and interventions from outside criminology may be more useful.

See Chapter 1.17 Deterrence

See Chapter 3.3 Critical criminologies; Chapter 3.9 Marxist criminologies

Many environmental problems are the result of small, repeated, seemingly innocuous behaviours that are not amenable to regulation. For example, nonpoint source pollution from many diverse sources (e.g., stormwater run-off from city streets or farms) presents a significant challenge for regulation because it is not linked to a single identifiable polluter. In this context, deliberate risk communication and behavioural nudges may be much more effective in encouraging cooperative behaviour among the public than traditional regulation.

When public concerns are misaligned with technical risk assessments, risk communication may be used to influence risk perceptions, and therefore behaviour. Any message or issue must be framed in some manner, and the manner chosen will influence how an audience interprets the subject (Chong and Druckman 2007). Theories from psychology and the risk and decision sciences can help us understand how different ways of communicating risk may influence public perception and behaviour. 'Nudges' may also be used to influence behaviours that damage or threaten the environment. Nudges are behavioural interventions that seek to influence, without limiting, choice (Thaler and Sunstein 2008). Nudges can take the form of behavioural feedback, changing the default choice to the desired choice or taking into account natural decision heuristics and biases. Constructing decision contexts in a way to encourage cooperative behaviour may provide an alternative way to mitigate widespread environmental risks.

Perspectives from disciplines outside the base of conservation criminology, such as psychology, can also offer opportunities to reduce environmental impacts that fall within the framework. Research on trust offers an important window into contemporary natural-resource management (Sharp et al. 2013), as trust is often implicated in facilitating effective and efficient resource management (Cvetkovich and Winter 2003). Trust is often linked to both compliance (Hamm et al. 2013) and cooperation in voluntary situations, such as the management of private property: both are critical for effective natural-resource management.

Given that environmental policy is moving toward systems of governance rather than a strict reliance on government institutions (Holley et al. 2011), understanding how trust and risk perceptions influence stakeholder behaviour will be increasingly important in securing compliance and cooperation with a variety of interventions needed to address environmental problems. Perspectives in psychology and the risk and decision sciences can help enrich current understanding of the role of each of these factors in natural-resource issues. Furthermore, the introduction of these perspectives through the conservation criminology framework can also suggest a range of interventions beyond the criminological domain.

Conservation criminology has provided a foundation for research on wildlife poaching and trafficking. It has proven to be robust in rural field settings (e.g., Madagascar) and contexts (e.g., with low literacy groups), as well as with a range of mixed methods of analysis (e.g., content analysis, community mapping). By integrating principles from **opportunity theories of crime**, animal behaviour, satellite data, risk perception and machine learning, new insights for policy and practice have been produced about why and how **wildlife crimes** occur and where they are likely to transpire in the future. The framework facilitates connections between conservation science and policy, providing decision-makers with unique interdisciplinary insights about how and why wildlife poaching occurs so that policy alternatives can be more precisely designed, implemented and evaluated.

See Chapter 6.6
Opportunity
theory

See Chapter 4.35
Speciesism and
theriocide

The framework has also been used to examine pollution-related risks/crimes, including the international trade in electronic waste and multiple dimensions of climate change (i.e., drivers, impacts, mitigation and adaptation). Additional studies have applied conservation criminology to Confined Animal Feeding Operations and fisheries depletion related to the vestiges of apartheid in South African natural-resource management and the behaviour of traditional abalone fishers in South Africa who have been labelled 'poachers'. In this body of work, case studies have been used to describe the potential improvement in our knowledge and interventions to address these issues through the use of a multidisciplinary and/or interdisciplinary approach. For example, in a recent manuscript entitled 'Applying a conservation criminology framework to common-pool natural-resource issues', the authors suggested that the combined use of theories from criminology (procedural justice, rational choice) and risk and decision sciences (theories of risk perception) could increase understanding of the behaviour of traditional abalone fishers in South Africa and support a new collaborative management regime that involves the meaningful participation of all stakeholders, including the normally disenfranchised local fishers (Rivers and Gibbs 2011).

Due to the relative recency of the conservation criminology framework, formal assessments in the literature are limited. The primary published critique is of the term 'conservation', which has been wrongly interpreted as setting aside certain places for environmental and species protection while allowing others to be completely exploited, as though one compensates for the other (Halsey 2013). As conservation criminologists apply it, the term 'conservation' actually refers to the wise use and management of all natural resources. In the conservation arena, some have also indicated discomfort with the term 'criminology' when it is assumed to indicate that the behaviour of minor players in major natural-resource crimes should be addressed through criminalization. The use of the term 'criminology,' however, is not meant to indicate that criminalization is an appropriate solution to all (or any) environmental problems. The framework is based on a governance approach that supports tailoring interventions (e.g., alternative livelihoods, nudges, participatory decision-making) to specific problems.

Future research could expand upon the current studies to further test the framework. Case studies are the primary methodology used in the current conservation criminology framework, as this method is consistent with the principle of inductive reasoning upon which the framework is built. Future research could build on this initial work to include mixed methods and both cross-sectional and longitudinal designs.

As the framework matures, the introduction of criminological theories to issues that have traditionally lacked insight from criminology represents another valuable contribution. For example, the development and assessment of environmental policy has been dominated by physical scientists, political scientists, sociologists and law and policy experts. A byproduct of this approach is the neglect of insights from criminology about enforcement processes and structures (see e.g., Gibbs et al. 2010). The conservation criminology framework can help address this gap in the literature, and potentially in the development of policy.

References

Chong, Dennis, and James N. Druckman. 2007. Framing Theory. *Annual Review of Political Science* 10(1): 103–26.

Cvetkovich, George, and Patricia Winter. 2003. Trust and Social Representations of the Management of Threatened and Endangered Species. *Environment and Behavior* 35(2), 286–307.

Gibbs, Carole, Meredith Gore, Edmund McGarrell, and Louie Rivers III. 2010. Introducing Conservation Criminology: Toward Interdisciplinary Scholarship on Environmental Crimes and Risks. *British Journal of Criminology* 50(1): 124–44.

Halsey, Mark. 2013. Conservation Criminology and the 'General Accident' of Climate Change. In *Routledge International Handbook of Green Criminology*, Nigel South and Avi Brisman, eds, pp. 107–19. New York: Routledge.

Hamm, Joseph A., Lisa M. Pytlik Zillig, Mitchel N. Herian, Alan J. Tomkins, Hannah Dietrich, and Sarah Michaels. 2013. Trust and Intention to Comply with a Water Allocation Decision: The Moderating Roles of Knowledge and Consistency. *Ecology and Society* 18(4): art. 49.

Herbig, F.J.W. and Joubert, S.J. 2006. Criminological semantics: Conservation criminology – vision or vagary? *Acta Criminologica* 19(3): 88–103.

Holley, Cameron, Neil Gunningham, and Clifford Shearing. 2011. *The New Environmental Governance*. New York: Earthscan.

Kasperson, Roger E., Ortwin Renn, Paul Slovic, Halina S. Brown, Jacque Emel, Robert Goble, Jeanne X. Kasperson, and Samuel Ratick. 1988. The Social Amplification of Risk: A Conceptual Framework. *Risk Analysis* 8(2): 177–87.

Rivers, Louie, and Carole Gibbs. 2011. Applying a Conservation Criminology Framework to Common Pool Natural Resource Issues. *International Journal of Comparative and Applied Criminal Justice* 35(4): 327–46.

Sharp, Emily A., Rik Twaites, Allan Curtis, and Joanne Millar. 2013. Trust and Trustworthiness: Conceptual Distinctions and their Implications for Natural Resources Management. *Journal of Environmental Planning and Management* 56(8): 1246–65.

Thaler, Richard H., and Cass R. Sunstein. 2008. *Nudge: Improving Decisions about Health, Wealth, and Happiness*: New Haven, CT: Yale University Press.

Further reading

Gibbs, Carole, Edmund F. McGarrell, Mark Axelrod and Louie Rivers III. 2011. Conservation Criminology and the Global Trade in Electronic Waste: Applying a Multi-Disciplinary Research Framework. *International Journal of Comparative and Applied Criminal Justice* 35(4): 327–46.

Gibbs, Carole, Michael Cassidy and Louie Rivers III. 2013. A Routine Activities Analysis of White-Collar Crime in Carbon Markets. *Law and Policy* 34(4): 341–74.

Gore, Meredith L. 2011. The Science of Conservation Crime. *Conservation Biology* 25(4): 659–61.

Gore, Meredith L., Jonah Ratsimbazafy, and Michelle L. Lute. 2013. Rethinking Corruption in Conservation Crime: Insights from Madagascar. *Conservation Letters* 6(6): 430–38.

McGarrell, Edmund F., and Carole Gibbs 2014. Conservation Criminology, Environmental Crime and Risk: An Application to Climate Change. *Oxford Handbooks Online*. 3 November 2014. Oxford University Press. www.oxfordhandbooks.com/view/10.1093/oxfordhb/9780199935383.001.0001/oxfordhb-9780199935383-e-54. Accessed 7 November 2014.

Convict criminology

Jeffrey Ian Ross

Convict criminology emerged in the early 1990s and has been variously referred to as a school, movement, group, organization and/or network, with its primary concern being the belief that the convict voice was not adequately acknowledged (i.e., was ignored, minimized or misinterpreted) in both academic and policy-related research. It also expressed difficulty with scholarship in the field of corrections (the study of prisons, jails, convicts, correctional officers and administrators) that was disproportionately statistical in nature and divorced from the lived realities of the carceral experience. The following addresses six interrelated questions:

- What is convict criminology?
- Who is a convict criminologist?
- What is the history of convict criminology?
- What has it accomplished?
- What have been the criticisms?
- And, what are its future directions?

Since its beginnings, convict criminology has drawn attention to a range of problems created by the criminal justice apparatus and defenders of the status quo. It is anchored theoretically in the fields of corrections and **critical criminology**. Although the location in corrections is understandable, the connection to critical criminology is reflective of a concern for marginalized voices, the dispossessed and powerless, and a historical interest in critical inquiry. Convict criminology also emphasizes the role of auto-ethnography

See Chapter 3.3
Critical
criminologies

as a favoured method for understanding the lived experiences of convicts and ex-convicts.

The question of who is a convict criminologist has been debated and is open to interpretation. In general, a convict criminologist is an individual who:

- has spent a significant amount of time in jail or prison, and is in possession of a PhD in criminology/criminal justice or a related field, or is on his/her way to earning a PhD in these academic disciplines;
- self-identifies as a convict criminologist;
- believes that the convict voice is underrepresented; and
- to varying degrees, participates in corrections-based research/scholarship, mentorship and activism.

Although most of these criteria are self-evident, the earning of a PhD means that the individual has been subjected to the rigors of academic training and analysis, and hopefully can speak with authority when it comes to scholarly research. One exception to this description includes critical criminologists and activists who possess PhDs who are committed to the goals of the groups.

Given this definition, it is inappropriate to label someone else a convict criminologist unless he/she has self-identified as such (Ross et al. 2016). Related to this, convict criminologists respect individual choices about revelations of personal histories and decisions to be publicly identified as a convict criminologist. Moreover, unlike most formal organizations, convict criminology does not have an official membership list. Convict criminology is a diverse collection of individuals whose interests range across scholarly research, mentoring and activism.

The history of convict criminology has been the subject of a number of reviews, highlights of which can be summarized as follows.

The first formal expressions of the idea of a convict criminology were put forward in the 1990s, although the underpinning sentiments and beliefs can be traced to a handful of criminologists who were ex-convicts. These include Frank Tannenbaum (1893–1969), Gwen Nettler (1913–2007), John Irwin (1930-2010) and Edward D. Tromanhauser (1932–) (although convict criminologists have never applied arbitrarily or inferred the convict criminology identity to any living social scientist).

Jeffrey Ian Ross and Stephen C. Richards were founders of a group of like-minded scholars and graduate students in the 1990s, and encouraged participation in meetings and as writers and presenters at the American Society of Criminology (ASC) conference and elsewhere. With the publication of *Convict Criminology* (Ross and Richards 2003) and the use of social media, convict criminology expanded beyond North America. One of the first initiatives was an international conference, 'Global Perspectives on Re-entry' (with a focus on convict criminology), held at the University of Tampere, Finland. Shortly thereafter, a British Convict Criminology group that organizes panels at the British Society of Criminology emerged (Ross et al. 2014).

Convict criminology is a growing movement, as evidenced by the number of panels held at national criminology conferences, publications and the adoption of this perspective by international scholars. This is probably related to the pace of mass incarceration in the United States and recognition of convict criminology as a viable explanation for this state of affairs.

Convict criminology has made a number of contributions to research, mentoring and activism, organizing sessions at criminology meetings, producing peer-reviewed journal articles, chapters and popular books (e.g., Ross and Richards 2002, 2009). In terms of methodology, convict criminology emphasizes auto-ethnography.

Convict criminologists have advised and mentored many convicts and ex-convicts at different stages of their prison and academic careers. These individuals (both men and women) are diverse in background, including African-Americans, Hispanics and members of the LGBT community. Some are in the process of earning their bachelor's degree; others have already earned their doctorates; and some are now professors of criminology/criminal justice or related fields. Some may be less active with the group because they are busy with civil-rights, social-justice and social-work activities. In addition, many members of the group have devoted considerable time to mentoring ex-convicts in areas not restricted to academia.

The convict criminology group has engaged in numerous examples of activist criminology (Richards et al. 2011). This includes helping to change Kentucky's sentencing policies, and offering classes and workshops within prisons (e.g., the Inviting Convicts to College programme). A convict-criminology website and Facebook page provide ways to communicate with other like-minded individuals to encourage mentoring and activism, and as contact points for ex-cons, family members of ex-cons and others seeking advice.

Throughout its history, convict criminology has sustained numerous criticisms, both internally and externally. These have included a perception that convict criminology lacks objectivity, that there is a tendency to over-generalize, and the possibility that contributors to convict criminology are mediocre in academic stature (see, e.g., Newbold and Ross 2013).

More recently, Joanne Belknap devoted three pages of a sixteen-page article, based on her speech as president of the ASC, to the subject of convict criminology, and criticized convict criminology for being predominately a collection of white men who have failed to include ex-convict women, African-Americans and lesbian, gay, transgender and bisexual individuals (Belknap 2015). The piece also took convict criminology to task for failing to include three individuals she considered to be convict criminologists. The speech and article, however, ignored the numerous efforts that convict criminology has engaged in to build a welcoming collective that includes the diverse voices of PhD-educated convicts and ex-cons. Belknap's comments can be seen as an example of a superficial understanding of the history, intent and activities of convict criminology (Ross et al. 2016).

Despite notable shortcomings, the auto-ethnographic approach is an appropriate methodology for uncovering the day-to-day realities, subtleties and nuances of living behind bars. So much occurs inside prisons that is not amenable to most quantitative research methodology: not every action can be easily operationalized; nor are survey methods the best way to delve into the heart of the prison experience. The auto-ethnographic approach is also therapeutic for those who have been incarcerated for long periods of time behind bars. Auto-ethnographic methods go beyond traditional prison memoirs and provide a self-conscious reflection on the experience of prison.

Members of the convict-criminology group are motivated to achieve their objectives, and often recognize the need to engage in more rigorous analysis. Other efforts include explaining to others their tireless attempts to recruit women, visible minorities and members of the LGBT community. Another aspect is to re-emphasize the need for people who claim to be 'convict criminologists' to have adequate/appropriate training. Finally, there is a need to emphasize the mentoring that the group undertakes.

Has convict criminology accomplished everything that it set out to do? No, but it is in the early stages of development. Convict criminology has been successful in bringing notice to the problems inherent in a carceral society. Raising public awareness is a worthy goal of any social movement, but there is more to do.

References

Belknap, Joanne. 2015. Activist Criminology: Criminologists' Responsibility to Advocate for Social and Legal Justice. *Criminology* 53(1): 1–22.

Newbold, Greg, and Jeffrey I. Ross. 2013. Convict Criminology at the Crossroads. *The Prison Journal* 93(1): 3–10.

Richards, Stephen C., Jeffrey I. Ross, Greg Newbold, Michael Lenza, Richard S. Jones, Daniel S. Murphy, and Robert S. Grigsby. 2011. Convict Criminology, Prisoner Re-entry, and Policy Recommendations. In *Global Perspectives on Re-Entry*, Ikponwosa O. Ekunwe and Richard S. Jones, eds, pp. 198–222. Tampere, Finland: University of Tampere Press.

Ross, Jeffrey I., and Stephen C. Richards. 2002. *Behind Bars: Surviving Prison*. Indianapolis: Alpha Books.

Ross, Jeffrey I., and Stephen C. Richards. 2009. *Beyond Bars: Rejoining Society after Prison*. Indianapolis: Alpha Books.

Ross, Jeffrey I., and Stephen C. Richards (eds). 2003. *Convict Criminology*. Belmont, CA: Wadsworth.

Ross, Jeffery I., Richard S. Jones, Michael Lenza, and Stephen C. Richards. 2016. Convict Criminology and the Struggle for Inclusion. *Critical Criminology* 24(4): 489–501.

Ross, Jeffrey I., Sacha Darke, Andy Aresti, Greg Newbold, and Rod Earle. 2014. The Development of Convict Criminology beyond North America. *International Journal of Criminal Justice* 24(2): 121–33.

Further reading

Jones, Richard S., Jeffrey I. Ross, Stephen C. Richards, and Daniel S. Murphy. 2009. The First Dime: A Decade of Convict Criminology. *The Prison Journal* 89(2): 151–71.

Leyva, Martin, and Christopher Bickel. 2010. From Corrections to College: The Value of a Convict's Voice. *Western Criminology Review* 11(1): 50–60.

Newbold, Greg, Jeffrey I. Ross, and Stephen C. Richards. 2010. The emerging field of convict criminology. In *Encyclopedia of Criminological Theory*, Francis Cullen and Pamela Wilcox, eds, pp. 2010–12. Thousand Oaks, CA: Sage.

Newbold, Greg, Jeffrey I. Ross, Richard S. Jones, Stephen C. Richards, and Michael Lenza. 2014. Prison Research from the Inside: The Role of Convict Auto-Ethnography. *Qualitative Inquiry* 20(4): 439–48.

Richards, Stephen C. 2013. The New School of Convict Criminology Thrives and Matures. *Critical Criminology* 21(3): 375–87.

Richards, Stephen C., Greg Newbold, and Jeffrey I. Ross. 2009. Convict criminology. In *21st Century Criminology: A Reference Handbook*, Vol. 1, J. Mitchell Miller, ed., pp. 356–63. Thousand Oaks, CA: Sage.

Ross, Jeffrey I., Miguel Zaldivar, and Richard Tewksbury. 2015. Breaking Out of Prison and into Print? Rationales and Strategies to Assist Educated Convicts Conduct Scholarly Research and Writing behind Bars. *Critical Criminology* 23(1): 73–83.

Ross, Jeffrey I., Stephen C. Richards, Greg Newbold, Michael Lenza, and Robert S. Grigsby. 2011. Convict criminology. In *Handbook of Critical Criminology*, Walter S. DeKeseredy and Molly Dragiewicz, eds, pp. 160–71. New York: Routledge.

Ross, Jeffrey I., Stephen C. Richards, Greg Newbold, Richard S. Jones, Michael Lenza, Daniel S. Murphy, Richard Hogan, and G. David Curry. 2011. Knocking on the Ivory Tower's Door: The Experience of Ex-Convicts Applying for Tenure-Track University Positions, *Journal of Criminal Justice Education* 22(2): 267–85.

Judith van Erp and Wim Huisman

See Chapter 4.12
Financial crime

See Chapter 4.16
Green criminology

See Chapter 6.4
Cybercrime

See Chapter 4.13
Genocide and
ecocide; Chapter
4.35 Speciesism
and theriocide

See Chapter 4.39
Victimology;
Chapter 4.11
Environmental
justice and
victimology

See Chapter 4.41
White-collar crime

See Chapter 2.7
Techniques of
neutralization

Corporate crimes are illegal and harmful acts, or omissions, committed by legitimate organizations or their members for the benefit of these organizations. Examples include **financial manipulation**, accounting fraud, corporate manslaughter or violence, **environmental harms** caused by corporate acts or negligence, corporate human rights violations, cartels, corporate bribery, corporate espionage, corporate **cybercrime** and, recently, software manipulation. These acts can result in enormous financial and social harm, as well as loss of trust, which is often difficult to quantify, and can bring about **environmental damage** affecting humans, non-human animals and ecosystems, which may be difficult to recognize. Corporate crime often results in mass **victimization**, in which victims are often unidentified and sometimes even unaware of the harm inflicted upon them.

The concept 'corporate crime' is generally reserved for crimes attributed to legal persons or corporate executives. In contrast to **'white-collar crime'**, which is associated with *individual offenders*, corporate crime draws attention to the opportunities and conditions related to the *organizational context* within which the crime occurs. Although corporate crimes are ultimately committed by individual members of an organization, the corporate crime concept emphasizes the decisive role of the corporate form in structuring opportunities for crime. Corporate crimes cannot be regarded purely as a result of individual decisions and motives, but are committed for, and justified by, the organization. Organizational norms, culture and socialization practices are essential explanations of corporate crimes: organizations provide individuals with **motives, beliefs and goals** to behave in ways that they would probably perceive as unethical as individuals separate from their organizational roles. Organizational strategy may impose goals and targets on (middle) managers that are impossible to realize with legal means. Organizational structures may result in irrationalities, 'group think', or dispersed information about risks or effects of organizational behaviour, resulting in flawed decision-making with harmful effects. Moreover, standard or automated operating procedures may instigate behaviour even without a real decision being made. Organizational hierarchy detaches those actually committing an offence from the responsibility for their behaviour, which may result in crimes of obedience. Finally, legal personhood can provide anonymity, legal protection, as well as a structure for avoiding blame for individuals acting in the name of these corporate bodies. In sum, paradoxically, it is often *conformity* to organizational norms and goals that can explain corporate deviancy.

Understanding the causes of corporate crime requires the integration of knowledge and theories from various disciplines concerning: organizational behaviour, organizational psychology and organizational sociology; the role of corporate governance, structure and culture; group decision-making and its flaws and irrationalities. Making sense of the aetiology of corporate crime also requires understanding the market and political economy, as well as the regulatory and enforcement context (or lack thereof) and its translation into organizational perceptions of risk. The criminological analysis of corporate crime therefore requires the realization of the interdisciplinary promise of criminology in full.

A particularly important topic in the analysis of corporate crime is the role of corporate power in shaping a legal environment beneficial to structural opportunities for profit. Corporations have the financial means, legal knowledge, economic power, connections and institutional access to create opportunities for influencing their regulatory and enforcement environment far beyond the potential of most individuals. A perennial debate in corporate-crime scholarship is whether the definition of corporate crime should be restricted to criminal offences or whether it should be broadened to include offences of administrative and civil law, or even corporate behaviour that is harmful but not illegal. A corporate-power perspective contends, however, that corporations are able to resist the law, to avoid criminalization, control and enforcement, and to define the law in favour of profit maximization. Limiting the object of study to criminal offences fails to take into account the fact that corporate crime is often enabled by ambiguous laws and regulations, which are closely related to corporate power. As such, the concept of 'corporate harm' has been suggested as a more suitable concept than corporate crime because it more naturally includes ambiguous behaviours such as loophole-seeking behaviour, tax evasion and gaming the law, as well as global harms that national laws fail to address or in which **state agencies** are involved. Corporate harm, however, includes unintended and unforeseen harms, whereas the concept of corporate crime better captures the responsibility of the corporation for the damage.

See Chapter 4.37
State-corporate
crime

A recurrent theme of corporate-crime scholarship has been the leniency of punishment – in particular, the failure of criminal prosecution of corporate crime. Remarkably, for example, the destructive behaviours of financial corporations that caused the global financial crisis have rarely been investigated as offences, and have not led to significant forms of punishment. Sanctions for corporate crime can be imposed on the responsible individual managers, but corporate criminal-liability laws enable prosecutors to also put blame on the legal entity for the acts of its individual employees, if the responsibility should be attributed to the corporation as a whole. Whereas corporate criminal liability developed in the US since the early 1900s, it was only very recently introduced in most of continental Europe. But, despite its massive adoption since 1999 – with now only Germany, Greece and Latvia not having introduced some kind of corporate criminal liability – criminal prosecution of corporations in Europe is also rare. In the US, deferred prosecutions are now the common answer to corporate crimes, but are also often criticized as lacking transparency, not bringing justice to the victims, lacking stigma and failing to

See Chapter 1.17
Deterrence

adequately **deter corporate crime**.

Remarkably, whereas criminologists tend to advocate against punitiveness with regard to street offenders, they have frequently called for more severe

See Chapter 5.16
Retribution

punishments for corporate crime. **Retributive** arguments left aside, the empirical evidence for the deterrent effect of sanctions on businesses is weak (Simpson et al. 2014). Moreover, criminal law is obviously not the only source of control. The majority of corporate behaviour is governed by administrative regulations, and at the same time, private regulation of business activity is increasing: the majority of business regulation actually stems from markets now. The actual impact of civil liability, administrative fines and reputational damage arising out of non-legal sanctions, in comparison to criminal judgment, is an empirical question. In some cases, civil liability may result in higher financial damage to a corporation than a criminal fine, in particular

See Chapter 4.14
Globalization

in a **globalizing** context. Likewise, the immense administrative sanctions imposed, for example, by the European Commission against cartel offences, may in reality be more of a deterrent than a criminal fine in one European Union (EU) member state. In other words, as much as we know about the limited impact of sanctions on regular offenders, we know little about the impact of sanctions on businesses.

The relative impact of various types of social control (criminal, administrative, civil, professional, reputational, societal) and their interplay is therefore one of the most important subjects for future research contributing to the prevention of corporate crime. The dominant criminological theory for effective corporate social control is 'responsive regulation' (Ayres and Braithwaite 1992). Responsive regulation argues that state sanctions should be the tip of a pyramid in which the majority of enforcement activity is exercised by third-party governance by private market regulators, professional auditors, local communities and non-governmental organizations (NGOs). In situations with strong social control, state enforcement authorities can 'speak softly' while carrying severe sanctions as the big stick that is only rarely used. Although responsive regulation and, in particular, the regulatory pyramid have been adopted widely across the globe, their main premise – that strong sanctions and eventually incapacitation are available as a last resort against recurrent offenders – is often not met in practice. Much remains to be done, therefore, with regard to understanding the complex interplay of various types of social control with the aim of combining them in a smart mix of instruments for a strong and effective web of control. For corporate crime theory, which has tended to be mainly state-centred, this means that it should adapt to a more pluralistic regulatory practice.

Increasingly, corporate crime scholarship addresses the relation between globalization and corporate crime and, in particular, the opportunities created by globalization and the increasing global effects of corporate acts. Corporations and markets globalize, but regulation and institutions do not globalize at the same pace. Therefore, monitoring and enforcement are still carried out at national or sometimes even local level, although the harm caused by illegal or irresponsible corporate behaviour may affect communities in several countries. Corporations based in the global north, sometimes more economically powerful than entire developing states, can also exploit opportunities created by weak oversight in these states. One of the most exciting current developments in corporate crime scholarship is the emergence of research on corporate human rights violations in developing countries and corporate green crimes against natural resources in, mainly, the global south.

See Chapter 4.16
Green criminology

A final question is whether criminology itself keeps pace with the globalization of the corporate world by extending the scope of research from the Anglo-Saxon world to globalizing markets, emerging economies and developing countries. European corporate crime scholarship is strengthening (Van Erp et al. 2015) and, recently, Asian research, in particular on China, is emerging (Pontell and Geis 2010), but corporate crime in Africa and Latin America is still understudied.

References

Ayres, Ian, and John Braithwaite. 1992. *Responsive Regulation: Transcending the Deregulation Debate*. Oxford: Oxford University Press.

Erp, Judith van, Wim Huisman, and Gudrun Vande Walle (eds). 2015. *The Routledge Handbook on White-Collar and Corporate Crime in Europe*. Abingdon and New York: Routledge.

Pontell, Henry, and Gilbert Geis. 2010. Introduction: White-Collar and Corporate Crime in Asia. *Asian Journal of Criminology* 5(2): 83–8.

Simpson, Sally, Melissa Rorie, Mariel Alper, and Natalie Schell-Busey. 2014. Corporate Crime Deterrence: A Systematic Review. *Campbell Systematic Reviews*: 4.

Further reading

Barak, Gregg (ed.). 2015. *Routledge International Handbook of the Crimes of the Powerful*. London: Routledge.

Cullen, Francis, Gray Cavender, William Maakestad, and Michael Benson. 2015. *Corporate Crime under Attack: The Fight to Criminalize Business Violence* (2nd edn). Abingdon: Routledge.

Pontell, Henry, and Gilbert Geis (eds). 2007. *International Handbook of White-Collar and Corporate Crime*. New York: Springer.

White, Rob (ed.). 2010. *Global Environmental Harm: Criminological Perspectives*. Cullompton, UK: Willan.

Will, Susan, Stephen Handelman, and David Brotherton. 2012. *How They Got Away With It. White Collar Criminals and the Financial Meltdown*. New York: Columbia University Press.

Crimmigration

Ben Bowling and Sophie Westenra

The concept of 'crimmigration' refers to the intertwinement of crime control and immigration control. It represents the distinct laws and legal processes that states employ as a means of exerting control over a sector of our **global society**. As US legal scholar Juliet Stumpf (2013:59) explains, the integration of immigration and criminal spheres 'tends to generate more severe outcomes, limit procedural protections, and encourage enforcement and adjudication processes that segregate non-citizens'. Yet what is emerging is not only differential treatment, but also an independent, specialized penal system – what we call a 'crimmigration control system'. Authorized by a unique panoply of 'crimmigration law', the crimmigration control system harnesses all the elements of the crime control industry: physical defences; mechanisms for intelligence gathering and **surveillance**; policing and law enforcement; a specialized legal process, courts and tribunals; and a 'secure estate' of detention centres. Recent developments in the UK, such as the Immigration Act 2014 and the Immigration Bill 2015, exemplify what is a global trajectory towards transnational social control. The use of these laws, institutions and practices, divorced from the criminal justice system, demands our scrutiny.

Crimmigration law lays the foundations for the system. It is an umbrella term for the interweaving of administrative immigration law and criminal law 'under conditions of interchangeability and mutual reinforcement' (Aas 2014:525). This convergence produces an instrumental panoply of laws geared towards the exclusion of undesirable non-citizens from which immigration officials may 'cherry-pick', depending on their objectives and resources.

See Chapter 4.14
Globalization

See Chapter 5.19
Surveillance

There are four different elements to crimmigration law: immigration offences, deportation, accessorial liability and creative civil exclusions. The creation of immigration offences for what were formerly administrative breaches of immigration law has proliferated in recent years. As the UK Home Office asserts, there is now a corresponding criminal offence for almost every breach of immigration law. This provides immigration officers with an armoury of powers to enforce compliance, with disregard for basic principles of criminalization, such as the requirements of harm and culpability.

The deportation of a non-citizen as a result of a criminal conviction is a second key element of crimmigration law. Since the UK Borders Act 2007, all non-European Economic Area (non-EEA) offenders sentenced to 12 months in custody or more, and EEA offenders sentenced to 24 months in custody or more, face automatic deportation at the end of their sentence. The classification of deportation as 'a measure taken in pursuance of "the law of aliens" not the criminal law' (*AT (Pakistan) v Secretary of State for the Home Department* [2010] EWCA Civ 567) allows for a departure from the evaluative approach to sentencing applied by the criminal courts. Issues relating to the proportionality of the sanction and the principle that no one should be punished twice for the same offence are similarly avoided.

A new kind of 'accessorial liability', utilizing both civil and criminal sanctions, has also developed. There are now criminal sanctions for facilitating a breach of immigration law, and there are civil penalty regimes, supported by criminal sanctions, for employers, airline carriers and private landlords who offer jobs, flights or housing to an undocumented migrant or overstayer.

Finally, creative civil exclusions have been introduced by the Immigration Act 2014 to further create a 'hostile environment' for migrants who are not entitled to be in the United Kingdom. Banks are not permitted to open a current account for migrants without leave to remain, and driving licences can be revoked. The Immigration Bill 2015 will lead to many of these creative civil exclusions being intertwined with criminal sanctions. Driving without a regular immigration status, for example, is to become an offence carrying up to 51 weeks' imprisonment.

With the development of crimmigration law, an independent form of policing and law enforcement has also emerged. As Ian MacDonald QC observes in *MacDonald's Immigration Law and Practice* (2010:1192), the UK Border Force is 'a true immigration police force'. The UK Border Force is responsible for immigration and customs controls at 138 ports in the UK, France and Belgium, and has a full-time staff of 7,600. Officers have powers of arrest, search, entry and seizure, and the power to use reasonable force if necessary in carrying out any of their functions. They have dark-blue, police-style uniforms to broadcast their authority, and their broad mandate is 'public protection'.

At a wider level, national border controls are bolstered by multiple agencies, such as the Border Policing Command – a new specialist unit within the National Crime Agency. The 2015 announcement of a British taskforce to be based with Europol in Sicily and The Hague, which will work with the Border

Force, GCHQ and MI6 to disrupt the operations of those attempting to cross the Mediterranean Sea, indicates just how far border control has moved from being an administrative enterprise (see Chorley 2015).

The crimmigration control system also parallels the criminal justice system through its physical segregation of 'undesirables'. Defensive technologies such as fences with razor wire and electricity continue to be exploited to their fullest extent, for both instrumental and symbolic reasons. Among recent UK developments, a 2-mile, high-security fence has been sent to France to increase **security** around the Channel Tunnel.

See Chapter 5.17
Security and
counter-security
See Chapter 5.19
Surveillance

An increasingly sophisticated transnational system of **surveillance** has developed as a vital aspect of the crimmigration control system. It acquires intelligence from public and private data sources, across borders and institutions. It is characterized by increasingly automated controls through the use of computer systems and databases, biometrics and automated border systems. Notably, it employs digital 'social sorting' mechanisms, which classify passengers as a precursor to differential treatment.

Broeders and Hampshire (2013) have identified three distinct processes of categorization. 'Blacklisting' leads to exclusion. Immigration offenders are now included on the criminal and terrorist watch lists with Eurodac (European Dactyloscopy) – the European fingerprint database for identifying asylum seekers – being the most developed example of migration blacklisting in the EU.

In the case of blacklisted persons, decision-making comes very close to being automated. Due to pre-embarkation checks, private carriers such as airlines play a central role in the practice of blacklisting. With heavy carrier sanctions, they are unlikely to listen to the explanations of travellers if they are flagged in a watch-list check prior to departure. 'Greylisting' involves risk-profiling from Advanced Passenger Information and Passenger Name Records, with little human agency, which will then lead to intervention by the Border Force if the National Border Targeting Centre issues an alert. 'Greenlisting' equates to facilitated inclusion. These are the 'desirables' – the 'registered travellers' who can pass, unsupervised, through E-borders after an initial check and screening at time of registration. By fast-tracking the border passage of wanted passengers, tighter controls can be levied on unwanted passengers.

The crimmigration control system also has its own system of appeals and tribunals. A two-tier independent tribunal with an immigration and asylum chamber hears appeals on 'administrative' immigration decisions, including deportation and detention. While criminal cases are heard in the criminal courts, immigration status is a 'pervasively important factor in almost every aspect of a criminal proceeding' (Aliverti 2013:107), from the refusal of bail to the systematic administering of custodial sentences. Both criminal and administrative immigration cases alike are processed in a highly bureaucratic manner. Appeal rights are tightly confined under the Immigration Act 2014, and – in an extension of the 'deport first, appeal later' regime – the Immigration Bill 2015 will make all immigration appeals, except asylum cases, exercisable out-of-country only.

Finally, the crimmigration control system includes a large 'secure estate' made up of immigration removal centres, prisons, short-term holding facilities at airports and ports, a special pre-departure facility for families at Gatwick Airport, and police cells. While there is significant variation in the physical estate and the restrictions imposed on detainees, there exists a consistent concern about security that mirrors the prison system. Some are built to restrictive Category B prison security standards, while several Immigration Removal Centres are situated in former or current penal institutions, or are run by former prison governors. Detention is nevertheless held up to be a matter of administrative convenience, thus circumventing the automatic judicial oversight that imprisonment attracts.

The various aspects to the 'crimmigration control system' have been observed and addressed by numerous scholars across a range of fields in many Western countries. What is emerging, however, is a global trend towards a transnational crimmigration control system that immobilizes the purportedly 'undesirable' sector of our global society. The institutionalized use of crime control techniques within a regulatory system of population management demands critical analysis. In the current political environment, this theoretical, empirical and practical project is all the more pressing.

References

Aas, Katja F. 2014. Bordered Penality: Precarious Membership and Abnormal Justice. *Punishment and Society* 16(5): 520–41.

Aliverti, Ana. 2013. *Crimes of Mobility: Criminal Law and the Regulation of Immigration*. Abingdon: Routledge.

Broeders, Dennis, and James Hampshire. 2013. Dreaming of Seamless Borders: ICTs and the Pre-Emptive Governance of Mobility in Europe. *Journal of Ethnic and Migration Studies* 39(8): 1201–18.

Chorley, Matt. 2015. British Spies and Police Sent into North Africa to Target Criminal Gangs Smuggling Thousands of Migrants across the Med. *Mail Online*, 24 June. www.dailymail.co.uk/news/article-3137214/British-spies-police-sent-North-Africa-target-criminal-gangs-smuggling-thousands-migrants-Med.html. Accessed 23 January 2017.

MacDonald, Ian. 2010. *MacDonald's Immigration Law and Practice in the United Kingdom*. London: LexisNexis.

Stumpf, Juliet. 2013. The process is the punishment in crimmigration law. In *The Borders of Punishment: Migration, Citizenship, and Social Exclusion*, Katja F. Aas and Mary Bosworth, eds, pp. 58–75. Oxford: Oxford University Press.

Further reading

Aas, Katja F., and Mary Bosworth (eds). 2013. *The Borders of Punishment: Migration, Citizenship, and Social Exclusion*. Oxford: Oxford University Press.

Aliverti, Ana. 2012. Making People Criminal: The Role of the Criminal Law in Immigration Enforcement. *Theoretical Criminology* 16(4): 417–34.

Bosworth, Mary. 2008. Governing through Migration Control: Security and Citizenship in Britain. *British Journal of Criminology* 48(6): 703–19.

De Giorgi, Alessandro. 2010. Immigration Control, Post-Fordism, and Less Eligibility: A Materialist Critique of the Criminalisation of Immigration across Europe. *Punishment and Society* 12(2): 147–67.

Michalowski, Raymond. 2007. Border Militarization and Migrant Suffering: A Case of Transnational Social Injury. *Social Justice* 34(2): 62–76.

See Chapter 3.3
Critical
criminologies

See Chapter 4.32
Queer criminology

4.7 Critical race theory

Lee E. Ross

Critical race theory concerns the study and transformation of the relationship between race, racism and power. The theory questions the very foundations of the legal order, including equality theory, legal reasoning, enlightenment rationalism and neutral principles of constitutional law (Delgado and Stefancic 2001). Building on the work of **radical criminologists**, critical race theorists believe that the disproportionate criminalization of persons of colour is a product of criminal definitions exercised by those in power seeking to protect their own interests. This chapter presents an overview of critical race theory and its explanation of the effects of racism and racially disparate outcomes throughout various stages of American justice systems. The inability of conflict and related theories to address subtle and covert forms of racism (i.e., petit apartheid) is a severe limitation on their usefulness, and therefore a critical-race theoretical perspective is heralded as more theoretically relevant than competing perspectives that view social and economic forces as fundamental causes of crime.

Conceived in the arena of critical legal studies, pioneers in the area of critical race theory include Derrick Bell, Richard Delgado and Alan Freeman, among others. European influences included important figures like Jacques Derrida and Antonio Gramsci. The American tradition is exemplified by César Chávez, Frederick Douglass, W.E.B. DuBois, Martin Luther King Jr, Sojourner Truth and the Black Panther and Chicano movements of the 1960s and early 1970s. Critical race theory is credited with various spin-off movements that include an emerging Asian-American jurisprudence, a powerful Latino-critical (LatCrit) contingent, a spirited **queer-crit interest group** and Native-American scholars who address **indigenous peoples' rights,** sovereignty and land claims. Collectively, these pioneering efforts have recognized that overt practices of racism often yield to more subtle and covert forms of racism that make it far more difficult to discern. Moreover, the ordinariness and prevalence of racism renders it harder to recognize, much less address.

See Chapter 4.18
Indigenous
criminology

Critical race theory has various underpinnings that easily distinguish it from other mainstream criminological theories. For instance, critical race scholars view racism as endemic in US society – deeply ingrained legally, culturally and even psychologically. Moreover, racism is ordinary, not aberrational 'normal science'. Contrary to claims of a post-racial society, racism is not only alive and well, but also experienced daily by most people of colour in the USA. Borrowing from several traditions – including liberalism, law and society, feminism and Marxism – critical race theory transcends many epistemological and disciplinary boundaries. The origins of critical race theory can be traced to a reinterpretation of civil rights (and its limitations) to illustrate that laws to remedy racial inequality are often undermined before they are fully implemented. Perhaps its most salient feature is that it exposes legal claims of neutrality, objectivity, colour-blindness and meritocracy as mere camouflages for the self-interest of powerful entities in society.

A litany of concepts captures the spirit of critical race theory, including the social construction thesis, differential racialization, **intersectionality** and anti-essentialism, among others. Two of the more powerful concepts are those of *legal indeterminacy* and *first-person narrative* (i.e., storytelling). Legal indeterminacy refers to the idea that not every legal case has one correct outcome. A classic example of legal indeterminacy can be witnessed in an examination of the 1985 Supreme Court case of *Tennessee v. Garner*, 471 U.S. 1 (1985). There, the Court held that the police may not invariably use deadly force on a fleeing suspect, even though they have probable cause to authorize an arrest (a 'seizure' of the person under the Fourth Amendment.) Yet, the law – even in its finest hour – is a function of time, place and circumstance. Ross (2010:396) noted:

See Chapter 4.20
Intersectionality

See Chapter 4.22
Narrative
criminology

> Assume for the moment that Garner was a suspected terrorist in possession of an incendiary device. He refuses to halt when ordered by police and deadly force was used to make his arrest. We soon realize there is little to prevent a court from validating police use of deadly force on a 'fleeing terrorist'. Hence, the indeterminacy thesis serves as an unpleasant reminder of the precariousness of criminal law.

The principle of legal indeterminacy is also seen in any US Supreme Court case involving a split (5–4) decision that is overturned on appeal and retried resulting in a different verdict. In these instances, deficient legal reasoning in the absence of compelling arguments leaves the door open for reversal.

With first-person narrative, critical race theory recognizes the experiential knowledge of people of colour as legitimate, appropriate and critical to understanding, analysing and teaching about racial subordination (Yosso 2005). Drawing explicitly on the lived experiences of people of colour, critical race theory includes various methods, such as storytelling, family histories, biographies, scenarios, parables, testimonials, chronicles and narratives designed to counter other historical accounts (Yosso 2005:74). Delgado and Stefancic (2001:144) define counter-storytelling as 'a method of telling a story that aims to cast doubt on the validity of accepted premises as myths, especially ones held by the majority'. This concept maintains that because of their different histories and experiences with oppression, Asian, black, Indian and Latino/a writers and thinkers may be able to communicate to their white counterparts matters that white writers are unlikely to know about or have experienced.

Just as other theories are inadequate to explain all social phenomena, critical race theory has its shortcomings. Near the end of the 1990s, Solórzano expressed doubts that critical race theory had achieved its goals, especially in its ability to understand forms of subtle discrimination: 'Indeed, we know very little about whom, where, and how these microaggressions are initiated and responded to. Without careful documentation and analysis, these racial and gender microaggressions can easily be ignored or downplayed' (1998:132).

Admittedly, measuring 'racism' has always proven problematic simply because it is often calculated by historical standards of positivism and its inability to discern more subtle and hidden forms of racism. Critical race theory appears to use a different standard of measurement to capture the experiences and perceptions of oppressed people who are typical victims of social injustice. As for critical race scholarship, its most common criticism is that it 'fails the test for rational discourse'. For example, Farber and Sherry (1997:24) characterized critical race theorists in the following manner: 'their disdain for standards, objectivity, and truths leads [the] radical scholars to indulge in a form of writing that is blatantly subjective. Instead of offering theoretical or doctrinal analysis, radical multiculturalists tell stories'.

Farber and Sherry's statement insinuates that 'storytelling' is one of the weaker linkages in critical race theory given its challenge to traditional notions of epistemology that looks at how one knows reality. For scientists, the way of knowing reality is via the scientific method. Traditionalists claim that storytelling is inherently problematic because stories cannot be verified, are inevitably subjective and may be atypical of real-world experiences. Moreover, narrative methodology 'reject[s] the linearity, abstraction, and scientific objectivity of rational argument' (Levit 1999:798, quoting Farber and Sherry 1997:47). Therefore, for the traditionalists, storytelling is neither legal nor academic, and threatens the credibility of the scholarly enterprise. Yet many critical race theorists regard it as exceedingly useful and undeniably powerful in its effects. Fearing that some are missing the point, Murray (1996:1080–81) asserts: 'At hand is an attempt to transform the meritocratic ideal by including what has been up to now excluded: the valuable, concrete, lived experiences of oppressed peoples.' For Levit, the problem is not storytelling, per se, but a lack of dialogue. She reminds readers that using narrative to move toward inquiry is not only an obligation owed by a storyteller; it is also an obligation due by a reader.

Despite criticisms and controversy, critical race theory and its ability to dissect, illustrate and expose the subtleties of racism and its manifestations within justice systems continues to attract scholarly attention across disciplines.

References

Delgado, Richard, and Jean Stefancic. 2001. *Critical Race Theory: An Introduction.* New York: New York University Press.

Farber, Daniel, and Suzanna Sherry. 1997. *Beyond All Reason: The Radical Assault on Truth in American Law.* New York: Oxford University Press.

Levit, Nancy. 1999. Critical of Race Theory: Race, Reason, Merit, and Civility. *Georgetown Law Journal* 87(3): 795–822.

Murray, Yxta M. 1996. Merit-Teaching. *Hastings Constitutional Law Quarterly* 23(4): 1073–113.

Ross, Lee E. 2010. A Vision of Race, Crime, and Justice through the Lens of Critical Race Theory. In *The Sage Handbook of Criminological Theory*, Eugene McLaughlin and Tim Newburn, eds, pp. 391–409. London: Sage.

Solórzano, Daniel. 1998. Critical Race Theory, Race and Gender Microaggressions, and the Experience of Chicana and Chicano Scholars. *Qualitative Studies in Education* 2(1):121–36.

Yosso, Tara J. 2005. Whose Culture Has Capital? A Critical Race Theory Discussion of Community Cultural Wealth. *Race, Ethnicity and Education* 8(1): 69–91.

Further reading

Bell, Derrick A. 1987. *And We Are Not Saved: The Elusive Quest for Racial Justice.* New York: Basic Books.

California Law Review. 1994. Symposium: Critical Race Theory. *California Law Review* 82(4): 741ff.

Crenshaw, Kimberlé et al. (eds) 1995. *Critical Race Theory: The Key Writings that Formed the Movement.* New York: New Press.

Delgado, Richard. 1995. *The Rodrigo Chronicles: Conversations about America and Race.* New York: New York University Press,

Delgado, Richard, and Jean Stefancic (eds) 1997. *Critical White Studies: Looking behind the Mirror.* Philadelphia: Temple University Press.

Delgado, Richard, and Jean Stefancic (eds) 1998. *The Latino/a Condition: A Critical Reader.* New York: New York University Press.

Harris, Angela P. 1990. Race and Essentialism in Feminist Legal Theory. *Stanford Law Review* 42(3): 581–616.

Wing, Adrien K. (ed.). 2003. *Critical Race Feminism: A Reader.* New York: New York University Press.

4.8 Cultural criminology

Keith Hayward and Jonathan Ilan

Cultural criminology is a theoretical, methodological and interventionist approach to understanding crime and its control that views criminality and the agents of its control as cultural products, i.e. as creative constructs enmeshed within processes of meaning-making. Attentive to the realities of a deeply unequal world, cultural criminology seeks to highlight how power effects the upwards and downwards construction of criminological phenomena: how rules are made, why they are broken and the deeper implications of such processes. Recognizing this multi-dimensional nature of criminality, punishment and control, cultural criminology deploys a triadic framework (Hayward 2016) that simultaneously examines *power* (macro-level structural processes), *meaning* (meso-level group interpretations and interactions) and *existential concerns* (micro-level personal and subjective experiences). This multi-levelled analysis resonates with many, not least because of the way it actively seeks to situate the micro-specificities of crime and human agency within the complex backdrop of late modernity and its attendant processes of intense individualization, hyper-consumption, cultural flow and **globalization**.

See Chapter 4.14
Globalization

See Chapter 3.8
Labelling theory

See Chapter 3.18
Symbolic
Interactionism

See Chapter 3.17
Subculture;
Chapter 3.2
Birmingham
Centre for
Contemporary
Cultural Studies

Originally formulated in the United States in the mid-1990s, cultural criminology emerged as a synthesis of older theoretical traditions – including the **labelling perspective**, **symbolic interactionism**, and various media and **subcultural approaches**. The key text inaugurating this emergence was *Cultural Criminology*, a collection of essays edited by Jeff Ferrell and Clinton Sanders that sought to 'confound categories of "culture" and "crime"' and embark on a series of 'journeys beyond the conventional boundaries of contemporary criminology' (1995:16). Such concerns ensured that, in its early years, the focus of cultural criminology was largely on the production of meaning and (sub)cultural representation, including a strong interest in style, symbolism and criminal aesthetics. By the end of the 1990s and early 2000s, these works had been augmented by British and European contributions that focused more on the structural implications of late modernity, consumer capitalism and debates around spatiality (see e.g., Hayward 2004). Uniting these complementary analyses was an interest in the phenomenological work of Jack Katz and Stephen Lyng – in particular, the way these sociologists prioritized the powerful experiential and **emotional** aspects of offending, or what they called the existential 'foreground' of crime.

See Chapter 4.10 Emotions

Attentiveness to such *existential qualities* of crime and its control reveal the extent to which those who offend and those who combat offending engage in their activities – not as cold, calculating actors, but charged with emotion. By demonstrating, following Katz (1988), that crime and its control are variously animated by humiliation, rage, shame, desire, excitement, pleasure and disgust, cultural criminologists oppose the dry, emotionally neutered analyses that are a regular feature of other criminological perspectives. For example, the logic of joyriding and burning out a stolen car cannot be properly understood without recognizing the feelings generated within the body of the car-thief and how such acts transform their image of self. Likewise, harsh sentences for relatively harmless crimes cannot be properly understood without recognizing the role played by fear, disgust and the media within the legislating and sentencing processes.

One of the appeals of cultural criminology is that it often challenges existing, orthodox criminological approaches, which seek to 'manage' crime and criminals without asking fundamental questions about the nature of contemporary society. Here, cultural criminologists challenge the claims of those who fetishize 'scientific' inquiry over a more human approach to the study of crime (see Ferrell et al. 2015). Indeed, cultural criminology distinguishes itself from many other criminological perspectives through maintaining an open, eclectic and stridently interdisciplinary sensibility. For example, in terms of methodology, this means that cultural criminologists are not content with abstract quantitative studies alone (although they are recognized to have their place within a broad methodological toolbox). Instead, cultural criminologists embrace **ethnography**, **visual** and documentary methods, new forms of 'netnography' and media analysis to gain a more fulsome, complex and experiential sense of social reality (see Ferrell et al. 2015). By the same token, cultural criminology is not restricted to studying only one kind of crime or another, or one form of crime control or another, but instead seeks to track the flow of power, meaning and experience across a range of spaces (real, virtual and mediated; regional, local and global). Cultural criminology's analysis of two topics – everyday life and the media – provides examples of this kind of reasoning.

See Chapter 3.1 Appreciative criminology; Chapter 4.40 Visual criminology

A central feature of cultural criminology is the way it analyses **how power functions across different levels of society**. Accordingly, rather than

See Chapter 3.3 Critical criminologies

viewing power as existing solely as an abstract structure or as top-down state action/inaction, cultural criminology locates it within a range of seemingly mundane everyday experiences and momentary sensations. For example, something as seemingly innocuous as a pair of designer sneakers/trainers can tell us much about the relationship between **neoliberal capitalism** and street-level criminality. In the mid-1970s, many young people in the West might have found stable, unionized employment in the domestic footwear or garment industries. Trace the origins of the average training shoe today, though, and chances are that it will take you to the grim sweatshop factories of China or the tax-free economic zones of the global south. As countless urban manufacturing jobs migrated to countries where wages and labour-welfare standards are considerably lower, the economy of many Western inner cities became desiccated and poverty-ridden, and certain individuals came to see street-level criminality as one of the only opportunities to feel a sense of respect for themselves 'at work'. In a further irony, many street-level criminals came to view expensive designer trainers as key markers of identity and self-worth, often spending the proceeds of drug deals and robberies on 'box-fresh' trainers so that the strict mandates of street identity and cultural style could be upheld. On occasion, trainers even come to function as a direct cause of violence, as young excluded men fight each other over scuff marks on their new shoes (Ilan 2015).

See Chapter 4.24 Neoliberalism

This illustrates how in contemporary society criminal practices and socio-cultural dynamics come together to manufacture meaning and shape social reality. Thus, while cultural criminologists are naturally concerned with broad, structural issues – such as the crimes of the state and state actors, the social harms of environmental degradation, and mass incarceration – they are also keen to trace how these and other aspects of crime and crime control give rise to differential everyday experiences that seep into commonplace perceptions and saturate day-to-day social interactions.

Another ubiquitous feature of everyday life is the contemporary 'media-scape' – that bundle of media that manufactures information and disseminates images via an expanding array of digital technologies. Today's fast-moving, omnipresent and increasingly interactive media shapes relations between space, time and identity – and, in so doing, 'frames' how crime and its control come to be understood in society. For cultural criminologists, this mediascape is likened to a vast 'hall of mirrors' (Ferrell et al. 2015), where the images and realities of crime and control constantly reflect back onto each other: where perpetrators and witnesses post images of crime to YouTube; where criminal justice policy is formulated to ensure that it will 'play in the media'; and where media-savvy commentators and lobbyists compete with each other for air time on 24-hour TV news in a bid to peddle their own political or commercial solutions to the crime problem.

Under these circumstances, images of crime and punishment become almost as 'real' as what they represent – 'if by "real" we denote those dimensions of social life that produce consequences; shape attitudes and policy;

define the effects of crime and criminal justice; generate **fear**, avoidance and pleasure; and alter the lives of those involved' (Ferrell et al. 2004:4). Consequently, cultural criminologists assert that it no longer makes sense to study 'real-world' crime and its mediated representation separately. Instead, in a hyper-connected society where mass-mediated images of crime and deviance proliferate, and where crime and control reflect off the shiny face of popular culture, what is required are forms of criminological analysis that can make sense of the blurred line between the real and the virtual. And, as always, this focus is political as well as theoretical: in late modernity, with power increasingly exercised through mediated representation and symbolic production, battles over image, style and mediated meaning become essential in the contest over crime and crime control, deviance and normality, and the emerging shape of social justice.

See Chapter 5.7
Fear of crime

Cultural criminology has grown from an upstart intervention to a bustling sub-discipline in a short space of time, shifting its lens back and forth from the most excluded of street criminals to the seemingly unconquerable leviathans of state crime and the criminalization of exclusion. Its message, however, remains relatively straightforward: that power affects how different people interpret the world differently; that these interpretations affect the experience of situated moments of meaning; and that these processes all feed back onto each other with important consequences for how we should understand crime and its control.

References

Ferrell, Jeff, and Clinton Sanders (eds). 1995. *Cultural Criminology*. Boston: Northeastern University Press.

Ferrell, Jeff, Keith Hayward, and Jock Young. 2015. *Cultural Criminology: An Invitation* (2nd edn). London: Sage.

Ferrell, Jeff, Keith Hayward, Wayne Morrison, and Mike Presdee. 2004. Fragments of a Manifesto: Introducing Cultural Criminology Unleashed. In *Cultural Criminology Unleashed*, Jeff Ferrell, Keith Hayward, Wayne Morrison, and Mike Presdee, eds, pp. 1–11. London: Cavendish.

Hayward, Keith. 2004. *City Limits: Crime, Consumerism and the Urban Experience*. London: GlassHouse.

Hayward, Keith. 2016. Cultural Criminology: Script Rewrites. *Theoretical Criminology* 20(3): 297–321.

Ilan, Jonathan. 2015. *Understanding Street Culture: Poverty, Crime, Youth and Cool*. Basingstoke: Palgrave Macmillan.

Katz, Jack. 1988. *Seductions of Crime: Moral and Sensual Attractions in Doing Evil*. New York: Basic Books.

Further reading

Ferrell, Jeff, Keith Hayward, Wayne Morrison, and Mike Presdee (eds). 2004. *Cultural Criminology Unleashed*. London: Cavendish.
O'Neill, Maggie, and Lizzie Seal. 2012. *Transgressive Imaginations: Crime, Deviance and Culture*. London: Palgrave Macmillan.
Young, Jock. 1999. *The Exclusive Society*. London: Sage.

Deviant knowledge

Deborah Drake and Reece Walters

The ability to openly challenge and express criticism of governing authorities is a cornerstone of progressive democratic societies. To 'speak truth to power' generates accountability and transparency where elected and appointed officials, and their governing rationalities and ideologies, are questioned and held accountable. Critical voices of dissent are often marginalized, suppressed and threatened, however. Recent international headlines – such as 'World press freedoms have deteriorated . . . warning of a new era of propaganda' (Reporters without Borders 2016); 'Art is under Threat: Oppression against Freedom of Expression is Dangerously High' (Freemuse 2016); and 'The demise of academic freedom. When politically correct "speech police" are given the upper hand' (Walpin 2015) – all attest to the ways that democratic freedoms in speech and artistic expression are under attack and subjected to systematic censorship and erosion. Such attacks on thought and expression have been witnessed in various historical regimes underpinned by a politics of intolerance and fear. More recently, the post-9/11 period has seen commentators critical of the 'war on terror' silenced and neutralized and their comments 'dismissed as traitorous acts of sedition' (Walters 2003:132–4).

For some commentators, the demise of civil liberties is associated with heightened **terrorist threats** and the perceived need to regulate and monitor 'offensive speech'. For Schoenwald (2001), the 'authoritarian ascendency' or the 'rise of modern American conservatism' has had a pervasive influence on media, global economics, political party politics and the production of knowledge. Therefore, to offend with words or creative expression is seen as a catalyst that may incite radical fundamentalism and disrupt the social order.

See Chapter 4.19 Institutional and anti-institutional violence

267

This position is examined comprehensively in Mike Hume's influential book *Trigger Warning*, where he argues that:

> Everybody in Western public life claims to support free speech in principle. Yet in practice free speech is on the endangered list. Freedom of expression today is like one of those exotic animals that everybody says they love, but that still appear to be heading inexorably towards extinction. Everywhere from the internet to the universities, from football to the theatrical stage, from out on the streets to inside our own minds, we are allowing the hard-won right to freedom of expression to be reined in and undermined.
>
> (Hume 2015:12)

If academics, journalists, artists and other critical commentators are prevented from openly challenging and critiquing governing authorities, then how are the ruling elites held accountable for their decisions, policies and actions? Along these lines – how are notions of democracy, human rights, social justice and humanitarianism advanced and progressed for the global good? If, as Hume argues, free speech is becoming constructed as a form of 'extremism' – as a danger to social and political stability – then those who exercise democratic rights to critical free speech also become demarcated as 'extremists' or 'deviants', and the words and values they disseminate are indeed forms of 'deviant knowledge'.

Moreover, what is to be gained by suppressing and regulating those who question the status quo and advance alternative and unorthodox non-state narratives? Those with political and financial power will aim to minimize and suppress, and distort truth and knowledge in the process. There are numerous historical examples of totalitarian and dictatorial regimes that have acted in this way. The justifications for mediating and synthesizing truth are often entangled in the narratives of the 'dangerous other' or the new terrorist threat. Such threats are often amplified, however, and used to legitimate censorship for a perceived greater good – at the expense of robust and transparent public discourse.

Within criminology, deviant knowledge seeks to promote critical voices and challenge the priorities and policies of conservative and socially unjust state and corporate enterprises. It is a project of resistance and dissent: one that promotes critique, challenges political power and certain concepts of social order; and one that pursues truth from a position of intellectual autonomy and as both critic and conscience of society (Scraton 2001; Walters 2003). It is a term that originates with the writings of Manfred Brusten, who described the ways in which deviant knowledge (criminological discourses that challenged the existing political and social order) was being systematically neutralized, marginalized and 'policed' by what he called offensive and defensive controls of criminological research (see Walters 2003; Brusten 1981).

See Chapter 3.3 Critical criminologies

Scraton (2001) argues that deviant voices are found in **critical criminological** narratives that must serve contemporary society as a form of 'knowledges of resistance'. Such knowledges, he argues, cannot be generated under government or corporate contract, where they are often silenced or neutralized. They require criminologists to stand outside the often lucrative and profitable domains of commercial criminology and actively assert a position of resistance. Correspondingly, Christie's (1973) *quarrelling society* thesis serves to remind us that effective and productive policy often emerges from the contestations and struggles between individuals, governments, interest groups and communities when debating responses to complex social problems. It is the contestations of those unafraid to challenge and critique governing authorities that provoke and stimulate creative and socially progressive social policy (Drake and Walters 2015). Christie argued that the post-World War II era created a period of 'intellectual tranquillity' that was counterproductive and regressive. It was a time that exacerbated the decline in social quarrelling, the political and social conflicts, contestations and turmoil involving widespread citizen participation that sparked intellectual innovation, creativity and social change. Central to Christie's argument is that a society is not living unless it engages in healthy quarrelling and intellectual conflict.

In a similar vein, Stan Cohen advocated the need for deviant criminological knowledges in *States of Denial* as a way to avoid the risk of 'intellectual denial', where:

> well-functioning minds become closed, and the gaze is averted from the uglier parts of their ideological blueprints and experiments. Or they allow themselves – for tangible rewards or an eagerness to please the powerful – to be duped into pseudo-stupidity. These shameful records of collusion go way back.
>
> (Cohen 2001:280)

In sum, if academics are to become mere information gatherers for government – and not prepared, or encouraged, to critique the role of the state, or challenge new modes of conservative governance, or address questions relating to social and political order in fear of losing contracts – then the academic criminologist is reduced to a co-conspirator in the policing of knowledge.

The promotion of new narratives in **cultural criminology**, **green criminology** and other critical criminologies – and with their attention to patriarchy and power, human rights and transnational justice, as well as state and corporate crime – provides important voices of resistance against embedded criminology. If criminology is to survive and be more relevant, it must embrace diverse knowledges of resistance – indeed, criminology must become a knowledge of resistance (see Walters 2003). This calls for a politics of engagement that is often prohibited by the proscriptive and regulated culture of government and corporate-led research that many academics are seduced by in the name of income-generation or evidence-based decision-making.

The ongoing development and diversity of critical criminological narratives sparks optimism. This – combined with the increasingly large and vocal

See Chapter 4.8
Cultural
criminology

See Chapter 4.16
Green criminology

number of social movements – suggests that people are hungry for critical voices: voices that represent the struggles of everyday lived experiences and that systematically challenge the increasingly untruthful and abusive powers that govern us. The critical voice is constantly under threat and engaging in critical scholarship can be a bruising experience. In an environment where income-generation dominates the academic agenda; where government bodies are purchasing and shaping university courses to meet their needs; where corporations are funding academic projects and personnel to maximize their profits; where corporate-style conferences discourage robust and critical dialogue; and where public servants more and more determine and regulate the type and nature of academic scholarship – it is high time to be buccaneers and to resist existing trends. Just as C. Wright Mills' *The Sociological Imagination* challenged the 'inhibitions, obscurities and trivialities' of mainstream social science, it is vital that a critical 'deviant' criminology continues to challenge mainstream discourses on crime and criminal justice in the construction of a criminological imagination.

To be critical in an academic context does not mean restricting one's research and scholarly activities to debates within an intellectual discipline. It also involves questioning the paradigms within which the discipline sits – the assumptions, concepts and categories through which it frames its concerns – and the methods by which it seeks to arrive at an understanding of the world. To be a critical criminological scholar who produces deviant knowledge(s) is to look beyond official crime statistics and criminal justice policies and practices that are constructed through seemingly unquestionable mechanisms of state governance and control. It means challenging knowledge(s) about crime and criminal justice that might seem unquestionable. It also means upholding the values of free speech – taking risks and holding those in power to account when others will not.

References

Brusten, Manfred. 1981. Social control of criminology and criminologists. In *State Control of Information in the Field of Deviance and Social Control*, Manfred Brusten and Paul Ponsears, eds, n.p.. Leuven: European Group for the Study of Deviance and Social Control.

Cohen, Stanley. 2001. *States of Denial: Knowing about Atrocities and Suffering*. Cambridge: Polity Press.

Christie, Nils. 1973. A living society is a quarrelling society. In *Law and Social Change*, Jacob Ziegel, ed., pp. 103–24. Toronto: Osgoode Hall Law School, York University.

Drake, Deborah, and Reece Walters. 2015. Crossing the Line: Criminological Expertise, Policy Advice and the Quarrelling Society. *Critical Social Policy* 35(3): 414–33.

Freemuse. 2016. Art is under Threat: Oppression against Freedom of Expression is Dangerously High. www.widewalls.ch/freemuse-art-censorship-report-2015. Accessed 23 January 2017.

Hume, Mick. 2015. *Trigger Warning: Is the Fear of Being Offensive Killing Free Speech?* London: HarperCollins.

Reporters without Borders. 2016. 2016 World Press Freedom Index: Leaders Paranoid about Journalists. https://rsf.org/en/news/2016-world-press-freedom-index-leaders-paranoid-about-journalists. Accessed 23 January 2017.

Schoenwald, Jonathan. 2001. *A Time for Choosing: The Rise of American Conservatism*. New York: Oxford University Press.

Scraton, Phil. 2001. A Response to Lynch and Schwendingers. *Critical Criminologist* 11(2): 1–3.

Walpin, Gerald. 2015. The Demise of Academic Freedom: When Politically Correct 'Speech Police' Are Given the Upper Hand. Washington Times, 19 November. www.washingtontimes.com/news/2015/nov/19/gerald-walpin-the-demise-of-academic-freedom. Accessed 23 January 2017.

Walters, Reece. 2003. *Deviant Knowledge: Criminology, Politics and Policy*. Cullompton, UK: Willan.

Further reading

Mills, C. Wright. 1959. *The Sociological Imagination*. New York: Oxford University Press.

Emotions

Jackie Turton

See Chapter 4.39
Victimology

See Chapter 4.17
Hate crime

See Chapter 5.7
Fear of crime

The heartfelt outpouring of emotions from **victims**, public outrage and indeed the provocative media campaigning after some crimes are impossible to ignore, as are the implications and effects of these emotional moments on the police, judiciary and general public more broadly. Examples include public moral outrage in response to **hate crime**, current debates around the perpetrators and victims of child sexual abuse, and policymakers' concerns regarding public **fear of crime**. While these examples may suggest the need for an emotional perspective to understanding crime, the tales of perpetrators have tended to be ignored, however. There are some exceptions, such as crimes of passion. In such cases it is assumed that emotions play a significant part, so it does seem logical that consideration of other crimes may benefit from a closer analysis to create an understanding of how perpetrators perceive and experience their activities.

See Chapter 1.8
Learning
theory; Chapter
1.15 Forensic
psychology

See Chapter 3.1
Appreciative
criminology

In the past, when perhaps the barriers between disciplines were more clearly defined, any hint of emotional behaviour associated with irrationality was deemed to belong to the **psychological discourses**. So understanding emotional outbursts or indeed emotional relief in deviant behaviour was not considered a relevant line of enquiry for the criminologist, and any attempts to investigate the emotional content of criminal acts were rather marginalized. This is not to say that emotional perspectives were totally ignored. Since Matza (1969) first revealed **the excitement and intoxication of deviant acts** experienced by young gang members, criminology has slowly but surely built an important body of work that supports and enhances a more complex and contextualized understanding of deviance and crime.

One of the key questions for criminologists pursuing the 'emotional' in their research is the question 'What leads offenders to offend'? So rather than considering the social background of the offender, or indeed the type of offence itself, these academics have turned the traditional criminological paradigm on its head, focusing on the emotional enticement and response felt by the deviant in the commission of a criminal act – in other words, how these acts are experienced. We can see this in the seminal work of Jack Katz (1988), who, inspired by Matza's early research, wrote *Seductions of Crime* in which he discusses the exciting and enticing nature of crime and how these emotional responses can lead to compulsive criminal behaviour. Although Katz's work has been criticized as sometimes lacking structural analysis, for concentrating on the foreground of action solely and for being rather descriptive, its significant contribution lies in challenging the complacency of the criminological estate for their lack of consideration of emotional perspectives. This was a very reasonable challenge as theories about emotions had been incorporated into the broader sociological discipline since at least the early works of Scheff (1979) and others.

Alongside Katz's concept of excitement as an enticement to acts of deviance, Braithwaite (1989) highlighted the emotional effects of **shame on the offender** within the criminal justice system. In some ways, the work of these two academics among others led criminology to begin to take more interest in this new approach. Subsequently, the links drawn with the **psychosocial** approaches and **cultural criminologists** have allowed the discipline to address the social-cultural process and practice of both criminal acts and the criminal, and, more importantly, to take into account the experiences of the deviant.

See Chapter 5.14
Reintegrative
shaming

See Chapter 4.30
Psychosocial
criminology

See Chapter 4.8
Cultural
criminology

In terms of the criminal there are a number of emotional responses that have been discussed, aside from just the thrill, excitement and seduction of crime. Presdee's (2000) work on joyriding, for example, recognizes that the pleasure for the deviant was linked to danger – the danger of the high-speed chase and the danger of being caught by the police. In his analysis, Presdee suggests that, due to their economic and social disadvantages, these deviants are unable to engage in legitimate 'risky' behaviours such as skydiving or motor racing, so they select an illegal substitute.

The work of Katz, Presdee and others has suggested that it is the response to boredom (Ferrell 2004) or maybe the thrill and challenge of the offending that gives some meaning to the lives of deviant individuals. Sometimes these high-risk activities can be interpreted as acts of resistance – resistance to the drudgery of everyday life or to a violent or abusive domestic situation. In other words, these deviants are making attempts to take back control of their lives or identities. Where dreams, hopes and expectations are curtailed, alternative routes are used to re-establish identity and a sense of belonging to at least part of society.

Anderson (1999) adds a different dimension to this emotional melting pot by considering the earning of *respect* and deference that he found was highly valued among urban youth gang members. The racism and alienation felt by these groups led to the formation of what Anderson terms *codes of the street* – an informal set of, often violent, social codes used by the gangs to assess members' rights to respect. These rights are hard to achieve, and the competition to win and maintain them is hard-fought. But the lack of self-esteem available within mainstream society for these youths makes the gang route an appealing necessity.

It is the concept of self-esteem and shame that Scheff takes up in much of his work (e.g., 1979). Scheff considers the interplay between shame, self-esteem and violence, and acknowledges that shame is an emotion we try to avoid: it is painful and he suggests that how well we manage it is measured by the level of our self-esteem. A failure to 'manage' shame, according to Scheff, results in a display of rage or uncontrollable anger; and it is by these responses that the deviant can, at least temporarily, remove the emotional discomfort of shame.

While Braithwaite (1989) offers a similar analysis of shame as an emotion – in so much as he recognizes the importance of shame to understanding identity – he also suggests that shame could be harnessed to reintegrate offenders back into the community. This process is not based upon piling more shame onto the *offender* but onto the *offence* – requiring the support of both the community and the family. While Braithwaite is not without critics, his principles of **restorative justice** have gathered some popular credibility as offering an alternative to modern penal systems.

See Chapter 5.15
Restorative justice

All of this work has lingered on the periphery of mainstream criminology, and the questions to consider are whether and how it will become a core part of the field. While changes in criminal justice policy now offer a more **victim-focused approach**, which might signal a more 'emotionally intelligent' legal system, even here there remain some unresolved emotional ambiguities between victims' (and sometimes the public's) desire for **retribution** and the 'softer' option of a community-led reintegrative justice. This mismatch is further exacerbated by the current actuarial focus on **risk**, and some have questioned whether a risk approach to crime is in fact based on emotional responses, such as fear of crime. So the emotional effect of fear of crime and assumptions about what might create public concerns persist despite falling crime rates. This suggests the need for more academic debate around the role and effect of emotions in criminal justice.

See Chapter 4.39
Victimology

See Chapter 5.16
Retribution

See Chapter 6.7
Risk

Recently, de Haan and Loader initiated some debate by suggesting that criminology faces a new 'aetiological crisis' reflecting a lack of consideration about the motivation of offenders. They have proposed that mainstream criminology has been unable to add significantly to criminological debates because it has failed to take a more measured approach to the experiences of offenders. As de Haan and Loader (2002:245) state: 'We need to insist that perpetrators of crime are moral subjects striving reflexively to give meaning to their actions before, during and after the crime.' They raise a number of points suggesting the importance of emotional interaction. For instance, on a macro level, the rise in penal populations in the Western world, given the diminishing crime rate, needs to be better understood beyond political rhetoric. It may be possible to tackle some of these issues by exposing, analysing and interpreting the emotions and feelings of offenders in order to understand the resulting social conduct. They leave little room for doubt that the experiences of offenders and others are shaped by both social and cultural practices. Therefore, deviant acts cannot be considered in isolation. Criminology needs to incorporate a more in-depth understanding of the effect of emotions on deviant social interaction.

References

Anderson, Elijah. 1999. *Code of the Street: Decency, Violence and the Moral Life of the Inner City*. New York: Norton.

Braithwaite, John. 1989. *Crime, Shame and Reintegration*. Cambridge: Cambridge University Press.

de Haan, Willem, and Ian Loader. 2002. On the Emotions of Crime, Punishment and Social Control. *Theoretical Criminology* 6(3): 243–53.

Ferrell, Jeff. 2004. Boredom, Crime and Criminology. *Theoretical Criminology* 8(3): 287–302.

Katz, Jack. 1988. *Seductions of Crime: Moral and Sensual Attractions of Doing Evil*. New York: Basic Books.

Matza, David. 1969. *Becoming Delinquent*. Englewood Cliffs, NJ: Prentice Hall.

Presdee, Mike. 2000. *Cultural Criminology and the Carnival of Crime*. London: Routledge.

Scheff, Thomas. 1979. *Catharsis in Healing, Ritual and Drama*. Berkeley: University of California Press.

Further reading

Butler, Judith. 2008. Violence, mourning, politics. In *Emotions: A Social Science Reader*, Monica Greco and Paul Stenner, eds, pp. 439–42. London: Routledge.

Cottee, S., and K. Hayward. 2011. Terrorist (E)Motives: the Existential Attractions of Terrorism. *Studies in Conflict and Terrorism* 34(12): 963–86.

Freiberg, Arie. 2008. Affective versus effective justice. In *Emotions: A Social Science Reader*, Monica Greco and Paul Stenner, eds, pp. 405–10. London: Routledge.

Karstedt, Susanne. 2008. Emotions and criminal justice. In *Emotions: A Social Science Reader*, Monica Greco and Paul Stenner, eds, pp. 418–24. London: Routledge.

Karstedt, Susanne. 2011. Handle with care: emotions, crime and justice. In *Emotions, Crime and Justice*, Susanne Karstedt, Ian Loader, and Heather Strang, eds, pp. 1–20. Oxford: Hart.

Rajah, Valli. 2007. Resistance as Edgework in Violent Intimate Relationships of Drug-Involved Women. *British Journal of Criminology* 47(2): 196–213.

Seidler, Victor J. 1998. Masculinity, violence and emotional life. In *Emotions in Social Life: Critical Themes and Contemporary Issues*, Gillian Bendelow and Simon J. Williams, eds, pp. 193–210. London: Routledge.

4.11 Environmental justice and victimology

Matthew Hall

See Chapter 4.16
Green criminology

See Chapter 4.39
Victimology

The development of **green criminology** as a distinct subject area has in recent years prompted a number of commentators from the field of **victimology** to focus their attention on 'green' questions. This has stimulated its own subfield, sometimes called 'green victimology', in which victimologists have contributed insights into the impacts of environmental harms and how those harms are managed/addressed by civil society from the perspective of so-called 'environmental victims'. Such commentators have often drawn on notions of 'environmental justice', which has been variously defined. Lynch and Stretesky (2003) understand environmental justice as not just a single movement, but a combination of at least three different perspectives. First, the authors draw on eco-feminists writers (e.g. Daly 1978) who, from the mid-1970s, began arguing that the effects of environmental degradation fall disproportionately on women compared to men.

On a similar theme, Lynch and Stretesky attribute the second foundation of environmental justice to growing discussions of what has come to be known as 'environmental racism'. This is the suggestion that the impact of environmental degradation falls disproportionately on some races, with early literature throwing particular light on the siting of large industrial processes in areas predominantly inhabited by ethnic minorities in the US (Bullard 1990). Finally, the authors draw on what they term 'red/green alliances', by which they mean forms of ecological socialism, the adherents of which sought to emphasize the inequalities of wealth and power in society which lead to increased environmental degradation while also ensuring it is the poor and socially excluded who bear the brunt of its negative effects (South 2010).

In all cases, these environmental justice perspectives represent an understanding that the effects (victimizations) of environmental harm at all levels do not fall equally on all parts of the world, or indeed on all groups of humans or animals within a country; and, as such, the authors in this field tend to prioritize the involvement of people and communities in decisions that might impact human health and their environment. Environmental justice is also often considered to include notions of intergenerational justice whereby present generations owe a duty to ensure subsequent generations can enjoy and benefit from the environment in the same manner they have (Hiskes 2008). White (2011), in following a more holistic approach, has criticized this understanding of environmental justice as ignoring the wider issues of *ecological* justice (acknowledging that humans are just one part of a complex ecosystem) and also *animal* and *species* justice (acknowledging the intrinsic right of non-human animals to be free of abuse).

The first call for the development of what was then termed 'environmental victimology' came in an article by Williams, which characterized victimology as a field 'broadly concerned with human rights, abuse of power, and human suffering irrespective of whether the circumstances are within the ambit of law' (1996:202). He thus argued that the victimological approach would provide a more objective alternative to developing concepts of environmental justice, which he saw as overly subjective and swayed by activism. For similar reasons, Williams restricted his conception of 'environmental victimization' to the notion of 'injury' rather than encompassing wider 'harms', arguing that this was the most useful starting point if the goal was to develop functioning legal systems to meet the challenges of such victimization.

More recently, White (2011) has emphasized the socio-cultural context of understanding and responding to environmental harm. Spencer and Fitzgerald (2013) also offer insight into environmental victims by essentially taking the field beyond its (predominantly, they argue) Marxist roots and applying more **post-structuralist** thinking – using the 2010 BP oil spill in the Gulf of Mexico as a case study. Thus, the authors argue, this 'victimization event' can be understood in terms of environmental, social and mental ecologies. In so doing, the authors expose the complex and multifaceted nature of such victimization itself both in human terms and in terms of the environment and non-human animals. Likewise, Hall (2013) has conceptualized the impacts of environmental harm on (human) victims in terms of: health impacts; social and cultural impacts; economic impacts; and impacts on security.

See Chapter 4.29
Post-structuralism
and criminology

As green criminology has challenged the predominantly anthropocentric bias of mainstream criminology, so too have green criminologists sought to encompass the victimization of non-humans within their theorizing. Like criminology, victimology has traditionally been almost exclusively anthropocentric in its outlook. Indeed, even the more recent discussions of

See Chapter 4.35
Speciesism and
theriocide

environmental victims have largely failed to consider in any depth the victimization of non-human animals. Williams' discussion of environmental victims, for example, was restricted to humans. From a criminological and public-policy perspective, it seems clear that the **victimization of non-human animals**, as well as the environment itself, is not being recognized in the same manner as human victimization, and thus as worthy of the 'criminal' label. Given the extension of criminology by green criminologists to *some* environmental harms, South (2010) argues that this continued anthropocentric bias is unjustified; animals live in environments, and their own physical, emotional and psychological well-being is absolutely and intimately linked to the health and good standing of those environments. As a matter of *law* (in most jurisdictions) non-human animals cannot be classed as victims of crime. That said, some crimes exist that involve non-human animals as direct targets, for example (in the United Kingdom): docking of dogs' tails (Animal Welfare Act 2006, s6); causing, attending or videoing dog-fighting (s8); illegal hunting, for example of foxes under the Hunting Act 2004. In terms of theory, some criminologists have approached the issue as one of animal rights, although on this point it can be argued that while often 'the environment' and 'non-human animals' are amalgamated into a single issue in green-criminological writings, in fact there are wide conceptual differences between the development of the animal rights (or 'animal abuse') movement on the one hand and 'environmentalism' on the other.

From an ecocentric perspective, we have already noted that animal and plant life is often seen as an 'acceptable' cost of industrial and commercial practices. Even among humans, however, South (2010) reflects upon the unequal impact of climate change on various groups of (usually poor) victims, and the possibility that some 'environmental rights' are being breached, which contradicts one of Williams' views that the impacts of environmental harm are more evenly spread between rich and poor. Certainly, the *geographically* unequal impact of environmental degradation is well recognized by the international legal order, with the preamble to the 1992 UN Framework Convention on Climate Change (UNFCCC) acknowledging the particular vulnerability of 'low-lying and other small island countries, countries with low-lying coastal, arid and semi-arid areas or areas liable to floods, drought and desertification, and developing countries with fragile mountainous ecosystems'. Beyond climate change, the unequal distribution of environmental harm has been commented on by South (2010), who sees this as reflecting wider tendencies towards 'social exclusion', which have long been a topic of research and discussion in mainstream criminology as well.

It is clear that development of victimological study in the environmental area has been slow to progress, even as green criminology as a whole has gathered pace. Given the difficulties of applying reforms intended to address and assist the victims of more orthodox criminal harms to the victims of environmental harms, more research is sorely needed. Hall (2013) has expanded on the difficulties of adapting standard mechanisms and redress of criminal justice to the environmental sphere, and to meeting the needs of environmental victims in particular. As in mainstream criminology, in more recent years there have therefore been moves to embrace more restorative and mediation-based mechanisms to resolve environmental conflicts, although detailed research into such options is still forthcoming.

References

Bullard, Robert D. 1990. *Dumping in Dixie: Race, Class, and Environmental Quality*. Boulder, CO: Westview.

Daly, Mary. 1978. *Gyn/Ecology: The Metaethics of Radical Feminism*. Boston: Beacon.

Hall, Matthew. 2013. *Victims of Environmental Harm: Rights, Recognition and Redress under National and International Law*. Abingdon: Routledge.

Hiskes, Richard. 2008. *The Human Right to a Green Future: Environmental Rights and Intergenerational Justice*. Cambridge: Cambridge University Press.

Lynch, Michael, and Paul Stretesky. 2003. The Meaning of Green: Contrasting Criminological Perspectives. *Theoretical Criminology* 7(2): 217–38.

South, Nigel. 2010. The ecocidal tendencies of late modernity: Transnational crime, social exclusion, victims and rights. In *Global Environmental Harm: Criminological Perspectives*, Rob White, ed., pp. 236–40. Cullompton, UK: Willan.

Spencer, Dale, and Amy Fitzgerald. 2013. Three Ecologies, Transversality and Victimization: The Case of the British Petroleum Oil Spill. *Crime, Law and Social Change* 59(2):209–23.

White, Rob. 2011. *Transnational Environmental Crime: Towards an Eco-Global Criminology*. Abingdon: Routledge.

Williams, Christopher. 1996. An Environmental Victimology. *Social Science* 23(1): 16–40. Reprinted in *Environmental Crime: A Reader*, Rob White, ed., pp. 200–22. Cullompton, UK: Willan, 2009.

Further reading

Beirne, Piers, and Nigel South (eds). 2007. *Issues in Green Criminology: Confronting Harms against Environments, Humanity and Other Animals*. Cullompton, UK: Willan.

Lynch, Michael, and Paul Stretesky. 2001. Toxic Crimes: Examining Corporate Victimization of the General Public Employing Medical and Epidemiological Evidence. *Critical Criminology* 10(3): 153–72.

Skinnider, Eileen. 2011. *Victims of Environmental Crime: Mapping the Issues*. Vancouver: International Centre for Criminal Law Reform and Criminal Justice Policy.

Spencer, Michael, Amanda Garratt, Elaine Hockman, Bunyan Bryant, and Laura Kohn-Wood. 2011. Environmental Justice and the Well-being of Poor Children of Color. *Communities, Neighborhoods and Health* 1(3): 219–33.

Financial crime

Vincenzo Ruggiero

See Chapter 4.19
Institutional and
anti-institutional
violence

The finance industry plays a significant role in facilitating crime (Platt 2015). Drug-trafficking, human smuggling, piracy and **terrorist activity**, for example, would be unthinkable without financial institutions making investment capital available and without their being prepared to receive the subsequent illegitimate proceeds. By exclusively focusing on this role, however, the conclusion might be drawn that financial crime is an aspect of conventional criminality, and the finance industry an ancillary to organized crime. While it can be argued that the financial sphere offers criminal groups a key 'service', other conduct found in this sphere belongs to the area of **white-collar and corporate crime**. These include money-laundering, tax-evasion, rate-rigging, mis-selling and fraud. The financial crisis of 2008 showed a combination of behaviours and practices straddling the areas of conventional and white-collar crime. It also showed that the ambiguity, ubiquity and evolving nature of financial crime makes the separation between acceptable and unacceptable practices extremely problematic.

See Chapter 4.41
White-collar
crime; Chapter 4.5
Corporate crime

The 2008 financial crisis, involving institutions which were deemed 'too big to fail', proved that such institutions are also 'too big to jail'. Scarce or shrinking resources resulted in criminal prosecutors avoiding complex financial irregularities committed by powerful actors. Many cases were regarded as unwinnable, also because offenders relied on a legal defence community closely associated with government departments. In the USA, by the end of 2011, the federal prosecution of financial fraud had fallen to a twenty-year low. Agreements were established to avoid indictments when financial firms offered to investigate and report their own crimes, while banking and related investment frauds were often regarded as beyond incrimination because to pursue them 'would not only potentially bring about the demise of these financial institutions but in the process would also certainly hurt investors' (Barak 2012:3). The crisis, in brief, revealed how the network of political and economic elites avoided any liability for the millions of people **victimized**, the funds illegally appropriated and the capital destroyed worldwide.

See Chapter 4.39 Victimology

Criminological analysis of these events leans on classical explanatory categories adopted in the domain of white-collar crime. **Learning theories**, for example, suggest that the techniques and justifications for committing crime are acquired through long-term socialization within specific occupational groups (Sutherland 1983). The pioneering work of Sutherland has been expanded by authors who have focused on the economic sphere, such as Pearce's (1976) analysis incorporating elements of the sociology of deviance alongside variables and concepts belonging to classical **Marxism**, such as mode of production, surplus value and class struggle. **Conflict** as an explanatory variable remains paramount for the analysis of the crimes of the powerful, including crimes perpetrated in the financial sphere.

See Chapter 1.8 Learning theory

See Chapter 3.9 Marxist criminologies

See Chapter 3.3 Critical criminologies

Anomie and control theory have also been mobilized to explain financial crime. The former posits that the settings in which the financial elite operate are already largely normless, thus encouraging experimental conduct and allowing for the arbitrary expansion of practices. Passas (2009:153), for instance, argues that **pressure to attain goals** is constantly experienced by people in the upper social reaches and that therefore 'they are far from immune to pressures towards deviance'. Control theory, in turn, has suggested that a number of characteristics belonging to offenders may explain all types of crimes, whether in the streets or in the suites. In this view, financial crime is committed by individuals characterized by **psychological** traits ranging from impulsivity and recklessness, to the inability to delay gratification, to a propensity to blame others first and themselves last. Sykes and Matza's **techniques of neutralization** appear to lend themselves ideally to explanatory efforts addressed to financial crime. For instance, such techniques may be used to deny that powerful offenders cause harm or victimize specifically identifiable subjects; to claim that other conducts are far more harmful than those one adopts; or that in any case whatever conduct one engages in is an expression of loyalty to one's social group and, therefore, it is permissible.

See Chapter 2.3 Anomie; Chapter 2.6 Control theories

See Chapter 2.8 Market society and crime

See Chapter 1.8 Learning theory

See Chapter 2.7 Techniques of neutralization

An important strand of analysis focuses mainly on micro-sociological factors, for example observing the dynamics guiding the behaviour of organizations and their members. As organizations become more complex, responsibilities are decentralized, while their human components inhabit an increasingly opaque environment in which the goals to pursue – and the modalities through which one is expected to pursue them – become vague and negotiable. Illegalities in the financial sphere, according to this perspective, are the outcome of this vagueness, as firms incessantly seek to devise new ways of achieving their ends and, consequently, endeavour to innovate by reinventing or violating rules (Keane 1995).

In further developments, attempts have been made to merge macro- and micro-levels of analysis, leading to the growing inclusion in the study of the crimes of the powerful of formal and complex organizations. These types of crimes, including financial crimes, are equated to manifestations of 'situated action', and explanatory efforts have addressed how contextual cultures affect decisions to violate laws (Vaughan 2007). Cultural rules, it is argued, define legitimate goals and determine action and meaning. In the financial sphere, actors experience a relative autonomy whereby agency determines whether obligations to obey the law or to follow business norms justifying violations will prevail. Organizations and their members, however, may not simply follow a **rational-choice model,** but find motivation for offending within the uncertain position in which they feel they are situated. More than sheer greed or striving for success, financial offenders experience anxiety and 'fear of falling' or 'status panic', as organizations and their members try to rise, remain the same or avoid falling in the rank of the organizational system (Vaughan 1983). It is within this culture of anxiety and panic that offenders are made to feel conformist, rather than deviant, in relation to their professional setting. Offending, in this sense, is not the result of calculated choice, but the routine outcome of an organizational culture which tends to normalize deviance.

See Chapter 1.18
Rational choice

The brief outline presented above situates financial crime within the larger area of white-collar criminality. The contributions examined, therefore, adopt well-established analytical concepts which have proved satisfactory vis-à-vis a variety of elite crimes. This is constructive but perhaps may also be unhelpful in that the specificity of financial crime is thus lost amid an enormous array of criminal conducts displayed by powerful individuals and groups. An alternative strategy to study financial crime is outlined as follows.

Pope Francis, while denouncing the incapacity of governments to reduce poverty and fight the exploitation of cheap labour, has on many occasions condemned greed, repeating several times the old medieval adage: *money is the excrement of the devil*. The distinction between clean and excremental, pure and impure, informs the symbolic order of many traditional and contemporary societies, and engenders rites of separation that pursue the constant dream of purification by warding off contagion (Douglas 1966). This distinction might also be useful to separate acceptable from unacceptable practices in the financial domain. A way of looking at crime committed in this domain would be to identify the process whereby the excrement of the devil was slowly 'freed' from both its sinful and criminal character.

The ideological arguments accompanying this process are of crucial importance as they are promptly mobilized whenever 'crises' occur in the financial world. Crises, bubbles and crashes have taken on 'natural' features, as if they were unpredictable meteorological events occurring in a sphere of human action whose logic is impermeable to lay cognitive skills. In fact, financial 'crises' hide a struggle juxtaposing criminalization and decriminalization processes in that specific arena of economic initiative. How did greed and sin, to use the Pope's categories, manage to turn into 'crises'? Only an exhaustive archaeological inquiry could attempt to furnish an answer, one examining the trajectory of financial misconduct through the centuries. According to Saint Paul, 'You cannot make profits while sleeping', and yet 'crises' are often caused exactly by that: from the 'Dutch tulip mania' in the 1620s and 1630s, to the contemporaneous Mississippi and South Sea bubbles; from John Law's grandiose attempt to establish modern monetary systems in Scotland and in France, to the 'railway mania' in the UK and the US in the nineteenth century; from the 'ultimate financial meltdown', namely the crash of 1929, to the contemporary examples of crimes and crises in the financial arena. The analysis of these events and their justification may provide criminology with supplementary tools when facing the ambiguity and evasive nature of financial delinquency.

References

Barak, Gregg. 2012. *Theft of a Nation: Wall Street Looting and Federal Regulatory Colluding.* Lanham: Rowman & Littlefield.

Douglas, Mary. 1966. *Purity and Danger: An Analysis of Concepts of Pollution and Taboo.* London: Routledge & Kegan Paul.

Keane, Carl. 1995. Loosely coupled systems and unlawful behaviour: Organization theory and corporate crime. In *Corporate Crime: Contemporary Debates*, Frank Pearce and Laureen Snider, eds, pp. 168–78. Toronto: Toronto University Press.

Passas, Nikos. 2009. Anomie and corporate deviance. In *Crimes of the Powerful: A Reader*, David Whyte, ed., pp. 153–6. Maidenhead: Open University Press.

Pearce, Frank. 1976. *Crimes of the Powerful: Marxism, Crime and Deviance.* London: Pluto.

Platt, Stephen. 2015. *Criminal Capital: How the Finance Industry Facilitates Crime.* Basingstoke: Palgrave Macmillan.

Sutherland, Edwin. 1983. *White Collar Crime: The Uncut Version.* New Haven: Yale University Press.

Vaughan, Diane. 1983. *Controlling Unlawful Organizational Behavior.* Chicago: University of Chicago Press.

Vaughan, Diane. 2007. Beyond macro- and micro-levels of analysis, organizations, and the cultural fix. In *International Handbook of White-Collar and Corporate Crime*, Henry Pontell and Gilbert Geis, eds, pp. 3–24. New York: Springer.

Further reading

Barak, Gregg (ed.). 2015. *The Routledge International Handbook of the Crimes of the Powerful.* London and New York: Routledge.

Ruggiero, Vincenzo. 2013. *The Crimes of the Economy.* London and New York: Routledge.

Ruggiero, Vincenzo. 2015. *Power and Crime.* London and New York: Routledge.

Genocide and ecocide

Damien Short

The neologism 'ecocide' – *eco* meaning ecosystem and *cide* meaning destruction – has been around since the time of the Vietnam War, when a group of scientists coined and propagated the term to denounce the environmental destruction and potential human health catastrophe arising from the herbicidal warfare programme known as Operation Ranch Hand. Ecocide is conceptually, historically and institutionally linked to the more famous term: genocide. Ecocide is, however, somewhat under-theorized in comparison, and has a much shallower intellectual history. The nucleus of the concept of genocide can be traced back to 1933 when Raphael Lemkin, a Polish jurist, spoke at the International Conference for Unification of Criminal Law in Madrid and urged the international community to ban the physical and cultural destruction of human groups, invoking the linked concepts of 'barbarity' and 'vandalism'. In later years, Lemkin formed a new, more comprehensive concept – *genocide* – by combining the Greek word *genos* (meaning tribe or race) and the Latin *cide*, which, as noted above, means destruction. For Lemkin, it was vital that his new concept be criminalized in international law.

Lemkin envisioned a comprehensive law addressing the deliberate destruction of a nation or ethnic group in the following ways: a) by killing its individual members, i.e. physical genocide; b) by undermining its way of life, i.e. cultural genocide. Lemkin's original definition envisaged the destruction of a culturally distinct people by methods other than direct physical killing, such as via cultural assimilation. Because a social group exists by virtue of its common culture, Lemkin argued that it was culture that animated the *genos* in genocide. Thus, during the construction of the draft United Nations

Convention on the Prevention and Punishment of the Crime of Genocide (the 'Genocide Convention'), Lemkin argued that 'Cultural Genocide is the most important part of the Convention' (Moses 2008). In his 1958 autobiography, Lemkin subsequently wrote:

> I defended it [cultural genocide] successfully through two drafts. It meant the destruction of the cultural pattern of a group, such as the language, the traditions, the monuments, archives, libraries, churches. In brief: the shrines of the soul of a nation. But there was not enough support for this idea in the Committee . . . So with a heavy heart I decided not to press for it.
>
> (Docker 2004:3)

Lemkin was forced to drop an idea that, in his words, 'was very dear to me' (ibid.).

The Genocide Convention was stripped of its coherence and conceptual integrity, and a major *method* of genocide envisaged by Lemkin was not fully criminalized. As such, its applicability to a whole range of colonial and settler-colonial contexts was thereby denied. This political dilution of the concept led to a preoccupation, in legal and scholarly realms, with establishing *perpetrator* intention rather than genocidal harms to the **victims**, and to the popular (mis)understanding of the crime of genocide as racially motivated mass killing.

See Chapter 4.39 Victimology

Prior to the mass killings in Rwanda in 1994, and the international tribunal that followed, the Genocide Convention was rarely invoked let alone used, which led to institutional reviews of its effectiveness. One of the first major UN discussions on this subject also led to one of the first attempts in international law to criminalize **environmental destruction**. A draft International Convention on the Crime of Ecocide (the 'Ecocide Convention'), prepared by Richard A. Falk, was considered by the United Nations Sub-Commission on Prevention of Discrimination and Protection of Minorities (the 'Sub-Commission'). In 1978 Falk recognized what many still fail to acknowledge today: 'that we are living in a period of increasing danger of ecological collapse' and 'that man has consciously and unconsciously inflicted irreparable damage to the environment in times of war and peace' (Gauger et al. 2013:6). Even so, in spite of the recognition that environmental damage can be caused consciously and unconsciously, the majority of the draft Ecocide Convention primarily focused on ecocide as a 'war crime with intent' and did not set out similar peacetime provisions. Within the Sub-Commission, there was support for criminalizing ecocide: 'any interference with the natural surroundings or environment in which ethnic groups lived was, in effect, a kind of ethnic genocide because such interference could prevent the people involved from following their own traditional way of life' (ibid.).

See Chapter 4.16 Green criminology; Chapter 4.11 Environmental justice and victimology

Although there was significant support for ecocide being included in an amended Genocide Convention, it was eventually dropped from the Sub-Commission's agenda. Even if ecocide had progressed via this route, it would have been *a method of genocidal* practice and would not have offered individuals or ecosystems any protection in their own right, in and of themselves, because genocide as a concept was formulated to protect only certain *human* groups. Following these discussions, from 1984 to 1996, there was extensive engagement in the UN's jurisprudential International Law Committee about the inclusion of environmental damage and ecocide in the list of 'Crimes against Peace' so that it could stand alongside such crimes as genocide in the draft Code of Offences against the Peace and Security of Mankind ('Draft Code') – the precursor to the Rome Statute. The Special Rapporteur, Doudou Thiam of Senegal, had included the crime based on precedence in international law.

Such post-1984 discussions centred on whether to include 'acts causing serious damage to the environment' as a Crime against Peace. Following numerous discussions, it was determined that the draft Article 26 would include the element of intent and read: 'wilful and severe damage to the environment'. Despite this narrowing, the draft Article 26 was eventually removed altogether (in 1996), with little consensus in the various committees and working groups.

The final Article 26, adopted by the International Law Commission (ILC), which was further amended by the Drafting Committee, refers to intentionally causing 'widespread, long-term and severe damage to the natural environment' within a war context (Gauger et al. 2013). This was the final reference to a crime against the environment that made it into the Rome Statute. And so, contrary to the prevailing mood at the time, 1996 saw the crime of ecocide suddenly removed from all draft documents.

A full picture of exactly how and why this happened is not available from the UN documentation, but the research conducted has discovered two important points. First, the Special Rapporteur on the Draft Code stated in his thirteenth report that the removal was due to the comments of a few governments that were largely opposed to any form of inclusion of Article 26 ('wilful and severe damage to the environment'). Second, Christian Tomuschat – who was a long-term member of the ILC from 1985 to 1996 and a member of the Working Group on the issue of wilful damage to the environment – published a brief article in 1996 where he reflected on the development of the provisions regarding crimes against the environment during the drafting and codification process of the Draft Code. In a telling passage he writes:

> One cannot escape the impression that nuclear arms played a decisive role in the minds of many of those who opted for the final text which now has been emasculated to such an extent that its conditions of applicability will almost never be met even after humankind would have gone through disasters of the most atrocious kind as a consequence of conscious action by persons who were completely aware of the fatal consequences their decisions would entail.
>
> (Tomuschat 1996:243)

In recent years a campaign to criminalize ecocide in its own right, and as a strict liability offence, was instigated by international lawyer and environmental activist Polly Higgins (Higgins et al. 2013). The *Eradicating Ecocide* campaign draws attention to the numerous examples of ecocide and its human consequences worldwide, at a time when preventing further ecological destruction could not be more pressing. While there is an international crime of environmental destruction – as a 'war crime' – this has no applicability in times of peace. Moreover, 'environmental destruction' does not capture our environmental embeddedness, the full scale of our predicament or the role of capitalism and resource extraction in its development.

The Eradicating Ecocide campaign's preference for the concept of 'ecocide' rather than 'environmental destruction' invokes a holistic understanding of the problem as an *ecological* crisis, and the concomitant need for the protection of ecosystems, rather than an abstract and external 'environmental' crisis. Indeed, Higgins et al. (2013) define 'ecocide' as: 'the extensive damage to, destruction of or loss of ecosystem(s) of a given territory, whether by human agency or by other causes, to such an extent that peaceful enjoyment by the inhabitants of that territory has been severely diminished.'

This definition is the basis of the Eradicating Ecocide campaign's proposed amendment to the Rome Statute – the treaty that established the International Criminal Court (ICC) and entered into force on 1 July 2002. In short, it is envisaged that any extensive damage, destruction to or loss of an ecosystem can constitute ecocide.

Under the Rome Statute, the ICC can investigate and prosecute only the core international crimes where states are unable or unwilling to do so themselves: the existing four Crimes against Peace (genocide, crimes against humanity, war crimes and the crime of aggression). As such, ecocide is sometimes referred to as 'the missing fifth Crime against Peace' (Gauger et al. 2013).

Leaving aside the thorny issue of likely political opposition, the process of revision of the Rome Statute is remarkably simple in that one member state can propose the amendment to the UN Secretary-General, who must then distribute the proposal to the other member states during a general assembly or at a revision conference. It remains to be seen whether or not a potential crime of ecocide can progress further within the international system the next time around, when the need is much more urgent and pressing than it was in the preceding decades. Because the need for a crime of ecocide is more acute than ever before, the likely opposition forces are now much stronger: corporate power and influence has grown, and the relationships between industry and governments have become even closer.

References

Docker, John. 2004. Raphael Lemkin's History of Genocide and Colonialism. Paper for United States Holocaust Memorial Museum, Center for Advanced Holocaust Studies, Washington DC, 26 February 2004. www.ushmm.org/m/pdfs/20040316-docker-lemkin.pdf. Accessed February 2017.

Gauger, Anja, Mai Pouye Rabatel-Fernel, Louise Kulbicki, Damien Short and Polly Higgins. 2013. Ecocide Is the Missing 5th Crime Against Peace. London: Human Rights Consortium. http://sas-space.sas.ac.uk/4830/1/Ecocide_research_report_19_July_13.pdf. Accessed February 2017.

Higgins, Polly, Damien Short, and Nigel South. 2013. Protecting the Planet: A Proposal for a Law of Ecocide. *Crime, Law and Social Change* 59(3): 251–66.

Moses, A. Dirk. 2008. Empire, colony, genocide: Keywords and the philosophy of history. In *Empire, Colony, Genocide: Conquest, Occupation, and Subaltern Resistance in World History*, A. Dirk Moses, ed., pp. 3–54. Oxford: Berghahn.

Tomuschat, Christian. 1996. Crimes against the Environment. *Environmental Policy and Law* 26(6): 242–3.

Further reading

Crook, Martin, and Damien Short. Marx, Lemkin and the Genocide–Ecocide Nexus. *International Journal of Human Rights* 18(3): 298–319.

Eradicating Ecocide. Closing the Door to Dangerous Industrial Activity: A Concept Paper for Governments to Implement Emergency Measures. http://eradicatingecocide.com/wp-content/uploads/2012/06/Concept-Paper.pdf. Accessed 7 February 2017.

Short, Damien. 2016. *Redefining Genocide: Settler Colonialism, Social Death and Ecocide*. London: Zed Books.

Zierler, David. 2011. *The Invention of Ecocide: Agent Orange, Vietnam, and the Scientists Who Changed the Way We Think about the Environment*. Athens: University of Georgia Press.

Globalization

4.14

Gary W. Potter

In its common usage, globalization refers to the increasing interdependency and interconnectedness of individuals, social groups, states and economies across the world. It is a complex process, but the single most compelling force behind globalization is the movement of capital and credit resulting from investment, and resource and profit extraction by multinational corporations in global markets.

There are many factors that have contributed to globalization as a process. Some writers point to the end of the Cold War (late 1980s/early 1990s) as the defining moment, with the collapse of the Soviet Union and its Eastern European allies and subsequent military, economic and cultural dominance by the United States and its allies (Ruccio 2010). Others have pointed to the proliferation of new means and faster methods of communication as an accelerant of globalization (Hart-Landsberg 2013). The argument is that new modalities of communication, such as 24-hour news channels, have made the world seem much smaller through their coverage of international events (Aas 2013). In addition, technological changes such as the Internet, email and mass social media have made what were once distant events, which may have been ignored outside their particular locality, part of our common day-to-day experiences. What happens in one remote part of the world now has profound cultural impacts across the entire globe. This process has been described by Ritzer (1998) as the 'McDonaldization' of society in which there is a global homogenization of cultures.

Some scholars argue that 'globalization' is an imprecise and not terribly useful term, rejecting the argument that it is simply another, necessary stage in a linear progression of capitalist development. Instead, they focus on a non-rationalist, materialistic ontology as a more useful perspective that places globalization in the contexts of imperialism and colonization. Calling attention to forced colonization and resource extraction by early European explorers and the subsequent military occupation of colonies by the United States and European nations, they see globalization as a simple extension of **imperialism**. The new aspect of globalization, in the context of this argument, is the addition of worldwide economic domination to the continued use of military force in order to extract both **resources** and inexpensive labour from what these nations still see as colonies (Ruccio 2010).

See Chapter 4.27
Postcolonial
criminology

See Chapter 4.16
Green criminology

Most commentators agree that globalization and the increased prominence and power of transnational corporations and their worldwide chains of production are the direct result of deliberate political decisions made at the highest levels of power among the strongest economic nations in the world, aimed at increasing profits by exploiting the cheapest sources of labour and raw materials. The impacts for both the economically powerful nations and for those nations subject to exploitation have been profound, with marked increases in inequality and poverty, austerity programmes which have eviscerated social welfare policies and weakened labour unions – all with criminogenic implications, and the creation of a highly erratic global capitalist economy prone to continual, rapid and unending crises (Hart-Landsberg 2013).

Globalization has created a myriad of new opportunities for new kinds of crime, and made familiar types of crime infinitely more profitable. The massively increased mobility of people, the ease with which cash can be moved, and the relaxation of trade and tariff restrictions have made criminal enterprise easier and safer (Aas 2013).

Types of crime and patterns of criminality have been impacted by globalization in every society across the world. There are very few countries on earth that are able to close borders to the massive economic, political and cultural changes attendant to globalization. While the impact of globalization may be somewhat mediated by local social, cultural and political circumstances, globalization touches everyone on the planet (Young 2007:38).

Globalization affects what kind of work people do, or if they work at all. It dictates where people live and defines the cultures of communities worldwide. Not only does globalization influence virtually every social factor relevant to crime and criminalization, but also the very international institutions, such as the World Bank and the International Monetary Fund (IMF), which propel globalization, commit crime themselves (Friedrichs and Friedrichs 2008).

See Chapter 4.13
Genocide and
ecocide; Chapter
4.18 Indigenous
criminology

See Chapter 4.12
Financial crime

A specific case involved a World Bank-financed dam in Thailand that exacerbated ethnic conflicts, increased poverty, caused widespread **environmental damage** and displaced **indigenous populations** in violation of international treaties and laws concerning human rights (Friedrichs and Friedrichs 2008). Another example involves the synergy between **finance policies** implemented by the World Bank and the IMF in sub-Saharan Africa, all of which required severe austerity measures and other stipulations reducing social welfare spending and increasing the power of the military.

Young (2007:38–40) points to six criminogenic outcomes of globalization. First, globalization has massively widened the income differential between rich and poor nations, and between the very wealthy and the rest of society in highly developed nations. Second, through its encouragement of **mass consumption**, globalization creates desires and hopes among masses of people that can never be realized because of structural inequalities; globalization thus creates and extends relative deprivation worldwide. Third, globalization plays a key role in exacerbating uncertainty about individual identities. Rising unemployment and poverty levels, the evisceration of communities and the instability of families have become commonplace and epidemic. The poor and others who have been socially excluded are victims of severe economic and political marginalization. Fourth, globalization creates **ontological insecurity** and feelings of **deprivation**. Economic, social and political insecurity, combined with pervasive feelings of unfairness and disrespect, become rationalizations for violence, for blaming 'othered' peoples for personal problems and subsequently dehumanizing them. Fifth, Young points to the 'narcissism of minor differences'. The identity and security concerns fuelled by globalization exacerbate minor cultural differences between and among ethnic and racial groups. Often these differences play out in violent conflict around issues of masculinity, religion or customs. Finally, globalization inexorably leads to identity wars. These violent outbreaks centred on culture, lifestyle and hopelessness are seen worldwide.

A significant outcome of globalization has been the growth of transnational crime, usually defined as crimes committed across national boundaries. Transnational crime usually involves a criminal organization or syndicate providing illicit goods or services. Looking only at illicit enterprises conducted across borders, most valid estimates place the annual revenue of transnational crime at $870 billion, or about 1.5 per cent of the world's gross domestic product (United Nations 2010). The variety of transnational crime in a globalized world is immense and includes: drug trafficking; **cybercrimes**; environmental crimes; trafficking of persons, endangered animals, plants and human organs; money-laundering and other financial crimes; industrial espionage; art and antiquities theft; and the illegal sale of gems, metals, timber and the like.

Often transnational crime involves the direct complicity of transnational corporations and the very states designated with the responsibility to control those crimes (Bowling and Sheptycki 2012). Many students of globalization have argued that transnational corporations have become more powerful and exercise greater control over social, political and economic life than governments themselves. In an era of globalization, we exist in a 'borderless world' where transnational capital is far more **powerful than states** (Ohmae 1995).

Other scholars are more hesitant to see globalization as a force diminishing state power. In fact, they point to the United States and its government as a principal engine of globalization, suggesting that the United States has

See Chapter 4.8
Cultural
criminology

See Chapter 5.17
Security and
counter-security

See Chapter 2.10
Relative
deprivation

See Chapter 6.4
Cybercrime

See Chapter 4.37
State-corporate
crime

become the most powerful empire in world history. This idea of 'globalization from above' argues that, through military and economic power, the United States has established worldwide hegemony (Kellner 2003). The unilateral use of military power, it is argued, establishes a regime of globalization by force which some contend is in direct violation of international law and constitutes state terrorism (Kramer and Michalowski 2005).

Globalization has also had a profound impact on mechanisms of social control worldwide. Social-control regimes have increasingly become reliant on rhetoric related to 'zero tolerance', 'pluralized' and fragmented policing, and increasing dependence on advanced technology related to surveillance. The aim of policing has shifted from 'crime control' to social exclusion. The result is paradoxical in that these regimes of social control reinforce societal and individual alienation, which creates a greater sense of insecurity, which results in amplified efforts to establish ever more systems of control. Thus, globalization has resulted in an insecurity–control spiral (Bowling and Sheptycki 2012). Closely associated with this exportation of Western crime-control logics and technologies has been the widespread emergence of paramilitary policing, heavily promoted by the United States, which threatens to become irreversible.

References

Aas, Katja. 2013. *Globalization and Crime* (2nd edn). London: Sage.

Bowling, Ben, and James Sheptycki. 2012. *Global Policing*. London: Sage.

Friedrichs, David, and Jessica Friedrichs. 2008. The World Bank and Crimes of Globalization: A Case Study. In *Global Criminology and Criminal Justice*, Nick Larsen and Russell Smandych, eds, pp. 81–114. Calgary: Broadview Press.

Hart-Landsberg, Martin. 2013. *Capitalist Globalization: Consequences, Resistance and Alternatives*. New York: Monthly Review Press.

Kellner, Douglas. 2003. *From 9/11 to Terror War: The Dangers of the Bush Legacy*. New York: Rowman & Littlefield.

Kramer, Ronald, and Raymond Michalowski. 2005. War, Aggression and State Crime: A Criminological Analysis of the Invasion and Occupation of Iraq. *British Journal of Criminology* 45(4): 446–69.

Ohmae, Kenichi. 1995. *The End of the Nation State*. New York: Free Press.

Ritzer, G. 1998. *The McDonaldization Thesis: Explorations and Extensions*. London: Sage.

Ruccio, David. 2010. *Development and Globalization: A Marxian Class Analysis*. New York: Routledge.

United Nations. 2010. *The Globalisation of Crime: A Transnational Organized Crime Threat Assessment*. New York: United Nations.

Young, Jock. 2007. *The Vertigo of Late Modernity*. London: Sage.

Further reading

Strange, Susan. 1996. *The Retreat of the State: The Diffusion of Power in the World Economy*. New York: Cambridge University Press.

Gothic criminology

4.15

Cecil E. Greek

Gothic criminology was developed as an interdisciplinary approach to create a dialogue between the humanities and the social sciences in exploring contemporary visualizations of the Gothic and the monstrous in film and the mass media. The ongoing fascination with evil as simultaneously repellent and irresistibly attractive – in Hollywood films, criminological case studies, popular culture and even public policy – points to the re-emergence of the Gothic, with its focus on themes such as blood-lust, compulsion, fear, godlike vengeance, greed, preposterous violence, and power and domination.

While the phrase 'Gothic criminology' may be new, its theoretical components can be gleaned from the writings of sociologists, criminologists and social philosophers describing the ever-present problem of human evil in ways that can be interpreted as Gothic. The roots of Gothic criminology may be seen in a number of early sociological sources (e.g., Ross 1907). Social philosophers (Arendt 1973) and criminologists (Katz 1990) also discuss evil in Gothic ways. Lyman (1978) has made the most significant effort to date to return the discussion of evil to the social sciences.

Gothic criminology does not draw upon classic and contemporary criminological and sociological works alone; it is also dependent on critical examination of themes and concepts apparent in both the Gothic literary tradition and how this tradition has embedded itself into certain film genres such as *film noir* as well as in television. Gothic scenes are heavily populated with images of decay, decadence, disease and death: crumbling architectural remains, rotting old houses, ancient relics, dark and dangerous urban spaces, and decrepit people. The human mind is depicted as similarly in turmoil.

See Chapter 1.2
Classical
criminology

See Chapter 4.13
Genocide and
ecocide; Chapter
4.16 Green
criminology

Death is attractive because of its absolute finality and for its return to primordial chaos. **Nature** also threatens to take its revenge on humanity for the systematic destruction and pillaging of the planet.

As Gothic criminology is predominantly about film (and its comparison to television drama and other mass-media accounts, such as televised news) rather than just literature, it is important to trace the transformation made by the Gothic from the page to the screen. Film offered the ability to recreate Gothic mood through the use of moving **visual imagery** and sound techniques, becoming an effective vehicle for re-envisaging Gothic stories. Over time, a set of stock techniques for lighting, camera locations, depth of field and angles, set design, music and sound, special effects and editing were developed, most famously associated with the Hollywood horror/terror genre pictures and *film noir*. Both frequently contain elements of the Gothic and maintain their ability to instil anxiety, fear and dread in audiences.

See Chapter 4.40
Visual criminology

Gothic criminal-justice films often depict a world similar to those in the *film noir* tradition, in which corruption is pandemic and heroes and villains are virtually indistinguishable. One of the most controversial aspects of the Gothic crime film is its depiction of criminals as monstrous, while one of the hallmarks of the Gothic view of evil is that it frequently maintains the humanity of its monsters. Thus, werewolves shift from human to monster and back again, while Count Dracula is a vampire depicted as an aristocratic sophisticate. Similarly, Hannibal Lecter would make a fascinating guest lecturer.

Several significant studies have employed Gothic criminology, often showing the overlap of various monstrous themes and memes. Examining serial-killing, Picart and Greek (2003) demonstrate the overlap of 'vampiric' themes in serial-murder films. Like vampires, serial killers develop a bloodlust that can be satiated only through repetitive killing. While 'sympathy' is not precisely the word to describe the response encouraged by serial-killer films, there is often a certain ambivalence in the representations of modern murdering monsters. Rather than being the demonic other that must be exorcised from mainstream society, the serial killer was identified explicitly as that society's logical and inevitable product. In a follow-up study, Picart and Greek (2009) looked at the female serial killer. The most well-recognized real-world example is Aileen Wuornos, played by Charlize Theron in the docudrama *Monster* (2003).

See Chapter 4.2
Chaos criminology

A proliferation of Gothic discourses can also be applied to the most feared contemporary monster: the terrorist. Here, the Gothic nuance focuses on the perceived unleashing of **'chaos'** in the world and the responding efforts to restore control and order.

Finally, Britto and Greek (2016) focus on the Gothic elements embedded in contemporary horror film and serial television, and their implied implications for the rule of law, such as questions about the role of law when faced with the possibility of monstrous, supernaturally induced evil. In fact, paradoxically, the cinematic treatment of law and law enforcement serves to validate the presence of ongoing supernatural evil. In a post-apocalyptic world, like that depicted in *The Walking Dead*, law cannot exist if the population does not recognize the symbols of law, or respect the persons that attempt to employ them.

Given the growing overlap between mass-media accounts of real-world examples of monstrous evil and their fictionalized counterparts in film and television, it would appear that there is a growing need for theoretical models that attempt to seriously analyse this phenomenon that go beyond 'fear'. Fiddler (2007) has focused on dark spaces, particularly prisons, as depicted in film. His discussions of *The Shawshank Redemption* (1994) and other films build upon Gothic criminology, and he enriches his analysis with additional concepts such as Freud's notion of the uncanny. Another significant application of Gothic criminology has been to combine it with various green and **cultural criminologies** to 'illuminate one of the primary horrors produced by modernity – the currently prevailing ecocidal destruction of our landscapes, seas, atmosphere and planet' (South 2017). The Enlightenment effort to rationalize human domination of the planet and also to use its natural resources for commercial purposes threatens 'an eventual revolt of nature' from which global warming and resulting human unsustainability appear inevitable. The Gothic imagination draws attention to our fears regarding the dystopian future which may follow from nature's revenge on humanity.

See Chapter 4.8
Cultural
criminology

References

Arendt, Hannah. 1973. *The Origins of Totalitarianism*. New York: Harcourt, Brace.

Britto, Farah, and Cecil Greek. 2016. A depiction of evil, order and chaos: The symbiotic relationship of law and the supernatural in film and television. In *Framing Law and Crime: An Interdisciplinary Anthology*, Caroline Picart, Michael Jacobsen and Cecil Greek, eds, pp. 371–99. Lanham, MD: Rowman & Littlefield.

Fiddler, Michael. 2007. Projecting the Prison: The Depiction of the Uncanny in *The Shawshank Redemption*. Crime, Media, Culture 2(2): 192–208.

Katz, Jack. 1990. *Seductions of Crime: Moral and Sensual Attractions in Doing Evil*. New York: Basic Books.

Lyman, Stanford. M. 1978. *The Seven Deadly Sins: Society and Evil*. New York: St. Martin's.

Picart, Caroline, and Cecil Greek. 2003. The Compulsion of Real/Reel Serial Killers and Vampires: Toward a Gothic Criminology. *Journal of Criminal Justice and Popular Culture* 10(1): 39–68.

Picart, Caroline, and Cecil Greek. 2009. When women become serial killers: Sexuality, class and gender in the case of Eileen Wuornos. In *Draculas, Vampires and Other Undead Forms: Essays on Gender, Race and Culture*, John E. Browning and Caroline J. Picart, eds, pp. 37–62. Lanham, MD: Scarecrow Press.

Ross, Edward A. 1907. *Sin and Society*. New York: Houghton Mifflin.

South, Nigel. 2017. Monstrous nature: A meeting of gothic, green and cultural criminologies. In *The Routledge International Handbook of Visual Criminology*, Michelle Brown and Eamonn Carrabine, eds, Chapter 42. Abingdon: Routledge.

Further reading

Arendt, Hannah. 2006. *Eichmann in Jerusalem: A Report on the Banality of Evil*. New York: Penguin.

Picart, Caroline and Cecil Greek. 2012. Profiling the terrorist as a mass murderer. In *Speaking of Monsters*: *A Teratological Anthology*, Caroline J.S. Picart and John E. Browning, eds, Chapter 15. New York: Palgrave Macmillan.

Picart, Caroline, and Cecil Greek (eds). 2007. *Monsters In and Among Us: Towards a Gothic Criminology*. Madison, NJ: Fairleigh Dickinson University Press.

Picart, Caroline, Michael H. Jacobsen, and Cecil Greek (eds). 2016. *Framing Law and Crime: An Interdisciplinary Anthology*. Madison, NJ and Lanham, MD: Fairleigh Dickinson University Press/Rowman & Littlefield.

Green criminology

4.16

Avi Brisman and Nigel South

Green criminology refers to the study of environmental crimes and harms affecting human and non-human life, ecosystems and the biosphere. The origins of the precise term – 'green criminology' – are in **critical criminology** (e.g., Lynch 1990; South 1998) and much research in the field examines environmental harms that may not be proscribed by law and result from **state–corporate collusion** in the propagation of environmental harm. A broad notion of a 'green' criminological perspective, however, can be seen in work conducted by criminologists across a wide range of research interests and varying **theoretical, methodological and eco-philosophical orientations** – e.g., anthropocentric, biocentric, ecocentric (see White 2013). Regardless of approach or perspective, the broad spectrum of green criminological scholarship includes research on local, regional, international and transnational dimensions of: air pollution and water issues (access, pollution, scarcity); **animal abuse, animal rights and animal welfare; environmental justice** and the disproportionate impact of environmental harms on marginalized populations; food and **agricultural crimes**; harm stemming from global warming and climate change; harm caused by the hazardous transport of e-waste; illegal disposal of toxic waste; poaching and the legal and illegal trade in non-human animals; and violations of workplace health and safety regulations that have environmentally damaging consequences.

Early work in green criminology was mostly concerned with making the case for the study of environmental issues within criminology and for exposing instances and patterns of environmental harm, ranging from the micro to the macro. The first published use of the term 'green criminology' seems to

See Chapter 3.3
Critical
criminologies

See Chapter 4.37
State-corporate
crime

See Chapter 4.3
Conservation
criminology;
Chapter 4.11
Environmental
justice and
victimology;
Chapter 4.13
Genocide and
ecocide; Chapter
4.35 Speciesism
and theriocide

See Chapter 6.9
Rural criminology

297

have been made by Lynch in 1990 (reprinted 2006). In Lynch's use of the term, the objective was to reveal and respond to a 'variety of class related injustices that maintain an inequitable distribution of power while destroying human life, generating hunger, uprooting and poisoning the environment of all classes, peoples and animals' (Lynch 1990/2006:3) Over time, green criminology has come to contemplate not just the individual-, group- and societal-level *causes* of various behaviours, patterns and practices *resulting in* environmental degradation, despoliation and destruction, but also the range and (in)efficacy of *responses* to such environmentally harmful acts and omissions (including law, regulation and resistance), as well as the constructions and representations of environmental crime and harm (see, e.g., Brisman and South 2014).

More specifically, green criminology now endeavours to:

- illuminate environmental risks and threats to specific places, localities and nation-states, as well as larger regions in and across geopolitical boundaries;
- identify and understand the aetiology of environmental harm (drawing upon existing and emerging mainstream and radical criminological theories), including violations of existing environmental law and regulation designed to protect the health, safety and vitality of humans, animals other than human and ecosystems, as well as environmental harms that may not be statutorily proscribed;
- analyse and assess existing and proposed environmental law and regulation (as well as failures and inadequacies), and avoidance of corporate, state and personal responsibility regarding environmental crimes, harms and threats;
- predict or otherwise anticipate environmental disaster and degradation, and propose measures for avoiding or mitigating such destruction;
- investigate grassroots and institutionalized resistance and opposition to environmental crimes and harms; and
- explore and critique the depictions and representations of non-fictional and fictional environmental crimes, harms, disasters and threats in newspapers, film, television, on the Internet, and in other media outlets.

Methodologically, various approaches contribute to the collection of data, both quantitative and qualitative, from surveys to observation, experimental designs to ethnography, and secondary analysis of existing sources. Scientific data, concerning climate change or toxic spillage, for example, are important and, while acknowledging limitations and bias, can be essential for the development of credible critique and argument. Where environmental crimes or harms are 'invisible' – as is often the case – they present particular challenges related to ease or legality of access, scope for examination, and health and safety questions for the researcher. As with research in other 'sensitive' areas, such work can also raise ethical dilemmas of various kinds.

Green criminology addresses the classic criminological questions of how to deal with: (i) harmful actions that are not criminalized but arguably should be; and (ii) actions that do break laws or regulations but which do not receive effective or rigorous responses. In the latter case, green criminology has highlighted emerging evidence about the value of specialist environmental courts. Attempts to identify and sanction key responsible individuals have had only rare success, so alternatives such as 'shaming' and restorative justice approaches seem promising based on the vulnerability to public criticism of heavily promoted corporate images and the principle that 'making good' may be more beneficial than imposing immaterial fines or trying to identify a 'culprit' to receive a prison sentence.

See Chapter 5.14
Reintegrative
shaming

See Chapter 5.15
Restorative justice

Green criminology has also drawn on theories of risk society (Beck 1992), globalization, the treadmill of production and cultures of consumption in thinking about the escalation of environmental harms as risks, and consequences of modernity and transnational production and reproduction. One conclusion would be that criminology must maintain awareness of new directions in, for example, biosciences and nanotechnology, as well as pay attention to the legacy of technologies, such as the challenges of disposal of radioactive waste and e-waste.

See Chapter 4.14
Globalization

The accelerating exploitation of the earth and consequent exhaustion of resources and damage to the planet has been described as a process of ecocide (Higgins et al. 2013), and the responsibility of humanity for this has led to the characterization of a new epoch in earth's history as the Anthropocene. Perhaps the dominant manifestation of these developments has been climate change. The evidence that this is occurring is overwhelming, with energy consumption the principal cause and rich consumer societies being disproportionate contributors to the problem. Criminologists have suggested that climate change will stimulate a number of deeply criminogenic forces. Agnew (2012), for example, examines linkages between climate change and crime in terms of theories such as strain and social control – e.g. climate change will create 'new' reasons for individuals to commit crime(s). Others, such as Kramer (2013), argue that climate change denial and regulatory failure constitute a state–corporate crime.

See Chapter 2.9
General strain
theory

See Chapter 2.6
Control theories

See Chapter 4.37
State-corporate
crime

Green criminology is still evolving, offering a flexible and inclusive framework orientated toward particular problems (harms, offences and crimes related to the environment, different species and the planet) and often borrowing from and seeking connections with other academic disciplines and governmental and non-governmental organizations. Future directions will probably elaborate on studies of the relationship between environment and culture, and environment and conflict, as well as the exploitation of nature and links to human rights issues in the global south.

See Chapter 4.34
Southern theory

Environmental challenges are both local and global, and criminological thinking has to respond correspondingly. It is important to acknowledge that some writers may feel that their scientific credibility will be questioned if they are associated with an explicitly 'green' position, group or body of work, and so are wary of the term; others may embrace the term as a political statement.

Some others point to confusion arising from the appropriation and misuse of the 'green' label by corporate interests. More neutrally, however, 'green' can be seen as simply a well-understood expression of concern about environmental matters.

'Green criminology' has certainly been an important development, encouraging criminology to examine crimes and harms that are often overlooked or excluded from its more traditional concerns and to illustrate how significant, wide-ranging and widespread these are. The term itself, 'green criminology', is useful and has provided a stimulus to a considerable body of work, but it is only a symbol or expression regarding a perspective or orientation toward certain crucially important concerns. What matters is that criminology continues to engage with these concerns.

References

Agnew, Robert. 2012. Dire Forecast: A Theoretical Model of the Impact of Climate Change on Crime. *Theoretical Criminology* 16(1): 21–42.

Beck, Ulrich. 1992. *Risk Society: Toward a New Modernity*. London: Sage.

Brisman, Avi, and Nigel South. 2014. *Green Cultural Criminology: Constructions of Environmental Harm, Consumerism, and Resistance to Ecocide*. London: Routledge.

Higgins, Polly, Damien Short, and Nigel South. 2013. Protecting the Planet: A Proposal for a Law of Ecocide. *Crime, Law and Social Change* 59(3): 251–66.

Kramer, Ronald C. 2013. Carbon in the Atmosphere and Power In America: Climate Change as State-Corporate Crime. *Journal of Crime and Justice* 36(2): 153–70.

Lynch, Michael J. 1990. The Greening of Criminology: A Perspective on the 1990s. *Critical Criminologist* 2(3): 1–4, 11–12. Reprinted in Nigel South and Piers Beirne, eds. 2006. *Green Criminology*. Pp. 165–9. Aldershot: Ashgate.

South, Nigel. 1998. A Green Field for Criminology? A Proposal for a Perspective. *Theoretical Criminology* 2(2): 211–33.

White, Rob. 2013. *Environmental Harm: An Eco-Justice Perspective*. Bristol: Policy Press.

Further reading

Hall, Matthew. 2013. *Victims of Environmental Harm: Rights, Recognition and Redress under National and International Law*. London and New York: Routledge.

Hall, Matthew. 2015. *Exploring Green Crime: Introducing the Legal, Social and Criminological Contexts of Environmental Harm*. London: Palgrave Macmillan.

Lynch, Michael J., and Paul B. Stretesky. 2014. *Exploring Green Criminology: Toward a Green Criminological Revolution*. Farnham: Ashgate.

Rodríguez Goyes, David, Hanneke Mol, Avi Brisman and Nigel South (eds). 2017. *Environmental Crime in Latin America: The Theft of Nature and the Poisoning of the Land*. Basingstoke: Palgrave Macmillan.

Sollund, Ragnhild (ed.). 2008. *Global Harms: Ecological Crime and Speciesism*. New York: Nova Science Publishers, Inc.

South, Nigel, and Avi Brisman (eds.) 2013. *Routledge International Handbook of Green Criminology*. London: Routledge.

White, Rob, and Diane Heckenberg. 2014. *Green Criminology: An Introduction to the Study of Environmental Harm*. London: Routledge.

Hate crime

Scott Poynting

The use of the designation 'hate crime' is widely agreed to have arisen in the United States in the 1980s in the context of campaigns for public awareness and policy responses to the incidence of crimes victimizing 'racial', ethnic and religious minorities. From the beginning, therefore, the concept was political, and remains unavoidably so.

Hate crime may be defined as a type of crime, typically violent, threatening or humiliating, in which the **victim or victims** are selected – or believe they are selected – because they belong to a group which is the subject of prejudice, bias or hatred on the part of the perpetrator(s). They are crimes committed against those 'different' from those who take themselves to be the measure of difference, and are in some position to do so.

See Chapter 4.39
Victimology

It is not merely a matter of difference, however, but of power. Barbara Perry (2001:10) makes the point that hate crime is '"doing" difference', but this form of difference is constituted in inequality:

> Hate crime involves acts of violence and intimidation, usually directed towards already stigmatised and marginalised groups. As such, it is a mechanism of power and oppression, intended to reaffirm the precarious hierarchies that characterise a given social order. It attempts to recreate simultaneously the threatened (real or imagined) hegemony of the perpetrator's group and the 'appropriate' subordinate identity of the victim's group.

Hate crime is thus produced by the **power relations** in which it is committed, and it operates to reproduce these power relations. As Levin and McDevitt

See Chapter 3.3
Critical
criminologies

(2002:6) observe, 'hate crimes . . . target not only a primary victim, but everyone in the victim's group'. Hate crime, therefore, is a 'message' crime: 'it sends a message to the entire group to which the victim belongs that they are "different" and that they "don't belong"' (Hall 2005:4).

Hate crimes may be categorized by the type of 'bias' or 'prejudice' that motivates the perpetrator and determines the targeting of victims. Thus, the US Federal Bureau of Investigation (FBI) defines hate crime as a: 'criminal offense against a person or property motivated in whole or in part by an offender's bias against a race, religion, disability, sexual orientation, ethnicity, gender, or gender identity.' Similarly, in the UK, the Association of Chief Police Officers and the Crown Prosecution Service (CPS) together define hate crime as:

> [A] criminal offence which is perceived by the victim or any other person, to be motivated by hostility or prejudice based on a person's race or perceived race; religion or perceived religion; sexual orientation or perceived sexual orientation; disability or perceived disability and any crime motivated by hostility or prejudice against a person who is transgender or perceived to be transgender.

See Chapter 4.13 Genocide and ecocide; Chapter 4.36 State crime; Chapter 4.37 State-corporate crime

Disagreements over the definitions of hate crime involve not only the long-standing debates over what constitutes a 'crime' (**can a state commit hate crime**, for example?), but also divergence between those who rely on inferred motivation and those who depend on the subjective experience of the victim(s). Do we need to demonstrate a causal connection between threats that are racist, xenophobic, anti-Semitic, Islamophobic, homophobic, transphobic, anti-disability and so on, and attacks on victims thus targeted, in order to categorize this as 'hate crime'? Or is the experience of the victims (where surviving) or perception of witnesses sufficient to define it thus? The British decision to define a hate incident in terms of the perception of victims or observers – a stance adopted following the Macpherson Report (1999) after the racist murder in 1993 of Stephen Lawrence and the deficiencies of bias and neglect in the police investigation – has been cause of much resentment among police.

Legislative responses to hate crime – a key objective of those who originated the term – are varied. One approach is to provide for augmentation of sentences where there is found to be the exacerbating factor of the offender(s) being motivated wholly or in part by hostility towards a group of persons who have an enduring common characteristic or perceived characteristic, with the characteristics often being listed as above. Here, the hatred, bias or prejudice is viewed as an aggravating factor which renders the crime a more serious one deserving of a harsher punishment; it does not constitute the crime in itself. A second approach involves rendering unlawful particular manifestations of hatred, prejudice or bias – such as discrimination against or vilification of a group with an enduring common characteristic, or incitement of hatred or violence against such a group. An example might be the placing of a burning cross on the lawn of an African-American family. In such cases, the offence is inherent in the act of hate or discrimination itself (or incitement towards one). Various anti-discrimination and anti-vilification laws, specifying proscribed types of bigotry (e.g., racial, religious, gender-based, sexuality-based, age-based) are included in this response to hate or bias crime. These legal prohibitions are often mandated by international law. They are also enforced infrequently in most jurisdictions, and provisions for punishment often lack teeth – or else the prescribed means of redress are often ineffectual. This is to be expected where the structured 'hate' in question reflects the interests of dominant groups in a society.

Freedom of speech and other civil liberties' principles are often raised in opposition to both forms of hate crime legislation – often by right-wing libertarians. For example, in proposing in 2014 to repeal section 18 of Australia's Racial Discrimination Act, then Attorney-General George Brandis asserted that people had a 'right to be bigots'. Opponents of this argument counter that all civil liberties are circumscribed by principles of preventing harm to others, and that fetishizing the 'free-speech' aspects overlooks the harm that hate crime does to victimized groups.

On the left, critics of the first (aggravation/sentence-enhancement) type of law against hate crime argue that it is a 'blunt instrument' – that it is ineffectual both as a deterrent and as a means of educating the public about the harmfulness of hate crime. They also observe that the legal provisions are in practice often used against the socially marginal and the less powerful: this contradicts the often-stated aims of hate-crime law – to protect the vulnerable and subordinated from crimes of prejudice (see, e.g., Gadd and Dixon 2011). A disadvantaged black woman, for example, using a deeply offensive gendered term against a white male police officer while resisting arrest, may be technically a hate crime, but this is hardly in the spirit of the legislation. The systemic discrimination in the criminal justice system, from policing to courts, is compounded rather than ameliorated by such application of the law. Hate-crime statistics – notoriously blunt instruments in themselves – will not tell us much about how often this happens; but the preventative inefficacy of the laws may be attributed to the differential exercise of discretion and judgement that has been well observed in the criminal justice system.

Another point of contention in legislating against hate crime is the often minor or even trivial nature of the offence. The majority of hate crime is not committed by associates of far-right and other organized hate groups; most hate crime is a much more ordinary, everyday occurrence. Is it right or even effective for a society to attempt to criminalize and punish everyday offences against civility, especially when their biases are widely shared among the population? In practice, there is not much stomach to do so, in most jurisdictions, most of the time. Yet, it is not necessary to draw a dichotomy between mundane hate crime and that of racist (and other hate-mongering, such as homophobic) organizations. The former can be encouraged by the latter. The study of hate crime, therefore, needs to pay attention to the ideology and institutional practices of prejudice and bigotry in everyday life, as well as to the politics in which they are organized and propagated.

One of the challenges in researching the motivation and causation of hate crime – beyond the fact that statistics do not tell us much about causal mechanisms – is the difficulty of access to credible qualitative data from perpetrators. This has nevertheless been attempted with considerable insight by Gadd et al. (2005), but more needs to be done in this area.

An example of a promising contribution in understanding the production of hate crime is Perry's (2001) notion of 'permission to hate'. This grasps the mechanisms by which the state – through indulgence of perpetrators, the incitement of some official and political rhetoric, and even modelling of discriminatory violence – confers upon potential hate-crime perpetrators a sense of rectitude and entitlement in hateful speech and actions. The mass media often engage in similar inducement of hate-based violence through blaming, scapegoating and vilificatory stereotyping. The wave of attacks on immigrants and ethnic minorities in Britain in 2016 following a divisive and 'dogwhistling' campaign for the London mayoralty, and then outright xenophobic hostility in the 'Brexit' campaign and the presidential candidacy of Donald J. Trump in the United States, are strong examples of 'permission to hate' from both the state and the popular mass media.

The wave of right-wing nationalist racist movements sweeping across Europe (and the US and Australia) contemporaneously leaves much to be researched about racist 'permission to hate'. Some have argued that conservative campaigns against **gay marriage and LGBTQI rights** educational materials have a similar effect. Yet there is always resistance, and movements against all forms of hatred, bias and prejudice (criminalized or not) will continue to struggle – in the state, the media and civil society – to deny permission to hate.

See Chapter 4.32
Queer criminology

References

Gadd, David, and Bill Dixon. 2011. *Losing the Race: Thinking Psychosocially about Racially Motivated Crime*. London: Karnac.

Gadd, David, Bill Dixon, and Tony Jefferson. 2005. *Why Do They Do It? Racial Harassment in North Staffordshire*. Staffordshire: Keele University.

Hall, Nathan. 2005. *Hate Crime*. Cullompton, UK Willan.

Levin, Jack, and Jack McDevitt. 2002. *Hate Crimes Revisited: America's War on Those Who Are Different*. Boulder, CO: Westview.

Perry, Barbara. 2001. *In the Name of Hate*. New York and London: Routledge.

Further reading

Chakraborti, Neil, and John Garland. 2015. *Hate Crime: Causes, Impact and Responses* (2nd edn). London: Sage.

Hall, Nathan, Abbee Corb, Paul Giannasi, and John Grieve (eds). 2014. *The Routledge International Handbook on Hate Crime*. London: Routledge.

Iganski, Paul. 2008. *Hate Crime and the City*. Bristol: Policy Press.

Levin, Jack, and Jack McDevitt. 1993. *Hate Crimes: The Rising Tide of Bigotry and Bloodshed*. New York: Plenum.

Perry, Barbara (ed.). 2009. *Hate Crimes* (5 vols). Westport, CT and London: Praeger.

4.18 Indigenous criminology

Chris Cunneen and Juan Tauri

See Chapter 4.27
Postcolonial
criminology

After centuries of colonization, indigenous peoples in the settler-colonial states – including Australia, New Zealand, Canada and the USA – still experience profound socio-economic disadvantage and political marginalization. Nowhere is the impact of **colonialism** more obvious than with Indigenous peoples' encounters with criminal justice, which are typically characterized by high rates of victimization, arrest, conviction and imprisonment. While the significant over-representation of Indigenous peoples in settler-colonial systems of crime control is acknowledged by both policymakers and mainstream criminologists and has resulted in significant research and policy recognition, overall the situation has worsened in recent decades. Critical Indigenous commentators and non-Indigenous collaborators argue that the failure to address over-representation in part rests with the paternalistic tendencies of settler-colonial governments and the Eurocentric bias of many within mainstream criminology. Dominant explanations of the causes of this problem, and policies and interventions designed to alleviate it, tend to **pathologize** Indigenous peoples, presenting them as individuals prone to criminality, and their cultural knowledge, philosophies and social practices as deviant and criminogenic. Furthermore, some prominent criminologists have suggested that Indigenous knowledge, at least that which impacts the development of crime control policy, is an impediment to the development of effective interventions for reducing Indigenous over-representation (see, e.g.,

See Chapter 1.6
Pathology

Weatherburn 2014; for a critique of these approaches, see Cunneen and Tauri 2016).

An Indigenous approach to criminological inquiry has emerged within settler-colonial contexts, partly in response to the perceived weaknesses and bias of the policy sector and the mainstream criminological approaches described above (Cunneen and Tauri 2016). The antecedents of this criminological movement were provided by Indigenous political and social activists from the early 1970s which focused on the role of the criminal justice system in the subjugation of Indigenous peoples. Activist critiques of criminal justice, supported by standpoint **feminist and restorative justice** denunciation of settler-colonial justice, centred on the colonial foundations of its core institutions and practices, including the role of policing, courts and prison (e.g., Jackson 1988). Building on the work of this group since the mid-1990s, Indigenous scholars such as Ross (1998) and Tauri (2012) and a group of critical, non-Indigenous collaborators such as Blagg (2008) and Cunneen (2001) have begun to construct a distinctly *Indigenous criminology* – an Indigenous approach to explaining and responding to social harm in the contemporary settler-colonial context. A further contribution of Indigenous activism to the development of an Indigenous criminology was made by the establishment and findings of a number of national inquiries, including the Canadian Royal Commission into Aboriginal Peoples and the Australian Royal Commission into Aboriginal Deaths in Custody.

See Chapter 3.6 Feminist criminologies; Chapter 4.26 Patriarchy and crime; Chapter 3.13 Radical feminism; Chapter 5.15 Restorative justice

When we speak of an Indigenous criminology we are talking more of an analytical and epistemological approach to examining relations between Indigenous peoples, the criminal justice system and the criminological academy than a fully elaborated theory of the causes of Indigenous criminality, Indigenous victimization and the over-representation and disempowerment of Indigenous peoples in the criminal justice system. An Indigenous-criminological approach can be distinguished by the following key analytical frameworks.

First, an Indigenous approach is one that is based firmly in historical and contemporary conditions, especially the impact of colonialism on the present relationship between Indigenous peoples, the settler-colonial state and criminal justice. Such an approach privileges the Indigenous perspective and requires a meaningful analysis of colonialism as an explanatory factor in Indigenous peoples' experiences of settler-colonial justice. It is a theoretical and practical necessity for understanding the antecedents of contemporary levels of over-representation and for developing meaningful solutions.

Second, of fundamental importance to the study of Indigenous experiences of crime control is the ideal that Indigenous knowledge and the processes for gathering, analysing and disseminating it are vital for understanding the Indigenous context and Indigenous experience of settler-colonial crime control.

Third, Indigenous criminological research gives back by 'speaking truth to power'. A principle that is common to Indigenous-inspired ethics for conducting Indigenous research is the need to give back to the communities from which knowledge is taken, even if one is a member of that community. Some of the ways in which Indigenous researchers have given back include taking on a political role as agents of change and unmasking dominant ideologies and colonizing practices of the state and other institutions, including the academy.

Fourth, Indigenous criminological research with Indigenous peoples should be 'real'. Arguably, some members of the Western academy have become adept at 'faking' the appearance of respectful consultation/research. Of late, Indigenous scholars have exposed the nature and extent of this problem as it recurs in criminological research on the 'Indigenous problem'. More importantly, the negative impact of deceptive or dishonest consultation and engagement – in terms of meaningless Indigenous strategies, biculturalized interventions and such like – is *very real* and often damaging for the Indigenous communities upon whom they are forced. Therefore, it is essential that we ensure that the knowledge about Indigenous peoples that we assemble and disseminate reflects their experiences and has a positive impact on their lives. For this to happen, we need to ensure that our work is 'real', meaning that it must come *from within* Indigenous peoples and their communities.

Fifth, the importance of Indigenous rights forms a cornerstone of criminological research and policy development. The *Declaration on the Rights of Indigenous Peoples* elaborates these rights. Of particular relevance to Indigenous criminology are self-determination; participation in decision-making and free, prior and informed consent; non-discrimination and equality; and respect for and protection of culture. Each of these principles provides a guide for both assessing contemporary criminal justice systems and respecting Indigenous demands for reconceptualizing justice.

The added value of an Indigenous approach to criminological analysis can be identified through the case study of the Māori jurist and activist Moana Jackson's (1988) exploration of Indigenous experiences of crime-control policy in New Zealand, which represents the only significant empirical project of its kind undertaken in New Zealand to date. The study was carried out over three years and involved individual interviews and focus groups with a range of Māori with experience of the justice system. To understand Māori offending, Jackson argued that theoretical explanations and policy responses had to contextualize Māori experiences in relation to a history of colonization. This approach emphasizes the importance of understanding how colonization shapes contemporary social relations and contexts, rather than seeking to limit analyses to that of individual pathology decontextualized from the wider social, political and economic relations of New Zealand society.

Jackson recommended referring cases to Māori providers; holding meaningful hearings on *marae* (meeting-houses); creating cultural advisory groups for justice agencies; practising affirmative action to secure employment of those with knowledge of *te ao Māori* (Māori culture and language); and developing meaningful bicultural training. Many of these recommendations, however, were ignored or dismissed by the government at the time as being 'separatist'. Indeed, the primary policy response largely revolved around the controlled integration of 'acceptable' Māori concepts and cultural practices into confined areas of the justice system. Government officials expressly recommended against transferring criminal justice-centred processes into distinctly Indigenous settings, such as *marae*. Officials argued that court trials could not be easily transposed to Indigenous cultural settings while ensuring the integrity of the state process remained 'intact'.

In the intervening 30 years, however, the majority of these recommendations have in some form or other been implemented. The state has moved to utilize *marae* to deal with Indigenous justice matters: first, as a site for the delivery of rehabilitation programmes and restorative justice interventions; and, of late, through the establishment of the *rangatahi* (youth) courts. The key point is that Jackson's highly politicized research changed the criminal justice landscape in New Zealand immeasurably and opened the space for Indigenous-centred research and responses to issues of crime control.

With respect to the future of Indigenous criminology, Cunneen and Tauri (2016) have recently identified a number of issues that require the theoretical and empirical attention of the evolving **Indigenous criminology movement**. Paramount is the development and empirical investigation of a 'theory of colonization' of the impact of colonial and neo-colonial policies of settler-colonial government on Indigenous communities. Also of importance for an Indigenous critique of crime-control policies is the reinvigoration of Indigenous social and political activism, such as Canada's *Idle No More* movement, and the ongoing battle of members of the Indigenous academy to centre Indigenous experiences, knowledges and methodologies as essential to criminological explorations of the Indigenous world.

See Chapter 4.7 Critical race theory; Chapter 4.34 Southern theory

References

Blagg, Harry. 2008. *Crime, Aboriginality and the Decolonisation of Justice*. Sydney: Hawkins Press.

Cunneen, Chris. 2001. *Conflict, Politics and Crime*. Sydney: Allen & Unwin.

Cunneen, Chris, and Juan Tauri. 2016. *Indigenous Criminology*. Bristol: Policy Press.

Jackson, Moana. 1988. *The Maori and the Criminal Justice System: He Whaipaanga Hou*. Wellington: Department of Justice.

Ross, Luana. 1998. *Inventing the Savage: The Social Construction of Native American Criminality*. Austin: University of Texas Press.

Tauri, Juan. 2012. Indigenous critique of authoritarian criminology. In *Crime, Justice and Social Democracy: International Perspectives*, Kerry Carrington, Matthew Ball, Erin O'Brien, and Juan Tauri, eds, pp. 217–33. Basingstoke: Palgrave Macmillan.

Weatherburn, Don. 2014. *Arresting Incarceration: Pathways Out of Indigenous Imprisonment*. Canberra: Aboriginal Studies Press.

Further reading

Agozino, Biko. 2003. *Counter-Colonial Criminology: A Critique of Imperialist Reason*. London: Pluto Press.

Kitossa, Tamari. 2012. Criminology and Colonialism: Counter Colonial Criminology and the Canadian Context. *Journal of Pan African Studies* 4(1): 204–26.

Milward, David. 2012. *Aboriginal Justice and the Charter*. Vancouver: UBC Press.

Porter, Amanda. 2016. Decolonizing Policing: Indigenous Patrols, Counter-Policing and Safety. *Theoretical Criminology* 20(4): 548–65.

Institutional and anti-institutional violence

4.19

Vincenzo Ruggiero

Extreme forms of political violence have mainly solicited the analytical efforts of political scientists and international-relations experts. When, particularly after the war in the former Yugoslavia, the interest of criminologists in these forms of violence grew, the impression was conveyed that their own disciplinary area had always neglected the subject matter. This contribution attempts to demonstrate otherwise, offering a brief journey through a variety of schools of thought within criminological theory and their contribution for our understanding of political violence. A preliminary distinction is, however, necessary.

There are forms of authorized and forms of unauthorized violence: the former is perpetrated by the authority (usually the nation-state or its agents), while the latter is deployed against the authority. Authorized force can be law-making violence, when it establishes new systems and designates new ruling elites, but can also be law-conserving violence, when it protects systems and reinforces the power of ruling elites. We can refer to both these types of violence as *institutional violence* (or violence from above). On the other hand, we can term unauthorized force, addressed against the ruling elites, *anti-institutional violence* (or violence from below). Let us see how criminology deals with these kinds of violence.

See Chapter 1.2
Classical
criminology

See Chapter 4.1
Anarchist
criminology

See Chapter 1.4
Positivism

See Chapter 1.11
Biosocial theory

See Chapter 2.1
Chicago School

See Chapter 4.25
Organized crime

On the front cover of one of the early editions of *On Crimes and Punishments*, we see Justice turning away in horror from a man holding three heads he has just cut off. That man is a thug, the personification of a brutal state whose violence is epitomized by the cruelty of punishment. **Cesare Beccaria** (1995) focuses on institutional violence and equates it to cold-blooded atrocity. In the last pages of his celebrated book, however, he does address anti-institutional violence when he shifts from the examination of crimes that undermine the personal security of individuals to those that directly destroy society or its representatives. The latter are deemed 'the greatest crimes', also termed crimes of *lèse-majesté* or sedition. It has seldom been noted that acts of sedition are the only ones, in Beccaria's view, that deserve capital punishment. The killing of citizens, he argues, becomes necessary 'in periods of **anarchy**, when disorder replaces the laws' (Beccaria 1995:67). Jeremy Bentham, echoing this view, completes the 'enlightened' picture of classical criminology, asserting that rational, useful and proportionate punishments do not apply to the 'crimes against the state'.

Almost totally neglected is also the contribution of the **positive school of criminology** to the analysis of political violence. Enrico Ferri (1967) coins the term 'evolutionary criminality', which in his opinion characterizes violent collective action bringing social change – a criminality, therefore, instrumental for progress and increasingly just societies. This he distinguishes from '**biosocial criminality**', which designates common interpersonal violence. Lombroso and Laschi (1890) admire the conspirators who fought violently for the unification of Italy, and from their portraits displayed in the Museo del Risorgimento evince their noble, altruistic nature. The atavistic type of criminal, in their view is only found in 'rebellions', not in 'revolutions' (Lombroso 1894).

This distinction returns in Durkheim (1958) in the form of the separate characteristics he sees in socialism and communism respectively. The former responds to the need for economic regulation, which comes about through social evolution assisted by a benevolent state and a variety of other moral agents. Communism, on the other hand, is a pathological, abnormal movement, and its violent manifestations indicate that it is tantamount to a mere programme of social destruction. If social effervescence is a crucial trait of socialists, it is 'morbid effervescence' that characterizes communists. Not all social manifestations are functional, therefore, and Durkheim regards the systematic use of political violence as an aberration: 'Once a social organization is destroyed, it takes centuries before building another one. Meanwhile, there will be a new Middle Ages' (Durkheim 1970:290).

With the **Chicago School**, the focus returns to institutional violence, which is expressed by political groups through the strong arm of **organized crime**. The study conducted by Landesco describes how the wealth accumulated by criminal groups during the 1920s cements strong partnerships with businessmen, law enforcers and politicians. While gangsters become politicians, politicians find in gangsters new allies who can mobilize voters and intimidate competitors or enemies. Landesco concludes that the alliance between official politics and organized crime rests on the mutuality of their services, and that institutional violence, therefore, reaps the fruits of conventional criminal violence.

Definitions of political violence, and for that matter of crime in general, can be understood if related to the uneven distribution of power and resources within society. Inequality, in other words, allows the powerful to criminalize acts committed by the powerless and to define their own conduct as legitimate. Conflict theory in criminology revolves around this notion, which leads to what Quinney (1971) describes as the 'politicality' of crime. In Quinney's view, disadvantaged groups express their desire for political change through law-breaking, while institutional agencies respond with definitions and measures that are just as political in nature. Demonstrations, for instance, manifest the need for social justice, and only become 'riots' when violence is provoked by the authorities charged with controlling the participants: police intimidation and brutality, therefore, are seen as their main characteristics. Political violence, in this perspective, is mainly equated to institutional violence: 'Increased use of police power has been justified as necessary to combat violence. But the paradox is that the violence that the police attempt to control is inspired in many cases by the police themselves' (Quinney 1971:315).

This interactionist logic returns in subsequent work by Becker, Lemert and Blumer. **Labelling theory and symbolic interactionism**, when applied to the analysis of political violence, would suggest that every action is 'joint action' in that it cannot be separated from the action which caused it and which will respond to it. Similarly, political violence from below cannot be broken down into the separate acts comprising it, namely the violence from above that it elicits and to which it responds. In this sense, the violence displayed by the Black Panther Party in the United States, the Red Brigades in Italy or the Red Army Faction in West Germany (active during the 1960s and 1970s–1980s) can be interpreted only as the result of an interaction between these armed groups and the violence of the system against which they fought, along with the violent institutional responses these groups elicited.

See Chapter 3.8 Labelling theory; Chapter 3.18 Symbolic interactionism

Readers may by now be aware that the word 'terrorism' has not been used so far. This is because there exists a monopoly of sorts in the definition of behaviour, and before defining a behaviour as 'terrorist', definitions must be filtered through the discourses of official politics and the media. Only then may such behaviour become worthy of criminological analysis. Manifestations of political dissent, extreme though they may be, should be seen against social and institutional processes, tentatively exemplified by Ferracuti (1982:130) in the following words: 'Terrorism could be defined as what the other person does. What we, or the state, do is anti-terrorism. But obviously the positions can be reversed by shifting side, or simply by the flow of history.' A definition incorporating such social and institutional processes might be: a terrorist act is any act carried out during the course of political struggle, aimed at influencing, conquering or *defending* state power, implying the use of extreme violence against innocent, non-combatant persons. This definition includes both institutional and anti-institutional violence, namely acts against a state and acts by states against their internal or external enemies. Terrorism, therefore, is a form of 'pure' violence exercised by organized forces inflicting mass violence on civilians. It is random: it does not target specific actors whose conduct is regarded as wrongful, but general populations which are hit because of their nationality, ethnicity, religious or political creed. Terrorism adopts a concept of collective liability against its victims. Note that contemporary wars waged by Western countries contain all of these definitional elements. This type of violence contains elements of what is known as **hate crime**, namely the recognition that victims are perceived as representatives of specific communities, and that they are not attacked in their capacity as individuals, but as individuals belonging to a real or imagined, alien group. Hatred may also be based on identities, lifestyles, cultural-religious values and tastes, and constitute a reservoir of bitter memories that can trigger violent antagonism.

See Chapter 4.17
Hate crime

In conclusion, both institutional and anti-institutional violence are extreme forms of political violence and include what we call 'terrorism', a morally and politically over-charged concept to be used with caution and defined with precision. All these forms of political violence are methods of struggle that can and have been employed by an infinite variety of actors, including governments, political factions, criminal gangs, and religious and civic movements.

References

Beccaria, Cesare. 1995/1765. *On Crimes and Punishments*. Cambridge: Cambridge University Press.
Durkheim, Émile. 1958. *Socialism*. Edited by Alvin W. Gouldner. New York: Collier.
Durkheim, Émile. 1970. *La science sociale et l'action*. Paris: Presse Universitaire de France.
Ferracuti, Franco. 1982. A Socio-Psychiatric Interpretation of Terrorism. *Annals of the American Academy of Political and Social Science* 463: 129–40.
Ferri, Enrico. 1967/1884. *Criminal Sociology*. New York: Agathon Press.
Landesco, John. 1973/1929. *Organized Crime in Chicago*. Chicago: University of Chicago Press.
Lombroso, Cesare. 1894. *Gli anarchici*. Turin: Bocca.
Lombroso, Cesare and Rodolfo Laschi. 1890. *Il delitto politico e le rivoluzioni*. Turin: Bocca.
Quinney, Richard. 1971. *The Problem of Crime*. New York: Dodd, Mead & Co.

Further reading

Becker, Howard. 1963. *Outsiders: Studies in the Sociology of Deviance*. New York: Free Press.
Bentham, Jeremy. 1954/1791. Anarchical fallacies. In *Works*. New York: Bowring.
Blumer, Herbert. 1969. *Symbolic Interactionism*. Berkeley: University of California Press.

Lemert, Edwin. 1964. *Human Deviance*. Englewood Cliffs, NJ: Prentice Hall.

Ruggiero, Vincenzo. 2006. *Understanding Political Violence*. Maidenhead: Open University Press.

Ruggiero, Vincenzo. 2015. War and the death of Achilles. In *Criminology and War*, Sandra Walklate and Ross McGarry, eds, pp. 21–37. London and New York: Routledge.

4.20 Intersectionality

Kathryn Henne and
Emily I. Troshynski

See Chapter 3.6
Feminist
Criminologies;
Chapter 4.26
Patriarchy and
crime; Chapter
3.13 Radical
feminism

See Chapter 3.3
Critical
criminologies;
Chapter 4.7
Critical race
theory

Intersectionality is an influential **feminist paradigm** that aids in analysing instances of oppression that arise out of a combination of marginalizing forces – namely, but certainly not limited to, **race, class and gender**. In particular, intersectionality offers a useful approach to explain how the interaction of these factors results in forms of discrimination that are fundamentally different from any of these considerations on their own. For example, women of colour stand at the intersection of raced and gendered axes of oppression (among likely others) and thus experience a form of oppression that is distinct compared to men of colour or white women. Although criminologists have called for a stronger commitment to intersectional studies of crime and deviance (Burgess-Proctor 2006; Potter 2015), they are, as Kathleen Daly (2010:237) points out, 'more an aspiration for the future than a research practice today'. The challenge for studies of crime is not simply to *apply* the term, but to *adapt* intersectionality for criminological inquiry.

As articulated by legal scholar Kimberlé Crenshaw (1991), intersectionality captures the structural and discursive effects of two or more axes of subordination interacting in tandem. Through an analysis of violence against black women in the United States, she outlines three primary foci: 1) structural intersectionality, that is, structural marginalization and forms of class disadvantage; 2) political intersectionality, or the more discursive practices of marginalization; and 3) representational intersectionality – those imaginary practices that render women of colour invisible in discourse. These three foci offer a guide to account for how individuals can endure the effects of inequality and law in distinct ways. Intersectionality, explain Sumi Cho, Kimberlé Crenshaw and Leslie McCall (2013:787), not only unpacks 'dynamics of difference' and 'solidarities of sameness' – particularly as applied to anti-discrimination and social-movement politics – but it also highlights how 'single-axis thinking undermines legal thinking, disciplinary knowledge production, and struggles for social justice' more broadly.

Intersectionality is not without its shortcomings, which Kate Henne and Emily Troshynski (2013) describe further in their work. First, many feminists acknowledge that Crenshaw's notion of intersectionality is but one way to study multiple marginalization – one that is rooted in a US-based context that privileges identity as the standpoint for knowledge about oppression. Second, in focusing on identity, Crenshaw's formulation of intersectionality is not well equipped to capture the many globalized shifts that shape forces of oppression. Third, the proliferation of intersectional analyses has actually undermined intersectionality's critical impetus: that is, intersectionality is increasingly reworked to 'fit' mainstream methodological approaches that fail to adequately capture its theoretical robustness. Fourth, and almost ironically, intersectionality, by offering such a comprehensive analytic, often emerges as a simplistic reference to the triad of 'race–class–gender', which skirts a milieu and myriad of concerns that intersectionality intends to expose and unpack. Thus, in trying to explain dilemmas of misrepresentation, the concept posits one of its own: intersectionality can be used as a stand-in term for multifaceted social relations that require in-depth analysis.

In light of these strengths and limitations, criminologists have adapted intersectionality in different ways. To date, criminological applications both build upon and extend Crenshaw's original framework. Hilary Potter (2015), for example, posits intersectionality as a way to address how identities are both raced and gendered. Moreover, identities take shape constitutively. In accounting for these interactive relationships, intersectionality, she argues, offers criminology an important framework for understanding *why* people of colour are over-represented in the US criminal-legal system and have higher offending and victimization rates than their white counterparts.

Amanda Burgess-Proctor (2006:27) proposes intersectionality as a broader intervention for criminology, suggesting that its use can achieve 'universal relevance and is free from the shortcomings of past ways of thinking'. She contends that intersectional criminology should draw on multiracial feminism as its 'theoretical orientation' in order to address 'issues of power and privilege without assuming a monolithic women's experience' (Burgess-Proctor 2006:28–5). Both Burgess-Proctor and Potter call for looking at how identities take shape through a lens of difference. Their recommendations, although important, fail to address the notable criticisms that intersectionality has received for privileging individuals and their experiences as the primary sites for understanding oppression. In other words, using individuals as the starting point from which to understand marginalization renders axes of oppression as stable characteristics, not as interconnected forces that can become destabilized and shift in different contexts.

Criminologists do acknowledge the potentially problematic implications of focusing on identity and seeking universal claims about difference. Henne and Troshynski (2013) warn that the awareness of globalized changes, namely in relation to the dynamism of crime categories and notions of deviance, poses important yet under-theorized tasks for criminologists. Following feminist criminologists who have long questioned disciplinary claims to know and explain crime through positivistic measures, they argue that there are (still) tenuous concerns regarding issues of representation embedded in criminology. That is, criminology may claim to know crime, but the basis of that knowledge relies on empirical claims about crime's *representation*, not its *enactment*. Crime is a recited event (through narratives, statistics and/or reports), and the *act* of crime remains a space that criminologists cannot fully know – a concern shared with cultural criminologists. Despite these observations, criminology still tends to utilize empirical tools that naturalize crime as an object, limiting the discipline's overall ability to deconstruct the political, representational and symbolic forces informing its construction. Intersectionality, however, is particularly attuned to such concerns, giving it the potential to radically impact how we generate criminological knowledge – even in transnational spaces.

Feminists, both within and beyond criminology, have employed intersectionality to shift analyses from the pursuit of truth-claims about marginalized identities to concerns of representation, including the limits of trying to represent those whose experiences are not captured by traditional empirical measures or broader discourse. Following these lines of inquiry reveals that axes of oppression are not stable formations themselves, but contextually and historically contingent. Henne and Troshynski (2013) use Crenshaw's metaphor of the intersection as a way to think about the events of crime: not only must the researcher account for actors standing and colliding in the intersection, but also for rules and patterns of traffic, the markings and conditions of the interchange, the policing of the area and the nature of the crossing itself. Crenshaw's notion of an accident in a road, with cars and people crossing, to describe discrimination in the United States does not – and cannot – capture sites of crime in other parts of the world. By attending critically to the structural, political and imagery dimensions of oppression in relation to our limited ability to know crime, intersectionality offers a corrective tool that can help criminologists move away from universalist explanations to more carefully considered representations of people of colour and acts of crime.

Feminist criminological calls for an intersectional criminology vary in focus and scope. Potter makes it clear that employing an intersectional analysis in criminological research should not simply involve the assurance of a diverse study sample, while Burgess-Proctor gives specific recommendations, including the use of mixed-methodological approaches that combine both qualitative and quantitative methods, to provide a more comprehensive picture of crime. In contrast, Henne and Troshynski (2013) suggest that intersectionality offers criminologists a tool to analyse how crime is reflective of constitutive relationships between inequality and representation that require closer, contextually specific interrogation. 'What makes an analysis intersectional', as Cho et al. (2013:795) suggest, is 'its adoption of an intersectional way of thinking about the problem of sameness and difference and its relation to power', which can apply to individuals, groups, institutions and tacit beliefs. Thus, intersectionality can enhance criminology by scrutinizing how knowledge about crime and deviance is situated; that is, it is, at best, partial in nature.

In sum, intersectionality enables an informed understanding of how axes of power and inequality operate to our individual and collective disadvantage as well as the differences between them. As intersectionality begins to inform criminological inquiry, then, it opens a space in which to engage different feminist methodologies that, although diverse, share a common commitment to better understanding how forms of difference come to affect various groups and their relationships to and experiences with crime. In doing so, this development also enables criminology, with its explicit focus on crime and deviance, to contribute to longstanding and emerging questions in the field of intersectionality studies in at least two ways. First, it highlights the many concerns of representation that underpin criminological analysis and theorizing, including, but not limited to, how crime and its context are understood – and not simply serving as a metaphor for people of colour standing at the crossroads of multiple axes of subordination. An intersectional criminology cannot focus exclusively on identity; it should also attend to the representations of criminal acts, including through an empirical investigation their (re) appropriation via larger cultural narratives (i.e. based on a specific time and space, historically). Second, in its commitment to empiricism, intersectionality has the potential to offer new insights into existing methodological debates about how to do intersectional research. In sum, despite being a specialized focus, intersectional criminology has the potential to have a far-reaching interdisciplinary influence.

References

Burgess-Proctor, Amanda. 2006. Intersections of Race, Class, Gender, and Crime: Future Directions for Feminist Criminology. *Feminist Criminology* 1(1): 27–47.

Cho, Sumi, Kimberlé W. Crenshaw, and Leslie McCall. 2013. Toward a Field of Intersectionality Studies: Theory, Application And Praxis. *Signs: Journal of Women in Culture and Society* 38(4): 785–810.

Crenshaw, Kimberlé W. 1991. Mapping the Margins: Intersectionality, Identity Politics, and Violence against Women of Color. *Stanford Law Review* 43: 1241–99.

Daly, Kathleen. 2010. Feminist perspectives in criminology: A review with Gen Y in mind. In *The SAGE Handbook of Criminological Theory*, Eugene McLaughlin and Tim Newburn, eds, pp. 225–46. London: Sage.

Henne, Kathryn, and Emily Troshynski. 2013. Mapping the Margins of Intersectionality: Criminological Possibilities in a Transnational World. *Theoretical Criminology* 17(4): 455–73.

Potter, Hillary. 2015. *Intersectionality and Criminology: Disrupting and Revolutionizing Studies of Crime*. New York and London: Routledge.

Further reading

Choo, Hae Y, and Myra M. Ferree. 2010. Practicing Intersectionality in Sociological Research: A Critical Analysis of Inclusions, Interactions, and Institutions in the Study of Inequalities. *Sociological Theory* 28(2): 129–49.

Daly, Kathleen. 1993. Class-Race-Gender: Sloganeering in Search of Meaning. *Social Justice* 20(1–2): 56–71.

Falcón, Sylvanna M., and Jennifer C. Nash. 2015. Shifting Analytics and Linking Theories: A Conversation about the 'Meaning-Making' of Intersectionality and Transnational Feminism. *Women's Studies International Forum* 50: 1–10.

McCall, Leslie. 2005. The Complexity of Intersectionality. *Signs* 30(2): 1771–881.

Mohanty, Chandra T. 2013. Transnational Feminist Crossings: On Neoliberalism and Radical Critique. *Signs* 38(4): 967–91.

Nash, Jennifer C. 2008. Re-thinking Intersectionality. *Feminist Review* 89(1): 1–15.

Patil, Vrushali. 2013. From Patriarchy to Intersectionality: A Transnational Feminist Assessment of How Far We've Really Come. *Signs* 38(4): 847–67.

Yuval-Davis, Nira. 2006. Intersectionality and Feminist Politics. *European Journal of Women's Studies* 13(3): 193–209.

Masculinities, structure and hegemony

James W. Messerschmidt and Stephen Tomsen

Criminologists consistently have advanced biological sex as the strongest predictor of criminal involvement: it explains more variance in crime cross-culturally than any other variable. As an explanatory factor, then, more developed accounts of gender as the social and cultural differences between men and women – rather than mere bodily difference – would seem to be critical. Yet early theoretical works in the sociology of crime were gender-blind. That is, although acknowledging that the vast majority of those who commit crime were men and boys, the gendered content of their legitimate and illegitimate behaviour was virtually ignored (Messerschmidt 1993). The rise of second-wave **feminism** – originating in the 1960s – challenged this masculinist nature of criminology by illuminating the patterns of gendered power that had been all but ignored. As a result of feminism, not only is the importance of gender to understanding crime more broadly acknowledged but it has also led to the critical study of masculinity and crime (see Messerschmidt and Tomsen 2015). The major theoretical perspective in this endeavour is James W. Messerschmidt's (2014) structured-action theory.

See Chapter 3.6 Feminist criminologies; Chapter 4.26 Patriarchy and crime; Chapter 3.13 Radical feminism

Following the work of feminist ethno-methodologists (West and Fenstermaker 1995), structured-action theory (Messerschmidt 2012, 2014) argues that gender is a situated social and interactional accomplishment that grows out of social practices in specific settings and serves to inform such practices in reciprocal relation: we coordinate our activities to 'do' gender in situational ways. Crucial to this conceptualization of gender as situated accomplishment is West and Zimmerman's (1987) notion of accountability. Because individuals realize that their behaviour may be held accountable to others, they configure their actions in relation to how these might be interpreted by others in the particular social context in which they occur. Within social interaction, then, we facilitate the ongoing task of accountability by demonstrating we are male or female through concocted behaviours that may be interpreted accordingly. Consequently, we do gender (and thereby crime) differently, depending upon the social situation and the social circumstances we encounter. Doing gender renders social action accountable in terms of normative conceptions, attitudes and activities appropriate to one's sex in the specific socially structured situation in which one acts (West and Zimmerman 1987).

Doing gender does not occur in a vacuum, but is influenced by the social structural constraints we experience. Social structures are regular and patterned forms of interaction over time that constrain and enable behaviour in specific ways; therefore, social structures exist as the reproduced conduct of situated actors (Giddens 1976). Following Connell (1987, 1995) and Giddens, structured action theory argues that these social structures are neither external to social actors nor simply and solely constraining; on the contrary, structure is realized only through social action, and social action requires structure as its condition. Thus, as people do gender they reproduce and sometimes change social structures. Not only then are there many ways of doing gender – we must speak of masculinities and femininities – but also gender must be viewed as *structured action*, or what people do under specific social structural constraints. In this way, gender relations link each of us to others in a common relationship: we share structural space. Consequently, shared blocks of gendered knowledge evolve through interaction in which specific gender ideals and activities play a part. Through this interaction, masculinity is institutionalized, permitting men (and sometimes women) to draw on such existing, but previously formed, masculine ways of thinking and acting to construct a masculinity for specific settings. The particular criteria of masculinity are embedded in the social situations and recurrent practices whereby social relations are structured.

Structured-action theory owes much of its inspiration to the theoretical contributions by the well-known Australian sociologist Raewyn Connell, who developed a key explanatory model of different forms of masculinity. Connell's concept of *hegemonic masculinity* – which has been integrated into structured-action theory – has been defined not as a particular character type, but as an entire complex of historically evolving and varied social practices in societies that either legitimate or attempt to guarantee the shoring up of

See Chapter 3.3
Critical
criminologies

patriarchy and male domination of women. Hegemonic masculinities then are those forms of masculinity in particular social settings that structure gender relations hierarchically between men and women, between masculinity and femininity, and among masculinities. This relational character is central in that it embodies a particular type of masculinity in hierarchical relation to a certain form of femininity and to various non-hegemonic masculinities.

Arguably, hegemonic masculinities have no meaning outside their *relationship* to femininity – and non-hegemonic masculinities – or to those forms of femininity that are practised in a complementary, compliant and accommodating subordinate relationship with hegemonic masculinity. And it is the legitimation of this relationship of superordination and subordination whereby the meaning and essence of hegemonic masculinity is revealed. Moreover, any attainment or approximation of this empowered hegemonic form by individual men is highly contingent on the uneven levels of real social power in different men's lives.

Structured-action theory is not without its critics, who centre their criticisms primarily on the concept of hegemonic masculinity. First, critics have raised concerns over the underlying concept of masculinity itself (Hearn 2004). Second, questions have been expressed regarding who actually represents hegemonic masculinity (Donaldson 1993). Third, some scholars have asked whether hegemonic masculinity simply reduces in practice to a reification of power or toxicity (McMahon 1993; Collier 1998). Fourth, some critics have discussed the concept's alleged unsatisfactory theory of the masculine subject (Wetherell and Edley 1999). Fifth, a few commentators have suggested that the concentration on masculinity downplays social class and race and, therefore, reflects a degrading view of working-class and racial-minority men as maintaining an inherently violent and destructive form of masculinity (Hall 2002). Finally, Jefferson (2002) suggests that, when applied to crime, hegemonic masculinity results in a narrow view of true masculinity as a wholly negative set of personal attributes. Each of these criticisms however has been robustly addressed (Connell and Messerschmidt 2005) and, consequently, the relationship between structured action, varieties of masculinities and crime has been and continues to be displayed in a rich and widening range of criminological studies that examine the full spectrum of masculine offending – from street crime, to violence against women and sexual minorities, to corporate and political crime (Messerschmidt and Tomsen 2015).

References

Collier, Richard. 1998. *Masculinities, Crime and Criminology: Men, Heterosexuality and the Criminal(ised) Other*. London: Sage.

Connell, Raewyn. 1987 *Gender and Power*. Sydney, Australia: Allen & Unwin.

Connell, Raewyn. 1995. *Masculinities*. St Leonards: Allen & Unwin.

Connell, Raewyn, and James Messerschmidt. 2005. Hegemonic Masculinity: Rethinking the Concept. *Gender and Society* 19(6): 829–89.

Donaldson, Mike. 1993. What is Hegemonic Masculinity? *Theory and Society* 22: 643–57.

Giddens, Anthony. 1976. *New Rules of Sociological Method*. New York: Basic Books.

Hall, Steve. 2002. Daubing the Drudges of Fury: Men, Violence and the Piety of the 'Hegemonic Masculinity' Thesis. *Theoretical Criminology* 6(1): 35–61.

Hearn, Jeff. 2004. From Hegemonic Masculinity to the Hegemony of Men. *Feminist Theory* 5(1): 49–72.

Jefferson, Tony. 2002. Subordinating Hegemonic Masculinity. *Theoretical Criminology* 6(1): 63–88.

McMahon, Anthony. 1993. Male Readings of Feminist Theory: The Psychologization of Sexual Politics in the Masculinity Literature. *Theory and Society* 22(5): 675–95.

Messerschmidt, James W. 1993. *Masculinities and Crime: Critique and Reconceptualization of Theory*. Lanham, MD: Rowman & Littlefield.

Messerschmidt, James W. 2012. *Gender, Heterosexuality, and Youth Violence: The Struggle for Recognition*. Lanham, MD: Rowman & Littlefield.

Messerschmidt, James W. 2014. *Crime as Structured Action: Doing Masculinities, Race, Class, Sexuality, and Crime* (2nd edn). Lanham, MD: Rowman & Littlefield.

Messerschmidt, James W., and Stephen Tomsen. 2015. Masculinities and crime. In *Sisters in Crime Revisited: Bringing Gender into Criminology: In Honor of Freda Adler*, Francis T. Cullen, Pamela Wilcox, Jennifer L. Lux, and Cheryl L. Jonson, eds, pp. 281–302. New York: Oxford University Press.

West, Candace, and Sarah Fenstermaker. 1995. Doing Difference. *Gender and Society* 9(1): 8–37.

West, Candace, and Don H. Zimmerman. 1987. Doing Gender. *Gender and Society* 1(2): 125–51.

Wetherell, Margaret, and Nigel Edley. 1999. Negotiating Hegemonic Masculinity: Imaginary Positions and Psych-Discursive Practices. *Feminism and Psychology* 9(3): 335–56.

Further reading

Baumeister, Roy F., Laura Smart, and Joseph M. Boden. 1996. Relation of Threatened Egotism to Violence and Aggression: The Dark Side of High Self-Esteem. *Psychological Review* 103(1): 5–33.

Bourgois, Philippe. 2003. *In Search of Respect: Selling Crack in El Barrio*. New York: Cambridge University Press.

Mullins, Christopher. 2006. *Holding Your Square: Masculinities, Street Life, and Violence*. Portland, OR: Willan.

Rios, Victor. 2012. *Punished: Policing the Lives of Black and Latino Boys*. New York: New York University Press.

Tomsen, Stephen. 2009. *Violence, Prejudice, and Sexuality*. New York: Routledge.

Winlow, Simon. 2001. *Badfellas: Crime, Tradition, and New Masculinities*. New York: Berg.

Narrative criminology 4.22

Lois Presser and
Sveinung Sandberg

Stories are open to interpretation – that is part of their appeal; but even as ambiguous forms they give direction to individuals, institutions, organizations and nations. Narrative criminology (NC) highlights the ways that stories influence crime and other harm. NC is a theory (rooted in social constructionism) that implicates a method (narrative analysis). NC joins psychology, sociology, history, literature and cultural studies in its view of experience as constituted discursively. Among discursive forms, the story – with its attention to temporal and moral order – is especially consequential. To name just a few examples: persecution narratives about Jews in post-WWI Germany surely shaped the motivation for the Holocaust, and contemporary stories of an anti-Muslim global war inspire young men to join jihadist extremist organizations; stories of honour and respect construct a violent street culture, and exotic stories of drugs fashion use of these substances. In this chapter, we summarize NC's key ideas and inspirations, and review studies explicitly set out as NC. We conclude with a forecast of research in this burgeoning field.

Lois Presser (2009) first coined the expression 'narrative criminology'. Within criminology, stories had mostly been taken as valuable representations of things relevant to offending, although leading figures Hans Toch and Jack Katz had observed that perpetrators of crime enacted some moral tale. The most important forerunner of NC within criminology was Shadd Maruna, who, in *Making Good* (2001), set out the influence of narrative on persistence in offending, for the stories of desisting and persisting property-offenders had

See Chapter 4.29
Post-structuralism
and criminology

See Chapter 4.19
Institutional and
anti-institutional
violence

See Chapter 4.8
Cultural
Criminology;
Chapter 3.17
Subculture

See Chapter 5.6
Desistance

different plotlines. Narrative criminology also has empirical forebears beyond criminology, in case studies of mass violence. Several studies reveal that certain narrative genres and themes – for example, a looming epic apocalypse – have directed groups to attack other groups, and nations to execute criminals and wage war on other nations.

Narrative criminology follows critical criminology in the latter's probing take on power as constituted ideologically – that is, through discourse. But NC is particular about the nature of (hegemonic) discourse. Moreover, criminologies influenced by **postmodern thought** – **constitutive criminology and cultural criminology** – are close cousins of the narrative criminology perspective, but NC is more specific about how harm is acculturated. Given that specificity, NC also builds upon but goes beyond criminological concepts such as **neutralizations** and situational interpretations, which attend only to the offence and not to a lifetime of (criminal *and* non-criminal) actions. In the NC view, stories fundamentally shape our life-worlds.

See Chapter 4.28
Postmodern
and constitutive
criminologies

See Chapter 2.7
Techniques of
neutralization

Within the last few years, several studies explicitly framed as narrative criminology have been launched. Lois Presser (2012) analysed the story told by Jim David Adkisson, a mass murderer in Tennessee, United States. This story emphasized Adkisson's scripted need to overcome despised social groups who undermined a fabled social order. In her book *Why We Harm*, Presser (2013) analysed similarities across the stories told by perpetrators of such different harms as penal harm, mass violence, meat-eating and interpersonal violence. Sveinung Sandberg has developed NC in his work on binge-drinking, illegal drug use and sale, violent crime and terrorism, most importantly in several articles about the Norwegian terrorist Anders Behring Breivik (e.g., Sandberg 2013). He critiques the assumption that stories are necessarily coherent, emphasizing their essentially ambiguous nature. He also argues that narrative can be discovered in events. That is, actions take the shape of a story; people transgress when certain situations and periods of their lives seem to demand certain stories.

The recent volume, *Narrative Criminology: Understanding Stories of Crime* (Presser and Sandberg 2015), presents the narrative criminological approach theoretically and via application to specific empirical cases, including mass atrocities, drug crime and tax evasion. For example, in that volume Robert M. Keeton reveals the impact of religious narratives on Indian removal policies and related atrocities in nineteenth-century America. Sveinung Sandberg and Sébastien Tutenges discuss the similarities between contemporary stories of addiction and bad trips and ancient folk-tales and myths, arguing that even tragic drug stories can motivate drug use. Patricia O'Connor clarifies the discursive devices that drug-users and maximum-security prisoners use to change their storylines and their lives. Carlo Tognato describes the shifting cultural conception of tax evasion. Other chapters – such as those by Thomas Ugelvik, Jennifer Fleetwood, Jody Miller et al., Janice Victor and James B. Waldram – deconstruct the stories with which ex-offenders re-establish dignity and agency as members of a vilified and/or incapacitated subpopulation. Finally,

Kester Aspden and Keith Hayward describe the relationship between cultural and narrative criminology using (Aspden's) autobiography.

A body of work by psychologists Donna Youngs and David V. Canter is also firmly within the NC tradition. They present and apply a Narrative Role Questionnaire (NRQ), which directs analytic attention to particular roles a person perceives her/himself as adopting while committing a crime. Although coming from psychology, the NRQ research follows NC's fundamental de-centring of criminal propensity, as narrative roles, not person types, align with offending. Contemporary studies in NC also include explorations of the story-ing of criminal-justice practice, including rehabilitation and profiling. These studies suggest that a variety of governmental, non-governmental and civilian actions, helpful and hurtful, might be illuminated in a novel way through NC analysis. Recent studies have also highlighted stories that oppose terrorism. The identification of effective counter-narratives towards radicalization takes NC in a new and practically useful direction. The embedding of narratives within socio-economic and gender structures has also been emphasized, most comprehensively in the work of Jennifer Fleetwood (2014).

Some key tasks and challenges await narrative criminology. Researchers should clarify the mechanisms by which narrative affects troublesome action. Clearly, we do not fulfil our prophecies unthinkingly. We do not simply act out our stories. Narratives may motivate criminal action or they may set the parameters for socially acceptable action. Other harms, those allegedly done out of desperation, seem more like an unhappy ending to one's story. Close attention to the structuring of stories can help reveal connections to action. Moreover, studying the social 'distribution' of stories – how different stories resonate among audiences and relations to power and privilege – can further our understanding of the complex link between stories and crime.

Narrative criminology is not a standpoint of **appreciation for stories** told by those we come to know in the field; nor is it only a method for ana-lysing qualitative data. From the perspective of NC, social life is altogether storied. Circumstance and incident make sense to us as elements of evolving plotlines, and the resulting stories shape our actions. NC thus can frame stud-ies of offenders' stories and media narratives, the meta-narratives that shape various harm-doing policies including but not limited to criminal-justice pol-icy. At a time when criminologists are taking on large-scale phenomena such as mass violence, **state harm** and **environmental degradation**, NC can make a sizeable contribution to understanding, probing direct harm and com-placency and bridging micro- and macro-levels of inquiry. In striving to nail down (narrative) causes, researchers necessarily bracket the fact that stories are always situationally constructed. That is, they provisionally treat stories as static, whereas an interdisciplinary theoretical heritage teaches us that they are anything but.

See Chapter 3.1
Appreciative
criminology

See Chapter 4.36
State crime;
Chapter 4.37 State-
corporate crime

See Chapter 4.3
Conservation
criminology;
Chapter 4.11
Environmental
justice and
victimology;
Chapter 4.13
Genocide and
ecocide; Chapter
4.16 Green
criminology

References

Fleetwood, Jennifer. 2014. *Drug Mules: Women in the International Cocaine Trade*. London: Palgrave Macmillan.

Maruna, Shadd. 2001. *Making Good: How Ex-Convicts Reform and Rebuild Their Lives*. Washington, DC: American Psychological Association.

Presser, Lois. 2009. The Narratives of Offenders. *Theoretical Criminology* 13(2): 177–200.

Presser, Lois. 2012. Getting on Top through Mass Murder: Narrative, Metaphor, and Violence. *Crime, Media, Culture* 8(1): 3–21.

Presser, Lois. 2013. *Why We Harm*. New Brunswick, NJ and London: Rutgers University Press.

Presser, Lois, and Sveinung Sandberg (eds). 2015. *Narrative Criminology: Understanding Stories of Crime*. New York: New York University Press.

Sandberg, Sveinung. 2013. Are Self-Narratives Strategic or Determined, Unified or Fragmented? Reading Breivik's Manifesto in Light of Narrative Criminology. *Acta Sociologica* 56(1): 65–79.

Further reading

Joosse, Paul, Sandra Bucerius, and Sara K. Thompson. 2015. Narratives and Counternarratives: Somali-Canadians on Recruitment as Foreign Fighters to Al- Shabaab. *British Journal of Criminology* 55(4): 811–32.

Presser, Lois, and Sveinung Sandberg. 2015. Research strategies for narrative criminology. In *Qualitative Research in Criminology: Advances in Criminological Theory*, Vol. 20, Jody Miller and Wilson Palacios, eds, pp. 85–100. Piscataway, NJ: Transaction.

Sandberg, Sveinung. 2010. What Can 'Lies' Tell Us about Life? Notes towards a Framework of Narrative Criminology. *Journal of Criminal Justice Education* 21(4): 447–65.

Sandberg, Sveinung, Sébastien Tutenges, and Heith Copes. 2015. Stories of Violence: A Narrative Criminological Study of Ambiguity. *British Journal of Criminology* 55(6): 1168–86.

Youngs, Donna and David V. Canter. 2012. Narrative Roles in Criminal Action: An Integrative Framework for Differentiating Offenders. *Legal and Criminological Psychology* 17(2): 233–49.

(Neo)-conservative criminology

Russell Hogg

(Neo)-conservatism refers to a tradition of *political* thought rather than to a discrete body of criminological ideas or theory. All criminological theory carries political implications, but it was only in the 1970s that a self-consciously neo-conservative criminology appeared and was embraced by politicians of the right like Margaret Thatcher and Ronald Reagan. Neo-conservative criminology was authored by academics who were often themselves involved in conservative policy-making circles, and it coincided tellingly with the rising salience of crime as a political issue.

It is not easy to tie down the meaning of conservatism or identify a single, coherent conservative theory or world-view. The French Revolution in 1789 is often regarded as the watershed event that gave rise to the development of a modern conservative tradition of thought. Edmund Burke, author of the most famous critique of the revolution, *Reflections on the Revolution in France*, is often credited as the pivotal figure, although he never used the term conservative and was aligned with the Whigs in English politics. A subtle thinker and a master stylist, Burke's fundamental distrust of abstract theory of any kind defined one of the enduring traits of conservative thought ever since – one which helps explain why conservatism eludes simple definition. For Burke, there could be no abstract, universal principles divorced from a concrete social context that gave them meaning. Societies do not conform to rational designs but are historically contingent social formations, complex and subtle accretions of practice and custom over ages. They defy complete and rational understanding, let alone efforts to politically re-engineer them from above. The forms and meanings of conservatism will thus vary according to local and national context.

This idea animated Burke's scepticism towards all efforts to distil the principles of the eighteenth-century Enlightenment into a body of revolutionary doctrine aimed at overthrowing the existing political order. It also made him a critic of the abstract individualism of classical liberalism. For Burke, individuals were by nature social creatures and liberty, rights and justice were meaningful only when understood in the context of established institutions, traditions and relationships. Destroy these, as revolutionary movements sought to do, and it would not be the good society that rose from the ashes. The suspension of all moral restraint would instead unleash violence, social breakdown and tyranny.

Burke, however, was no defender of political absolutism. He was a champion of the 1688–89 settlement (that limited the powers of the English monarchy and led to the Bill of Rights) and he supported American independence and Catholic rights in Ireland. He was also acutely sensitive to arbitrary rule and government abuses of power, including in respect of British colonial rule in India. Burke (1993/1790:21) excoriated revolution but he believed in reform, arguing that 'A state without the means of some change is without the means of its conservation.'

See Chapter 4.24
Neoliberalism

Wary of political tyranny, conservatives in the Burkean mould are scarcely less critical of the abstract market principles at the heart of the economic liberal tradition (or what is now **neoliberalism**) and the vision they have of a world of sovereign individuals making atomized choices, dis-embedded from culture and context. Politically conservative participants in contemporary crime debates reflect some of these ideas and concerns, but they typically draw very selectively on the conservative tradition. A conservative political agenda on crime was advanced in the Anglo world from the 1970s by influential thinkers like J.Q. Wilson (a Harvard political scientist and advisor to President Ronald Reagan on crime policy), Richard Herrnstein (a Harvard psychology professor) and Patricia Morgan (a British policy commentator).

See Chapter 4.1
Anarchist
criminology;
Chapter 5.18
Social control

See Chapter 1.2
Classical
criminology;
Chapter 1.18
Rational choice

See Chapter 1.5
Biological
criminology;
Chapter 1.8
Learning theory;
Chapter 1.7
Psychopathy;
Chapter 1.16
Neurocriminology

In *Thinking about Crime* (1977:3), Wilson observed the 'paradox of the 60s', 'crime amidst plenty'. Soaring crime rates at a time of rising affluence undercut claims that poverty and disadvantage were the major causes of crime. Whilst he acknowledged the coming of age of the baby-boomers as a factor, he indicted the emerging 'cult of liberation' (1977:20) and the growing disrespect for authority as major causes of crime. The solution was not more freedom, but stricter **control**.

New Deal liberals and welfare-state criminologists (along with 1960s' radicals) seriously misdiagnosed the crime problem when they focused on poverty and disadvantage, and their remedies made it worse. Crime was a matter of **human choice**, albeit conditioned by **biological and psychological factors** (Wilson and Herrnstein 1985). They maintained that crime ran in families and that criminals tended to have low IQs and poor impulse control. These individual and family traits explained both their greater predisposition to crime and their higher rates of poverty, disadvantage and poor educational performance. Social policies that aimed to ameliorate these conditions reinforced the abdication of personal and family responsibilities and promoted entrenched welfare dependency. And, by offering excuses for crime, such policies encouraged it. The problem, then, was not one of constrained freedom, but undue personal licence.

Wilson rejected the search for deep causes of crime because it offered nothing useful to the urgent policy question of what to do about rising crime rates. It was difficult if not impossible to influence biological, psychological and social factors that lay behind crime. Practically minded policymakers must eschew the attempt to influence causes, structures and attitudes and concentrate on the policy instruments that directly affected behaviour. That meant simply increasing the costs and risks of crime by enhancing the deterrent force of the law and using it more effectively to **incapacitate** offenders through increasing apprehension rates and lengthening prison sentences. Wilson's later work, with George Kelling, calling for a 'zero-tolerance' approach to minor street offences and incivilities, was also rooted in **deterrence theory** (Wilson and Kelling 1982).

See Chapter 5.9
Incapacitation

See Chapter 1.17
Deterrence

On the other side of the Atlantic, similar themes were rehearsed in the politically and ideologically engaged criminology of Patricia Morgan. In her book *Delinquent Fantasies* (1978), she pinpointed youth crime, violence, vandalism and other forms of street crime and disorder as central to the breakdown of community and the social compact in 1970s' Britain. But the underlying problem lay with the erosion of moral restraints caused by the social-democratic state and progressive legal and social reforms of the recent past. Welfare ideology and policy, child-centred psychologies and progressive educational philosophies highlighted social deprivation and preached a gospel of social need. The reality of evil was denied and personal responsibility derided.

Although there is no conservative academic school of criminology as such, it is possible to talk about a conservative or neo-conservative criminology in the contemporary Anglophone world because these arguments fed directly into the politics of the era. In Chapter 15 of her political memoir, Margaret Thatcher, British prime minister from 1979 till 1990, makes clear her debt to these ideas and their authors for her own tough stance on law and order. She rejects the 'idea that poverty was a cause rather than a result of various kinds of irresponsible or deviant behaviour' (1995:547), and links crime with welfare dependency, single-parenthood and the abandonment by the poor of the virtues of thrift, effort, independence and respectability.

Burke's conservatism finds an echo in neo-conservative arguments around crime that took root in parts of academe and in the mainstream of American and British politics from the late 1970s. Margaret Thatcher even expressly invokes his argument that freedom, if it is not to destroy society, must be exercised within a framework of moral restraints. But the cardinal neo-conservative lesson – to reduce crime simply increase the risk and burdens of punishment and remove the crutch of welfare from the poor – reflects a crude, mechanistic and decontextualized reading of Burke. The idea of law and control as formally rational instruments of deterrence (the counterpart to abstract market incentives) is alien to Burke's concern for the particularities of circumstance, culture, sentiment and moral suasion. There is also a yawning disconnect between calls for the re-moralization of society and the essentially amoral conception of social life underpinning the free-market economic policies undertaken by contemporary conservative governments whose destructive effects on community, family and employment (and consequential impacts on crime, security and social cohesion) are simply ignored.

The grafting of neo-conservative ideas on crime, family and morality onto the neo-liberal political agenda creates a deeply unstable mix that sits uncomfortably with the Burkean tradition of conservative thought. Indeed, John Gray (2007:131), a political theorist with Burkean sympathies, has argued that the hegemony of neo-liberalism within contemporary conservative thought has destroyed conservatism as a viable political project for the foreseeable future.

References

Burke, Edmund. 1993/1790. *Reflections on the Revolution in France*. Oxford: Oxford University Press.
Gray, John. 2007. *Enlightenment's Wake*. London: Routledge.
Morgan, Patricia. 1978. *Delinquent Fantasies*. London: Temple Smith.
Thatcher, Margaret. 1995. *The Path to Power*. London: HarperCollins.
Wilson, James Q. 1977. *Thinking about Crime*. New York: Vintage.
Wilson, James Q., and Richard Herrnstein. 1985. *Crime and Human Nature*. New York: Simon & Schuster.
Wilson, James, and George Kelling. 1982. Broken Windows: The Police and Neighbourhood Safety. *Atlantic Monthly* March: 29–38.

Further reading

Gamble, Andrew. 1988. *The Free Economy and the Strong State: The Politics of Thatcherism*. Basingstoke: Macmillan.
Scruton, Roger. 1984. *The Meaning of Conservatism* (2nd edn). London: Macmillan.
Stenson, Kevin, and David Cowell (eds). 1991. *The Politics of Crime Control*. London: Sage.
Young, Jock. 1994. Incessant chatter: Recent paradigms in criminology. In *The Oxford Handbook of Criminology*, Mike Maguire, Rodney Morgan, and Robert Reiner, eds, pp. 69–124. Oxford: Clarendon.

Neoliberalism

Rob White

Neoliberalism describes a broad political and economic orientation that emphasizes the individual responsibility for one's own actions – and individual accountability for the consequences of those actions – within the institutional framework of strong private property rights and unfettered commodity markets. All of this has implications for crime and criminology both in terms of profit, competition and **greed** as motives of and contexts for criminal activity and in terms of the deregulation and weakening of certain domestic and international criminal laws that deal with social and **environmental harms** and the damage wrought by them.

See Chapter 4.5 Corporate crime; Chapter 4.12 Financial crime

See Chapter 4.16 Green criminology; Chapter 4.11 Environmental justice and victimology

See Chapter 1.3 Utilitarianism

Although related, neoliberalism is not the same as *liberalism*. Liberalism is an ideology that incorporates varying conceptions of liberty, individualism, equality, justice, rights, **utilitarianism** and rationality. Fundamentally, liberalism privileges the ideas of individual liberty and democracy – encapsulated in the notion 'liberal democracy' – as benchmarks for a free and just society. Important to this concept, as well, is the idea of rule of law under which all people should be treated alike, without fear or favour. The law is to apply universally to all classes of people.

Liberty, a central concept of liberalism, can refer to 'freedom to' (maximize capacities) or 'freedom from' (state intervention). A **politically right-wing version of liberty** advocates that each individual has and should have an equal chance to become unequal. A politically left-wing version asserts that the role of social institutions is to maximize each person's creative energies. There is, however, a basic incompatibility between these two concepts of the

See Chapter 4.23 (Neo)-conservativism

human essence, both of which are present within liberal democratic theory (Macpherson 1977):

- a concept of persons as consumer, desirer and maximizer of utilities; and
- a concept of persons as doer, exerter and developer of their uniquely human attributes.

The incompatibility stems from the difficulty of reconciling the liberal property right (i.e., private ownership, acquisition and accumulation) and the effective equal right of all individuals to use and develop their capacities (i.e., a central ethical principle of liberal democracy). The problem is that the liberal system of market incentives and rights of free contract leads to and supports a concentration of ownership and a system of power relations between individuals and classes which negates the ethical goal of free and independent individual development. This latter observation is central to understanding both the development of neoliberalism and the **critiques of it**.

See Chapter 3.3
Critical
criminologies;
Chapter
3.9 Marxist
criminologies

The use and definition of the term 'neoliberalism' has changed over time. In the 1930s in Europe, for example, it was associated with what became known as the 'social market economy'. The market failure of the 1930s, evident in the Great Depression, were responded to by attempts to trace a middle way between laissez-faire economic liberalism (in which key economic decisions are left entirely to the market) and socialist planning (in which major economic decisions are decided upon by the state) (Mirowski and Plehwe 2009). By the 1980s, however, the term had shifted in meaning, back toward the classical laissez-faire model. Intellectually this shift was advocated by economists such as Friedrich Hayek (1944, 1960) and Milton Friedman (2002), and tested in practice during the dictatorship of Augusto Pinochet in Chile. Over the next few decades, traversing different countries and encompassed by varied terminological labels – for example, it was known as 'economic rationalism' in Australia in the mid- to late-1980s (see Pusey 1991) – neoliberalism became

See Chapter 4.14
Globalization

part of the common sense of **global economic discourse** and practice.

Contemporary neoliberalism ostensibly favours market forces over state intervention, and it views inequality as a natural outcome of competition between individuals. At an abstract level, each person is seen to be personally responsible for his or her own welfare and life chances. In practice, economic power tends to already be monopolized and concentrated in ways that foreclose any possibility of fair or free competition. Nonetheless, the idea dominates the reality. The main economic policy and practical trends associated with neoliberalism include reduced trade protection, user-pays, privatization and deregulation (Harvey 2005). Contemporary notions of 'human nature' are expressed in terms of competition, self-interest and possessive individualism. Institutionally, the policies and ethics of neoliberalism are reflected in: reliance upon the market for the allocation of goods and services; the shrinking of the welfare state; assertion of the role of the state as 'night watchman' (albeit with little government oversight for those at the top); and an emphasis on strong law and order and defence of private property (that includes strict control over those at the bottom).

Historical analysis demonstrates empirically that social inequality is intrinsic to the capitalist system (Piketty 2014). This has been exacerbated and further entrenched over the past three decades of aggressive neoliberalization. The net result of neoliberalism is impoverishment for many at the same time that social privilege has skyrocketed for the few. This is occurring on a global level and is related to the dominance and major push of the 'Washington Consensus' concerning political economic policies and practices since the 1970s. This involves the collusion of international corporate elites working in conjunction with high-level political leaders in the USA and other hegemonic nation-states in order to drive public policy toward worldwide privatization and diminishment of public services (Beder 2006). Accompanying this has been a deterioration in public services, increased costs associated with fees and co-payments, and feelings of a democratic deficit and political disenfranchisement. By contrast, social privilege has been on the rise, as manifest in the further concentration of wealth and power; and powerful interests have been served through the cutting-back of state regulation designed to protect present and future generations of citizens, consumers, workers and the environment.

As applied to criminology and criminal justice, the context within which concern about adult crime and juvenile offending is occurring and perceived to be a growing problem is defined by this reconfiguration of economic and political relations – one consequence of which is the increasing polarization of rich and poor, both between and within countries. Neoliberalism is now an ingrained aspect of public policy and material provision. Institutionally, each individual is being forced to fend for himself or herself, and this has been elevated to the level of moral good – to fail at getting a job, an income, suitable welfare and an education is construed as personal failure *in* the **marketplace**, not a failure *of* the marketplace. For people living in vulnerable communities, this makes them even more susceptible to the attractions, benefits and dangers of crime, as well as providing a context for **antisocial behaviour**.

See Chapter 2.8
Market society and crime

See Chapter 5.2
Antisocial behaviour

Entrenched economic adversity has been accompanied by state attempts to intervene in the lives of marginalized groups, usually by coercive measures, which is itself a reflection of a broader shift in the role of the state, from concerns with 'social welfare' to renewed emphasis on the 'repressive'. States that have the greatest levels of inequality also tend to be the most punitive in their criminal justice responses (Wilkinson and Pickett 2009). Thus, those states that have most fully embraced the neoliberal agenda – like the USA, Australia, New Zealand and the UK – have simultaneously adopted more punitive penal policies, particularly compared to some European jurisdictions that have sustained more social democratic and corporatist forms of government and more moderate criminal justice policies.

The individualized framing of **risk**, responsibility and reward has occurred in the context of significant social, economic and political changes since the mid-1980s. The 'crime problem' has likewise been re-cast as part of these broad

See Chapter 6.7
Risk

changes. For instance, an emphasis on the exercise of individual agency has been fostered through the neoliberal reorganization of institutions (school, family, welfare, criminal justice): the key focus now is on personal responsibility for 'success/failure', doing 'good/bad' and 'advantage/disadvantage', rather than shared structural conditions, opportunities and experiences. Accordingly, the crux of state intervention is how best to manage the problem of disadvantaged groups (their presence and activities), rather than to eradicate disadvantage.

The key ideas and sentiments of neoliberalism include: the individual is the basis of social order; personal responsibility is the basis of accountability; and self-interest is the basis of morality. These ideals can be contrasted with those that emphasize the collective good, communal responsibility and solidarity, and the importance of addressing general welfare and social needs.

The critique of neoliberalism, then, is twofold. First, philosophically, neoliberalism is criticized because it tends to reduce the human condition to one of market exchanges, within which instrumental use of people and environments is acceptable and where personal wealth and capital accumulation are seen as the highest goods that define human success. It is a highly competitive moral universe. Alternative ideals to neoliberalism are based on the notion that society is more than a mere collection of individuals, and that freedom from want is the platform for freedom to develop one's capacities to the fullest. It is the positive interconnection between people and their mutual well-being that ought to count most in any moral hierarchy.

The second critique argues that neoliberalism as a practice, policy and ideal is basically built upon a falsehood. Powerful sectional interests already substantially own and control the bulk of the world's resources (including natural, financial and technical capital). There is no 'free market' as such. Land, water, food and energy are under the control of a small and shrinking number of private firms, and the community outside is both growing and increasingly powerless in the face of this concentrated ownership and control.

Resistance to neoliberalism is possible, especially given the decline in material provision and narrowing of creative opportunities for the majority of the Earth's population. In some instances, for example, popular sentiment has been harnessed in support of measures that benefit everyone (universal provision of health care, education, welfare, clean environments), while, by contrast, selective provision undermines this sentiment and reinforces the targeting of 'at-risk' populations in ways which end up treating them as if *they* are the problem and a social drain. In the alternative scenario, meeting social need and acknowledging the public good implies solidarity, collective responsibility and shared input – ideas that run counter to dominant neoliberal themes.

References

Beder, Sharon. 2006. *Suiting Themselves: How Corporations Drive the Global Agenda.* London: Earthscan.

Friedman, Milton. 2002. *Capitalism and Freedom.* Chicago: University of Chicago Press.

Harvey, David. 2005. *A Brief History of Neoliberalism.* Oxford: Oxford University Press.

Hayek, Friedrich. 1944. *The Road to Serfdom.* Chicago: University of Chicago Press.

Hayek, Friedrich. 1960. *The Constitution of Liberty.* New York: Routledge.

Macpherson, C.B. [Crawford Brough]. 1977. *The Life and Times of Liberal Democracy.* Toronto: Oxford University Press.

Mirowski, Philip, and Dieter Plehwe. 2009. *The Road from Mont Pèlerin: The Making of the Neoliberal Thought Collective.* Cambridge, MA: Harvard University Press.

Piketty, Thomas. 2014. *Capital in the Twenty-First Century.* Cambridge, MA: Belknap Press of Harvard University Press.

Pusey, Michael. 1991. *Economic Rationalism in Canberra: A Nation Building State Changes Its Mind.* Cambridge: Cambridge University Press.

Wilkinson, Richard, and Kate Pickett. 2009. *The Spirit Level.* New York: Bloomsbury.

Further reading

Klein, Naomi. 2008. *The Shock Doctrine: The Rise of Disaster Capitalism.* London: Picador.

Wacquant, Loïc. 2009. *Punishing the Poor: The Neoliberal Government of Social Insecurity.* Durham, NC: Duke University Press.

4.25 Organized crime

Dick Hobbs

Organized crime is a contested concept (see Von Lampe n.d.) and is best understood as an umbrella term for a multiplicity of local and global concerns. Although the concept of organized crime has only come to prominence relatively recently, there are historical precedents. The concept of organized crime has long been associated with urban enclaves where regimentation of the poor was most ineffective, and both smuggling and poaching required elements of organization – and networks of professional criminals pervaded an increasingly urbanized society.

The state found nascent elements of organized crime useful: for instance, the establishment and maintenance of British colonies was, in Elizabethan times, largely the prerogative of an early form of organized criminality in the form of state-sponsored piracy. Their licence to plunder was exploited to the full, and, while pirate culture was a clear and distinct phenomenon, success was rewarded by legitimation and an entry into polite society. In time, piracy was seen as a threat to the comportment of legitimate trade, and this led to a decline in the supporting structures, havens and, above all, the markets upon which piracy relied.

In urban Britain, criminal cultures flourished within some key parts of the emergent working class, and neighbourhood crime firms based upon extortion and commercial theft created the foundations of urban underworlds populated by professional criminals where 'the business of crime is planned, contacts are made, some crimes are carried out, the fruits of crime are often enjoyed, and the methodologies for the integration of organized criminals into civil society are established' (Block 1991:15). In the UK, the notion of 'professional' as opposed to 'organized' crime was imprinted upon police and popular discourses until as recently as the 1990s.

While in the UK criminal networks remained hidden in increasingly urban underworlds, in the USA key characteristics of organized crime were being implemented in the establishment of many of the industrial and commercial empires upon which modern America was founded. As Bell (1953:152) explains: 'The early settlers and founding fathers, as well as those who "won the west" and built up cattle, mining and other fortunes, often did so by shady speculations and not an inconsiderable amount of violence.'

Along with the corruption of urban American politics – with its violence, graft and vote-rigging – this was the environment that existed long before the term 'organized crime' entered common usage. Organized crime was a catch-all term for both the established criminal cultures of the new urban centres and the innovative groups exploiting opportunities offered by the prohibition of alcohol, which lasted from 1919 to 1933. Vast profits emanated from this unpopular law, which prohibited the manufacture, transportation, sale and importation of intoxicating liquor. Prohibition embedded criminality into everyday life, and its repeal enabled gangsters and corrupt officials to merge seamlessly into the American mainstream, as the distinction between the 'underworld' and the 'upperworld' became vague and easily crossed.

Both Prohibition and the post-World War II Senate investigations stressed the role of ethnicity in organized crime, and this emphasis has been exploited by Hollywood – from *Little Caesar* to the *Godfather* trilogy and to *Goodfellas* and beyond. Indeed, despite a number of the iconic 'brands' of organized crime – such as the Italian Mafia or the Japanese Yakuza – emerging respectively from the indigenous population, the perception that foreigners constitute the primary organized-crime threat by conspiring to pervert an otherwise pure society remains a feature of anti-organized crime policies across the globe. Critical scholars considered crime to be an essential component of American society that is essentially functional in offering an alternative mode of upward mobility to ethnic groups who found more traditional paths blocked by the rigid stratification of conventional society (Bell 1953). This succession thesis, however, is contradicted by the multi-ethnic networks that emerged as a result of Prohibition.

From the 1950s onward, a series of high-profile commissions and investigations were formed to investigate organized crime, which was presented as a national conspiracy run by the Mafia and imported via Italian immigrants. This threat was built upon America's obsession with conspiracy and post-war fear of alien subversion. A meeting featuring a number of organized-crime figures in Apalachin (New York) in 1957 reinforced the public's growing belief that 'forces outside of mainstream American culture are at work which seek to pervert an otherwise morally sound, industrious, and democratic people' (Potter 1994:10). The public's voracious appetite for conspiracy received a further boost in 1963 when a gangster appeared before a Senate sub-committee declaring the existence of the Cosa Nostra, and so proved a godsend for government officials seeking to promote the existence of a national conspiracy of organized criminality that exhibited many of the structural features of legitimate corporate enterprise (Cressey 1969).

Although scholars have exposed the alien conspiracy theory as an over-elaboration founded on myth (Smith 1975), as we will see below, the theory has proved to be a popular device amongst politicians and law-enforcement personnel. **Globalization** has enabled local organized crime to mutate into entities that are increasingly indistinguishable from legitimate enterprise, which in turn has contributed to the erosion of traditional criminal territories. As a result, the old urban underworld of professional criminals has either entered the economic mainstream or fragmented and dispersed along with the traditional working class into which they were once embedded. These new criminal collaborations operate across national boundaries and, as a consequence, have inspired transnational law-enforcement innovations on a scale unthinkable just a generation ago.

See Chapter 4.14
Globalization

It should be stressed that to highlight the role of globalization is not the same as making a claim for 'transnational organized crime'. The term 'transnational' is essentially misleading in referring to organized crime, for it is a term that is normally assigned to cross-border activity involving the explicit exclusion of the state – and the relationship between the state and organized crime is ambiguous. The state utilizes criminality for a variety of ends, but particularly as an alternative means of implementing foreign policy

Despite the ability of organized-crime groups to operate across national boundaries, organized crime remains an essentially local phenomenon grounded in highly specific historical practices and relationships. Even the Sicilian Mafia are restricted by traditionalism and territoriality and the Mafia's relationship with the state is not as problematic as its relationships with other Mafia groups, where market confrontations are dominated by rules of engagement dictated by traditional territorial values rather than market prerogatives (Arlacchi 1986).

Although recent changes in both business practice and the status of the nation-state are responsible for the infiltration of organized crime into legitimate state structures, criminal collaborations remain rooted in multiple indicators of disadvantage. When articulated within local trading networks, albeit linked by networks spanning national boundaries, organized crime is able to mutate while remaining 'local at all points' and constituting 'continuous paths that lead from the local to the global, from the circumstantial to the universal, from the contingent to the necessary' (Latour 1993:117).

The organization of criminal labour mirrors trends in the organization of its legitimate counterpart, resulting in criminal business taking place within networks of small, flexible firms featuring short-term contracts and lack of tenure – 'flexible, adaptive networks that readily expand and contract to deal with the uncertainties of the criminal enterprise' (Potter 1994:12).

A community of practice – embracing a far wider population than either that of the old urban underworld or the rigid hierarchies of semi-institutionalized organized crime 'brands', such as the Mafia and other demons of transnational organized crime – has emerged, characterized by fluctuating networks of individuals and groups committed to entrepreneurial action. The notion of a community of practice enables us to break down the mystique of transnational organized crime, with its monolithic alien threat. Most importantly, the notion of a community of practice recognizes the manner in which entrepreneurial networks make full use of market society's embedded legal and economic infrastructures to normalize the concept of organized crime.

References

Arlacchi, Pino. 1986. *Mafia Business: The Mafia Ethic and the Spirit of Capitalism*. London: Verso.

Bell, Daniel. 1953. Crime as an American Way of Life. *Antioch Review* 13(2): 131–54.

Block, Alan. 1991. *Masters of Paradise*. New Brunswick, NJ: Transaction.

Cressey, Donald. 1969. *Theft of the Nation: The Structure and Operations of Organized Crime in America*. New York: Harper & Row.

Latour, Bruno. 1993. *We Have Never Been Modern*. London: Harvester Wheatsheaf.

Potter, Gary. W. 1994. *Criminal Organizations*. Prospect Heights, IL: Waveland.

Smith, Dwight. 1975. *The Mafia Mystique*. New York: Basic Books.

Von Lampe, Klaus. n.d. Organized crime research. www.organized-crime.de/contactpage.htm. Accessed 23 January 2017.

Further reading

Hobbs, Dick. 2015. *Lush Life: Constructing Organized Crime in the UK*. Oxford: Oxford University Press.

Karraker, Cyrus. 1953. *Piracy Was a Business*. Rindge, NH: Richard R. Smith.

Naylor, R.T. [Tom]. 1995. From Cold War to Crime War. *Transnational Organised Crime* 1(4): 37-56.

Rawlinson, Patricia. 2010. *From Fear to Fraternity: A Russian Tale of Crime, Economy and Modernity*. London: Pluto.

Shore, Heather. 2015. *London's Criminal Underworlds, c. 1720–c. 1930: A Social and Cultural History*. Basingstoke: Palgrave Macmillan.

Patriarchy and crime

Elizabeth Whalley and Joanne Belknap

Patriarchy is the hierarchical legal, political and social structure that promotes masculine dominance and privileges men and males while subordinating other sexes and genders. The term *patriarchy* has its origins in Greek and Latin, which, taken together, means 'the rule of the father'. As employed in early Western legal systems, it became understood as the rule of the father or the rule of the husband. In the 1970s, feminist theorists began to interrogate the connections between patriarchal structures and crime: challenging sexism in the judicial system; bringing sex- and gender-based abuse into focus; and highlighting the exclusion of women/girls from criminological research and theory. In the following decades, such analyses would provide the foundation of **intersectional** feminist criminology and feminist pathways theory. These groundbreaking challenges to **masculine power and knowledge-creation** faced serious marginalization in traditional criminology.

The first major scholarly contributions to the study of criminal behaviour and patriarchal power emerged during the second wave of feminism (the early 1960s to early 1980s) as activism created new space for women's knowledge and experiences, including in academia and, in particular, law schools. Historically, criminological research and theories were dominated by the masculine construction of knowledge. Women were invisible both in research and as researchers, omitted from theories of crime and marginalized by academia. Feminist research revealed the persistent and prevalent forms of sex- and gender-based abuse and **victimization** in women's/girls' lives, including

See Chapter 4.20
Intersectionality

See Chapter 4.21
Masculinities, structure and hegemony

See Chapter 4.39
Victimology

child and adult sexual abuse, partner abuse, sexual harassment and stalking – all primarily perpetrated by men well known to the victims. Feminist scholarship conceptualized this abuse as *political acts* representative of and resulting from patriarchy, not **psychopathy**. Simultaneously, feminist theorists of colour described the connections between crime and patriarchy from an intersectional perspective. More specifically, black feminist scholars, such as Angela Y. Davis and bell hooks, challenged mainstream criminology and white feminists in their publications on the histories of institutional forced reproduction, the legal rape of women of colour and racist cultural tropes that vilified black men.

See Chapter 1.7
Psychopathy

In her classic 1976 book *Women, Crime and Criminology*, Carol Smart addressed the powerful lens of patriarchy in criminology. In this book, Smart critiqued the patriarchal focus of the classical criminological studies on female offenders – primarily studies by **Cesare Lombroso** and William Ferrero, W.I. Thomas and Otto Pollak. In addition, Smart documented:

See Chapter 1.4
Positivism; Chapter
1.5 Biological
criminology

- the almost invisible scholarship on female offenders;
- the gendered nature of offending (i.e., crimes that are more likely to be committed by and/or associated with women/girls);
- the politics of how crimes that are disproportionally committed by women (i.e., prostitution) and that disproportionately victimize women (with a focus on rape) are legally defined and processed, and how this is related to the incarceration of convicted women and girls;
- the complex relationship between women's offending and mental illness; and
- how to begin to redress these sexist limitations in research, laws and responses to offending women and girls.

Since the 1990s, feminist pathways theory has become increasingly popular in understanding individual risks for offending. In brief, pathways theory scholarship has documented the significant risk of victimizations and other adverse life events for subsequent offending, and how offending can also influence subsequent victimization. The development of feminist pathways theory centres on the influence of meso-level patriarchal forces in women's and girls' offending, where previously mainstream criminology either ignored or masculinized their crimes. Stated alternatively, the pathways perspective provides crucial insight into how sex- and gender-based abuse and institutional failings shape girls'/women's criminal trajectories.

Although publications dating back to the early 1900s associate women's and girls' offending as stemming from trauma, this phenomenon was not labelled 'pathways' until 1992, in Kathleen Daly's classic article 'Women's pathways to felony court', analysing court personnel's pre-sentence investigation reports (PSIs). Other landmark pathways research by African-American feminist scholars Regina Arnold (1990) and Beth Richie (1996) centred on in-depth life-history interviews with incarcerated women about their victimization and offending – including not only the impacts of patriarchal families and family and intimate partner violence, but also the structural impacts of poor and racist schools and communities, and sexist, racist and classist criminal legal system responses.

Additionally, pathways scholarship typically explores the criminalization girls and women face in their help-seeking, primarily through leaving abusive parents and partners. According to pathways theory, these girls' and women's exit and survival strategies – such as self-medicating with drugs, selling drugs, theft and sex work – are often criminalized. Mental health is also an important factor within pathways theory, as mentally ill women are more at risk of victimization and criminalization, and victimization and criminalization can exacerbate mental illness. Thus, the pathways perspective highlights patriarchal abuses, both interpersonal and institutional, in understanding women's and girls' criminal trajectories (DeHart et al. 2014).

See Chapter 3.6 Feminist criminologies; Chapter 3.13 Radical feminism

Feminist criminology emerged very much from the proliferation of second-wave patriarchal crime analysis, and was strengthened by the foregrounding of explicit intersectionality in the decade following. Scholars such as Richie (1996, 2012) argue that patriarchal analyses underestimated the dynamics between violence and other demographic locations such as race and socio-economic class. Within an intersectional approach to both sex/gender and crime, feminist criminology examines patriarchy as a system enmeshed within many interconnected structures of oppression. Primarily these are class, gender and race/ethnicity, but also include health, immigration status, sexuality and other significant social locations of oppression. From this intersectional framework, feminist analyses have been and continue to provide major contributions to criminological scholarship, including but not limited to: macro-level analyses of sex and gender in relation to mass incarceration; meso-level examinations of women's criminogenic pathways; and micro-level analysis of the enactment of masculine violence. For example, feminist criminological approaches reveal that:

- Parents are more likely to call the police when concerned about their daughters than they are in relation to similar concerns regarding their sons.
- School officials treat young people differently based on sex and gender.
- Police responses, detention systems (such as jails, prisons and other systems incarcerating youth and adults) and sentencing decisions all reflect bias based on sex and gender.
- Official responses to sex- and gender-based abuse can also be discriminatory.

Recent feminist criminological research has advocated for the continued use of structural power analyses to understand both old and new typologies of cultural violence. In her book *The New Jim Crow* (2012), Michelle Alexander uses analysis of systems of oppression to delineate how then President Ronald Reagan constructed crack cocaine as a gendered and racialized **moral panic**.

See Chapter 3.10 Moral panic

During the midst of the War on Drugs, Reagan hired a publicity team to generate fear around crack, hoping that public alarm would increase support for his campaign and political party. While cocaine use was culturally understood as a drug of the white upper class, crack was a cheaper drug more commonly associated with the black community. Reagan's campaign against crack engaged tropes with a long historical lineage: the Jezebel, or hyper-sexualized and dehumanized black woman. Beth Richie (2012) described this policy manipulation as a technique of a 'prison nation' – a government that reifies structural power using unilateral policies that erode the safety of marginalized communities and black women. The hyper-policing of crack cocaine in urban neighbourhoods and institution of mandatory minimum sentencing caused massive increases in drug-related incarceration, and the rates of female incarceration spiked. These increases have continued for women, despite the overall decline in incarceration (for men). While governmental reports and criminologists alike have heralded perceived prison reform, patriarchal analysis indicates important caveats in recent trends in incarceration rates. Moreover, Richie's work documents profoundly the intensity of class, gender, race and sexuality intersections in the lives of the women and girls she describes and in the 'offending' for which they are convicted, but which appear far more to be offences against them by individuals, often including professionals working in the criminal justice system.

While the anti-rape movement of the second wave moved away from patriarchal criticism, contemporary scholarship has resumed the task. In her reformulation of previous theoretical understandings of rape, Mardorossian (2014) discusses masculinity as a *structural position* rather than a *sexual difference*, and violence as caused by gendered hierarchies of subordination and domination, not women's relation to men. Rape disproportionately impacts women not because of their sex and gender, but because of patriarchal structuring of power. By centring patriarchal structures, abuse is understood as a crime that saturates all of culture.

Patriarchal power analysis also lends itself to examining new cultural phenomena of violence. While mental illness and/or gun availability may have played a role in recent mass shootings in the United States, an analysis of such events through the lens of patriarchy as relevant to crime reveals that the perpetrators have been overwhelmingly white men/boys who are displaying or performing their **masculinity** during their attacks. The common motivations of perpetrators of mass shootings exemplify white masculine power: a desire for dominance, control over women's bodies, fear, respect and belief in white supremacy. By highlighting the racist and sexist motivations common in such violence, the crimes can be understood as violent defences of slighted masculinity or patriarchal challenges.

See Chapter 4.21 Masculinities, structure and hegemony

References

Alexander, Michelle. 2012. *The New Jim Crow: Mass Incarceration in the Age of Colorblindness*. New York: New Press.

Arnold, Regina A. 1990. Women of Color: Processes of Victimization and Criminalization of Black Women. *Social Justice*, 17(3): 153–66.

Daly, Kathleen. 1992. Women's Pathways to Felony Court. *Southern California Review of Law and Women's Studies* 2(1): 11–52.

DeHart, Dana, Shannon Lynch, Joanne Belknap, Priscilla Dass-Brailsford, and Bonnie Green. 2014. Life History Models of Female Offending: The Roles of Serious Mental Illness and Trauma in Women's Pathways to Jail. *Psychology of Women Quarterly* 38(1): 138–51.

Mardorossian, Carine M. 2014. *Framing the Rape Victim: Gender and Agency Reconsidered*. New Brunswick, NJ: Rutgers University Press.

Richie, Beth E. 1996. *Compelled to Crime: The Gender Entrapment of Battered Black Women*. New York: Routledge.

Richie, Beth E. 2012. *Arrested Justice: Black Women, Violence, and America's Prison Nation*. New York: New York University Press.

Smart, Carol. 1976. *Women, Crime and Criminology: A Feminist Critique*. London: Routledge & Kegan Paul.

Further reading

Belknap, Joanne. 2015. *The Invisible Woman: Gender, Crime, and Justice* (4th edn). Stamford, CT: Cengage.

Potter, Hillary. 2015. *Intersectionality and Criminology: Revolutionizing Studies of Crime*. New York: Routledge.

Walby, Sylvia. 1990. *Theorizing Patriarchy*. Cambridge, MA: Blackwell.

Postcolonial criminology

Biko Agozino

Criminology is the discipline that served colonialism more directly than most, having been deliberately designed as a technology for the control of others. Partly as a result of this historical collusion, the discipline continues to blossom in former centres of imperialism and in places of settler colonialism, while the former colonized locations have almost unanimously refused to develop the disciplinary criminological fetishes of Western modernity. Accordingly, the history of Western criminology follows the example of Foucault by locating the emergence of the discipline at the height of Western slavery and colonialism or at the birth of sadism as a libertine tradition in Europe, but with hardly any mention of the historically specific concrete conditions that shaped the discipline into a fetish of the control-freak state – slavery, colonialism and anti-colonial struggles.

Agozino (1997) is credited with launching a 'decolonization paradigm' in criminology with an explicit call to criminologists to contribute to the ongoing project of decolonization and development of a 'postcolonial criminology'. One question that arises from the term 'postcolonial' is what is the 'post' in postcolonial? Is it suggesting that colonialism is passé, even though the symbols of colonial oppression and authority persist? As in **postmodernism** and **post-structuralism**, which presuppose the continuation of modernist and structuralist tendencies in discourse, postcolonialism does not take for granted an abrupt end to colonialism in lineal historiography. The very term,

See Chapter 4.28
Postmodern
and constitutive
criminologies

See Chapter 4.29
Post-structuralism
and criminology

'postcolonial', invokes the living ghosts, haunting spectres and enduring legacies of colonialism, while hinting at ongoing resistance to attempts to recolonize the world.

Stuart Hall and colleagues (1978) provide a pivotal example of postcolonial criminology by calling for scholars and intellectuals concerned about the criminological and colonialist crises of law and order politics in Europe to remember the history of slavery and colonialism when explaining phenomena such as the amplification of deviance as a control strategy targeting minorities in Europe. A postcolonial criminology would argue against the conventional criminological assumption that punishment is reserved only for offenders. For example, during slavery, colonialism and apartheid, black women did not have to offend in order for punitive measures to be directed against them – in line with colonialist policing tactics based on 'guilt by association' which then continued in the internal colonies of inner-city Australia, Belgium, Brazil, Britain, Canada, Colombia, France, Jamaica, Mexico and the United States (Agozino 1997). This suggests that postcolonial criminology is relevant to the whole of criminology, and not just to those who used to be colonized by Europe.

See Chapter 3.9
Marxist
criminologies

Elsewhere, Hall (1980) employed the **Marxist political economy** notion of the articulation of modes of production that was applied to the context of apartheid South Africa, where the distinction between rural peasantry and urban industrial worker had proved unhelpful because rural immigrants were exploited as cheap labour by apartheid mining industries. It would be ridiculous to say that only class exploitation was going on under apartheid, given that there was also racism and sexism simultaneously. Hall (1980) extended the concept of articulation to the social relations of race and class, and by implication to gender. He concluded that these different social relations are not separate and cannot be understood separately, especially in contexts such as the authoritarian populism of Thatcherism, which attempted to define Britishness in terms of an original English culture being swamped by waves of immigrants, or the regime of apartheid South Africa, where a white-male-bourgeois minority futilely attempted to defend white supremacy with the support of the white working class that sought to protect white privileges.

See Chapter 3.2
Birmingham
Centre for
Contemporary
Cultural Studies

Compared to both Habermas and Foucault – who theorized the history of power and democracy in Europe but without saying anything about colonial power as the antithesis of democracy – Hall helped found the **Birmingham Centre for Contemporary Cultural Studies** by placing emphasis on the drift towards a law and order state in postcolonial Europe at the expense of the working class that was weakened through racial and gender divisions in societies structured in dominance. Similarly, Edward Said (1993) questioned why Habermas and Foucault maintained complete silence about colonialism and anti-colonial struggles and implicitly rejected the potential defence that scholars have every right to narrow down their topics to a manageable area – say, Western Europe. Said suggested that even if the focus is narrowly Eurocentric, there is no way to explain conditions in modern Europe without reference to the history of Orientalism during slavery and colonialism that produced the enormous wealth that 'smothers' Europe, as Fanon put it, at the expense of the underdeveloped regions of the world and at the expense of the European working class. Said held Fanon up as the model for explaining the colonial and postcolonial conditions under which a phantom bourgeoisie replaced the European colonizers but continued to be answerable to the colonial authorities under the new imperialism or hegemony of finance capital.

A puzzle for postcolonial criminology, then, is the passion with which neocolonial and postcolonial authorities continue to embrace repressive laws introduced during slavery, colonialism and apartheid, rather than allow them to wither away – especially as the European colonizers who introduced such laws have since abolished them in their own countries. A further foundation for postcolonial criminology can be identified in the work of W.E.B. Du Bois (1895), who devoted his doctoral dissertation at Harvard University to the explanation of why slavery was seen by many as a perfectly legitimate business despite early attempts to legislate against it in parts of the USA, and why the USA continued with slavery long after Britain had abolished slavery and the slave trade. Du Bois' subsequent work, *The Philadelphia Negro* (1897), explained that the reason African-Americans were over-represented in the criminal justice system was not that they were more crime-prone, but that law-enforcement agents racially profiled people of African descent while turning a blind eye to the wrongdoing of the white higher-economic classes; he also showed how the convict-lease system helped return the newly freed enslaved Africans back into chains at a high rate. This suggests that the conditions of the African diaspora in the Americas could be understood as postcolonial conditions and benefit from the development and application of postcolonial criminological theories.

Today, postcolonial criminology is capable of contributing to the critique of the high rates of killing of unarmed African-Americans and other people of colour by the police and by vigilantes across the USA. It is also relevant to understanding why large numbers of unarmed white Americans are killed annually by the police, who, in turn, also suffer high rates of fatalities in the line of duty while trying to police the crises of imperialism on the home front.

It would be an error to look at postcolonial criminology as a 'special case' applying only to former colonial countries because colonialism is a crime against *humanity*. Colonialism is a general form of criminality because every crime has in common the invasion of the spaces of the victimized with attempts to colonize the resources of others. Hence, power is more of a causal explanation for crime than poverty, given that the vast majority of the poor remain overwhelmingly law-abiding while many of the rich are able to act as if they are above the law. The solution to abusive power relations is not disempowerment but the increasing democratization of all power relations at all levels.

A 2014 special issue of the *African Journal of Criminology and Justice Studies* honoured the 10th anniversary of the publication of Agozino's *Counter-Colonial Criminology* (2003) and extended the theory to the development of

See Chapter 4.18
Indigenous
criminology

Indigenous criminology. This subject is gradually gaining more attention, especially among critical young scholars who see in postcolonial criminology the promise of justice for all. South African students launched a massive campaign for the decolonization of higher education in 2015. A 2016 symposium at the University of Wollongong focused on Indigenous perspectives on decolonising criminology and criminal justice, and a seminar series in 2016 at the University of Padua, Italy, focusing on the decolonization of the social sciences, featured a session on Gramsci and the decolonization paradigm in criminology.

As Derrida (2001) maintained in his essay about forgiveness as the 'forgiving of the unforgivable', Western criminology can benefit from postcolonial criminology by abandoning the control-freak criminology of imperialism (with its fantasies of punitive expeditions against erring natives) and embracing the Southern African philosophy of Ubuntu, which states that there is no one who does not deserve to be forgiven and there is nothing that cannot be forgiven. Derrida reviewed the Abrahamic religions of the book and found that each of them teaches forgiveness but that each also reserves the right to identify things that are unforgiveable, whereas Africans went through 400 years of slavery, 100 years more of colonialism and many more years of apart-

See Chapter 3.12
Peacemaking in
criminology

heid without obsessing about vengeance. **Criminology as peacemaking** borrows from the postcolonial tradition of nonviolence by advocating the enrichment of communities through a commitment to build peace and love rather than seek punitiveness – which, wherever in the world it is employed, has a tendency to make bad people worse.

References

Agozino, Biko. 1997. *Black Women and the Criminal Justice System: Towards the Decolonization of Victimization*. Aldershot: Ashgate.

Agozino, Biko. 2003. *Counter-Colonial Criminology: A Critique of Imperialist Reason*. London: Pluto.

Derrida, Jacques. 2001. *On Cosmopolitanism and Forgiveness*. New York: Routledge.

Du Bois, W.E.B. [William Edward Burghardt]. 1895. *The Suppression of the African Slave Trade*. Cambridge, MA: Harvard University Press.

Du Bois, W.E.B. 1897. *The Philadelphia Negro*. Philadelphia: University of Pennsylvania Press.

Hall, Stuart. 1980. Race, articulation and societies structured in dominance. In *Sociological Theories: Race and Colonialism*, UNESCO, ed., pp. 305–45. Paris: UNESCO.

Hall, Stuart, Chas Critcher, Tony Jefferson, John Clarke, and Brian Roberts. 1978. *Policing the Crisis: Mugging, the State, and Law and Order*. London: Macmillan.

Said, Edward. 1993. *Culture and Imperialism*. New York: Penguin.

Further reading

Fanon, Frantz. 1963. *The Wretched of the Earth*. New York: Penguin.

Garland, David. 1990. *Punishment and Modern Society*. Oxford: Clarendon.

Kitossa, Tamari. 2014. Authoritarian Criminology and the Racial Profiling Debate in Canada: Scientism as Epistemic Violence. *African Journal of Criminology and Justice Studies* 8(1): 63–88.

Lywak, Joey. 2014. Biko Agozino and Justice for All. *African Journal of Criminology and Justice Studies* 8(1): 125–32.

Tutu, Desmond, and Mpho Tutu. 2014. *The Book of Forgiving: The Fourfold Path for Heeling the World and Ourselves*. New York: HarperOne.

4.28 Postmodern and constitutive criminologies

Nigel South

See Chapter 4.29
Post-structuralism
and criminology

Both postmodernism and **post-structuralism** present a critical challenge to modernism and articulate critiques of the assumptions and frameworks that shaped modern criminology. Criminology was a product of the claims of certainty of modernity, its goals and values. What then, might a 'criminology' for a complex postmodern world of fluid values and unstable systems look like? There is – appropriately – no definitive answer to this question, but various writers and developments have been suggestive.

As a starting point, it may be helpful to contrast what might be seen as the characteristics of modernity, late-modernity and post-modernity. *Modernity* offered grand theoretical overviews (e.g., Marxism, functionalism) regarding society and social structure, subjectivity and agency, knowledge, discourse and social change. It promised a certainty of explanation that, according to some, has now collapsed into fragmented and competing narratives and the end of deference and embrace of difference. Such overviews can be seen in the distinctions drawn between traditional and modern society in the classic accounts of Marx, who described the transition in terms of capitalism, conflict and exploitation; of Durkheim and his notion of a move from mechanical to organic society; and of Weber, in his analysis of bureaucratization, calculability and control.

The idea of *late-modernity* has been explored by various writers (e.g., Young 1999) in terms of social divisions, such as economic exclusion from the labour market, social exclusion and the over-inclusion of some within an expanded criminal justice system (thereby resulting in penal exclusion). Beck (1999:165) describes late-modernity as an 'age in which the social order of the national state, class, ethnicity and the traditional family is in decline' and, looking to the future, observes that: 'Any attempt to create a new sense of social cohesion has to start from the recognition that individualism, diversity and scepticism are written into Western culture.' Stones (1996:22) therefore suggests that postmodernists would argue:

> for respecting the existence of a plurality of perspectives, as against a notion that there is one single truth from a privileged perspective; local, contextual studies in place of grand narratives; an emphasis on disorder, flux and openness, as opposed to order, continuity and restraint.

From a postmodernist perspective, meanings, contexts, influences, intentions all differ from person to person and place to place. In terms of implications for the criminological field, this challenge to the search for certainties is not new, and in many ways echoes elements of **symbolic interactionism** and **labelling** perspectives as well as **social constructionism** and **chaos theory**. Postmodernism suggests that the search for explanatory causes is a way of subscribing to belief in grand meta-narratives that no longer stand as credible. A postmodern world is one of diversities and differences: a turn from structures to cultures; from grand claims of truth to multiple narratives; from foundational 'truths' arrived at through the scientific method to notions of knowledge as partial, fractured (or fragmented) and contingent; and from assumptions of linear development in historical change to order and disorder/ continuity and discontinuity co-existing contemporaneously.

Flux and change in structures and politics, readjustments to social align-ments and popular feeling have corresponding implications for forms of crime as reflections of culture, economy and values. For example, consumerism and commodification, aspiration and desire shape forms of related crime – such as fraud and credit crimes, counterfeiting and exploitation of cheap labour to produce cheap goods. Changes in demographics, labour markets and rela-tionships increase the use of casual and informal labour arrangements in the workplace and fluidity in the experience of time (as in the growth of informal and night-time economies), weaken traditional **controls and bonds** and encourage more focus on the individual, the self and simulations and repre-sentations, as multiplied by a world of media and accelerating technologies of shallow communication. Desire for immediate experience overshadows long-term thinking, so considerations regarding environmental harm and climate change (as considered by **green criminology** and by those con-cerned about **ecocide** and **environmental injustice**) are compromised by unwillingness to take action that might undermine a consumption lifestyle.

See Chapter 3.18
Symbolic interactionism

See Chapter 3.8
Labelling theory

See Chapter 3.15
Social constructionism

See Chapter 4.2
Chaos criminology

See Chapter 2.6
Control theories

See Chapter 4.16
Green criminology

See Chapter 4.13
Genocide and ecocide

See Chapter 4.11
Environmental justice and victimology

353

All these can be seen as characteristics of a postmodern society which Sennett (1998:27), for example, sees as corrosive of 'qualities of character which bind human beings to one another and furnishes each with a sense of sustainable self'.

Postmodernism challenges the 'absolute truths' purportedly achieved through science, and postmodern criminologists call into question modernist faith in the availability of explanations for, and solutions to, crime. A postmodern assessment would thus criticize the whole modern criminological project as misguided; and one of the most incisive critiques along these lines was provided by Smart (1990), who queried whether a male-dominated criminology, preoccupied with the theories and methods of modernity, held anything of value for **feminism**. The faith in aetiology, causality and explanation is misconceived, according to the postmodern criminologist: there is no single, universal, determining factor regarding criminal behaviour – or even combination of factors.

Unsurprisingly, if a postmodern view can be so critical of criminology and eschews the usual features of a 'scientific' approach to problems, then the development of a 'postmodern criminology' presents challenges, if it is possible at all. 'Constitutive criminology', as promulgated by Henry and Milovanovic, seeks to articulate a version of a postmodern criminology animated by different notions of 'crime', 'offender', 'victim' and 'control'. Henry and Milovanovic (1996:53) begin by 'abandoning . . . the futile search for "the causes of crime"' and calling for a focus on 'genealogies, drift, seductions, chaos, discourse, social constructions, structuration and structural coupling' as ways of thinking about crime. The social world – and hence 'crime' – is a construction of human beings, drawing on symbols and language. But this is also a world of inequalities in power and vulnerability:

> Constitutive theorists argue that the co-production of harmful relations occurs through society's structure and culture, as these are energized by human actions. These actions come not only from offenders, but also from victims, criminal justice practitioners, academics, commentators, media reporters and producers of film and TV crime shows, and most generally, as investors, producers, and consumers in the crime business.
>
> (Henry and Milovanovic 2003:58)

In this way, constitutive criminologists' claims regarding the ways in which society's structure and culture produce harmful relations bears resemblance to **cultural criminology**.

Henry and Milovanovic define crime in terms of 'the power to deny others their ability to make a difference' (1996:116) and as 'harm resulting from humans investing energy in harm-producing relations of power' (2003:58), thereby demonstrating an affinity with **zemiological and social-harm perspectives**. Essentially, constitutive criminology divides crime into two types:

See Chapter 3.6
Feminist
criminologies;
Chapter 4.26
Patriarchy and
crime; Chapter
3.13 Radical
feminism

See Chapter 4.8
Cultural
criminology

See Chapter 4.33
Social harm/
zemiology

- 'crimes of reduction', which occur when those who have been offended against experience the loss of some quality relative to their present standing; and
- 'crimes of repression', occurring when people experience a limit or restriction that prevents them from achieving a desired position or standing, or which prevents their realizing an accomplishment (e.g., sexism, racism).

Henry and Milovanovic (2003:59) emphasize that:

> Where attempts to achieve a desired position or standing are . . . limiting to others, then the repression of those attempts might be more correctly called control. Such control [is] always a crime of repression, but the manner in which control is done can be more or less harmful and more or less justified.

Some describe constitutive criminology as a significant 'new' criminology, but critics argue that it is not underpinned by research and that its arguments are too complex to translate into a form that can revitalize traditional criminology or policy and practice. While constitutive criminology's argument that crime and crime control cannot be divorced from the contexts (cultural, structural) in which they are produced remains salient – and its ideas regarding the ways in which harmful relations stem from unequal power relations are compelling – it is a perspective that has not gained much traction beyond its progenitors. One might also argue that its greatest limitation lies in its aspiration to (still) be (a) 'criminology'.

References

Beck, Ulrich. 1999. *World Risk Society*. London: Wiley.

Henry, Stuart, and Dragan Milovanovic. 1996. *Constitutive Criminology*. London: Sage.

Henry, Stuart, and Dragan Milovanovic. 2003. Constitutive criminology. In *Controversies in Critical Criminology*, Marty Schwartz and Suzanne Hatty, eds, pp. 57–69. Cincinnati, OH: Anderson.

Sennett, Richard. 1998. *The Corrosion of Character: The Personal Consequences of Work in the New Capitalism*. New York: Norton.

Smart, Carol. 1990. Feminist approaches to criminology, or postmodern woman meets atavistic man. In *Feminist Perspectives in Criminology*, Loraine Gelsthorpe and Allison Morris, eds, pp. 70–84. Milton Keynes: Open University Press.

Stones, Rob. 1996. *Sociological Reasoning*. Basingstoke: Macmillan.

Young, Jock. 1999. *The Exclusive Society*. London: Sage.

Further reading

Arrigo, Bruce A., and Dragan Milovanovic (eds). 2010. *Postmodernist and Post-Structuralist Theories of Crime*. Farnham: Ashgate.

Henry, Stuart, and Dragan Milovanovic. 1991. Constitutive Criminology: The Maturation of Critical Theory. *Criminology* 29(2): 293–316.

Henry, Stuart, and Dragan Milovanovic (eds). 1999. *Constitutive Criminology at Work: Applications to Crime and Justice*. Albany: State University of New York Press.

Morrison, Wayne. 1995. *Theoretical Criminology: From Modernity to Post-Modernism*. London: Cavendish.

South, Nigel 1987. Late-modern criminology: 'late' as in 'dead' or 'modern' as in 'new'? In *Sociology after Postmodernism*, David Owen, ed., pp. 81–102. London: Sage.

Post-structuralism and criminology

Adam J. Duso and Bruce A. Arrigo

Post-structuralism (PS) exists as a loose collection of anti-foundational theories and anti-essentialist methods that interrogate forms of thinking and destabilize ways of knowing. Ontologically, PS intends to reveal hidden biases, expose epistemological assumptions and dismantle hierarchical claims to social-reality construction – especially with respect to identity categories such as race, class, gender and their **intersectional** standpoints. The intellectual history of PS is traceable primarily to the works of French and other continental philosophers of the early to mid-twentieth century. In part, PS is a deliberate response to the philosophy of structuralism; in part, it is an evolving critique of radical movements or heterodox currents, such as postmodernism, ultra-modernism and cosmopolitanism. Within the realm of criminological theory, post-structural insights have furthered deconstructionist, **psychoanalytic** and semiotic theorizing. These insights have produced novel forms of critical and textual discourse analysis with relevance for legal change and social justice. More specifically, post-structural theorizing has produced a number of critiques concerning the nature of both crime and the criminal justice system. These critiques argue against the **positivistic** (and post-positivistic) means by which the assessment of crime, the calculation of criminal prevention and the decisional science of punishment and justice find their ends.

PS is often cited as a response to structuralism, which posits that all of social life (e.g., its artefacts of community, its cultural representations, its

See Chapter 4.20
Intersectionality

See Chapter 1.10
Psychoanalytic
perspectives

See Chapter 1.4
Positivism

ritualized histories) can only ever be understood through its relationship to all-encompassing a priori systematic structures. Thus, these structures are assumed to be the foundation of things such as community, culture and history. Although PS advocates differ substantively in their critique of structuralism, several commonalities do exist. Perhaps chief among them is the 'perspectivist' philosophical position regarding the nature of human existence and social life. Specifically, PS proponents seek to explore knowledge-generation and knowledge-building (as systems of thought) through the lens of their human producers, arguing that the constitution of both (knowledge and human producers) emerges from the ongoing dialectical exchanges and the recurring dialogical elaborations that breathe meaning and purpose into both. These interactions and elaborations co-shape the world 'out there' and those who define it as such. Often, Eurocentric and Western narratives of historical fact and presumed significance prevail, and these narratives (as power/knowledge truth regimes) typically support status quo dynamics and the logic of capital. As such, PS adherents also endeavour to shatter and increase knowledge, and with it human productivity, through a critical re-reading of the imperatives (i.e., system-based policies, programmes and practices) that politicize

See Chapter 3.13
Radical feminism

truth (e.g., **phallocentric** justice) and normalize its human agents (e.g., heteronormative ethics).

A number of critical theorists and social philosophers are generally understood to be aligned with PS or otherwise responsible for its intellectual development. Luminaries such as Jacques Derrida, Michel Foucault and Jacques Lacan have been particularly influential within criminology and legal studies. Others such as Roland Barthes, Drucilla Cornell, Gilles Deleuze, Felix Guattari and Julia Kristeva have also been the source of post-structural insights with import for criminological and socio-legal theorizing. The use of post-structural concepts in criminology is most readily associated with Foucault, whose works such as *Madness and Civilization* (1965) and *Discipline and Punish* (1977) establish genealogical views of psychiatric disease and criminal punishment, derived from the systems of thought that constitute their respective histories and corresponding bodies of knowledge. Recent works from scholars such as Arrigo and Milovanovic (2010), as well as Crewe and Lippens (2015), have drawn attention to the intersections of PS, postmodernism and criminology, emphasizing the importance of pursuing academic border-crossing that develops and integrates the epistemological and ontological contributions of constitutive, psychoanalytic semiotic, complexity/non-linear systems theorizing and related forms of sociocultural critique and heterodoxy.

PS's approach to knowledge and its human producers forms the basis of its anti-foundational and anti-essentialist framework. The nature of discourse and the constitution of human agency are its principal conceptual concerns. According to PS, material objects (e.g., phenomena, events) are not discrete in their existence; rather, they are discursive in disposition. What this means, then, is that *how* these objects are experienced (i.e., witnessed, processed and evaluated) establishes their discursive (intra/intersubjective) character. For post-structuralists, because our experiences assume the form and content of a language, this begs the question: whose perspective and which way(s) of knowing define (and govern) our experiences? Proponents of PS maintain that even the thoughts that we think assume the form and content of a language (a system of what to know, a regime of how to be). Thus, they (these powerful thoughts) can never be neutral, represent only one rendition of social reality, and can be the source and product of the subject's existential captivity or human freedom.

For adherents of PS, the nature of discourse both informs and is shaped by the construction of human agency. Historically, although ontology (the study of agency, being or subjectivity) has been minimized within the post-structural framework, its re-emergence is worth noting. Drawing inspiration from Deleuze, often in collaboration with Guattari (1984, 1987), post-structural criminology has called for a vision of ontology that is in process, dynamic, local, contingent and open to change. Indeed, if discourse and knowledge are themselves the source of 'undecidability' (multiple re-readings and inexhaustible revisions), it follows that the human agent's possible existence (and all of humanity's) can be reconceptualized – and, with it, potentially revitalized and even transformed. For post-structural criminologists, this is a nomadic journey and a mutual struggle for a just people yet to be.

The influence of PS, as both an assemblage of theories and a set of deracinating methods, extends to a number of critical currents and epistemological standpoints within criminology. One topical example is **convict criminology** as social-change movement and as anti-subordination theory. Convict criminologists exemplify the PS paradigm through their direct experiences with and within the criminal justice system. These experiences, and the perspectivism from which they are derived, rewrite and reproduce knowledge and human agency as praxis (the convict criminologist as a valued and pertinent identity category) and transpraxis (the convict criminologist as a researcher/scholar, college educator and public intellectual). These are the narratives of shared change – of collective becoming. But the influence of post-structural thought on convict criminology also reaches into theory development. To illustrate, the problem of mass incarceration is about **essentializing PRISON as a 'complex'**. This includes fetishizing its institutional logics and professional rhetoric; its mechanisms of security and apparatuses of control; its privatization projects and community initiatives; its commercialized industries and culturalized simulations – as much as it is about the kept and their keepers, administrators and watchers (i.e., their human producers/participants). For proponents of PS, the essentializing of prison – existentially, materially and corporeally – *is* mass incarceration. This is the point at which a society of captives morphs into the captivity of society. In the extreme, this is a 'clinical' condition in which discourse, knowledge and human agency are themselves all finalized.

A strand of complementary critique developed by post-structural theorists is the problem of modern-day **surveillance** and its use in creating a **panoptic**

See Chapter 4.4
Convict
criminology

See Chapter 5.5
Decarceration;
Chapter 5.17
Security and
counter-security;
Chapter 5.18
Social control

See Chapter 5.19
Surveillance

See Chapter 5.11
Panopticism

(Foucault), synoptic (Thomas Mathiesen) and banoptic (Didier Bigo) society (Lyon 2006). This trajectory conveys the transition from the few who see the many, to the many who see the few, to the coding and classifying of the many and the few for the purpose of profiling all. Excessive investments in these conditions contribute to what some post-structural criminologists define as 'total confinement' (Arrigo et al. 2011). This condition constitutes systemic **pathology** or societal disease in which all are held captive by control society. In control society, human experience is reduced to and repressed by the encoded and informational data that signify everyday life in the service of the surveillant assemblage that society itself has become. For post-structural adherents, this serializing of our humanity, then, represents the creeping/creepy criminalization (i.e., crime analytics) of veritable existence.

See Chapter 1.6
Pathology

PS is not without its limitations and criticisms. Some opponents raise semantic arguments, taking exception to what is perceived to be incessantly obtuse and needlessly convoluted prose whose ultimate end seemingly produces nothing more than ideological nihilism, ethical relativism and ontological fatalism (i.e., the 'death' of the subject and with it the social). Additional concerns draw attention to the dearth of policy goals, directives or recommendations arising from PS-related research. These criticisms notwithstanding, precisely because PS functions as 'outsider jurisprudence' in its theoretical and methodological approach to knowledge, discourse, agency and the like, it stands in stark contrast to the conventional criminological canon. These investigations focus on the human condition as a series of objectively verifiable empirical truths to data mine. For positivists and post-positivists alike, these truths are an approximate stand-in for human experience in which the parts (revealed through data manipulations) can (and should) be disconnected (disaggregated) from the communities, cultures and histories from which each manipulation is already and always inscribed with pluri-signification. Such is the order of things in the structural episteme. For post-structuralists, this empiricized order is a fiction – a site of contestation and resistance – and emblematic of the ongoing struggle to reclaim, transform and revolutionize a people to come.

References

Arrigo, Bruce. A., Heather Y. Bersot, and Brian G. Sellers. 2011. *The Ethics of Total Confinement: A Critique of Madness, Citizenship, and Social Justice.* New York: Oxford University Press.

Arrigo, Bruce. A., and Dragan Milovanovic (eds). 2010. *Postmodernist and Post-Structuralist Theories of Crime.* Farnham: Ashgate.

Crewe, Don, and Ronnie Lippens (eds). 2015. *What Is Criminology About? Philosophical Reflections.* London: Routledge.

Deleuze, Gilles, and Felix Guattari. 1984. *Anti-Oedipus: Capitalism and Schizophrenia.* Minneapolis: University of Minnesota Press.

Deleuze, Gilles, and Felix Guattari. 1987. *A Thousand Plateaus: Capitalism and Schizophrenia.* Minneapolis: University of Minnesota Press.

Foucault, Michel. 1965. *Madness and Civilization: A History of Insanity in the Age of Reason.* New York: Pantheon.

Foucault, Michel. 1977. *Discipline and Punish: The Birth of the Prison.* New York: Pantheon.

Lyon, David (ed.). 2006. *Theorizing Surveillance: The Panopticon and Beyond.* Cullompton, UK: Willan.

Further reading

Arrigo, Bruce A., and Dragan Milovanovic. 2009. *Revolution in Penology: Rethinking the Society of Captives.* Lanham, MD: Rowman & Littlefield.

Arrigo, Bruce A., Dragan Milovanovic, and Robert C. Schehr. 2005. *The French Connection In Criminology: Rediscovering Crime, Law and Social Change.* Albany: State University of New York Press.

Deleuze, Gilles, and Felix Guattari. 1994. *What Is Philosophy?* New York: Columbia University Press.

Psychosocial
criminology

David Gadd

See Chapter 2.5
Control theories;
Chapter 2.9
General
strain theory;
Chapter 1.12
Developmental
criminology

See Chapter 4.39
Victimology

See Chapter 4.8
Cultural
criminology;
Chapter 4.10
Emotions

See Chapter 1.2
Classical
criminology;
Chapter 1.18
Rational choice

Definitive of the psychosocial approach to criminology is the premise that human subjectivity is constituted through both biographical and historical experience and fundamentally split between conscious thoughts, values and attitudes and unconscious desires. For psychosocial criminologists, it is critical to conceptualize sociological and psychological phenomena as in dynamic interaction with each other. Consequently, when psychological phenomena (e.g., dispositions, personalities, emotions) and sociological phenomena (e.g., culture, gender, poverty) are reduced to each other – as they sometimes are in orthodox approaches to crime causation (i.e., **control theory**, **strain theory**, **developmental criminology**) – criminological theorizing becomes over-generalizing. Hence, one should not simply assume that because someone is a **victim of crime**, or from a particular class or ethnic background, that he/she will think or feel the same as others with similar backgrounds. Likewise, the criminological notion of a 'propensity' derived from the sum of a series of risk factors is, from a psychosocial perspective, overly reductionist – both in its tendency to read subjectivity off from criminal histories without regard for the **meaning of the events** within them and for its presumption of a unitary, **rational** subject.

Within criminology the psychosocial approach is most commonly associated with the work of Gadd and Jefferson (2007), whose book *Psychosocial Criminology* highlighted the lost legacies of psychoanalytic thinking in criminology and revealed what the discipline might gain from re-engaging with concepts derived from Kleinian and object-relational **psychoanalysis**. Using case studies, Gadd and Jefferson illustrated the potential of the psycho-social approach to explain anomalous features of the perpetration of domestic and sexual violence, the fear of crime and racist crime, as well as the homo-phobic hate crimes of Clifford Shaw's infamous Jack-Roller, 'Stanley'. Earlier articulations of psychosocial criminology can be found in Jefferson's (1994, 1997) writing on the subject of masculinities and in Hollway and Jefferson's (2001) *Doing Qualitative Research Differently*.

See Chapter 1.10
Psychoanalytic
perspectives

Hollway and Jefferson's book problematized why some of those most at risk of criminal victimization (either because they were young and male or because they lived in high-crime areas) sometimes reported the lowest fear levels in crime surveys, while those at least risk (older adults living in low-crime areas) sometimes presented as the most fearful. In order to resolve this conundrum, Hollway and Jefferson proposed a new approach to qualitative research that adopted techniques from psychoanalytic practice, which encour-aged their research participants to 'freely associate' in in-depth interviews. In order to expose the unconscious defences mobilized in response to much everyday concern about crime, Hollway and Jefferson also attempted – both in their interviews and in their subsequent data analysis – to probe beyond the rationalizations research participants offered for viewpoints that seemed not to fit their experiences.

Outside of criminology an expansive field of psychosocial studies attends to the merits of the various ways of conceptualizing the interrelation between social and psychodynamic phenomena, especially that which is not fully con-scious. Within criminology, however, three key ideas have been central to the psychosocial approach.

1. *The defended subject.* Within criminology, the psychosocial approach pre-sumes that we are all anxious beings and that the insecurities we live with are usually rooted both in current life challenges and previous strug-gles, including childhood conflicts. The source of these insecurities is not confined to issues of separation, sexuality and death, as it is in much classic psychoanalytic writing; it can also include, for example, the fear of ill-health, estrangement, redundancy, stigma and victimization, as well as being caught in a lie or accused of a crime – life crises that can easily reinvoke unresolved conflicts from earlier years. Rather than let such fears overwhelm us, psychosocial criminologists presume that most of us seek to keep our anxieties at bay using defence mechanisms of which we are not fully conscious. This renders us all 'defended subjects' to greater or lesser degrees. Mechanisms of defence can include splitting and projec-tion, through which others are attacked for qualities one person dislikes in himself/herself – explaining why scapegoating often has such a hypocriti-cal feel to it, and also why some people feel menaced by those they blame for social problems. (Our demons remind us of the parts of ourselves we

hoped to have disowned.) Repression, or burying troubling feelings deep inside oneself, is another commonly used defence mechanism. Unsettling feelings that suddenly return to consciousness can threaten to overwhelm the person engaged in repression and/or be rearticulated in rage, sudden or festering, as well as sadistic sentiment that facilitates the vicarious enjoyment of seeing others suffer instead. More commonly in research settings, anxieties reveal themselves in slips of the tongue, awkward body language, incomplete sentences, overgeneralizations, jokes and sarcasm.

See Chapter 4.29
Post-structuralism
and criminology

2. *Investment in discourse.* While **post-structuralism** posits a subject shaped primarily by the power/knowledge configurations of discourse, psychosocial criminologists presume that people are motivated, not fully consciously, to take up positions in discourse that help them fend off feelings of vulnerability. So, for example, someone accused of being a 'racist' might insist that they never judge people by their skin colour but have qualms about migrants who 'take our jobs' or do not respect 'our values'. This could be conceived of as a discursive repositioning that protects the individual from the stigma of being labelled an 'unthinking bigot' by representing them as 'informed but reflexive on issues of economy and diversity'. Discourses are the means by which the stories people tell about their lives – including their involvement in, and reactions to, crime – get reproduced in socially familiar ways. Deconstructing the individual's particular positioning within social discourses can often reveal the complexity of the person behind socially familiar attitudes: the fearful citizen who calls for harsh punishment but has limited experiences of victimization; the perpetrator of hate crime who presents as multicultural; the domestic abuser who criticizes other men for their sexism.

3. *Identification.* In order to make sense of such anomalies psychosocial criminologists have drawn attention to the concept of 'identification' – the inter-psychic processes through which we take parts of others, in the first instance our primary carers, into the self. Identification can involve a complex dynamic, entailing the perception of shared likenesses, as well as a desire for the other's recognition, neither of which are likely to be fully conscious. Identifications can be a source of resilience that enables people to empathize with the feelings of another who has been hurt or experienced loss. Accounts of desistance that hinge upon a valued mentor seeing something good within an ex-offender who has been labelled 'bad' invoke reciprocal processes of identification. But identifications are also at stake in many forms of bullying behaviour. Through projective identification the person who feels crazy makes another feel that madness is actually part of them – that they are being driven 'crazy' – and attacks them verbally or physically for it. Likewise, identification with the aggressor occurs, for example, when a child identifies with the power of a father who is abusive while repressing his or her identification with the vulnerability of a mother who is being abused. Noting how such identifications operate is crucial if we are to better understand the contingencies that

make change possible but difficult to secure, whether in terms of working with persistent offenders or shifting unforgiving social reactions to crime more generally.

Take-up of the psychosocial approach to criminology has, to date, been piece-meal. The psychosocial approach is often identified as a key perspective in writing about hate crime, domestic violence and desistance because it is conceptually well equipped to critically interrogate issues of context and motive without requiring the researcher to side with those whose politics they do not agree with, whose social demographic characteristics they cannot share, or whose behaviour they cannot condone. Gadd and Dixon's book *Losing the Race* (2011) attempts this by exploring how losses of community, employment and cultural homogeneity intersected with losses of love, family, health and mental well-being in a community where racially aggravated crime presented itself as a pressing social problem.

Other articulations of the approach can be found in Robinson and Gadd's (2016) attempt to map out the criminological contours of contemporary annihilation anxiety, and in Maruna and colleagues' (2004) analysis of the defensive underpinnings of punitiveness. These works also reveal the extent to which concepts derived from the classic approaches to psychoanalysis evident in the works of Freud, Fromm and Adorno continue to be deployed metaphorically to explain cultural reactions to crime without addressing sufficiently their connection to individual manifestations of psychopathology evidenced in clinical practice. These questions are being addressed in the wider field of psychosocial studies, where some are exploring how organizational defences against anxiety inhibit the delivery of welfare, care and justice (Armstrong and Rustin 2015).

The following four international networks have contributed to book series addressing psychosocial approaches to these issues: *The Association for Psychosocial Studies*; *The Psychosocial Studies and Psychoanalysis Study Group* within the *British Sociological Association*; *The International Research Group for Psycho-Societal Analysis* and the *Association for the Psychoanalysis of Culture and Society*. In tandem, a small number of universities in the UK offer undergraduate and postgraduate degrees in psychosocial studies that address a range of social problems and policy issues, including criminological ones.

References

Armstrong, David, and Michael Rustin (eds). 2015. *Social Defences against Anxiety*. London: Karnac.

Gadd, David, and Bill Dixon. 2011. *Losing the Race*. London: Karnac.

Gadd, David, and Tony Jefferson. 2007. *Psychosocial Criminology: An Introduction*. London: Sage.

Hollway, Wendy, and Tony Jefferson. 2001. *Doing Qualitative Research Differently: Free Association, Narrative and the Interview Method*. London: Sage.

Jefferson, Tony. 1994. Theorising masculine subjectivity. In *Just Boys Doing Business? Men, Masculinities and Crime*, Tim Newburn and Elizabeth A. Stanko, eds, pp. 10–31. London: Routledge.

Jefferson, Tony. 1997. Masculinities and crime. In *The Oxford Handbook of Criminology* (2nd edn), Mike Maguire, Rodney Morgan, and Robert Reiner, eds, pp. 535–58. Oxford: Clarendon.

Maruna, Shadd, Amanda Matravers, and Anna King. 2004. Disowning Our Shadow: A Psychoanalytic Approach to Understanding Punitive Public Attitudes. *Deviant Behavior* 25(3): 277–99.

Robinson, Robin, and David Gadd. 2016. Annihilation Anxiety and Crime. *Theoretical Criminology* 20(2): 185–204.

Further reading

Chancer, Lynn, and John Andrews (eds). 2014. *The Unhappy Divorce of Sociology and Psychoanalysis: Diverse Perspectives on the Psychosocial*. Basingstoke: Palgrave Macmillan.

Clarke, Simon, and Paul Hogget (eds). 2009. *Researching Beneath the Surface: Psycho-Social Research Methods in Practice*. London: Karnac.

Frost, Liz, and Stuart MacLean. 2013. *Thinking about the Lifecourse: A Psychosocial Introduction*. Basingstoke: Palgrave Macmillan.

Public criminology

4.31

Gordon Hughes

The idea of a public criminology emerged as a powerful yet contested rallying call in the 2000s, expressing widespread concerns regarding criminology's decline in both political influence and wider public engagement, and deliberations seeking to reverse this decline.

Since the mid-2000s the debate on public criminology has stimulated a growing body of organized controversy associated with:

- deliberations about the declining influence of criminological research and analysis on politics and policymaking about crime and crime control, at the very time of its growth in the academy;
- claims that a public criminology needs to prioritize engaging deliberatively with wider 'publics' than that of the state and, in particular, with 'progressive' social movements generated within civil society concerned with questions of social justice and human rights;
- what it is to be a criminologist (scientist, activist, policy adviser, teacher, etc.) and thus the nature of the contribution made by major forms of criminological 'labour' and its expertise to the crime question.

Like many 'new' innovations in criminology, the notion of a public criminology entered from 'without' – as a result of a debate that developed initially within the discipline of sociology. This debate was associated with the challenge laid down by the president of the American Sociological Association, Michael Burawoy (2005), regarding contemporary sociology's failure to engage sufficiently and critically in the key public issues and challenges of the period.

Of course, expressions of concern as to the wider public relevance and social purpose of the social sciences ('knowledge for what?') is nothing new, and we would do well to remember and reprise Mills' (1959) programme for a 'sociological imagination' in any current debate on the 'public' place and purpose of social scientific practice.

To briefly summarize Burawoy's call for a public sociology and its application to criminology's own debate on its public roles, he contends that there is a growing 'gap' between the increasingly 'inward-looking' professional ethos of sociology (and by implication sociological work on the problem of crime and crime control) and the world 'out there'. The challenge opened up by this gap is thus to develop public knowledge which is capable of engaging 'multiple publics in multiple ways'. Burawoy, not forgetting his intellectual commitment to Gramscian 'sociological-Marxism', is suspicious of too close a relationship between the academy and both the state and the market; instead of these two dominant forces, he argues that social scientists need to forge closer working relations with the forces of civil society and its progressive social movements. The call for a public sociology thus envisages social scientists intervening in public life, using their particular knowledge and skills to both inform and influence public discourses about social problems.

It may be contended that Burawoy's call for a public social science speaks to some of the most urgent challenges also facing criminology as a social-scientific field of study. Hughes (2007:201–8), for example, adapts much of Burawoy's argument to the contemporary criminological field and, in particular, his four-fold characterization of the division of labour in the discipline of sociology in terms of 'professional', 'policy', 'critical' and 'public' forms of intellectual production. Although often ignored in many of the contributions to the debate on public criminology, the importance of this heuristic four-fold typology lies in not overstating the centrality of public criminology over that of the core labour and vocation of professional criminology in particular (Hughes forthcoming). To summarize each mode of work:

- First, 'professional' criminology occupies the centre of the discipline's division of labour. Its goal is to produce rigorous and reliable methods of research; accumulate collective bodies of knowledge; and create clear conceptual frameworks, education and training and so on – all institutionalized in a culture of peer-review testing and public scrutiny. It represents specialist knowledge concerned with solving puzzles. As exponents of social-scientific enquiry, members of the professional academic community interact first and foremost with one another in search of internally generated intellectual problems rather than external set agendas (Loader and Sparks 2010). This is what Max Weber (1948) famously termed 'science' or 'academic life' as a vocation. None of the three other types of criminological labour can exist without professional criminology.

- Second, 'policy' criminology is constituted largely by problem-solving in the service of a goal defined primarily by, or in negotiation with, a client – usually that of government. Its *raison d'être* is to provide solutions to problems presented to the criminologist, although there is no reason why policy criminology cannot play a key role in defining and redefining problems itself because this is often how policy in the real world is made. There is a rich, if increasingly forgotten, history to such criminological labour whose 'public' influence is all too easily dismissed as being 'administrative' (see Rock (2014:414) on the 'virile, if perhaps limited, public criminology' existing in Britain from the late 1950s to the 1970s).

▨ Third, 'critical' criminology (shorn of its all too often almost mythical aura) may be defined as the reflexive form of knowledge focused on examining the foundations – explicit and implicit, normative and political – of the disciplinary field and the research programmes associated with the other modes of criminological labour. In turn, such critical labour argues for a more activist and engaged 'public' assertiveness in countering dominant forces of oppression and injustice (Currie 2010).

▨ Fourth and finally, 'public' criminology may be defined as a form of reflexive criminological labour which aims to create a dialogic relation between the criminologist and various publics in which the agenda of each is brought to the table and in which each adjusts to the other. It may be viewed as: building on and complementing professional knowledge of criminology as a field of study; producing 'systematic back-translation'; taking knowledge back to those from whom it came; making public issues out of private troubles; and regenerating criminology's moral fibre (Burawoy 2005). Crucially, **public criminology would not privilege the conversation with the state and its crime-control agencies**, but would instead also seek to support work beyond the state, for example, with movements for social justice and human rights (Carrabine et al. 2000).

See Chapter 3.11 Newsmaking criminology

This typology of different ways of doing public-criminological labour is helpful in further clarifying the different roles available to – and different challenges facing – practitioners of the craft and science of criminology. Of course these heuristic distinctions should not be viewed as fixed roles, but rather represent specific aspects or phases of the academic career around which criminologists should be able to move with relative ease.

That the debate on the public roles of social science that emerged in sociology has gained such traction in contemporary criminology also appears to be because of a growing concern among practitioners in its Anglo-American heartland that the public influence of criminology on crime and control policymaking has declined paradoxically at the time of its expansion in the academy. It has also been widely noted that the crime problem has become 'heated up'; that the policy environment is now more volatile and unstable than in previous 'cooler' policy times; and, more broadly, that the late-modern culture of crime and fear has marginalized criminological reasoning (Garland 2001).

Although criminology has always had a very strong applied tradition, geared to an intensive research relationship with government, any 'public criminology' is confronted with exceptional problems, given both party-political and mass-media interest in issues of crime control and, relatedly, 'security'. Electoral and media interest thus generates a 'hot' policy environment, alongside popular crime-saturated sensibilities, that together inhibit the communicative rationality of social science. Insofar as criminologists adopt a scientific vocation, their communication of their research interests is filtered, if not distorted, by the formative intentions of public-policymakers to advance political manifestos, cultivate electoral support, deliver policy successes within electoral cycles, manage pressure group and mass-media criticism and so on.

Given these external problems confronting criminology, it may be argued that the criminological community needs to engage more positively with public debates in both the mass media and policy circles, though this seems little different from the work of 'mainstream' policy-oriented criminology in the social-democratic period (see, for example, Rock 2014, on British criminology), and may indeed represent just normal practice of any policy-relevant social science. More significantly, Loader and Sparks (2010:117) contend that criminology has too often assumed or accepted that governmental bodies are the principal audience for criminological research and that criminologists should play a more engaged role in contributing to 'a better politics of crime and its regulating' – although exactly what this 'better politics' is remains unstated by Loader and Sparks. Less ambitiously, and more concretely, there is also an increasing interest in deliberative methods that can structure dialogue between criminologists, policymakers and interested non-governmental actors around the experience of and expertise about what is, or could be, known about particular problems rather than around a priori political commitments (for a discussion of these challenges and opportunities with regard to the problem of urban security in Europe, see Edwards et al. 2013).

The concept of public criminology is not without its detractors and dissidents. Whilst there is a broad consensus among criminologists that they have a professional and public duty to engage in the interconnected spheres of politics and policymaking, the exact ways in which this should happen is open to deep contestation, and many may doubt whether we need a new term to describe this very old dilemma. For some, criminologists are at best able to produce modest but practical policy recommendations for 'evidence-based' crime control for national governments, whilst for others, the much broader but less tangible ambition should be that of working with social movements beyond the state endeavouring to improve social justice and enhance human rights across the globe and beyond state borders.

It is probable that the collective deliberation and organized controversy stimulated by the idea of a public criminology for our field of study has been more important than the soundness of the concept itself. In generating more open and frank discussion about the purpose of criminology beyond the confines of the academy than has been commonplace, this 'sensitizing concept' has most importantly highlighted the often different and at times competing logics underpinning criminology as a predominantly 'applied' branch of the social sciences. One of the unintended consequences of leading international criminologists running with Burawoy's original challenge for US sociology may be greater clarification of and humility regarding what criminological research-based expertise is able to offer the various publics with whom we can have potentially productive conversations. In particular, it has helped stimulate challenging questions as to what is the 'vocation' of the criminologist (artisan? partisan? scientist?) and what types of contributory expertise does the academic community bring to the 'crime question'.

References

Burawoy, Michael. 2005. For Public Sociology. *American Sociological Review* 70: 4-28.

Carrabine, Eamonn, Maggy Lee, and Nigel South. 2000. Social Wrongs and Human Rights in Late Modern Britain: Social Exclusion, Crime Control and the Prospects for a Public Criminology. *Social Justice* 27(2): 193–211.

Currie, Elliott. 2010. Against Marginality: Arguments for a Public Criminology. *Theoretical Criminology* 11(2): 175–90.

Edwards, Adam, Gordon Hughes, and Nicholas Lord. 2013. Urban Security in Europe: Translating a Concept in Public Criminology. *European Journal of Criminology* 10(3): 260–83.

Garland, David. 2001. *The Culture of Control: Crime and Social Order in Contemporary Society*. Oxford: Oxford University Press.

Hughes, Gordon. 2007. *The Politics of Crime and Community*. Basingstoke: Palgrave Macmillan.

Hughes, Gordon. Forthcoming. *Sociological Criminology: Connecting Classical and Modern Practice*. London: Sage.

Loader, Ian, and Richard Sparks. 2010. *Public Criminology?* London: Routledge.

Mills, C. Wright. 1959. *The Sociological Imagination*. New York: Oxford University Press.

Rock, Paul. 2014. The Public Faces of Public Criminology. *Criminology and Criminal Justice* 14(4): 412–33.

Weber, Max. 1948. Science as a vocation. In *From Max Weber: Essays in Sociology*, Hans H. Gerth and C Wright Mills, ed. and trans., New York: Free Press.

Further reading

Bosworth, Mary, and Carolyn Hoyle (eds). 2011. *What Is Criminology?* Oxford: Oxford University Press.

4.32 Queer criminology

Matthew Ball

Historically, criminology has contributed to the regulation of supposedly 'deviant', non-normative sexualities and genders, leading to a failure to accord the criminal justice experiences of lesbian, gay, bisexual, transgender, intersex and queer (LGBTIQ) communities a serious place in its purview. The shadow of the supposed 'deviancy' of LGBTIQ people looms large (Woods 2014), and they continue to experience injustice at the hands of criminal justice institutions and agents, and neglect within criminological scholarship. As such, there is significant scope for criminology to engage with bodies of knowledge produced by and for LGBTIQ communities, such as queer theory, in order to address these issues.

Queer theory is notoriously difficult to pin down. It developed in the 1980s alongside critical studies of sexuality and gender politics, which challenged the limitations, exclusions and assumptions of existing **feminist** and homosexual liberation movements. These movements, they argued, often essentialized women and gay and lesbian people – that is, they ascribed 'essential' or 'natural' characteristics to them which presented these identities as relatively stable, thereby overlooking the complex array of differences among them (such as those based on race and class), and often perpetuating the marginalization of some within that group. Drawing from **post-structural insights** – notably Michel Foucault's (1998) argument that sexuality is a product of historical power–knowledge relations – these movements sought to produce a politics around sexuality and gender that avoided the use of essentializing identity categories (and thus eschewed identity politics that reproduced the exclusions mentioned above), and which was based on an understanding of the regimes

See Chapter 3.6
Feminist
criminologies;
Chapter 4.26
Patriarchy and
crime; Chapter
3.13 Radical
feminism

See Chapter 4.29
Post-structuralism
and criminology

of power and knowledge through which sexuality and gender are produced, regulated and maintained. Two early queer theorists – Judith Butler and Eve Kosofsky Sedgwick – set the scene for queer theory's exploration of these issues. Butler identified the normative orders through which gender and heterosexuality come to seem natural and inevitable, while Sedgwick highlighted the effects of binary constructions (such as heterosexual/homosexual) in language and thought where one term is privileged over the other.

In line with broader post-structural insights, queer theory interrogates normative orders regulating sexuality and gender (and not just by considering the *non*-normative but also by taking the norm itself as an object of analysis). In addition, queer theory challenges normative orders that govern subjectivity more generally. As Halperin suggests, 'queer' 'acquires its meaning from its oppositional relation to the norm. "Queer" is by definition *whatever* is at odds with the normal, the legitimate, the dominant. *There is nothing in particular to which it necessarily refers*' (1995:62, original emphases). Queer theory is about challenging the very *idea* of the normal.

The radical challenge to, and deconstruction of, normative orders that queer signifies also explains the use of the term 'queer' itself. Previously a term of abuse, 'queer' has been reclaimed and resignified by (particularly LGBTIQ) scholars and activists as a way of not only acknowledging but also *celebrating* one's distance from, and challenge to, normative orders. This reclamation and resignification has also led to 'queer' being used in a variety of ways in related scholarship. For example, it has been used as a noun – that is, as a shorthand umbrella category to refer to LGBTIQ communities – because any initialism that seeks to be inclusive quickly becomes unwieldy; it has also been used as a verb to describe either the introduction of LGBTIQ perspectives on an issue or deconstructive critiques that challenge normative orders. While this definitional slipperiness has been productive in extending the presence of 'queer' analyses in a variety of fields, the incompatibility of some of the projects assembled under the term 'queer' can be problematic and lead to misunderstandings. In particular, as mentioned above, the post-structural insights into subjectivity underpinning queer theory mean that queer theorists generally avoid using 'queer' as a noun, given that this makes the identity categories relating to sexuality and gender more 'solid' than they are.

In recent years, a body of scholarship engaging with the notion of 'queer' has emerged within criminology. Developing from the work of scholars such as Stephen Tomsen and Nic Groombridge (among others), such criminological scholarship has grown since the mid-1990s into a discernible sub-field often referred to as 'queer criminology', with some key publications now establishing the parameters of the field (Ball et al. 2014; Dwyer et al. 2015; Peterson and Panfil 2014). This work is quite diverse, drawing from a range of different schools of criminological thought, and reflecting the numerous ways that 'queer' can be utilized and understood.

For example, many of these works approach queer as a noun and explore LGBTIQ experiences of a range of traditional criminological problems or criminal justice issues. By considering queer experiences as victims or offenders, and their interactions with the institutions of criminal justice, these studies make a 'corrective' contribution, addressing the absence of such discussions from criminology. Many such contributions focus on issues of homophobic and transphobic hate crime, intimate partner violence, bullying and interactions between LGBTIQ people and the police (see Dwyer et al. 2015; Peterson and Panfil 2014). By virtue of the fact that they focus on overlooked and marginalized communities, seek to open a criminological space in which their experiences can be understood and considered, and hope to ensure that crime and justice policy is reformed in order to reduce injustice, these studies clearly align with critical criminologies. Such scholars can also align with the tasks of 'mainstream' criminology, however, given that the inclusion of LGBTIQ experiences in these traditional concerns of criminological research does not necessarily lead to a thorough deconstruction of criminology and the forms of regulation and normativity that it produces.

Other studies have engaged more closely with queer theory, aligning with the deconstructive aspects of 'queer'. These studies have examined critically the way in which LGBTIQ people are represented in criminological and criminal justice discourse and practice; unpacked the regulation of sexuality and gender through criminal justice institutions; and identified the essentialized understandings of LGBTIQ people that continue to permeate these disciplines and practices, in order to challenge the forms of normativity inherent in those understandings (see Dwyer et al. 2015; Peterson and Panfil 2014). While perhaps not as widespread as the more 'corrective' approaches mentioned above – due no doubt to the relatively slow pace with which critical concepts from outside the discipline are taken up, and the limited presence of deconstructive approaches within criminology generally – these critical discussions offer substantial promise for further 'queering' criminology.

Since its emergence in the 1980s, queer theory has been declared dead a number of times, yet it continues to provoke insightful work across the humanities and social sciences. In doing so, it has garnered its share of criticisms, some of which have filtered into considerations about the directions that queer criminology ought to take. Many such criticisms relate to the importance of post-structural thought and deconstructive approaches to queer theory. These critiques suggest that the focus of deconstructive queer work on analysing discourses occurs at an abstract level, and at the expense of an interest in the material – that is, in material relations that produce injustice in a person's life. Relatedly, concerns have been raised about the way in which the deconstruction of identity categories 'may discount the experiences of people who identify with, and experience marginalisation on the basis of, those differences' (Woods 2014:30). Despite the fact that queer theorists analyse the discursive precisely *because of* its role in shaping the material and in mediating the way in which we think about and interact in the world, and also take very seriously the power and importance of identity categories in people's lives, these critiques persist and often stem from a clash of the conceptual and theoretical assumptions underpinning the work of researchers in these areas. Nevertheless, such critiques ought to be addressed in the development of queer criminology.

As this field is still in its early stages of development, criminological engagements with queer theory can only increase. It can be argued that the silence surrounding the experiences of LGBTIQ people in criminal justice is so loud, and their lack of visibility such a pressing concern, that effectively *all* attention paid to these issues is urgent and necessary. While not all such work will necessarily engage explicitly with queer theory, it will nevertheless contribute to the increasing deployment of 'queer' (and the variety of ideas brought together by that term) within criminology, and thus the development of greater discursive space for such engagements. A key question that scholars must consider in developing this body of work is whether queer criminology ought to become part of the mainstream of criminology or remain on the margins, continually deconstructing criminological objects of knowledge in order to unearth the forms of normativity embedded within crime and criminal justice, and the existence and operation of binaries within these knowledges and institutions. While either path is productive, it would seem that for many queer criminological scholars the answer to this question depends largely on which path is more likely to lead to greater justice for LGBTIQ people.

References

Ball, Matthew, Carrie L. Buist, and Jordan B. Woods. 2014. Queer/ing Criminology: New Directions and Frameworks. *Critical Criminology* 22(1): Special issue.

Dwyer, Angela, Matthew Ball, and Thomas Crofts (eds). 2015. *Queering Criminology*. Basingstoke: Palgrave Macmillan.

Foucault, Michel. 1998. *The Will to Knowledge: The History of Sexuality*, Vol. 1. London: Penguin.

Halperin, David. 1995. *Saint Foucault: Towards a Gay Hagiography*. Oxford: Oxford University Press.

Peterson, Dana, and Vanessa R. Panfil (eds). 2014. *Handbook of LGBT Communities, Crime, and Justice*. New York: Springer.

Woods, Jordan B. 2014. 'Queering criminology': Overview of the state of the field. In *The Handbook of LGBT Communities, Crime, and Justice*, Dana Peterson and Vanessa R. Panfil, eds, pp. 15–42. New York: Springer.

Further reading

Ball, Matthew. 2016. *Criminology and Queer Theory: Dangerous Bedfellows?* London: Palgrave Macmillan.

Buist, Carrie L., and Emily Lenning. 2015. *Queer Criminology*. London: Routledge.

Groombridge, Nic. 1999. Perverse Criminologies: The Closet of Doctor Lombroso. *Social and Legal Studies* 8(4): 531–48.

Stanley, Eric A., and Nat Smith (eds). 2011. *Captive Genders: Trans Embodiment and the Prison Industrial Complex*. Oakland, CA: AK Press.

Sullivan, Nikki. 2003. *A Critical Introduction to Queer Theory*. New York: New York University Press.

Tomsen, Stephen. 1997. Was Lombroso a queer? Criminology, criminal justice, and the heterosexual imaginary. In *Homophobic Violence*, Gail Mason and Stephen Tomsen, eds, pp. 33–45. Annandale, NSW: Hawkins Press.

Social harm/zemiology

Lois Presser

It was only a matter of time before scholars would conceptualize a discipline centred on harm rather than crime. Radical criminologists since the 1970s have observed that government-defined 'crime' is a biased designation for activities that threaten the (capitalist) status quo and not necessarily those that cause harm. Schwendinger and Schwendinger (1970) called for a definition of crime as violation of human rights. **Feminist and critical-race scholars** have exposed justice systems that reproduce current social hierarchies through selective criminalization and enforcement. They have also made clear that the criminal justice system itself causes tremendous suffering that is perfectly legal. Studies of **environmental harm** have shown that actions and arrangements immeasurably destructive of ecological, non-human and human health and well-being are beyond the reach of the state. In short, a fair consensus exists that whereas some crime is not harmful, much harm is not crime, and that criminal justice is a morally stained enterprise.

The social harm perspective, or zemiology (from *zemia*, Greek for harm), was formally launched in 1999 at a meeting of social scientists at the University of Bristol in England. A landmark book titled *Beyond Criminology: Taking Harm Seriously* followed. Its editors presented an incisive critique of criminology:

> Our argument is that a number of consequences arise as a direct result of the bracketing of crime from other harms and focusing extensively on

See Chapter 3.6 Feminist criminologies; Chapter 4.26 Patriarchy and crime; Chapter 3.13 Radical feminism; Chapter 4.7 Critical race theory

See Chapter 4.11 Environmental justice and victimology; Chapter 4.13 Genocide and ecocide; Chapter 4.16 Green criminology; Chapter 4.35 Speciesism and theriocide criminal harm. It provides a highly partial, biased and distorted view of the nature and extent of harms people experience during their lifetime and makes any attempt to explain the origins of criminal harms suspect. Moreover, it helps to perpetuate the belief that the solution to many different forms of social harm is by criminalizing them and ratcheting up and broadening the aims of the criminal justice system. More fundamentally, it leads to a neglect of much more damaging and dangerous forms of harm.

(Hillyard et al. 2004:2)

Against the 'distorting and distorted approach of criminology' (p.9), Hillyard and colleagues envision an interdisciplinary and policy-relevant field concerned with physical, financial/economic, emotional/psychological and cultural injuries. Hence, their volume contains chapters on poverty, emotional abuse of children and heterosexuality as harm, among other issues. More recent books in a Studies in Social Harm series, and others in progress or in press, suggest that the approach has taken root.

See Chapter 5.15
Restorative justice

In addition, the **'restorative justice' philosophy**, which has received international attention as the framework for such varied practices as victim–offender meetings and national truth and reconciliation commissions, stands ready to partner with zemiology. According to that philosophy, crime is harm and justice necessitates the repair of harm (Zehr 1990). Interventions based on restorative justice seek to meet the needs caused by offending behaviour, as well as the needs that give rise to it by engaging the capacities of victims, offenders and supportive community members. In effect, restorative justice is zemiology in practice.

See Chapter 3.3
Critical
criminologies

If zemiology is a logical next step in the progression of **critical criminology**, it is also a logical framework for the problems of contemporary life on the planet which victimize *and* implicate multitudes. Accordingly, Hillyard and colleagues focus on the myriad harms produced by a contemporary global neoliberal regime, while others have indicted certain modes of capitalism. In *Why We Harm*, Presser (2013) does not situate her arguments historically, but devotes a good deal of attention to harm from ignorance and knowledge avoidance, which are undoubtedly nurtured by today's frenetic pace, information fatigue, hyper-reality and free-agent/irresponsible ethos. A discipline focused on social harm is right for these times. But is it feasible? And is it warranted? The rest of this chapter entertains these critical questions.

How feasible is a discipline (or a sub-discipline) centred on harm? Hillyard and colleagues (2004:19) observe that a 'possible problem with a social harm approach is with its broadness, its encompassing nature'. The field seems boundary-less: even relatively mundane actions are proper subjects of study. In a related vein, the designation of some action as harm is highly subjective. People call different things 'harmful' depending, among other things, on their social position and relation to the event – hence perpetrators' denials of injury and allegations of false memories concerning childhood sexual abuse. Competing harm claims are common in civil society and public-policy debates, such as alleged jobs versus environment conflicts.

Zemiology, as a field, can police trivial topics: this is nothing new in academia, and scholars can grapple empirically with contested harms. A bigger problem, it would seem, is that zemiology opens floodgates to unintended harms. One may cause harm without meaning to do so; operational distinctions between more and less and not at all responsible parties are clearly necessary (see, e.g., Pemberton 2007). Some of the aforementioned problems plague 'crime' as well. Crime is the term for a broad category of activities, and crime is highly subjective – although in many studies, especially those using official data, researchers gloss over the fact that the data are based on someone's discretion. It remains subject to debate whether breadth is a problem for a discipline: consider how biology, philosophy or physics examine a breathtaking (and growing) array of phenomena.

Regarding the value of zemiology, the question we must ask is: Do we even need it? Hughes maintains that critical criminology already provides ample space for the study of non-criminalized harms. He wonders: 'is the figure of a singular criminology at best a convenient but simplifying "straw(wo)man"?' (2006:158). No doubt criminology is now complex and heterogeneous. But a distinct zemiology has something unique to contribute.

Zemiology is potentially broader than critical criminology, encompassing, for example, teasing and the hurt experienced by straight white men. These topics could be scrutinized within contexts of political economy and ideology to yield general insights. The fact is that they have not been within the confines of any sort of criminology. On this point, Pemberton's (2007:29) point that 'even critical criminology has neglected significant examples of human suffering', not to mention nonhuman suffering, becomes even more salient. In addition, more than a few critical criminologists pine for 'getting tough' on corporate criminals, whereas zemiologists' sensitivity about doing harm affords scrutiny to that impulse as well.

Specific harms aside, zemiologists using quantitative data can produce new understandings of social factors in offending. For example, criminologists consistently observe that young people offend more often than older people; that males offend more and commit more serious crimes than females; that African-Americans commit certain conventional crimes at higher rates than do white people; and that most offending behaviour targets people of the same race and class. Such knowledge is shaken up when the phenomenon under investigation is harm, potentially overturning taken-for-granted ideas about (causes of) 'misconduct'.

Finally, zemiology demands a reflexive stance that is much talked about but seldom achieved (or, if achieved, sustained) in criminology or other social sciences. Criminologists generally ask why other people do the bad or deviant things they do. Whereas critical criminologists emphasize structural and cultural arrangements, when they turn attention to someone's agency, it is the agency of (elite) others and not themselves. Yet most of us, including scholars, have done and do both direct and indirect harm. Given their charge, zemiologists must turn at least some attention to their own involvement in harm.

It is for this reason that Presser titled her book *Why We Harm* and analysed discourses of meat-eating, including the ones that she deploys as a meat-eater. Bibbings (2004:235) warns against the 'danger of being overly reductive by describing a concept as solely harmful', following an analysis of heterosexuality causing harm via its reduction of sexuality to person categories.

In sum, 'social harm' or zemiology offers a hub for studies of diverse injuries in the world. Zemiology is most usefully located within criminology, as a productive thorn in the side of the discipline. Wherever it is located, by staking a territory explicitly and nominally we can move beyond talking about mainstream criminology and talk about and theorize harm instead. The work can be altogether productive: we can grow the field.

References

Bibbings, Lois. 2004. Heterosexuality as harm: Fitting in. In *Beyond Criminology: Taking Harm Seriously*, Paddy Hillyard, Christina Pantazis, Steve Tombs, and Dave Gordon, eds, pp. 217–35. London: Pluto.

Hillyard, Paddy, Christina Pantazis, Steve Tombs, and Dave Gordon (eds). 2004. *Beyond Criminology: Taking Harm Seriously*. London: Pluto.

Hughes, Gordon. 2006. Book Review: Beyond Criminology: Taking Harm Seriously. *Social Legal Studies* 15(1): 157–9.

Pemberton, Simon. 2007. Social Harm Future(s): Exploring the Potential of the Social Harm Approach. *Crime, Law and Social Change* 48(1): 27–41.

Presser, Lois. 2013. *Why We Harm*. New Brunswick, NJ and London: Rutgers University Press.

Schwendinger, Herman, and Julia Schwendinger. 1970. Defenders of Order or Guardians of Human Rights? *Issues in Criminology* 5(2): 123–57.

Zehr, Howard. 1990. *Changing Lenses: A New Focus for Crime and Justice*. Scottsdale, PA: Herald Press.

Further reading

Faludi, Susan. 1999. *Stiffed: The Betrayal of the American Man*. New York: HarperCollins.

Kowalski, Robin M. 2003. *Complaining, Teasing, and Other Annoying Behaviors*. New Haven, CT and London: Yale University Press.

Kramer, Ronald C. 1985. Defining the Concept of Crime: A Humanistic Perspective. *Journal of Sociology and Social Welfare* 12(3): 469–87.

Michalowski, Raymond J. 1985. *Order, Law, and Crime: An Introduction to Criminology*. New York: Random House.

Pemberton, Simon A. 2015. *Harmful Societies: Understanding Social Harm*. Bristol: Policy Press.

Reiman, Jeffrey. 2006. Book Review: Beyond Criminology: Taking Harm Seriously. *British Journal of Criminology* 46(2): 362–4.

White, Rob. 2014. *Environmental Harm: An Eco-Justice Perspective*. Bristol: Policy Press.

Southern theory

Albert de la Tierra and Kathryn Henne

Criminology, like most social sciences, has imperialist roots and has received notable criticism for its treatment of difference. The discipline has been charged with disavowing difference even as it romanticizes 'others' in significant ways. Southern theory aids in understanding how this seemingly paradoxical treatment of difference has emerged, and still persists, because it confronts the **postcolonial** implications at the core of social-science scholarship.

See Chapter 4.27 Postcolonial criminology

Southern theory draws critical attention to periphery–centre relations, with a focus on how knowledge takes shape amid power dynamics that are marked by authority, exclusion and inclusion, hegemony and appropriation. It emphasizes the unequal relations between intellectuals and institutions in the North Atlantic, a hegemonic centre, and the world periphery – those places and spaces in which ways of thinking are often discredited, subordinated, ignored or granted no intellectual authority. Accordingly, Southern theory, as an intellectual project, questions and challenges the privileging of the North Atlantic within the realm of knowledge production.

In *Southern Theory*, Australian sociologist Raewyn Connell contends that Northern theory often makes universal claims, even though the global periphery generates significant and distinct social theories. Claims asserted and buttressed by Northern beliefs are thus likely to serve hegemony rather than liberation, especially when such claims ignore the experience of the majority world (Connell 2009:x). Connell argues that theory at the margins of the social sciences deserves serious and unprejudiced engagement because it offers important insight overlooked by mainstream social science. Whereas Northern theory makes broad claims to knowledge based on ontologies of the North Atlantic, Southern theory illuminates the limits of Northern theory by underscoring how it reflects a particular position of privilege.

Southern theory calls for countering the skewed nature of Northern-dominated scholarly values. According to Connell, knowledge production reflects colonial structures. The birth of sociology, for example, took place in 'the urban and cultural centres of the major imperial powers at the high tide of modern imperialism. They were the "metropole," in the useful French term, to the larger colonial world' (Connell 2009:9). She reminds us that most contemporary social-scientific claims stem from nineteenth-century efforts to deal with the anxieties underlying modernity. Founding figures of social-scientific canons sought to explain global difference, but they did so from the position of the metropole and a gaze preoccupied with distinguishing the metropolitan citizen from the colonial Other. In short, European imperialism enabled the genesis of contemporary social science. Thus, the weaknesses of modern social theory do not simply lie in its North Atlantic centrality; they also stem from its enduring colonial features.

Although most present-day social science does not explicitly adopt an imperialist gaze, it does present a skewed vision of the world. As Connell (2011:288) explains further:

> Much of current sociological thought is based on a great fantasy – that the world of the metropole is all there is, or all that matters, so that theories developed from the social experience of the metropole are all that sociology needs.

More specifically, the widespread privileging of Northern frameworks reveals four core tendencies (Connell 2009:44–8):

1. *The claim of universality*: Knowledge produced in the North Atlantic is tacitly assumed to hold universal relevance. Moreover, Northern intellectuals assume that all societies are not only knowable, but also knowable through their vantage point. Knowledge generated in the periphery is thus challenged for its relevance outside of its specific context.
2. *Reading from the centre*: Most Northern theory emerges as a resolution for antinomies, problems or weaknesses in previous Northern theories; it responds to a Northern canon, in turn either dismissing other knowledges or pushing them to the margins.
3. *Gestures of exclusion*: Social thought of colonized cultures is treated as irrelevant to the 'real' theoretical debates or surpassed by metropolitan thinking.
4. *Grand erasure*: The core of theoretical conversations is in dialogue with empirical realities. Empirical knowledge is increasingly focused on or concerned with metropolitan society's problems, the effect of which is an erasure of the majority of the world's experience.

Taken together, these four tenets reveal that both theoretical and empirical forms of knowledge retain embedded postcolonial contours, as well as geopolitical and epistemological assumptions of the North Atlantic. In order to expose and challenge the assumptions embedded in knowledge, Southern theory demonstrates how so-called 'peripheral' societies, many of which are former colonies, produce knowledges with as much intellectual power as metropolitan social thought.

How can Southern theory inform contemporary criminology and future inquiry? Meaningful criminological engagement with Southern theory first requires the acknowledgement that criminology itself is a consequence of imperialist anxieties. This is a step beyond the recognition that criminological theories posit universal claims to understanding crime and deviance that are not devoid of context or politics. In making such assertions, criminological theory undermines other forms of knowledge, particularly those that reflect ideas and worldviews of places outside the North Atlantic. The second step requires identifying the ways in which those anxieties are manifest in current paradigms, including both those that are mainstream and those that are critical in nature. This approach also demands the consideration of relationships that at first seem beyond the scope of criminology: for example, posing questions about citizenship, belonging, disenfranchisement and inequality that inform who and what becomes accounted for in notions of crime and deviance. Southern theory also requires criminologists to take seriously, work with and value ideas from the periphery. While a growing number of criminologists have acknowledged this need, few have proposed pathways for building periphery–centre connections (e.g., Braithwaite 2013; Carrington et al. 2015).

In light of these critical imperatives, criminologists face three immediate problems when it comes to employing Southern theory. First, there is a professional challenge. Given the Northern bias of criminology, Southern theorizing is likely to happen outside disciplinary boundaries and professional channels of scholarly dissemination. The perspectives of the periphery are often out of reach as metropolitan forms of knowledge production and communication place little value on the intellectual labour necessary to adopt alternative epistemologies and research questions. Braithwaite states that this reflects criminology's growing internal obsession, which lends to asking 'narrower questions, using a narrower set of methodologies about a narrow set of institutions', and which he warns can yield a 'cross-cultural wasteland' and a 'pile up of theoretical dead wood'. 'In this context,' he explains, 'even being a critical criminologist might suggest that you are not a very critical scholar at all because criminology is such a narrow thing to be critical about' (2013:9).

Second, treating vast geographic spaces under a single umbrella term puts the neophyte global theorist at risk of overlooking constellations of cultures and their varying relationships to the metropole. Southern theory is not intended to homogenize the perspectives of the periphery. It is intended to highlight long-lasting patterns of inequality in power, wealth and cultural influence that grow out of historical and material experiences with North Atlantic imperialism.

Third, criminologists attentive to Southern theory inevitably must grapple with the ways in which alternative perspectives are also produced within Northern contexts. Newton (1970) expressed this in an address to the Revolutionary People's Constitutional Convention in Washington, DC, in the mid-1960s: 'We are aware that many of us are the descendants of those who were captured and enslaved so that their labor could build the wealth of this nation.' Those legacies too carry over into the North Atlantic and its world position, highlighting complex Southern standpoints that exist within geographic territories putatively understood as the privileged North.

In sum, Southern theory requires the recognition and interrogation of broader postcolonial relationships, a task that Carrington and colleagues (2015) elaborate upon as essential to creating new criminologies. Some criminologists suggest the need for more ethnographies of the periphery so as to better grasp the nuances of understudied spaces and the distinct contributions of Southern ideas. Others call for greater support of **Aboriginal and First Nations scholars** in order to bolster their numbers in the ranks of criminology and to build collaborative networks in parts of the world with few criminologists, such as Pacific Island nations. Periphery–centre partnerships, in particular, offer opportunities for new insight into interconnected global problems. For instance, as Braithwaite (2013:10) states, 'Northern market economies might learn from Western Pacific gift economies in the process of Pacific criminologists becoming more ambitious about their special niche in the invigoration of the social sciences.' These strategies alone, however, do not guarantee the institutionalization of Southern theoretical perspectives into criminology: rethinking the dilemmas of difference at the discipline's core is imperative.

See Chapter 4.18 Indigenous criminology

The experiences of scholars of colour in other fields illustrate how the kind of reflexive engagement required by Southern theory can disrupt the foundations of social science. For example, anthropologists of colour in the United States have drawn attention to how their discipline posits a narrow notion of difference – one that tends to rely on a binary distinction between a (Northern) researcher and a (Southern) Other. As anthropologists of colour often offer alternative vantage points, their scholarship is often not legible to a traditional anthropological gaze. In contrast, interdisciplinary fields – such as ethnic, gender and cultural studies – are more inclusive of ethnographers of colour (Navarro et al. 2013:445).

Although fraught with challenges, criminology might do well to follow the lead of other fields in accounting for how it perpetuates particular notions of difference. The difficult task of pursuing Southern theory offers possibilities of new, even counter-hegemonic, modes of generating knowledge. Doing so, however, arguably requires rethinking criminology as a broader interdisciplinary project that questions the place of crime and deviance in a postcolonial world.

384

References

Braithwaite, John. 2013. One Retrospective of Pacific Criminology. *Australian and New Zealand Journal of Criminology* 46(1): 3–11.

Carrington, Kerry, Russell Hogg, and Máximo Sozzo. 2015. Southern Criminology. *British Journal of Criminology* 56(1): 1–20.

Connell, Raewyn. 2009. *Southern Theory: The Global Dynamics of Knowledge in Social Science*. Cambridge: Polity.

Connell, Raewyn. 2011. Sociology for the Whole World. *International Sociology* 26(3): 288–91.

Navarro, Tami, Bianca Williams, and Attiya Ahmad. 2013. Sitting at the Kitchen Table: Fieldnotes from Women of Color in Anthropology. *Cultural Anthropology* 28(3): 443–63.

Newton, Huey P. 1970/2009. Resolutions and declarations. In *To Die for the People: The Writings of Huey P. Newton*, Toni Morrison, ed., pp. 39–43. San Francisco: City Lights.

Further reading

Aas, Katja. 2012. 'The Earth Is One but the World Is Not': Criminological Theory and Its Geopolitical Divisions. *Theoretical Criminology* 16(1): 5–20.

Blagg, Harry, and Thalia Anthony. Forthcoming. *Decolonising Criminology*. London: Palgrave Macmillan.

Cain, Maureen. 2000. Orientalism, Occidentalism, and the Sociology of Crime. *British Journal of Criminology* 40(2), 239–60.

Fraser, Alistair. 2013. Ethnography at the Periphery: Redrawing the Borders of Criminology's World-Map. *Theoretical Criminology* 17(2): 251–60.

Lee, Maggy, and Karen J. Laidler. 2013. Doing Criminology from the Periphery: Crime and Punishment in Asia. *Theoretical Criminology* 17(2): 141–57.

Speciesism and theriocide

Martine Synnøve Bergersen Lie and Ragnhild Sollund

Speciesism concerns normalized repressive attitudes and practices of humans towards other species, and it relates to other forms of oppression, such as sexism and racism. The term, 'speciesism', was coined by Richard Ryder in a leaflet circulated at Oxford University in 1970, and was further developed by Peter Singer in *Animal Liberation* (1975). Speciesist attitudes and practices are shown to be extensive, with deep historical and cultural roots, and held and practised by most humans (Nibert 2002; Singer 1975; Sollund 2012). This makes speciesism more of a description and diagnosis of the human–animal relationship than a theory. Speciesist practices often involve or lead to 'theriocide', a term coined by Piers Beirne (2014) to describe human killing of non-human animals.

See Chapter 4.16
Green criminology

Speciesism is a central concept in **green and eco-global criminologies**, which include not only environmental harms and human **victimization**, but also non-human animals as victims of harm and foci of study. The concept of speciesism is based on **a broad definition of harm** (legal and illegal, intentional and unintentional, and direct and indirect actions causing harm), reveals disproportionate power structures, and pays attention to marginalized groups and individuals.

See Chapter 4.11
Environmental justice and victimology;
Chapter 4.39
Victimology

See Chapter 4.33
Social harm/
zemiology

Speciesist practices, such as meat-eating, can be described as *doxic* – taken for granted and unquestioned, and part of most people's habitus and daily lives. These practices are facilitated and justified both consciously and unconsciously through 'techniques of neutralization' and mechanisms of 'denial' (Sollund 2012). These techniques and mechanisms justify and conceal the discriminatory basis of certain acts, and are used by individuals and public and private corporations and institutions (Sollund 2012; Nibert 2002). Due to the hegemonic character of speciesist practices, abstinence from them often breaks the social continuum and is often met with discomfort and little understanding by people partaking in the practices (Sollund 2012).

See Chapter 2.7
Techniques of
neutralization

Singer's framework of speciesism (1975) is utilitarian, comparing the consequences of similar actions carried out towards humans and other animals, and their shared ability to feel pain. According to Singer, conducting and tolerating harmful actions against animals that would not be accepted if they were directed towards humans is illogical and discriminatory because individuals of other species clearly feel and express pain. In addition, animals of other species have abilities and cognitive skills that exceed some humans' (such as those of newborns or some disabled persons), so attitudes about, and practices directed at, them are not grounded in the mental or physical capabilities of these species, but rather in their classification as *not human*.

See Chapter 1.3
Utilitarianism

The publication of Singer's *Animal Liberation* in 1975 sparked the modern animal rights movement and has had a significant impact on attitudes towards animals. This is reflected in academic literature and in animal rights activism, whether in relation to the food industry, animal experimentation or other forms of systemic animal abuse. Because much animal abuse is driven by capitalist interests (Nibert 2002), protest movements are also often oppressed by the criminal justice system, and animal rights activists (such as the Animal Liberation Front) have been harshly punished.

Academic advocates for animal rights criticize Singer for condoning the infliction of harm and the killing of non-human animals by humans if the benefits outweigh the costs to the victims. Tom Regan's (1983) conceptualization of animals as 'subjects-of-a-life' implies that if we want to ascribe value to all human beings regardless of their capacity to be rational agents, then we must similarly ascribe it to non-human animals because they too have the ability to suffer and have the same interest in a continued and a pain-free life.

The focus on speciesism as an oppressive social phenomenon has created a tension between the animal welfarist movement and animal rights advocates and activists. For the former, using animals is acceptable as long as they are 'humanely' kept and killed, while the latter believe that animal exploitation will not end until animals are accorded legal rights.

See Chapter 3.6
Feminist
criminologies;
Chapter 4.26
Patriarchy and
crime; Chapter
3.13 Radical
feminism; Chapter
4.21 Masculinities,
structure and
hegemony

Singer has also been challenged by feminists, who emphasize that humans should use their empathy and what can be called their 'emotional compasses' to determine how animals should be treated. Furthermore, feminist scholars connect speciesism to male power and oppression of women (Donovan and Adams 1996). David Nibert similarly holds that it springs from an all-encompassing hierarchical culture in modern Western states, built on capitalism and market economies. This repression is economically beneficial for humans, and is therefore furthered by the state, through its social institutions, and by big corporations which have considerable influence on human values and choices (Nibert 2002).

Nibert understands speciesism to be part of a repressive ideology that sustains industrialized exploitation and the increased use of nonhuman animals that far exceeds practices pre-industrialization. For him, this culture and ideology of domination and subordination means that nonhuman animals and marginalized groups of human animals are seen and treated as 'the other'. This is due to a binary distinction in which animals are understood to be different and inferior to human animals, women as different and subordinate to men, and persons with darker skin tones as different and lesser than white people.

Central to speciesism is the 'categorization' by human animals of groups and individuals of other animals according to their ascribed 'utility'. Attitudes regarding acceptable treatment of species that are bred as food for human animals differ greatly from the ways in which species that are kept as pets are viewed. Individuals in the same 'category' are also differentiated: golden retrievers, for example, have a different status from pit bull terriers. Speciesism also permeates human–animal relations that are close, loving and nurturing; the human animal is still 'at the centre' (Sollund 2012:93) as the owner/'boss', while the other animal is captive and must obey her or his demands.

This discriminating hierarchy is also evident when it comes to the act of killing. The murder of a person belonging to an elite class by a socially disadvantaged person will garner much more media, police and popular attention than the murder of a disadvantaged person by another disadvantaged person. The same holds true for humans killing other animals, which is often accepted, legal and institutionalized. Both culturally and in legislation, other animals are mostly considered property, things without agency – not beings, persons, who can be murdered (Beirne 2014:55). The killing of a companion animal might elicit some indignation, albeit minimal compared to the attention directed towards human murder victims.

The connection between attention garnered and a murder victim's social status is especially obvious when it comes to the unimaginable number of animals killed daily and without remorse in the food, clothing and pet industry, and for research, sport and entertainment. The number is inconceivable partly because many of these killings are never registered; nor are they perceived as murders, because the victims are usually considered expendable. These killings are made possible and concealed, especially by spatial and linguistic distancing: in the case of the former, locating slaughterhouses far from residential areas and city centres, and only involving a small percentage of slaughterhouse workers in the actual physical killing moment; in the case of the latter, using euphemisms such as 'beef' and 'ham' to describe the flesh and muscle of cows and pigs for human consumption (see Beirne 2014).

While the term 'homicide' covers all murders of humans, there is no parallel word for the murders of other animals, even though they are much more common. Words such as 'speciecide' or 'ecocide' also relate to the large-scale killing of animals, but are either expressions of speciesism or not exclusively applied to animals other than humans. In this respect, Beirne has proposed 'theriocide' as a term to cover the diverse human actions that cause the deaths of animals – a way of naming and acknowledging all the killing of nonhuman animals by humans, and creating a more honest way to talk about these killings than the euphemisms often used. The derivation of the term is explained in Beirne (2014).

As with the killing of one human by another, a theriocide can be socially acceptable or unacceptable, legal or illegal, intentional or unintentional. It can involve active maltreatment or passive neglect and 'may occur one-on-one, in small groups or in large-scale social institutions. The numerous sites of theriocide include intensive rearing regimes; hunting and fishing; trafficking; vivisection; militarism; pollution; and human-induced climate change' (Beirne 2014:55).

Both speciesism and theriocide are concepts that express 'opposition to human dominion over animals' (Beirne 2014:56). They are theoretical concepts taking a stand, acknowledging and highlighting the situation for marginalized and discriminated groups in modern societies – animals other than humans. This, together with their broad definitions of harm, makes them part of a critical criminological research tradition, invested in critically analysing the status quo, revealing disproportionate power structures and aiding disadvantaged groups.

References

Beirne, Piers. 2014. Theriocide: Naming Animal Killing. *International Journal for Crime, Justice and Social Democracy* 3(2): 50–67.

Donovan, Josephine, and Carol J. Adams. 1996. *Beyond Animal Rights: A Feminist Caring Ethic for the Treatment of Animals*. New York: Continuum.

Nibert, David. 2002. *Animal Rights/Human Rights: Entanglements of Oppression and Liberation*. Lanham, MD: Rowman & Littlefield.

Regan, Tom. 1983. *The Case for Animal Rights*. Berkeley: University of California Press.

Singer, Peter. 1975. *Animal Liberation: A New Ethics for Our Treatment of Animals*. New York: Random House.

Sollund, R. 2012. Speciesism as doxic practice versus valuing difference and plurality. In *Eco-Global Crimes: Contemporary Problems and Future Challenges*, Rune Ellefsen, Ragnhild Sollund, and Guri Larsen, eds, pp. 91–113. Farnham: Ashgate.

Further reading

Adams, Carol J. 2010. *The Sexual Politics of Meat: A Feminist Vegetarian Critical Theory*. New York: Bloomsbury Academic.

Agnew, Robert. 1998. The Causes of Animal Abuse: A Social Psychological Analysis. *Theoretical Criminology* 2(2): 177–210.

Beirne, Piers. 1999. For a Nonspeciesist Criminology: Animal Abuse as an Object of Study. *Criminology: An Interdisciplinary Journal* 37(1): 117–49.

Benton, Ted. 1998. Rights and Justice on a Shared Planet: More Rights or New Relations. *Theoretical Criminology* 2(2): 149–75.

Dunayer, Joan. 2001. *Animal Equality: Language and Liberation*. Derwood, MD: Ryce.

Francione, Gary. 1998. *Animals as Persons*: *Essays on the Abolition of Animal Exploitation*. New York: Columbia University Press.

Noske, Barbara. 1997. *Beyond Boundaries: Humans and Animals*. Montreal: Black Rose.

State crime

Phil Scraton

What constitutes 'state crime' appears self-evident: acts or omissions that breach a state's own criminal law or international criminal law. All states – monarchic, totalitarian, oligarchic, democratic – claim authority for the power to govern, legislate and regulate their subjects. In exercising state power, legitimacy is derived and maintained through regulatory processes underpinned by the 'rule of law'. Clearly, the degree to which a state is considered 'authoritarian' depends on where it is situated on a continuum ranging between dictatorial regimes presided over by military juntas or ruling oligarchs and participatory advanced democracies in which citizens have the right to vote for their political leaders.

Whatever their formation, all 'modern states' claim legitimacy for their *'monopoly of the legitimate use of physical force* within a given territory' (Weber 2009:77–8, emphasis in original). This assumes a fundamental relationship between geographical boundaries, political autonomy and legal jurisdiction. Territories, however, are contested terrains, their complexity locked into histories of invasion, annexation and colonization. Each of these aggressive processes of dominance generated power and authority, wielded initially by a colonizing ruling state, eventually transitioning to neo-colonial state forms. Consequently, states are neither easily mapped nor easily categorized by their internal structural relations or by external political allies. Given this complexity, defining 'state crime' is not straightforward.

The International State Crime Initiative (http://statecrime.org) recognizes that identifying 'serious crimes' committed 'by governments and their officials – genocide, war crimes, torture and corruption' – should be 'uncontroversial'.

Yet, a 'purely legal definition' of state crime is limited as it excludes institutionalized 'mass violations of human rights', invariably supported by embedded processes of truth concealment. As Kramer and Michalowski (2005:446) note, the study of state crime must extend beyond harms that states choose to criminalize. States 'rarely criminalize the social harms they commit', or acknowledge their own 'violations of international law'. The category of state crime should also include crimes committed, but excused as legitimate, during periods of internal armed conflict. Finally, it must be recognized that the due process of criminal law privileges and protects the state by emphasizing personal liability rather than interrogating the culpability of state institutions.

See Chapter 4.13
Genocide and
ecocide

In Germany in the 1930s, the rise and consolidation of the Third Reich, using state powers and authority to impose a programme of selective internment, and to then legitimate systemic **genocide** – eliminating Jews, Roma, communists, homosexuals and others labelled 'alien' – remains the starkest contemporary illustration of institutionalized state crime directed *inward* towards its citizens. Its occupation and annexation of neighbouring states, exporting terror, torture and the Holocaust, remains an unequivocal demonstration of state crime directed *outward* across sovereign borders.

Complexity in defining state crime, however, is well illustrated by the long-running debate concerning the British and Allied forces' orchestrated bombing of Dresden in the last months of World War II. Much of a defenceless city was razed to the ground, killing over 20,000 civilians. Alongside the US bombing of Nagasaki and Hiroshima, the bombing of Dresden was described initially by the British prime minister, Winston Churchill, as an act of 'terror', thus questioning the legitimacy of targeting a civilian population as an act of reprisal rather than war.

More recently, the long-term incarceration of men captured by US military forces in Afghanistan and Iraq as part of its ongoing 'war on terror' has caused international concern about the legitimacy of military offensives conducted from the air and on the ground, using extraordinary rendition, commissioning torture by third-party states and imprisoning without charge those categorized 'enemy combatants' (Scraton 2007). The use of Guantanamo Bay, a US military prison in Cuba outside US jurisdiction, has allowed successive US administrations a thread of legitimacy in contesting the claim that incarceration without trial constituted an egregious breach of international criminal law. The US Government's commitment to overthrowing regimes in Afghanistan and Iraq by means of a self-styled international 'coalition of liberation' was complemented by introducing 'special' legislation, particularly the 2000 PATRIOT Act. This legislation identified, policed and interned individuals considered a threat to state security within its own borders.

These examples, among many, illustrate the dynamics of state power, authority and legitimacy that constitute the foundations of policing and regulation within and beyond territorial borders. Whatever authority is claimed by advanced democratic states in deploying 'exceptional' force or imprisonment against their citizens or those of other states, it is a fine line between lawful and unlawful state actions, and claiming legitimacy for unlawful interventions. Critical reflection on the history of **colonialism**, for example, exposes genocide, slavery and torture as vehicles of subjugation, a legacy evident on US and Canadian reservations, Australian and African settlements and post-apartheid townships in South Africa.

See Chapter 4.27
Postcolonial
criminology

'Crimes' are also perpetrated against citizens or non-citizens by democratic states *within* their borders. Reflecting on the emergence of critical social analysis, Krisberg (1975:20) argued that 'the study of crime' should be situated 'within the broader quest for social justice', exposing the 'relationship of crime to the maintenance of privilege' and addressing the 'context of the structures of injustice created by the powerful to further their domination'. Developing this proposition, Quinney (1980:51) explored how, on several interlocking levels, advanced democratic states facilitate class-based 'public policy' extending to 'coercive oppression'. The maintenance and reproduction of capitalism, he argued, generates *crimes of domination* carried out 'by corporations, ranging from price-fixing to pollution of the environment' (Quinney 1980:57-8). Such activities include '*crimes of individual businessmen* [sic] *and professionals*' and the industry–state nexus of **state-corporate crime** and **organized crime**. Further, *crimes of government*, protecting and reinforcing political administrations, extend to unlawful monitoring and regulation of 'persons and groups who would seemingly threaten national security'. Finally, beyond state borders, are *crimes of warfare*, at their most extreme, including the political assassination of foreign and domestic leaders (Quinney 1980:58).

See Chapter 4.37
State-corporate
crime

See Chapter 4.25
Organized crime

In the operation of state power, *crimes of control* encompass the institutionalization of unlawful behaviour, violence and brutality by police, prison guards and other state agents. These acts extend to civil liberty violations through non-sanctioned 'surveillance, the use of provocateurs and the illegal denial of due process'. Finally, *social injuries* occur as a consequence of 'systemic actions involving the denial of human rights' (Quinney 1980:59). Such manifestations of control and domination are 'necessary features and natural products of a capitalist political economy', components of the structural relations of inequality and unequal access to justice.

Quinney's analysis provided a comprehensive typology through which the complexity of the state's involvement in crime could be understood. In his influential text *Power, Crime and Mystification*, Box (1983:14) implicated the state's 'control agencies, criminologists, and the media' in 'conceptualiz[ing] a particular and ideological version of serious crime and who commits it', not least by 'concealing and hence mystifying its own propensity for violence and serious crimes on a much larger scale'. Defined exclusively by the state, 'crime' formed only part of the story: 'the powerful commit devastating crimes and get away with it, whilst the powerless and "potentially dangerous" commit less serious crimes, and get prison' (Box 1983:222).

Chambliss (1989) agreed, warning that criminologists had neglected 'state-organized crime' and crimes of the powerful in their persistent preoccupation with community-based organized crime and crimes of the poor. While there was a well-established pattern of state officials, including the police, exploiting professional discretion for personal gain, Chambliss targeted practices imbedded deep within state institutions: drug-dealing, money-laundering, state-sanctioned killings and the arms trade.

Despite these significant contributions, Green and Ward (2004:1) note that 'criminology as a discipline has never regarded state crime as an integral part of its subject matter'. Their work has developed analysis of state crime beyond the parameters of criminal law violations. Criminology, they propose, 'cannot be neutral between human rights violators and their victims', for state crime is '*state organisational deviance involving the violation of human rights*' (Green and Ward 2004:2, emphasis in original). Extending the scope of analysis beyond law-breaking *within* jurisdictions, they include universally accepted harms caused by acts that compromise principles of justice established by internationally agreed human rights standards.

Green and Ward map state crime's diversity across the spectrum of advanced democratic, transitional and authoritarian states. Their detailed, complex analysis of different and distinctive state forms reveals:

- 'political and administrative' corruption;
- state-corporate crime involving the 'criminal actions of corporations' that 'produce massive human rights and environmental violations' (2004:28);
- 'police deviance in fundamental, and apparently universal, features of policing' (2004:69);
- organized crime and collusion with covert, corrupt state practices; and
- systemic forms of state terror, extending to the use of torture and genocide.

In addition, they identify states' contributions to, and responsibility for, so-called 'natural disasters' – including 'criminal actions and negligent practices' behind 'catastrophic floods, famines, earthquakes, and so on' (Green and Ward 2004:52).

See Chapter 4.33
Social harm/
zemiology

Hillyard and Tombs (2004:19-20) challenge the limitations of a 'crime' focus, arguing that **corporate and state 'harms'** should be analysed within the context of pervasive, enduring structural inequalities. These include: all forms of physical harm from negligence and neglect through to state-sanctioned brutality; financial and economic harms from poverty through to misappropriation of funds; emotional and psychological harm; and access to cultural, educational and information resources.

Expanding the focus of 'state crime' to include 'harms' that occur as a consequence of acts or omissions by those whose interventions carry state authority has been a significant advance. In addition to extending the scope of definition, critical analysis has exposed harmful behaviours and practices, not necessarily criminal acts, that are deeply institutionalized in agencies operating with state authorization and legitimacy (see Scraton 2007).

References

Box, Steven. 1983. *Power, Crime, and Mystification*. London: Tavistock.

Chambliss, William J. 1989. State organized crime. In *Organized Crime*, Nikos Passas, ed., London: Dartmouth.

Green, Penny, and Tony Ward. 2004. *State Crime: Governments, Violence and Corruption*. London: Pluto.

Hillyard, Paddy, and Steve Tombs. 2004. Beyond criminology? In *Beyond Criminology: Taking Harm Seriously*, Paddy Hillyard, Christina Pantazis, Steve Tombs and Dave Gordon, eds, pp. 10–29. London: Pluto.

Kramer, Ronald C., and Raymond J. Michalowski. 2005. War, Aggression and State Crime: A Criminological Analysis of the Invasion and Occupation of Iraq. *British Journal of Criminology* 45(4): 446–69.

Krisberg, Barry. 1975. *Crime and Privilege: Toward a New Criminology* Englewood Cliffs, NJ: Prentice Hall.

Quinney, Richard. 1980. *Class, State and Crime* (2nd edn). London: Longman.

Scraton, Phil. 2007. *Power, Conflict and Criminalisation*. Abingdon: Routledge.

Weber, Max. 2009/1985. *From Max Weber: Essays in Sociology*. Edited by Hans J.H. Gerth and C. Wright Mills. Abingdon and New York: Routledge.

Further reading

Coleman, Roy, Joe Sim, Steve Tombs, and David Whyte (eds). 2009. *State, Power, Crime*. London: Sage.

Kauzlarich, David, Christopher Mullins, and Rick Matthews. 2003. A Complicity Continuum of State Crime. *Contemporary Justice Review* 6(3): 241–54.

Ross, Jeffrey Ian, and Dawn L. Rothe. 2008. Ironies of Controlling State Crime. *International Journal of Law, Crime and Justice* 36(3): 196–210.

Rothe, Dawn L. 2009. *State Criminality: The Crime of All Crimes*. Lanham, MD: Lexington.

Tombs, Steve, and David Whyte (eds). 2003. *Unmasking the Crimes of the Powerful: Scrutinising States and Corporations*. New York and London: Lang.

4.37 State-corporate crime

Penny Green

The concept of state-corporate crime refers to crimes that result from the specific relationship between the state and commercially motivated corporations. The term was developed by Kramer and Michalowski in 1990 and employed in the 'integrated model' which encouraged a multilayered approach to understanding corporate offending within a framework of state complicity – an approach by which the structural, organizational and psychological interrogation of a deviant event was essential for its understanding (Kramer et al. 2002). The model is based on the proposition that criminal behaviour at the organizational level results from a coincidence of pressure for goal attainment, availability and perceived attractiveness of illegitimate means, and an absence of effective social control (Kramer et al. 2002:274).

A distinction was drawn between what Kramer and colleagues described as 'state-initiated corporate crime' and 'state-facilitated corporate crime'. State-initiated corporate crime occurs when corporations, employed by the government, engage in organizational deviance at the direction of, or with the tacit approval of, the government. State-facilitated corporate crime, on the other hand, occurs when government regulatory institutions fail to restrain deviant business activities, either because of direct collusion between business and government or because they adhere to shared goals whose attainment would be hampered by aggressive regulation (Kramer et al. 2002:271–2).

This approach, however, failed to recognize the existence of state crimes that have been either initiated or **facilitated by corporations**. 'Corporate-initiated state crime' occurs when corporations directly employ their economic power to coerce states into engaging in deviant actions. 'Corporate-facilitated

See Chapter 4.5
Corporate crime

state crime', on the other hand, occurs when corporations either provide the means for a state's criminality (e.g., weapons sales) or when they fail to alert the domestic/international community to the state's criminality because these deviant practices benefit the corporation concerned.

The emphasis of the integrated model is on what state crimes and other kinds of crime have in common. Crimes are rarely, if ever, committed without a motive, an **opportunity** and the failure of some form of control to prevent them (if no control mechanism at all is at work, it hardly makes sense to speak of a crime). Importantly, however, when dealing with crimes of the powerful, it is essential to understand that these are not mere individual acts. They are acts committed by people working for organizational units that in turn are part of overarching organizations – states and corporations. Thus, a criminological explanation of state crime needs to study motives, opportunities and failures of control at the structural and organizational level as well as the individual.

See Chapter 6.6
Opportunity
theory

The most persuasive and indeed emblematic case study in this model remains Kramer's powerful investigation into the organizational processes that led to the Space Shuttle *Challenger* explosion, which he argued was 'the collective product of the interaction between a government agency, the National Aeronautics and Space Administration (NASA), and a private business corporation, Morton Thiokol, Inc., (MTI)' (Kramer 1992:214). Here, however, a concentration on the confluence of interests evinced by both state and capital results in both forms being interrogated as effectively discrete entities. As Tombs (2012:175) has argued:

> despite the clearly-stated, and genuinely innovative, conceptual intentions of Michalowski and Kramer – that the focus should be on relationships not acts – the work which has utilized and indeed sought to develop this concept has overwhelmingly focused upon discrete acts and paid inadequate attention to the nature and dynamics of state-corporate relationships.

The case-study model, with its template for analysis and narrative sureties, has resulted in successive and latterly uninspiring reproductions, particularly in US scholarship – with little change in the case-study analysis save the nature of the deviant corporate entity and minor rearrangements of goals, opportunities and social control (Lasslett 2010).

The contours of state-corporate crime scholarship are, however, changing; and this change can be credited to the exciting and challenging work of UK scholars associated with the International State Crime Initiative (ISCI), in particular that of Kristian Lasslett, Thomas MacManus, Steve Tombs and Dave Whyte. Underpinning this new work is an understanding that the corporation is not independent of the nation-state but rather its creation, and that the nation-state plays a central role in supporting and maintaining the corporate form to ensure 'the mobilization, utilization and protection of capital' (Tombs 2012:176). Moreover, state-corporate crime is not atypical but routine and endemic.

In a powerful critique of the extant literature on state-corporate crime, Tombs (2012:177) captures the essence of the new direction in which state-crime scholarship is travelling:

> just as states create and sustain markets, so too can and do they create and sustain criminogenic markets, that is, markets that are conducive to, or facilitate, the production of harms and crimes. With this obviousness to the fore, what appear at first sight to be discrete events brought into view by the lens of state-corporate crime are in fact better understood as processes, that is, ongoing, enduring and complex relationships between public and private actors.

One of the key texts capturing this shift is Lasslett's (2014) seminal work on the Bougainville War – a largely hidden war that decimated the South Pacific island of Bougainville during the 1990s. At its epicentre, Lasslett exposes the mining giant Rio Tinto, which colluded with the Papua New Guinea and Australian governments to violently suppress indigenous landowner resistance against one of the world's largest copper mines. Employing unparalleled access to senior state-corporate officials and leaked records, *State Crime on the Margins of Empire* uncovers and theorizes this conspiracy from the inside, including the enduring international effort to deny survivors justice and erase their struggle from memory:

> Internment camps, the mortaring of homes, aerial bombardment, extra-judicial killings, the torture and humiliation of prisoners, rape, and the denial of humanitarian aid, these are just some of the criminal state practices endured by Bougainville residents during 1988 and 1997. Even on the margins of Empire, retribution was cruelly and indifferently applied to those who challenged 'pax Capital'.
>
> (Lasslett 2014:178)

By focusing on the conditional relationship that binds states and corporations, the field of state-corporate criminality has become both wider and more nuanced. The following two examples are further indications of this new wave of scholarship.

The role of public-relations (PR) corporations in state-crime denial presents one of the most significant new developments in state-corporate crime scholarship. In response to civil-society claims of crimes against humanity and war crimes, the Sri Lankan government hired the British PR firm Bell Pottinger to write the speech of President Mahinda Rajapaksa delivered at the UN General Assembly in September 2010, in which he vehemently denied the allegations. Similarly, in the face of public outcry in 1998, the same PR firm assisted in the campaign for the release of, and continued impunity for, Chile's Augusto Pinochet, with the slogan 'reconciliation not retribution'. Pioneered by MacManus, this area of criminological research explores and describes the interrelationship between the unveiling of state and state-corporate crime by civil society and the counter-campaigning and state-crime denial of PR firms on behalf of states. More specifically, MacManus's work aims to understand the combative relationship between civil-society organizations and PR firms in the public-arena process of labelling and counter-labelling state and state-corporate crime (MacManus 2016).

A second new area of study is that presented by **land-grabbing** and related forced evictions. Forced eviction occurs when the state uses its power – often in the service of speculative capital and regularly under conditions of corruption – to displace residents or farmers who are generally poor and often have no formal title to land. The forced migration of urban and rural populations is intimately linked with the intensity and conditions under which capital comes to accumulate in and through landed property. How capital circulates, in this respect, is of course mediated in a significant way by the organization of state power within the particular regional context. Through the conduit of urban and rural development strategies, physical planning and property regimes, states can stimulate the character, pace and conditions under which capital circulates through land (Green et al. 2014).

See Chapter 4.11 Environmental justice and victimology; Chapter 4.16 Green criminology

Rapid urbanization, enhanced transnational capital flows and shifting patterns of growth in emerging **market countries** have provoked a noticeable rise in development-based, forced evictions in countries as diverse as Azerbaijan, Brazil, Burma, Colombia, India and Papua New Guinea (Green et al. 2014; Harvey 2012). Such development-induced, mass forced evictions tend to be highly organized events, underpinned by a range of illicit processes, for instance: illegal land transactions, corruption, security-force violence, illegal use of firearms, the destruction of property and the displacement of civilians, including vulnerable groups such as children.

See Chapter 2.8 Market society and crime

References

Green, Penny, Kristian Lasslett, and Angela Sherwood. 2014. Enclosing the commons: predatory capital and forced evictions in PNG and Burma. In *The Routledge Handbook on Migration and Crime*, Sharon Pickering and Julie Ham, eds, pp. 329–50. London: Routledge.

Harvey, David. 2012. *Rebel Cities: From the Right to the City to the Urban Revolution*. London: Verso.

Kramer, Ronald C. 1992. The Space Shuttle *Challenger* explosion. In *White Collar Crime Reconsidered*, Kip Schlegel and David Weisburd, eds, pp. 214ff. Boston: Northeastern University Press.

Kramer, Ronald C. and Raymond J. Michalowski. 1990. State-corporate crime. Paper presented at the annual meeting of the American Society of Criminology, November, Baltimore, Maryland.

Kramer, Ronald C., Raymond J. Michalowski, and David Kauzlarich. 2002. The Origins and Development of the Concept and Theory of State-Corporate Crime. *Crime and Delinquency* 48(2): 263–82.

Lasslett, Kristian. 2010. Scientific Method and the Crimes of the Powerful. *Critical Criminology* 18(3): 211–28.

Lasslett, Kristian. 2014. *State Crime on the Margins of Empire*. London: Pluto.

MacManus, Thomas. 2016. The Denial Industry: Public Relations, 'Crisis Management' and Corporate Crime. *International Journal of Human Rights* 20(6): 785–97.

Tombs, Steve. 2012. State-Corporate Symbiosis in the Production of Crime and Harm. *State Crime* 1(2): 170–95.

Further reading

Green, Penny, and Tony Ward. 2004. *State Crime: Governments, Violence and Corruption*. London: Pluto.

Tombs, Steve, and David Whyte. 2009. The state and corporate crime. In *State, Power, Crime*, Roy Coleman, Joe Sim, Steve Tombs, and David Whyte, eds, pp. 103–15. London: Sage.

Ultra-realism

Steve Hall and Simon Winlow

Ultra-realism is one of the first new criminological paradigms to emerge in the twenty-first century. Its advocates argue that, without neglecting the intersectional injustices that pervade the criminal justice system and broader society, criminology must return to its fundamental question: why do some individuals and groups risk harm to others as they pursue their instrumental and expressive interests? Criminology must be able to offer convincing explanations of mutating forms of crime and harm in today's world. To do this, the discipline requires a new theoretical paradigm and the adoption of ethnography as its principal research method.

As a first step towards theoretical reconstruction, proponents of ultra-realism contend that criminology must look beyond the slippery socio-legally constructed concept of crime towards the more ontologically grounded concept of **harm**. Ultra-realism remains on the critical side of the fence but responds to the inadequacy of the **social constructionism** that dominates older critical criminologies. The moves towards social constructionism and **intersectionality** since the mid-1960s have fragmented criminology into a matrix of closed positions that are resistant to evaluation and appraisal. Ultra-realism's advocates argue that twenty-first-century criminology should frame its analyses of harm in a coherent critique of the whole advanced capitalist way of life, its competitive-narcissistic culture, its subjectivities and its harms.

To do this, criminology must escape the narrow parameters of right-wing and left-wing liberalism – political groups that limit criminological thought to their own agendas and degenerative research programmes. Thus older paradigms constructed within these parameters – such as **strain theory**,

See Chapter 4.33
Social harm/
zemiology

See Chapter 3.15
Social
constructionism

See Chapter 4.20
Intersectionality

See Chapter 2.9
General strain
theory

See Chapter 3.8
Labelling theory

See Chapter 3.17
Subculture

labelling theory, subcultural theory and so on – are less worth keeping than we once thought. Researchers thus need to get back out into the real world to construct theory anew. Ethnography is the most effective method for this purpose; but, as ultra-realist theory develops, it will be able to supply researchers with new and more advanced concepts to test in the field.

The current discipline is a hierarchy. So-called 'seminal' thinkers from the past continue to be revered despite their intellectual failings and time-limited views. Alternative thinkers from the past and present have been rejected for reasons that are not discussed openly. This has encouraged intellectual laziness as academics reproduce sacred ideas. New ethnographic research conducted by younger academics is either ignored or forced into traditional theoretical frameworks. Thus, new thinking fit for purpose in the twenty-first century is discouraged.

Ultra-realists argue that criminology should encourage theory and research that can open up new or previously proscribed and obscured *parallax views*. By generating rich and conceptually advanced qualitative data from various spaces and different sections of the population, views from multiple observational positions can be used to displace standard views of objects and events. To undercut orthodox political and cultural positions, these views must be based on the experiences and understandings of situated individuals. The problems of generalizability and the ecological fallacy that plague the ethnographic method can be overcome by constructing ethnographic networks (see Hall and Winlow 2015: Chapter 7). Networked ethnographers working in multiple geographical spaces can use observations and in-depth ethnographic interviews (Treadwell et al. 2012) to amass data and search for *concrete universals* that connect these experiences to broad socio-economic structures and processes. Individuals' understandings of their experiences and situations – and indeed understandings offered by the media, politicians and criminologists representing positions from across the political spectrum – can subsequently be evaluated by using concepts emerging from new philosophical and theoretical frameworks.

Initially, ultra-realists are using the new framework of *transcendental materialism* (Ellis 2015), which provides an updated concept of ideology that explains how subjectivities emerge in the neoliberal context, but this could change as new ideas fit for purpose appear in philosophy and social science. The overall aim is to create open, dialectical, forward motion in criminological research and theory (Hall and Winlow 2015).

See Chapter 4.39
Victimology

See Chapter 3.6
Feminist
criminologies;
Chapter 4.26
Patriarchy and
crime; Chapter
3.13 Radical
feminism

See Chapter 3.14
Realism and left
idealism

Ultra-realism is partially influenced by some previous criminological schools of thought, but also seeks to break away from them. For instance, it looks to diverge from institutionalized qualitative work, which pays too much attention to prisoners and young offenders rather than active criminals and thus gives a one-dimensional picture. It is also influenced by **victimological** and **feminist research**, but not their theoretical positions, which are largely restricted to intersectional power relations. Its primary influence is **left realism**, but this position produced little qualitative research, failed to engage with the concept of harm and neglected consumer culture as a criminogenic environment. Instead, ultra-realism seeks to advance left realism's determination to get underneath discourse and language: crime is not simply a social construction used by right-wing politicians to justify an authoritarian state. It is defined as an act that breaks rules, but various acts defined as crime impact on real individuals, their environments and their social norms in various ways as harm.

'Harm' is defined as an act that leaves what it affects in a worse condition. How well crime represents real harm depends on how well rules and laws have been made, and ultra-realism – using a core–periphery model of harm (Hall 2012) and the concept of trauma (Winlow 2014) – seeks to untangle this relationship. Ultra-realism acknowledges the theory that a lack of social recognition creates the conditions for harm, but it adds the point that **neoliberal** capitalism has virtually severed the master–slave relation. As such, victims of harmful relations and acts now have very little influence or bargaining position in relation to their exploiters. Ultra-realism's explanation of the exploiters themselves, who can appear in any position throughout the social structure, is informed by the concept of *special liberty* (Hall 2012). This is a sense of entitlement felt by individuals as they pursue business, wealth and enjoyment, driven by the obscene desires of narcissism and jouissance.

See Chapter 4.24 Neoliberalism

In search of a new realist model that can explain the drives behind *special liberty*, ultra-realists reject cynical forms of right-wing realism and move beyond the administrative pragmatism of left realism. Ultra-realism is influenced by critical realism's ontological and epistemological model, which is based on three layers of reality and our ability to know about it:

- empirical – knowledge of events and their patterns;
- actual – events and subjective experiences;
- real – underlying generative mechanisms that probabilistically cause the events.

In criminology, of course, because crime carries penalties, offenders put a lot of effort into concealing their crimes, which is why it needs the penetrative ethnographic method. Statistics and surveys are of very limited use and too susceptible to political manipulation by governments and the media. For critical realists, **positivism** is descriptive and correlational and simply cannot reveal enough about the world. Interpretivism is interminably wrapped up in the pluralistic construction of meanings that can never be firmly established, which does not help us to theorize cultural influences that can act like causes by encouraging and justifying actions with real consequences. Socioeconomic structures and processes are not just theoretical concepts, but systems of possibilities and constraints which impact on us in our everyday lives as 'natural necessities' that allow or deny thought and action. Thus, structures and processes are generative and degenerative mechanisms, creating and destroying our fundamental conditions of existence.

See Chapter 1.4 Positivism

Ultra-realism adds a fourth layer to the critical-realist model, however. By fetishistically disavowing the system and our part in it – we know a lot about its exploitation and harms but systematically avoid the issue while we act out its imperatives every day – we choose what goes into our unconscious to become habitual, unspoken action (Hall and Winlow 2015). Transcendental materialist philosophers argue that these imperatives and the ideology that justifies them are not genetically hard-wired but become emotionally accepted and neurologically 'real' as we adapt to them over generations (Johnston 2008). Because no feasible alternative system exists, subjects emerge from the terrifying Lacanian 'Real' – the human world in a state of nature underneath language, culture and politics – to become default active members of the current system, whether they believe in it or not.

The absence of a feasible alternative system is causative. It locks the individual into active engagement with the current neoliberal system's imperatives. For Johnston (2008), this is today's variation of the process of *deaptation*, in which continuing commitment to an obsolete ideology becomes dysfunctional in an environment no longer suitable for it. For instance, Parenti (2011) exposes the effects of global warming, drought, neoliberal economic restructuring and cheap arms dumping in the tropical convergence zone. In the presence of a culture of competitive individualism and special liberty, but in the absence of a stable economy and nurturing states and social systems, this process promotes criminality and violence rather than the politics of solidarity. This is the type of criminogenic process ultra-realism seeks to investigate and bring to the foreground in criminology.

References

Ellis, Anthony. 2015. *Men, Masculinities and Violence: An Ethnographic Study*. London: Routledge.

Hall, Steve. 2012. *Theorizing Crime and Deviance: A New Perspective*. London: Sage.

Hall, Steve, and Simon Winlow. 2015. *Revitalizing Criminological Theory: Towards a New Ultra-Realism*. London: Routledge.

Johnston, Adrian. 2008. *Žižek's Ontology*. Evanston, IL: Northwestern University Press.

Parenti, Christian. 2011. *Tropic of Chaos: Climate Change and the New Geography of Violence*. New York: Nation.

Treadwell, James, Daniel Briggs, Simon Winlow, and Steve Hall. 2012. Shopocalypse Now: Consumer Culture and the English Riots of 2011. *British Journal of Criminology* 53(1): 1–17.

Winlow, Simon. 2014. Trauma, Guilt and the Unconscious: Some Theoretical Notes on Violent Subjectivity. *Sociological Review* 62(S2) 32–49.

Further reading

Raymen, Thomas. 2015. Designing-In Crime by Designing-Out the Social? Situational Crime Prevention and the Intensification of Harmful Subjectivities. *British Journal of Criminology* 56(3): 497–514.

Reiner, Robert. 2007. *Law and Order: An Honest Citizen's Guide to Crime and Control.* Cambridge: Polity.

Smith, Oliver, and Thomas Raymen. 2016. What's Deviance Got to Do With It? Black Friday Sales, Violence, and Hyper-Conformity. *British Journal of Criminology* 56(2): 389–405.

The Deviant Leisure Research Group. https://deviantleisure.wordpress.com.

Yar, Majid. 2012. Critical criminology, critical theory and social harm. In *New Directions in Criminological Theory*, Steve Hall and Simon Winlow, eds, pp. 52–65. London: Routledge.

Victimology

Pam Davies

Broadly understood, 'victimology' is the study of victims of crime. Those contributing to this field of academic inquiry are variously concerned with theory, research, policy and practice as related to the topic of criminal – and for some – non-criminal victimizations and **harms**. Although the work of Von Hentig and Mendelsohn in the late 1940s and 1950s focused on victims, in the 1960s Steven Schafer (1960:8) could still describe the 'crime victim' as the 'Cinderella' of the criminal justice system. Only recently has there been a growing emphasis on meeting the needs and rights of victims of crime and harm across the globe. Today, criminal justice policies are increasingly framed and justified in terms of the needs and rights of the victim. This growth of interest in the victim of crime has seen victimology emerge as a specialist area of study, to the point where it is on the verge of becoming an established discipline in its own right rather than a sub-discipline of criminology, and there is now a wealth of international scholarship reflecting the global nature of many of the issues surrounding justice for victims of crime and social harm.

While there have been victims as long as there have been crimes and harms, the intellectual heritage of victimology was stimulated by thinkers who were inspired by the social and political context immediately after World War II. These writers were interested in the dynamics and processes of victimization. We now recognize a victim movement gradually taking shape – that is, a move towards victim-oriented policies and services in different countries. The victims' lobby emerged independently in Britain and the USA, while other countries introduced services that were to some extent based on policies developed elsewhere. A major landmark in the growth of interest in the victims of

See Chapter 4.33
Social harm/
zemiology

crime was the advent of the criminal victimization survey. First developed in the United States and disseminated in 1972, national victim surveys were followed by international and local surveys, some taking a specific geographical and crime-type focus, all making a significant contribution to our knowledge of the nature and extent of victimization and to our understanding of the patterns to victimization. The reasons why victim-oriented policies were supported in the latter half of the twentieth century vary according to different historical and socio-economic factors, as well as governmental/political pressures in countries such as the Netherlands and Australia, France and Germany. The victim-oriented shift in different sovereign states has also been influenced by global and European pressures towards convergence of victim support brought about by international bodies.

See Chapter 3.14 Realism and left idealism

The World Society of Victimology – a non-governmental organization (NGO) that now commands consultative status within Europe – was instrumental in the adoption in 1985 by the United Nations General Assembly of the *Declaration of Basic Principles of Justice for Victims of Crime and Abuse of Power*. Within Europe, the European Court of Human Rights, the Council of Europe, the European Forum for Victim Services, the European Forum for Restorative Justice and the European Union have all been vital to harmonizing policy and practice. The historical and socially situated contexts in which provisions for the victimized were extended remain important in understanding contemporary responses to victims today. Victim support has found a place on the human rights agenda, and concerns about the environment and non-human species as victims are also increasingly impacting the victimological agenda. For example, there is a distinct subset of victimological inquiry devoted to people, communities, environments and ecosystems suffering the effects of toxic gases and pollutants, greenhouse gases and carbon emissions (Beirne and South 2007; White 2010).

See Chapter 4.11 Environmental justice and victimology; Chapter 4.16 Green criminology

Marked differences in the victim services adopted in various countries are derived from the contrasting priorities espoused by those engaged in the victims' movement around the world. Overall, the impact that the feminist movement has had is particularly noteworthy. The impact of feminist-inspired thinking and activism has been enormous in making domestic and intimate partner violence more widely reported and in drawing attention to its highly gendered nature. Other key drivers have come from those keen to secure prosecutions; thus, for some, enticing and supporting victims and witnesses to give their most compelling or 'best evidence' in court has been a priority. Justifying tougher sentences and – in contrast – advocating rehabilitation, mediation or restorative justice as well as financial imperatives to reduce costs have also been notable priorities.

See Chapter 3.6 Feminist criminologies; Chapter 4.26 Patriarchy and crime; Chapter 3.13 Radical feminism; Chapter 4.21 Masculinities, structure and hegemony

See Chapter 5.15 Restorative justice

The emergence of services for crime victims has been subject to scholarly review and comparison. Traditionally, Western societies have paid scant regard to the needs of victims of crime. Those suffering interpersonal violence, especially rape victims, were often twice victimized: first by their offender, and a second time by the offender-oriented criminal justice system. While this still occurs, it is now commonplace to observe that victims of crime play a rapidly changing role in the criminal justice system in England and Wales. Many changes have been introduced, particularly since 1990, aimed at rebalancing the system in favour of victims. Some of the changes made in recent years, such as measures to protect witnesses in court, have apparently been effective in improving victims' position; yet victimological research continues to be sceptical in its conclusions about the extent to which policies advocated in the name of the victim are inevitably a good thing (Davies 2015; Duggan and Heap 2014).

Topics that have been the subject of considerable victimological inquiry pertain to the form of support that victims of crime might receive during their experience in the criminal justice process and in their longer-term recovery and survival. The range of services available and forms of redress or compensation are often topics under victimological scrutiny (see for example Hall 2013). These include:

- support that victims might receive after the offence, which may be given by the police, a generalist victim assistance programme (such as Victim Support in England) or a specialist agency (like a rape crisis agency);
- help at the court stage aimed at integrating victims into the prosecution and post-court processes; and
- assistance in the form of financial or other forms of compensation, through compensation orders, criminal injuries compensation or – more recently – mediation or restorative justice programmes.

Victimology has accrued its own intellectual terminologies, key concepts and different perspectives to inform the study of the victim of crime, and which variously explain the dynamics and processes of victimization. Most famously, Norwegian author Nils Christie employed the term 'ideal victim' to denote the major attributes belonging to a model or ideal-type victim, while a number of controversial phrases and concepts can be traced back to the work of scholars referred to above in the 1940s–1960s. One of the key terms commonly drawn upon within victimology is 'victim blaming'. This refers to the extent to which a person might be viewed as in some way responsible for the experience they have suffered. In the context of criminal victimization, this involves perceptions of how blameworthy or culpable the victim is for the harm, pain and suffering he/she experiences. Victim blaming is closely associated with a range of similarly controversial terms – including 'victim precipitation', 'victim provocation' and 'victim culpability'. Each of these terms has variously been used to attempt to understand how people become victims of crime, to conceptualize the dynamics of victimization and to illustrate how victimhood is a process.

Some are highly critical of the manner in which victims have been politicized, leading to a position where victims find themselves increasingly burdened in the pursuit of justice. In England and Wales, the *Code of Practice for Victims of Crime* (2013) was probably the last most significant victim-related publication emanating from the Ministry of Justice. This code is perhaps best summarized as the twenty-first-century version of the Victim's Charter, which was originally published in Britain in 1990 (Home Office 1990). This code is broadly indicative of the current state of victim-oriented policy and, as such, it seems that victims of crime continue to occupy a position defined by their need rather than by any notion of rights.

The concerns of victims are at the heart of victimology, with central issues for the field being:

▦ the historical and socio-political influences and intellectual thinking that have given rise to the origins and development of victimology;
▦ the research methods and tools that have been adapted, developed, pioneered and used to develop a victimological evidence base;
▦ new directions in theorizing, policy and practice and the **interconnec-** See Chapter 4.31
tions between research and theory, policy and praxis. Public criminology

Victimological inquiry is ever more important in exposing the different varieties of harm and injustice that constitute victimization and in critiquing and steering victim policies to ensure they have a positive impact.

References

Beirne, Piers, and Nigel South (eds). 2007. *Issues in Green Criminology: Confronting Harms against Environments, Humanity and Other Animals*. Cullompton, UK: Willan.

Davies, Pamela. 2015. Victims: Continuing to Carry the Burden of Justice. *British Society of Criminology Newsletter* 76(Summer): 16–17.

Duggan, Marian, and Vicky Heap. 2014. *Administrating Victimization: The Politics of Anti-Social Behaviour and Hate Crime Policy*. Basingstoke: Palgrave Macmillan.

Hall, Matthew. 2013. *Victims of Environmental Harm: Rights, Recognition and Redress under National and International Law*. Abingdon: Routledge.

Home Office. 1990. *The Victims Charter: A Statement of Rights for Victims of Crime*. London: Home Office.

Ministry of Justice. 2013. *Code of Practice for Victims of Crime*. London: Ministry of Justice.

Schafer, Stephen. 1960. *Restitution to Victims of Crime*. London: Stevens.

White, Rob. 2010. Environmental Victims and Resistance to State Crime through Transnational Activism. *Social Justice* 36(3): 46–60.

Further reading

Davies, Pamela, Peter Francis, and Chris Greer (eds). 2017. *Victims, Crime and Society* (2nd edn). London: Sage.

Rothe, Dawn L., and David Kauzlarich (eds). 2014. *Towards a Victimology of State Crime*. Abingdon: Routledge.

Shoham, Shlomo G., Paul Knepper, and Martin Kett (eds). 2010. *International Handbook of Victimology*. Boca Raton, FL: CRC Press.

Vanfraechem, Inge, Anthony Pemberton, and Felix Muwiza Ndahinda. 2014. *Justice for Victims: Perspectives on Rights, Transition and Reconciliation*. London: Routledge.

Walklate, Sandra (ed.). 2007. *Handbook of Victims and Victimology*. Cullompton, UK: Willan.

Wilson, Dean, and Stuart Ross (eds). 2015. *Crime, Victims and Policy: International Contexts, Local Experiences*. London: Palgrave Macmillan.

Visual criminology

Eamonn Carrabine

The attention given to images in criminology is a recent development, but across the humanities and social sciences the visual has become a major feature of quite diverse research practices. These approaches are pursued from a plethora of disciplinary and theoretical positions, to the extent that there is no single, shared view on how images should be used or to what ends they might be put. Nevertheless, it is clear that the field of visual methodology is the site of innovative interdisciplinary scholarship, which is a telling indication of the increasingly prominent place images occupy in contemporary life. Yet it is only really since the 1990s that there has been a remarkable growth in scholarship on *visual culture*. In Britain, this was partly a result of an increasing specialization in cultural studies, where anthropological and sociological approaches have been especially influential, while in the United States, the emerging field has been more indebted to art history, and visual culture is now taught in most corners of the world from many different perspectives (Mirzoeff 2009).

Although there is a rich tradition of research on **crime and the media in criminology**, specific attention to the role and place of the *image* in crime, in crime control and in criminal justice has long been lacking. This omission is particularly surprising given just how deep-seated the cultural fascination with the iconography of crime and punishment is in the popular imagination. To understand more fully the emergence of a 'visual criminology' it is also important to note that the documentary photography tradition, which itself emerged in the nineteenth century, had its origins in social activism, investigative journalism, fine art, science and pseudoscience (including phrenology,

See Chapter 4.8 Cultural criminology

physiognomy and eugenics), as well as in public health and criminology itself (Sekula 1989; Tagg 1988).

The last few years have seen a remarkable visual turn in criminology; and the radical claim, made by cultural criminologists, is that a 'decisive moment' has now been reached – where it is no longer possible to divorce crime and control from how they are visually represented; they urge an end to the distinction made between 'real' crime and the 'unreal' image (Ferrell and Van De Voorde 2010:36). Yet, ever since the birth of the camera in the nineteenth century, photography has been accused of breaching the divide between public worlds and private selves, transforming the very act of looking and giving rise to a whole series of characterizations of this condition – e.g., the society of spectacle, the politics of representation and the gendered gaze. Indeed, photography was a vital element in the construction of the modern criminal subject, and has since become central to the dynamics of celebrity, criminality, desire, fame, trauma and voyeurism that continue to shape social practices in significant and often disruptive ways.

The growing popularity of visual methods across the social sciences is a striking development; but often the techniques are 'reinvented over and over again without gaining much methodological depth and often without consideration of long-existing classics in the field' (Pauwels 2011:3). Such ahistoric and dispersed treatments are unhelpful, implying that method can be divorced from theoretical issues and ignoring some of the fraught encounters that have shaped the use of visual material in and across disciplines. Once the roots are traced back to the nineteenth century, it becomes apparent that anthropologists and sociologists, for example, used photographs from the beginning to explore societies near and afar. Photographs gradually fell out of favour, however, as they were deemed too subjective, unsystematic and eccentric (Becker 2004).

From its earliest days, the status of photography as a medium drew from its ability both to offer an authentic record of the truth and to present a radically new way of seeing the world. Photojournalism originated in war reporting and provided a sobering counterpoint to the official battlefield art produced by 'war artists', which tended to glamorize and romanticize combat. War photography revealed to many the horrors of conflict and has since become integral to news reporting. All the characteristic photographic practices now associated with the documentary tradition were well established by the 1860s: aside from war photography, historical sites, sacred places and exotic natives each became subjects of the lens as colonial empires expanded.

See Chapter 1.4
Positivism

Cesare Lombroso's criminal anthropology is the most well-known example, to criminologists at least, of how photography was used to classify bodies into distinguishable types in this era. Alan Sekula and John Tagg have each argued that the photographs taken for police and prison records should be understood in relation to the boom in portraiture whereby people were encouraged to measure the respectable citizen against the criminal body and visualize social difference. It was not until the 1880s that a French bureaucrat, Alphonse Bertillon, developed 'anthropometric' techniques to systematically record and identify offenders. His filing-card system helped transform what had been an uneven and inconsistent practice into a disciplinary technology that rapidly expanded and remains pivotal to contemporary biometric databases devised to identify and classify increasingly mobile populations.

At the beginning of the twenty-first century a plethora of new tools – including biometrics, DNA analysis, digital imagery, surveillance systems and computer databases – provide new ways of representing, and watching, criminals and suspects. Jonathan Finn (2009) has described how the development of police photography in the nineteenth century laid the foundations for contemporary identification practices, including several that have been established after the terrorist attacks of September 11, 2001. Contemporary law-enforcement agencies, he argues, position the body as potentially criminal in his analysis of the use of visual representation in police practices. The collection and archiving of identification data – which today consists of much more than photographs or fingerprints – reflect a reconceptualization of the body itself.

See Chapter 5.19
Surveillance

Phil Carney (2010:27) has also examined how artists have played with the relationship between 'celebrity and desire in the criminal identification photograph': from Andy Warhol's 'Most Wanted Men' series of silk screens in 1964; through Marcus Harvey's enormous painting of Myra Hindley's infamous mugshot initially shown at the *Sensation* art exhibition in 1997; to the more recent work of Neil Hepburn and Russell Young that superimposes the faces of model Kate Moss and musician Pete Doherty on the mugshots of the child-killers Myra Hindley and Ian Brady to comment on contemporary tabloid culture. Others have argued that the documentary photography tradition offers much from which a visually attuned criminology can learn (Ferrell and Van De Voorde 2010; Carrabine 2012). For example, contemporary practitioners have become increasingly aware that they have certain social responsibilities towards the subjects they photograph, while remaining committed to anthropological exploration, moral commitment and political reform.

One of the best examples of visual criminology is the collaboration between anthropologist Philippe Bourgois and photographer Jeff Schonberg (2009) in their ethnography of homelessness and drug addiction in San Francisco. *Righteous Dopefiends* is the result of a twelve-year project chronicling the suffering, friendships and betrayal that characterize survival among the destitute, while also analysing the structural forces and institutions (police, welfare and hospital) that they negotiate in their daily lives. The book is composed of vivid excerpts from field notes, stark black-and-white photography and critical social theory (drawing on Bourdieu, Foucault and Marx to understand the systemic violence enveloping this social world). Here photography is used explicitly to expose unjust social relations, and Bourgois and Schonberg suggest different kinds of relationships between homeless addicts and those who appear devoted to their care (in public health work and emergency hospital services) via a detailed critique of the dysfunctional US medical system.

A new edited collection by Brown and Carrabine gives a sense of the wide range of approaches in visual criminology, and this diversity characterizes both the kind of visual materials they work with and the analytical procedures to which that material is subjected. A key distinction can be made between a detailed interpretation of an aspect of visual culture (whether this be a photograph, a piece of film, internet design, a television series or the practices of visualization deployed in scientific representation) and the use of visual methods in social research (such as photo-elicitation, virtual ethnography, spatial mapping, video diaries and other kinds of explicitly collaborative documentary making). Some scholars work with visual material 'made' in the research situation – whether these are generated by the researcher or in collaboration with participants – while others work with 'found' images. Although visual social science is nearly as old as photography, it is hard to dispute the view that 'we are really still at the beginning, with a lot of work yet to do' (Becker 2004:197).

References

Becker, Harold. 2004. Afterword: Photography as evidence, photographs as exposition. In *Picturing the Social Landscape: Visual Methods and the Sociological Imagination*, Caroline Knowles and Paul Sweetman, eds, pp. 193–7. London: Routledge.

Bourgois, Philippe, and Jeff Schonberg. 2009. *Righteous Dopefiend*. Berkeley: University of California Press.

Carney, Phil. 2010. Crime, punishment and the force of photographic spectacle. In *Framing Crime: Cultural Criminology and the Image*, Keith Hayward and Mike Presdee, eds, pp. 17–35. London: Routledge.

Carrabine, Eamonn. 2012. Just Images: Aesthetics, Ethics and Visual Criminology. *British Journal of Criminology* 52(3): 463–89.

Ferrell, Jeff, and Cécile Van De Voorde 2010. The decisive moment: Documentary photography and cultural criminology. In *Framing Crime: Cultural Criminology and the Image*, Keith Hayward and Mike Presdee, eds, pp. 36–52 London: Routledge.

Finn, Jonathan. 2009. *Capturing the Criminal Image: From Mug Shot to Surveillance Society*. Minneapolis: University of Minnesota Press.

Mirzoeff, Nicholas. 2009. *An Introduction to Visual Culture* (2nd edn). London: Routledge.

Pauwels, Luc. 2011. An Integrated Conceptual Framework for Visual Social Research. In *The SAGE Handbook of Visual Research Methods*, Eric Margolis and Luc Pauwels, eds, pp. 3–23. London: Sage.

Sekula, Allan. 1989. The body and the archive. In *The Contest of Meaning*, Richard Bolton, ed., pp. 343–89. Cambridge, MA: MIT Press.

Tagg, J. 1988. *The Burden of Representation: Essays on Photographies and Histories*. Basingstoke: Macmillan.

Further reading

Brown, Michelle, and Eamonn Carrabine (eds). 2017. *Routledge International Handbook of Visual Criminology*. London: Routledge.

Carrabine, Eamonn. 2014. Seeing Things: Violence, Voyeurism and the Camera. *Theoretical Criminology* 18(2): 134–58.

Hayword, Keith J., and Mike Presdee (eds). 2010. *Framing Crime: Cultural Criminology and the Image*. London: Routledge.

White-collar crime

Wim Huisman and Judith van Erp

When company managers, politicians or public officials are accused of committing crimes, such behaviour is often referred to as 'white-collar crime'. This concept was introduced in 1939 by the criminologist Edwin Sutherland in his presidential address to the American Sociological Association. Sutherland accused his colleagues of looking only at deviant behaviour of members of the lower social classes – the 'blue-collar' working class – neglecting the harmful behaviours of the 'white-collar' social elite. (The 'collars' referred to the occupational clothing associated with different social classes.) Although the concept of white-collar crime became widely known, Sutherland was not the first criminologist to call attention to the crimes of the elite. In 1905, the **Dutch criminologist Willem Bonger** made a distinction between 'crimes in the streets' and 'crimes in the suites' in his study on crime and economic conditions (see also Van Erp et al. 2015).

See Chapter 3.9
Marxist
criminologies

While lauded for introducing the concept of white-collar crime, Sutherland was also criticized for not clearly defining its meaning or delineating its contours. Although he provided several definitions in various publications, the following definition of white-collar crime by Friedrichs (2009:3) is commonly accepted: 'Crime committed by a person of respectability and a high social status in the course of his occupation'. This definition has three central elements, each of which has been subject to criticism.

First, Sutherland explicitly embraced a wide interpretation of 'crime'. Because of their high social status and networks, white-collar offenders are frequently able to keep their conduct out of the reach of criminal law. When their acts or omissions are subject to criminal law, they may be overlooked by enforcement agencies. If and when harmful business conduct is regulated by law, it is likely to be civil or administrative regulation for which the violation thereof carries less social and moral stigma than criminal prosecution. Sutherland's approach was criticized heavily by Tappan, who argued that 'crime' should be limited to those acts that have been criminalized in penal codes. Sutherland, in turn, responded that under such a narrow definition, hardly any white-collar crime would be identified (Friedrichs 2009:251).

Second, 'white-collar' reflects the element of 'a person of respectability and a high social status', in contrast to regular 'street' crime. The social status of the offender, however, is often difficult to operationalize in empirical research. It is clear that the CEO of a company listed on a stock exchange who is guilty of anti-trust violations is a 'white-collar offender', as is the minister or state secretary accused of taking bribes. But when does the colour of the collar change from white to blue? At the level of a manager of a department of 20 employees? At the level of the alderman of a small municipality? In one of the first large research projects on 'white-collar crime', the term was defined by the nature of the offence (non-violent property crime). Researchers found that social backgrounds were quite heterogeneous (subsequently labelling them as 'crimes of the middle classes' [Weisburd et al. 1991]). Critics of this so-called offence-based approach, however, argued that this takes away the central element of white-collar crime: the social and occupational status of the offender.

Third, the element, 'in the course of his occupation', implies that the crime is committed in a professional role, not as a private person. A politician having sex with minors would then not be an example of someone committing a white-collar crime. Nevertheless, the occupational context can create two different motives for committing crimes: one can commit crimes in the execution of organizational tasks and one can abuse the occupational role to enrich oneself illicitly, often to the detriment of the employing organization. Because these motivations bring different explanations for the crimes, new concepts have been introduced to differentiate these two forms of white-collar crime: **corporate crime** is committed on behalf of and primarily for the benefit of the organization, while *occupational crime* is committed using the occupational profession for personal gain (Friedrichs 2009). It bears mention that when he introduced the general concept of white-collar crime, Sutherland studied corporate crime. Indeed, ten years after proposing the concept, Sutherland (1949) published his study of the crimes of the 70 largest corporations in the United States. Furthermore, when committing crimes is not incidental and becomes standard operating practice, producing the principal part of a company's revenue, a similarity to the criminological concept of **organized crime** appears.

See Chapter 4.5
Corporate crime

See Chapter 4.25
Organized crime

Besides the social status of the offender, white-collar crime has several other characteristics. Most crucial is the abuse of trust that comes with the occupational role and social status of the offender. Certain positions present opportunities to commit certain crimes; and, because of the status of the individuals in these positions, victims do not expect to be victimized. Furthermore, a certain level of complexity is generally attributed to white-collar crime.

Because these crimes are committed in the context of an organization and of legitimate business practices, the illicit nature of these particular acts may prove difficult to identify. For instance, expertise in business accounting is required to detect accounting frauds.

Because of this, and unlike most types of crime, white-collar crime is often discovered neither by reports by victims to the police nor by criminal investigation activities. Rather, white-collar crime is often exposed by insiders. These might be whistle-blowers or informers who were involved initially in the commission of the crimes and decided to 'go public' because senior-management was not willing to intervene in illegal business practices, or because they were involved in the perpetration themselves. In addition, cases of white-collar crime are sometimes exposed by investigative reporters or public-interest groups, such as unions, consumer-interest organizations or environmental groups. Because many white-collar – and most corporate – crimes constitute violations of the regulation of business activities, regulatory agencies such as security and exchange commissions or environmental protection agencies have the duty to monitor compliance and detect non-compliance.

Measurement of the scale of white-collar crime is extremely difficult. Nevertheless, the few studies on the prevalence of white-collar crime reveal that it is widespread and is often considered 'normal' in the settings in which it has been exposed. For the same reasons, the material and immaterial costs of white-collar crime are hard to quantify although available calculations, and estimates suggest it exceeds the costs of street crime multiple times (Friedrichs 2009). Furthermore, the indirect costs of white-collar crime – due to the loss of societal trust in economy, politics and government – have consequences. The well-established correlation between a country's high level of corruption and low level of economic and human development is an illustration of this.

White-collar crime is mostly explained by the situational characteristics that are related to the white-collar position, such as an unethical corporate culture, an attractive illicit business opportunity or **financial strain**. However, some contemporary studies do suggest some individual traits in which white-collar offenders differ from their law-abiding peers or colleagues, and that might contribute to explaining white-collar crime (Benson and Manchak 2014).

See Chapter 4.12
Financial crime

The characteristics and causes of white-collar crime make this form of crime less susceptible to criminal justice interventions. The status of offenders and the context of legitimate organizational practices create moral and legal ambiguities that impact on enforcement priorities and create problems in proving the illegal nature of the acts and the *mens rea* of the offenders (Nelken 2012). According to a criminal investigator quoted in Friedrichs (2009:278): 'In normal crime cases, the police are searching for the criminal, in white-collar crime cases they are searching for the crime.' The result is that prosecution and criminal conviction of white-collar crimes are rather scarce. Cases often end in settlements. This difference to the criminal justice responses to street crime is sometimes perceived as 'class justice'.

See Chapter 6.2
Community safety

As the causes of white-collar crime are strongly attributed to criminogenic opportunity structures, reducing these opportunity structures by **situational crime prevention** techniques is seen as a promising alternative to law enforcement. Organizational codes of conduct and policies aimed at safeguarding integrity in public service and politics and promoting ethical business practices are also seen as fruitful tools to prevent white-collar crime. The effectiveness of these alternatives to a criminal justice response to white-collar crime is yet to be determined, however.

References

Benson, Michael L., and Sarah Manchak. 2014. The psychology of white-collar crime. In *Oxford Handbooks Online in Criminology and Criminal Justice*. DOI: 10.1093/oxfordhb/9780199935383.013.008. Accessed 23 January 2017.

Bonger, Willem A. 1905. *Criminalité et conditions économiques*. Amsterdam: G.P. Tierie.

Friedrichs, David O. 2009. *Trusted Criminals: White-Collar Crime in Contemporary Society* (4th edn). Belmont, CA: Wadsworth.

Nelken, David. 2012. White-collar and corporate crime. In *The Oxford Handbook of Criminology* (5th edn), Mike Maguire, Rodney Morgan, and Robert Reiner, eds, pp. 623–59. Oxford: Clarendon.

Sutherland, Edwin H. 1949. *White Collar Crime*. New York: Dryden.

Van Erp, Judith, Wim Huisman, and Gudrun Vande Walle (eds). 2015. *The Routledge Handbook of White-Collar and Corporate Crime in Europe*. Abingdon: Routledge.

Weisburd, David, Stanton Wheeler, Elin Waring, and Nancy Bode. 1991. *Crimes of the Middle Classes: White Collar Offenders in the Federal Courts*. New Haven, CT: Yale University Press.

Further reading

Benson, Michael L., and Francis T. Cullen (eds). 2016. *The Oxford Handbook of White-Collar Crime*. New York: Oxford University Press.

Benson, Michael L., and. Sally S. Simpson 2015. *White-Collar Crime: An Opportunity Perspective* (2nd edn). New York: Routledge.

Pontell, Henry, and Gilbert Geis (eds). 2007. *The International Handbook of White-Collar and Corporate Crime*. New York: Springer.

Simpson, Sally S., and David Weisburd (eds). 2009. *The Criminology of White-Collar Crime*. New York: Springer.

Part 5

Punishment and security

Part 5 Introduction

The essays in this part of the book address criminological thinking on punishment and security – two distinct sub-fields in the discipline – although it is only really since the beginning of the twenty-first century that the latter has come to the fore. Since 9/11, the topic has been mobilized in a number of ways: 'governing security', 'governing through security', 'selling security', 'civilizing security', 'imagining security' and tackling 'insecurity', as well as through 'security management systems', 'private security' and the 'security industry'. These are just some of the examples that have been identified and have preoccupied criminologists, and that speak to some of the wider troubles facing twenty-first-century societies.

In contrast to this new interest in security, criminologists have long highlighted the institutional complexity of punishment, emphasizing how it plays a range of penal and social functions in which crime control is only one objective – albeit an important one. It is convenient to distinguish between three very different approaches. One is best described as an *administrative penology* primarily concerned with the implementation of particular sanctions and monitoring their effectiveness. Consequently, the kind of issues it addresses is narrow in scope and tends to ignore the deeply social character of punishment. Although proponents of it can and do criticize particular institutions, penal policies and legal processes, administrative penology is largely concerned with identifying the best ways of running prisons, organizing probation or enforcing fines, rather than critically examining why these measures exist in the first place. In other words, it is a *reform-oriented project* with practical goals in mind, rather than an endeavour challenging the state's power to punish. Such matters are more to the fore in the other two distinctive traditions exploring the *philosophy of punishment* and the *sociology of control*.

Because the punishment of offenders causes pain, suffering and harm, it requires some form of moral justification, as the power to punish is ultimately derived from the legal authority of the state to do things that would otherwise be plainly wrong (if undertaken by private citizens against each other). Modern *philosophical* thinking treats punishment as a crucial dynamic in the classic liberal problem of how the individual should relate to the state. The key issue that immediately arises is: what gives any social institution the moral right to inflict deliberate suffering on offenders? There are a number of competing justifications, which have come to revolve around the central problem of reconciling punishment as state coercion alongside a valuing of individual autonomy. Each seeks to explain why it is 'right' to punish in morally acceptable ways, or highlight the greater 'good' that can be achieved through inflicting further harm. Consequently, justifications of punishment are firmly rooted in broader moral and political philosophies that often conflict.

Sociological perspectives on punishment, on the other hand, focus on the wider aspects of social control to reveal the underlying structures of penal systems. Although there is a tendency to evade complex normative issues, this approach does raise fundamental questions over how to understand punishment as a social phenomenon, which generates webs of cultural meaning and is determined by political forces that would otherwise remain hidden. As each of the essays that follow very ably demonstrates, inevitably there are different theoretical perspectives, each shedding significant light on some aspects of punishment while neglecting others. In many respects, the current preoccupations with security in criminology can be traced from the increasing significance of risk assessment and prudentialism associated with the 'new penology' project, which has been transforming criminal justice and the very nature of democracy itself. Today, the securitization of the state, across both private and public spheres, is an enterprise in its own right with a dynamic and a momentum distinct from crime rates, explaining why it is attracting so much criminological attention.

5.1 Abolitionism

Joe Sim

Abolitionism emerged from the political schisms that gripped Western Europe and North America in the late 1960s. It was a 'social movement, a theoretical perspective and a political strategy' (de Haan 1991:203). Abolitionists not only challenged the dominant discourses surrounding crime and punishment but also argued for the abolition of the prison. They maintained that the institution was less concerned with the rehabilitation and social integration of the offender and was more concerned with the delivery of punishment and pain. In practice, the discourses of rehabilitation and reform were chimeras that masked and mystified the capacity of the institution to deliver punishment. Prisons not only failed to rehabilitate; they also failed in their other goals in terms of individual and collective **deterrence**, **crime prevention** and **incapacitation**. In short, the prison was indefensible (Mathiesen 2000).

See Chapter 1.17
Deterrence

See Chapter 6.2
Community safety

See Chapter 5.9
Incapacitation

Abolitionists also critiqued the contention that the crisis in prisons – and the social problems in the wider society – could be solved by introducing progressive, incremental reforms designed to improve the operation of the institution in order to ensure that it worked more efficiently and effectively. Rather, abolitionists asserted that the prison, and the criminal justice system more generally, needed to be transformed radically and replaced with social and welfare policies which emphasized care and empathy towards, and the social integration of, the offender. Abolitionists contrasted this vision of confinement with the brutality, dehumanization, terror and alienation that, despite some honourable exceptions, were intrinsic to the everyday operation of penal institutions. Contemporary abolitionists have pointed to the levels of self-harm and self-inflicted deaths in penal institutions, historically and contemporaneously, as an example of this point (Sim 2009).

Abolitionists argue that prisons are not concerned with crime control but function as institutions of **a coercive, capitalist state whose role is to defend an inequitable social order**. For over two hundred years, prisons have helped defend this social order which is built on systemic inequalities generated by social divisions around class, race, gender, sexuality, age and ability/disability (Ryan and Sim 2016). Prisons contain, confine, regulate and punish those on the economic and political margins of capitalist society: the unemployed, the poor, the powerless, those with mental-health issues and the sexually abused. The state criminalizes the activities of these groups and classifies them as unproductive members of society.

See Chapter 3.3
Critical
criminologies

At the same time, **the state** has failed to respond to the criminal behaviour of, and the systemic harms generated by, the powerful. Abolitionists argue that by focusing on the imprisoned as *the* source of criminal behaviour, the prison functions ideologically to distract attention away from crimes of the powerful while socially constructing potent symbols of good (the law-abiding outside prisons) and evil – those inside prisons (Mathiesen 1974).

See Chapter 4.36
State crime;
Chapter 4.37
State-corporate
crime

Abolitionists campaign for 'negative reforms' (Mathiesen 1974:202) that are strategically designed to compete with, and contradict, the existing system in order to undermine and eventually abolish it. This strategy can be contrasted with the destructive, devastating and hypocritical penal policies pursued by the state whose emphasis on piecemeal change ultimately leads to compromise and incorporation, as exemplified by the history of liberal prison-reform groups. Liberal reforms, in principle and in practice, have merely reinforced and extended penal power while failing to address the destructive impact of the power to punish on the confined, their families and their communities. Nor do liberal reformers question the wider role of the prison in maintaining a capitalist society. What is required are *not* liberal reforms but **fundamental change**, including: stopping prison-building; closing existing institutions; introducing well-funded, radical alternatives to imprisonment; decriminalizing a range of offences; and radically reducing the length of prison sentences. Ultimately, the prison, in its present form, needs to be abolished as it has little impact on the crime rate and offers little in the way of public protection. The vast majority of women in prison could be released without either the crime rate rising or the public being put in danger. Abolishing these institutions *would* help those women detained within them whose pain is intensified though their incarceration (Carlen 1990).

See Chapter 5.5
Decarceration

Abolitionists have been criticized for being idealistic and utopian. They have been erroneously labelled as individuals who want to abolish prisons and free dangerous offenders. Powerful institutions such as the mass media, together with politicians and state servants, construct abolitionists as being pro-crime and **anti-victim**. Abolitionists would respond by arguing that the criminal justice system does little, if anything, to protect victims of crime, while the image of the victim has been hypocritically exploited and

See Chapter 4.39
Victimology

manipulated by politicians and the media for their own narrow, political interests – principally to reinforce the discourse of law and order that has dominated the debate around crime since the mid-1970s (Sim 2009).

In addition, abolitionists contend that while there are some individuals who are clearly dangerous in conventional, legal terms, they have *not* advocated that such individuals should walk free. Rather, they should be confined in places that are very different to the destructive system that currently prevails. In the UK, institutions such as the Barlinnie Special Unit, Parkhurst C Wing and Grendon Underwood can be understood as 'abolitionist alternatives' (Davis 2003:109) in that they are built on a radically different model of confinement and stand in direct contradiction to the painful and destructive system that currently operates, which harms more than it helps (Sim 2009).

See Chapter 3.6 Feminist criminologies; Chapter 4.26 Patriarchy and crime; Chapter 3.13 Radical feminism

Abolitionists also argue that those who defend the prison on the grounds that it protects the public from dangerous individuals ignore one key issue: **the institution does little to protect women from male violence**, as the official criminal statistics, victimization surveys and self-report surveys indicate. In practice, given the culture of **masculinity** prevailing in prisons, misogynistic attitudes towards women are reinforced rather than challenged. Furthermore, the widespread nature of violence against women indicates that they do little to deter men outside prisons from committing such violence.

See Chapter 4.21 Masculinities, structure and hegemony

Abolitionists raise questions about how dangerousness is defined, and argue for a definition that extends beyond its legal definition to include activities which are **socially harmful** and which can also lead to deaths and injuries but which are rarely policed and punished. This would include deaths at work, which far outstrip the conventional murder rate, and **environmental harms and pollution**, which lead to many more deaths annually, again compared with the conventional murder rate.

See Chapter 4.33 Social harm/ zemiology

See Chapter 4.16 Green criminology; Chapter 4.11 Environmental justice and victimology

Angela Davis has argued that abolitionists have also failed to think about the role of anti-racist struggles in delivering a radically transformed penal system. This point has become particularly important in the context of the political economy of **neoliberalism** which has been underpinned by the emergence of a penal-industrial complex, the privatization of criminal justice institutions and the detention of increasing numbers of black and ethnic-minority men and women in prisons and immigration detention centres. For abolitionists, these places are designed not to control crime but to regulate the socially bereft and politically powerless while defending and reproducing a **globalized**, exploitative, capitalist, international social order.

See Chapter 4.24 Neoliberalism

See Chapter 4.14 Globalization

Contemporary abolitionists continue to point to the destructive power of penal institutions that, as noted above, have become integral to the armoury of the neoliberal state in the regulation and punishment of the poor, nationally and internationally. They have also argued for extending the philosophical and political basis of abolitionism so that it links to broader social issues and concerns:

Abolitionism is a movement to end systemic violence, including the inter-personal vulnerabilities and displacements that keep the system going. In other words, the goal is to change how we interact with each other and the planet by putting people before profits, welfare before warfare, and life over death.

(Berger 2014:vii–viii)

Nearly half a century after the movement emerged in the late 1960s, the ongoing influence of abolitionist thought can be seen across the political land-scape. The interventions made by abolitionist groups in Australia, Canada, England and Wales and Scandinavia have: challenged the state's definition of 'truth' around confinement; impacted hegemonically on traditional, liberal reform groups by dragging them onto a more critical terrain with respect to critiquing penal policy; intervened in the deliberations of official inquiries while influencing their policy recommendations; and affected state policies around deaths in custody. Furthermore, in England and Wales, contemporary abolitionists – working with radical organizations such as INQUEST – have highlighted the lack of democratic control of penal institutions and the need make state servants more accountable for their actions if the high levels of self-harm and deaths in custody are to be reduced and, eventually, eliminated. Given this history, the pejorative labels attributed to abolitionists – that they are out of touch, idealistic and utopian – are misplaced. For abolitionists, radical interventions will break the endless cycle of liberal reforms that have dominated penal policy developments in the last 200 years. These interven-tions will contribute to the eventual abolition of *all* penal institutions as well as the inequitable and unjust social order they help to legitimate, sustain and reproduce.

References

Berger, Dan. 2014. *Struggle Within: Prisons, Political Prisoners, and Mass Movements in the United States*. Montreal: Kersplebedeb.

Carlen, Pat. 1990. *Alternatives to Women's Imprisonment*. London: Sage.

Davis, Angela. 2003. *Are Prisons Obsolete?* New York: Seven Stories Press.

de Haan, Willem. 1991. Abolitionism and crime control: A contradiction in terms. In *The Politics of Crime Control*, Kevin Stenson and David Cowell, eds, pp. 203–17. London: Sage.

Mathiesen, Thomas. 1974. *The Politics of Abolition*. London: Martin Robertson.

Mathiesen, Thomas. 2000. *Prison on Trial*. Winchester: Waterside Press.

Ryan, Mick, and Joe Sim. 2016. Campaigning for and campaigning against prisons: Excavating and reaffirming the case for prison abolition. In *The Handbook on Prisons* (2nd edn), Yvonne Jewkes, Jamie Bennett, and Ben Crewe, eds, pp. 712–33. Abingdon: Routledge.

Sim, Joe. 2009. *Punishment and Prisons: Power and the Carceral State*. London: Sage.

Further reading

Carlton, Bree. 2007. *Imprisoning Resistance*. Sydney: Institute of Criminology Press.

CR10 Publications Collective (eds). 2008. *Abolition Now! Ten Years of Strategy and Struggle against the Prison Industrial Complex*. Oakland, CA: AK Press. See also www.criticalresistance.org on the abolitionist group Critical Resistance.

Hartnett, Stephen J. (ed.). 2011. *Challenging the Prison-Industrial Complex*. Urbana: University of Illinois Press.

Mogul, Joey L., Andrea J Ritchie, and Kay Whitlock. 2011. *Queer (In)Justice: The Criminalization of LGBT People in the United States*. Boston: Beacon.

Piché, Justin, and Mike Larsen. 2010. The Moving Targets of Penal Abolitionism: ICOPA, Past, Present and Future. *Contemporary Justice Review: Issues in Criminal, Social and Restorative Justice* 13(4): 391–410.

West, W. Gordon, and Ruth Morris (eds). 2000. *The Case for Penal Abolition*. Toronto: Canadian Scholars' Press.

Antisocial behaviour

Peter Squires

The focus on antisocial behaviour (ASB) management, arising in the mid-1990s in the UK, reflected concerns about community, class, identity, crime and disorder. The phenomenon can be seen as a distant cousin of the psychological conception of *anti-social personality disorder* (Rutter et al. 1998) – although more socially and morally framed, and centred especially on the irresponsibility, disrespect and lack of discipline of the poorest (especially their children). In this sense, in approaching the modern phenomenon of ASB, we need to engage with Pearson's (1983) 'history of respectable fears' and other efforts to either moralize or demonize the poorest in Britain.

Tony Blair, first as Shadow Home Secretary and later as Labour leader and Prime Minister, made much of the political running on the issue, describing his 'passion' for tackling ASB as a 'crusade'. By contrast, American criminologist Michael Tonry felt the emphasis placed on ASB was a political and criminological error, 'making a small problem larger' (2004:57) and creating the impression that social problems are amenable to *enforcement solutions*. Yet while political targeting of ASB had a populist edge, it also resonated with public concerns and rapidly became accepted as an interpretation of Britain's late twentieth-century condition.

A wider series of ideas were also significant. First, although the idea of ASB was initially most prominent in the UK, it drew upon Wilson and Kelling's (1982) 'broken windows' perspective and crime-prevention thinking, more generally, in that in order to prevent communities sliding into cycles of decline, it was essential to tackle lower-level harms and incivilities. Early intervention was key to preventing antisocial youth turning into career criminals.

See Chapter 6.1
Broken windows

See Chapter 6.2
Community safety

Second, the idea of 'zero tolerance' shaped responses to certain 'demonized' groups whose existence and behaviour represented both real and symbolic challenges to the community. Third was the idea that, while crime itself appeared to be falling, in the poorest and most disadvantaged areas, daily experiences of ASB were adversely affecting people's quality of life. Acts and behaviours that, in themselves, were unlikely to be regarded as serious – or a priority for the police, for that matter – when experienced continually, undermined community life in fundamental ways.

Campbell's research (2002) also highlighted a sense of 'impunity' associated especially with younger offenders; and, in due course, ASB came to be closely associated with the behaviour of young people, hanging around and misbehaving in urban and residential areas. In response, many of the new ASB interventions aimed to provide quick enforcement solutions, 'fast-tracked' through police and legal 'due process' in a performance culture driven by 'results'.

Section 1 of the 1998 *Crime and Disorder Act* introduced perhaps the most notorious ASB innovation – the Anti-Social Behaviour Order (or ASBO) – which was a form of civil injunction that could be awarded by magistrates courts regarding anyone acting in a manner that 'caused or was *likely to cause* harassment, alarm or distress to one or more persons not of the same household' (S1: CDA, 1998). Breach of an ASBO could result in a sentence of imprisonment of six months to five years (for adults). A particularly controversial aspect concerned the burden of proof – initially set at the civil standard for injunctions (the 'balance of probabilities') until the courts subsequently established that the criminal threshold, 'beyond reasonable doubt', should apply. ASBOs could be issued in respect of behaviour that was not in itself criminal; moreover, interim ASBOs could be granted (without those named being given the opportunity to defend themselves) and court-reporting restrictions could be waived in respect of ASBO proceedings against those under 18. Some commentators (Simester and von Hirsch 2006) have regarded the ASBO as a form of 'two-step criminalization': the first step attaches the order to a group of 'culpable' individuals; the second step, for *breach* of an order, permits a swift punitive upgrade to apply in the case of repeat offenders. Others have seen the ASBO as a flexible aspect of 'preventive justice' which could apply at the 'pre-criminal' stage (Ashworth and Zedner 2014).

By the time of the 2003 Anti-Social Behaviour Act, the ASBO had become one of a range of flexible interventions, including: Penalty Notices for Disorder; Acceptable Behaviour Contracts ('pre-crime' interventions which could be used in respect of misbehaviour by children as young as eight); Closure Notices; Dispersal Orders; Parenting Orders and Contracts; and Curfew Orders – which, taken together, transformed the landscape of routine crime and disorder management. Later, drawing upon US experience, 'gang injunctions' (or 'GangBos') were added to the repertoire of powers.

As Crawford (2009) has argued, new regulatory ideas – including 'pre-crime', early intervention, risk management and precautionary measures – have been used to short-circuit, sidestep or undermine established precepts of criminal justice, especially due process, proportionality and the special protections (anonymity, non-reporting) usually afforded to young people within the system. ASB management opened up new areas of community life and conduct to behavioural **surveillance** and criminal justice scrutiny, establishing patterns of enforcement action strongly oriented around established social inequalities and divisions, and frequently driven by ideological judgements reflecting social divisions of class, ethnicity and identity. Insofar as 'unattached youth' came to be seen, above all, as the primary subjects of ASB management, it was claimed that ASB had effectively 'turned public policy into a form of pest control' (Squires 2014).

See Chapter 5.19
Surveillance

The 2010 Conservative-led coalition government gave ASB policy further practical and ideological twists. A 2012 White Paper, *Putting Victims First*, spoke of the need for swifter supportive action for the most vulnerable victims and for putting communities at the centre of ASB management. In due course, the *Anti-Social Behaviour, Crime and Policing Act 2014* installed a newer, more flexible series of powers and orders addressing a wide range of criminal and pre-criminal behaviours, many of which would be determined at the lower, 'balance of probabilities', standard of proof.

In addition, a new *Criminal Behaviour Order* could be issued following a criminal conviction that would add banning or treatment conditions with which an offender would have to comply. Civil injunctions could be issued (on application by a variety of agencies: police, local authorities, social-housing agencies), assessed at the civil standard of proof, to prevent future ASB and harassment – breach being 'contempt of court' punishable by up to two years' imprisonment. Community Protection notices, for use against both individuals and organizations, could be introduced to prohibit behaviour likely to have a persistent, detrimental and unreasonable impact upon community life. Finally, and perhaps closest in spirit to the old ASBO, the new Public Space Protection Order (PSP) could be applied to individuals and groups in public spaces. Breach of this order is a criminal offence punishable by a £100 fixed penalty notice or a fine on conviction. Liberty, amongst other critics, has complained that the PSP is too vaguely drawn and open-ended, while the grounds for appeal are particularly narrow.

In terms of process, these new powers have been combined with what have been called the 'community trigger' and 'community remedy'. The former is designed to *require* an official response when three or more related ASB complaints are received over the course of a six-month period; the latter is intended to give victims a say in community resolutions. How frequently these measures will be employed is not clear.

The notion of 'anti-social behaviour' has been firmly planted in the lexicon of British crime control but, just as regulating misbehaviour has become a truly international phenomenon, it is no longer a novelty. Perhaps the chief legacy of the 'ASBO era' is the flexible array of graduated new 'police' enforcement powers, welfare sanctions, injunctions and orders designed to target, risk-manage, discipline, exclude, criminalize and 'pre-criminalize'. ASB has made the terrain of social control wider and the measures employed increasingly more insidious making it all the more important to examine how and against whom these powers are being employed.

References

Ashworth, Andrew, and Lucia Zedner. 2014. *Preventive Justice*. Oxford: Oxford University Press.

Campbell, Siobhan. 2002. *Implementing Anti-Social Behaviour Orders: Messages for Practitioners*. London: Home Office.

Crawford, Adam. 2009. Governing through Anti-Social Behaviour: Regulatory Challenges to Criminal Justice. *British Journal of Criminology* 49(6): 810–31.

Pearson, Geoffrey. 1983. *Hooligan: A History of Respectable Fears*. Basingstoke: Macmillan.

Rutter, Michael, Henri Giller, and Ann Hagell. 1998. *Anti-Social Behaviour By Young People*. Cambridge: Cambridge University Press.

Simester, A.P., and Andrew von Hirsch. 2006. Regulating offensive conduct through two-step prohibitions. In *Incivilities: Regulating Offensive Behaviour*, Andrew von Hirsch and A.P. Simester, eds, pp. 115–32. Oxford: Hart.

Squires, Peter. 2014. Anti-social behaviour: Marginality, intolerance and the 'usual suspects'. In *Anti-Social Behaviour in Britain: Victorian and Contemporary Perspectives*, Sarah Pickard, ed., pp. 214–24. Basingstoke: Palgrave Macmillan.

Tonry, Michael. 2004. *Punishment and Politics: Evidence and Emulation in the Making of English Crime Control Policy*. Cullompton, UK: Willan.

Wilson, James, and George Kelling. 1982. Broken Windows: The Police and Neighborhood Safety. *Atlantic Monthly* 249(3): 29–38.

Further reading

Bottoms, Anthony E. 2006. Incivilities, offence and social order in residential communities. In *Incivilities: Regulating Offensive Behaviour*, Andrew von Hirsch and A.P. Simester, eds, pp. 239–80. Oxford: Hart.

Cohen, Stanley. 1985. *Visions of Social Control*. Cambridge: Polity.

Flint, John. 2002. Social Housing Agencies and the Governance of Anti-Social Behaviour. *Housing Studies* 17(4): 619–37.

Mannheim, Hermann. 1946. *Criminal Justice and Social Reconstruction*. London: Routledge & Kegan Paul.

Pickard, Sarah (ed.). 2014. *Anti-Social Behaviour in Britain: Victorian and Contemporary Perspectives*. Basingstoke: Palgrave Macmillan.

Squires, Peter. 2006. New Labour and the Politics of Anti-Social Behaviour. *Critical Social Policy* 26(1): 144–68.

Squires, Peter (ed.). 2008. *ASBO Nation: The Criminalisation of Nuisance*. Bristol: Policy Press.

Squires, Peter, and Dawn Stephen. 2005. *Rougher Justice: Anti-Social Behaviour and Young People*. Cullompton: Willan.

Community corrections

Anne Worrall

'Community corrections' is a widely used generic term for the delivery of court sentences and programmes of rehabilitation, reparation and deterrence that do not involve incarceration There is no agreed definition of the term, however, and little consistency in its use. It is more popular in countries such as the USA, Canada, South Africa, China, Australia and New Zealand than it is in Europe, where the word 'corrections' sometimes has unacceptably negative connotations – and terms such as 'offender supervision', 'community sanctions' or 'offender management' are preferred (McNeill and Beyens 2013). Nor is there a consensus about which measures should be included under this umbrella term. Some argue that all non-custodial sentences – including financial penalties and suspended prison sentences – should be included, while others favour only those sentences that involve some form of professional supervision, such as probation and unpaid community work. A further complication is whether or not parole supervision following early release from a prison sentence should be included in the definition, since this is a post-custody measure rather than one that does not involve imprisonment at all. Increasingly, courts impose sentences that involve *both* a period in prison and a period of supervision in the community, thus blurring the boundaries of what constitutes community corrections. Community corrections are administered and delivered by public, private and voluntary sector staff with a range of titles – such as 'community corrections officer', 'probation officer', 'parole officer' or 'offender manager'.

For the purposes of this chapter, community corrections will be taken to include the following:

See Chapter 5.15
Restorative justice

- probation and multi-agency supervision
- unpaid community work
- curfews and electronic monitoring
- parole
- **restorative justice**

Some community corrections have long histories, while others have been introduced more recently. For example, the origin of probation can be traced back to the middle of the nineteenth century, whereas unpaid community work and electronic monitoring were introduced in the late twentieth century, partly as a result of prison overcrowding and as a means to find 'alternatives to prison' that were less expensive but equally demanding. The concept of parole has a long history, while restorative justice is a relatively recent innovation.

See Chapter 5.6
Desistance

See Chapter 3.8
Labelling theory;
Chapter 3.16
Stigma

Community corrections have many advantages over imprisonment. They allow offenders to retain the family, work and social ties that contribute to social capital and **desistance**. At the same time, they give offenders the opportunity to repair the damage they have done to the community and to resolve the personal and social problems that may have led to their offending in the first place. They enable an offender to avoid the **stigma of imprisonment** and the risk of becoming embedded in a criminal culture as a result of constant association with other criminals in prison. On the whole, community corrections are also far less costly to administer than imprisonment, and their reoffending rates are no worse.

Despite these advantages, community corrections have an 'image' problem. Although many more offenders receive some form of non-custodial sentence than are imprisoned, penal debates and policies focus overwhelmingly on prisons and neglect other forms of punishment. Attempts to raise the profile of community corrections have encountered a number of obstacles.

First, and of most significance, is the public and media perception that community corrections are but a poor substitute for the 'real punishment' of prison. Viewed as *soft options*, such sentences are often represented as being weak and undemanding 'let-offs' which do not command public confidence. There is, therefore, a constant search by advocates of community corrections to include more, and more demanding, conditions which distance such sentences from old-fashioned 'welfare' approaches.

Second is the obstacle of *net-widening* – a term that entered criminal justice vocabulary in the 1960s in the wake of labelling theory. With the proliferation of alternatives to custody comes the danger that, instead of keeping people out of prison, community corrections will simply draw more and more people into the 'net' of the criminal justice system, and thereby increase the likelihood that they will eventually end up in prison. With net-widening comes the concept of the 'dispersal of discipline' (Cohen 1985), which proposes that community corrections extend the restrictions of liberty experienced in prison to the community outside the prison walls. Curfews and the electronic monitoring of offenders are concrete examples of this.

The third major obstacle is that of *enforcement*. Ensuring compliance with community sentences – especially those with multiple and demanding conditions – is notoriously difficult, and courts have the right to send to prison any offender who breaches the conditions of their order. Consequently, it is difficult for community corrections to function other than 'in the shadow' of imprisonment.

Since the early 1990s, community-corrections interventions have been dominated by an umbrella approach known as *What Works*. This phrase is an explicit rejoinder to pessimistic earlier claims that 'nothing works' (that no intervention can be shown to be more effective than any other). The 'discovery' of cognitive **behavioural programmes** (initially in Canada and the USA) that focus on an offender's thinking and attitudes gave rise to a series of conferences and subsequent programmes that caught the imagination of politicians and professionals. Evaluation research has given cause for cautious optimism that such programmes can reduce reoffending – although critics have argued that enthusiasm for this approach should not result in the neglect of other provision such as basic literacy skills, social skills, drugs treatment, housing, employment and debt-counselling. The recognition that rehabilitation depends not only on changes in offenders' thinking and attitudes but also on fair access to opportunities has been supported by findings from desistance research (Weaver 2014). Criminal justice interventions may contribute to 'primary' desistance – to temporary but increasing gaps in criminal behaviour. Stopping offending altogether and continuing to lead a law-abiding life, however, depends on individuals coming to see themselves no longer as an 'offender' but as a different kind of person.

See Chapter 1.8
Learning theory

Partly in response to criticisms of the highly focused What Works interventions – and partly in response to ever-increasing managerialism and risk-assessment in the governance of criminal justice – multi-agency approaches to community corrections have developed since the mid-1990s whereby the police, prison and probation services explicitly work together, often being physically co-located in their premises. Alongside health, education, housing and employment agencies, offenders are offered an 'integrated' package of assistance and monitoring in return for their commitment to reduce their reoffending. The balance between care and control is constantly under review and dependent on the dynamic nature of offenders' **'risk'**, as calculated by various computerized systems. In the UK, the best-known of these partnerships are: Multi-Agency Public Protection Arrangements (MAPPA) for serious and high-risk offenders, and Integrated Offender Management (IOM) for medium- and low-risk offenders.

See Chapter 6.7
Risk

For reasons described earlier, it is even more difficult to undertake comparative research into community corrections than into prisons. Indeed, much has been written about the problems related to the transportation of penal ideas between countries and between communities. Although the broad principles underpinning community corrections may appear to be the same, specific interventions are often most effective when they respond to local or regional needs. For example, programmes designed for Canadian or Australian Aboriginal offenders are able to take account of the varying social, economic and cultural circumstances that are often disregarded by large commercially produced programmes that claim to be more or less universally applicable (Worrall 2004). Similarly, much has been written about the inappropriateness of interventions designed for male offenders for use with women, who are more likely to have been the victims of intimate violence and therefore to respond in different ways to the demands of the programmes (Sheehan et al. 2011).

The term 'corrections' is contested because of its multiple interpretations, ranging from the highly punitive to the psychologically manipulative to the politically Orwellian (presaging a utopia of 'corrected' ex-offenders). But the addition of the word 'community' creates a phrase that increasingly offers a future for criminal justice that can be civilized, rational, proportionate and fair in a way that prison so often is not.

References

Cohen, Stanley. 1985. *Visions of Social Control*. Cambridge: Polity.

McNeill, Fergus, and Kristel Beyens. 2013. *Offender Supervision in Europe*. Basingstoke: Palgrave Macmillan.

Sheehan, Rosemary, Gill McIvor, and Chris Trotter (eds). 2011. *Working with Women Offenders in the Community*. Abingdon: Willan.

Weaver, Beth. 2014. Control or Change? Developing Dialogues between Desistance Research and Public Protection Practices. *Probation Journal* 61(1): 8–26.

Worrall, Anne. 2004. What works and the globalization of punishment talk. In *What Matters in Probation*, George Mair, ed., pp. 327–45. Cullompton, UK: Willan.

Further reading

Hanser, Robert D. 2014. *Community Corrections* (2nd edn). Thousand Oaks, CA: Sage.

Latessa, Edward J., and Paula Smith. 2015. *Corrections in the Community* (6th edn). Abingdon and New York: Routledge.

Mair, George, and Lol Burke. 2012. *Redemption, Rehabilitation and Risk Management: A History of Probation*. Abingdon: Routledge.

Worrall, Anne, and Canton, R. 2013. Community sentences and offender management for adults. In *Criminology* (3rd edn), Chris Hale, Keith Hayward, Azrini Wahidin, and Emma Wincup, eds, pp. 493–512. Oxford: Oxford University Press.

Community policing

5.4

Victor E. Kappeler

Community policing is a philosophy that embraces a number of organizational principles and strategies designed to expand public participation in the co-production of crime control – reducing the fear of crime, lessening the perception of public disorder, and enhancing the quality of life of communities. The philosophy seeks to broaden the police mission from a narrow focus on 'law enforcement' and 'crime-fighting' to a broader one that encourages the exploration of creative, community-driven solutions for a host of social problems (Kappeler and Gaines 2015). The philosophy suggests the use of meaningful partnerships and problem-solving techniques; and, in its ideal form, strives to change policing from an authoritarian exercise of unilateral state power to a more democratic method of policing. In this sense, community policing seeks to empower people in the decision-making process such that the **police derive their agendas, role and practice** *from the community*, rather than vice versa.

See Chapter 5.3 Community corrections

Ideally, the community-policing philosophy values people and their concerns, relegating the police institution and its law-enforcement agenda to a secondary consideration. The idea is that, by paying attention to human and social problems as well as tailoring the police service to those problems, communities may be transformed into safer places with improved quality of life for all people – not just those with political or economic power. Solving human problems and making communities safer places in which to live is achieved by giving average people control over the police agenda. This means a radical redistribution of the power that has traditionally marked the divide between government, police and the population. From this perspective, the average citizen is no longer a passive actor in the practice of policing: he/she is an active participant in determining both what constitutes a community problem and how best to address it.

In an historic sense, community policing can be understood as a social and political response to the progressive reform efforts that took place at the beginning of the twentieth century. Social reformers sought to reduce corruption among the police and depoliticize the institution by narrowing its mandate from broadly construed 'public service', which was driven by local political leaders, to a narrower 'law-enforcement' directive devoted to crime control. Such a reform was to be achieved by the bureaucratization of the institution; the introduction of technology and ostensibly scientific practices; and the professionalization and training of occupational members. The institution's inability to achieve this reformed crime-control mandate – and a growing isolation of police from the communities they served, however – set the stage for a crisis in police legitimacy which led to the emergence of the community-policing movement.

See Chapter 5.17
Security and
counter-security

In the 1970s and early 1980s, as crime rates in the US climbed, police executives and political leaders came under increasing public pressure to address crime. At the same time, the **private security industry** was growing dramatically, challenging the police institution's near monopoly on crime control, and there was a general loss of trust and confidence in the police institution. Public policing had steadily lost ground to private policing, though few outside police circles realized that there were far more people employed in private security than there were public police officers. While it would be an exaggeration to say that policing was on the brink of extinction, the institution faced a direct threat to its occupational mandate, with private security firms waiting eagerly to make a quick profit and the general public withdrawing much of its traditional support from the police institution. Largely as a result of these pressures and a lack of police responsiveness to the needs of the public, police officials, political leaders and many scholars embraced the idea of community policing.

By the 1990s, select aspects of community policing had become institutionalized and it was a publicly accepted, if confused, form of policing. The Violent Crime Control and Law Enforcement Act of 1994 and its provision to fund 100,000 more community-policing officers during the presidency of William Jefferson Clinton further popularized the philosophy. At the close of the twentieth century, most police departments in the United States said they subscribed to community policing, and many included some form of the philosophy in their mission statements.

While the phrase 'community policing' became very popular during this period, and significant government funding was provided for the development of such initiatives, the substantive and systemic changes required to enact the philosophy never truly emerged. Several countervailing trends in policing contributed to the lack of substantively advancing community policing. The War on Drugs continued to be waged throughout the 1980s and well into the twenty-first century, which kept policing fully involved in its historic roles of law enforcement and crime-fighting. In a related trend, the police institution also embarked on a clear and dramatic movement toward the militarization of its ranks. These trends, coupled with the prevalence of competing policing strategies – such as 'broken windows' (Wilson and Kelling 1982), 'zero tolerance' (Kelling et al. 1994), 'problem-solving' and 'location-based' policing – better fit an aggressive law enforcement culture and contributed to the supplanting of community policing. Following the September 11, 2001 terrorist attacks in the United States, community policing faded from the political discourse, only to resurface occasionally in the form of rhetoric when the police institution faced a crisis – such as in late 2015 in the wake of the deaths of a number of unarmed African-American men by law-enforcement officials.

See Chapter 6.1
Broken windows

Confusion about what actually constitutes community policing has abounded almost from its inception. The philosophy of community policing is often, perhaps intentionally, confused with two of its component organizational strategies: 'community-oriented policing' and 'problem-oriented policing'. The former tends to engage the community, but, unlike community policing, it does not surrender authority, control or decision-making; rather, it merely *takes into consideration* the community when police and public officials set their agendas. Problem-oriented policing, a strategy designed to apply ostensibly scientific methods to social problems without community control of police agendas, retains the traditional authoritarian top-down approach to policing, and does not involve the power-sharing necessary to constitute community policing (Goldstein 1990).

While a community orientation and problem-solving are both necessary to enact community policing, neither captures the essential shift in occupational ethos and values necessary to move away from authoritative policing. Further confounding the meaning of community policing is that police executives and political leaders alike have conjoined the language of the philosophy with a wide array of aggressive strategies, programmes and practices that have very little to do with the philosophy itself. At the strategic level, these rhetorical slights of hand have conjoined strategies that range from broken windows to zero tolerance; at the programme level, community policing has been confounded with public-relations (PR) gimmicks to 'crime-prevention' initiatives; and, at the practice level, community policing has been comingled with tactics from foot patrol to aggressive field interrogations. Today, community-policing rhetoric is used to garner public support for almost any crime-control strategy, programme or practice that local political leaders and police officials want to advance.

See Chapter 6.2
Community safety

Community policing has been criticized for a number of reasons. Perhaps the most compelling critique is the observation that the philosophy was never fully implemented in the vast majority of police agencies. Like many philosophies, the abstraction became troubled when attempts were made to put the philosophy into practice. Both the authoritarian nature of policing and the need to deploy state power, coupled with the nature of police culture, resulted in many compromised implementations of the philosophy.

A related critique of the difficulty of abstraction is the fact that 'community' is a fraught term – one that often suggests a degree of consensus, homogeneity or unanimity among people living in an area that is lacking in most geographies in the US in the twenty-first century. Community policing has also been criticized as a rhetorical means to assist circumvention of the rule of law by allowing the police to expand their powers, infiltrate formerly insulated social space and restrict social practices that would not be permissible with strict adherence to the rule of law. In this sense, the philosophy has contributed to the development of a post-9/11 security state where police powers have been expanded well beyond the rule of law.

Finally, the select ways in which community policing has been implemented have resulted in a co-joining of economic elites with state use-of-force entities, which has the potential to enlist 'communities' in the marginalization of some of their own members. In this sense, the most vocal sectors of the community may violate the rights or civil liberties of others in the pursuit of what they imagine to be a 'safer community'. The community-policing movement thus has led not to the more democratic form of policing envisioned by its proponents, but to a whole new set of tensions and contradictions.

References

Goldstein, Herman. 1990. *Problem Oriented Policing*. New York: McGraw-Hill.

Kappeler, Victor E., and Larry K. Gaines. 2015. *Community Policing: A Contemporary Perspective* (7th edn). London: Routledge.

Kelling, George, Michael Julian, and Steven Miller. 1994. *Managing 'Squeegeeing': A Problem-Solving Exercise*. New York: New York Police Department.

Wilson, James, and George Kelling. 1982. Broken Windows: The Police and Neighborhood Safety. *Atlantic Monthly* 249(3): 29–38.

Suggested reading

Crank, John P. 1994. State Theory, Myths of Policing, and Responses to Crime. *Law and Society Review* 28: 325–51.

Eck, John E., and Dennis P. Rosenbaum. 1994. The new police order: Effectiveness, equity, and efficiency in community policing. In *The Challenge of Community Policing: Testing The Promise*, Dennis P. Rosenbaum, ed., pp. 3–24. Thousand Oaks, CA: Sage.

Klockars, Carl. 1988. The rhetoric of community policing. In *Community Policing: Rhetoric or Reality*, Jack Greene and Stephen Mastrofski, eds, pp. 239–58. New York: Praeger.

Manning, Peter K., 1988. Community policing as a drama of control. In *Community Policing: Rhetoric or Reality*, Jack Greene and Stephen Mastrofski, eds, pp. 27–45. New York: Praeger.

Skogan, Wesley G. 2004. *Community Policing: Can it Work?* Boston: Cengage.

Skogan, Wesley G., and Susan M. Hartnett. 1999. *Community Policing, Chicago Style*. New York: Oxford University Press.

Decarceration

Judah Schept

Decarceration is a concept that eludes essential definition. As Scull (1984:3) pointed out in one of the first scholarly treatments of the subject, the term 'decarceration' does not appear in general dictionaries. At its broadest level of agreement, decarceration refers to the process of closing down prisons, jails and other carceral institutions and releasing their populations back to their communities. The concept is contested rhetorical terrain, however, and very different visions have been projected through it (Cohen 1985). Depending on the context in which it is used, decarceration may imply the treatment or captivity of formerly incarcerated people in various forms of community supervision or confinement; in other situations, it may signify a broader systemic critique of the carceral state, including the role of community social-control systems; in still others, the term may be employed to suggest a commitment to **abolition**.

See Chapter 5.1
Abolitionism

Foundational work on decarceration emerged during an historical period marked by broad distrust of state institutions and a growing embrace of control in the community. This early work on decarceration critically considered this process and engaged deeply with the politics, political economies and lived experiences of carceral regimes stretched across both institutions and their so-called alternatives in communities. One major study acutely considered how movements to close down prisons and asylums and instead treat people in community settings have often failed on their own terms, providing neither the cost savings nor the more humane treatment they had promised (Scull 1984).

The orientation of this early work locates the study of decarceration in the broader tradition of revisionist historical treatments of punishment. This tradition – associated with works such as Michel Foucault's *Discipline and Punish*, David Rothman's *Conscience and Convenience* and Anthony Platt's *The Child Savers* – pushes against the argument that approaches to punishment have evolved progressively. Instead, this work argues that efforts to reform penal practices have often resulted in expanding carceral infrastructure, essentially shifting the emphasis within a given system of punishment – akin to what Michel Foucault calls 'the carceral archipelago' and what a number of scholars have referred to as 'net-widening' (see broadly Cohen 1985). In addition, this work considers both punishment and its reform as central to reproductions of class relations, racial control and the exercise of state power. Still other work has cautioned against the 'impossibilist stance' of this vision, and instead suggests that community **social-control** efforts can operate outside of the coercive and punitive logics of the prison and serve, in this way, as a legitimating force for decarceration (McMahon 1992).

See Chapter 5.18
Social control

This decarceration literature from the 1980s and early 1990s may seem quaint, obsolete or even naïve when read in the context of mass incarceration in the United States. After all, in the intervening decades between much of that literature and the present volume, the number of people under some form of correctional control has grown exponentially. This has involved both a massive rise in the number of people incarcerated and an expansion in the scope of community corrections. At present in the United States, 2.3 million people are imprisoned and close to 5 million are under some form of community supervision. And yet the concept of decarceration is not an intellectual relic from a time before the project of the carceral state was realized; in fact, it is alive and well and the tension from its early days is productive for a consideration of its contemporary contradictions as well as its political potential.

Decarceration has been an important plank in the larger platform of prison-abolitionist activism for decades. Associated in the United States with critical resistance and in North America and globally with the International Conference on Penal Abolition, the abolitionist movement organizes to dismantle societal reliance on penal institutions and logics. Decarceration figures importantly in these visions. Evidence of this can be found in the growing number of both state- and municipal-level organizations and coalitions that preface their regional focus with the word 'decarcerate' – including groups such as Decarcerate PA, Decarcerate the Garden State, Decarcerate STL and Decarcerate Monroe County (IN). Importantly, the movement has long recognized and struggled over the connection between the prison and community forms of social control, pushing essential analysis to conceptualize both as part of the present carceral regime. Noting that the words 'incarceration' and 'cancel' share the same root, activist and scholar Maya Schenwar (2014:119) notes: 'Decarceration, then, is also a movement toward un-canceling people – not just by fighting for their release, but by recognizing and supporting their humanity.'

Decarceration is a living and dynamic concept. While its origins are in critical scholarly traditions and activism, in recent years the term has come to embody some of the contested intellectual and political terrain of the current moment of reform. As state governments partner with public-policy think tanks in the name of justice reinvestment, reducing recidivism and sentencing reform, decarceration – as a principle if not as a political position – has entered the lexicon of bipartisan politics. 'Justice reinvestment' illuminates this complicated landscape. Conceived by reformers as a mechanism by which to reinvest in the welfare, social and health services of low-income communities that had been abandoned under neoliberalism and the growth of the carceral state, in practice, justice reinvestment has included the redistribution of money from state departments of correction to municipal jails, police departments and **community corrections**, shifting more of the weight of the carceral state to the city and county level (Gottschalk 2015:98-116). That this project could conceivably be called decarceration by some reformers demonstrates the instability of the concept as well as the continuing resonance of earlier scholarship to considerations of its particular salience in this historical moment.

See Chapter 5.3 Community corrections

The bipartisan consensus on prison reform belies the ways in which the carceral state may re-form through a number of shifts: from the rhetoric and politics of 'tough on crime' to those of rehabilitation and 'smart on crime' – and, importantly, from overcrowded state prisons to a more diffuse network of carceral and community-based institutional settings across several spatial scales (Gottschalk 2015). Ironically, then, decarceration may serve as one of the central concepts through which the reconfiguration of the carceral state occurs, a process the historian of punishment Heather Ann Thompson (2014) has called 'the Decarceration Dodge'. At the same time, however, growing scholarly attention to non-carceral communities and transformative justice also demonstrates that the concept of decarceration remains firmly grounded in its radical and abolitionist roots (Brown 2014; Schept 2015).

References

Brown, Michelle. 2014. Visual Criminology and Carceral Studies: Counter-Images in the Carceral Age. *Theoretical Criminology* 18(2): 176–92.

Cohen, Stanley. 1985. *Visions of Social Control: Crime, Punishment, and Classification.* Malden, MA: Polity.

Gottschalk, Marie. 2015. *Caught: The Prison State and the Lockdown of American Politics.* Princeton: Princeton University Press.

McMahon, Maeve. 1992. *The Persistent Prison? Rethinking Decarceration and Penal Reform.* Toronto: University of Toronto Press.

Schenwar, Maya. 2014. *Locked Down, Locked Out: Why Prison Doesn't Work and How We Can Do Better.* Oakland, CA: Berret-Koehler.

Schept, Judah. 2015. *Progressive Punishment: Job Loss, Jail Growth and the Neoliberal Logic of Carceral Expansion.* New York: New York University Press.

Scull, Andrew. 1984. *Decarceration: Community Treatment and the Deviant – A Radical View* (2nd edn). New Brunswick, NJ: Rutgers University Press.

Thompson, Heather. 2014. Dodging Decarceration: The Shell Game of 'Getting Smart' on Crime. *Huffington Post*, 9 July. www.huffingtonpost.com/heather-ann-thompson/ dodging-decarceration-the_b_5485361.html. Accessed 25 January 2016.

Further reading

Foucault, Michel. 1977. *Discipline and Punish: The Birth of the Prison*. Translated by Alan Sheridan. New York: Random House.

Miller, Jerome. 1998. *Last One over the Wall: The Massachusetts Experiment in Closing Down Reform Schools* (2nd edn). Columbus: Ohio State University Press.

Platt, Anthony M. 1977. *The Child Savers: The Invention of Delinquency*. Chicago: University of Chicago Press.

Rothman, David. 1980/2002. *Conscience and Convenience: The Asylum and Its Alternatives in Progressive America*. New York: Walter de Gruyter.

Desistance

Ben Hunter

The study of desistance from crime is concerned with how and why individuals stop offending. Despite this seemingly simple description, defining what constitutes desistance has proved a difficult enterprise. As a result of various definitional ambiguities, there are nearly as many different ways of defining desistance as there are studies devoted to the topic.

Part of the reason for the definitional difficulty relates to the problems of conceptualizing what desistance represents. After all, in defining and measuring desistance, we are attempting to identify the *absence* of an event – in this instance, crime. How much time must pass before an offender can be considered to have desisted from crime? Must we wait for the death of the offender to declare with confidence that he/she ceased his/her criminal activities? A related challenge concerns the fact that conceptualizations of desistance must square with existing research observations of how offenders spend their time. Even the most prolific offenders spend a large portion of their time not offending, and the period between offences can often be quite long. Similarly, how do we account for those individuals who continue to offend but do so less frequently over time before finally stopping altogether, thus exhibiting a gradual decline in offending behaviour rather than a sudden stop? (For elaboration on the above see Laub and Sampson 2001.) These realities of offender behaviour caution us against trying to develop hard and fast definitions of desistance.

In an effort to reconcile these difficulties, researchers have largely abandoned efforts to identify desistance as a specific event in an offender's life, i.e. efforts indicating the 'moment' when offending stops. Such attempts risk leading to arbitrary cut-off points differentiating desisters from persisters – e.g. two years without offending, no convictions after a certain age. In contrast to this emphasis on desistance as an *event* then, attention has shifted to desistance as a *process*. One way of differentiating these two conceptualizations of desistance is to consider the questions each prompts us to ask. A concern with desistance as an event encourages a focus on 'why'? For example, why did an individual stop offending? In contrast, in conceptualizing desistance as a process, one is more interested in the 'how?' of offending and its cessation. For example, how do individuals live in such a way as to achieve a goal of a crime-free life? How do they cope with obstacles they may encounter as they construct an ex-offender identity? Emphasizing desistance as a process recognizes that reforming one's character and building an identity as an ex-offender frequently takes time, and can involve considerable and deliberate effort on the part of the individual.

Early desistance work emphasized the specific correlates of desistance from crime. As a result, ageing (Farrington 1986), gaining employment (Laub and Sampson 2003) and forming romantic partnerships (Uggen 2000) have all been identified as important for desistance. Explanations for the impact of ageing on offending were frequently grounded in maturation processes that led to a re-evaluation of the appropriateness of offending behaviour or a decline in the physical ability needed to commit many crimes. The power of employment and partnerships in their ability to inspire desistance was often explained as result of the changes they heralded in **routine activities of offenders** or the increased **social control** that engagement with these opportunities implied (Laub and Sampson 2003). Although useful, however, a focus on the correlates of desistance tended to – at least implicitly – emphasize desistance as something that occurred externally to the individual, with particular structures exerting their influence to 'cause' desistance. What such understandings lacked was an appreciation of *individuals* as active participants in their own change.

See Chapter 6.8
Routine activity
theory

See Chapter 2.6
Control theories

Reflecting in part a desire to understand the 'inner' world of desistance, and sympathetic to a more desistance as process-oriented account, later desistance scholarship has sought to understand not just the correlates of desistance, but also the subjective experience of desistance from crime – that is, what it is like to desist (for examples see, e.g. Giordano et al. 2002; Paternoster and Bushway 2009). This work, which might be termed a 'phenomenology of desistance', has highlighted, among other things:

- the importance of attending to offenders' goals;
- their reaction to obstacles faced;
- the way in which they make sense of their offending pasts;
- the decisions they make to live lives in keeping with who they want to be; and
- the contribution of this cognitive work to changes in values and beliefs.

It has served to consider the internal – we might say 'agentic' – world of desistance. This research has also emphasized the importance of offenders being cognitively ready to change in order for such change to happen.

Naturally, it is important not to set up a false dichotomy between structural and agentic factors. Instead it is important to appreciate the interplay between them. So an (internal) desire to desist from crime and do something productive with one's life might prompt a search for employment. Conversely, the forming of intimate relationships might lead to a desire to change for the sake of the new relationship. This appreciation therefore stresses that occurrences such as marriage or employment do not just happen to people; they are frequently sought out for the advantages and opportunities they bring, and often involve commitment on the part of the would-be desister.

As the above implies, the study of desistance is concerned not only with change over time, but also individuals' understanding of such change. Consequently, longitudinal designs are perhaps best suited to studying desistance. Earlier work did attempt to argue against the necessity of longitudinal designs in criminology (e.g. Gottfredson and Hirschi 1987) and there are some excellent desistance studies employing cross-sectional designs. Nevertheless, the ability of longitudinal designs to account for the dynamic nature of desistance highlights their usefulness in tracking how offenders come to desist.

Desistance research has progressed steadily since the mid-1980s. More recent efforts have argued for making criminal justice interventions and offender supervision in particular more desistance focused. Thus, there has been a desire to inform criminal justice practice with observations gleaned from research. Such research has also suggested the importance of criminal justice interventions taking time to 'bed in' and impact offending behaviour. In addition, desistance research has indicated the role that seemingly small interventions can make in the lives of offenders. Interventions need to focus on helping offenders build and maintain social capital – the goal being to assist offenders in strengthening the relationships they have that are important to them.

Despite the wealth of desistance research and its vibrancy as an area of study, there are a number of shortcomings with the existing literature. Our understanding of how the process of desistance might operate for female and ethnic minority offenders is poor when compared to more general understandings of desistance (but see Sheehan et al. 2013; Calverley 2014 for respective exceptions). Nor has there been extensive consideration of how desistance might operate in the context of certain types of offending, such as white-collar crime or for groups of high-risk offenders (but see Hunter 2015; Weaver 2014). More broadly, there is a need to develop a body of work that seeks to marry desistance research with wider understandings of how social inclusion might be promoted, bringing in insights from social-capital literature for example.

References

Calverley, Adam. 2014. *Cultures of Desistance*. London: Routledge.

Farrington, David. 1986. Age and Crime. *Crime and Justice: An Annual Review of Research* 7: 189–250.

Giordano, Peggy C., Stephen A. Cernkovich, and Jennifer L. Rudolph. 2002. Gender, Crime and Desistance: Toward a Theory of Cognitive Transformation. *American Journal of Sociology* 107(4): 990–1064.

Gottfredson, Michael, and Travis Hirschi. 1987. The Methodological Adequacy of Longitudinal Research on Crime. *Criminology* 25(3): 581–614.

Hunter, Benjamin. 2015. *White-Collar Offenders and Desistance from Crime: Future Selves and the Constancy of Change*. London: Routledge.

Laub, John H., and Robert J. Sampson. 2001. Understanding Desistance from Crime. *Crime and Justice: An Annual Review of Research* 28: 1–78.

Laub, John H., and Robert J. Sampson. 2003. *Shared Beginnings, Divergent Lives: Delinquent Boys to Age 70*. Cambridge, MA: Harvard University Press.

Paternoster, Ray, and Shawn Bushway. 2009. Desistance and the 'Feared Self': Toward an Identity Theory of Criminal Desistance. *Journal of Criminal Law and Criminology* 99(4): 1103–56.

Sheehan, Rosemary, Gill McIvor, and Chris Trotter (eds). 2013. *What Works with Women Offenders*. Cullompton, UK: Willan.

Uggen, Christopher. 2000. Work as a Turning point in the Life Course of Criminals: A Duration Model of Age, Employment and Recidivism. *American Sociological Review* 65(4): 529–46.

Weaver, Beth. 2014. Control or Change? *Probation Journal* 61(1): 8–26.

Further reading

Farrall, Stephen, Ben Hunter, Gilly Sharpe, and Adam Calverley. 2014. *Criminal Careers in Transition: The Social Context of Desistance from Crime*. Oxford: Oxford University Press.

Maruna, Shadd. 2001. *Making Good: How Ex-Convicts Reform and Rebuild Their Lives*. Washington, DC: American Psychological Association.

Presser, Lois, and Sveinung Sandberg. 2015. *Narrative Criminology: Understanding Stories of Crime*. New York and London: New York University Press.

Weaver, Beth, and Fergus McNeill. 2015. Lifelines: Desistance, Social Relations and Reciprocity. *Criminal Justice and Behaviour* 42(1): 95–107.

Fear of crime

Lynn Hancock

'Fear of crime' emerged as a focus for criminological inquiry and policy concern in the USA in the mid- to late 1960s. Influenced by developments in
various criminological perspectives in the 1970s and 1980s, and taken up
as political issue for parties, governments and media outlets, fear of crime
soon became an object of investigation and political intervention in the UK
and some other English-speaking nations (Lee 2007). What exactly is meant
by 'fear of crime', however, has been and remains the subject of debate. As
Jackson (2004:20, cited in Lee 2007:108) explains, fear of crime is 'a complex,
diffuse, "catch all" phrase referring to a range of inter-related but theoretically
distinct perceptions and responses to crime and risks of victimisation'. Given
the difficulties associated with defining the concept, it is not surprising that
contestation and debate arise with regard to, for example: the techniques used
to assess the extent of 'fearfulness' in populations; the tools used to discover
who fears more than others (and why); how the cues that are said to generate
fear are examined; and the effects of fear on individuals' daily lives.

Most writers trace the emergence of the concept in the USA to the report
The Challenge of Crime in a Free Society (President's Commission on Law
Enforcement and the Administration of Justice 1967). Lee (2007), however,
points to a confluence of factors emerging in the late eighteenth and early
nineteenth centuries which laid the groundwork upon which criminological
interest in the fear of crime as a focus of study could arise. These included; the
rise of **classicist criminology**; the growing importance of empirical data
and social statistics for understanding and governing populations; and concerns about urban squalor and the 'dangerous classes' in the rapidly growing

See Chapter 1.2
Classical
criminology

industrial cities. In the USA in the 1960s, expanding interest in public-opinion polling, concerns about rising rates of crime and, again, social unrest – especially in the context of the civil rights struggles of that decade –provide the background to the President's Commission report. The coming together of political, media and government interests – along with academic criminologists' interest in quantifying **victimization**, the 'dark figure' of unreported crimes and public 'fear' – created what Lee refers to as a 'feedback loop' which produced and reproduced the concept of fear of crime and furthered its ongoing development.

See Chapter 4.39
Victimology

In the UK, the first of a series of the (then) biennial British Crime Survey (BCS) sweeps (actually focused on England and Wales) was undertaken in 1982. This followed Sparks and colleagues (1977) first victimization study for the Home Office and efforts to promote situational **crime prevention** (under Ronald Clarke in the Home Office's Research and Planning Unit) – with these developments taking place against the general backcloth of campaigns for 'law and order' preceding and following the 1979 General Election. This is not to say that 'administrative criminology' drove the agenda, as it is generally accepted that **radical, feminist and realist criminologies (left and right)** also played important roles in shaping fear-of-crime discourses in different ways; but all had the same effect of foregrounding fear of crime as an object of scrutiny and intervention (Walklate 1998; Lee 2007).

See Chapter 6.2
Community safety

See Chapter 3.3
Critical
criminologies;
Chapter 3.6
Feminist
criminologies;
Chapter 3.13
Radical feminism;
Chapter 4.26
Patriarchy and
crime; Chapter
3.14 Realism and
left idealism;
Chapter 4.23
(Neo)-conservative
criminology

Debates about how fear of crime could best be identified and the problems of measuring 'fear' have surrounded the concept from the beginning. Criticisms of national victimization surveys (of the like mentioned above) have produced methodological refinements and the identification of conditions (beyond 'crime') that shape public attitudes and perceptions. The central problem of measuring 'objectively' what is a varying, **emotional** and subjective response ('fear') using a large-scale victimization survey has been highlighted by many writers. Disapproval has frequently focused on the use of scenario questions and hypothetical situations to assist respondents with their assessments of their levels of 'fear' (Lee 2007). The preferred notion of 'worry' (rather than fear) about crime in the Crime Survey for England and Wales (CSEW, formerly the British Crime Survey) retains rather than dispenses with some of these problems. Academic disputes about what exactly is being 'feared' or worried about are also longstanding. National surveys such as the CSEW ask respondents about a narrow range of crimes – such as burglary, car crime and interpersonal violence; but academic criminologists have considered and critiqued a wider range of conditions that have been said to shape public responses. These include (but are not limited to) the question of whether fear of crime may be used as a proxy for fear of strangers; respondents' perceptions of their vulnerability to personal victimization; the influence of neighbourhood context (change, instability, **organization** and perceived levels of social control); prior experience of victimization or knowledge about local victims; the role of print and broadcast media; and rapid social change in society.

See Chapter 4.10
Emotions

See Chapter 2.2
Social
disorganization
theory

The relationship between 'fear' and 'risk' has bedevilled fear of crime debates over a long period, especially when survey results have suggested (or have been construed to suggest) that sections of the population have 'irrational fears' (Lee 2007:90). Surveys such as the CSEW situate findings about worry about crime against respondents' perceptions of national and local crime levels. Data on levels of worry are presented for different demographic groups (by sex, age and ethnicity) in contrasting **spatial settings** (urban and **rural**, private and social housing) and local environments (whether a high level of 'disorder' is said to be present, for example). These 'variables' have been a staple of the BCS and the CSEW since 1982, with only slight variations.

See Chapter 6.10
Space, place and
crime

See Chapter 6.9
Rural criminology

In the 1980s and 1990s, understandings of fear of crime that had been derived from national victimization survey findings faced challenges from various perspectives. For example, local crime surveys promoted by left realists aimed to offer a more nuanced and complex understanding of fear of crime in urban areas, while feminist criminologists disputed the idea that women's fear was out of step with their risk of victimization (Lee 2007). During the 1990s further conceptual, methodological and empirical work (qualitative as well as quantitative) challenged and shaped fear-of-crime debates. In the UK, a range of projects funded through the Economic and Social Research Council's (ESRC) Crime and Social Order Initiative (1993–97) supported innovative critical inquiry and interdisciplinary work that subsequently shaped further transformations, with human-geographers, psychologists and, later, cultural criminologists, among others, stimulating discussion and debate.

The rise of 'critical voices' (Farrall and Lee 2009) in this period also coincided with initiatives that augmented government interest in the fear of crime. In England and Wales, under New Labour, the BCS was expanded and extended to be administered annually. The Crime and Disorder Act (1998) required that Crime Audits, often including public perceptions of fear of crime, be undertaken in Community Safety Partnership areas. While the Home Office promoted 'tool kits' to assist with data collection and analysis in this period, there remained weaknesses associated with the definition of concepts and their operationalization (Lee 2007). Furthermore, media outlets displayed no concerns about accurate measurement, and increasingly invited viewers and readers to respond with their views on simplistic questions, reflecting and sustaining public opinion and political interest regarding fear of crime (and related 'law and order' matters), as the media marketplace became more competitive (Lee 2007).

Academic preoccupation with measuring the extent of 'fearfulness' in (various) populations, the conditions that generate 'fearful' responses and the impact on the well-being of individuals and communities continues. More critical work has placed attention on understanding fear of crime alongside a wider range of 'risks' and harms in people's everyday sensemaking in different settings. Others have explored the work that fear of crime performs in generating a marketplace for home-security devices and personal protection, thus perpetuating inequalities in the distribution of 'safety', with the extension and

See Chapter 4.24
Neoliberalism

See Chapter 4.14
Globalization

See Chapter 5.17
Security and
counter-security

See Chapter 4.19
Institutional and
anti-institutional
violence

consolidation of **neoliberal** rationalities and **globalization** giving further rise to expanding markets for 'security'. The fear-of-crime discourse moulds compliant citizens for governments, and this has become another focus for critical academic work. In particular, 'fear of terrorism', and its role in statecraft, has become a major theme in this vein following the attacks on the World Trade Center in New York in 2001 (Lee 2007).

References

Farrall, Stephen, and Murray Lee. 2009. Critical voices in an age of anxiety: a reintroduction to the fear of crime. In *Fear of Crime: Critical Voices in an Age of Anxiety*, Murray Lee and Stephen Farrall, eds, pp. 1–11. Abingdon: Routledge.

Lee, Murray. 2007. *Inventing Fear of Crime*. London: Routledge.

President's Commission on Law Enforcement and the Administration of Justice. 1967. *The Challenge of Crime in a Free Society*. Washington, DC: United States Government Printing Office. Available at: www.ncjrs.gov/pdffiles1/nij/42.pdf.

Sparks, Richard, Hazel G. Genn, and David J. Dodd. 1977. *Surveying Victims: A Study of the Measurement of Criminal Victimization, Perceptions of Crime, and Attitudes to Criminal Justice*. Chichester: Wiley.

Walklate, Sandra. 1998. Excavating the Fear of Crime: Fear, Anxiety or Trust? *Theoretical Criminology* 2(4): 403–18.

Further reading

Hale, Chris. 1996. Fear of Crime: A Review of the Literature. *International Review of Victimology* 4(2): 79–150.

Hope, Tim, and Richard Sparks (eds). 2000. *Crime, Risk and Insecurity*. London: Routledge.

Lee, Murray, and Stephen Farrall (eds). 2009. *Fear of Crime: Critical Voices in an Age of Anxiety*. Abingdon: Routledge.

Walklate, Sandra, and Gabe Mythen. 2008. How Scared Are We? *British Journal of Criminology* 48(2): 209–25.

Governmentality

Randy K. Lippert

'Governmentality' is an analytical concept that refers to methodical ways of thinking about how to govern conduct. Used in criminology and other disciplines, the portmanteau 'governmentality' was coined by French philosopher and historian Michel Foucault by combining 'government' and 'mentality' – to refer not only to state practices but also more broadly to the 'conduct of conduct'. 'Government', in this context, means any effort to lead, guide or shape behaviour – including criminal conduct but also that of police and various other authorities. Government thus includes criminal justice and crime-control policies and practices of the state; it also includes systematic efforts to prevent or react to criminal and immoral conduct among private authorities and agents (e.g. corporations, churches and volunteer organizations) and those that are neither obviously private nor public in character. Criminologists have used governmentality concepts and themes to make sense of a wide range of crime-control and criminal-justice policies and practices – and a significant, if varied, body of work has emerged.

Foucault was certainly not a criminologist (and was actually disdainful of the field), but his ideas on governmentality became widely influential in critically oriented criminology, although an English translation of the 'Governmentality' lecture that appeared in 1979 only gained popularity a decade later when republished in an widely distributed anthology. Thereafter, governmentality ideas became more accessible to Anglo-American scholars, including criminologists.

Three concepts distilled from Foucault's work became central: *mentalities* (also termed 'governmentalities' or 'rationalities'), *program(me)s* and *technologies* (or 'techniques'). A 'mentality' is a methodical means of thinking about government. Mentalities tend to raise doubt about existing governmental arrangements targeting crime or crime control, and are based on seeing conduct as a problem to modify in some manner. Mentalities demand forms of knowledge, including mainstream criminology, but also accounting, **forensics, geography, medicine and psychology**. The questions mentalities raise allow thinking about how to reconfigure governmental arrangements. **Neoliberalism** is one such mentality.

See Chapter 1.8 Learning theory; Chapter 1.15 Forensic psychology

See Chapter 4.24 Neoliberalism

'Programmes' are prescriptions and plans for acting on criminal conduct or on authorities' practices that seek to respond to it. Programmes imagine addressing problems raised by mentalities to improve the way this conduct is managed. These are informed by criminological knowledge about how to overcome particular problems deemed to require a response (e.g. a rash of robberies on an urban retail strip or an unaccountable police force). Again, programmes are not limited to state schemes, but instead include those conceived by private and other agencies and agents. They can include everything from neighbourhood **crime-prevention** schemes to zero-tolerance policing programmes, to prison rehabilitation to police cultural diversity training programmes. The common denominator is an effort to manage criminal conduct or the conduct of those initiating crime-control and criminal justice measures.

See Chapter 6.2 Community safety

'Technologies' are devices, methods and means that make this government possible. Technologies become arranged within programmes by mentalities, while technologies simultaneously allow mentalities to be implemented. These practical elements help install mentalities and effect programmes. Technologies are in principle infinite but include crime statistics and rewards/incentives for crime 'tips', as well as broader 'technologies' such as **community policing** and private insurance (Garland 1997).

See Chapter 5.4 Community policing

By the 1990s, these concepts were informing **critically oriented criminology**, especially in Australia, Britain and Canada, with Garland (1997:173) arguing that 'the governmentality literature offers a powerful framework for analyzing how crime is problematized and controlled'. This wider embrace of the governmentality analytic in criminology's critical circles coincided with the ascendency of sweeping political economic changes particularly evident in the 1990s and most often termed 'neoliberalism' (sometimes called advanced liberalism, a related but not identical term). These developments were complex and uneven, but typically involved a reduction of welfare-state arrangements. With this came private forms of crime control epitomized by private security firms and gated communities, empowerment of persons previously seen as deserving of state services, and the introduction of entrepreneurialism and marketization mechanisms in the state, especially in advanced Anglophone countries.

See Chapter 3.3 Critical criminologies

Two key themes emerging from these and related engagements with governmentality are noteworthy: 'responsibilization' (Garland 1997:188) and 'governing through' (Simon 2007:4). The former refers to a technique consistent with neoliberal governmentality involving shifting responsibility for security or crime reduction from the state to its lower levels, private agencies or individuals. It is a hallmark of neoliberal governmentality. The latter refers to those occasions when populations (or subpopulations) are governed through a desire to avoid the risky 'criminal other' revealed by criminological knowledge (e.g. criminal-profiling). Here institutions and authorities use crime categories to justify 'interventions that have other motivations' (Simon 2007:4).

Governmentality-informed criminology has three key features distinguishing it from much criminology. First, governmentality is not a theory of crime, criminalization, governance, power or society. Rather, it is a set of conceptual tools, a perspective or analytic. Criminology informed by governmentality concepts and themes is not expected to reduce findings to theories of crime or crime control or broader theories involving capitalist society, network society, postmodernity or risk society (Garland 1997). The governmentality analytic calls instead for detailed analyses of governmental programmes involving crime and its control using its concepts to render them at once more intelligible and less self-evident by unearthing their (often historical) component parts (see Lippert and Stenson 2010). Second, whilst mainstream criminologies tend to focus more on patterns of *criminal conduct*, governmentality-informed criminology tends to focus instead on programmes and practices of *authorities* (e.g., police, prison personnel, private-security professionals) that seek to prevent, reduce and otherwise control conduct. Exploring the role of knowledge is thus deemed essential here. Governmentality-informed criminology sees mainstream criminology (e.g., routine activities theory) as a way to govern populations.

A third feature is an attention to **language or discourse** rather than to reality: a criminology informed by governmentality thus tends to correspond, in principle, with post-structuralist assumptions. A key focus is the language of texts (e.g., policy statements, operational manuals), which is seen neither as representing reality nor as a form of ideology that obscures real (political or economic) interests underlying criminal justice or crime-control reforms or authorities' actions (e.g., state domination, racism, capital accumulation). Rather, language is constitutive; it makes up ways of acting upon crime and criminals as well as the spatial and temporal dimensions in which this occurs. Discourse is presumed to structure what can be experienced and to limit what can be done or said, including by public, private and other authorities concerned about crime and related behaviour.

See Chapter 4.29
Post-structuralism
and criminology

The current status of governmentality-informed criminology is uncertain. Governmentality concepts and themes still appear in criminology's top journals; and responsibilization and governing through, especially, continue to resonate with critically oriented criminologists. Through them, governmentality's influence lives on. Yet, other Foucault-related themes – such as brute exercises of exceptional sovereign power or 'exceptionalism' since 9/11 by the US and other Western states – have seemingly garnered scholarly attention at the expense of analyses of mentalities and technologies (Lippert and Walby 2016). Thus, among other required refinements, such as greater engagement

See Chapter 4.19
Institutional and
anti-institutional
violence

with 'the real' (see Lippert and Stenson 2010), for revitalization of this analytic in criminology is more systematic consideration of governmentality in relation to sovereign power and associated exceptionalism. Certainly Foucault had not suggested sovereign power had passed us by with governmentality's ascendency: in closing his governmentality lecture, Foucault (1991:102) made clear that sovereignty had not been historically replaced by discipline or government, but instead remained intimately tethered to them and stood of equal conceptual importance. Recall too that Foucault's (1979) 'spectacle of the scaffold' account in *Discipline and Punish*, well known to criminologists as underscoring the sovereign's exceptional power to put subjects to death, also, crucially, noted a sovereign's capacity to decide the exception – that is, the last-minute pardon that could spare the condemned. In the twenty-first century, the peculiar coexistence of forms of governmentality and sovereign power in crime control and criminal justice – as well as the ongoing 'war on terror' and their real effects – need closer consideration if governmentality and its concepts are to fulfil their analytical promise in criminology.

References

Foucault, Michel. 1979. *Discipline and Punish: The Birth of the Prison*. New York: Vintage.

Foucault, Michel. 1991. Governmentality. In *The Foucault Effect: Studies in Governmentality*, Graham Burchell, Colin Gordon, and Peter Miller, eds, pp. 87–104. Chicago: University of Chicago Press.

Garland, David. 1997. Governmentality and the Problem of Crime: Foucault, Criminology, Sociology. *Theoretical Criminology* 1(2): 173–214.

Lippert, Randy, and Kevin Stenson. 2010. Advancing Governmentality Studies: Lessons from Social Constructionism. *Theoretical Criminology* 14(4): 473–94.

Lippert, Randy, and Kevin Walby. 2016. Governing through Privacy: Authoritarian Liberalism, Privacy Law, and Privacy Knowledge. *Law, Culture, and the Humanities* 2(2): 329–52.

Simon, Jonathan. 2007. *Governing through Crime: How the War on Crime Transformed American Democracy and Created a Culture of Fear*. New York: Oxford University Press.

Further reading

Gordon, Colin. 1991. Governmental Rationality: An Introduction. In *The Foucault Effect: Studies in Governmentality*, Graham Burchell, Colin Gordon, and Peter Miller, eds, pp. 1–51. Chicago: University of Chicago Press.

Hunt, Alan, and Gary Wickham. 1994. *Foucault and Law: Towards a Sociology of Law as Governance*. London: Pluto.

Rose, Nicholas, Pat O'Malley, and Mariana Valverde. 2006. Governmentality. *Annual Review of Law and Social Sciences* 2: 1–22.

Incapacitation

Helen Johnston

To incapacitate a person means to stop or prevent him/her from doing something; in the case of punishment, incapacitation is used to physically prevent people from committing crime. At the most basic level, offenders are incapacitated by being temporarily or permanently stopped from committing additional offences; this is achieved by killing them or by removing body parts (e.g., cutting off the hands of thieves to prevent further thefts) or, most commonly across the Western world, by placing them in prison to stop them committing further crimes against wider society (though not against other prisoners or prison staff). In 2015, 25 countries across the world executed offenders. Most executions took place in Iran, Pakistan and Saudi Arabia, but this does not include figures for China or North Korea, two countries that are thought to execute large numbers of offenders but for which accurate data remains secret (Amnesty International 2016).

Incapacitation has long been used as a justification for punishment, and its use can be traced to early forms of physical punishments, such as banishment, and to the use of prisons either as places of detention or punishment. Rooted in **classical theory and in utilitarianism**, incapacitation is a forward-looking justification for punishment that operates to prevent further crimes from being committed by the offender. The focus of incapacitation is the removal of the offender from society in order to prevent repeat offences; it is not concerned with why the offender committed the crimes or with trying to address any reasons for offending. Nor is it concerned with rehabilitating the offender. As a theory, it also appealed to early **positivists** who were interested

See Chapter 1.2 Classical criminology; Chapter 1.3 Utilitarianism

See Chapter 1.4 Positivism

in trying to predict who might commit offences and in identifying the supposed physical and moral traits of criminality as they saw them.

The practice of incapacitation can vary, and criminal justice systems may employ various tactics to achieve this aim. For example, authorities might ban a drunk or dangerous driver from driving for a period of time, or place restrictions or curfews on offenders to ensure they do not visit a victim or a particular location associated with their offending. In most Western societies, however, when it comes to serious offending and punishment, incapacitation is usually discussed in relation to the use of long sentences of incarceration based on an assessment of the risk posed to the public by the individual. For example, in the UK, mandatory life sentences are given for crimes of murder (even though the offender may not be incarcerated for the whole of his/her life but released on life licence or parole), and discretionary life sentences are given for other serious offences. In the UK, there are also a small number of offenders who have 'whole-life' tariffs and will never be released from prison. Another well-known example of incapacitation in sentencing is the 'three-strikes' laws introduced in the US state of California in 1994, which provided for a life sentence for any third offence committed: no matter how serious the third offence, if the offender had been convicted twice before for previous serious or violent offences, he/she would automatically receive a life sentence.

Since the development of long-term imprisonment for the punishment of serious offenders from the mid-nineteenth century onwards, we can observe the use of other sentences based on incapacitation that provide some historical context for more recent policies. Fundamentally, incapacitation has been used to selectively incapacitate those offenders who are deemed, in their various ways, to be dangerous or pose a risk or threat to wider society. In England, the passing of the Penal Servitude Act 1864 and habitual offenders legislation in 1869 and 1871 resulted in minimum sentences of seven years for repeat offenders, registers of offenders and police supervision for up to seven years after release. Similarly, 40 years later, in England, the 1908 Preventive Detention Act aimed to incapacitate those offenders who were deemed to be dangerous or at risk of committing crimes; offenders would serve their sentence of penal servitude for the crime committed and, once this had been completed, could be subject to a further five to ten years of 'preventive detention'.

Most recently, incapacitation has underpinned the use of various sentencing policies and legislation to ensure long determinate or indeterminate sentences for certain offenders and to address the perceived threat that these individuals pose in terms of risk to the public. This is evident in recent penal policies such as three-strikes legislation in the US (noted above), as well as the Indeterminate Public Protection (IPP) sentencing framework in the UK (Criminal Justice Act 2003), which combined long, indeterminate sentences with minimum tariffs to ensure certain offenders were locked away from the rest of society to prevent them from committing further offences.

See Chapter 5.10
The new penology

See Chapter 6.7
Risk

It has been observed that in the last 20 to 30 years we have shifted towards a **'new penology'**, one based on **risk management**, actuarial justice and, as part of this, a greater use of sentences based on incapacitation (Feeley and Simon 1992). Scholars have also argued that we can observe a 'new punitiveness' or 'punitive turn' since the mid-1990s. They see this shift as being characterized by a number of different features. In terms of punishments this has manifested itself in shifts toward policies of indefinite detention and the use of 'supermax' security imprisonment and sentencing policy based on incapacitation, like the 'three-strikes' legislation. There has also been increased use of 'shaming' or ostentatious punishments, examples of which include requiring offenders to wear placards in public places referring to their crime (e.g., 'I am a thief') or requiring them to undertake community work while wearing brightly coloured jumpsuits or badges declaring their criminal status. These penal strategies have been underpinned by the use of zero-tolerance policing and electronic surveillance. These policies are justified and influenced by those who claim to be representing public opinion (Pratt et al. 2005).While the IPP sentence in the UK has since been abolished, many thousands of offenders are still under the sentence in prison, with a significant proportion past their minimum tariffs. Instead of the IPP, repeat offenders in the UK receive mandatory life sentence for their 'second strike' if they commit one of 45 listed offences in the Legal Aid, Sentencing and Punishment of Offenders Act 2012 (Cavadino et al. 2013).

Punishment based purely on incapacitation can be criticized on a number of fronts. First, imprisoning someone for long periods of time may be considered unjust or undeserved depending on the offence committed. For example, offenders under three-strikes legislation in the US may be serving a life sentence even though their third offence could be considered a minor one, like a theft of small monetary value. Therefore, sentences of incapacitation may be viewed as disproportionate to the actual offence committed. Second, there is also the problem of false positives and false negatives: we might judge an offender low risk and release him/her on parole, only for him/her to commit further crimes; conversely, we might keep someone in prison, viewing him/her as high risk even though he/she may have aged out of crime. In an often-cited example, it is estimated that we would have to increase the prison population by 25 per cent to achieve a 1 per cent reduction in crime rates (Tarling 1993). Accordingly, incapacitation can work only when it is used on large numbers of the population, and even then its effects are generational as older repeat offenders are replaced with younger ones (Scott and Flynn 2014). While incapacitation as an aim for punishment is most effective in the use of the death penalty, predicting the dangerousness or risk of reoffending remains a challenge.

References

Amnesty International. 2016. Dramatic Rise in Executions in 2015: The Most in One Year for a Quarter of a Century. www.amnesty.org.uk/death-penalty-2015-numbers-figures-rise-executions-death-sentence. Accessed 29 June 2016.

Cavadino, Michael, James Dignan, and George Mair. 2013. *The Penal System: An Introduction* (5th edn). London: Sage.

Feeley, Malcolm M., and Jonathan Simon. 1992. The New Penology: Notes on the Emerging Strategy of Corrections and its Implications. *Criminology* 30(4): 449–74.

Pratt, John, David Brown, Mark Brown, Simon Hallsworth, and Wayne Morrison (eds). 2005. *The New Punitiveness: Trends, Theories, Perspectives*. Cullompton, UK: Willan.

Scott, David, and Nick Flynn. 2014. *Prisons and Punishment* (2nd edn). London: Sage.

Tarling, Roger. 1993. *Analysing Offending: Data, Models and Interpretations*. London: HMSO.

Further reading

Morris, Norval. 1994. 'Dangerousness' and incapacitation. In *A Reader on Punishment*, Anthony Duff and David Garland, eds, pp. 238–60. Oxford: Oxford University Press.

Walker, Nigel. 1991. *Why Punish? Theories of Punishment Reassessed*. Oxford: Oxford University Press.

The new penology

5.10

Michelle Brown

The new penology is a perspective that plots the rise of actuarial justice in understandings of crime and criminal justice in late-modern, neoliberal capitalist societies. Viewing crime as now normal and no longer a site for **social reformation**, the new penology positions criminality as a problem of **risk-management** and a primary mechanism of governance. Based upon **discourses**, technologies and practices that enhance the identification and management of 'high-risk,' 'dangerous' or unruly groups, the new penology marks the rise of technocratic forms of knowledge no longer concerned with the rehabilitation or disciplinary transformation of individual offenders. Instead, the model is concerned with the production of aggregate categories and classification schemes that presume to locate, track and **incapacitate** actual and potential offenders. Scholars of the new penology argue that this formation focuses on the management of the system in a manner that expands the scope of crime control and the managerial tactics of criminal justice agents, institutions and crime policies across social life.

See Chapter 5.12
Penology

See Chapter 6.7
Risk

See Chapter 4.29
Post-structuralism
and criminology

See Chapter 5.9
Incapacitation

Sociolegal scholars Malcolm Feeley and Jonathan Simon introduced the term 'new penology' in a widely read 1992 *Criminology* article, later revising and further developing their propositions in a series of works (Feeley and Simon 1998; Simon and Feeley 2003). Their claims continue to serve as a critical building point within the field of criminology and the sociology of punishment. They argue that the new penology marks a predominant transformation in punishment centred on a series of shifts:

The emergence of new discourses: In particular, the language of probability and risk increasingly replaces earlier discourses of clinical diagnosis and retributive judgment.

The formation of new objectives for the system: The objectives we have in mind are not simply new to the system (some of them have old antecedents) but are in some sense newly 'system.' We are especially interested in the increasing primacy given to the efficient control of internal system processes in place of the traditional objectives of rehabilitation and crime control. Goals like reducing 'recidivism' have always been internally shaped in important ways . . . but in the contemporary setting the sense that any external social referent is intended at all is becoming attenuated.

The deployment of new techniques: These techniques target offenders as an aggregate in place of traditional techniques for individualizing or creating equity.

(Feeley and Simon 1992:450)

Under the new penology, risk, in the form of 'dangerous' populations, is most effectively managed not through normalization but through a spatialization that primarily functions to isolate and exclude. The rise of mass incarceration, for instance, with its focus on removing potentially dangerous individuals from society and warehousing them in prison for long periods of time – largely disconnected from the larger aims of crime control or rehabilitation – reflects this kind of risk-management emphasis. This actuarialist model emerges as a complex mixture of styles of thought, discourse and vocabulary, as well as sets of practices, strategies and technologies. Grounded in efficiency, new-penology actors value a certain technicism where system streamlining on the basis of cost-benefit analysis and risk assessments are foregrounded. These new-penology actors are driven by an economy of management centred on the distribution of aggregate numbers of individuals across the justice system and an extension of these patterns of control across the everyday life of offenders and system professionals. Their primary tools are prediction instruments, classification schemes of 'at-risk' populations, distribution grids and technology – all of which are conducive to the production of emergent, wider networks of control.

Mapping its application to all manner of criminal justice agencies and institutions – juvenile justice, policing, courts, probation and parole, and incarceration – scholars of the new penology have analysed how it serves as a lens through which to understand a variety of shifting sociolegal landscapes. These include workplace regulation, sex-offender registries, **immigration** and border control, homeland security and **the war on terror**. Furthermore, one of the new penology's primary contributions is tracing how current configurations of crime and social control operate in a manner which extends beyond criminal justice into families, communities, schools and other primary social institutions and practices of everyday life – a phenomenon Simon refers to as 'governing through crime' (2007). Materializing as a symptom of a larger crisis

See Chapter 4.6
Crimmigration

See Chapter 4.19
Institutional and
anti-institutional
violence

within **governance**, the new penology seeks to *regulate* rather than *explain* or *change* contemporary social problems – and thereby risks in its dissemination the widespread loss of social thinking, or the ability to understand social issues in collective and political terms. The privileging of actuarial techniques in relation to problems of crime, poverty and power risks erasing the moral, political and social significance of the historical markers of vulnerability and inequality – race, class, gender, sexuality and disability. Instead, these differences are positioned as no longer problematic, closing off significant social debates a priori. Out of this framework, critics argue, emerges a new and dangerous kind of social collectivity, one that is defined not by a deep sense of shared bonds or experiences but by exclusion.

See Chapter 5.8
Governmentality

The new penology has been subject to a wave of critical revision by punishment scholars. Some have argued that the 'new-ness' of the new penology is more or less a repackaging to some extent of pre-existing theoretical frames with its emphasis on classical Marxist terms like the dangerous class. Others argue that the new penology is unable to account for the rise of populist understandings of punishment centred on retribution, harshness and an emotive turn in law and order politics (Pratt 2000). Similarly, it is not entirely clear how the new penology marks a fundamental rupture from disciplinary to actuarial modes, or from modern punishment to something postmodern or otherwise, with critics pointing to the presence of actuarial logics historically in criminal justice as well as the persistence of individualistic, rational actor orientations that privilege retribution and expressive modes of populist sentiment in contemporary contexts (O'Malley 1999).

Some of the more compelling critiques of this model have emerged at the level of the field of practice. In assessments of the degree to which front-line actors and professionals in the criminal justice system have internalized the actuarial logic of the new penology, scholars find conflicting evidence. In a classic article examining a California parole field office, sociolegal scholar Mona Lynch writes of the importance of micro-level jurisdictional penal change in assessing the new penology's broad claims:

> One site for examining whether the new penology is indeed emerging as a distinct penological operating system is at the place where strategy is put into penal practice: at the level of implementation. There is reason to think that the contact point between the institution (and its new penological policies) and the outside world (with its old-fashioned 'modern' take on criminality) is one battleground where the sustainability of the new penology may be tested.
>
> (Lynch 1998:842)

Her findings point to the manner in which features of old and new penology meld in the everyday settings of criminal justice agencies, with actors reaffirming conventional law-enforcement roles, including an individualistic focus, even as upper management developed policies framed by actuarial logics of risk management. Others make a case for the unpredictable aspects of human agency within institutional frameworks as a check upon the totalizing, systematizing tendencies of a new penology (Cheliotis 2009).

See Chapter 4.14
Globalization

The weakening of social-welfare frameworks for governance has led to an expansion and **exportation of punitive carceral strategies by the United States** – a new mode from which to regulate racial minorities, the poor and myriad groups defined more so by vulnerability than criminality. The new penology has played a pivotal role in understanding the nature of that expansion, contributing to a number of key areas of study, including sociolegal scholarship; the sociology of punishment and risk; and governmentality and actuarial critiques. While its primary contributions have since morphed into larger dialogues about governance and the carceral state, the new penology remains an important marker in understanding the history of criminology and the force of penality at the turn of the millennium.

References

Cheliotis, Leonidas. 2009. How Iron is the Iron Cage of New Penology? The Role of Human Agency in the Implementation of Criminal Justice Policy. *Punishment and Society* 8(3): 313–40.

Feeley, Malcolm, and Jonathan Simon. 1992. The New Penology: Notes on the Emerging Strategy of Corrections and Its Implications. *Criminology* 30(4): 449–74.

Feeley, Malcolm, and Jonathan Simon. 1998. Actuarial justice: the emerging new criminal law. In *Crime and the Risk Society* Pat O'Malley, ed., pp. 375ff. Brookfield, VT: Ashgate.

Lynch, Mona. 1998. Waste Managers? The New Penology, Crime Fighting, and Parole Agent Identity. *Law and Society Review* 32(4): 839–69.

O'Malley, Pat. 1999. Volatile and Contradictory Punishment. *Theoretical criminology* 3(2): 175–96.

Pratt, John. 2000. Emotive and Ostentatious Punishment: Its Decline and Resurgence in Modern Society. *Punishment and Society* 2(4): 417–39.

Simon, Jonathan, and Malcolm Feeley. 2003. The Form and Limits of the New Penology. *Punishment and Social Control* 2: 75–116.

Simon, Jonathan. 2007. *Governing Through Crime*. New York: Oxford University Press.

Further reading

Baker, Tom, and Jonathan Simon (eds). 2010. *Embracing Risk: The Changing Culture of Insurance and Responsibility*. Chicago: University of Chicago Press.

Hannah-Moffat, Kelly. 2005. Criminogenic Needs and the Transformative Risk Subject: Hybridizations of Risk/Need in Penality. *Punishment and Society* 7(1): 29–51.

Harcourt, Bernard. 2007. *Against Prediction: Punishing and Policing in an Actuarial Age*. Chicago: University of Chicago Press.

Hudson, Barbara. 2003. *Justice in the Risk Society: Challenging and Re-Affirming 'Justice' in Late Modernity*. London: Sage.

Wacquant, Loïc. 2009. *Punishing the Poor: The Neoliberal Government of Social Insecurity*. Durham, NC: Duke University Press.

Panopticism

Michael Fiddler

Panopticism is centrally concerned with visibility. As derived from Jeremy Bentham's 1791 architectural plans for the Panopticon, the term refers to that which is 'all-seeing'. As such, panopticism relates to the mechanisms that facilitate that visibility. To unpack this, we must examine Michel Foucault's seminal 1977 text *Discipline and Punish*, which famously begins with the prolonged and graphic description of the execution of Damiens for the attempted assassination of Louis XV. Pages pass on the unflinching details of the punishment wrought on Damiens' body. This is then juxtaposed with the minute detail of a prison timetable some 80 years later. The movement, the microgestures, of the prisoner were precisely mapped out and regimented. They were to be observed, recorded and categorized. The 'punishment–body relation' shifted. Punishment had moved away from pain inflicted upon a body. The body itself became 'an instrument or intermediary', while punishment led the 'soul to become the prison of the body' (Foucault 1977:11, 30). The body was to be rendered 'docile' by an ever-present surveillant gaze. Vision and visibility were central to both displays of punishment. The former was concerned with spectacle. The latter occluded the act of punishment from public view, yet had its subject under close surveillance behind the prison walls. This is our point of departure for a discussion of panopticism: the importance of vision on the path to a 'state of conscious and permanent visibility' (Foucault 1977: 201).

Foucault used Bentham's Panopticon as a device to explore these overlapping ideas of vision and visibility. The building itself was proposed by Bentham and drawn up by the architect William Reveley in 1791. The plans were published as *Panopticon; or The Inspection House*. Two decades of political wrangling eventually led to the end of the project, and a different design was used in the construction of Millbank Prison on its proposed site. Whilst the prison was not constructed per Bentham's vision, Illinois Stateville Correctional Center and the Presidio Modelo on Cuba's Isle of Pines have definite echoes. The Panopticon design itself was derived from a textile mill that Samuel Bentham (Jeremy's brother) had constructed for Prince Potemkin's estate in Krichev in what is now Belarus. Both factory and prison were premised on an asymmetry of sight. In the prison, cells were to be located on the inner perimeter of a circular tower. An observation tower rose in the centre allowing a single observer to see into each of the cells. Thick curtains draped the observer's vantage point. The observer could look out through pinpricks in the curtain, but, in the cell, the prisoners would never know if they were being observed. They would come to internalize the seemingly ever-present **surveillant** gaze of the observer. They would discipline themselves. Today, the all-seeing eye of the panopticon refers to that privileged central observer. It is he/she who sees the many, while the observer is shrouded in permanent invisibility.

See Chapter 5.19
Surveillance

The extraordinary efficiency of the panoptic design is such that it merges geometry, economy and morality. In Bentham's phrasing, the Panopticon was intended to offer 'morals reformed – health preserved – industry invigorated – instruction diffused'. The Panopticon was rooted in physical architecture. If we reframe it as a diagram of disciplinary power, however, its continued influence can be felt beyond the material.

The asymmetry of vision within the Panopticon merits further analysis. As Brighenti (2007) puts it, asymmetries transform visibility into a site of strategy. The differential between observer and observed is clear. The observed becomes 'the object of information, never a subject in communication' (Foucault 1977:200). Furthermore, in being unable to return the gaze, in being denied 'the reciprocity of the eye-to-eye relation', there is a 'dehumanization of the observed' (Brighenti 2007:337). The 'axial' visibility of margin from the centre allows for examination, categorization and division whilst inhibiting a lateral visibility at the margins. '[T]o impose a particular conduct on a particular human multiplicity', however, does not require a physical apparatus (Deleuze 1988:29). The 'distribution of bodies, surfaces, lights, gazes' can be effected through more intangible mechanisms (Foucault 1977:202). This theatre of discipline – this 'virtual assemblage' and 'luminous environment' (Deleuze 1988:28) – finds effect in its 'imaginary intensity' (Foucault 1977:205).

In *Discipline and Punish* Foucault (1977:205) states that the Panopticon 'is the diagram of a mechanism of power reduced to its ideal form; its functioning . . . must be represented as a pure architectural and optical system.' Deleuze (1988:28) extrapolates from this point to see the Panopticon as a 'system of light before being a figure of stone.' The Panopticon becomes, then, a diagram of power. Stripped of its physicality, it becomes an 'abstract machine' (Deleuze 1988:30). It exists as both a 'system of light' and a system of discourse. It is at once a system of surveillance based on the visual *and* the collection of information gathered about its subjects. For Brighenti, this still places a primacy on (the asymmetry of) vision. Where the idealized physical building provided a first order of asymmetry between observer and observed, a diagram of power offers a second-order asymmetry in as much as there are those who are cognizant of the diagram and those who are not. Alternatively, Deleuze (1988:44) suggests that thinking of the Panopticon as a diagram of power should, instead, be reframed as 'several superimposed maps.' Rhizomic in nature, these maps overlap and interpenetrate one another. In so doing, they provide 'points of creativity, change and resistance' (ibid.). This multiplied way of examining the flows of power pushes us in the direction of critiques and alternatives that reframe panopticism in terms of simulations within wider surveillant assemblages.

Critiques of Foucauldian panopticism are largely premised on the notion that Foucault took historical discussions of the practice of punishment for the reality. For example, Alford (2000:134) suggests that Foucault 'presents the utopian ideals of eighteenth-century prison reformers . . . as though they were the actual reforms of the eighteenth and nineteenth centuries.' In *Discipline and Punish*, however, Foucault (1977:205) stated that the 'Panopticon must not be understood as a dream building . . . it is in fact a figure of political technology that may and must be detached from any specific use.' It was a diagram of power, not a statement of the real. Indeed, he counsels against developing a general theory from a singular institutional example. That the Panopticon was not built adds to its imaginative force. Its applicability to contemporary imprisonment speaks to other factors. For Alford (2000:127), 'prison authorities don't look because they don't have to.' There is no need for the 'warehouse' prison to produce docile bodies. Clearly, this relates to broader changes at the level of political economy, culture and technology.

Critics also argue that a panoptical model is simply too reductive for advanced Western societies. Alford proposes that the trajectory of 'power' is rather more subtle than a unidirectional flow from centre to margin. An alternative might look to 'sousveillance'. This inverts the top-down surveillance of the powerful and, instead, makes them the subject of a 'look' from those at the margins. There is also Mathiesen's (1997) *synopticon*. This describes the many watching the few. Mathiesen suggests that the rise of the modern mass media developed alongside panopticism. The growth of print media, followed by radio and then television, led to a 'viewer society'. There is a sense of passivity within Mathiesen's formulation, however, that has subsequently been problematized by the interactivity of social media. If we can fold this turn towards interactivity into Mathiesen's synopticon, we see that it remains a fundamentally *visual* phenomenon. This is a relationship mediated by screens. Yet, as implied by Mathiesen's suggestion (1997:230), this is a mechanism encouraging the masses to 'acquiesce'. They are seduced into looking.

It is perhaps best to talk of panopticism and synopticism working in parallel. The contemporary post-panoptical subject acquiesces and consents to be watched, volunteering information whilst also watching the few. On top of this, we can also layer previsualization and prevention. Here surveillance takes on a diagnostic character. This 'actuarial gaze' (Brighenti 2007:337) peers into networks, connections and interstices. It is a surveillance of meta-data. The surveillant assemblage has shed the physical. This architecture of power has moved beyond the carceral. Rather, it has come to embrace phone records, Internet browser histories and the contents of shopping carts.

References

Alford, C. Fred. 2000. What Would It Matter If Everything Foucault Said about Prison Were Wrong? *Discipline and Punish* after Twenty Years. *Theory and Society* 29(1): 125-46.

Brighenti, Andrea. 2007. Visibility: A Category for the Social Sciences. *Current Sociology* 55(3): 323–42.

Deleuze, Gilles. 1988. *Foucault*. London: Continuum.

Foucault, Michel. 1977. *Discipline and Punish*. London: Penguin.

Mathiesen, Thomas. 1997. The Viewer Society: Michel Foucault's 'Panopticon' Revisited. *Theoretical Criminology* 1(2): 215–32.

Further reading

Bentham, Jeremy. 1843. *The Works of Jeremy Bentham*, Vol. 4: *Panopticon, Constitution, Colonies, Codification*. Available at: http://oll.libertyfund.org/titles/bentham-the-works-of-jeremy-bentham-vol-4. Accessed 29 January 2016.

Boyne, Roy. 2000. Post-Panopticism. *Economy and Society* 29(2): 285–307.

de Lint, Willem. 2001. Arresting the Eye: Surveillance, Social Control and Resistance. *Space and Culture* 4(7–9): 21–49.

Elmer, Greg. 2003. A Diagram of Panoptic Surveillance. *New Media and Society* 5(2): 231–47.

Gane, Nicholas. 2012. The Governmentalities of Neoliberalism: Panopticism, Post-Panopticism and Beyond. *Sociological Review* 60(4): 611–34.

Smith, Philip. 2008. *Punishment and Culture*. Chicago: University of Chicago Press.

Penology

Leonidas K. Cheliotis

The birth of penology is commonly associated with the penal theories produced by **utilitarian** legal philosophers Cesare Beccaria and Jeremy Bentham in the eighteenth century. Over time, penology has come to assume a range of other, not necessarily mutually incompatible forms. The most important of these are usefully described by Spanish scholar Manuel López-Rey (1964) in his typology of penologies, which he defined according to the interests, aims, moral ideals and scientific theories reflected in each of them.

See Chapter 1.3
Utilitarianism

The first major type is what López-Rey calls 'administrative penology'. As the name itself suggests, administrative penology is managerial in nature, and as such is focused on efforts to increase the efficiency and effectiveness of the penal system, without any particular substantive attachment to the moral or other roles the penal system may be thought to perform in society. Thus, the privileging that administrative penology has historically accorded to institutionalized 'treatment' as a means of dealing with lawbreakers has had little if anything to do with adherence to some moral ideology or social function, and has rather been reflective of the relationship of dependent subservience that administrative penology bears to the penal system. In contemporary times, the most acute expression of administrative penology is what Feeley and Simon (1992) critically refer to as **'the new penology'** – the increased emphasis penal systems have been placing on the effective control of actuarially designated risk groups and the efficient management of internal system processes through continuous audits, at the expense of pursuing the traditional objectives of **retribution, deterrence** or, indeed, rehabilitation.

See Chapter 5.10
The new penology
See Chapter 5.16
Retribution
See Chapter 1.17
Deterrence;
Chapter 1.2
Classical
criminology

See Chapter 1.4
Positivism

See Chapter 1.5
Biological
criminology

The second major type in López-Rey's account is what he terms 'scientific penology'. Here penology consists of attempts by experts to promote the successful individualized 'treatment' of lawbreakers inside penal institutions, based on theories, mostly drawn from clinical psychology and psychiatry, which either are or purport to be scientifically grounded. The most famous proponent and practitioner of this approach is Italian physician **Cesare Lombroso**, whose work in the late nineteenth century sought to advance a scientific method for identifying the **biological** causes of crime and addressing them under conditions of incarceration; indeed, by dint of its tightly controlled regime and cellular architecture, the prison lent itself ideally both as a kind of laboratory where large amounts of data could be gathered systematically about individual criminals and their offending, and as a clinical environment where diagnosed character pathologies could be 'treated' by specialists (see further Garland 1985). Over time, Lombrosian and cognate branches of scientific penology have come under severe criticism, not only for their actual lack of scientificity and their harmful consequences for lawbreakers (not least of which has been the legitimation of indefinite detention until 'treatment' is deemed complete), but also for their self-serving tendency to produce the need for clinical interventions that they themselves are specially equipped to supply. The 'treatment' ideology has never fully waned, however. New and popular versions of it have emerged over recent decades; and, while some are arguably more sophisticated and respectful towards lawbreakers than their predecessors were, there has also been an alarming resurgence of interest in Lombrosian-style perspectives.

The third major type in López-Rey's discussion is 'analytical penology'. Substantively, its core task is two-pronged: on one hand, to ascertain whether, and the degree to which, penal systems, policies and practices perform their formally ascribed functions; on the other hand, to identify the array and relative significance of the reasons why punishment manifests itself the way it does, qualitatively as well as quantitatively. What this implies is that analytical penology may as well pass judgement on the contributions made by the administrative and scientific strands of penology to the scope and delivery of punishment. At the same time, in seeking to account for levels and patterns of punishment, analytical penology is in contact with a range of disciplines (sociology, history and political science, for example) through which it engages with thematic fields transcending narrowly penological concerns as such. Indeed, as the degree and depth of engagement with those disciplines and fields have risen over time, so the role of analytical penology has extended beyond that reserved for it by López-Rey – namely, beyond merely proposing policy and practical interventions in the penal system with a view to improving its performance.

Broadly perceived, analytical penology has shed light on a wide range of substantive issues. Key amongst them is the role of state-sanctioned punishment as a carrier of cultural meaning, and especially the latent symbolic functions it may perform from the perspectives of individual and group

468

psychology. Research in this area has examined, for instance, the ways in which dominant cultural values and prevalent emotions influence the degree and intensity of punishment, and how the rituals of punishment express collective sentiments and enhance social cohesion. Under the rubric of the political economy of punishment, another major concern of analytical penology has been the links between penal policy and different forms of economic organization, from preindustrial capitalism to welfare capitalism and **neoliberalism**. Relevant studies here have explored such themes as:

See Chapter 4.24
Neoliberalism

- the functional equivalence and aggregate effect of seemingly unrelated state policies regarding matters of welfare, employment and criminal punishment insofar as they bolster, simultaneously as well as cumulatively, exploitability in the labour market;
- the ways in which criminalization and punishment of weak minorities may help to manage the insecurities caused amongst mainstream publics by unjust socio-economic policies;
- the role played by the so-called **'prison industrial complex'** in the expanded use of custodial punishment; and
- the specific institutional arrangements (e.g., legislation and bureaucratic structures and cultures) that filter the effects of economic forces on penal policy and practice.

See Chapter 5.5
Decarceration

In recent years, analytical penology has also shown growing interest in the relationship between political systems and punishment, both in terms of whether certain levels and patterns of punishment are distinct to particular political systems, and in terms of the politico-institutional and other factors that account for any observed similarities or differences. Pertinent research has addressed a range of themes: from the effect different democratic features are thought to exert on the use of punishment; to the role played by electoral politics in fuelling punitive policies and practices; to the detrimental implications punishment has for the quality and reach of structures and processes of political participation; to how democracies and non-democracies compare in terms of their use of the power to punish; to how legacies of authoritarianism may affect penal policy and practice in the ensuing democratic environment.

Although analytical penologists have usually focused their attention on single jurisdictions (typically democracies of the global north), they have increasingly paid due recognition to the need for international comparisons (and for greater diversity in the selection of comparators at that) as the most appropriate means of replicating, validating and falsifying extant arguments in the field (see further Nelken 2009). In a similar vein, a small but growing throng of analytical penologists have been calling for research stretching beyond the standard use of imprisonment as a measure of state punishment to include, amongst others, policing, **surveillance** and civil and criminal law (see, for example, Tonry 2007). This as yet underused approach promises not only to help capture the punitive consequences other, non-carceral institutions

See Chapter 5.19
Surveillance

may have in their own right, but also, ultimately, to facilitate better gauging the magnitude of state punishment as a whole – as a process carried out cumulatively and simultaneously by an ensemble of different institutional forces.

References

Feeley, Malcolm M., and Jonathan Simon. 1992. The New Penology: Notes on the Emerging Strategy of Corrections and Its Implications. *Criminology* 30(4): 449–74.

Garland, David. 1985. The Criminal and His Science: A Critical Account of the Formation of Criminology at the End of the Nineteenth Century. *British Journal of Criminology* 25(2): 109–37.

López-Rey, Manuel. 1964. Analytical penology. In *Studies in Penology*, Manuel López-Rey and Charles Germain, eds, pp. 138–83. The Hague: Martinus Nijhoff.

Nelken, David. 2009. *Comparative Criminal Justice*. London: Sage.

Tonry, Michael. 2007. Determinants of Penal Policies. *Crime and Justice: A Review of Research* 36(1): 1–48.

Further reading

Brooks, Thom. 2012. *Punishment*. London: Routledge.

Cavadino, Michael, and James Dignan. 2013. *The Penal System: An Introduction* (5th edn). London: Sage.

Garland, David. 1990. *Punishment and Modern Society: A Study in Social Theory*. Oxford: Clarendon.

Hudson, Barbara. 2003. *Understanding Justice* (2nd edn). London: Sage.

Scott, David. 2008. *Penology*. London: Sage.

Simon, Jonathan, and Richard Sparks (eds). 2012. *The SAGE Handbook of Punishment and Society*. London: Sage.

Recidivism

Mark Halsey

5.13

Recidivism derives 'from the Latin *recidere*, which means to fall back' (Payne 2007:4). In criminological terms, it describes the occurrence of *re*offending following official attempts by the state to prevent crime. A pivotal question has long been, and remains: What should count as recidivism? More specifically: Is recidivism best understood in terms of an individual's behaviour (or refusal to comply with the law) or as something that, at least in part, is produced or constituted by particular actions (or inactions) of key institutions of criminal justice (police, courts, prisons, post-release supervision) and society generally (e.g., public opinion and mythology, media stereotypes)? These questions are explored below.

It is difficult to pinpoint when the concept of recidivism first received explicit and sustained critical attention. Mayhew and Binny's *The Criminal Prisons of London and Scenes of Prison Life* mentioned rates at which prisoners returned to custody. For example, of the 7,743 commitments of 1855 to Coldbath Fields House of Correction in central London, Mayhew and Binny note that one-third (32.5 per cent) had served time previously in that institution during that year. Speaking to the idea of a smaller 'intractable' core of repeat offenders, nearly 5 per cent of admissions had been recommitted to Coldbath Fields on *three or more* occasions within a 12-month period (Mayhew and Binny 1862:343). Such statistics are firm evidence of the historical interest in those who 'fall back' into crime.

The question of how criminal justice interventions relate to recidivism (i.e. how they impact on an offender's motivation or need to reoffend) is complicated. Most often, recidivism is calculated in relation to two points of contact with the criminal (or juvenile) justice system: 1) following sentence and conviction for an offence or series of offences where the punishment involves *non*-custodial options (such as a good-behaviour bond or probation order); and 2) following a term of imprisonment. Some would argue that recidivism should also be examined in relation to those who receive a police warning (i.e., who are not convicted of any crime) and/or who are diverted from the 'deeper' end of the system via a restorative-justice conference, drug court or other specialized court designed to address criminogenic needs. Being convicted of a criminal offence has traditionally been the formal legal indicator of 'criminality', however, and has therefore tended to act as the point from which **desistance** from crime, or persistence in offending, is measured.

*See Chapter 5.6
Desistance*

Research on recidivism (and there are literally dozens of studies proclaiming to measure recidivism over different time periods, for various cohorts, using an array of methodologies) illustrates a few common findings. In order to simplify matters, such commonalities are discussed in relation to the 'deep' end of recidivism – that is, in relation to prisoners convicted of at least one crime and who have been released from prison and 'tracked' for a number of years.

First, the majority of people who reoffend after being incarcerated do so within two years of release. The exact proportion varies but typically falls within the 35–50 per cent range, depending on jurisdictional factors (Sentencing Project 2010; Payne 2007:55–7).

Second, for every year an ex-prisoner is *not* rearrested, it becomes more likely that rearrest (and therefore reconviction) will be avoided over the longer term. For example, of 404,638 prisoners released across 30 US states in 2005 (and tracked until 2010), 109,186 (27 per cent) avoided arrest for four years. Just 13 per cent of that sub-cohort was rearrested in the fifth year, and this contrasts with the 43 per cent rearrested in the first year of release and the 29 per cent who faced arrest in the second year out of prison (Durose et al. 2014:7). As the time since release from custody increases, so does the *total* percentage of persons reincarcerated. However, the percentage rearrested in each year decreases through time.

Third, recidivism rates vary according to class (socio-economic location) and ethnicity, suggesting that statistics about reoffending (whether events become known to police and are counted as crime) likely reveal as much about policing tactics and possible biases against certain groups as they do about the *actual* level of recidivism. In Australia, for example, the proportion of

*See Chapter 4.18
Indigenous
criminology*

Aboriginal prisoners who report experience of prior incarceration is 50 per cent higher than non-Aboriginals (67 v 43 per cent) (ABS 2015:Table 29). Such persons account for just 2 per cent of the national general population, so there is good reason to examine the way policing impacts recidivism rates in this instance.

Fourth, some types of offenders are less likely than others to recidivate post-imprisonment. Defying popular (mis)conceptions, sex offenders tend to be rearrested at comparatively low rates when viewed next to those convicted of property crime or non-sexual violent crime. This again might have to do with the capacity to detect sex offences (the 'invisibility' of such crimes, especially in the age of the Internet) and the (un)willingness of victims to report them. That said, a study of 9,691 sex offenders released from prison in 15 US states in 1994 showed that just 5.3 per cent reoffended within three years in accordance with their index offence (i.e., the most serious offence for which they were previously incarcerated). The same study showed, however, that the recidivism rate for *other* violent crimes committed by this cohort post-imprisonment was 17.1 per cent, and that 43 per cent were rearrested for any offence within three years of release (Przybylski 2015:2).

The debate surrounding whether recidivism rates should be measured only against someone's 'index' (most serious) offence is an important one. To illustrate, some argue that programmes undertaken in prison targeting illicit drug use cannot be expected to prevent someone from committing, say, domestic violence (i.e. a different class or type of offence). Therefore, if someone is imprisoned for illicit drug use and completes all relevant programmes addressing *that* particular crime type, it is only proper to count them as recidivating if their subsequent most serious charge and conviction is for illicit drug use. If that person commits armed robbery or rape they should not be counted in recidivism statistics. Jurisdictions that define recidivism in very narrow ways will end up reporting lower rates of reoffending. Conversely, those that take a broader view of recidivism will count *any rearrest*, additional conviction(s) and time in prison as examples of recidivist behaviour. In such circumstances, the recidivism rate will (appear to) be much higher. The key to getting a more accurate picture of repeat offending is to be absolutely consistent in the definition used.

A fifth and final issue concerning recidivism concerns the 'blunt' nature of the concept. Studies of recidivism tend to result in a binary view of the social and criminal justice fields. Either one is or is not an offender, or one has or has not recidivated (Halsey and Deegan 2015). There is good evidence to say that few studies of recidivism build in the variables of offence severity and frequency when reporting rates of reoffending. 'Gary's' situation – based on the study *Generations Through Prison* funded by the Australian Research Council – is a good case in point (see Further reading). At 20 years of age, Gary was sentenced to 14 years' imprisonment for multiple armed robberies and aggravated assaults. After eight and half years he was paroled but was reincarcerated many times for *comparatively minor* offences over subsequent years.

> I did eight and a half years non-parole, and I got out . . . [But] I've been back in 17 times since then. . . . Seventeen times over five years.
> *What have been the main reasons that you have been brought back in?*
> [I]t's been breaches for dirty [urine] tests and for changing my address . . . I can't stop smoking pot. It's just not going to happen. I will smoke pot until the day I die.
> *So basically . . . they're bringing you back in for smoking pot?*

Yeah, that's it. Then you're in for another couple of months and they let you back out again. You're out for a couple of weeks and then you're back in for another dirty [urine] test.

Is Gary a recidivist? By any standard his latest 'crimes' pale against the violent offences for which he was originally incarcerated. And yet many jurisdictions would label Gary a repeat offender.

In sum, it is critical to know what kind of behaviour should be used to signal recidivism and what should be called a lapse (as opposed to relapse) after release from custody, or from court, or even while on police bail. In an era dominated by key performance indicators, appropriate definition and measurement of recidivism has probably never been more important.

References

ABS. 2015. *Prisoners in Australia*, publication 4517.0. Canberra: Australian Bureau of Statistics.

Durose, Matthew R., Alexia D. Cooper, and Howard N. Snyder. 2014. *Recidivism of Prisoners Released in 30 States in 2005: Patterns from 2005 to 2010*. Washington, DC: Office of Justice Programs, US Department of Justice.

Halsey, Mark, and Simone Deegan. 2015. *Young Offenders: Crime, Prison, and Struggles for Desistance*. Basingstoke: Palgrave Macmillan.

Mayhew, Henry, and John Binny. 1862. *The Criminal Prisons of London and Scenes of Prison Life*. London: Griffin, Bohn, & Co.

Payne, Jason. 2007. *Recidivism in Australia*. Canberra: Australian Institute of Criminology.

Przybylski, Roger. 2015. *Recidivism of Adult Sexual Offenders*. Washington, DC: Office of Justice Programs, US Department of Justice.

Sentencing Project. 2010. State recidivism database. www.sentencingproject.org/detail/Publication.cfm?Publication_id=311. Accessed 18 March 2016.

Recommended reading

Australian Research Council. 2012–15. *Generations Through Prison: A Critical Exploration of the Causes, Experiences and Consequences of Intergenerational Incarceration*. Funded by the Australian Research Council, Project Number FT120100284.

Brisman, Avi. 2004. Double Whammy: Collateral Consequences of Conviction and Imprisonment for Sustainable Communities and the Environment. *William & Mary Environmental Law and Policy Review* 28(2): 423–75.

Halsey, Mark. 2007. Assembling Recidivism: The Promise and Contingencies of Post-Release Life. *Journal of Criminal Law and Criminology* 97(4): 1209–60.

Maruna, Shadd. 2001. *Making Good: How Ex-Convicts Reform and Rebuild Their Lives*. Washington, DC: American Psychological Association.

Presser, Lois, and Sveinung Sandberg. 2015. *Narrative Criminology: Understanding Stories of Crime*. New York and London: New York University Press.

Sellin, Thorsten. 1958. Pioneers in Criminology. *Journal of Criminal Law, Criminology, and Police Science* 48(5): 481–90.

Reintegrative shaming 5.14

Meredith Edelman and Nathan Harris

Reintegrative shaming theory (RST), introduced in Braithwaite's (1989) *Crime, Shame and Reintegration*, predicts that societies in which the censure of offending is reintegrative will experience lower rates of such offences than in societies where censure is stigmatizing. RST draws from various disciplines to explain crime rates, recidivism and deviant behaviour generally. It was developed in response to a general sense that theory in the field was stagnant, and sought to reconcile theoretical traditions previously seen as competing within a single framework.

See Chapter 5.13 Recidivism

Braithwaite argues that to understand crime rates, we need to look beyond official mechanisms – beyond those penalties imposed by criminal justice systems – toward a broader understanding of how societies express disapproval of crimes. This is captured through the concept of *shaming*, which is defined as 'all societal processes of expressing social disapproval which have the intention or effect of invoking remorse in the person being shamed and/or condemnation by others who become aware of the shaming' (Braithwaite 1989:100). This definition does not limit shaming to demeaning or humiliating forms of disapproval. Rather, it includes the full spectrum of ways in which disapproval might be expressed. Expressions of disapproval can be formal or informal, direct or indirect, and can involve personal or impersonal forms of expressing disapproval. Examples of shaming include: burning the doors of criminals' houses in republican Rome; verbal denunciation of wrongdoing in people's courts in Cuba and China; informal talks between doctors when one is engaging in wrongful behaviour; gossip which eventually gets back to an offender; and even a slight shaking of the head or a laugh (Braithwaite 1989:100).

This broad definition of shaming is important because, while shaming is a necessary form of **social control** in all societies, the forms of shaming are not equal in the effect that they have on subsequent offending. The crucial distinction RST makes is between *stigmatization* and *reintegration*, which can be viewed as opposite ends of a continuum. Drawing on **labelling theory**, Braithwaite argues that shaming can be **stigmatizing**, and that this response to offending is criminogenic. Stigmatization is characterized by humiliation, communication of disrespect and ceremonies to certify deviance for which there is no counterpart terminating such certification. Stigmatizing, or disintegrative shaming, has the effect of allowing deviance to become a master status trait. As described by labelling theory, where a person is deemed deviant and comes to identify with a criminal or deviant status, such identity, alongside any pre-existing or imposed marginalization, acts to foreclose the willingness and ability to access legitimate opportunities. A person so labelled is less willing to seek legitimate opportunities because such opportunities will be more difficult to find; because the person may feel that he or she has been treated unjustly; and because deviant subcultures may become more attractive as fitting with the imposed deviant identity.

Where RST diverges from labelling theory, however, is in its argument that shaming is also crucial in the reduction of offending. Reintegrative shaming occurs when expressions of disapproval communicate respect for and acceptance of the person while simultaneously condemning deviant behaviour. According to Makkai and Braithwaite (1994), reintegrative shaming involves the following:

■ disapproval while sustaining a relationship of respect;
■ ceremonies to certify deviance terminated by ceremonies to decertify deviance;
■ disapproval of the evil of the deed without labelling the person as evil; and
■ not allowing deviance to become a master status trait.

Reintegrative shaming often occurs as a sequential process in which expressions of disapproval of the act are followed by efforts to reintegrate the offender back into society, which can include words or gestures of forgiveness.

Considerable store is placed in the ability of reintegrative shaming, as a form of moral persuasion, to reform individual offenders. While shaming is regarded as having a **deterrent effect** through the threatened loss of respect from valued community members, this effect is considered secondary to shame's moralizing function. Emphasis is on the development or engagement of conscience. As Braithwaite (1989:9) puts it, reintegrative shaming is 'conceived as a tool to allure and inveigle the citizen to attend to the moral claims of the criminal law, to coax and caress compliance, to reason and remonstrate with him over the harmfulness of his conduct'. Reintegrative shaming

See Chapter 5.18
Social control

See Chapter 3.8
Labelling theory

See Chapter 3.16
Stigma

See Chapter 1.17
Deterrence

is seen as having distinct advantages in moralizing because it allows concerns about behaviour to be communicated effectively to offenders without the counterproductive effects of stigmatization. Affirmation and inclusion of the individual allows moralizing and denunciation of the act to occur in a way that invites the offender to acknowledge guilt and express remorse. This is because the offender knows that he or she will not be outcast – that decertification of his/her deviant status will occur.

A distinctive characteristic of the theory is its emphasis on the notion of shaming. Braithwaite's use of this term, rather than simply disapproval, is significant because it suggests that the response to disapproval is also emotional. It is argued, particularly in Braithwaite's 2001 restatement of the theory, that reintegrative shaming engages offenders in ways that allow individuals to manage feelings of shame more effectively (Ahmed et al. 2001). Evidence suggests that when shaming is reintegrative, individuals are more likely to acknowledge or resolve feelings of shame and guilt. On the other hand, stigmatization leaves the individual with unacknowledged or unresolved feelings of shame, which are associated with externalization of anger towards others (ibid.). It is suggested that shame involves a threat to the individual's ethical identity that demands resolution. One way in which an individual might resolve feelings of shame that stem from offending is to perceive his/her offending as a mistake or aberration that can be repaired. Research on **desistance** suggests that offenders who desist are more likely to identify with a law-abiding identity that they perceive as distinct from the previous self who offended (Maruna 2001).

See Chapter 5.6
Desistance

The theory's faith in moral persuasion at the individual level stems from a broader social premise which Braithwaite draws from **control theorists**: that the reason individuals do not commit crime is that they have commitments to shared moral norms and social institutions. Braithwaite argues that punishment, for most people, is not the primary deterrent when it comes to serious criminal behaviour because they find such behaviour morally repugnant – for the vast majority of individuals, performing such acts would be unthinkable. Socialization of children about moral norms leads to a broad consensus about what acts should be crimes. While **subcultures** that support alternative cultural values exist, support for the criminal law is, in most societies, much greater. Indeed, Braithwaite states that RST is only valid to the degree there is a consensus that certain acts are, and should be, criminalized.

See Chapter 2.6
Control theories

See Chapter 3.17
Subculture

Accordingly, while RST is relevant to understanding the effect of censure on secondary deviance, the theory is also concerned with explaining primary deviance. It predicts that societies with strong shared norms and lower crime are those that engage in reintegrative shaming more often. Shaming is important not just because of its effect on the individual subject of disapproval, but also because it reinforces commitments to norms among those who witness it. Mechanisms such as gossip are significant because of their role in socializing children and adults about what Braithwaite calls the 'curriculum of crimes'. Commitment to social norms will be strongest in societies that are communitarian and have high levels of interdependency between individuals.

Interdependencies include social bonds, attachments and commitments between individuals, as emphasized in control theories. Communitarianism refers to a culture in which group loyalties and personal obligations to others in one's community are emphasized. Both interdependency and communitarianism are predicted to increase the likelihood that communities will be reintegrative, as well as the significance that shaming has for individuals. Examples of reintegrative shaming can be identified in multiple forms in various societies and locations.

See Chapter 5.15
Restorative justice

Worldwide, emerging forms of **restorative justice** are designed to facilitate reintegrative shaming. Restorative justice presents an alternative approach to the traditional criminal justice system that is defined by its distinct philosophy and practices. It posits that justice is best achieved when an offender repairs the harm caused by his or her offence rather than simply being punished. It includes practices – such as family group conferences, offender mediation and healing circles – which seek to empower affected parties to come together to decide how the harms can be repaired. Reintegrative practices within restorative conferences involve the inclusion of people who will offer the offender support, a focus on the offence and its consequences rather than on the offender (even denunciation of the offence is often eschewed in favour of less confronting discussions about the harms that were caused) and the aim of finding ways in which to restore harm rather than punish the offender. Consequently, restorative justice represents the strongest implementation of reintegrative shaming to date, and is certainly the implementation that has received most attention. Reintegrative shaming theory has become an important justification for the use of restorative justice as far as its potential to reduce recidivism is concerned, and has been widely used in the development of practices.

References

Ahmed, Eliza, Nathan Harris, John Braithwaite, and Valerie Braithwaite. 2001. *Shame Management Through Reintegration.* Melbourne: Cambridge University Press.

Braithwaite, John. 1989. *Crime, Shame and Reintegration.* Cambridge: Cambridge University Press.

Makkai, Toni, and John Braithwaite. 1994. Reintegrative Shaming and Regulatory Compliance. *Criminology* 32(3): 361–85.

Maruna, Shadd. 2001. *Making Good: How Ex-Convicts Reform and Rebuild Their Lives.* Washington, DC: American Psychological Association.

Further reading

Ahmed, Eliza, and John Braithwaite. 2005. Forgiveness, Shaming, Shame and Bullying. *Australian and New Zealand Journal of Criminology* 38(3): 298–323.

Harris, Nathan. 2011. Shame, ethical identity and conformity: Lessons from research on the psychology of social influence. In *Emotions, Crime and Justice*, Susanne Karstedt, Ian Loader, and Heather Strang, eds, pp. 193–210. Oxford: Hart.

Hay, Carter. 2001. An Exploratory Test of Braithwaite's Reintegrative Shaming Theory. *Journal of Research in Crime and Delinquency* 38(2): 132–53.

Kim, Hee Joo, and Jurg Berber. 2012. The Effectiveness of Reintegrative Shaming and Restorative Justice Conferences: Focusing on Juvenile Offenders' Perceptions in Australian Reintegrative Shaming Experiments. *International Journal of Offender Therapy and Comparative Criminology* 56(7): 1063–79.

Losoncz, Ibolya, and Graham Tyson. 2007. Parental Shaming and Adolescent Delinquency: A Partial Test of Reintegrative Shaming Theory. *Australian and New Zealand Journal of Criminology* 40(2): 161–78.

Restorative justice

Emily Gaarder

Restorative justice (RJ) emerged as a response to the limitations of the Western criminal/legal system. The field of RJ developed primarily through innovative experiments in justice by those who questioned the reliance on crime–punishment systems and their professional employees to solve problems. Proponents of RJ suggest that ordinary people affected by crime should be given the means to define and participate in responses aimed at repairing harmful action. The process of accountability for those who cause harm is redefined as taking responsibility for one's actions and repairing harm, not merely taking punishment.

Descriptions of restorative justice vary. There is little agreement on whether RJ is a set of values, a set of practices or an outcome. The term 'restorative justice' derives from a central concern with repair – that of **victims**, offenders and the damage done to communities. Tony Marshall's working definition of RJ, now adopted by the United Nations, states: 'Restorative justice is a process whereby all the parties with a stake in a particular offence come together to resolve collectively how to deal with the aftermath of the offence and its implications for the future' (1996:37).

Howard Zehr (2002) names the three central concepts as:

See Chapter 4.39
Victimology

See Chapter 6.2
Community safety

1. RJ focuses on harm, understanding crime as **harm done to people and communities**.
2. Harms result in obligations, so RJ emphasizes the need for the wrongdoer to take responsibility and make things as right as much as possible.
3. RJ promotes participation by the parties affected by the crime.

Zehr was among the first to outline a vision that was explicitly called restorative justice. His influential book, *Changing Lenses* (1990), argued that the criminal justice system did not meet the needs of victims *or* offenders. He made the case for a new model of justice that viewed *crime* as a violation of people and relationships, and *justice* as a process that involved victims, offenders and the community in the search for solutions and repair.

The development of RJ victim–offender mediation programmes in Scandinavian countries was influenced by Nils Christie's (1977) argument that government, through the criminal justice system, steals conflict from those most directly affected by it: victims and offenders. Other criminological perspectives linked to RJ include: peacemaking criminology; John Braithwaite's concept of **reintegrative shaming**, which helped form the basis for the police conferencing model developed in Wagga Wagga, New South Wales, Australia; and Lawrence Sherman's **defiance theory**.

See Chapter 5.14
Reintegrative
shaming

See Chapter 3.4
Defiance theory

Some advocates see RJ as much more than an alternative to the criminal justice system. Gerry Johnstone views it as a broad political project and fundamental challenge to conventional notions of crime, victims, offenders and justice. Dennis Sullivan and Larry Tifft (2005) envision RJ as a **theory of social justice** that aims to transform social arrangements and consider the basic needs of all.

See Chapter 4.1
Anarchist
criminology

Restorative justice programmes have emerged in many countries, often in conjunction with **traditional legal justice** or as an alternative to court sanctions. In New Zealand, RJ operates as the basis for the entire juvenile justice system. Practices that set RJ apart from normal judicial processes include the following: offenders have admitted to the crime; the parties affected communicate face to face; and there is a focus on the injuries done to victims with a response geared toward repairing the harms. The dialogue and decision-making are guided by values such as respect and non-violence.

See Chapter 4.18
Indigenous
criminology

Harm and its remedy are central concerns of RJ; thus its use is not limited to situations defined by law as criminal. It is used to resolve conflict in schools and workplaces, and also for **large-scale injustices enacted by nation-states** (e.g., truth and reconciliation commissions, such as the case of South Africa following the end of apartheid).

See Chapter 4.36
State crime

What constitutes RJ practice is contested terrain. Indeed, the term 'restorative justice' has been attached to a dizzying array of justice interventions, some of which lack key elements associated with RJ. The following describes the three most commonly agreed upon restorative practices in the context of criminal justice: mediation, conferencing and circles. Restorative justice is commonly equated with a singular activity – *victim–offender mediation* or *conferences* – where victim and offender speak to each other about the crime with a facilitator present. Victim–offender mediation in North America began in the 1970s as an effort to help offenders understand the harm they caused victims and to find ways to repair the damage.

Family group conferencing and *circles* typically expand the group of participants to family, friends and community members. Family group conferencing, commonly used in juvenile cases in New Zealand and Australia, includes family members as an integral part of determining an appropriate response to problem behaviour. Conferencing in New Zealand began as a response to Māori political challenges to the juvenile justice system, particularly its impact on indigenous Māori and other minority groups. The resulting family group conference model incorporates certain Māori values and decision-making practices, though it remains connected to a government process quite different from indigenous justice.

Similarly, RJ circles draw from certain traditions of indigenous groups in Canada and the United States. Circles generally use a form of ceremony to mark the opening and closing of the circle and a talking piece to regulate discussion. They address underlying causes of harmful behaviour rather than focusing on a single incident. Circles take many forms, including **sentencing, re-entry, peacemaking, healing and victim support**.

See Chapter 3.12
Peacemaking
criminology

In addition to indigenous justice practices, formative influences on RJ include victim advocacy groups, the restitution movement, informal justice proponents, **prison abolitionists**, social justice groups and religious communities such as the Mennonites in North America. The research on restorative justice may be categorized by three types of outcomes:

See Chapter 5.1
Abolitionism

- procedural justice – perceptions of fairness, inclusion and respect;
- restorativeness – the amount of harm repaired and the degree to which participants acknowledged and responded to each other's needs; and
- recidivism – the prevention of further harm or offences.

Restorative programmes rank highly on measures of procedural justice. High levels of satisfaction and fairness are typically reported among victim–offender mediation participants. A consistent finding across youth restorative justice conferences in Australia and New Zealand is that victims and offenders had a say in the outcome, and viewed the process and outcomes as fair and respectful. This may have important implications for crime reduction, as procedural justice theory suggests that people are more likely to follow rules when they view justice officials and the law as fair.

Certain measures of restorativeness emerge as strong in the research literature: offenders who participate in RJ programmes are much more likely to complete restitution and other agreements. Studies also report that victims who meet offenders in a restorative setting can experience lasting benefits, such as a reduction in fear and anger, and a sense of recovery or closure. Yet victim advocates also note that some RJ programmes are designed primarily to address offender-based outcomes (e.g., recidivism) rather than victim needs. And some victims do not experience restorativeness (e.g., a sense of empathy, a sincere apology) in their encounters with offenders. On average, however, victims of crime who participate in RJ fare better on a wide range of outcomes than those who do not.

The question of how RJ affects recidivism is less certain. Like all interventions, RJ works differently according to context and person. While many studies demonstrate that RJ is more successful in lowering recidivism than traditional court approaches, others report no difference. A common problem in assessing the effect of restorative programming is self-selection bias – the voluntary nature of RJ means that many participants already display a motivation to change. Studies of mandatory RJ programmes, however, such as youth conferencing in Australia and New Zealand, also demonstrate positive effects on recidivism. While RJ has been more commonly used for minor offences, especially as a method of diversion from the formal justice system, tests of RJ also find reductions in repeat offending for more serious and violent crimes.

A clear limitation of RJ is that it relies on a person admitting to an offence. It does not employ fact-finding or discovery of guilt or innocence, and cannot fully replace the existing legal system. It is questionable whether elements of crime causation, such as structural inequities, can be changed through restorative processes. Critics argue that RJ simply creates new forms of governance rather than challenging state power or oppressive justice systems (Cuneen and Hoyle 2010). Daly further notes that 'it is easier to achieve fairness than restorativeness in an RJ process'. She warns against 'nirvana' stories of RJ, arguing instead that RJ processes rely on the capacities and interests of the involved parties to express empathy and remorse and 'act in ways we may define as restorative' (2006:138, 143).

Despite these critiques, RJ practices continue to grow in number and popularity. Sherman and Strang's (2007:8) review of 36 quantitative RJ studies concluded:

> There is far more evidence on RJ, with more positive results, than there has been for most innovations in criminal justice that have ever been rolled out across the country. The evidence now seems more than adequate to support such a roll-out for RJ, especially if that is done on a continue-to-learn-as-you-go basis.

The future development of RJ will depend on further study of its effects, debate over what constitutes restorative practice, and the political will necessary to change systems of justice.

References

Christie, Nils. 1977. Conflicts as Property. *British Journal of Criminology* 17(1): 1–15.
Cuneen, Chris, and Carolyn Hoyle. 2010. *Debating Restorative Justice*. Oxford: Hart.
Daly, Kathleen. 2006. The limits of restorative justice. In *Handbook of Restorative Justice: A Global Perspective*, Dennis Sullivan and Larry Tifft, eds, pp. 134–45. New York: Routledge.
Marshall, Tony. 1996. The Evolution of Restorative Justice in Britain. *European Journal on Criminal Policy and Research* 4(4): 21-43.
Sherman, Lawrence W., and Heather Strang. 2007. *Restorative Justice: The Evidence*. London: Smith Institute.

Sullivan, Dennis, and Larry Tifft. 2005. *Restorative Justice: Healing the Foundations of Our Everyday Lives* (2nd edn). Monsey, NY: Willow Tree Press.

Zehr, Howard. 1990. *Changing Lenses: A New Focus for Crime and Justice.* Scottdale, PA: Herald Press.

Zehr, Howard. 2002. *The Little Book of Restorative Justice.* Intercourse, PA: Good Books.

Further reading

Johnstone, Gerry (ed.). 2005. *A Restorative Justice Reader: Texts, Sources, Contexts.* Cullompton, UK: Willan.

Ptacek, James (ed.). 2010. *Restorative Justice and Violence against Women.* New York: Oxford University Press.

Van Ness, Daniel W., and Karen H. Strong. 2014. *Restoring Justice: An Introduction to Restorative Justice* (5th edn). New York: Routledge.

Retribution

Rob White

The concept of retribution is used in a criminological context to refer to a specific purpose of punishment. The purpose of retribution is to express public disapproval of a specific criminal act (or omission) through the use of punitive measures. The emphasis is on punishment as moral desert – that is, offenders deserve to be punished – as offenders are viewed as being solely responsible for their actions and thus their punishments. There is meant to be a direct connection between crime and punishment, both in the sense that only those who actually commit an offence ought to be punished, and in regard to the notion that each crime should be punished in proportion to the seriousness of the offence.

The concept of retribution is linked to the *classical school* of criminological thought, which has at its core a utilitarian philosophy of crime and punishment. According to classical theory, humans are considered equally capable of reason, and hence are deemed responsible for their actions. All individuals are considered to have free will, which enables them to act in their own best interests. In recognition of the possibility of predation from others, however, individuals agree to forego some of their freedoms in exchange for protection by the state. An individual who engages in crime either acts irrationally or knowingly makes a bad choice. The purpose of punishment within the law is therefore to deter individuals from impinging upon and violating others' rights and interests, thereby affirming the legitimacy of the social contract (the implied agreement between state and the individual that laws and rules are reasonable, based upon consensus and binding for all). The two leading figures in the development of classical criminology were Cesare Beccaria and Jeremy Bentham (see White et al. 2012).

See Chapter 1.2
Classical
criminology

See Chapter 1.3
Utilitarianism

See Chapter 1.17
Deterrence

485

Retribution is justified according to two general rationales (Feinberg 1991). A moral justification imbues punishment with terminology such as 'wrong-doing', 'morally fitting' and 'merits'. It argues that punishment is just because wrongdoers deserve to be punished. A *legal justification*, by contrast, focuses on the lawbreaking. The imposition of a prescribed penalty is in response to a legal transgression (that is, someone is found legally guilty of committing an offence) and the application of the sanction occurs irrespective of whether the offender incurs moral guilt.

Fundamentally, punishment has a symbolic character, which is oriented toward drawing the lines of acceptable behaviour or conduct by denouncing activities deemed to be morally harmful, transgressing of legal rules or socially repugnant. Through public censure of an offender and/or his or her offensive behaviour, punishment functions to reaffirm the legitimacy of established rules demarcating 'right' and 'wrong' behaviour through branding such as legal and illegal or criminal. Retribution, therefore, functions to reaffirm certain forms of authority and belief.

Generally speaking, retribution calls for vengeance to be exacted in proportion to the seriousness of the offence committed and the degree of offender culpability. Superficially, this can be summed up in the phrase 'do the crime, do the time'. This, however, glosses over important political and analytical differences in the use of the concept.

See Chapter 4.24
Neoliberalism

For example, from a **politically right-wing libertarian position** – where the emphasis is on personal responsibility and individual freedoms ('freedom to do') – retributive punishment should only ever be used as a restricted form of 'just deserts', tailored to the unique circumstances of the specific individual in question. The punishment should fit the crime but should not be excessive. An offender who steals a loaf of bread, for example, does not deserve the death penalty. Parsimonious state intervention should also apply to the administration of criminal justice. Punishment should be meted out, but in proportion to the specific harm only.

By contrast, from a conservative political position – where the emphasis is on upholding social order and privileging a particular overarching moral universe ('adherence to core values') – retribution is not only about punishing the individual but also setting an example in doing so. This opens the door to the use of exemplary sanctions, regardless of whether these are proportional to the crime. Seriousness of offence in this instance is not conceptualized in terms of proportionate response to the specific offence/offender *per se* (for example, being caught with one illegal marijuana joint = small fine), but is framed as escalating punishments that mirror the broader deterrent purposes of retributive punishment (one joint = 10 years; 1 ounce of 'weed' = 20 years). The public denunciation and punishment of offenders thus serves as a symbolic means to an end, for in the process of delivering these more generalized 'just deserts', the offender is sacrificed: he or she is made an example of to others – for the greater good of society.

Beyond these two broad approaches, there are in fact many different ways in which retribution is conceptualized and operationalized in practice (White and Perrone 2015). For instance, included among the approaches that have been banded under the retributivist banner are:

- *Repayment theory*: The act of punishment serves as a means by which the offender repays a debt, not just to the victim(s) of his or her crime but also to society generally.
- *Placation theory*: By punishing an offender, a wrathful God (who might otherwise remain angry) is appeased.
- *Annulment theory*: As long as an offender escapes punishment, the crime is permitted to remain in force and flourish. Punishment acts in a restorative capacity – to somehow cancel out or annul the evil intention embodied in the crime.
- *Satisfaction or vengeance theory*: Punishment is seen to vindicate the retaliatory desire of the wronged individual (whether the immediate victim or others injured or insulted by the crime). An evil is acknowledged and repaid in kind; in so doing, the harm caused is avenged.
- *Denunciation theory*: Punishment is justified on the grounds that it represents an emphatic expression of moral public outrage and a formal admonition of the conduct in question.
- *Desert theory*: Under this approach, it is a simple measure of justice that the offender be punished, and it is on the basis of the offender's moral culpability that he or she is deserving of punishment.
- *Penalty theory*: This follows from desert theory in that the appropriate measure of punishment is linked directly to the harm or suffering inflicted upon the victim, rather than the nature of the conduct itself.

Despite the diversity in form, retribution is essentially predicated on a view of punishment that holds that the state has a right and duty to inflict punishment on the offender, solely on the grounds of their moral and/or legalistic desert. The act of punishment serves to restore equilibrium by counterbalancing the unfair advantage gained by the wrongdoer. It also provides a strong public statement that these are the consequences for those who transgress the moral order. Thus, punishments – and, in particular, severe punishments – while rationalized on the grounds of offence seriousness, simultaneously serve to symbolically reflect public indignation.

Retribution as a purpose of punishment has been critiqued at both a philosophical level and in regard to specific practical consequences. At a philosophical level, for example, a restorative justice approach emphasizes the restoration of dominion (or 'liberty') to the **victim**, the offender and the community, and situates the purposes of punishment in terms of repairing the harm (Braithwaite and Pettit 1990). This perspective, which **promotes non-adversarial forms of justice**, refers to ideas such as reconciliation between victim and offender, recompense for the harm inflicted and reassurance that the offence will not happen again by consideration of the specific attributes of the offender. Retribution has also been criticized by those who view

See Chapter 4.39
Victimology

See Chapter 5.15
Restorative justice

rehabilitation as both more important than, and undermined by, punitive punishment practices. In a similar vein, therapeutic jurisprudence – a perspective that emphasizes the importance of courtroom decision-making in the promotion of positive behaviour – has been accompanied by the development of problem-oriented courts (such as drug courts and mental-health courts), which seek to promote offender accountability and preparedness for, and participation in, rehabilitation.

At the level of practice, retribution has been criticized for the massive rise in the number of people imprisoned since the mid-1980s (as it is punishment oriented rather than restorative or rehabilitative in its orientation), as well as for the substantive inequalities embedded in this expansion of punitive sanctioning (because poor people, people of colour and other marginalized groups are over-represented in the harshest parts of the criminal justice system). Mass

See Chapter 4.18
Indigenous
criminology

imprisonment and hyperincarceration of **Indigenous people**, for example, reflect the uneven application of penality, and the fact that 'just deserts' in its legal and criminal justice manifestations inevitably has meant that it is the vulnerable and the marginalized who are deemed to 'deserve' punishment (Cunneen et al. 2013).

Many jurisdictions exhibit hybrid mixes of punishment that incorporate

See Chapter 6.2
Community safety

See Chapter 5.9
Incapacitation

elements of retribution, deterrence, rehabilitation, **community safety**, **incapacitation** and restorative justice. The key question pertinent to this, and involving retribution specifically, is who is selected for restorative justice and so-called 'soft' responses and who is dealt with retributively, and why? At the bottom end of the criminal justice system, for example, Indigenous young people are generally and disproportionately shunted into retributive parts of the criminal justice process, while white, middle-class children benefit from juvenile conferencing and the like. At the top end, businesses and corporate leaders receive the benefit of the doubt and are rarely dealt with retributively. Yet, the culpability of white-collar and corporate offenders is frequently related to greed rather than need, and the deed is far greater in terms of social, economic and environmental impact.

A synthesis of retributive and restorative approaches to punishment is potentially possible and attractive. While it makes sense to deal with individual offenders and small firms via restorative justice processes – because there is greater scope for offender change of conscience and understanding, as well as behaviour – this is less relevant with respect to large companies. Here it is proposed that a form of *reparative justice*, with an emphasis on repairing harm within a generally more punitive context, would be more appropriate and effective. Company personnel, including senior managers, change. But to change company practices, especially those that pertain to the economic profit margin, requires regulatory and enforcement systems that penalize and sanction in ways that are tailored to the size and activities of the corporation. Retribution in this context, and used in this way, would indeed be revolutionary.

References

Braithwaite, John, and Philip Pettit. 1990. *Not Just Deserts: A Republican Theory of Criminal Justice*. Oxford: Oxford University Press.

Cunneen, Chris, Eileen Baldry, David Brown, Mark Brown, Melanie Schwartz, and Alex Steel. 2013. *Penal Culture and Hyperincarceration: The Revival of the Prison*. Farnham: Ashgate.

Feinberg, Joel. 1991. The justification of punishment: The classic debate. In *Philosophy of Law*, Joel Feinberg and Hyman Gross, eds, pp. 646ff. Belmont, CA: Wadsworth.

White, Rob, and Santina Perrone. 2015. *Crime, Criminality and Criminal Justice*. Melbourne: Oxford University Press.

White, Rob, Fiona Haines, and Nicole Asquith. 2012. *Crime and Criminology* (5th edn). Melbourne: Oxford University Press.

Further reading

Ashworth, Andrew. 2010. *Sentencing and Criminal Justice* (5th edn).New York: Cambridge University Press.

Beccaria, Cesare. 1764. *Dei delitti e delle pene* [*An essay on crimes and punishments*]. www.constitution.org/cb/crim_pun.htm. Accessed April 2014.

Bentham, Jeremy. 1789. *An Introduction to the Principles of Morals and Legislation*. http://oll.libertyfund.org/titles/bentham-an-introduction-to-the-principles-of-morals-and-legislation. Accessed April 2014.

Paternoster, Raymond. 2010. How Much Do We Really Know about Criminal Deterrence? *Journal of Criminal Law and Criminology* 100(3): 765–823.

Pettit, Philip, and John Braithwaite. 1993. Not Just Deserts, Even In Sentencing. *Current Issues in Criminal Justice* 4(3): 225–39.

Zehr, Howard. 1990. *Changing Lenses: A New Focus for Crime and Justice*. Scottsdale, PA: Herald Press.

Security and counter-security

Phil Carney

Today, 'security' is an odd word because it functions in a monstrous couple with the word 'insecurity'. In a dialectical descent toward the abyss, 'security' (*se cura*) means 'without care', while 'insecurity' effectively means 'without-without care'. Security and insecurity are essentially empty vessels, driven first and foremost by absence. How did this nihilistic couple arise?

Three kinds of security are found in the history of political theory and practice: 1) 'security from' threats such as enemies; 2) 'security to' – or access to – basic goods and rights; 3) 'security of' states of being, such as certainty or peace. Today, we are anxious about the first kind of security, born in the early modern age under the shadow of Hobbes' (1651) *Leviathan* state: the 'coldest of all cold monsters', according to Nietzsche (1883–85). Here, security is an imaginary deal between subject and state, where obedience is exchanged for protection. Rights are given up for the sake of release from a state of nature characterized by unremitting danger, hostility and violence. Hobbesian security is thus motivated by the politically problematic sentiments of fear and enmity.

Nietzsche (1887) provides a genealogical analysis of the power relations from which the state of security emerges. Attended by the affects of *ressentiment* (resentment), a servile morality is carefully cultivated among the 'flock' by a priestly governing class, the first form of pastoral power later to be analysed by Foucault (2009). Traversed by demonic danger and spiritual insecurity, the world, according to Nietzsche, is a war between Good and Evil – where a 'fallen' flock always vulnerable to sin must choose between the pure and the impure, the righteous and the sinful. Through pulpit and confessional, priestly power inserts a fearful, self-observing, ever-vigilant, self-punishing and guilty subjectivity. Self-enforced servility now enters new governmental relations and the flock is rendered docile and governable. Pastoral power cultivates self-surveillance and self-punishment. Subjects become the agents of their own subjection. Foucault's (1995) genealogical analysis of **surveillance**, discipline and punishment now comes into view, not so much a repressive apparatus and more as a 'productive' technology creating docile bodies.

See Chapter 5.19
Surveillance

Following Nietzsche's understanding of how power relations work, Foucault (2009) conceives of security as a technology of government, analytically distinct from, though interacting with, the mechanisms of **panoptic discipline and sovereignty**. Foucault's analysis of security can be confusing, for he mixes the forms of 'security from', 'security of' and 'security to', mentioned above. Though he deals with the 'security of' and 'to' in the new liberal, capitalist order, he also touches on the 'security from' treated here. Foucault finds a genealogical source for the modern power relations of security in the pastoral principle of salvation. In order to make sense of Foucault, we should always consider security in its articulation with the forces of sovereignty and panopticism.

See Chapter 5.11
Panopticism

In this way, Foucault questions the opposition between 'freedom' and 'security' set up by Hobbes. A modernity characterized by the ascent of capitalism requires a form of pastoral government that also ushers in the discourse and practices of security. For Foucault, freedom is not released by emancipation from oppression, the conventional discourse of the Enlightenment; rather, it is a discourse produced in various ways through social practices that have a relationship with security. Haunted by all kinds of menace, the liberal nineteenth century is involved in an 'entire education and culture of danger'. Foucault refers to the discourses of crime, disease and degeneration – to which we can add the associated fears and dangers of perversity, conspiracy, spies, foreigners and colonial underlings. Liberalism as a discourse of freedom is by the very same token a 'political culture of danger' in which proliferate 'procedures of control, constraint, and coercion' (Foucault 2009:66, 67), especially those he describes as panoptic. If sovereign security is centralized at the heart of the state, in liberal **governmentality** it is articulated with multiple forces distributed across the social field, associated with a panoply of fears producing desires and values in the hearts of those who are governed. As in Nietzsche's priestly–pastoral power, the outcome, according to Foucault (2009:239), is 'a specific subject, who is subjected in continuous networks of obedience', where obedience is a micropolitics of self-enslavement.

See Chapter 5.8
Governmentality

In the liberal order, a biopolitically constructed national population – called 'society' (a nationalistic society) – finds itself in a state of everlasting war in defence against actual or potential enemies, whether internal or external. These threats have often been constructed in terms of 'race', something readily deployed in our various wars on poverty, crime and drugs, as well as in defence against the figure of the migrant. Thus we understand the discourses energized by the mass media, in which today's populist right and far right are haunted by enemies from without and within, including migrants, foreign criminals, multiculturalism, Islam and the cosmopolitan European Union – often articulated with the **general spectre of terrorism**. We encounter again the affective complex of fear and enmity, theorized by Nietzsche as *ressentiment*, which so readily joins calls for well-functioning apparatuses of security, among which we see the increasingly normalized technologies of prerogative decision (Zedner 2009), pre-emptive detention and military-security action such as drone strikes, as well as the power of mass surveillance.

See Chapter 4.19 Institutional and anti-institutional violence

How do we respond to the problem of security? Molotch (2012) draws our attention to the way in which what he calls the fear system has informed the implementation of security architectures, technologies and other practices in public space. Underpinning these measures is a top-down command-and-control model of surveillance and security management by the authorities, with no evidence that a strategy of this kind has any efficacy. Indeed, anxieties are amplified rather than allayed: the surveyed are turned into dehumanized suspects, and governed communities are weakened in their erosion of trust rather than strengthened. Molotch calls for a complete rethink, beginning with a cultivation of the capacities of communities to care for their own safe-keeping. We can add that, even more fundamentally, we should consider a positive or productive ethics of security, an ethics and micropolitics of security that seeks to overcome the traditional affective investment of security in fear and enmity (Carney and Dadusc 2014).

Should we resist security altogether? In the end, Foucault (2009) circumvented the problem of resistance itself and elaborated instead the idea of counter-conduct, a productive practice that escapes the perils of transgressive refusal found in disobedience, dissent and insubordination. Foucault's work thus also points to present-day experiments in various kinds of autonomous social movements. Such movements should attend to possibilities in the counter-conduct of security, a counter-security, rather than re-energize the dialectic of the security–insecurity monster in the service of 'anti-security'. Instead counter-security offers a different kind of security, one in which the nihilism of the security–insecurity couple evaporates – perhaps to the extent that the very word security will one day dissolve itself in front of our eyes.

References

Carney, Phil, and Deanna Dadusc. 2014. Power and servility. an experiment in the ethics of security and counter-security. In *Positive Criminology: Reflections on Care, Belonging and Security*, Marc Schuilenburg, Ronald van Steden, and Brenda Oude Breuil, eds. The Hague: Eleven.

Foucault, Michel. 1995/1975. *Discipline and Punish: The Birth of the Prison*. New York: Vintage.

Foucault, Michel. 2009. *Security, Territory, Population: Lectures at the Collège de France 1977–1978*. New York: Picador.

Hobbes, Thomas. 2008/1651. *Leviathan*. Oxford: Oxford University Press.

Molotch, Harvey. 2012. *Against Security: How We Go Wrong at Airports, Subways and Other Sites of Ambiguous Danger*. Princeton: Princeton University Press.

Nietzsche, Friedrich. 1967/1887. *On the Genealogy of Morality* and *Ecce Homo*. New York: Random House.

Nietzsche, Friedrich. 1969/1883–85. *Thus Spoke Zarathustra*. Harmondsworth: Penguin.

Zedner, Lucia. 2009. *On Security*. London: Routledge.

Further reading

Ericson, Richard V. 2007. *Crime in an Insecure World*. Cambridge: Polity.

Hallsworth, Simon, and John Lea. 2011. Reconstructing Leviathan: Emerging Contours of the Security State. *Theoretical Criminology* 15(2): 141–57.

Johnston, Les, and Clifford Shearing. 2003. *Governing Security: Explorations in Policing and Justice*. London: Routledge.

Loader, Ian, and Neil Walker. 2007. *Civilizing Security*. Cambridge: Cambridge University Press.

Neocleous, Mark. 2008. *Critique of Security*. Edinburgh: Edinburgh University Press.

Neocleous, Mark, and George S. Rigakos (eds). 2011. *Anti-Security*. Ottawa: Red Quill.

Schuilenburg, Marc. 2015. *The Securitization of Society: Crime, Risk and Social Order* (trans. George Hall). New York: New York University Press.

Shearing, Clifford D., and Philip C. Stenning. 1983. Private Security: Implications for Social Control. *Social Problems* 30(5): 493–506.

5.18 Social control

Robert Reiner

The concept of social control has been prominent in social theory since its classic nineteenth-century origins, and continues to be influential (Innes 2003). Paradoxically, however, the term has rather passed out of fashion since the mid-1990s, even as the phenomena and problems it seems to point to have arguably become more pronounced.

The term 'social control' originally achieved prominence through a 1901 book by American sociologist Edward A. Ross. Ross did not coin the term (he attributed it to Herbert Spencer), but he was the first to make it the mainstay of an analysis of society. In the hands of Ross and many other celebrated American social theorists of the first half of the twentieth century, social control was a major conceptual tool answering what they saw as the key problem for sociology, politics and indeed philosophy: the 'problem of order'.

Ross's work encapsulated certain quintessential features of the first phase of the usage of social control in sociological theory, which also echo down through its later key representatives, notably Robert Park and Talcott Parsons. Above all, the perspective was concerned with the *social* component of 'social control'. Although often castigated as such, none of these thinkers was politically conservative. The problem of order was not so much an eternal consequence of human nature but of the rapid and unsettling tumult of industrial, urbanized capitalism. Massive inequality, poverty and class conflict, and an egoistic, anomic culture, generated social problems of many kinds – including, but not limited to, crime and deviance. *Social* control, then, was the project of identifying and developing institutional and policy responses to alleviate and hopefully ultimately tame the pernicious problems of unregulated and unrestrained capitalism: 'All social problems turn out finally to be problems of social control' (Park and Burgess 1924:209). It is important to note, however, that the criminal justice system, ultimately based on legalized coercion, is seen as having little if any part in this. Ross identified the roots of social control as sympathy, sociability, and the sense of justice (1901:Chaps 2–4), and devoted only one of his 33 chapters to law, focusing instead on a variety of cultural and social-psychological processes.

Social control was espoused as the humane, non-violent alternative to order maintenance through the criminal justice system because that rested ultimately upon the potential delivery of physical force and the pain of imprisonment. This remained true of its usage throughout the first half of the twentieth century, although the provenance of social control narrowed to those processes geared specifically to reactions against deviance. Thus, in Talcott Parsons' major exposition of structural functionalism, social control was defined as 'those processes in the social system which tend to counteract the deviant tendencies' (1951:297), contributing to social integration and pattern maintenance, alongside socialization, education, religion, media and other institutions, that figured as parts of Ross's more expansive notion of social control.

During the late 1950s and early 1960s, the development of **labelling theory**, and later **critical criminologies**, upended the moral/political evaluation of social control, and its causal significance. The common ground of these perspectives was the (tautological) claim that 'deviance is *not* a quality of the act the person commits, but rather a consequence of the application by others of rules and sanctions to an "offender"' (Becker 1963:9). The research focus thus shifted to the explanation of labelling rather than offending, for example in Becker's analysis of the origins of the 1937 Marijuana Tax Act in the moral entrepreneurship of the Federal Bureau of Narcotics (Chaps 7–8). Following Becker, many sociologists shifted their standpoint from identification with society as a whole (and in particular its respectable upper layers or the criminal law and justice system) to sympathy with the outsiders who were stigmatized and oppressed by the powers that be.

See Chapter 3.8
Labelling theory

See Chapter 3.3
Critical
criminologies

Formal social-control institutions were castigated as causes of the most seriously problematic behaviour that came to be criminalized. This was made most explicit in Lemert's (1967) concept of 'secondary' deviance, which resulted from the changes in self-identification and in perception by others following formal labelling of an offender. Thus, according to Lemert, social control actually *produced* deviance – a process distinct from the initial primary delinquency that young people might **drift** in and out of (Matza 1964). Far from being a solution to the problem of order, social control *was* the problem – intellectually, morally and causally.

See Chapter 3.5
Drift

The ideas developed by Lemert and others snowballed into radical critique of the wider processes that Ross and colleagues had celebrated as benign informal social control. The 1960s and 1970s produced many critical analyses of the repressive effects of apparently benign institutions such as education, family, media, religion and welfare.

Despite the value of many of these analyses, the underlying concept of social control as everything that contributed to the reproduction of a fundamentally unjust and repressive social order was problematic and tended to be tautological. Cohen (1985:1–2), dubbed the all-encompassing notion of social control a 'Mickey Mouse' concept and proposed a narrower, more specific definition: 'the organized ways in which society responds to behavior and people it regards as deviant, problematic, worrying, threatening, troublesome or undesirable'. While restricting the concept of social control to an intended and conscious reaction, Cohen certainly did not mean that the perspective of policymakers and control agents should be accepted. On the contrary, his book is perhaps best known for its analysis of the way that attempts to restrict the negative punitive impact of control often prove counterproductive, drawing in more marginally deviant behaviours and individuals (colourfully depicted in his fishing metaphor as 'net widening' and 'thinning the mesh').

Since the 1980s, discussions of social control have become bifurcated, reflecting more general destructuring impulses in criminology and social science. On the one hand, studies of specific formal control institutions, such as policing, prosecution and punishment, have proliferated. The majority are sponsored by and oriented towards the state and its control institutions, exploring 'what works?' and how to improve the system's crime control performance. On the other hand, there has also been a burgeoning critical literature on the liberty-threatening, and elite- and corporate-power-enhancing, consequences of the growth of **surveillance** and tougher (and smarter) **crime prevention** and sanctioning.

See Chapter 5.19
Surveillance

See Chapter 6.2
Community safety

A dominant influence has been Foucault, and the desire to avoid the deterministic and negative connotations of the earlier critical social-control theories. Instead, the emphasis shifted to the detailed way that discipline shapes human actions in creative as well as controlling ways.

The most influential overall analysis of crime-control trends in recent decades has been Garland's (2001) *Culture of Control*, which pays due weight to social, economic and cultural aspects of the development of crime-control practices in late-modern times. This had roots in macro-level transformations of political economy, social relations and culture; but Garland traces down the complex mediations shaping everyday perceptions and behaviour that then feed back into institutional and state policies.

More recent twenty-first-century developments in crime and its control, as well as in the broader political economy, can be seen as resuscitating the relevance of the older social-control perspectives. In particular, the big puzzle for contemporary criminological analysis is how to understand the crime drop since the mid-1990s throughout the Western world. Despite a proliferation of hypotheses to explain the crime decline, it largely remains a mystery. For present purposes, the crucial puzzle is how far can the crime drop be attributed to social control functioning more effectively, and what aspects have contributed to it? More broadly, the economic crisis since the 2007/08 financial crash did not only expose the fragility of the future; it also revealed the thin ice on which the apparent economic prosperity of the **neoliberal** era had been constructed. Beyond this, the project of restoring economic and social security, without exacerbating further the perilous environmental challenges threatening human existence, raises even more profound issues of social control than those that ushered in the concept in the wake of the dislocations of modernity.

See Chapter 4.24
Neoliberalism

References

Becker, Howard. 1963. *Outsiders*. New York: Free Press.

Cohen, Stanley. 1985. *Visions of Social Control: Crime, Punishment, and Classification*. Cambridge. Polity.

Garland, David. 2001. *The Culture of Control*. Oxford: Oxford University Press.

Innes, Martin. 2003. *Understanding Social Control*. Maidenhead: Open University Press.

Lemert, Edwin. 1967. *Human Deviance, Social Problems, and Social Control*. Englewood Cliffs, NJ: Prentice Hall.

Matza, David. 1964. *Delinquency and Drift*. New York: Wiley.

Park, Robert, and Ernest Burgess. 1924. *Introduction to the Science of Sociology*. Chicago: University of Chicago Press.

Parsons, Talcott. 1951. *The Social System*. Glencoe: Free Press.

Ross, Edward A. 1901. *Social Control: A Survey of the Foundations of Order*. New York: Macmillan.

Further reading

Becker, Howard. 1967. Whose Side Are We On? *Social Problems* 14(3): 239–47.

Reiner, Robert. 2007. *Law and Order: An Honest Citizen's Guide to Crime and Control*. Cambridge: Polity.

Reiner, Robert. 2016. *Crime*. Cambridge: Polity.

Tonry, Michael (ed.). 2014. *Why Crime Rates Fall and Why They Don't*. Chicago: University of Chicago Press.

5.19 Surveillance

Peter Fussey

Surveillance, a portmanteau of the French word *sur* ('over') and the verb *veiller* ('to watch'), has been defined as 'the focused, systematic and routine attention to personal details for the purposes of influence, management, protection or direction' (Lyon 2007:14). Yet one of the challenges of defining technologically mediated practices is the dynamic nature of both the subject and the context they operate within. The current ubiquity of digitally mediated life and the erosion of any meaningful boundary between online and offline living has led to an unprecedented abundance of digital information, all amenable to categorization, scrutiny and surveillance.

In the contemporary era of digital living online-hosted information and communications technologies operate with ubiquity across multiple scales of action. These range from the constellations of global governance – including planetary climate- and disease-monitoring processes – via urban management projects such as smart cities, to the comparatively quantum level of the individual body, and fragmented elements thereof, through personal health 'life-logging' and social communication. Information is confessed, offered up by users for external and unknowable scrutiny. Yet it is also externally imposed via 'biopolitical tattoos', subcutaneous inscriptions delivered by a ubiquitous 'technological apparatus [that] identifies and registers bare life', as Giorgio Agamben (2008:202) contends.

As such, surveillance practices reach beyond the corporal and temporal boundaries of life itself. Focus no longer rests on the individual as subject, but instead falls both within and beyond it. Surveillance aggregates the activities of populations and, as Foucault (2008) traces, the situation of individuals in relation to them. Paradoxically, surveillance also divides what was once deemed indivisible, dissecting the individual into 'dividual' (Deleuze 1995) elements, traits or categories. Moreover, such scales are not neatly delineated: surveillance practices extract, combine and reassemble fragments of selves into wider aggregate assemblages of information.

Concerning temporality, surveillance practices are episodic and ephemeral, yet also operate longitudinally. With advances in prenatal imaging and digital residues remaining beyond life itself, digital monitoring of individuals now extends and reaches beyond the womb-to-tomb boundaries of human existence. Human life increasingly bears the imprint of technology. Once evanescent, youthful transgressions become digitally remembered, freeing spectres of the past to continually stalk the present and erode any right to be forgotten.

Despite such complexity, surveillance remains unhelpfully characterized through a select few well-worn lenses. Among these, famous Orwellian tropes – replete with characterizations of concentrated sovereign power and its unidirectional top-down coercive dispatch – have proved irresistible to many. While Snowden's revelations remind us that the state matters, pluralities of security governance and the 'confessional' nature of much data-generation temper the applicability of this frame. Orwellian narratives, largely unfaithful to their literary origins, also mask how the surveillance gaze falls unevenly, with scrutiny heavily mediated by social location. Also concealed are the often more egregious incursions and unaccountable actions of non-state actors.

See Chapter 5.17
Security and
counter-security

Elsewhere, surveillance is regularly characterized by antagonistic couplets, including the binaries of 'nothing to fear, nothing to hide' or 'liberty versus security'. Both are excessively reductionist in their capacity to explain the complex operations and impacts of surveillance. The former, nothing to fear, is easily dismissed on the grounds that the right to privacy is a fundamental human right, enshrined in every international code of rights and valued in almost all human societies. Rights to privacy are not available for arbitrary renegotiation just because technological innovation holds the capacity for greater intrusion. The latter, liberty verses security, masks the broader social costs of surveillance (including chilling effects on expression, proportionality, categorization and deeper questions of social justice) whilst overstating its security benefits.

Prominent and enduring theoretical understandings of surveillance have relied on a triumvirate of French scholars: Michel Foucault, Gilles Deleuze and Bruno Latour. Taking these in turn, Foucault's canon is rich and varied; yet there has been a noticeable over-representation of work on discipline and panopticism. Drawing inspiration from a prison designed by Samuel Bentham – brother of the famous utilitarian often erroneously credited with the idea – Foucault used the panopticon to theorize micro-level articulations of regulatory power. Developed in the monograph *Discipline and Punish*, panopticism operates as a metaphor for subjects' self-regulation, and conformity to standards defined via power-knowledge webs of normalization, in response to self-perceived visibility before the gaze of authority. This technique was famously argued by Foucault (1977:298) as perfected in prisons before being

See Chapter 5.11
Panopticism

See Chapter 1.3
Utilitarianism

'transported . . . to the entire social body'. The rush to panopticize has been conspicuous among critical studies of surveillance, as the tedious regularity with which the 'opticon' suffix is applied to supposedly newly identified modes of surveillance attests.

Numerous critiques challenge this theorization of surveillance, including the uneven application of surveillance and its use to exclude and delineate, rather than 'retrain' and reintegrate, subjects. The overrepresentation of panopticism within surveillance studies is unfortunate given Foucault's much more cautious, detailed and nuanced treatment of the material. Often ignored is how, actually within the pages of *Discipline and Punish*, Foucault suggests panopticism as a blueprint, 'reduced to its ideal form' (1977:205), and warns against its over-literal application. More significantly, the attachment to panopticism remains puzzling given that by February 1978, just a few months after *Discipline and Punish* was published in English, Foucault (2007) had himself rejected the totality of the concept. Instead, he advocated for *dispositifs* comprising diverse registers of power operating simultaneously. Perhaps most problematic is the way panopticism has overshadowed other, potentially more fecund, contributions of relevant Foucauldian thought. This includes ideas of population and biopolitics (Foucault 2008), which potentially harmonize well with contemporary aggregated 'big-data' practices. Perhaps most significant are Foucault's (2007) examinations of 'security' during the development of his **governmentality** thesis that focuses on circulations, mobilities and movements – a *laissez-passer* to companion the growth of *laissez-faire* (see Fussey 2013 for an application of these ideas to surveillance).

See Chapter 5.8
Governmentality

Post-Foucauldian theorizations of surveillance have drawn heavily on the work of Deleuze, with his short essay *Postscript on the Societies of Control* (1995) holding greatest influence. There are perhaps three main strands of Deleuzian thought of particular relevance here. The first is his emphasis on the integration and merger of disparate forms of power into composite apparatuses or *assemblages*. Prominently captured in Haggerty and Ericson's (2000) concept of the *surveillant assemblage*, disparate forms of surveillance are seen to coalesce around mobile objects and subjects. In this sense, *assemblage* places emphasis on the connectivity, integration and interoperability of different forms of power. Other components of Deleuzian societies of control are also relevant, however. Particularly important here is the way power is seen to operate to continuously *modulate* subjects rather than seeking to *mould* them into a final normalized form as Foucault's disciplinary model suggests. This provides a theoretical vocabulary to accommodate the heterogeneous, partial and incomplete ambitions of many current surveillance practices.

Much of Deleuze's canon, particularly prominent in work with Felix Guattari (1987), is concerned with questions of *emergence*. Indebted to Foucault's view that power is something exercised rather than merely possessed, and is thus productive, emergence attends to the composition of something new, rather than merely describing a connectivity of formerly heterogeneous elements. It is in this sense that critics have argued that Anglophonic scholars have misunderstood important features of Deleuze's work. Here, *assemblage* has been translated from the French *agencement*, which, some critics argue, holds a broader meaning. This extends beyond the arrangement of things, to encompass the *act* of connecting them together, and development of new compositions and interdependencies that subsequently emerge.

Finally, recent years have witnessed an increasing influence of science and technology studies (STS) to understand surveillance, particularly through understandings of how technology is neither neutral nor passive. Instead, technological design is considered embedded with, and reproducing of, a range of normative and subjective values. Within this field, Latour's (2005) *actor network theory* is particularly influential. The central theme of this theory is that non-human objects, such as technology, hold agential influence and play an *active* role in shaping the social relations and practices in which they exist. Whilst the attribution of agency to non-animate objects has become one of the most controversial elements of Latour's approach, the idea may be applied in the sense that surveillance technologies may exert such influence by rendering some activities visible, and therefore actionable, whilst concealing others.

References

Agamben, Giorgio. 2008. No to Biopolitical Tattooing. *Communication and Critical/ Cultural Studies* 5(2): 201–2.

Deleuze, Gilles. 1995. Postscript on Control Societies. In *Negotiations 1972–1990*, pp. 177–83. New York: Columbia University Press.

Deleuze, Gilles, and Felix Guattari. 1987. *A Thousand Plateaus*. London: Continuum.

Foucault, Michel. 1977. *Discipline and Punish: The Birth of the Prison*. London: Penguin.

Foucault, Michel. 2007. *Security, Territory, Population, Lectures at the Collège de France 1977–1978*. Basingstoke: Palgrave Macmillan.

Foucault, Michel. 2008. *The Birth of Biopolitics, Lectures at the Collège de France 1978–1979*. Basingstoke: Palgrave Macmillan.

Fussey, Peter. 2013. Contested Topologies of UK Counterterrorist Surveillance: The Rise and Fall of Project Champion. *Critical Studies on Terrorism* 6(3): 351–70.

Haggerty, Kevin, and Richard Ericson. 2000. The Surveillant Assemblage. *British Journal of Sociology* 51(4): 605–22.

Latour, Bruno. 2005. *Reassembling the Social: An Introduction to Actor Network Theory*. Oxford: Oxford University Press.

Lyon, David. 2007. *Surveillance Studies: An Overview*. Cambridge: Polity.

Further reading

Gilliom, John, and Torin Monahan. 2013. *SuperVision: An Introduction to the Surveillance Society*. Chicago: University of Chicago Press.

Lyon, David, Kevin Haggerty, and Kirstie Ball (eds). 2012. *The Routledge International Handbook of Surveillance Studies*. London: Routledge.

Part 6

Geographies of crime

Part 6 Introduction

The relationships that obtain between crime and place have long been the focus of the criminological imagination. From Victorian explorations of urban squalor in London, through the moral mapping of modernity in Chicago, to recent excavations of postmodernity in fortress Los Angeles, it is clear that the city – as both a geographic space and a cultural concept – has preoccupied thinking about crime. Going further back in time, the idea of an 'underworld' has been a persistent trope in popular culture, and has often been depicted as a shadowy, deviant space of collaboration where sophisticated outlaw networks extend over many localities to form 'criminal areas'. Then, as now, mobility is key. Indeed, it was the nomadic rootlessness of vagabonds and rogues that enabled some to prosper amid the growing social complexities of urban life in the sixteenth century.

Also crucial was the role of the marketplace, which was at the centre of most towns and cities, and the pivotal point around which trade and commerce grew – both legal and illegal. All European cities, as they evolved from ancient Greece up to the medieval world, are a distinctive combination of fortress and market. Indeed, it was the economic function of the great trading towns that fuelled their growing power and led to political freedom. The defensive walls protected citizens, encouraging individual and collective liberation, but also spoke to the inherently authoritarian character of the urban condition.

The essays in this part of the book explore how geographies of difference and exclusion are crucial to understanding how problem places are constructed. Indeed, the popular view that a causal relationship exists between different settlement types and the quality of life in them can be traced back to antiquity, but took on a compelling mythologizing force during the Industrial Revolution. Here, an idealized, pastoral sense of rural community and solidarity is contrasted with the city – represented as bleak, alienating and degrading. But metropolitan living also offers a dynamic sense of possibility, of sociability and of movement, underlining the deep ambivalence of the urban experience. The vivid and vibrant contrasts of urban life have inspired a considerable body of writing on the city as a site of desire, fantasy and pleasure, as well as a space of anxiety, fear, insecurity and violence.

Many commentators have found in Los Angeles a paradigm of the postmodern metropolis: disorganized around a collage of many suburban nuclei; defined by the increasing militarization of urban space and the defence of luxury lifestyles through private policing, state-of-the-art electronic surveillance and the destruction of public space. This can be contrasted with Chicago as the epitome of the modern city organized around a single centre. The trend toward fortification and sequestration is most pronounced in the United States, but it is a process that can be found in more or less brutal form in cities around the world. In Britain, dystopian images of the city have tended to concentrate on the demonization of social housing. Council estates perform an ideologically important role as a signifier of 'problem' people and places.

In many of these estates across Britain, and also more broadly in Europe, there were and are heavy concentrations of unemployment and poverty that parallel processes of dereliction that have been in full flow in the United States since the early 1980s. This is not to imply that forms of marginality in Europe are exactly following the black American ghetto experience, but that social and spatial exclusion on either side of the Atlantic shares some significant features. These widely despised, blemished places are largely the product of state policies and result from uneven development in capitalist economies and neoliberal governance, where the formation of an enduring 'precariat' is one of the defining features of the post-industrial landscape.

Broken windows

Gareth Millington

See Chapter 4.23
(Neo)-conservative
criminology

'Broken windows' is a cornerstone of right realist or **neo-conservative crim-inology**. It attempts to account for why disorder and crime might escalate quickly within a neighbourhood, and suggests what should be done to prevent this. Right realism recommends decentralized, cost-effective, practical solutions to crime and disorder. Usually, these solutions are pragmatic, based upon a philosophy of 'what works' as opposed to left/liberal concerns with identifying and understanding the 'external' social factors that cause or sustain crime. Right realism does, however, appeal to tradition and community, and is critical of the permissive social revolutions of the 1960s for weakening the moral culture of Western societies. For Kelling and Coles (1996), the spread of disorder in American cities is due to: the growth of individual (or

See Chapter 4.39
Victimology

See Chapter 1.18
Rational choice

See Chapter
6.6 Opportunity
theory; Chapter
6.2 Community
safety; Chapter 6.5
Defensible space

See Chapter 5.7
Fear of crime

See Chapter 5.2
Antisocial
behaviour

victim) **rights**; the decriminalization of drunkenness and substance-abuse; the deinstitutionalization of the mentally ill; and the erosion of legal authority for controlling disorder (referring especially to the tendency to treat disorder as a problem of poverty or homelessness). Such political arguments, however, merely provide a context for broken windows, which rests wholly upon a **rational choice** approach to understanding the causes of crime and disorder.

The broken windows perspective has been extremely influential on public policy in relation to crime control, especially as part of a wider 'preventive turn' in criminology that advocates **opportunity-reduction strategies of situational crime prevention** (see Hughes 2007). Its influence can also be traced directly to issues/legislation relating to zero-tolerance policing, **fear of crime** and **antisocial behaviour**.

The two key texts that outline the broken windows perspective are the article published by James Q. Wilson and George L. Kelling in 1982 in *Atlantic Monthly*, titled 'Broken Windows', and *Fixing Broken Windows: Restoring Order and Reducing Crime in Our Communities*, the 1996 book by Kelling and Catherine M. Coles. Both works are written in the persuasive, rhetorical style that is a common feature of conservative US social scientists. The *Atlantic Monthly* article uses the image of the 'broken window' to explain how neighbourhoods descend into disorder and crime if no one attends to their maintenance. The broken window is an analogy to describe a simple relationship between disorder and crime: if a window in a building is broken and is left unrepaired, it is highly likely that the other windows will soon be broken. The unrepaired window is a signal that nobody in the neighbourhood cares. For the would-be vandal, there is no reason why he/she should not break more.

A crucial point is that the potential vandal need not already be a 'criminal'. Wilson and Kelling cite a famous experiment by Stanford psychologist Philip Zimbardo in 1969. Zimbardo placed comparable automobiles, without licence plates and with their bonnets raised, on streets in the Bronx borough of New York City and suburban Palo Alto, California. The car on a decayed street in the Bronx was attacked and completely stripped within 24 hours. The car in Palo Alto was left untouched for over a week. Zimbardo then smashed part of the car with a sledgehammer. Within an hour, the car had been turned over and destroyed by – in Wilson and Kelling's terms – 'respectable whites' (1982:3). This experiment is deemed important because it apparently reveals how possible social causes of crime such as poverty, 'race' or inequality are not as significant as a visible, public sign that 'nobody cares'.

In a now famous passage, Wilson and Kelling (1982:32) describe the developmental sequence of broken windows in concrete terms:

> A stable neighbourhood of families who care for their homes, mind each other's children, and confidently frown on unwanted intruders can change, in a few years or even a few months, to an inhospitable and frightening jungle. A piece of property is abandoned, weeds grow up, a window is smashed. Adults stop scolding rowdy children; the children, emboldened, become more rowdy. Families move out, unattached adults move in. Teenagers gather in front of the corner store. The merchant asks them to move; they refuse. Fights occur. Litter accumulates. People start drinking in front of the grocers; in time, an inebriate slumps to the sidewalk and is allowed to sleep it off. Pedestrians are approached by panhandlers.

The argument goes that visible signs of decline like weeds or abandonment can lead to a relaxing of informal neighbourhood controls. This can lead to disorder, or 'incivility, boorish and threatening behaviour' (Kelling and Coles 1996:12). When the first signs of disorderly behaviour go unregulated, this communicates to citizens that the area is becoming unsafe. Citizen fear then causes people to choose to stay at home and/or avoid public areas. Some will buy weapons or dogs. Others will choose to leave the neighbourhood completely. As citizens withdraw physically, they also withdraw from roles of mutual support with their neighbours. When the fabric of urban and community life is undermined in this way, it leads to an increased vulnerability to more serious crime (Wilson and Kelling 1982:20). The argument that disorder precipitates a drift towards serious crime is one of the most alarmist and contentious aspects of the broken windows perspective:

Serious street-crime flourishes in areas in which disorderly behaviour goes unchecked. The unchecked panhandler is, in effect, the first broken window. Muggers and robbers, whether opportunistic or professional, believe they reduce their chances of being caught or even identified if they operate on streets where potential victims are already intimidated by prevailing conditions (Wilson and Kelling 1982:34).

Here, the premise of broken windows is applied directly to conduct. The street beggar or panhandler – a recurrent figure in broken windows literature – is identified as the 'first broken window'. If the 'intimidating' behaviour of the panhandler goes unchecked – if he/she is not removed from the street or prevented from asking citizens for money – this sends a signal to would-be thieves that this is an area where menacing behaviour is permissible and where they, themselves, are unlikely to be apprehended or caught.

Kelling and Coles acknowledge that broken windows is viewed as controversial by civil libertarians. In response to charges of intolerance and brutality towards the homeless or 'outsider' groups such as ethnic or racial minorities, the authors turn to a populist line of defence, maintaining that 'despite assertions by many libertarians, attempts to restore order do not pit rich against poor or black against white' (1996:4). They suggest that, in relation to accepted standards and norms of public behaviour, a broad consensus exists that cuts across racial, ethnic and class differences. Actually, they contend, broken windows is *antithetical* to the use of heavy-handed 'streetsweeping' tactics (ibid.:22). Despite how the principles of broken windows were aggressively deployed by, say, the New York Police Department (NYPD) during the 1990s, what the proponents themselves endorse is collaboration between police and citizens in improving neighbourhood standards, primarily through the use of foot patrols. This 'soft' policing tactic, they argue, is concerned with 'order maintenance' and aims to support communities, build trust and lessen fear.

While broken windows has become almost 'folk wisdom' within crime control, it has also been subject to criticism. For example, Harcourt has argued that, despite widespread practical deployment, there remains scant empirical evidence to suggest that 'order-maintenance' approaches have brought about a decline in crime. He additionally points to how they can also lead to an 'uncritical dichotomy between disorderly people and law abiders' (Harcourt 2001:7). These categories are the product of the repressive nature of broken windows policing, and a preoccupation with them overshadows serious costs such as 'increased complaints of police misconduct, racial bias in stops and frisks, and further stereotyping of black criminality' (ibid.). Matthews takes a different angle, and uses British Crime Survey data to question the 'inextricable' link between crime and incivilities. He argues it is important to take a nuanced approach and 'consider the relations between different contexts and try to better understand the types of assessments which people make about their future victimisation' (1992:29). He also questions the simplistic link between disorder and neighbourhood decline, pointing to how high-crime neighbourhoods in sought-after urban locations can actually see property prices rise and experience an influx of middle-class residents, a process urban scholars call 'gentrification'. Matthews also highlights the potential danger of displacement, whereby order-maintenance in one neighbourhood occurs at the expense of others, the result being that crime and disorder consolidates in areas of the city in an already advanced state of neglect.

See Chapter 3.14 Realism and left idealism

References

Harcourt, Bernard E. 2001. *Illusion of Order: The False Promise of Broken Windows Policing.* Cambridge, MA: Harvard University Press.

Hughes, Gordon. 2007. *The Politics of Crime and Community.* Basingstoke: Palgrave Macmillan.

Kelling, George L., and Catherine M. Coles. 1996. *Fixing Broken Windows: Restoring Order and Reducing Crime in Our Communities.* New York: Touchstone.

Matthews, Roger. 1992. Replacing 'broken windows': crime, incivilities and urban change. In *Issues in Realist Criminology*, Roger Matthews and Jock Young, eds, Chapter 2. London: Sage.

Wilson, James Q., and George L. Kelling. 1982. Broken Windows. *Atlantic Monthly* 249(3): 29–38.

Further reading

Bratton, William J. 1997. Crime is down in New York: blame the police. In *Zero-Tolerance Policing: Policing a Free Society*, Norman Dennis, ed. London: Institute of Economic Affairs.

Brisman, Avi. 2011. The "Subculture Career" as a Challenge to Broken Windows: A Review of Gregory J. Snyder's *Graffiti Lives: Beyond the Tag in New York's Urban Underground. Crime, Law and Social Change* 56(2): 213–17.

Brisman, Avi. 2012. Coda: An Elevated Challenge to 'Broken Windows': The High Line (New York). *Crime Media Culture* 8(3): 381.

Lees, Loretta, Tom Slater, and Elvin Wyly. 2013. *Gentrification.* New York: Routledge.

6.2

See Chapter 6.5
Defensible space

See Chapter 6.6
Opportunity
theory

See Chapter 5.17
Security and
counter-security

6.2 Community safety

Karen Evans

The concept of community safety emerged in the early 1980s as a progressive alternative to the narrowly focused situational techniques associated with the term 'crime prevention', which had been developed to respond to rising levels of recorded crime in the post-World War II period. While **situational crime-prevention** measures were designed to limit **opportunities for criminal activity in particular localities**, community safety offered a broader approach that looked beyond the confines of crime-focused interventions and towards the active promotion of safe neighbourhoods. The perspective promoted by community safety appealed to the emotionally driven, engaged and active citizen rather than the cold and rationally calculating 'homo economicus' of traditional crime prevention theory. Where previous crime-prevention measures typically involved professional top-down interventions to control crime in a given local area, community safety imagined more inclusive policy and practice focused on the needs of local people, and engaging local people in the design and implementation of community-specific solutions to rising levels of fear and **insecurity**.

These solutions, it was envisaged, would be perceived as directly relevant to a neighbourhood, and therefore meaningful to its residents. In addition, the community safety perspective encouraged policymakers to look outside definitions of crime constructed through the frameworks of law and criminal justice to encompass a consideration of broader social harms, such as environmental degradation, inadequate housing, poverty, unemployment and discriminatory practices – all of which may contribute to the social circumstances in which lawbreaking takes place. While the situational crime prevention techniques employed to reduce crimes against property were not abandoned, the need for measures which tackled the social and economic conditions at the root of the problem of crime were considered equally, if not more, important under the community safety approach.

Community safety is associated with the theory of 'left realism' and the desire to take victimization seriously. As such, it has the **reduction of all types of victimization at its core**. In the UK, community safety was initially embraced by left-leaning and Labour-controlled local authorities – a number of which conducted local crime and community safety audits to measure the extent of criminal victimization and **fear of crime** in high-crime neighbourhoods. Some also employed community safety coordinators to work closely within local neighbourhoods to implement policies and support projects designed to tackle problems, such as domestic violence, racism and any community tension or division, as well as to reduce burglaries, to improve street-lighting and to work with young people to improve the quality of life for all. Central to community safety work was the idea of partnership, connecting an area's residents and businesses to the locally powerful in policing, local government, health and environmental services and so forth in order to ensure that residents' voices were heard and to encourage multi-agency responses to problems which were, after all, clearly related.

This perspective signalled a fundamental change in the discourse surrounding the prevention of crime. Henceforth, tackling crime was considered, as described by Home Office Circular 8/84 in the UK, 'a task for the whole community' rather than just the preserve and responsibility of official agencies of law enforcement. Indeed, at this time, community safety was steered by local-government practitioners working alongside the police, rather than driven by nationally-set police targets. Considered a useful but a marginal and largely local approach, the community safety perspective did not become institutionalised into national government discourses until the latter half of the 1990s.

During the 1980s and most of the 1990s, the community safety perspective was associated with a number of programmes that were largely welfarist in their approach. They combined urban regeneration projects with economic development, services for young people and community-building projects. While voluntary-sector organisations and the private sector were fully involved, these programmes were led by local and regional authorities, and funding was often found from national sources and, within Europe, from European Commission sources such as the URBAN initiative. Around the turn of the century, however, welfarist discourses were increasingly displaced by more punitive and risk-based approaches built upon a very different response to the problem of crime. In classic **neoliberal** style, responsibility for tackling the problem of crime shifted away from the state and towards the individual and the community. Under these conditions, community safety work was correspondingly altered in tone. In the UK, this shift became apparent under the New Labour administrations, which governed from 1997 to 2010. Their Crime and Disorder Act of 1998 took the community safety model as its starting point, requiring the

See Chapter 3.14
Realism and left idealism

See Chapter 5.17
Fear of crime

See Chapter 4.24
Neoliberalism

setting-up of statutory mechanisms to ensure partnership working to prevent crime in every local authority area in England and Wales – with a required sharing of data, regular audits of crime and reporting back to the community placed on a statutory footing.

More than this, however, the Crime and Disorder Act introduced new systems for working with young people which were punitive and focused on regulation of individual behaviour. This was a departure from the progressive ethos which had informed the early stage of the development of the concept of community safety. Henceforth, the outward trappings of the community-safety perspective were adopted and co-opted into a preventive framework, which was based on an assessment of future **risk** and averting potential problems. The community safety projects of old did not disappear immediately, but were gradually displaced by early-intervention programmes aiming to 'nip in the bud' future criminal careers. The emphasis correspondingly moved away from community-wide solutions and towards individually focused interventions and work with 'troubled families' and 'at-risk' individuals. The inclusion of 'disorder' as a major governmental concern reflects this new attention to 'pre-crime' (Zedner 2007), wherein disorder became an indicator of possible trouble ahead or a precursor to crime but not lawbreaking in itself.

See Chapter 6.7 Risk

While the vocabulary of community safety persisted in some areas, existing community safety partnerships were dissolved and replaced by the Crime and Disorder Reduction Partnerships (CDRPs) required by statute. Somewhere in this change of emphasis, the community voice was increasingly drowned out and community safety structures became more top-down and driven by national government and policing priorities rather than tailored to local concerns and issues. At the same time, the focus narrowed once again to the prevention of 'signal crimes and disorders' (Innes and Fielding 2002), and the more holistic agenda, which set out to promote multiple aspects of community safety, was lost to a crime-focused, preventive agenda.

The history of community safety is one which cannot be understood outside the political and economic context in which it was first developed and later promulgated. Envisaged as an approach which would give a voice to the most marginal and vulnerable in society and extend the focus of preventive work to hidden or forgotten areas of **victimization**, this approach could not be sustained in an era of responsibilization, victim-blaming and attacks on welfare. The problems which community safety work were meant to address have, as a result, been reconceptualized as individually rather than socially produced, and the solutions offered have consequently targeted individuals and their motivations, thereby abandoning the focus on community and local social relationships. The idea of 'community' itself has been harnessed in a variety of ways by different political administrations in a bid to reinforce their particular strategies and perspectives. In the 1970s and 1980s, when the concept of community safety was being developed, 'community' was considered as a significant buttress to the incessant march of depersonalized market forces. More recently, however, it has been reimagined as offering an alternative to state-centred models

See Chapter 4.39 Victimology

of provision, which have been perceived as out of touch and irrelevant. This rearticulation of community has been central to a redrawing of the relationship between the state, crime control and the maintenance of social order.

Consequently, the concept of community safety has been co-opted into a new governance of crime that looks beyond the traditional practitioners of law enforcement to place non-state actors at the centre of crime-control policy and as active in the management of risk and insecurity. Communities have therefore been drawn into government agendas in ways which were simply not envisaged in the early 1980s. Communities are now expected to play their part in **anti-terrorism** and anti-radicalisation agendas, for example, and are seen as a crucial element in **surveillance** strategies, collecting intelligence and passing information on to relevant government departments. At the same time, a growing intolerance towards the poor, which has become apparent in government rhetoric, paints high-crime, low-employment and struggling communities as dysfunctional and problematic, mitigating against a politics of engagement (Wacquant 2009). This hardening of attitude has become more apparent since the global economic and banking crisis of 2008 that has fostered a widespread agenda of 'austerity' – a further retrenchment from welfarism and a scaling-down of state interventions. It represents a significant departure from the progressive ideals of inclusion, recognizing the vulnerable and widening conceptions of victimization that informed early community safety theory and practice, and suggests that this concept of community safety has today been distorted beyond recognition.

See Chapter 4.19 Institutional and anti-institutional violence

See Chapter 5.19 Surveillance

References

Innes, Martin, and Nigel Fielding. 2002. From Community to Communicative Policing: 'Signal Crimes' and the Problem of Public Reassurance. *Sociological Research Online* 7(2). www.socresonline.org.uk/7/2/innes.html. Accessed 23 January 2016.
Wacquant, Loïc. 2009. *Punishing the Poor: The Neoliberal Government of Social Insecurity.* Durham, NC: Duke University Press.
Zedner, Lucia. 2007. Pre-Crime and Post-Criminology. *Theoretical Criminology* 11(2): 261–81.

Further reading

Crawford, Adam. 1997. *Local Governance of Crime.* Oxford: Clarendon.
Crawford, Adam. 1998. *Crime Prevention and Community Safety: Politics, Policies and Practices.* Harlow: Longman.
Gilling, Daniel. 1997. *Crime Prevention: Theory, Policy and Practice.* London: UCL Press.
Hughes, Gordon, Eugene McLaughlin, and John Muncie (eds). 2002. *Crime Prevention and Community Safety: New Directions.* Milton Keynes: Open University Press.
Squires, Peter. 2006. *Community Safety: Critical Perspectives on Policy and Practice.* Bristol: Policy Press.

6.3 Crime science

Gloria Laycock

The term 'crime science' first appeared in the public arena in 2001, when the Jill Dando Institute for Crime Science (JDI) was established at University College London. Crime science describes a distinctive approach to determining responses to crime problems. Using experimental approaches and scientific principles, it aims to inform crime-reduction policies and practices, including those relating to situational prevention, detection, disruption and treatment. Crime science is thus outcome-focused and can, in this respect, loosely be compared to medical science, which aims to inform preventive medicine, reductions in the transmission of diseases and the treatment of sick individuals. It addresses crime and is the science of so doing; it thus has a broader agenda than police science (Weisburd and Neyroud 2011). Crime science concerns itself with the scientific investigation of all aspects of crime control including pre-emptive action against crime; the design of crime products, places and processes to reduce crime opportunities and provocations; the operation of the criminal justice system; and the treatment of offenders. It also addresses all types of crime – from minor acts of vandalism to serious offending, including **terrorism** and **organized crime**.

See Chapter 4.19 Institutional and anti-institutional violence

See Chapter 4.25 Organized crime

See Chapter 1.15 Forensic psychology

Science can contribute to crime control in at least four possible ways (Laycock 2005). First, it can increase our understanding of crime and its causes – the domain of the social sciences including criminology. Second, it can help make crimes more difficult to commit: technologies derived from scientific development help here and have led to CCTV, deadlocks, immobilisers on vehicles and so on. Third, it can help catch offenders more quickly and bring them to justice, which is particularly the domain of **forensic science** but might also include CCTV technology and computer science. Finally, thinking and acting 'like scientists' by devising and testing hypotheses empirically can help us better understand crime and determine the efficacy of responses to it. For all these reasons, crime science takes a multidisciplinary approach to crime control and might draw upon, for example, chemistry, computer science, criminology, engineering, forensic sciences, geography, mathematics, political science, psychology and sociology.

The roots of crime science and many of its underlying theoretical approaches to crime control can be traced to the development of **environmental criminology**. Fundamentally, the reduction of opportunities for crime in the immediate situation is seen as a major means of **'primary crime reduction'**. Primary crime prevention aims to avert crime by stopping it from happening, and addresses the behaviour of the general population. It can be contrasted with 'secondary prevention', which targets those at risk of offending, and 'tertiary prevention', which is concerned with treatment of known offenders. Thus, **routine activity theory** (Felson and Ekert 2015) and situational crime prevention (Clarke 1997) – together with contributions from a number of scholars who have studied crime analysis and **crime mapping** (particularly Brantingham and Brantingham 1991) – all contribute to the theoretical infrastructure from which crime science draws. This background also accounts for the initial emphasis of crime scientists on primary crime prevention.

See Chapter 6.5
Defensible space;
Chapter 6.10
Space, place and
crime

See Chapter 6.2
Community safety

See Chapter 6.8
Routine activity
theory

See Chapter 6.11
Spatial crime
modelling and
analysis

The emphasis on **scientific method** and hypothesis testing permeates all aspects of crime science. Thus, defining a problem, speculating on a solution, implementing it and assessing its subsequent effect are important elements of the approach, and each involves testing hypotheses. This is sometimes termed the SARA process – Scanning, Analysis, Response and Assessment – which is the bedrock of **problem-oriented policing** and is the process through which the police are encouraged to take a problem-solving approach to their work. This, it is argued, will support the development of an evidence base for policing and crime reduction.

See Chapter 1.4
Positivism

See Chapter 5.4
Community
policing

Crime-science researchers have generated a number of interesting and important insights. These include providing advances in our understanding of the geography of crime, which has stimulated work on predictive policing and demonstrated that a domestic burglary could be predicted with about 80 per cent accuracy within a two-day time-window in an area small enough to patrol. Other crime-science research has demonstrated the use of agent-based modelling, which makes it possible to test crime theories using computer-simulated models, reducing risk to **victims** and without raising ethical issues. Crime science has also led to recent advances in forensic geo-science and the development of a practitioner-oriented framework for the translation of 'what works' in crime reduction. All of these activities are relevant to the crime-control aspirations of crime scientists, and therefore have an applied focus.

See Chapter 4.39
Victimology

Four major criticisms have been levelled at crime science. The first is that it is not a discipline in its own right. Although there may be some merit in this

See Chapter 1.14
Experimental
criminology

See Chapter 5.17
Security and
counter-security

See Chapter 1.8
Learning theory

view, in drawing on a very wide range of science and technology, crime science differs from both **experimental criminology**, which aspires to scientific rigour but is confined to the social sciences, and from criminology in general, some of which is sceptical about the applicability of certain scientific approaches. Crime science is also determinedly concerned with outcomes – specifically the reduction of crime and the delivery of **security**, which are narrower than the broad scope of criminology.

The second criticism is that scientific exploration is only marginally relevant to a socially defined construct such as 'crime'. Criminal behaviour is, however, but one category of human behaviour, albeit socially proscribed. **Psychology** is the scientific study of the behaviour of organisms, including humans, and there is no reason why scientific principles cannot be applied in the exploration of behaviours that have been socially defined as 'antisocial' or 'criminal'.

The third criticism is that crime science embraces situational determinism. Even if all human behaviour is not strictly or mechanically determined, however, there is a substantial body of evidence demonstrating that human behaviour is responsive to the immediate situation – and it is on this that crime science draws. What is termed the 'fundamental attribution error' is relevant here as it is widely found and lies behind the difficulty many have in recognizing the significance of situations in causing behaviour in general and crime in particular. The fundamental attribution error is revealed when we attribute other people's actions to their personal characteristics but draw on the immediate situation or other external factors when explaining our own behaviour. Moreover, it is change in the situation that has delivered some of the most striking reductions in crime over the past few decades, such as reductions in car crime and domestic burglary.

The final criticism is that crime science embraces naïve positivism. Positivism as an account of scientific method, however, has long been discredited and is certainly not embraced by crime science, which acknowledges that reality can only be known imperfectly and that the theories, assumptions and experience of the researcher will inevitably influence the conclusions drawn from a given experiment. The approach taken to evaluation in crime science is well described by Pawson and Tilley (1997), who do not subscribe to positivism but adopt a critical realist understanding of science, emphasizing the importance of identifying the mechanisms through which initiatives exert their effect in any given context. Thus, the outcome is a consequence of firing a given mechanism in a specific context. The extent to which a mechanism might be effective in any given context will depend upon the extent to which it can be implemented and fired there.

A number of universities now offer crime science as an option for study. Some of these tend to stress the forensic aspects of the subject; others stress intelligence and detection, whilst others are more closely aligned with traditional criminology. They all, nevertheless, include courses on experimentation and experimental methods in their programmes, thereby demonstrating growing interest in this area of study.

References

Brantingham, Paul J., and Patricia L. Brantingham (eds). 1991. *Environmental Criminology*. Prospect Heights, IL: Waveland.

Clarke, Ronald V. (ed.). 1997. *Situational Crime Prevention: Successful Case Studies* (2nd edn). Albany, NY: Harrow & Heston.

Felson, Marcus, and Mary Ekert. 2015. *Crime and Everyday Life* (5th edn). Los Angeles: Sage.

Laycock, Gloria. 2005. Defining crime science. In *Crime Science: New Approaches to Preventing and Detecting Crime*, Melissa J. Smith and Nick Tilley, eds, pp. 3–24. Cullompton, UK: Willan.

Pawson, Ray, and Nick Tilley. 1997. *Realistic Evaluation*. London: Sage.

Weisburd David, and Peter Neyroud. 2011. *Police Science: Toward a New Paradigm*. Washington DC: National Institute of Justice. Available from www.ncjrs.gov/pdffiles1/nij/228922.pdf. Accessed 1 January 2015.

Further reading

Cornish, Derek, and Ronald V. Clarke. 2003. Opportunities, precipitators and criminal decision: A reply to Wortley's critique of situational crime prevention. In *Theory for Situational Crime Prevention: Crime Prevention Studies*, Vol. 16, Martha J. Smith and Derek B. Cornish, eds, pp. 41–96. Monsey, NY: Criminal Justice Press.

Ekblom, Paul. 1997. Gearing up against Crime: A Dynamic Framework to Help Designers Keep up with the Adaptive Criminal in a Changing World. *International Journal of Risk, Security and Crime Prevention* 2(4): 249-65.

Goldstein, Herman 1990. *Problem-Oriented Policing*. New York: McGraw-Hill.

Smith, Melissa, and Nick Tilley (eds). 2005. *Crime Science: New Approaches to Preventing and Detecting Crime*. Cullompton, UK: Willan.

Tilley, Nick, and Gloria Laycock. 2002. *Working Out What To Do: Evidence-Based Crime Reduction*. Crime Reduction Research Series paper 11. London: HMSO. Available from www.ncjrs.gov/pdffiles1/nij/grants/193161.pdf. Accessed 23 January 2016.

Cybercrime

Craig Webber

Cybercrime is any crime that utilizes networked computer systems wholly, or in part, to undertake illegal activities. Such activities are diverse, ranging from theft of money, data or intellectual property to the distribution of illegal images, bullying, piracy and vandalizing websites, such as in hacktivism. The key to the uniqueness of cybercrime is that networked computers – such as those on the World Wide Web (the 'Web') – allow crimes to take place that are more automated, anonymous and unhindered by time and global barriers. Such activity can also be committed on a huge scale and for very little cost. Criminologists can ask questions about cybercrime in the same way that we approach any other form of criminal activity. Is it new, unique and a real social problem or **a moral or media-led panic**? We can ask questions about the cause of the various activities that might be encompassed within a definition of cybercrime, and we might even ask if the notion of cybercrime is a useful concept in the first place. Yet, many of these basic questions are only just being posed. The starting point, however, is what exactly is cybercrime?

If we are to define cybercrime as any computer-mediated criminal activity, then someone using a smartphone to google the address of the bank they wish to rob might be classified as a cybercriminal. This would greatly inflate the number of instances of cybercrime, and might not be very helpful in identifying the unique characteristics of these offences. We might also define cybercrime as crime that is enabled by the Web and the interrelated network of connected computers linking citizens, business, commerce and government. This has enabled the advent of *cracking*, *hacking* and *spoofing*. These three terms each refer to similar actions. A 'cracker' is the original term for someone who

See Chapter 3.10
Moral panic

maliciously breaks into a service. So, for example, originally telephone lines and exchanges were 'cracked' in order to make free calls. A 'hacker' tends to be the term we use today, but it has become associated with crime when it was originally a term to denote ingenuity in the manipulation of technology for purposes for which it was not originally intended. 'Spoofing' is the use of a system by someone pretending to be the person who lawfully has access to it, such as the spoofing of an email address to send to an unwitting recipient to defraud them or encourage them to click on a link or attachment containing a virus.

It is often suggested that the 'breaking-in' to a computer is unique to cyber-crime, but many of the activities associated with hackers and crackers share a traditional corollary. So, for example, hacktivists who are able to take over a website and change the pictures or text, or render it useless by bombarding it with requests, a denial of service (DoS) attack, are echoing traditional forms of protest (Brisman 2014). The DoS attack might stop a bank's website working in a similar way to a physical protest at a high-street branch. Changing the pictures or text to make a political point is akin to vandalism. The difference becomes one of scale and speed, rather than intention. One person can render a global company's computer systems redundant or defaced via the Web, and this can be felt in many different countries simultaneously.

Are there crimes that can only be committed with the advent of computers and the Web? The use of malware and viruses are perhaps the only 'cyber-dependent' crimes that could not take place without the advent of networked computer systems, and indeed connecting the latter to a botnet has further expanded and accelerated this form of crime (Wall 2008). Finally, and the most banal definition of all, is that cybercrime is any crime that is against the laws created to tackle cybercrime, such as the Computer Misuse Act of 1990 in the UK.

What do we know about cybercrime? Until a question was included in the Crime Survey for England and Wales (CSEW) and reported in 2015, we knew very little about cybercrime victimization beyond the frequent warnings from the cybersecurity industry itself. The CSEW showed that cybercrime and fraud were the most prevalent forms of **victimization**, but even these data are limited to the awareness of the general public about how to spot if you have been a victim. We also know something of the way that various 'cyber-enabled' or cyber-dependent crime takes place by visiting the many discussion forums devoted to it. Here one can find tutorials about the 'correct' way to commit crime, such as credit-card fraud. We can even 'lurk' on these forums and read people discussing how they first became involved in the crime, and their fears and reasons for taking part (Yip et al. 2013). Yet, very little research has been conducted face to face with cybercriminals due to the difficulties in gaining access. There are some notable exceptions that use interviews gained at hacker conferences, virtual ethnography and email interviews (Blevins and Holt 2009; Sugiura et al. 2012).

Cybercrime is a rapidly changing activity. As new technology is invented, with increasingly rapid public acceptance, and then equally rapid criminal

See Chapter 4.39
Victimology

exploitation, many doubt the ability of law enforcement to keep up with these changes. Stephen Spielberg's film, *Minority Report* (2002), presented a vision of the future in which large screens could be manipulated by touch – virtual objects pulled from one part of the screen to another. Most people now take their touch-screen tablets for granted, and the rapid advancement of 3D printing means that it is relatively straightforward to print a useable gun (Memmott 2013).

In the UK, cybercrime was regarded as a Tier One risk to the country in the 2010 National Security Strategy, meaning a cyber-attack by other states or cybercriminals is one of the top four risks threatening the UK. The risk of a cyber-attack is therefore as much of a priority as the threat posed by a nuclear, chemical or biological device being exploded, or by major accidents or natural hazards and international military crises.

There is, however, a contradiction at the heart of the cybersecurity debate. On the one hand, the public is increasingly going to be held responsible for individual and collective security failings. This is sometimes referred to as the *responsibilization thesis* (Garland 2001). For example, banks have compensated the victims of cyber-theft and businesses have tended towards overlooking the mistakes of staff if they inadvertently click on a virus-infected email or succumb to a phishing attack. This appears set to change, however, as potentially all organizations with a website face the call to take out cyber-insurance policies. The impact of this additional cost to an organization may well be passed on to customers and other users of those services. This relates not just to the cost of buying an insurance policy, but also to the enhanced security measures that may become part of the policy stipulations. In contrast to and appearing to contradict the quest for greater security, however, is the advent of contactless payment. This is where one can tap one's payment card on a terminal in a shop to pay for goods without entering a PIN or signing anything.

See Chapter 5.17
Security and
counter-security

What has driven this counterintuitive shift towards less secure systems of payment? Cybersecurity has grappled with the friction caused by **security** measures, more generally. The need to create and remember passwords has proliferated as the Internet has become the central system for almost every form of transaction, financial or otherwise. Almost everyone has forgotten a password and has needed to reset it. This is often time-consuming, meaning that for every forgotten password, a website is potentially losing business at the same time as causing the would-be customer frustration. So the trend may be towards a more frictionless form of security, using 'harder' forms of biometrics such as fingerprints or iris scans. The key to this development is making such systems hard to crack through forcing someone to touch the fingerprint pad or looking into the scanner. It is hoped that the end result will be a form of e-commerce that will not be frustrated by the human capacity to forget a password. One thing that we can confidently predict, however, is that these systems will still be cracked.

References

Blevins, Kristie R., and Thomas J. Holt. 2009. Examining the Virtual Subculture of Johns. *Journal of Contemporary Ethnography* 38(5): 619–48.

Brisman, Avi. 2014. In the garden with 'creative crime': Kudzu and the third branch. In *The Poetics of Crime: Understanding and Researching Crime and Deviance through Creative Sources*, Michael Hviid Jacobsen, ed., pp. 51–70. Farnham: Ashgate.

Garland, David. 2001. *The Culture of Control*. Oxford: Oxford University Press.

Memmott, Mark. 2013. Gun Made with 3-D Printer is Successfully Fired. *National Public Radio*, 6 May. www.npr.org/sections/thetwo-way/2013/05/06/181612663/gun-made-with-3-d-printer-is-successfully-fired. Accessed 23 January 2017.

Sugiura, Lisa, Catherine Pope, and Craig Webber. 2012. Buying Unlicensed Drugs from the Web: A Virtual Ethnography. Proceedings of the Web Science Conference 2012. Available at: http://eprints.soton.ac.uk/344878. Accessed 23 January 2017.

Wall, David S. 2008. *Cybercrime: The Transformation of Crime in the Information Age*. Cambridge: Polity.

Yip, Michael, Craig Webber, and Nigel Shadbolt. 2013. Trust among Cybercriminals? Carding Forums, Uncertainty and Implications for Policing. *Policing and Society* 23(4): 516–39.

Further reading

Holt, Thomas J., 2007. Subcultural Evolution? Examining the Influence of On- and Off-Line Experiences on Deviant Subcultures. *Deviant Behavior* 28(2): 171–98.

Poulsen, Kevin. 2011. *Kingpin: How One Hacker Took over the Billion-Dollar Cybercrime Underground*. New York: Crown.

Shalhoub-Kevorkian, Nadera. 2012. E-Resistance and Technological In/Security in Everyday Life. *British Journal of Criminology* 52(1): 55–72.

Webber, Craig, and Michael Yip. 2013. Drifting on and off-line: Humanising the cyber criminal. In *New Directions in Crime and Deviancy*, Simon Winlow and Rowland Atkinson, eds, pp. 191–205. London: Routledge.

Yar, Majid, 2013. *Cybercrime and Society* (2nd edn). London: Sage.

6.5 Defensible space

Ken Pease

Defensible space is a concept whose application in residential planning is intended to make human settlements less vulnerable to crime. Crime is a frequent reason for moving from one location to another, and newcomers seem to be disproportionately **victimized** relative to residents of longer standing. Stable communities are less vulnerable. Population churn is associated with elevated levels of crime. Sustainable development is facilitated when human settlements are internally cohesive (lack of internal conflict yields reduced carbon and human costs).

See Chapter 4.39
Victimology

Recognition of the malign effects of poor housing, at the individual dwelling and area levels, is not new. The nineteenth-century investigations of Henry Mayhew and colleagues, published in their four-volume study of the lives of the poor in London, provide a notable, though far from the earliest, description of the 'rookeries' where crime proliferated. The novels of Mayhew's contemporary, Elizabeth Gaskell – for example *North and South* – present often moving accounts of conditions in Manchester with which she was very familiar as the wife of an inner-city Manchester non-conformist minister.

See Chapter 6.10
Space, place and
crime

More recent scholarly attention to the criminogenic effects of **place design** is generally ascribed to the pioneering work of Jane Jacobs and of Oscar Newman, whose first relevant publications appeared in the same year, 1961, and whose combined influence has been immense in sensitizing the planning and architecture professions to the relevance of place characteristics to behaviour. Their key contribution lies in providing a lexicon of variables putatively relevant to crime. Although the present essay centres on the notion of defensible space pioneered by Newman, a respectful nod to Jacobs is fitting.

This essay will seek concisely to set out the core of defensible-space thinking and to trace, albeit briefly, the legacy left by Newman in what was badged by him as crime prevention through environmental design (CPTED), a term whose range of application has changed but which retains Newman's imprint.

Newman's first published perspective in 1961 was followed by a raft of publications: one in 1972 was devoted exclusively to defensible space and the most complete articulation of his fully fledged ideas appeared in 1996. In Newman's words (1972:3):

> 'Defensible space' is a surrogate term for the range of mechanisms – real and symbolic barriers, strongly defined areas of influence, and improved opportunities for surveillance – that combine to bring an environment under the control of its residents. A *defensible space* is a living residential environment which can be employed by inhabitants for the enhancement of their lives, while providing security for their families, neighbours and friends.

Early critics of defensible space seem more inclined to accept the premise, but criticize the way in which this is theorized. In particular, the relative safety of high-rise developments above the ground floor seems general and is contrary to the defensible-space formulation.

To return to Newman himself, the relevant mechanisms underpinning the core idea are:

- Territoriality: the subdivision of buildings and grounds into zones of influence, such that no one place has an obvious overseeing residence.
- Surveillance: the design of buildings to maximize surveillance opportunities.
- Image: the design of social housing to minimize stigmatization by dint of poor design.
- Juxtaposing social-housing developments with others deemed safe.

The four elements are not independent. For example, the zones of influence in 'territoriality' tend to be those where 'surveillance' is possible. Having a zone of influence is relevant only insofar as area 'image' does not evoke fear. Defensible space is not necessarily defended space. The juvenile population of an area seems a good predictor of crime, arguably reflecting decreased willingness of adults to exercise guardianship. Much recent work has focused on the psychology of place guardianship, teasing out the factors which make people more inclined to intervene.

See Chapter 5.19
Surveillance

See Chapter 5.7
Fear of crime

See Chapter 2.6
Control theories

To what extent can it be said that the idea of defensible space has been shown to be associated with lower levels of crime in developments adhering to Newman's core principles? The natural surveillance component of the defensible space theory has survived empirical test best. Early and ingenious studies showed that levels of bus-vandalism varied with lack of surveillance opportunities, and that vandalism to telephone kiosks declined as the number of windows overlooking the kiosk increased. These early tests adhered most closely to the notion of *design* rather than *add-on measures*, like closed-circuit television (CCTV) and street-lighting. These are, of course, enablers of surveillance and contributors to defensible space, albeit of less interest to planners – except in the negative sense that it may let the planners off the hook in devising security measures.

Assessment has been undertaken of the comparative effectiveness of two forms of surveillance in preventing crime in public space: *formal surveillance*, in the form of CCTV cameras; and *natural surveillance*, in the form of improved street lighting. They were found to be equally effective in reducing crime. Detailed analyses showed that improved street lighting was more effective in reducing crime in city centres; that both forms of surveillance were more effective in reducing property crimes than violent crimes; and that both measures were far more effective in reducing crime in Britain than in America. Road closures and targeted deployment of security guards also curb crime. In an emergent strand of research likely to be of immense importance, mathematical-network theory was used to demonstrate how connectivity of street segments with the street network generally is powerfully associated with presenting burglary rates.

In sum, surveillance – inbuilt or add-on – retains importance in controlling residential burglary, vandalism in multi-unit housing, and school break-ins. Employee surveillance is particularly relevant to public transport and school crime reduction. Yet Newman's contribution is not properly thought of narrowly in these terms, but in the way in which it has spawned a perspective and a literature. The title of Barry Poyner's (1983) book – *Design against Crime: Beyond Defensible Space* – captures the relationship. Even now, Newman remains the near-obligatory reference in any student essay about 'designing out' crime.

See Chapter 6.8
Routine activity
theory

A valid criticism of defensible space is that the complexity of **routine activities** and other variables of structure and use mean that optimizing design to reduce crime is formidably difficult, and a formulaic approach of any kind is inappropriate. Surely we should have thought otherwise. But Newman and Jacobs have set us on a route towards sustainable housing via housing security against crime. Neither are the fortress overtones of the phrase 'defensible space' appropriate. Aesthetic quality-of-housing developments appear to be independent of security levels. Thus we can design, indeed have designed, homes that are both attractive and secure. Human dwellings last for many years. Building crime opportunities into new developments casts a shadow that will endure for decades. Dwelling design is important in crime reduction. Much of the detail needs to be fleshed out, but the path on which Newman set us is important to follow.

References

Jacobs, Jane. 1961. *The Death and Life of Great American Cities*. New York: Random House (reissued with a new foreword in 1993).

Newman, Oscar. 1961. *New Frontiers in Architecture*. New York: Basic Books.

Newman, Oscar. 1972. *Defensible Space*. New York: Macmillan.

Newman, Oscar. 1996. *Creating Defensible Space*. Washington, DC: US Department of Housing and Urban Development.

Poyner, Barry. 1983. *Design against Crime: Beyond Defensible Space*. London: Butterworth-Heinemann.

Further reading

Davies, Toby, and Shane D. Johnson 2015. Examining the Relationship between Road Structure and Burglary Risk via Quantitative Network Analysis. *Journal of Quantitative Criminology* 31(3): 481–507.

Ellingworth, Dan, and Ken Pease. 2000. Movers and Breakers: Household Property Crime Against Those Moving Home. *International Journal of Risk, Security and Crime Prevention* 3(1): 35–42.

Reynald, Danielle. 2010. Guardians on Guardianship: Factors Affecting the Willingness to Supervise, the Ability to Detect Potential Offenders, and the Willingness to Intervene. *Journal of Research in Crime and Delinquency* 47(3): 358–90.

Welsh, Brandon C., and David P. Farrington. 2004. Surveillance for Crime Prevention in Public Space: Results and Policy Choices in Britain and America. *Criminology and Public Policy* 3(3): 497–526.

Welsh, Brandon C., Mark E. Mudge, and David P. Farrington. 2010. Reconceptualizing Public Area Surveillance and Crime Prevention: Security Guards, Place Managers and Defensible Space. *Security Journal* 23(4): 299–315.

6.6 Opportunity theory

Scott A. Hunt

Opportunity theory is a collection of related but conceptually distinct perspectives which claim to offer an alternative to offender-focused criminology (Wilcox and Gialopsos 2015:4). Rather than focusing on offender characteristics, opportunity theory traditionally has concentrated on the temporal and spatial distribution of crime events. Recent developments, however, have reincorporated the offender by positing a multilevel or integrated opportunity theory that represents a social-psychological explanation of crime events (see, e.g., Wilcox et al. 2003, 2014). This represents a significant shift in opportunity theory in that it suggests that differential offender characteristics actually matter. Further conceptual development of a multilevel opportunity theory will require problematizing core assumptions and concepts in rich social-psychological terms. This is particularly true for assumptions and concepts wrapped up in the agency-structure question.

Opportunity theory has emerged from the confluence of several simultaneous, yet independent and distinct, theoretical streams of thought (Wilcox and Gialopsos 2015:6). One stream is **situational crime prevention** or **rational choice theory**, which theorizes that potential offenders identify crime opportunities by rationally calculating risk, reward and effort inputs. Another theoretical stream is **victimization studies**, which argues that certain demographic groups (e.g., single men, younger adults, African-Americans) pursue lifestyles that put them in places and times correlated with greater victimization risk. Yet another strand of work stems from **routine activities theory**, which posits that criminal acts are the result of the temporal and spatial convergence of motivated offenders, suitable targets and a lack

See Chapter 6.2
Community safety;
Chapter 6.5
Defensible space

See Chapter 1.18
Rational choice

See Chapter 4.39
Victimology

See Chapter 6.8
Routine activity
theory

of effective guardians. In addition, social disorganization theory argues that criminal opportunities are created by breakdowns in social institutions, organizations and relationships. Opportunity theory has also benefited from work that examines particular physical and social characteristics of 'place', which lead to space–time concentrations of crime events (i.e., 'hotspots'). Most recently, opportunity theorists have integrated these various strands into a general multilevel opportunity theory, which incorporates social-psychological traits of actors in socially and temporally structured opportunity contexts.

See Chapter 2.2
Social
disorganization
theory

See Chapter 6.10
Space, place and
crime

The development of a multilevel opportunity theory has brought the offender to the forefront. It has introduced, albeit mainly implicitly, the idea that it is necessary to include a social-psychological treatment of the offender in order to have a truly *multilevel* theory. The introduction of this idea can be construed as problematic because it runs counter to what is commonly considered *the* defining trait of opportunity theory: namely, that offender characteristics as such are assumed away, giving exclusive attention to opportunity *per se*. From this view, individual-level characteristics may be relevant if they can be conceptualized as indicators of structural opportunity (e.g., when particular demographics are said to be indicators of lifestyle opportunities for victimization). Offender characteristics as such are believed to be extraneous, however, given opportunity theory's longstanding domain assumptions about motivation and rational calculations. Suggesting that a robust social psychology of the offender is warranted represents a significant challenge to the foundational metaphysical and theoretical assumptions established in the nineteenth century.

Opportunity theory's understanding of agency, motivation and rationality is grounded in Bentham's (1879) classical formulation. Bentham's view is highly deterministic and reductionist in that it insists that pleasure and pain alone govern all humans in all spatial-temporal contexts in all they do, in all they say and in all they think. According to Bentham, pain and pleasure are 'sovereign masters' that determine what we *shall* do and what we *ought* to do. Bentham's foundational ontological assumptions hold that rationality, reasoning, passion, morality and conscience – indeed, the entirety of human nature, thought and action – are reduced to and determined by pleasure and pain. From this foundational premise, there simply is no need to investigate motives, reasoning processes, rationality or criminality because all those things are assumed a priori. In classical and later neo-utilitarian formulations, the commission of a crime, by definition, is evidence of a rational act that held more pleasure than pain. This amotivational assumption simplified the utilitarian project. Given rational actors and ubiquitous motivated offenders, the task of explaining crime is narrowed to discovering the characteristics of 'opportunities' – i.e., those spatial-temporal attributes that make the likelihood of realized pleasure greater than the likelihood of realized pain. From this view, the characteristics of actors are simply irrelevant. There is no need for a social-psychology of the offender.

See Chapter 1.2
Classical
criminology

See Chapter 1.3
Utilitarianism

It seems clear that further advancement of a social-psychological, multilevel opportunity theory depends upon an explicit rejection of the amotivational assumption. Failure to do so will result in a un- or under-theorized actor and a rejection of a truly social-psychological level of analysis. As Cullen (2004:360) points out, 'the amotivational assumption ignores the wealth of evidence that there are substantial individual differences in criminality (that, when aggregated, account for compositional effects in population groups)'.

Cullen's criticism suggests that a social-psychological, multilevel opportunity theory must take up the agency-structure question anew. At the centre of the agency-structure question is a debate about the social-psychological causes of action. Philosophers over many centuries have staked out the parameters of the 'hard problem' of free will. There is no good reason for criminologists to enter into this particular philosophical arena, for which most are inadequately prepared. Criminologists can do what social scientists do best, however: identify what factors make actions more or less free. This would require theorizing on agency-opportunity. What social-temporal contexts inhibit or enable agency (e.g., economic inequality, availability of formal education, concentrated disadvantage, social networks, matrices of **surveillance**)? What person-level characteristics inhibit or enable agency (e.g., neurological disorders, impulse control, addiction, **life-course turning-points**, **social bonds**)? A social-psychological, multilevel opportunity theory could move forward by problematizing such things as motives, decision-making processes, self-regulation, personality traits, personality states and the plasticity of action. It could even explore less restricted conceptualizations of rationality than the utilitarian pleasure–pain reduction.

Seriously engaging the agency-structure question would create conceptual space to enrich the very notion of criminal opportunity itself. For example, Cullen suggests that a social-psychological, multilevel opportunity perspective could enrich its understanding of opportunity by incorporating more fully Cloward's (1959) 'illegitimate means' perspective. This effort would necessarily engage sociological and economic work that has examined the differential distribution of illegitimate means across time and space, but it would also need to consider the sociological and psychological treatments of how illegitimate means are differentially perceived and pursued. Cullen further suggests that it would be incumbent upon a social-psychological, multilevel opportunity theory to explore to what degree people *create* opportunities to offend. What social-structural characteristics facilitate or inhibit an actor's ability to create criminal opportunity? What psychological characteristics make one more or less likely to engage in the work of creating criminal opportunity?

The field of social psychology generally – encompassing all of its sociological, psychological and discursive variants – has much to offer a multilevel opportunity theory of criminal acts. Once the offender is brought back in, social psychological insights on motivations, social cognition, rationality, attitudes, violence, aggression, prosocial action, prejudice, discrimination, developmental psychology, personality, self-concept, identity, collective action, social influence, interpersonal relationships, embodiment, psychobiology and affect

See Chapter 5.19
Surveillance

See Chapter 1.13
Life-course theory

See Chapter 2.6
Control theories

(among other topics), seem eminently germane to understanding the structures and processes of multilevel opportunity.

Admittedly, some labouring in the various fields of opportunity theory will find the inherent social-psychology in the recent multilevel opportunity synthesis either not worth the trouble or something completely extraneous to opportunity theory. Still others will see this development as a corrective that brings back into focus the actor in a theory of criminal acts. To be a corrective, a social-psychological, multilevel opportunity theory must take on some hefty metaphysical and theoretical work – such as the kind found in Agnew's (2011) treatment of the ontological questions concerning determinism-agency, human nature, nature of society and the nature of reality. It must also be willing to dive deep into the abundance of riches found in social-psychological work that cuts across a variety of disciplines (e.g., anthropology, communications, criminology, psychology, sociology), as well as a variety of interdisciplinary programmes focused on age, class, gender and race. The degree to which a multilevel opportunity theory thrives over the coming years will largely depend on how fully it embraces the development of a robust social-psychology of the offender.

References

Agnew, Robert. 2011. *Toward a Unified Criminology: Integrating Assumptions about Crime, People and Society*. New York: New York University Press.

Bentham, Jeremy. 1879. *An Introduction to the Principles of Morals and Legislation*. Oxford: Clarendon.

Cloward, Richard A. 1959. Illegitimate Means, Anomie, and Deviant Behavior. *American Sociological Review* 24(2): 164–76.

Cullen, Francis T. 2004. Book Review: Criminal Circumstance: A Dynamic Multicontextual Criminal Opportunity Theory. *Contemporary Sociology: A Journal of Reviews* 33(3): 359–61.

Wilcox, Pamela, Kenneth C. Land, and Scott A. Hunt. 2003. *Criminal Circumstance: A Dynamic, Multicontextual Criminal Opportunity Theory*. New York: Walter de Gruyter.

Wilcox, Pamela, and Brooke Miller Gialopsos. 2015. Crime-Event Criminology: An Overview. *Journal of Contemporary Criminal Justice* 31(1): 4–11.

Wilcox, Pamela, Christopher J. Sullivan, Shayne Jones, and Jean-Louis van Gelder. 2014. Personality and Opportunity: An Integrated Approach to Offending and Victimization. *Criminal Justice and Behavior* 41(7): 880–901.

Further reading

Deryol, Rustu, Pamela Wilcox, Matthew Logan, John Wooldredge, and Glenn D. Walters. 2016. Crime Places in Context: An Illustration of the Multilevel Nature of Hot Spot Development. *Journal of Quantitative Criminology* 32(2): 305–25.

Janssen, Heleen J., Veroni I. Eichelsheim, Maja Dekovic, and Gerben J.N. Bruinsma. 2016. How is Parenting Related to Adolescent Delinquency? A Between- and Within-Person Analysis of the Mediating Role of Self-Control, Delinquent Attitudes, Peer Delinquency, and Time Spent in Criminogenic Settings. *European Journal of Criminology* 13(2): 169–94.

McNeeley, Susan, and Pamela Wilcox. 2015. Street Codes, Routine Activities, Neighbourhood Context and Victimization. *British Journal of Criminology* 55(5): 921–43.

Sampson, Robert J., and John D. Wooldredge. 1987. Linking the Micro- and Macro-level Dimensions of Lifestyle-Routine Activity and Opportunity Models of Predatory Victimization. *Journal of Quantitative Criminology* 3(4): 371–93.

Walters, Glenn D. 2013. Introduction to the Special Issue: Psychology of Crime. *Journal of Criminal Justice* 41(2): 61–3.

Wilcox, Pamela, Brooke Miller Gialopsos, and Kenneth C. Land. 2013. Multilevel criminal opportunity. In *The Oxford Handbook of Criminological Theory*, Francis T. Cullen and Pamela Wilcox, eds, pp. 579–601. New York: Oxford University Press.

Risk

6.7

Pat O'Malley

Risk came to the attention of social theorists in the 1980s, when governmental practices and discourses shifted from rehabilitation and punishment to prevention based on probabilistic prediction. While prevention had been central to medicine and insurance since the nineteenth century, in the 1980s, it expanded in prominence and scope. Indeed, in almost all areas of life, risk-based prevention became focal: diet and exercise, vehicle and road design, pregnancy, policing and justice, financial management, career choice – all became heavily influenced by discourses of, and invested in, practices of risk.

For criminologists, **crime prevention** became particularly prominent as police and justice departments fostered the growth of 'situational prevention' programmes that focused not so much on *criminals* as on statistically identified *opportunities* for offending. Urban planners began to '**design out**' crime by creating streetscapes that maximized **surveillance**, by improving street lighting and, most controversially, by creating gated communities to exclude strangers. Neighbourhood Watch programmes enlisted communities in active surveillance of suspicious activities, and encouraged increased **security** measures such as improving locks, avoiding high-risk situations and installing alarms.

Other aspects of crime control were also identified as coming under the sway of risk. Particularly prominent was '**actuarial justice**' (Feeley and Simon 1994), in which sentencing of offenders was based on the danger or threat they posed rather than the moral wrongness of their offence. Repeat offenders would be given lengthy terms of imprisonment as their risk of **reoffending** was statistically high. Accordingly, sentences came to be calculated on factors related to risk reduction rather than punishment and correction:

See Chapter 6.2
Community safety

See Chapter 6.6
Opportunity theory

See Chapter 6.5
Defensible space

See Chapter 5.19
Surveillance

See Chapter 5.17
Security and counter-security

See Chapter 5.10
The new penology

See Chapter 5.13
Recidivism

prisons became 'risk containers' in which correctional programmes gave way to secure confinement. At this time, electronic monitoring of offenders boomed, as did house arrest.

Concomitantly, police were arguably shifting away from traditional concerns with detection and capture of criminals and instead becoming information-brokers for security industries – notably insurance – providing data relevant to the prevention of crime and the minimization of its consequences (Ericson and Haggerty 1997). Electronic monitoring of traffic offences – through 'safety cameras' and computerized surveillance networks – helped create a new risk-based policing. As vehicle speed was identified as a risk to life and property, automated policing became both justified and enabled: computers could calculate speeds and, through sentencing algorithms, assess penalties and issue penalty notices that could, in turn, be paid electronically. In many respects, then, risk-based justice became virtual. Probation and parole were also restructured around risk. Decisions about release from prison, for example, became determined increasingly by risk schedules. Based on statistical data for reoffending, scores were assigned to offenders applying for parole, and these scores determined decisions to release.

Most controversially, the use of such data to identify 'pre-criminals' began to reshape discourses of dangerousness. Interventions against 'high-risk' individuals could be justified even before offences had occurred, as their identification no longer relied on the subjective judgement of experts – who could always be contradicted by other experts – but rather appeared as 'factual'. Individuals were allocated to various levels of risk groups on the basis of statistical data, just as insurers classified their risks with 'science'.

After the turn of the twenty-first century, events such as 9/11 ramped up the consciousness of risk even higher. For air travel, electronic scanning, no-fly lists, profiling of passengers, restrictions on what could be taken aboard – all these and more became the new 'risky' normal. **The permeability of borders became a governmental obsession**, and in the process, borders morphed into new preventive forms: a nation's borders could exist in the airports of other countries; border security practices and agencies could turn inward to risks already within national territory (Mythen 2014).

Such accounts are easily overdrawn, yet clearly a massive transformation has affected crime control and almost every field of governance. Several major approaches have addressed why this occurred. Originating with the work of Ulrich Beck (1992), the 'risk-society' thesis proposes that the emergence of risk-consciousness originates with the discovery of 'modernization risks'. These are risks of global reach, such as **global warming**, nuclear armament, international **terrorism** and global **financial crises**. While global and uncontainable, these risks are difficult or impossible to predict. Because they emerge quickly and usually are unprecedented, we have no statistical data upon which to build predictive risk models. Yet with rising risk consciousness, the demand for increased identification and management of risks spirals. While this theory has been influential across most sociology, it has had surprisingly limited impact

See Chapter 4.6
Crimmigration

See Chapter 4.11
Environmental
justice and
victimology;
Chapter 4.13
Genocide and
ecocide; Chapter
4.16 Green
criminology

See Chapter 4.19
Institutional and
anti-institutional
violence

See Chapter 4.12
Financial crime

on criminology. *Policing the Risk Society* (Ericson and Haggerty 1997) deployed it to explain the increasing influence of the insurance industry that, in turn, was seen to transform the police into a security-data brokerage. But while this classic work did much to promote the idea of risk-based policing, its foundation in Beck's work was not to become focal – although given much lip service – and indeed the authors immediately moved on to other approaches.

A radically different approach was adopted by the idea of 'govern- mentality'. Emerging from the work of Michel Foucault, it rejected grand transformational theories such as Beck's, and focused instead on more spe- cific and often contingent changes, especially those associated with shifts in governmental mentalities and techniques. The rise of 'actuarial justice', for example and noted above, was linked inter alia with emerging perceptions that the African-American population in the USA had become disconnected economically from the mainstream society, and had sunk below the threshold of deterrence. Reform and punishment thus gave way to containment: the removal of this risky population to prisons (Feeley and Simon 1994).

See Chapter 5.8
Governmentality

See Chapter 1.17
Deterrence

A second thesis focused on the nature of *risk regimes* rather than simply the growth of risk *per se*. The rise of risk was linked to the development of neoliberalism, and its preference for individual responsibility and market- led techniques of government. Thus, while the welfare state had been a *risk-minimizing assemblage*, neoliberals regarded this as producing multiple ills associated with the loss of competitive risk and individual risk-management. Criminologists argued that, accordingly, crime prevention should continue to shift from welfare-style interventions for high-crime areas toward interven- tions that 'empowered' communities and individuals to manage their risks. 'Welfare-state' therapeutic prison regimes were to be abandoned in favour of visions of offenders as rational choice risk-takers who simply needed to be punished in order to increase deterrence. Police would become more oriented to crime prevention in order to reduce risks to the 'customers' of justice; police resources would increase to raise the risk of capture, and thus rational choice deterrence (O'Malley 2010).

See Chapter 4.24
Neoliberalism

See Chapter 1.18
Rational choice

The principal approaches to crime and risk have tended to emphasize the negative aspects of ever-expanding risk-based justice, and have correspond- ingly ignored effective resistance and governmental failures. This has produced a pessimistic depiction of retreat into an unassailable 'culture of control'. Critics, however, have noted that many risk-based changes have had positive effects. Drug-harm minimization that pitted public-health risk management against the war on drugs set out to reduce demonization and criminalization of drug users, increase medical aid to drug users and provide access to less risky forms of drug administration. Risk-needs analysis, which became prominent in prison settings, was intended to displace punitive regimes and provide therapy and other services to prisoners that reduced their risk of reoffending. Parole officers were seen to resist using risk schedules and made these no more than one factor in parole decision-making. Police did not become risk-information brokers for the insurance industry, and traditional forms of crime-fighting policing have retained a high profile. Actuarial justice has been effectively opposed by judges, lawyers and others, and has generally became restricted to a limited array of mainly sexual and violence offences.

Much less prominent has been attention to risk in criminal behaviour. As risk has become more central culturally, certain 'risky' forms of offending have developed or expanded. Associated with **'edgework'** – exposing oneself to extreme risk at the edge of control – it is suggested that a new generation of financial crimes has emerged in which unauthorized individuals make high-risk investments for huge sums. In addition, the cultural centrality of excitement and risk-taking has been linked to the longer-term rise of offences such as illicit recreational drug use and illicit 'sports', such as street car-racing or rooftop riding on trains (O'Malley 2010). This aspect of crime and risk has received comparatively little attention, however.

See Chapter 4.8 Cultural criminology

While risk retains a high profile in criminological theory and crime control, two developments have become increasingly prominent. Consistent with Beck's theory has been an increased awareness of risk's preventive limits. Recently, 'resilience' has become markedly salient as an approach that emphasizes instead the ability of individuals, institutions and communities to survive and bounce back from the impact of harmful events. Even where prevention retains a high profile, less probabilistic techniques have come to prominence that work through imagining possible futurities and guarding against these – an approach that has become particularly prominent with respect to crimes of terror. Elsewhere in criminology, risk models have been retained, but new approaches focus more on emergent models of surveillance and control. In particular, Deleuze's (1995) 'control societies' thesis has drawn attention to the ways in which electronic monitoring – from credit and access cards to traffic cameras and monitoring drones – seek to govern illegalities by modulating distributions: allowing or preventing access, recording electronic trails, identifying risky behavioural patterns. As risk is beginning to morph into new forms and be put into effect through new technologies, so criminological concepts and approaches are shifting accordingly.

References

Beck, Ulrich. 1992. *Risk Society: Toward a New Modernity*. London: Sage.

Deleuze, Gilles. 1995. *Negotiations 1972–1990*. New York: Columbia University Press.

Ericson, Richard, and Kevin Haggerty. 1997. *Policing the Risk Society*. Toronto: University of Toronto Press.

Feeley, Malcolm, and Jonathan Simon. 1994. Actuarial justice: The emerging new criminal law. In *The Futures of Criminology*, David Nelken, ed., pp. 173–204. New York, Sage.

Mythen, Gabe. 2014. *Understanding the Risk Society: Crime, Security and Justice*. Basingstoke: Palgrave Macmillan.

O'Malley, Pat. 2010. *Crime and Risk*. London: Sage.

Further reading

Ericsson, Richard. 2007. *Crime in an Insecure World*. Cambridge: Polity.

Hudson, Barbara. 2003. *Justice in the Risk Society*. London: Sage.

Kemshall, Hazel. 2003. *Understanding Risk in Criminal Justice*. Buckingham: Open
University Press.

6.8 Routine activity theory

Martin A. Andresen and Olivia K. Ha

During the 1950s and 1960s, Western society underwent substantial social and economic improvements, particularly in the United States. Income levels were rising, education levels were increasing, particularly for women, poverty levels were decreasing, and unemployment was relatively low. Despite all these positive changes, crime rates were skyrocketing – by 150 to 250 per cent, depending on the measurements – which Cohen and Felson (1979) referred to as a 'sociological paradox'. Routine activity theory was developed to explain these co-occurrences in a way that sociological theories could not.

Routine activity theory begins by stating the importance of understanding the spatial component of crime patterns put forth by the **Chicago School**. We frequent particular places and not others, and visit those particular places at particular times. When we travel to the same place at the same time on a regular basis, these activities can be considered 'routine activities', defined by Cohen and Felson (1979:593) as 'any recurrent and prevalent activities which provide for basic population and individual needs, whatever their biological or cultural origins'. Because these activities will normally take us out of the relatively protective environment of the home, if we modify the frequency and/or timing of these routine activities, we will alter our risk of criminal victimization; if these routine activities change en masse at a societal level, we will impact crime rate trends.

In its original formulation, routine activity theory considered only direct-contact predatory violations in which the offender and the victim or target

See Chapter 2.1
Chicago School

were tangible; subsequent development of the theory, however, has extended it to other violations that include **white-collar crime**. In order for one of these violations/crimes to occur, Cohen and Felson stated that there must be a *motivated offender*, a *suitable target* and the *lack of a capable guardian*. They sought to explain the changes in the crime rate trends based on suitable targets, through one of two mechanisms: (1) changes in the routine activities of people; and (2) the presence of more suitable targets. They argued that post-war social and economic developments meant people had more time and money for shopping and recreation. Related to this was the increase in young adults leaving home for a post-secondary education, and, particularly for women, increases in the rates of working outside the home. This was also a time of rapid increases in the availability of valuable lightweight consumer electronics: some have stated we are seeing another, more subtle but comparable, crime wave from increases in mobile electronic devices (phones, tablets) (Mailley et al. 2008).

See Chapter 4.41
White-collar crime

These changes, though not present for all individuals and communities, were significant enough to impact societal levels of being outside the relatively protective environment of the home. Outside the home, an individual is more vulnerable to property and violent offences, and his/her home (and everything in it) is more vulnerable because no one is there guarding it. Cohen and Felson (1979) pointed out that economic conditions can impact crime in indirect ways: changes in disposable income have an impact on routine activities that then impact crime; increases in societal wealth lead to increases in the opportunities to steal from others. The resulting theory of crime trend changes is consistent with increases in social and economic development and crime. Therefore, if support was found for the theory, there would be no sociological paradox. Using national-level time-series data, Cohen and Felson found strong support for their theory, particularly for any variables that related to changes in routine activities for the following offence categories: aggravated assault, burglary, forcible rape, non-negligent homicide and robbery.

As developed, routine activity theory was an aggregate-level theory that sought to explain societal changes in crime rates. At the individual level, the classic evaluation of routine activity theory was conducted by Kennedy and Forde (1990), using data from the Canadian Urban Victimization Survey that considered routine activities and criminal victimization of individuals in major urban centres across Canada (from west to east: Vancouver, Edmonton, Winnipeg, Toronto, Montreal, Halifax-Dartmouth and St. John's). This study investigated the role of individual-level routine activities relative to the following crime types: assault, automobile theft, breaking and entering (residential burglary), and robbery. Kennedy and Forde not only took into account routine activity theory-based variables, but also a series of control variables that are considered important in sociological theories of crime, such as age, income, marital status, single-parent households and unemployment. These researchers found that:

See Chapter 4.39
Victimology

- Spending time in a bar or pub was positively associated with being a **victim** of all four crime types.
- Sporting activities, working or going to school, spending time walking or driving, and having a full-time job were all positively related to residential burglary.
- Working or going to school was positively associated with automobile theft.
- Working or going to school and spending time walking or driving was positively associated with assault.
- Spending time walking or driving was positively associated with robbery.

All of these results make perfect sense within routine activity theory. Essentially, spending time outside the relatively protective environment of the home increases the risk of one's home being burgled, as well as the risk of personal victimization outside one's home.

One aspect of routine activity theory that has gone relatively untested is the concept of capable guardianship, or the lack thereof. Capable guardians have the ability to prevent a crime from occurring, playing an important role in routine activity theory. Reynald (2011) has investigated this dimension of routine activity theory through the concept of *guardianship in action*. Guardianship in action measures the intensity of guardianship in a residential area using a three-stage typology: 1) occupancy, noting the actual presence of people in the residential space; 2) monitoring, noting whether or not residents in the area actually monitor local behaviour; and 3) intervention, noting whether or not residents actually directly intervene (saying or doing something) when they observe activities that are not approved.

See Chapter 6.5
Defensible space

In her research on this topic, Reynald directly observed these three aspects of guardianship in action at the street-segment level. She sought to investigate which factors in an area (demographic, physical, social and spatial) predicted the intensity of guardianship and, subsequently, how well guardianship in action predicted crime rates in an area. The empirical research found that guardianship intensity plays a significant role in predicting (decreasing) property crime in an area. Moreover, the traditional measures of guardianship – such as **target hardening and territoriality** – have positive relationships to property crime. This research suggests that the more traditional measures of guardianship (target hardening and territoriality) are largely reflections of areas with high crime rates. Consequently, *guardianship in action* is a better construct for measuring the ability of guardianship to repel crime. In sum, routine activity theory is a simple theory to understand, but contains many complex ideas that are still undergoing refinement. This theoretical framework worked well in understanding the changing crime-rate trends in the United States post-World War II, and continues to provide insight into today's changing nature of crime.

References

Cohen, Lawrence E., and Marcus Felson. 1979. Social Change and Crime Rate Trends: A Routine Activity Approach. *American Sociological Review* 44(4): 588–608.

Kennedy, Leslie W., and David R. Forde. 1990. Routine Activities and Crime: An Analysis of Victimization in Canada. *Criminology* 28(1): 137–52.

Mailley, Jen, Roni Garcia, Shaun Whitehead, and Graham Farrell. 2008. Phone Theft Index. *Security Journal* 21(3): 212–27.

Reynald, Danielle M. 2011. Factors Associated with the Guardianship of Places: Assessing the Relative Importance of the Spatio-Physical and Sociodemographic Contexts in Generating Opportunities for Capable Guardianship. *Journal of Research in Crime and Delinquency* 48(1): 110–42.

Further reading

Andresen, Martin A. 2014. *Environmental Criminology: Evolution, Theory, and Practice*. New York: Routledge.

Farrell, Graham, Andromachi Tseloni, Jen Mailley, and Nick Tilley. 2011. The Crime Drop and the Security Hypothesis. *Journal of Research in Crime and Delinquency* 48(2): 147–75.

Felson, Marcus. 2006. *Crime and Nature*. Los Angeles: Sage.

Felson, Marcus, and Ronald V. Clarke. 1998. *Opportunity Makes the Thief: Practical Theory for Crime Prevention*. London: Home Office.

Felson, Marcus, and Mary Eckert. 2016. *Crime and Everyday Life* (5th edn). Los Angeles: Sage.

Hawley, Amos H. 1950. *Human Ecology: A Theory of Community Structure*. New York: Ronald Press.

Reynald, Danielle M. 2009. Guardianship in Action: Developing a New Tool For Measurement. *Crime Prevention and Community Safety* 11(1): 1–20.

Rural criminology

Joseph F. Donnermeyer

See Chapter 2.1
Chicago School;
Chapter 2.2 Social
disorganization
theory

The development of criminology in the late nineteenth century and through much of the twentieth century was both theoretically and empirically **urban in its focus**. The transition of societies from rural and agricultural to urban and industrial provided a rich field for exploring and understanding criminal behaviour and criminal justice. The context was inevitably and overwhelmingly urban, with rural criminology lagging far behind.

This situation has changed considerably since the 1990s (Donnermeyer 2016), however, as the study of rural crime has grown conceptually and diversified empirically. The application of theory in rural criminology can be divided into three categories: (1) work which explicitly borrows from established criminological theories; (2) theoretical constructs that have an **'indigenously' rural context** but can be applied to urban locations as well; and (3) rural scholarship which critiques and revises established criminological theories.

See Chapter 4.18
Indigenous
criminology

See Chapter 6.8
Routine activity
theory

See Chapter 3.4
Defiance theory

See Chapter 4.16
Green criminology

Contributors to Donnermeyer's (2016) edited work demonstrate how much rural criminology has borrowed from established theory in criminology. For example, several contributors construct theoretical explanations of poaching that can be based on **routine activities theory** and **defiance theory**, and 'folk crime' is reconceptualized for the purposes of creating a more in-depth contextual analysis of violations against hunting and other **environmental regulations in rural settings**. These three examples demonstrate that rural crime in general, not merely wildlife violations, must be understood in terms of crime as conditional on shifting definitions of illegal behaviours vis-à-vis the political economies of countries and regions around the world.

There are numerous other examples of criminological theory that also have been applied to important issues in rural criminology. Donnermeyer and DeKeseredy (2014) have discussed the application of the **left-realist** concept of the 'square of crime' to the study of rural crime, including such diverse issues as agricultural crime, substance use and variations in crime rates among rural communities. Building from past work on farm **victimization**, Barclay and Donnermeyer (2011) use both **opportunity theory** and routine activities theory to specify factors associated with farm victimization, such as the physical relationship of the farm homestead to other outbuildings, which influences levels of visibility or **surveillance** of farm property – one aspect of guardianship. More recently, Brisman and colleagues (2014) have synthesized the frameworks of **green** and **cultural criminology** to examine the rural context of various issues: from the exploitative practices of agribusinesses to abuse of farm workers and others labouring in dominantly rural located industries, to environmental activism and rural protest movements.

See Chapter 3.14
Realism and left idealism

See Chapter 4.39
Victimology

See Chapter 6.6
Opportunity theory

See Chapter 5.19
Surveillance

See Chapter 4.16
Green criminology

See Chapter 4.8
Cultural criminology

Normally, the term 'indigenous' refers to people, but in this situation, it refers to theories that originate from the context in which rural scholarship occurs. There are two notable examples of new frameworks based primarily upon work on rural studies. The first is research on abusive relationships by DeKeseredy and Schwartz (2009), derived from their work in rural, southeast Ohio. Drawing on previous ethnographic work on violence in rural settings, their model of male peer-support systems is based on the idea that strong networks of **abusive men** in small, rural communities provide reinforcement for violence against their wives/partners.

See Chapter 3.6
Feminist criminologies;
Chapter 3.13
Radical feminism;
Chapter 4.26
Patriarchy and crime; Chapter
4.21 Masculinities, structure and hegemony

Whilst the theoretical foundations of violence against rural women is built on qualitative research (e.g., case study, ethnography), there is another 'indigenously rural theory' that is constructed from quantitative data analysis of large datasets derived from the census and official police data of arrest and offence rates: 'Civic community theory', as described by Matthew Lee (2008), is not a criminological theory per se, even though it bears a resemblance to social disorganization theory – especially the systemic model that considers the internal social and cultural dynamics of place. Instead, it is a theory of social control derived from the sociological sub-fields of rural sociology and community development. Its essential idea is that a strong social ecological infrastructure of civic engagement (as measured by voting patterns, membership in volunteer organizations, etc.) should affect the welfare of a community, including crime rates.

There is a large amount of rural criminological scholarship that is based on social disorganization theory (Donnermeyer and DeKeseredy 2014). Yet, a great deal of this research suggests that the theory's generalizability is limited. As such, while rural criminology has borrowed from existing criminological theory, it also (and crucially) poses a challenge to criminological theory – especially that of social disorganization. Specifically, Kaylen and Pridemore (2013) question the validity of both the structural antecedents and systemic versions of social disorganization theory based on their rural work. Donnermeyer and

DeKeseredy extend this critique by questioning the logic of both social disorganization theory and its derivative theory of collective efficacy. Contemporary versions of both assume that cohesive places are associated with less crime and less cohesive places with more crime. This is a type of linear reasoning that they find troubling for explaining the more complex realities of places.

Donnermeyer and DeKeseredy advocate that criminological theories of place must go beyond these one-dimensional conceptualizations to recognizing a multiplicity of social realities existing within the same social networks and within the same places. Hence, the same form of collective efficacy can constrain some types of crime even as it simultaneously facilitates the commission of other types of offence, based on considerations of power, inequality, discrimination and other social structural and normative forces as expressed at the local level. In addition, even at the micro-level, places exhibit a complexity that belies the idea that there is only one single, hegemonic form of collective efficacy that controls the behaviour of those who live there. In fact, there are multiple efficacies and each may well selectively constrain and facilitate different types of offending. Hence, **subcultural** dimensions are reinserted into the formulations of social disorganization theory and the theory of collective efficacy, considerations of which dimmed significantly in mainstream criminology as tests of both shifted to a dominant quantitative mode in the second half of the twentieth century and into the twenty-first century.

See Chapter 3.17
Subculture

Rural criminology is now more theoretically critical and international in its scope, with an ever-expanding cadre of scholars who are engaged with understanding the non-urban context of crime. *The International Journal of Rural Criminology* was established in 2011 and publishes articles by scholars on a wide range of topics and study sites from around the world. Green criminology and rural criminology display a significant overlap in their foci on environmental and wildlife crime, including the impact of energy development and other extractive industries on rural peoples and rural communities. The '**global south**' initiative (Carrington et al. 2016) – intended to expand the scope of criminology beyond its narrow Western, urban roots – has a significant rural dimension. In turn, rural criminology has much to offer the development of a more diverse and representative criminology, regardless of topic and the size and complexity of place.

See Chapter 4.34
Southern theory

References

Barclay, Elaine, and Joseph F. Donnermeyer. 2011. Crime and Security on Agricultural Operations. *Security Journal* 24(1): 1–18.

Brisman, Avi, Bill McClanahan, and Nigel South. 2014. Toward a Green-Cultural Criminology of 'the Rural'. *Critical Criminology* 22(4): 479–94.

Carrington, Kerry, Russell Hogg, and Máximo Sozzo. 2016. Southern Criminology. *British Journal of Criminology* 56(1): 1–20.

DeKeseredy, Walter S., and Martin D. Schwartz. 2009. *Dangerous Exits: Escaping Abusive Relationships in Rural America*. New Brunswick, NJ: Rutgers University Press.

Donnermeyer, Joseph F. (ed.). 2016. *The Routledge International Handbook of Rural Criminology*. London: Routledge.

Donnermeyer, Joseph F., and Walter S. DeKeseredy. 2014. *Rural Criminology*. London: Routledge.

Kaylen, Maria T., and William A. Pridemore. 2013. Social Disorganization and Crime in Rural Communities: The First Direct Test of the Systemic Model. *British Journal of Criminology* 53(5): 905–23.

Lee, Matthew R. 2008. Civic Community in the Hinterland: Toward a Theory of Rural Social Structure and Violence. *Criminology* 46(2): 447–78.

Further reading

Barclay, Elaine, Joseph F. Donnermeyer, John Scott, and Russell Hogg (eds). 2007. *Crime in Rural Australia*. Sydney: Federation Press.

Ceccato, Vania. 2015. *Rural Crime and Community Safety*. London: Routledge.

Chakraborti, Neil, and John Garland (eds). 2004. *Rural Racism*. Portland, OR: Willan.

Critical Criminology. 2014. Special Issue: Critical Rural Criminology 22, November. Edited by Joseph F. Donnermeyer, Kerry Carrington, and Walter S. DeKeseredy.

Donnermeyer, Joseph F. 2017. *The Criminology of Food and Agriculture*. London: Routledge.

Garriott, William. 2011. *Policing Methamphetamine: Narcopolitics in Rural America*. New York: New York University Press.

Harkness, Alistair, Bridget Harris, and David Baker (eds). 2016. *Locating Crime in Context and Places: Perspectives on Regional, Rural and Remote Australia*. Sydney: Federation Press.

Hogg, Russell, and Kerry Carrington. 2006. *Policing the Rural Crisis*. Sydney: Federation Press.

International Journal of Rural Criminology. 2016. Special Issue 3, July. Edited by Emmanuel Bunei and Joseph F. Donnermeyer.

Journal of Rural Studies. 2015. Special Issue 39, June. Edited by Vania Ceccato.

Mawby, Rob I., and Richard Yarwood. 2011. *Rural Policing and Policing the Rural*. Farnham: Ashgate.

Weisheit, Ralph, David Falcone, and Edward Wells. 2006. *Crime and Policing in Rural and Small-Town America* (3rd edn). Long Grove, IL: Waveland.

Space, place and
crime

Martin A. Andresen

The importance of space and place in criminology has been known for almost
200 years. The overarching pattern of this research is that, despite the various
motivations for crime, crime is patterned across space and those crime patterns
are stable over time. Consequently, understanding the nature of those spatial
patterns is critical for understanding crime.

This approach to the study of crime had its beginnings with the work of
Adolphe Quetelet, from Belgium, and André-Michel Guerry, from France, who
studied property-crime and violent-crime patterns in French departments
(regions) during the early 1800s. What they found was that southern France
had high rates of violent crime and northern France had high rates of property
crime. Moreover, with the time frame they had for data, these crime patterns
were relatively stable and, therefore, predictable (Andresen 2014).

Though most people who study criminology will come across the work
of Guerry and Quetelet, the early criminological work most often associated
with spatial criminology is **social disorganization theory** that came out
of the **Chicago School** of sociology in the 1920s and 1930s (Andresen 2014).
This research focuses on neighbourhoods and their relationship to delin-
quency/crime (with the early work focusing on juvenile delinquency). The
expected relationships within social disorganization theory are that places
that have high levels of population turnover and ethnic heterogeneity are less
able to produce social cohesion in a neighbourhood that will repel crime and

See Chapter 2.2
Social
disorganization
theory

See Chapter 2.1
Chicago School

delinquency. Population turnover contributes to this because places with high population turnover will have difficulties establishing social cohesion simply because people are not invested in the neighbourhood when they plan to leave after a short period of time. Ethnic heterogeneity contributes to social disorganization literally because people do not speak the same languages, but also because of cultural differences: ethnic heterogeneity at the time social disorganization theory was developed involved primarily varieties of Europeans. This theoretical approach dominated spatial criminology until the 1970s, with more recent advances that consider collective efficacy. Overall, social disorganization theory has strong empirical support.

Beginning in the late 1970s and early 1980s, a new set of theories emerged to explain the spatial patterns of crime: **routine activity theory**, geometry of crime and **rational choice theory** – collectively known as environmental criminology. Routine activity theory, developed by Lawrence Cohen and Marcus Felson, states that in order to have a criminal event, a motivated offender and a suitable target must converge in space and time in the absence of a capable guardian (Andresen 2014). Though this theory was not initially developed to understand spatial crime patterns – it was developed to explain long-run temporal-crime patterns, namely the increase in crime during the 1950s and 1960s while social indicators were improving – it became popular in the spatial criminology literature. The reason for this is quite simple: we undertake our routine activities (travelling to and from home to work, school and recreation activities) in a very restricted number of places. As such, the number of places where we will tend to be victimized is also small.

See Chapter 6.8
Routine activity theory

See Chapter 1.18
Rational choice

The geometry of crime emphasizes the importance of the underlying geography of a place to explain crime patterns: the street network, the type of land use, building types and so on all matter for understanding crime patterns – this is called the environmental backcloth. Subsequently, the geometry of crime identifies the places in which we spend our time (home, work, shopping, etc.) as our activity nodes, and the paths in between those activity nodes as our activity space – where we spend our time (Andresen 2014). Only when our activity spaces overlap with the activity spaces of offenders will we be a victim of crime.

Rational choice theory manifests itself in two ways. First, routine activity theory and the geometry of crime assume rational offenders; as such, rational choice theory is 'working' in the background. Second, rational choice theory seeks to understand criminal events from a rational perspective, such that offenders consider the risks and rewards of a potential criminal event when deciding whether to commit that criminal event or not (Andresen 2014). It is important to note here that rationality is in the eye of the beholder: just because one person believes a criminal event is worth the risk does not mean another person will.

There are a number of empirical regularities that have emerged from these theoretical perspectives: geographic profiling, repeat **victimization**, crime measurement, near-repeat victimization and the journey to crime. In short, because of this research, we know the following:

See Chapter 4.39
Victimology

- Based on where a serial offender commits his/her crimes, we can predict his/her home location.
- A relatively small percentage of victims account for a disproportionate percentage of all criminal victimizations.
- There are many ways to measure criminal activity, with some methods being superior to others.
- If a home is burgled, not only is it at a greater risk of re-victimization (repeat victimization) but so are the homes in its immediate vicinity, albeit for a short period of time.
- Offenders' journeys to crime tend to be relatively short, especially for violent crime types (see Andresen 2014 for a discussion of these research areas).

There are two aspects of research within space, place and crime, however, that deserve particular attention: (situational) crime prevention and crime concentrations, each discussed in turn.

See Chapter 6.2
Community safety

The origins of the contemporary theories within environmental criminology are largely related to, or became associated with, **crime prevention**. Crime prevention, in this context, refers to preventing crimes from occurring before they ever occur, rather than through the rehabilitation of offenders after the fact, for example. Generally speaking, it involves the removal of opportunities and is 'situational' because it varies from place to place and crime to crime (Clarke 2012). The number of strategies that is involved in crime prevention is too vast to discuss here, but generally involve increasing risks and decreasing rewards, such as making suitable targets not suitable and adding capable guardians. Research that investigates (situational) crime prevention initiatives has generally found that they are successful and reduce crime. Moreover, there is little evidence for crime displacement resulting from crime prevention activities (Guerette and Bowers 2009); rather, if anything occurs, there is a diffusion of crime prevention benefits such that areas near the crime prevention area also experience a reduction in crime because offenders are not able to identify clearly the spatial boundaries of the crime prevention initiative.

What is probably the most active and interesting aspect of space, place and crime at this time is the study of crime concentrations. Indeed, the history of spatial criminology has been about understanding crime concentrations, most often framed in the context of crime hotspots, but also the importance of spatial heterogeneity in crime patterns: spatial crime patterns are not uniform across entire neighbourhoods, but there are safe places in bad neighbourhoods, for example.

The most recent research that considers crime concentrations has done so at the micro-spatial unit of analysis – the micro-place: most often, street segments and intersections. The general result is that 5 per cent, or less, of street segments and intersections can account for 50 per cent of crime. This result has been found across many cities in the United States, but also in Brazil, Canada and Israel (Andresen et al. 2016; Weisburd 2015). In fact, when specific crime types are investigated, most often fewer than 5 per cent of micro-places can account for 50 per cent of crime. Moreover, while it is common for half of an entire city to be free from crimes reported to the police, elsewhere there can be concentrations of crime within already existing concentrations – hot spots within hot spots (Andresen et al. 2016). Finally, this research has shown that these patterns of concentration are relatively stable over long periods of time – over a decade, and almost 30 years in some cases.

Because of the high degree of concentration that is present in all places that have been investigated, understanding the nature of these micro-places has significant implications for the prevention of crime. Some research has begun to investigate the nature of these micro-places that have high levels of crime and found that the presence of high-risk juveniles, commercial land use and public facilities, such as community centres, arterial roadways, vacant land and the presence of public transit all increase the probability of high-crime areas. Although this research is instructive, and consistent with the expectations of the theories within environmental criminology, it has been undertaken only in one city – Seattle, Washington. As such, because of the importance of replication in the (social) sciences, much more research is necessary. In addition to replication, extensions to what have been undertaken thus far are also critical. Understanding the nature of these micro-places and their stability despite changes in the underlying nature of these cities will prove to be instructive research that may lead to a safer society.

References

Andresen, Martin A. 2014. *Environmental Criminology: Evolution, Theory, and Practice.* New York: Routledge.

Andresen, Martin A., Shannon J. Linning, and Nick Malleson. 2016. Crime at Places and Spatial Concentrations: Exploring the Spatial Stability of Property Crime in Vancouver BC, 2003–2013. *Journal of Quantitative Criminology* DOI: 10.1007/s10940-016-9295-8.

Clarke, Ronald V. 2012. Opportunity Makes the Thief. Really? And So What? *Crime Science* 1(1): article 3.

Guerette, Rob T., and Kate J. Bowers. 2009. Assessing the Extent of Crime Displacement and Diffusion of Benefits: A Review of Situational Crime Prevention Evaluations. *Criminology* 47(4): 1331–68.

Weisburd, David. 2015. The Law of Crime Concentration and the Criminology of Place. *Criminology* 53(2): 133–57.

Further reading

Cornish, Derek B., and Ronald V. Clarke. 1987. Understanding Crime Displacement: An Application of Rational Choice Theory. *Criminology* 25(4): 933–47.

Farrell, Graham. 2013. Five Tests for a Theory of the Crime Drop. *Crime Science* 2(1): article 5.

Felson, Marcus, and Mary Eckert. 2016. *Crime and Everyday Life* (5th edn). Los Angeles: Sage.

Rossmo, D. Kim. 2013. Geographic profiling. In *Encyclopedia of Criminology and Criminal Justice*, Gerben Bruinsma and David Weisburd, eds, pp. 1934–42. New York: Springer.

Weisburd, David, Elizabeth Groff, and Sue-Ming Yang. 2012. *The Criminology of Place: Street Segments and Our Understanding of the Crime Problem*. New York: Oxford University Press.

Weisburd, David, Laura A. Wyckoff, Justin Ready, John E. Eck, Joshua C. Hinkel, and Frank Gajewski. 2006. Does Crime Just Move around the Corner? A Controlled Study of Spatial Displacement and Diffusion of Crime Control Benefits. *Criminology* 44(3): 549–91.

Spatial crime modelling and analysis

Nick Malleson

The field of environmental criminology, as concerned with spatial crime patterns and crime theory, has a long history of employing mathematical models and statistical techniques to better identify and understand the underlying factors associated with high or low crime rates in particular areas. For example, a simple regression model of crime that is based on **routine activity theory** might hypothesize that crime rates are associated with levels of guardianship in an area and the abundance of attractive goods. If such a model is able to reliably predict the observed crime rates then it provides empirical evidence in support of the underlying theory or hypothesis. Models do not *prove* their hypotheses of course, but can help provide evidence for or against some theory.

See Chapter 6.8
Routine activity
theory

The main spatial modelling and analysis methods used in criminology are broadly broken down into: regression, hotspot mapping and simulation. Data, however, are an essential ingredient for any reliable model. 'Garbage in, garbage out' refers to the fact that models will operate on nonsensical data ('garbage in') in exactly the same way as they operate on reliable data. They will therefore produce meaningless nonsense ('garbage out') from poor input data. Models typically require data about crime occurrences – usually in the form of recorded crime or calls-for-service records – as well as data on the underlying factors that inhibit or facilitate crime, such as information about the physical environment of a neighbourhood or the socio-demographics of a community. There is a growing body of evidence in the *crime at places* literature (e.g., Weisburd 2015) that demonstrates that crime patterns exhibit substantial spatial variation, and hence high-resolution spatial data are required for small-scale spatial models. Population censuses are commonly used to represent socio-demographic characteristics, and these are often released at fine temporal scales (such as Census Blocks in the US or Output Areas in the UK). Furthermore, crime events are often now recorded with accurate spatial coordinates, so high-resolution spatial models are possible and becoming increasing popular.

Regression models are a family of mathematical models that estimate the relationships between a *dependent* variable – usually rates or counts of crime occurrences – and a number of *explanatory* variables that might include environmental or socio-demographic factors. Specifically, models can demonstrate how the dependent variable changes with respect to the explanatory variable, highlighting the factors that contribute to, or hinder, crime events. For example, the hypothetical routine activities theory model alluded to earlier might take the form:

$$y_i = \beta_0 + \beta_1 x_{i1} + \beta_2 x_{i2} + \varepsilon_i \tag{1}$$

where y_i is the crime rate in area i, x_{i1} is a variable that represents the degree of guardianship in the area and x_{i2} is a variable that represents the abundance of attractive goods. The purpose of the model is to estimate the β_1 and β_2 parameters (termed the *coefficients*). Positive coefficients suggest that increases in the variable will lead to an increase in crime in the area; negative coefficients suggest the opposite. Note that ε_i represents the error (no model will be perfect). If the model results in a low error term, it is able to explain more of the variation in the crime data than if the error were larger. β_0 is a constant and indicates what the crime rate would be if all input variables were 0. It does not necessarily have a meaningful interpretation, but 'anchors' the regression line in the right place.

There are numerous variations on the simple linear regression outlined above, and a wealth of examples of their application to studies in criminology. An important method to note here, because it has been designed explicitly to represent spatial phenomena, is Geographically Weighted Regression (GWR) (Brunsdon et al. 1998). GWR is a method that allows the regression coefficients to vary across space. This reduces the error in the model (such that the model is able to explain more of the variation in crime) but also provides information about how the impacts of different social/environmental factors may vary across a region. For example, in some areas the abundance of attractive goods might have a stronger influence on crime rates than in other areas.

Mapping is a useful technique for exploring spatial crime patterns. A seminal example in criminology was the mapping produced by Clifford Shaw and Henry McKay as part of their work in the **Chicago School** on **social disorganization** in the 1930s and 1940s. Early crime-mapping examples were

See Chapter 2.1
Chicago School

See Chapter 2.1
Social
disorganization
theory

relatively primitive, however. Advances in computer hardware and software – particularly in the field of Geographical Information Systems (GIS) – as well as the availability of high-resolution data have catalysed the development of more advanced mapping and spatial-analysis techniques.

A common mapping technique that is used to visualize large volumes of crime is kernel density estimation (KDE). KDE maps estimate the overall density of a phenomenon from a set of distinct points (i.e., crime occurrences) and are particularly effective at highlighting crime 'hotspots'. A drawback with KDE, however, is that it does not provide statistical evidence for the presence or absence of a hotspot. Although an area might *appear* to be a hotspot, this might simply be a consequence of how the density was calculated, or how the map was ultimately produced. As an alternative, the GI* statistic (Getis and Ord 1992), highlights areas with *statistically significant* high or low rates (see Figure 6.1). There is also a growing body of work that attempts to quantify more accurately the *population at risk*. This is important because, with a larger number of potential victims in an area, the potential for crime is greater. Quantifying the number of potential victims can be difficult, however, particularly for non-residential crimes where it becomes necessary to estimate the number of people who might be present on a street or in an area.

There is, of course, a very wide range of further crime-mapping/analysis techniques. Importantly, environmental criminologists have begun to adapt *spatio-temporal* techniques from other fields that are able to better account for the temporal dynamics of crime patterns. Examples include spatio-temporal scan statistics (STSS) and spatio-temporal KDE (STKDE) methods.

Although techniques such as regression or hotspot analysis have proven invaluable to criminologists, they inevitably have limitations. One major limitation is that they typically work at an *aggregate* level and, as such, must generalize across populations of individuals. Therefore, it can be difficult to tease out the various underlying factors that ultimately lead to crime events. As Liu and Eck (2008:xiv) put it: 'The central problem of empirical crime analysis, both applied and academic, is that many of the underlying processes that give rise to crime patterns are not visible, and so are not well understood.'

To overcome this limitation, there is a burgeoning interest in the use of computer-simulation techniques such as cellular-automata and agent-based modelling to simulate the behaviour of systems by modelling the individual components. 'Individuals' often include virtual people, such as victims, offenders or police officers. These individuals are placed in a 'virtual environment' that typically represents a spatial area (such as a city) and are equipped with behavioural rules that determine how they should behave. As the model runs, the individuals make decisions and perform actions, and in this manner, a *virtual crime system* emerges. Such models can be used to experiment with crime theory (Birks et al. 2012) or to forecast future crime patterns (Malleson et al. 2013).

It is worth pointing out that the development of reliable, easy-to-use software programs has made many of the techniques outlined here much more

Kernel Density Estimation
Residential Burglary Density

0   5   10   20 Miles

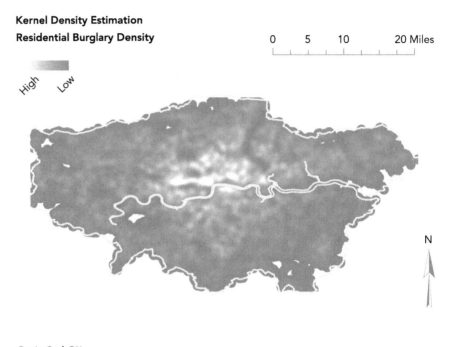

Getis Ord GI*

Statistically Significant Hot-Spots   1.96 – 2.58 Std. Dev.

Not Significant   > 2.58 Std. Dev.

1.65 – 1.96 Std. Dev.

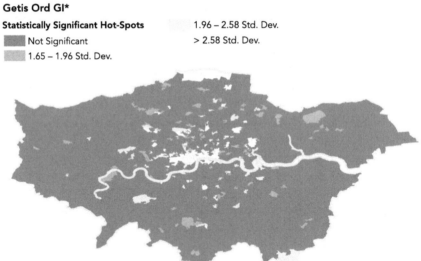

Figure 6.1 Crime Mapping Examples: KDE (kernel density estimation) and GI*.

The maps illustrate counts of residential burglary in London throughout 2015.

Crime data (publicly available) were sourced from http://data.police.uk.

accessible to both academics and practitioners. *CrimeStat* is one of the most popular packages. It is free and is able to perform a wealth of statistical and mapping techniques. For mapping in particular, as well as spatial analysis, geographical information systems, such as *ESRI ArcGIS* and *Quantum GIS* (which is also free), are popular. Finally, *NetLogo* software is an excellent starting place for those interested in developing simulations of crime.

There is an ongoing need to reliably model and analyse spatial crime patterns; hence, the field continues to develop rapidly. The 'Age of Big Data' is having a substantial impact on the analysis techniques. A wealth of new social data from mobile phone records, credit card payments, and social media are opening up new avenues in the analysis and prediction of crime. One of the most well-known, and controversial, developments is *predictive policing*, whereby statistical models are used to estimate the times and locations of new crimes in real time. These systems are being integrated into some police force operations and are even determining the patrol routes of officers. Here, in particular, academics have an important role to play in developing ethical frameworks for this kind of work.

References

Birks, Daniel, Michael Townsley, and Anna Stewart. 2012. Generative Explanations of Crime: Using Simulation to Test Criminological Theory. *Criminology* 50(1): 221–54.

Brunsdon, Chris, Stewart Fotheringham, and Martin Charlton. 1998. Geographically Weighted Regression: Modelling Spatial Non-Stationarity. *Journal of the Royal Statistical Society: Series D (The Statistician)* 47(3): 431–43.

Getis, Arthur, and J.K. Ord. 1992. The Analysis of Spatial Association by Use of Distance Statistics. *Geographical Analysis* 24(3): 189–206.

Liu, Lin, and John Eck. 2008. *Artificial Crime Analysis Systems: Using Computer Simulations and Geographic Information Systems.* Hershey, PA: Information Science Reference.

Malleson, Nick, Alison Heppenstall, Linda See, and Andrew Evans. 2013. Using an Agent-Based Crime Simulation to Predict the Effects of Urban Regeneration on Individual Household Burglary Risk. *Environment and Planning B: Planning and Design* 40(3): 405–26.

Weisburd, David. 2015. The Law of Crime Concentration and the Criminology of Place. *Criminology* 53(2): 133–57.

Further reading

Chainey, Spencer, and Jerry Ratcliffe. 2005. *GIS and Crime Mapping.* Chichester: Wiley.

Griffiths, Elizabeth. 2011. Geographic Information Systems (GIS) and Spatial Analysis. In *The SAGE Handbook of Innovation in Social Research Methods*, Paul Vogt and Malcolm Williams, eds, pp. 442–64. London: SAGE.

Gujarati, Damodar, and Dawn Porter. 2008. *Basic Econometrics* (5th edn). Boston: McGraw-Hill.

Hill, Joanna F., Shane D. Johnson, and Herve Borrion. 2014. Potential uses of computer agent-based simulation modelling in the evaluation of wildlife poaching. In *Situational Crime Prevention of Poaching*, Andrew M. Lemieux, ed., pp. 120–53. London and New York: Routledge.

Williams, Matthew L., Pete Burnap, and Luke Sloan. 2017. Crime Sensing with Big Data: The Affordances and Limitations of using Open Source Communications to Estimate Crime Patterns. *British Journal of Criminology* 57(2): 320–40.

Index

Note: page numbers in **bold type** indicate chapters relating to the subject.

The Routledge Companion to Criminological Theory and Concepts

A comprehensive one-stop reference text, *The Routledge Companion to Criminological Theory and Concepts* (the '*Companion*') will find a place on every bookshelf, whether it be that of a budding scholar or a seasoned academic. Comprising over a hundred concise and authoritative essays written by leading scholars in the field, this volume explains in a clear and inviting way the emergence, context, evolution and current status of key criminological theories and conceptual themes.

The *Companion* is divided into six historical and thematic parts, each introduced by the editors and containing a selection of accessible and engaging short essays written specifically for this text:

- Foundations of criminological thought and contemporary revitalizations
- The emergence and growth of American criminology
- From appreciation to critique
- Late critical criminologies and new directions
- Punishment and security
- Geographies of crime

Comprehensive cross-referencing between essays will provide the reader with signposts to later developments, to critiques and to associated theoretical developments explored within the book, and lists of further reading in every essay will encourage independent thinking and study. This book is an essential reference work for criminology students at all levels and is the perfect companion for courses on criminological theory.

Avi Brisman is an Associate Professor in the School of Justice Studies at Eastern Kentucky University and an Adjunct Associate Professor in the School of Justice at Queensland University of Technology.

Eamonn Carrabine is a Professor in the Department of Sociology at the University of Essex.

Nigel South is a Professor in the Department of Sociology at the University of Essex and an Adjunct Pro nd University of Technology.

The Routledge Companion to Criminological Theory and Concepts is a great conspectus of the different bloodlines, forms and uses of criminology, prepared by authors recruited from across the globe, many of them the principal experts in the areas they describe. It is, without doubt, remarkably comprehensive, nonpartisan and authoritative, and it will serve as an invaluable *vade mecum* for anyone engaged in the study of crime.

– **Paul Rock**, *Emeritus Professor of Sociology,*
London School of Economics and Political Science, UK

This Companion will undoubtedly leave its mark on criminology. The editors have brought together a remarkably thorough and comprehensive collection of essays by experts in their respective fields that will not only stand the test of time but at the same time captures the diversity and intellectual excitement of criminology. This is a clear and accessible collection that will enhance the understanding of the discipline by all those who read it: tutors and students alike. This is the 'must have' book for anyone claiming the label 'criminologist'.

– **Sandra Walklate**, *Eleanor Rathbone Chair of Sociology, University of*
Liverpool; Professor of Criminology, Monash University, Australia; and Adjunct
Professor School of Justice, Queensland University of Technology, Australia

An extraordinary achievement, breathtaking in its scope. A crucial resource, by some of the most insightful thinkers within criminology, that not only surveys what has been achieved but identifies and explores crucial new directions. A criminological milestone that will inspire and guide criminologists for decades to come.

– **Clifford Shearing**, *Professor at the University of Cape Town,*
South Africa; Griffith University, Australia; and Adjunct Professor
at the University of Montreal, Canada

This intellectual history of criminological theories comes at an important time, when we urgently need to re-think our understandings of deviance, transgression and wrongdoing. This is a generous, robust and wide-ranging collection of essays, and they are accessible, rigorous and critical. Many of these are reassuring contributions from key thinkers, and others represent welcome challenges to the field.

– **Katherine Biber**, *Professor of Law,*
University of Technology Sydney, Australia

The Routledge Companion to Criminological Theory and Concepts

Edited by Avi Brisman, Eamonn Carrabine and Nigel South

Routledge
Taylor & Francis Group

LONDON AND NEW YORK

First published 2017
by Routledge
2 Park Square, Milton Park, Abingdon, Oxon OX14 4RN

and by Routledge
711 Third Avenue, New York, NY 10017

Routledge is an imprint of the Taylor & Francis Group, an informa business

British Library Cataloguing in Publication Data
A catalogue record for this book is available from the British Library

Library of Congress Cataloging in Publication Data
Names: Brisman, Avi, editor. | Carrabine, Eamonn, editor. |
South, Nigel, editor.
Title: The Routledge companion to criminological theory and concepts /
edited by Avi Brisman, Eamonn Carrabine and Nigel South.
Description: 1 Edition. | New York : Routledge, 2017. |
Includes bibliographical references and index.
Identifiers: LCCN 2016055264| ISBN 9781138818996 (hardback) |
ISBN 9781138819009 (pbk.) | ISBN 9781315744902 (ebook)
Subjects: LCSH: Criminology.
Classification: LCC HV6018 .R686 2017 | DDC 364.01—dc23
LC record available at https://lccn.loc.gov/2016055264

ISBN: 978-1-138-81899-6 (hbk)
ISBN: 978-1-138-81900-9 (pbk)
ISBN: 978-1-315-74490-2 (ebk)

Typeset in Stone Serif and Rockwell
by Keystroke, Neville Lodge, Tettenhall, Wolverhampton

MIX
Paper from
responsible sources
FSC® C013056
www.fsc.org

Printed and bound in Great Britain by
TJ International Ltd, Padstow, Cornwall